So lernst du mit Green Line

Introduction

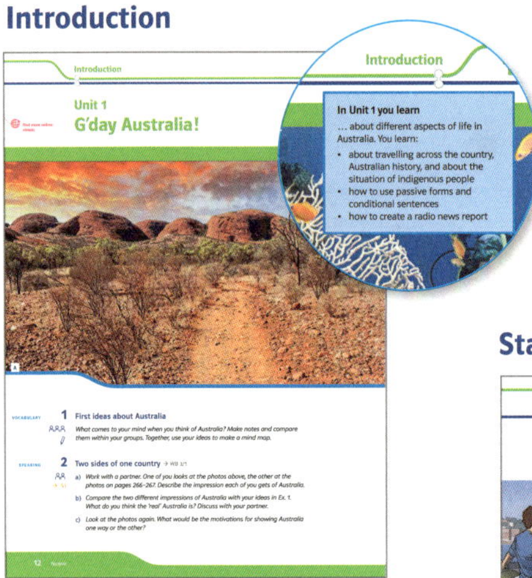

Die ersten beiden Seiten stimmen dich auf das Thema der Unit ein. In der blauen Kompetenzbox siehst du, was du in dieser Unit lernen wirst.

Die Aufgaben mit dem Puzzle-Symbol unterstützen dich besonders dabei, deine Lernziele zu erreichen und helfen dir bei der Vorbereitung der Unit task.

Stations

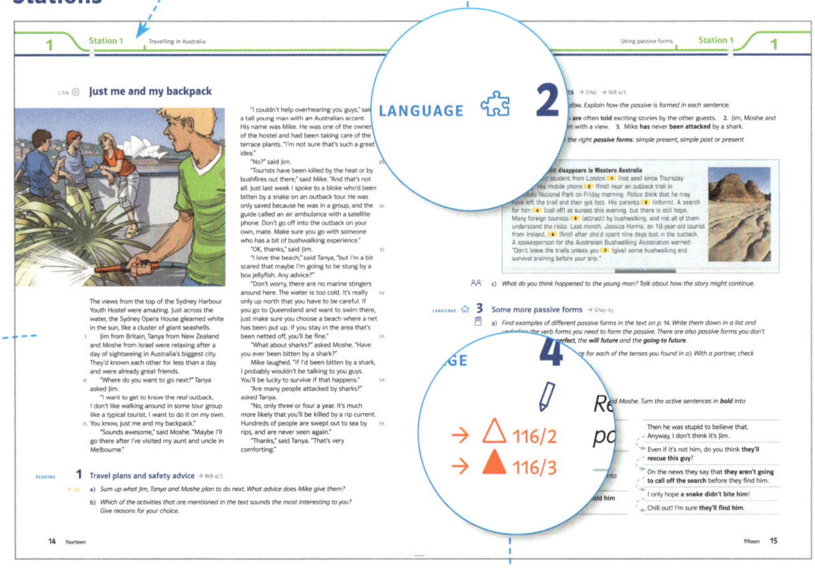

In den Stations jeder Unit findest du deinen neuen Lernstoff, tolle Texte und passende Aufgaben.

Die roten Dreiecke zeigen dir, dass du hinten im Diff pool Hilfen bzw. leichtere oder weiterführende Aufgaben findest.

Unit task

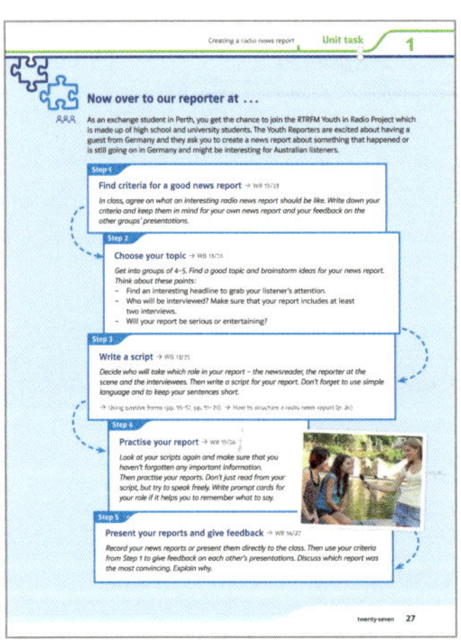

Und so kommt zum Schluss alles zusammen. Anhand der Unit-Aufgabe kannst du deine neu erworbenen Fähigkeiten schrittweise überprüfen und festigen und dabei auf kreative Weise zeigen, was du nun kannst.

Story

Hier findest du spannende Geschichten mit interessanten Aufgaben.

Viewing

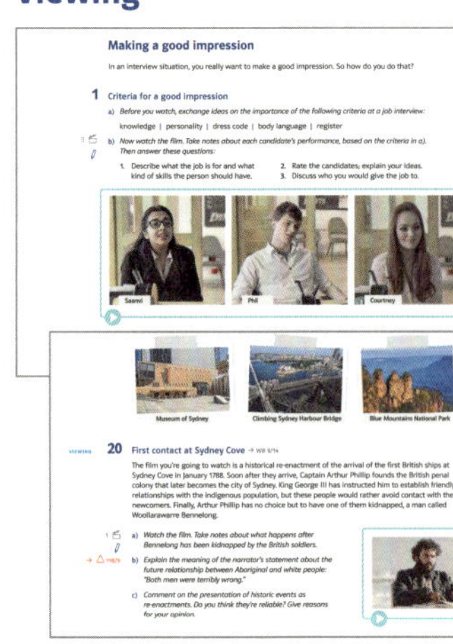

Zwischendurch findest du Aufgaben mit tollen Filmen zum Hör- / Sehverstehen.

Text smart

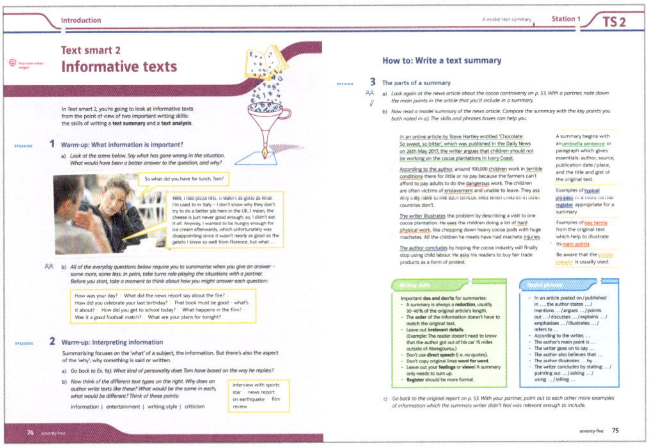

Auf den *Text smart*-Seiten lernst du, wie du mit verschiedenen Textsorten umgehst (z. B. Sachtexten, argumentativen Texten oder auch einem Kurzfilm) und sie im Anschluss für deine eigenen Arbeiten nutzen kannst.

Across cultures

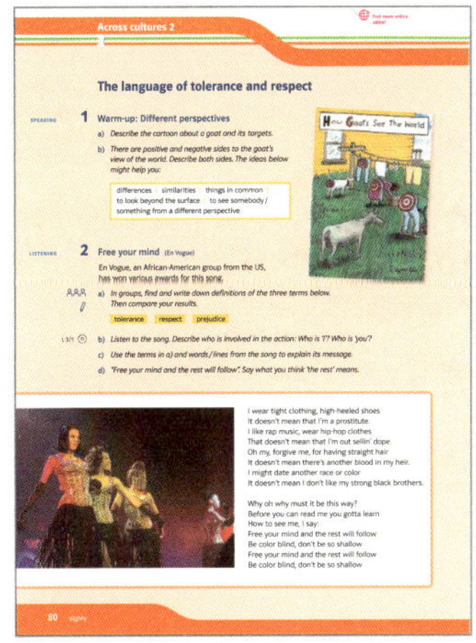

Hier kannst du Themen und Begegnungssituationen in der englischsprachigen Welt mit deinem Alltag vergleichen.

Diff pool

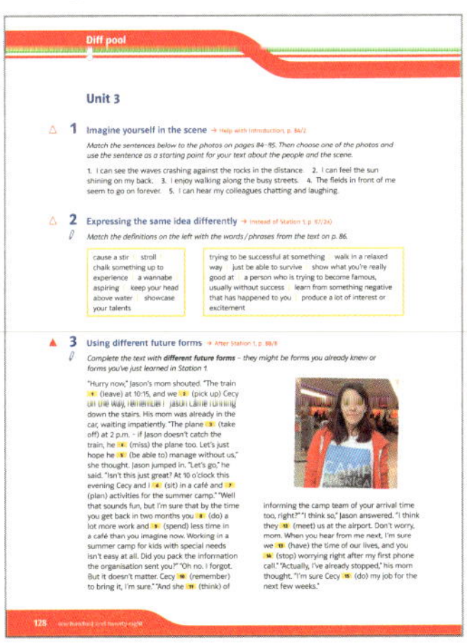

Skills

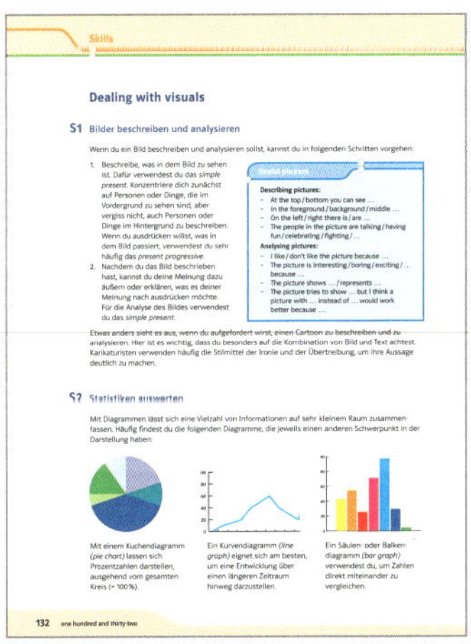

Grammar, Vocabulary

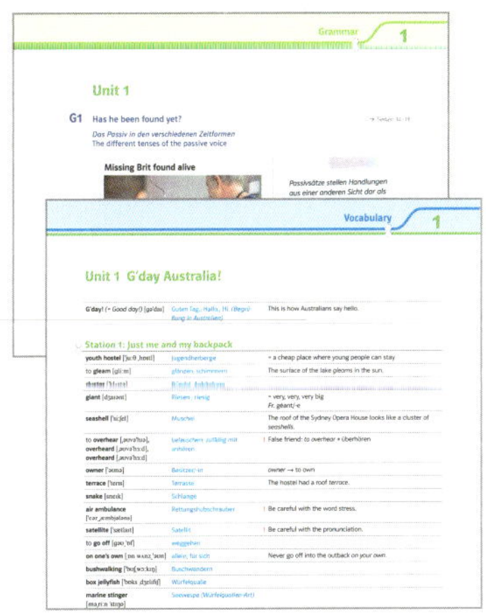

Im hinteren Buchteil stehen dir hilfreiche Anhänge zur Verfügung. Achte auf die Verweise in den Units, die dir sagen, in welchem Anhang du nachschlagen kannst.

Symbole

→ △ 116/1	Verweis auf leichtere Aufgaben / Hilfen im Diff pool
→ ▲ 116/3	Verweis auf anspruchsvollere Aufgaben im Diff pool
→ WB 7/4	Verweis auf eine Übung im Workbook
→ G2	Verweis auf die Grammatik im Anhang
→ S2	Verweis auf die Skills im Anhang
	Partnerarbeit
	Gruppenarbeit
‹ ›	Diese Übung ist fakultativ
[ ]	In Baden-Württemberg verpflichtend zu behandeln

	Schreiben (geschlossen / einfach)
	Schreiben (offen / kreativ)
	Hier entsteht ein Produkt für dein Portfolio.
S1/14	Verweis auf die Schüler-CDs im Workbook (Audio)
L1/19	Verweis auf die Lehrer-CDs (Audio)
	Verweis auf die Lehrer-DVD (Film)
	Code auf www.klett.de eingeben und Zusatzmaterial nutzen
	Übungen, die die Unit task vorbereiten
	Across cultures

Green Line 5 für Klasse 9 an Gymnasien

Herausgeber: Prof. Harald Weisshaar, Bisingen

Autorinnen und Autoren: Jennifer Baer-Engel, Göppingen; Carolyn Jones, Beckenham; Jon Marks, Ventnor; Alison Wooder, Ventnor sowie Cornelia Kaminski, Fulda; Elise Köhler-Davidson, Exeter

Beratung: Paul Dennis, Lahnstein; Cornelia Kaminski, Fulda; Nilgül Karabulut, Aachen; Hartmut Klose, Seevetal; Antje Körber, Merseburg; Jörg Nieswand, Berlin; Jörg Schulze, Dresden sowie Dr. Jan Kulok, Ostfildern

1. Auflage 1 7 6 5 4 | 2025 24 23 22

Alle Drucke dieser Auflage sind unverändert und können im Unterricht nebeneinander verwendet werden. Die letzte Zahl bezeichnet das Jahr des Druckes.

Redaktion: Michael Mattison; Martina Reckart; Lektorat editoria: Cornelia Schaller, Fellbach
Herstellung: Anita Bauch; Anne Leibbrand

Gestaltung: Petra Michel, Essen
Umschlaggestaltung: know idea, Freiburg; Koma Amok, Stuttgart
Illustrationen: Peer Kramer, Düsseldorf; jani lunablau, Barcelona
sowie Christian Dekelver, Weinstadt *(Karten)*; Denise Drews, Zürich *(Time line, Institutions)*
Satz: Satzkiste GmbH, Stuttgart
Reproduktion: Schwaben-Repro, Stuttgart
Druck: Mohn Media Mohndruck GmbH, Gütersloh

Printed in Germany
ISBN 978-3-12-834250-4 (fester Einband)
ISBN 978-3-12-834251-1 (flexibler Einband)

Green Line 5

von
Jennifer Baer-Engel
Carolyn Jones
Jon Marks
Alison Wooder
Cornelia Kaminski
Elise Köhler-Davidson

herausgegeben von
Harald Weisshaar

Ernst Klett Verlag
Stuttgart · Leipzig

Unit 2 The good life?

Text smart 2 Informative texts

Across cultures 2 The language of tolerance and respect

Unit 3 California dreaming

Text smart 3 Argumentative texts

Across cultures 3 Having a voice

Die in diesem Band aufbereiteten Inhalte stellen ein Angebot dar, sie sind nicht obligatorisch durchzunehmen. Maßgeblich für die Auswahl der Texte und Aufgaben ist der Lehrplan Ihres Bundeslandes bzw. Ihr schulinternes Curriculum.

Find more online: mb3js5

The world speaks English

READING

1 A look at three popular English-speaking countries → WB 2/1–2

What do you think people from popular tourist destinations like or dislike about their home countries? Read some personal views as well as the three fact boxes. Then:

1. Sum up the important information for each country. 2. Point out what you find interesting. 3. Give your opinion on positive / negative points that were mentioned. 4. Your turn: In a personal view about Germany, what likes / dislikes would you mention?

SOUTH AFRICA

Population: 55 mil. (25th in the world)
Area: 1.2 million sq. km (25th)
Independent from UK since: 1910
Interesting facts:
- There are 11 official languages, incl. English, Afrikaans, Zulu and Xhosa.
- South Africa has Africa's largest economy.
- 90 % of the world's platinum comes from here, 20 % of the world's gold.
- South Africa has three capital cities: Pretoria (home of the President), Cape Town (seat of the Parliament) and Bloemfontein (seat of the Supreme Court).

L1/1

😊 ❤ Where else can you get beaches AND safaris on the same holiday? I love what nature has given us! Beautiful.

😊 ❤ When I hear my parents talk about how bad the years of racial segregation (= apartheid) were, I'm really proud that their generation was able to forget the bitterness, forget the racism, and move forward. Of course it helped to have a real icon – Nelson Mandela – as the coolest civil rights leader any country could hope for! Proud that he became our first president in free elections back in 1994.

😊 ❤ A lot of people my age are part of a healthy black middle class here. Maybe the media could show more images like this one here of me and my friends: young blacks at a cool café, NOT in a slum.

☹ I don't like the way the rich whites and blacks build high walls around their big, expensive homes. Haven't we already had enough segregation in this country?!

☹ The water is never warm at our beaches. (Tourists, you can thank Antarctica for that!)

Dennis Chiku (student, Cape Town)

INDIA

Population: 1.3 billion (2nd)
Area: 3.3 million sq. km (7th)
Independent from UK since: 1947
Interesting facts:

- 80% of Indians are Hindu, 13% are Muslim, 7% practise other religions.
- The Indian film industry ('Bollywood') is the world's largest, not Hollywood.
- Varanasi is the world's oldest city.
- 2,600 years ago, the doctor Sushruta was the first to conduct plastic surgery.

L1/2

It's a big compliment for India that so many people from Western countries come here to enjoy our ancient culture with its beautiful monuments, colourful traditions and world-famous food. Often, they come to look for spirituality in our Hindu and Buddhist cultures. But sometimes I have to smile to myself when I talk to tourists: At the beginning of their trips, they still have a romantic image of India in their heads; when they leave, that image is mixed with much more reality.

They call India 'the world's largest democracy'. Well, yes and no. It's true that more people vote in free elections here than anywhere else. Something to be proud of!

But guess what: Child labour is still a huge problem, and so is the discrimination and widespread sexual harassment of women. Is that democratic? We still have lots of work to do in the area of human rights. But let's remember that India is an ancient culture with traditions that go back thousands of years. Change doesn't happen overnight in places like this! But it happens, slowly.

After work, I love meeting my friends at some of the cool bars in Delhi. Western visitors are often surprised to find such modern places. (Do they really expect everything to look like a Bollywood film cliché?!)

What I love the most about India? It's so intense! Whenever I return from a trip abroad, I can't help feeling that here, at home, somebody has turned the power back on: Everything is brighter, louder, more chaotic, more beautiful, simply more intense. I love it.

Rani Darshini (IT manager, New Delhi)

AUSTRALIA

Population: 24 million (51st)
Area: 7.7 million sq. km (6th)
Independent from UK since: 1901
Interesting facts:

- The name 'Australia' comes from the Latin word *australis*, meaning 'southern'.
- Most Australians have a British or Irish background (56%). There are also many ethnic Italians and Chinese (both 4.6%), but only 2.5% Aboriginal Australians.
- The world's largest crocodiles, Australia's 'salties', can grow to lengths of six metres!

L 1/3

I know it's a cliché for an Aussie guy to say he loves beaches, sun and surfing, but: that's my life! I turned my love of surfing into a job and now I'm a surf instructor. That's me in the photo, at Bondi Beach, Sydney's most famous beach.

As an instructor, I don't make a lot of money, but: I get a lot of phone numbers if you know what I mean. LOL!

Even though Australia seems to offer it all, I envy my European friends and my cousins from Italy: In Europe, you can get to so many countries so fast! Here, you're kind of stuck at the end of the world.

There's that saying in English: "You can look, but don't touch!" It usually applies to expensive shops, but it applies really well to Uluru (= Ayers Rock) too. The place is sacred to the Aboriginal people, so shouldn't we respect that? The tourists I give surf lessons to always tell me about their plans to see Uluru, and even though I'm not at all a political person, I always mention what this Australian symbol means to the original residents of our country.

You know a party must be good when people from all over the world come all the way to Oz for it! And Sydney's gay Mardi Gras is one AWESOME party. One of my best friends is gay and so I go with him and his mates every year. I'm proud of Australians for being so open to different lifestyles. I mean, why not?

I love heading out into the outback on road trips with friends.

But it seems like all the bushfires out there just get worse and worse each year.

Nick Battiato (surf instructor, Sydney)

READING

2 < What's the language of the future? > → Fact page, p. 268

→ S3, S13

a) *Read the book excerpt below about the English language. Sum up the author's main points.*

b) *Do you think English will remain the world's leading language, its 'lingua franca'? What makes you think so? Justify your opinion with information from the text or from your own personal experience.*

c) *Your turn: Describe changes in the German language you have noticed, e.g. between your grandparents' generation and yours, or between your parents' generation and yours.*

No language has spread as widely as English, and it continues to spread. In the twenty-first century the world is becoming more urban and more middle class, and the success of English is a symptom of this. Increasingly English serves as the lingua franca of business and popular culture. It is dominant in other areas such as shipping, diplomacy, computing, medicine and education. A recent study has suggested that among students in the United Arab Emirates "Arabic is associated with tradition, home, religion, culture, school, arts and social sciences," while English "is symbolic of modernity, work, higher education, commerce, and science and technology."

English has spread because of British colonialism, the technological advances of the Industrial Revolution, American economic and political dominance, and further (mostly American) technological developments in the second half of the twentieth century. Its rise has been assisted by the massive exportation of English as a second language, as well as by the growth of an English-language mass media.

But there may be challenges to the position of English as the dominant world language in the twenty-first century. The main ones could come from Spanish and Mandarin Chinese. Both have more first-language users than English. But at present neither is much used as a lingua franca. The majority of speakers of Mandarin Chinese live in one country, and most Spanish-speakers are in the Americas.

But the main challenges to English may come from within. Two challenges stand out:

First, the use of English in the world's two most populous countries (China and India) means that the language is changing. Some of the changes may prove to be unpleasant for its native speakers, with English losing more and more of its 'English-ness'.

Second, native speakers of English tend to assume that their ability in this language makes it unimportant to learn other languages. The reality is different. British companies often miss out on export opportunities because of a lack of relevant language skills. Also, there is a chance that, within twenty or thirty years, a command of English will be regarded as a basic skill for business, and native speakers of the language will no longer enjoy any competitive advantage.

Excerpt (abridged and adapted) from *The Language Wars: A History of Proper English*, by Henry Hitchings

Unit 1
G'day Australia!

Find more online: vh4e6c

A

VOCABULARY

1 First ideas about Australia

What comes to your mind when you think of Australia? Make notes and compare them within your groups. Together, use your ideas to make a mind map.

SPEAKING

2 Two sides of one country → WB 3/1

→ S1

a) *Work with a partner. One of you looks at the photos above, the other at the photos on p. 266. Describe the impression each of you gets of Australia.*

b) *Compare the two different impressions of Australia with your ideas in Ex. 1. What do you think the 'real' Australia is? Discuss with your partner.*

c) *Look at the photos again. What would be the motivations for showing Australia one way or the other?*

In Unit 1 you learn

… about different aspects of life in Australia. You learn:

- about travelling across the country, Australian history, and about the situation of indigenous people
- how to use passive forms and conditional sentences
- how to create a radio news report

B

C

D

E

SPEAKING

3 < Exciting facts about Australia: A gallery walk >

→ △ 116/1
→ S12

a) *In groups of 3–4, choose one of the topics below and do some research on the internet. The map at the back of your book can give you some ideas to start with.*

a dangerous animal | an interesting city | a remote place to live | an Aboriginal tribe | an interesting fact about Australia's past | a famous Australian actor / sportsperson / band | a popular sport

b) *Design a poster about your topic for a gallery walk. Make sure you include some interesting visuals and information to grab your classmates' attention.*

c) *Present your posters in the classroom. Choose a speaker from your group to answer your classmates' questions. Take turns.*

L1/4 ◎

Just me and my backpack

The views from the top of the Sydney Harbour Youth Hostel were amazing. Just across the water, the Sydney Opera House gleamed white in the sun, like a cluster of giant seashells.

Jim from Britain, Tanya from New Zealand and Moshe from Israel were relaxing after a day of sightseeing in Australia's biggest city. They'd known each other for less than a day and were already great friends.

"Where do you want to go next?" Tanya asked Jim.

"I want to get to know the *real* outback. I don't like walking around in some tour group like a typical tourist. I want to do it on my own. You know, just me and my backpack."

"Sounds awesome," said Moshe. "Maybe I'll go there after I've visited my aunt and uncle in Melbourne."

"I couldn't help overhearing you guys," said a tall young man with an Australian accent. His name was Mike. He was one of the owners of the hostel and had been taking care of the terrace plants. "I'm not sure that's such a great idea."

"No?" said Jim.

"Tourists have been killed by the heat or by bushfires out there," said Mike. "And that's not all. Just last week I spoke to a bloke who'd been bitten by a snake on an outback tour. He was only saved because he was in a group, and the guide called an air ambulance with a satellite phone. Don't go off into the outback on your own, mate. Make sure you go with someone who has a bit of bushwalking experience."

"OK, thanks," said Jim.

"I love the beach," said Tanya, "but I'm a bit scared that maybe I'm going to be stung by a box jellyfish. Any advice?"

"Don't worry, there are no marine stingers around here. The water is too cold. It's really only up north that you have to be careful. If you go to Queensland and want to swim there, just make sure you choose a beach where a net has been put up. If you stay in the area that's been netted off, you'll be fine."

"What about sharks?" asked Moshe. "Have you ever been bitten by a shark?"

Mike laughed. "If I'd been bitten by a shark, I probably wouldn't be talking to you guys. You'll be lucky to survive if that happens."

"Are many people attacked by sharks?" asked Tanya.

"No, only three or four a year. It's much more likely that you'll be killed by a rip current. Hundreds of people are swept out to sea by rips, and are never seen again."

"Thanks," said Tanya. "That's very comforting."

READING

1 Travel plans and safety advice → WB 4/2

→ S3 **a)** *Sum up what Jim, Tanya and Moshe plan to do next. What advice does Mike give them?*

b) *Which of the activities that are mentioned in the text sounds the most interesting to you? Give reasons for your choice.*

LANGUAGE

2 Revision: Passive forms → G1a) → WB 4/3

a) *Look at the sentences below. Explain how the passive is formed in each sentence.*

1. In a youth hostel, you **are** often **told** exciting stories by the other guests. 2. Jim, Moshe and Tanya **were given** a room with a view. 3. Mike **has** never **been attacked** by a shark.

b) *Complete the text with the right **passive forms**: simple present, simple past or present perfect simple.*

Bushwalking Brit disappears in Western Australia

A 19-year-old student from London **1** (not see) since Thursday morning. His mobile phone **2** (find) near an outback trail in Purnululu National Park on Friday morning. Police think that he may have left the trail and then got lost. His parents **3** (inform). A search for him **4** (call off) at sunset this evening, but there is still hope. Many foreign tourists **5** (attract) by bushwalking, and not all of them understand the risks. Last month, Jessica Harris, an 18-year-old tourist from Ireland, **6** (find) after she'd spent nine days lost in the outback. A spokesperson for the Australian Bushwalking Association warned: "Don't leave the trails unless you **7** (give) some bushwalking and survival training before your trip."

c) *What do you think happened to the young man? Talk about how the story might continue.*

LANGUAGE

3 Some more passive forms → G1a)–b)

a) *Find examples of different passive forms in the text on p. 14. Write them down in a list and underline the verb forms you need to form the passive. There are also passive forms you don't know yet: the **past perfect**, the **will future** and the **going-to future**.*

b) *Write a new passive sentence for each of the tenses you found in a). With a partner, check each other's sentences.*

LANGUAGE

4 Our Jim? → WB 4/4, 5/5

→ △ 116/2
→ ▲ 116/3

*Read the chat messages between Tanya and Moshe. Turn the active sentences in **bold** into passive ones.*

Hi Moshe. I heard a young Brit went into the outback, and **nobody has seen him** since. Do you think that's our Jim?

No, don't worry. There are lots of young British tourists around. **That guy at the hostel warned Jim** not to go off alone into the outback. Remember?

Yeah, but what if **somebody else told him** that it was safe before he left?

Then he was stupid to believe that. Anyway, I don't think it's Jim.

Even if it's not him, do you think **they'll rescue this guy**?

On the news they say that **they aren't going to call off the search** before they find him.

I only hope **a snake didn't bite him**!

Chill out! I'm sure **they'll find him**.

READING

5 Living in Australia: Town and country → Fact page, p. 269

Read the information in the box. With a partner, talk about things which are easy to do in Germany, but which would be difficult to do in Australia.

Across cultures

Australia is **one of the most urbanised countries** in the world. About 70 % of all Australians live in cities of more than 100,000 people. That is because there are large parts of the country with **extreme climatic conditions** – very high temperatures and little rain. About 40 % of Australia is said to be uninhabitable, mostly in the country's interior which is often referred to as 'the outback'.

Apart from being urbanised, Australia is the **most sparsely populated country** in the world. Germany would fit into Australia 20 times, but the Australian population is just about 24 million, compared to 80 million in Germany. Many Australians are used to travelling **huge distances**. The journey from Sydney to Perth, for example, takes about five hours by plane.

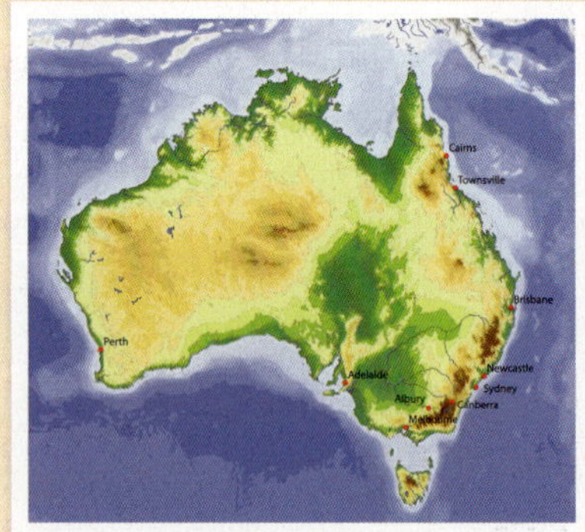

LANGUAGE

6 The passive infinitive → G1c) → WB 5/6

a) *Find the rule: Look at the sentences. How is the passive infinitive formed after modal verbs (can, must, should etc.) and after other verbs (hope, would like, want, expect etc.)?*

1. Some of the most dangerous animals **can be found** in Australia.
   Not all the stories about the outback **should be believed**.
2. If you**'d like to be invited** to a barbecue, be open and talk to Australians.
   I **don't want to be shown** around in a tour group. I'd prefer to look around on my own.

b) *It's a typical day at the Sydney Harbour Youth Hostel. Some guests tell Mike what they want / expect / would like / hope to be done. Later, Mike tells a friend about his day. Make sentences with the **passive infinitive**.*

Example: Some guests **would like to be shown** around the city.

LANGUAGE

7 Rules for Australia's national parks

→ △ 117/4

a) *Australia has more than 500 national parks, which have all introduced rules for visitors. Use the phrases in the box and the* ***passive infinitive*** *to say what must not / should not be done in these parks.*

Example: Dogs **must not be brought** into the park.

bring dogs ✔ | pick flowers | throw away litter | leave tracks | disturb animals | touch or walk on Aboriginal sites | use bush as toilet | damage trees and plants

b) *Explain why you think these rules were introduced.*

LANGUAGE

8 A message from Jim

Complete the text with the right ***passive forms****.*

Hey guys! Still hanging out in Sydney?! You won't believe what I [1] just [2] (tell): A young guy from London got lost in the outback! He [3] last [4] (see) by another tourist just before he started his tour. And guess what: He's my age! Isn't that weird?! Anyway, I hope he [5] (rescue). I'm on day five of my great train journey across Australia and I still love it! We saw some bushfires in the distance, and the smoke [6] (can – smell) from far away. Yesterday I went on my outback tour. You know I [7] (not want – show around) in a group, but then I decided to listen to what we [8] (tell) at the hostel. Lucky me! There was this pretty girl in my group. She was so impressed when I saved her from this weird-looking thorny devil lizard. I [9] (tell) by the guide that they aren't dangerous at all, but Julie thinks I'm her hero now! 😉 We saw lots of kangaroos and there are even camels around! They [10] (bring) to Australia a long time ago, and they seem to enjoy life in the outback. Have fun! – Jim

WRITING

9 How to: Write news headlines

a) *Look at two examples of news headlines and compare them to the sentences that give the same information. Find a rule for how news headlines are written.*

1. Some deadly spiders were found in a hotel in Sydney. → Deadly spiders found in Sydney hotel
2. The record heatwave sparks bushfires all around the country. → Record heatwave sparks bushfires

b) *With your partner, think of three things that happened in your hometown or region (they can be either real or fictional). Think of news headlines that grab the reader's attention.*

WRITING

10 What's in the news? → WB 6/7

→ △ 117/5
→ S5–6

a) *Look at the news photo. What might be the story behind it? Write down your ideas and compare them with your partner's.*

b) *Together, write a news story to go with the photo. Include passive forms and don't forget to think of an interesting headline!*

c) *Exchange your texts with another pair and give each other feedback.*

L1/6 When did your folks get here?

Moshe: Nice of you to let us come to your barbie, Mike.

Mike: No worries. Great you're here. – Hey Cam! Come and meet a couple of new mates. They're staying at the hostel.

Cam: Hey, how're you doing?

Tanya: Hi. I'm Tanya. Nice to meet you.

Cam: You're a Kiwi, right? From your accent? And you're, let me guess … American?

Moshe: No, I'm from Israel. Moshe.

Cam: OK, cool. You know Mike can trace his ancestors right back to the first British convicts in Australia?

Mike: Come on, Cam. Not that joke again! The story is: My ancestor Bill was walking down the road when a man bumped into him. The man was being chased by a police officer because he'd stolen a gold necklace from a jewellery shop. When the man ran off, the police officer stopped Bill and found the gold necklace in his pocket. Then Bill was arrested and given a sentence of 30 years in Australia.

Cam: OK, he was just a victim. But many of the convicts were *real* criminals.

Tanya: What about you, Cam? Where are your ancestors from?

Cam: My parents came here from Vietnam before I was born. Life used to be very hard in Vietnam back then. People were being oppressed, but a lot of them managed to leave, in tiny little boats. You want to talk to somebody whose family has been here a bit longer, try Clifton. – Hey Clifton!

Clifton: Hi. Are you guys bored by one of Cam's extra-long stories?

Cam: Very funny, Cliff. We were talking about when people's ancestors arrived in Oz. When did your folks get here?

Clifton: That'd be around 50,000 years ago, I guess. They call us 'Indigenous Australians' but we came from somewhere else too. Just got here a bit faster than everybody else.

Cam: So where do you guys plan to go next?

Moshe: Good question. I've got an aunt and uncle in Melbourne, and my parents made me promise I'd go there. But I also really want to see the outback, and I've only got a few days left. It's like I'm being pulled in two different directions.

Cam: That's hard! What about you, Tanya?

Tanya: Sydney is perfect for me. You've got beaches, culture, everything I want.

Mike: You should check out the Museum of Sydney, if you haven't already. It tells the whole story, from when some British sea captain had the first prison camp built up to the present day.

Tanya: Yeah, that's definitely on my 'to do' list, but it's being renovated at the moment. So I'll just hang out on the beach.

READING **11** **Understanding the text** → WB 6/8

→ S3

a) *Sum up when and why Mike's and Cam's ancestors came to Australia. What does Clifton tell them about his ancestors?*

b) *Why do you think Mike is irritated when Cam speaks about his ancestor?*

LANGUAGE

12 Find the rule: The passive progressive → G1d)

a) *Look at these examples from the text on p. 18. Explain how the* ***present*** *and* ***past progressive passive*** *are formed.*

1. It's like I'**m being pulled** in two different directions.
2. The man **was being chased** by a police officer.

b) *Find two more examples of the* ***passive progressive*** *in the text.*

LANGUAGE

13 Christmas barbie on Bondi Beach → WB 7/9–10

→ △ 117/6

Read what Fiona, a young Irish tourist, posted on social media. Then turn her post into a report about her trip. Change the ***active*** *progressive forms into* ***passive*** *ones.*

Start like this: When Fiona arrived in Sydney it was summer, but Christmas decorations **were being put up** everywhere …

When I arrived in Sydney it was summer, but people were putting up Christmas decorations everywhere. What a strange experience! Yesterday, on Christmas day, I went to Bondi Beach with some friends and there were already crowds of people. They were planting fake Christmas trees in the sand and they were cooking steaks on an open barbie. Next to us a group of young Australians were singing Christmas songs. Today people are still wearing Santa hats in the city, while on the beach they're cleaning up the leftovers of yesterday's barbie. I just love Christmas on the other side of the world!

LANGUAGE

14 Find the rule: *Let, allow, make* and *have* → G2

a) *Look at the pictures. Explain the difference between* ***let, allow, make*** *and* ***have (sth done)****.*

Moshe's parents **let** him go to Australia. / They **allowed** him **to** go to Australia.

Moshe's father **made** him read about the dangers of travelling in Australia.

Moshe **had** his photo taken by a photographer for his first passport.

b) *Translate the sentences from a) into German. Can you find a German verb with which you can translate all the examples? What other German verbs can you use to translate them?*

c) *Explain the difference between these two sentences:*

1. Moshe **had** his photo **taken**. 2. Moshe **had taken** his photo.

LANGUAGE

15 Preparing for the trip → WB 7/11

→ △ 118/7

*Read more sentences about Moshe's last days before his trip. Fill in **let**, **allow**, **make** or **have**.*

1. Moshe's parents ___ him have a big party with his friends. 2. Moshe ___ his hair cut. 3. His best friend ___ him promise to chat once a week. 4. His teacher ___ him present his tour to the class. 5. Moshe's friends ___ a farewell present made for him. 6. His parents ___ him to take their expensive camera on his trip. 7. His grandparents ___ him tell them everything about Australia. 8. Moshe ___ his new backpack delivered to his house.

READING

16 Australia: A multicultural country

Across cultures

As a nation of immigrants, Australia is **one of the most multicultural countries** in the world. Almost 25% of the population was born overseas – most of them in the UK, New Zealand and China. This is reflected in the country's food, lifestyle and cultural practices. So Sydney, for example, hosts a variety of multicultural festivals and events. One of the most popular ones is **Living in Harmony**, which is a month-long celebration in March, with workshops, talks, cultural tours and many other events.

Most immigrants are able to apply for a **Skilled Migration Visa** because their occupation is one that is needed in Australia. Refugees, however, who come to Australia without a valid visa, are often brought to **immigration detention centres** where they have to wait until their case is cleared. Since Australia's immigration policy is very restrictive, most of them will be sent back to their home countries sooner or later.

a) *Can you imagine why a country like Australia wants to restrict immigration in the way they do?*

b) *Do you know of any multicultural events in your hometown? If so, talk about them with your partner. If not, discuss if you think such events would be a good idea for your hometown.*

LANGUAGE

17 From active to passive: Verbs with two objects → G3 → WB 8/12–13

→ △ 118/8

a) *As you already know, active sentences can have an **indirect object** and a **direct object**. When you change these sentences into the **passive**, the indirect object is often placed at the beginning of the passive sentence. Look at these examples:*

1. The travel agency sent **me brochures** with useful information about Australia.
   → **I** was sent **brochures** with useful information about Australia (by the travel agency).
2. They gave **my ancestor** a **sentence** of 30 years in Australia.
   → **My ancestor** was given a **sentence** of 30 years in Australia.

b) *Change these sentences into the **passive**.*

1. Somebody had told me exciting stories about Bondi Beach before I left for Australia. 2. The people at the hostel offered Moshe a free drink. 3. When I got lost in Sydney, a really friendly guy showed me the way. 4. Nobody has ever told Tanya anything about her ancestors. 5. I don't think they'll give us an invitation to the barbie tonight.

VOCABULARY

18 < Understanding Australian English: No worries, mate! >

L1/8

a) *Listen to the conversation between an Australian and a British teenager. Then match the Australian English words / phrases on the left with their British English equivalents on the right.*

b) *Explain why you think Australian English has developed new words, and also differences in pronunciation, grammar and spelling.*

Aussie | Cheers. | No worries. | Oz | saltie | lollies | tucker | Good on ya! | barbie | mate | G'day! | marine stinger | thongs | How ya going?

sweets | Well done! | saltwater crocodile | friend | food | box jellyfish | Thanks. | Australia | flip-flops | How are you? | You're welcome. | barbecue | Australian | Hello.

SPEAKING

19 Your own special Sydney tour

→ S9

Imagine you're in Australia on a school exchange. Together with other exchange students, you have the chance to organise a tour in and around Sydney. Do some research on the internet about what to see and do there. Include at least five sights / activities inside and two outside the city. Then present your tour to the class. After the presentations, vote on your 'Top 3' highlights in and around Sydney. Give reasons for your choice.

Museum of Sydney

Climbing Sydney Harbour Bridge

Blue Mountains National Park

VIEWING

20 First contact at Sydney Cove → WB 9/14

The film you're going to watch is a historical re-enactment of the arrival of the first British ships at Sydney Cove in January 1788. Soon after they arrive, Captain Arthur Phillip founds the British penal colony that later becomes the city of Sydney. King George III has instructed him to establish friendly relationships with the indigenous population, but these people would rather avoid contact with the newcomers. Finally, Arthur Phillip has no choice but to have one of them kidnapped, a man called Woollarawarre Bennelong.

1

→ △ 118/9

a) *Watch the film. Take notes about what happens after Bennelong has been kidnapped by the British soldiers.*

b) *Explain the meaning of the narrator's statement about the future relationship between Aboriginal and white people: "Both men were terribly wrong."*

c) *Comment on the presentation of historic events as re-enactments. Do you think they're reliable? Give reasons for your opinion.*

L 1/9

The land owns us

Cindy Carter is an artist who helps to run an Aboriginal arts centre.

Sue: You have some amazing pictures here. If I hadn't seen them for myself, I wouldn't have believed how beautiful they are. Can you tell me a little about what's so special about Aboriginal art?

Cindy: Well, it looks great, of course, but its true value is its cultural meaning. The pictures tell the Dreaming stories we're told by our mothers and fathers about the land and how to live on it.

Sue: So these stories pass on important knowledge and cultural values to later generations. What can you tell me about this picture?

Cindy: This is a bush potato Dreaming. The lines here show how the plant grows underground. When the soil is wet, the potatoes are close to the surface, but when the soil is dry, you have to dig deeper to find them.

Sue: What about this painting?

Cindy: This is an emu Dreaming, which the artist learned from his grandfather. You can see the emu's tracks right here. The men used to hunt the emu by following these tracks. If I wanted to, I could use this information to help me hunt emus now.

Sue: So did these stories and paintings use to teach people how to survive in the harsh landscape of Australia?

Cindy: That's right. And if my ancestors hadn't had them, they also wouldn't have been able to communicate with people who spoke different languages. People travelled across the country and understood the stories, landscapes and traditions of other people from their pictures. They didn't need a common language, like English is now. – This is Charlie, another of our artists.

Charlie: I'm painting my father's land. The lines here between the mountains are Dreaming tracks. These dark parts here are the living water.

Sue: Is this your land here then, in your painting?

Charlie: Understand that for us, we don't own the land. The land owns us. So I belong to this land here and these stories belong to my land. This Dreaming belongs to my family. If I don't pass on the art to our children, they won't learn the Dreaming.

Sue: So if you hadn't been taught this, you wouldn't have been able to start painting it?

Charlie: That's right. I see you got the idea.

READING

21 Understanding the text

→ S3

a) *In your own words, sum up the reasons why Aboriginal art is so important.*

b) *Explain what Charlie means when he says, "The land owns us."*

c) *Compare what you've learned about Dreaming stories with the way we pass on important knowledge and cultural values in Germany.*

LANGUAGE

22 Conditional sentences → G4 → WB 10/15

a) *Look at the examples of conditional sentences types 1, 2 and 3. Say what the verb forms for the **if-clause** and the **main clause** are.*

1. If you **want** to buy some Aboriginal art, you**'ll find** many different styles to choose from.
2. If an Indigenous Australian from 1,000 years ago **saw** a modern Aboriginal painting, she**'d understand** it. 3. If Australia **hadn't been** a British colony, English **wouldn't have become** the main language.

b) *Compare the sentences and explain why you need each type of conditional sentence.*

c) *Find more examples of conditional sentences in the text on p. 22.*

READING

23 The Stolen Generations

Read the information in the box. With a partner, talk about what effects the white policy might have had on the 'Stolen Generations'.

Across cultures

From the beginning of the 20th century right into the 1970s, a large number of Aboriginal children of mixed descent – most of them with a white father – were taken away from their families and brought up by white foster families, in orphanages or church missions. Their names were often changed, and they were forbidden to speak their traditional languages. With this policy, the Australian government wanted to stop the children's families and communities from passing on their Aboriginal culture and identity. It was only in 2008 that Australian Prime Minister Kevin Rudd made a **formal apology** to the Stolen Generations.

"I grew up feeling alone, a black girl in a white world, and I resented them for trying to make me white but they couldn't wash away thousands of years of Dreaming." – *Aunty Rhonda Collard*

LANGUAGE

24 An artist from the Stolen Generations → WB 10/16

→ △ 119/10

a) *Read the article about the artist Carrie McDonald, who was a member of the Stolen Generations. Use the right verb forms to make **conditional sentences type 3**.*

"My art is very important to me because it helps me to find connections to the land and to my own family history. If I **1** (not join) the arts centre and met the people here, I **2** (not find out) about where I really come from. If I **3** (know) my mother and my grandmother, they **4** (teach) me so much. But I was taken away when I was very young and was placed with a white foster family. I didn't get the chance to learn about my family's Dreamings, but the senior community members here have given me permission to paint the stories as I imagine them. If I **5** (not have) that permission, I **6** (not start) painting. I think it would have been disrespectful. I paint the Dreaming of the crocodile. I've been told by the elders that the crocodile is a guardian of its territory. It may travel away but it'll always come back. So that's why I paint it. I've come back to the place of my family. I'm sure that if I **7** (not return) to this place, I **8** (not be able) to start painting."

b) *Explain how art has helped Carrie to deal with her childhood experiences.*

LISTENING 25 A radio news report: Protests on Australia Day

Every year on 26 January, Australia Day, which marks the anniversary of the arrival of the British in 1788, is celebrated with outdoor concerts, barbecues, sports competitions, festivals and fireworks. Not all Australians, however, think it's right to celebrate – among them many Aboriginal people.

L1/10

a) *Listen to a radio news report and take notes on what is said about protests on Australia Day.*

→ S7

b) *Can you understand the reasons for protesting against Australia Day or do you think everybody should celebrate their country together? Justify your opinion.*

LANGUAGE 26 Find the rule: *Used to* + infinitive → G5 → WB 11/17–19

→ 119/11

a) *Look at the sentences with* ***used to*** *below. Explain what it means and how you use it.*

1. How **did** the Aboriginal people **use to live** before the arrival of the British? – They **used to live** as nomads.
2. What language **did** they **use to speak**? – They **didn't use to have** a common language. There were more than 250 different languages, but most of them are no longer spoken today.

b) *Your turn: With your partner, talk about things you used to do or like, but don't any more, and what you do or like now.*

Examples: I **used to listen** to music a lot, but now I prefer to play computer games.
I **didn't use to like** healthy food, but now I think it's OK.

READING 27 ‹ A poem: If it wasn't for the footprints › Zelda Quakawoot → WB 12/20

L1/11

If it wasn't for the footprints
we wouldn't know about 'before'
Australia's history we have today
would not make sense any more.

If it wasn't for the footsteps
which created the path we share
our survival in this landscape
would lead us to nowhere.

If it wasn't for the footpaths
still here from long ago
our heritage in writing
would still reflect our woes.

If it wasn't for the footprints
which were made into the sand
the footprints of first Australians;
our Aboriginal clans.

If it wasn't for their footsteps
which carved the land and lore
Australians could not know a history
from this land that was 'before'.

a) *What do you think is the main message of the poem? Talk about your ideas with a partner; then share them in class.*

b) *Read the poem again. Explain each verse in your own words.*

MEDIATION

28 Discovering Aboriginal Australia

→ S10

a) *You're planning a holiday in Australia with your family. In an online forum, you find useful tips about where to go and what to do. You've just read an interesting article on the internet and you want to share it with the other users in the forum. Write a post in English with the most important information.*

5 Tipps für Backpacking in „Aboriginal Australia“

1 Es gibt viele Webseiten und Bücher über das Australien der Aborigines. Informiere dich über die Geschichte der Orte, die du besuchen möchtest. Schärfe auch deinen Blick für das heutige Leben der Aborigines. Viele Reiseseiten stellen Aborigines anders dar, als sie sind. 60 Prozent der Aborigines leben in Städten, es gibt Probleme mit der gesellschaftlichen Gleichstellung und es gibt auch die traditionell lebenden Aborigines. Mach dir bewusst, dass viele Seiten Stereotype erschaffen, warum auch immer.

2 Viele Aborigines bieten Touren und Führungen an, die besonders spannend sind, weil du das Land aus den Augen der Ureinwohner kennenlernst. Nutze die Zeit und stelle den Menschen alle deine Fragen, die dir unter den Nägeln brennen – wo bekommst du bessere Antworten als hier?

3 So, wie du in Berlin „echte“ Mauerstückchen kaufen kannst, wird auch in Australien viel Geld mit „echten“ Aborigine-Souvenirs gemacht. Wenn du also ein Andenken kaufen möchtest, tue dies bei Aborigines. Du bekommst dann originale Kunst der Ureinwohner und unterstützt ihre Arbeit.

4 Ein Wasserfall zum Reinspringen, ein Felsen zum Sonnen? Schnell begehen Touristen Fehler, die die Ureinwohner verärgern und heilige Stätten entweihen. Informiere dich deshalb vorher, was erlaubt ist. Nicht nur bekannte Naturdenkmäler wie der Uluru gehören zu den heiligen Stätten der Aborigines. Auch unscheinbare Fleckchen Erde, auf denen du am liebsten die Picknickdecke ausbreiten würdest, könnten kulturelle Bedeutung haben.

5 Die Aborigines folgen einer Art Naturreligion, die mit dem englischen Wort „Dreamtime“ bzw. dem deutschen Wort „Traumzeit“ übersetzt wird. Dies sind aber irreführende Begriffe, da dies alles mit dem nächtlichen Träumen nichts zu tun hat. Das „Träumen“ bezeichnet hier viel mehr ein Begreifen und Nutzen der Welt und ihrer Zusammenhänge. Das Weltverständnis der Aborigines zu kennen stellt eine echte Bereicherung beim Reisen durch Australien dar. Viele Dinge wirst du anders sehen und erleben als Reisende, die diesen Teil Australiens gar nicht kennen.

Source: Reiseblog „Travelicia“ (abridged)

b) *Research a place that is important for Indigenous Australians. Collect information about where it is and why it's so important. Prepare a 3-minute talk about your place.*

SPEAKING

29 ‹ Looking back at Unit 1: An Australia quiz › → WB 12/21

a) *Write down ten questions you want to ask about Australia. You can use the information you learned in the unit and do some internet research too.*

b) *Now divide your class up into two groups. Take turns to ask your questions from a). For each correct answer your group gets one point. Make sure that nobody asks the same question twice!*

How to structure a radio news report

For the unit task you're going to create your own radio news report. This page will give you some useful phrases and help you with the structure of a radio news report.

1 Shark attack on Australian beach

L1/12

a) *Listen to the headline of a news report about a shark attack on Australia's East Coast. Does it make you want to listen to the report? Explain why, why not.*

b) *Now listen to the full report. Take notes about the following topics:*

what happened | when, where and why it happened | who was involved

c) *Write down how a news report is structured. Include information on the different roles in a report (newsreader, etc.).*

d) *Look at the useful phrases box. Then listen to the news report again. Write down which phrases you can hear.*

Writing skills

- While the headline for a written news report needs to be short and give the key words of the story, the headline for an oral news report is often a full sentence. **Headlines for radio news reports** are most effective when the voice and words really grab the listener's attention.
- Remember to follow the **three C's** of news writing: being clear, concise and correct. Use simple language and keep your sentences short.

2 Write a short interview

→ △ 119/12

Work with a partner. Each of you takes one of the roles below. Then write another interview for the report in Ex. 1 and present it to the class.

Reporter at the scene: Ask the lifeguard what can be done about the shark attacks.

Lifeguard: Tell the reporter what can be done, e.g. nets to prevent sharks from coming to the beach.

Useful phrases

Newsreader: Hello / Good morning to all our listeners out there. | Welcome to … news. | You won't believe what happened … | We've just received news of … | Our reporter at the scene has the full story. | Let's hear from (name), who is reporting live at the scene. | Now over to you, (name). | That's all for now. Thanks for listening / staying with us.
Reporter at the scene: Here I am at … | With me here is … | Back to you in the studio, (name).

3 ‹ Same story, different radio station ›

L1/13

a) *Listen to the beginning of another report about the same news story. Point out how it is different from the first report.*

b) *Talk about the advantages and disadvantages of each style of news report. Explain which you prefer.*

Now over to our reporter at ...

As an exchange student in Perth, you get the chance to join the RTRFM Youth in Radio Project which is made up of high school and university students. The Youth Reporters are excited about having a guest from Germany and they ask you to create a news report about something that happened or is still going on in Germany and might be interesting for Australian listeners.

Step 1

Find criteria for a good news report → WB 13/23

In class, agree on what an interesting radio news report should be like. Write down your criteria and keep them in mind for your own news report and your feedback on the other groups' presentations.

Step 2

Choose your topic → WB 13/24

Get into groups of 4–5. Find a good topic and brainstorm ideas for your news report. Think about these points:

- Find an interesting headline to grab your listener's attention.
- Who will be interviewed? Make sure that your report includes at least two interviews.
- Will your report be serious or entertaining?

Step 3

Write a script → WB 13/25

Decide who will take which role in your report – the newsreader, the reporter at the scene and the interviewees. Then write a script for your report. Don't forget to use simple language and to keep your sentences short.

→ Using passive forms (pp. 15–17; pp. 19–20) → How to structure a radio news report (p. 26)

Step 4

Practise your report → WB 13/26

Look at your scripts again and make sure that you haven't forgotten any important information. Then practise your reports. Don't just read from your script, but try to speak freely. Write prompt cards for your role if it helps you to remember what to say.

Step 5

Present your reports and give feedback → WB 14/27

Record your news reports or present them directly to the class. Then use your criteria from Step 1 to give feedback on each other's presentations. Discuss which report was the most convincing. Explain why.

Nona and me

S1/3–6 L1/14–17

WRITING

1 Before you read

Have you ever had a guilty conscience because you didn't stand up for a friend? What were your reasons for not doing so? Take five minutes to write a short letter to yourself (real or fictional) in which you describe your experience. Put your letter in an envelope and give it to your teacher. Your teacher will give you back your letter, unopened, after you've read and discussed the following story.

I see her across the school yard. It's like a ghost passing. One second she's there and then she's gone, following Mrs Reid around the corner in the direction of the front office. Was it really her? I replay the moment. That glimpse of her determined, upright walk. Her quiet strength. A lot about her has changed, but that hasn't. It has to be her. Something jabs me in the ribs. "Hello, Miss Daydream!" Selena is waving her hand in front of my face. "Rosie, you with us?"

"Sorry."

We are sitting in our usual spot, on the benches near the basketball court. Just close enough to see the boys playing, not so close that we seem desperate. It is May; the wet season has just ended, and everything glows green. Selena sighs, as if having to repeat herself for a small child. "I was saying, do you want to get ready at my house?"

Anya chimes in. "For Libby's party."

"What time?"

"Whenever your mum can drop you into town."

I hate living out at Yirrkala. It's only a twenty-minute drive from town but it might as well be a different planet. "I probably can't get there till after five. Mum will be working."

"Okay, but no later than that if we want to you-know-what."

Selena grins conspiratorially. She wants to go fridging before the party. She's tried to persuade us before, but this time she's got an address: the house of some government guy who travels for work. He doesn't have a dog. She's sure we won't get caught, but even the idea of it makes me nervous. I've never drunk alcohol before, let alone stolen it. I look away.

"So, are you in?"

Anya says, "I am." She looks smug. We used to be good friends, before Selena.

They're both looking at me now, waiting. My stomach churns, but I say, "Yeah. Of course."

The bell goes. We pick up our bags and reluctantly walk to class. We move into the History classroom and take our seats. It goes Anya, Selena, me.

Miss Fuller writes in big letters on the board, then turns to face us. "Federation." Why do teachers always do that? It's up there in capital letters. We can read.

There's a knock at the door. And then Mrs Reid is showing her in. It *is* her. I knew it. It's Nona. I want to jump up and hug her but I stay glued to my seat. Nona raises her dark eyes and locates me in the sea of uniformed students. She gives me a shy smile. I feel Selena turn in the seat next to me. I don't need to look to see her disbelieving expression: *You know her?*

Nona is wearing a basketball singlet, stretchy purple shorts and worn white thongs. Her legs are tall, black and skinny. Her feet look strong. On her arms, I notice a few dark scars near her shoulders, and wonder what they're from. Her long wavy hair is freshly washed and tied back in a careful ponytail. She could be any Yolnu girl in this school. But she's not.

There's only one desk empty so she sits up the front. Mrs Reid smiles warmly at the class. "Everyone, this is Nona. She's joining 10B. She's just moved back here from Elcho Island. Please make her feel welcome." She gives Nona a reassuring nod. "You need anything, just come and see me." Nona nods back and Mrs Reid heads out.

Miss Fuller smiles at Nona, then starts an endless talk about federation. It's obvious she's practised this at home. Miss Fuller is young and enthusiastic, probably came straight from university to Nhulunbuy.

Miss Fuller hands out comprehension sheets, telling us to pick out the key dates and put them on a timeline. She hesitates at Nona's desk, then squats down next to her, lowering her voice. "Do you want to do this? If you don't want to I can give you an exercise to do with Luke and Ali."

Ali has just arrived here. He's from Iraq. Until now, Luke has been the only Yolnu kid in our class. Miss Fuller gives them special tasks because their English isn't great. Half the time Luke's away. The rest he sits there, silent. Sometimes he just walks out. Miss Fuller never asks him where he's going or tells him to come back. She doesn't know how to deal with Luke.

Ali smiles at Nona, but Luke just keeps staring out the window. I can see one of his skinny feet tapping to a silent beat. I wonder if Nona and Luke are related and, if so, how.

Nona reaches out and takes the comprehension sheet. Miss Fuller smiles nervously. "Okay, great." She gives Nona a pen and paper. Nona's voice used to be full of laughter, like even her insides were grinning. But now it comes out soft and flat. "You got a pencil?"

"Sorry?"

"Pencil."

"Oh. Yes. Sure."

Miss Fuller gets her one. Selena smirks. She writes on the side of her exercise book, nudging it over so I can read. *What are we – in primary school?* I force a smile. I tell myself the words are harmless, just a joke.

I watch Nona as she starts to work. She begins by colouring in the holes in the letters – the a's, the o's, the d's, the e's. By the end of the lesson they are all filled in. I lean forward and see she's also drawn in the left margin, decorating it with swirls and … are they turtles? I can't quite make it out from my desk. It's beautiful, though.

Selena catches me looking and underlines her previous words: *primary school*.

Miss Fuller passes Nona and sees what she's doing. I wait for a reaction but our teacher just nods and smiles and walks on.

Selena whispers, "Can you imagine if one of us did that?" Selena always talks like that. Us and them. Näpaki and Yolnu. She's right, though. If a Näpaki kid – a non-Aboriginal kid – did that Miss Fuller would be telling them to start working or stay and do it in detention.

Selena articulates the question this time. "You know her?" I want to say yes. I want to say, *She's my sister. She was my best friend.* But I know Selena would find that crazy and I don't want to explain. So I say, "She knows my mum."

"From the art centre?"

I nod, convincing myself it's easier this way.

The bell goes and we throw our timelines onto Miss Fuller's desk as we stream out to our next classes. I feel someone touch my arm. I look down and see a dark-brown hand. Long fingernails. A pale palm.

I hear her voice say, *"Yapa."* Sister. And suddenly I'm six years old again. We're in my bedroom holding hands. I look up at Nona. "Mum said you were back."

"Got here last week."

"Are you living at your grandma's?"

Nona shakes her head. "In Birritjimi. My auntie's house. You remember Tina? She just had a baby, a little boy. We're living with them – me, my mum and the smalls."

I smile at the mention of her two little sisters; they're only a couple of years younger than us, but we always called them the smalls

to make ourselves feel bigger. Nona smiles shyly back at me. There is so much to say. So much I want to know. But I can feel Selena and Anya watching us. They're standing outside their classroom, waiting to go in. Selena makes eye contact and frowns, as if to say, *What are you doing?* I remember what school was like before she came. Me and Anya, always on the periphery. Not a real group, just two loners clinging desperately together. It was years ago but it was yesterday. I feel sick. I turn back to Nona. My words come out abruptly. "I'd better go. See you around."

I see Nona's face fall, a crumple of confusion. And then I'm walking away. I can hear a voice in my head. *Chicken-shit.* But I keep walking.

The school bus is a cool, air-conditioned bubble. There's only one road from town to Yirrkala. I must drive down it a thousand times a year, but today every patch of scrub is etched with memories. There's the turn-off to Rainbow Cliff, where we painted ourselves in gapan, smearing the white and orange clay on our bodies in made-up designs. And the airport road that took us to weekend swims at Goanna Lagoon. And the spot where I first tasted guku, sweet bush honey scooped straight from the tree into my waiting mouth. Like the road, all my memories lead in one direction. Nona. We're close to home now. The parade of signs begins.

Welcome to Yirrkala.
Don't drink and drive.
You are now on Aboriginal land – do you have your access permit?

The bus slows as we turn left into the community. We lurch to a stop outside Yirrkala School. I thank Tony, the driver, and get off. The heat engulfs me. I walk home, over the crest of the hill.

Before I know it, I'm down the hill and I'm home. In the lounge room I turn the ceiling fan on to three and sink into my favourite armchair. I close my eyes. Nona's face appears again, her features etched with hurt.

"Hey, darling."

My eyes flick open to see Mum ducking in the back door. She moves through the kitchen, to the lounge, and turns the fan down. "It's not that hot."

I sit up, guiltily. "Shouldn't you still be at work?"

"Forgot my lunch so I just popped home. Lucky we live next door, hey?"

I check the clock on the wall. "Mum, it's three o'clock."

"Yeah, it'll be a late lunch."

Mum picks up her forgotten sandwich. "I've had the craziest day, driving all over looking for Waltjan. She was supposed to come in and sign these prints, but she's nowhere to be found. I went out to Ski Beach and Birritjimi … oh, I saw Gulwirri there."

The mention of Nona's mum grabs my attention.

"She seems much better. Well, better than before they left. She said Nona's back at school. Did you see her there?"

"Yeah."

"It's great she's studying again."

I think of Nona's coloured-in letters and swirly margin. "Yeah, it is."

"Do you want to have her over one day? She could catch the bus home with you after school."

"Maybe."

I can feel Mum's eyes on me, questioning. She glances at the clock. "I'd better run."

The screen door bangs shut behind her. I'm grateful she's gone. I turn the fan back up to three again.

by Clare Atkins (abridged and adapted)

READING

2 Understanding the story

a) *In groups of three, say if you like or don't like the story. Then compare your first reactions in class. Is there a difference in the reactions of girls and boys?*

b) *Divide up the story into three parts. Each of you finds a heading for your part and sums up what happens in your own words.*

READING

3 Difficult relationships

→ S3

a) *Point out what the story tells you about the relationship between Rosie and Nona. Why does Rosie feel awkward when she meets Nona at school for the first time?*

b) *Read your letter from Ex. 1 again. From what you've experienced yourself, can you understand Rosie's behaviour and feelings? Take five minutes to consider any differences or parallels; then comment on Rosie's behaviour in class.*

c) *How does Miss Fuller, the teacher, treat Aboriginal and non-Aboriginal students differently? Contrast her behaviour with Selena's reaction towards Nona.*

WRITING

4 Rosie and Selena

a) *What impression do you get of Rosie's and Selena's characters? Each of you writes a characterisation about one of the girls. Look at the skills box if you need help.*

b) *Exchange texts with your partner and give each other feedback. Do you agree with your partner's characterisation of Rosie / Selena?*

c) *Role play: Rosie wants to talk to Selena about her conflict. How do you think Selena will react? Make notes. Then one of you is Rosie and one of you is Selena. Practise your role play and present it in class.*

Writing skills

These steps can help you to write a **characterisation**:

1. Read the text carefully. Remember that we know about the characters not only from what's said about them in the text, but also from how they act and behave towards other people.
   Example: *My words come out abruptly. "I'd better go. See you around."* (lines 175–176) → You see that Rosie is insecure because she doesn't dare to talk to Nona when her friends are around.
2. Write a **short introduction** in which you present the character and his / her situation.
3. Organise your notes into **short paragraphs**. Every paragraph should deal with one characteristic feature. Don't forget to refer to or quote the text.
4. Write a **conclusion** that sums up the results of your analysis.

WRITING

5 ‹ Write the next scene › → WB 15/28

→ S5-6

a) *How do you think Rosie will behave towards Nona when they meet at school the next day? Will she talk to her or stick with Selena and Anya? Make a plan for the next scene. Keep in mind what you found out about the characters in Ex. 3 and 4. Then write your version of the scene.*

b) *Present your texts in small groups. Choose the version you all like best and improve it further. Then read out your text to the class.*

c) *If possible, read the whole novel and compare your ideas with the original version.*

LISTENING

1 The missing bag

L 1/19

a) *Listen to the conversation about a missing bag in Port Arthur. Take notes and write the report that the security man gives his boss about what happened. Use* ***passive forms****.*

Start like this: This young woman says her bag **was stolen** when she went on a ghost tour. It's bright red and new. She …

b) *Write a different ending for the story. Where else could the woman's bag have been?*

LANGUAGE

2 Port Arthur, Tasmania[1] → WB 18/1

a) *Fill in the correct* ***passive forms****: simple present, simple past or present perfect simple.*

Port Arthur **1** (found) in the 1830s as a penal colony for Britain's worst criminals. The conditions under which convicts **2** (keep) there were very harsh. During the day they **3** (force) to do heavy work such as cutting down huge trees; at night they **4** (lock up[2]) in their cells[3], alone and without light. Port Arthur **5** (also know) as a prison from which nobody could escape.

More than 30 of the original buildings, many of which **6** (build) by the convicts, **7** (save). Some of the buildings **8** (even renovate) so that they look just like they did in the 1800s. Guided walking tours for tourists **9** (offer) during the day and at night visitors **10** (show) around on mysterious ghost tours. Fresh Tasmanian food **11** (serve) in the bistro.

b) *Do you know any other prisons that are now tourist destinations? Have you ever visited one? Give your opinion on former[4] prisons as tourist destinations.*

LANGUAGE

3 Warning! → WB 19/2

a) *Put in the* ***passive infinitive*** *after modals and after other verbs.*

Are you planning on going to Australia for a few weeks or months? Then you should **1** (warn) because you may fall in love with the country! When you arrive, expect **2** (welcome) by warm, sunny weather even in the winter. Winters are usually short and not too cold. Aussies love sports so you can hope **3** (include) in everything from surfing to horseback riding to tennis. You should **4** (prepare) to try out all kinds of new things because there are so many things that can **5** (do) and sights that should **6** (see) on the world's largest island. Remember – it's lined by 7,000 beaches! If you hope **7** (invite) to a party, you probably will be because the Australian lifestyle is very relaxed. And if you want **8** (give) a job, it should be easier in Australia than in many other countries. After a few weeks in Oz, you might ask your parents to send you the rest of your belongings because you don't want to leave!

b) *What 'good warnings' can you give to people who visit Germany? Write three sentences with the* ***passive infinitive****.*

1 Tasmania [tæz'meɪniə] Tasmanien *(größte Insel Australiens und australischer Bundesstaat)* | **2 to lock sb up** [ˌlɒk 'ʌp] jmdn. einschließen | **3 cell** [sel] Zelle | **4 former** ['fɔːmə] frühere/-r/-s

LANGUAGE

4 What did she use to do? → WB 19/3

Linda stopped doing some things and started doing others. Write sentences about her.

She stopped: arguing with the elders | ignoring stories about her ancestors | being lazy at school | fighting with her younger brothers and sisters | making music | **She started:** passing on her family's stories | getting involved in an indigenous association | hosting bushwalks for other indigenous teens | helping her mother with her brothers and sisters | doing sports

Example: Linda **used to** argue with the elders. She never **used to / didn't use to** …

LANGUAGE

5 At the Melbourne International Film Festival

a) *Alice Ashton was discovered as Australia's best new actress in 2017. Look how her life has changed since then. Use the* ***present progressive passive*** *to write sentences about her.*

Example: A: In this picture from last year, I'm driving myself to the festival.
But this year you can see me as …

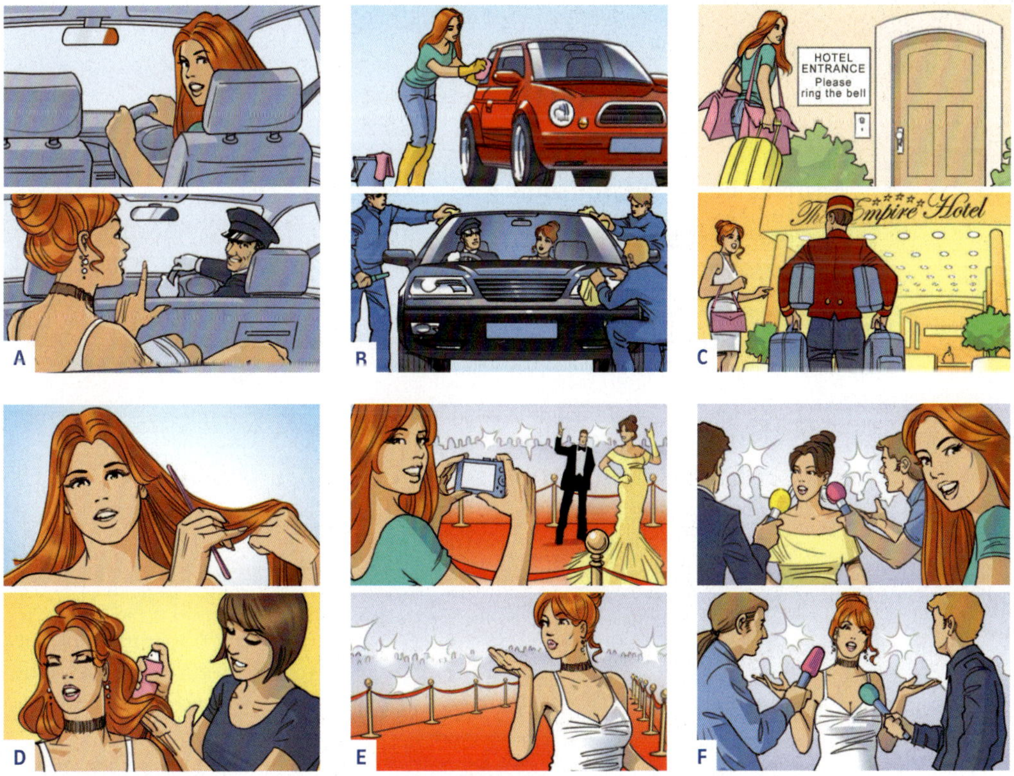

b) *What was happening before the festival? Change the sentences into the* ***past progressive passive****.*

1. Some people were hanging up posters. 2. Others were setting up the lights. 3. Some people were preparing the foods and drinks. 4. Some people were rolling out the red carpet. 5. Others were giving interviews. 6. People from the media were taking lots of photos.

WRITING

6 The latest news!

a) *In groups of four, choose one of the photos and think of the news story behind it:*

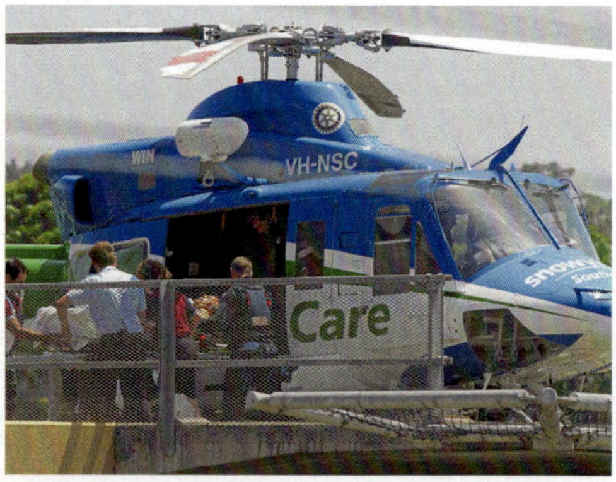

b) *Each of you takes one of these roles for a radio news report: the newsreader, the reporter at the scene, interviewee 1, interviewee 2. Together, think of an introduction that grabs the listener's attention and write the interviews.*

c) *Practise your news report and present it in class.*

LANGUAGE

7 Simon's bushwalking tour → WB 20/4

a) *Read what happened to Simon, a young American tourist, on his tour in the Australian outback. Complete the sentences with the right tenses to make* ***conditional sentences type 3****.*

1. Simon got to the meeting place on time. If he ___ (be) late, he ___ (miss) the bushwalking tour.
2. Simon was glad that he'd been warned to bring enough water. He ___ (be) very thirsty if the guide ___ (not remind) him.
3. Simon went off on his own. If he ___ (stay) with the group, he ___ (not cause) so much trouble.
4. Simon bumped into Amy, a young Australian woman with bushwalking experience. If he ___ (not lose) his way, he ___ (not meet) her.
5. Simon didn't know it, but the guide called off the bushwalk. If Simon ___ (find out), he ___ (have) a guilty conscience.
6. The guide called the air ambulance to help Simon if he was hurt. He ___ (call off) the search immediately if he ___ (know) that Simon was safe.
7. The whole day ___ (be) disastrous if Amy ___ (not return) her new friend to the meeting place.
8. Simon ___ (feel) even more awkward when he returned if the guide ___ (not be) so relieved to see him.

b) *Think back on Unit 1 and make sentences about what would have been different in Australia if something else hadn't happened. One of you starts with an if-clause, the other finishes with a main clause.*

Start like this: If the Europeans **hadn't landed** in Australia … / If the Aboriginal children **hadn't been taken away** from their families …

c) *Your turn: Now write three sentences about yourself. What would have been different if something else hadn't happened?*

LANGUAGE

8 Aboriginal history → WB 20/5

a) *Put in **let**, **make** or **have**. Make sure you use the correct tense.*

1. For several decades[1], the British didn't ___ Aboriginal children of mixed descent stay with their families. 2. The British ___ many of them put in orphanages. 3. There they ___ them live like white children. 4. The government also ___ the Aboriginal people leave their land. 5. If they didn't want to go, the British ___ them removed. 6. Finally in the 1960s, the British ___ the Aboriginal people vote. 7. Since 1976 the Aboriginal people ___ some of their land returned to them. 8. The Prime Minister ___ Australians rethink their history when he apologised to the Aboriginal people in 2008.

b) *What do your parents let or make you do? Think of three examples with a partner. Then think of three things you've had done for yourself this week.*

Examples: At the weekend my parents **let** me **go out** until 10 p.m. / They **make** me **clean up** my room once a week. / I **had** shoes **delivered** to my house last week.

SPEAKING

9 Rural Australia

a) *In England there are 1,005 people per square mile, in the EU 297 and in Australia 7. Point out the advantages and disadvantages of a low population density[2].*

b) *First describe the cartoon, then analyse it. What's the cartoonist making fun of?*

c) *Explain how this cartoon would be different for Germany.*

LANGUAGE

10 A tour through the Sydney Opera House

*What happened at the Sydney Opera House? Copy the text and turn the underlined **active sentences** into **passive ones**.*

<u>A travel agency sent me two free tickets for a tour of the Sydney Opera House.</u> When my best friend and I arrived in Sydney, we caught a glimpse of the Opera House, but we couldn't find our way there. <u>Finally a friendly police officer helped us. At the ticket office they offered the last two tickets for the day to the people in front of us. The lady in the office promised us the first two tickets for the first tour the next day.</u> That didn't help because our flight was leaving the next morning. Someone must have heard us <u>because suddenly the lady gave us special backstage tickets</u>. It all happened very abruptly. We walked down a long corridor and then we were on the stage – with real opera singers who were rehearsing for their next performance! <u>And guess what, they asked us to sing a song with them!</u> We weren't happy because we're terrible singers. When they saw how awkward we felt, <u>they taught us a simple song instead</u>. What a great experience!

1 decade [ˈdekeɪd] Jahrzehnt | **2 population density** [pɒpjəˈleɪʃn ˌdensɪti] Bevölkerungsdichte

VOCABULARY

11 My trip to Australia

a) *Use these words from Unit 1 to replace the words and phrases in **bold**.*

barbie | clusters of | foster family | to gleam | glimpse | No worries. | outback | rip current | spokesperson | a variety of

I like Australia for **many different** reasons. I knew I'd like it from the first **quick look** I got of it from the plane. From the air I could see that the bigger cities like Sydney, Melbourne, Perth and Adelaide all have **groups of** similar buildings and houses along the coasts. The skyscrapers **shine softly** in the Australian sun, while in the middle of the country it's almost all **countryside where few people live**. And the Australians are just great! I know that every country has its problems, but wherever I went in Australia people seemed to be laid-back. Whenever I had a problem, someone offered to help me. And when I thanked them, the answer usually was **"You're welcome."** I almost felt like I had a **substitute family**. With the help of my new Aussie friends, I even defeated my fear of sharks because they taught me that the **pull of the water below the surface** is even more dangerous! That's why now I usually stay out of the water and take care of the **grill** for everyone. Don't you think I'd be the right **person who could speak officially** for Australia?

b) *Choose four of the words below and use them each in a sentence. Then replace the words in your sentences with other words or with phrases that explain them. Exchange your sentences with a partner's. Your partner then needs to guess which words you chose.*

ancestor | awkward | comforting | convict | desperate | disastrous | to glance | guilty conscience | indigenous | previous | to protest | to be related

LANGUAGE

12 Australian dangers

a) *Complete these sentences with the right **passive forms**.*

1. He was in hospital because he ___ (bite) by a poisonous[1] snake.
2. The Australian authorities[2] hope that fewer people ___ (attack) by crocodiles this year.
3. I know the sun in Australia is dangerous, so I'm sure sunscreen[3] ___ (sell) in every shop there.
4. Don't worry. Nobody ___ (kill) by the Sydney funnel web spider these days.
5. I was afraid of the water because I ___ (tell) that Australia is surrounded by waters that are full of sharks.
6. Of course Australia is on the other side of the world, but they still speak English and you ___ (understand) by your host family with the English you speak!

b) *What real and imaginary dangers are there where you live? Change two of the sentences from a) to match the dangers around you.*

1 poisonous ['pɔɪznəs] giftig | **2 authorities** [ɔ:'θɒrətiz] Behörden | **3 sunscreen** ['sʌnskri:n] Sonnenschutzmittel

MEDIATION

13 Dos and don'ts in Australia

a) *Your exchange partner from Australia is interested in the kind of intercultural tips you get in Germany when you read about their country. You find this article on the internet and in your next video chat you tell him / her about what you've read.*

Auch in einer Kultur wie der australischen, die der unseren gar nicht so unähnlich scheint, gibt es für Besucher einige Fallstricke. Wer nicht weiß, welches Verhalten erwartet wird, merkt vielleicht gar nicht, warum die Person gegenüber so merkwürdig reagiert. Deshalb kommen hier einige Verhaltenstipps, die helfen sollen, Fettnäpfchen zu umgehen.

Die Australier sind bekannt für ihre Aufgeschlossenheit und Freundlichkeit. Deshalb sollten Besucher sich in Australien ebenso freundlich und offen verhalten. Die Freundlichkeit und verbale Kumpelhaftigkeit, sowie die Anrede „mate" sollte man jedoch nicht mit einer schnell geschlossenen Freundschaft verwechseln. Genau wie in Deutschland braucht es auch in Australien in der Regel Zeit, bis sich Freundschaften entwickeln.

Hilfsbereitschaft und Humor gelten für Australier als typisch und sind auch gern gesehen. Ganz anders übrigens als direkt vorgebrachte Kritik, zu der viele Deutsche neigen, ohne es böse zu meinen. In Australien fallen sie damit jedoch unangenehm auf. Zum guten Ton gehört es, Kritik möglichst nett zu verpacken.

Genau wie in den USA ist auch in Australien die Frage „How are you?" meist nicht mehr als eine Begrüßungsformel. Niemand sollte daraufhin sein Herz ausschütten. Die gemeinhin erwartete Antwort ist: „Fine, thanks." Überhaupt sind Probleme kein gern gesehenes Thema für Smalltalk. Das gilt übrigens auch für die Tatsache, dass Australien aus einer Sträflingskolonie heraus entstanden ist, sowie die mit der Kolonialisierung verbundene Situation der Aborigines.

Beim Ausgehen in einen Pub ist es oft üblich, Runden zu trinken. Das heißt, innerhalb einer Gruppe sollte jeder einmal ein Getränk ausgeben. Wer auf Einlass, beispielsweise in Clubs, oder etwa auf Bedienung an Serviceschaltern wartet, sollte in Australien geduldig in der Schlange anstehen. Sich vorzudrängeln kommt gar nicht gut an. Gäste eines Barbecues, umgangssprachlich auch „barbie" genannt, bringen üblicherweise Getränke und manchmal auch Grillfleisch oder andere Lebensmittel mit. Bei einer Einladung zu einem Abendessen ist es üblich, Wein oder Schokolade als Gastgeschenk zu überreichen. Es gilt als höflich, die Gastgeber zu fragen, ob man selbst eine Speise beisteuern soll, und beim Abräumen zu helfen.

Mit Gesten, die hierzulande positiv gemeint sind, können Ausländer in Australien auch schnell anecken. Handzeichen wie „peace" oder „victory" haben (wenn die Handfläche dabei nach innen zeigt) in Australien und einigen anderen Ländern nicht dieselbe Bedeutung wie in Deutschland, sondern stellen eine Beleidigung dar. Die kulturellen Unterschiede zwischen Australien und Deutschland zeigen sich also sogar in Form von Handzeichen.

Source: College Contact (abridged)

b) *Find an article that gives intercultural tips for travelling in Germany. Do you agree with the article?*

Find more online: ta5ie3

Text smart 1
A short film

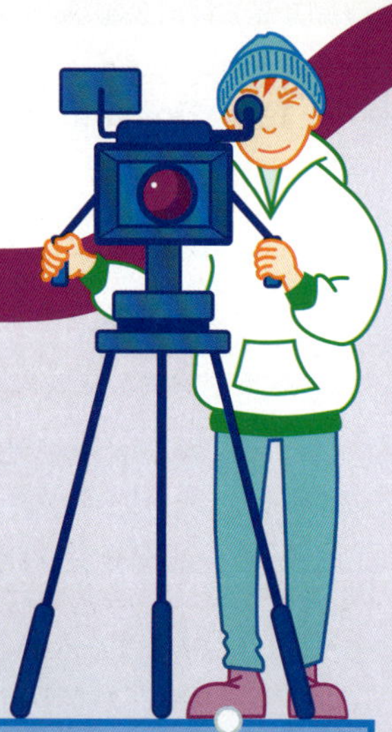

In Text smart 1, the 'text' is actually a short film, a musical comedy. But it isn't just a question of watching the film and understanding its content. Learn about the film's key features and the effect they achieve together.

SPEAKING

1 Motivations for watching a film

What are your motivations for watching a film at the cinema or maybe just a short clip online? Use the elements on the right to explain why you watch a film. Discuss your ideas in small groups.

Word bank

action | actors | genre | interesting characters | message | music | plot | setting | special effects

Start like this:

A: I like films with … That's my main motivation for watching …
B: Whenever there's a new film with …, I always …
C: I just like anything visual. I don't care if it's …

VOCABULARY

2 Vocabulary for discussing films → WB 21/1

To talk about films, you need some basic vocabulary. This exercise revises words you already know and introduces new vocabulary too.

a) *Look at the word cluster for 'film set' below. Then divide up into groups of 5–6. Each group chooses **one** of the five categories on the other card. Make a word cluster for your category, as a poster. Use words in the yellow box below and other words you might know too. (Some words belong to more than one category.) Put all the posters up on the wall for a classroom vocabulary display.*

equipment camera props
actors director FILM SET
film crew costumes

- genres
- camera
- actors / acting
- audio / visual elements
- plot

action | appearance | background noises | body language | camera shots | cast | characters | climax | close-up shot | comedy | conflict | costume | dialogue | director | facial expression | first-person narrator | horror | humour | location | main role | make-up | medium shot | music | mystery | plot | props | roles | romance | scene | science-fiction | setting | shot sizes | sound effects | special effects | stage directions | supporting role | third-person narrator | turning point | use of voice | wide shot | to zoom in on sb / sth

<b)> *Start a glossary of film terms by writing down short definitions for all the words on your posters.*

A first look

On the next two pages, you're going to deal with the storyline and content of the short film ***College Romance – The Musical*** (by Isabelle Sieb) before analysing how the film works.

SPEAKING

3 Before you watch: A first look at Penny

→ △ 120/1

In the still below, the girl on the right is Penny, the film's main character.
Exchange ideas with a partner as you answer these questions:

1. **People:** Use adjectives to describe the emotion Penny is feeling at the moment. And what about the other girl?
2. **Plot:** Say what you think might have happened to cause a reaction like this in public.
3. **Location:** Say where you think the action might take place.

VIEWING

4 Getting from picture A to picture B

2

a) *Watch until 00:55. Describe what happens to make the boy's mood change from A to B.*

b) *How would you have reacted if you were the boy or Penny?*

→ △ 120/2

c) *Your turn: In small groups, think of situations you think are equally embarrassing. They can be real or invented. Then decide which situation is the* ***most*** *embarrassing!*

VIEWING

5 Penny's problem

a) *Go back to the beginning of the film and watch until 03:13. Share your first reactions.*

b) *Sum up the action in the three scenes which involve Penny and a different college boy.*

Boy 1

Boy 2

Boy 3

c) *Now describe Penny's overall problem. In your answers, refer to these words and phrases that Penny uses:*

booboo | ouchie | misery | uncomfortable | true love

the tears I try to fight | I let myself go | I can't hold back | someone who understands | I did it again

d) *Think-pair-share: Exaggeration is a key element in this comedy. But do you feel the film is too exaggerated in showing teenagers' lives and problems? If yes, what is being exaggerated, and why?*

VIEWING

6 Penny as master of her own fate?

Watch from 03:14 till 03:56, the scene in which Penny says the following key lines: "Now I've had enough. I'm the master of my own fate."

1. What adjectives would you use to describe her mood in this scene?
2. Explain what Penny means with her statement. What is her new approach to her old problem? Name the key line that tells you *exactly* what her new approach is.

VIEWING

7 The ending

a) *Now watch from 03:14 till the end. Describe the action. Point out what is similar to the previous scenes with the three college boys and what is very different this time.*

b) *Sum up the overall message of the film. In your explanation, give the words and lines from Penny's first song (00:56–01:56) which you feel are the most important for understanding the message. (The whole text is on p. 267 at the back of your book.)*

Key elements of films

Now have a closer look at different elements of films, and how they are combined to support a film's storyline, create atmosphere and show the characters' personalities.

VIEWING

8 Understanding genre: The romantic teen comedy

a) *In class, have a discussion about the idea of 'light entertainment': Is it a good idea for films to combine real problems with humour?*

→ △ 121/3

b) *Read the skills box. Before you watch the film again, divide up into groups. Each group chooses element 1, 2 or 3 from the box. While viewing, think of these questions:*

- When is your element used? Give 1–2 examples.
- How *effectively* do you think your element is featured?

Share your results with the class.

Film skills

Most teen comedies feature serious topics, but packaged in a way that can be considered 'light entertainment'. Typical elements:

1. **humour**
2. **exaggeration**
3. **romance and dating**

And if it's a *musical* teen comedy, there will of course be music, singing and dancing.

VIEWING

9 A closer look at the music: Comparing two scenes

a) *Compare the **library scene** (02:30–02:45) and the **basketball scene** (02:46–03:13):*

1. Describe how the lines below reflect a difference in Penny's mood and actions in the two scenes:

A And now I'm dancing with books in the library! What's become of me?

B Maybe it's not too late. Maybe he's worth the wait.

2. Do you think Penny's style of singing and her movements match the scenes well? Explain.
3. What do you like / dislike in each scene?

A

B

b) *In class, go to the text on p. 267 and read the lines from the two scenes aloud. What sounds better to you: the spoken or the sung lines? Give your opinion.*

VOCABULARY

10 Facial expressions

a) *Get into groups of 4–6. Read the adjectives for facial expressions in the word bank. What situations cause people to make faces like that? Take turns to describe situations.*

→ S1

b) *Now describe the emotions that are shown in stills A–H.*

c) *A facial expression can show lots of things: a small change in the action, or maybe even a major turning point in the plot. Which moments below tell you that something is changing? Describe those moments.*

Drama skills

Films live from their **characters**, and it helps when the viewer can see a character's personality. That's why **facial expressions** and **body language** are so important. The 'cool guy / girl' has to look cool, etc.

Word bank

more positive: confident | cool | flirty | friendly | (extremely) happy | hopeful | sexy | surprised

more negative: afraid | annoyed | awkward | bitchy | confused | disgusted | embarrassed | mean | nervous | shocked | turned off

A 02:29

B 03:03

C 02:05

D 00:13

E 02:20

F 01:10

G 02:56

H 00:20

d) *Your turn. How good are you at showing facial expressions? In your same group, do the following:*

1. On cards, each person writes down two different situations that would require a certain facial expression as a reaction. You can use your ideas from a), or new ones.
2. Put all the cards together; take turns choosing one. Make the face on the card you chose.
3. The classmates in your group have to tell you which emotion you're trying to show.

VOCABULARY

11 Camera shots and their functions

The Birds, a 1963 film by the legendary director Alfred Hitchcock, is one of the most famous films ever made and a classic of the horror genre.

a) *Read the skills box and then look at the example stills from* The Birds. *Below the stills, read about the different functions of the three most common camera shots. Match the shots to their functions. Then add the terms to your folder.*

Film skills

Films, whether short clips or full-length cinema films, depend on a mix of different **camera shots** for dramatic effect. The most common three are the following:
- the **close-up**
- the **medium shot**
- the **wide shot** (also called 'long shot')

A

A scary bird attack
(close-up)

B

Waiting for the next attack
(medium shot)

C

Trying to escape
(wide shot)

- often used to start and / or end a film
- shows the entire person, groups of people and objects in the context of their complete surroundings / location
- often used in sequences where a small group of people are acting
- usually shows outdoor spaces like street scenes or landscapes
- often used to show a person's scared / happy / sad face
- often used to establish main characters
- gives the viewer information about atmosphere / setting by showing some of the background
- shows the actors' facial expressions in the context of their body language
- important for showing detail, like a character's emotions

b) *Now find examples of the three different camera shots on pages 39–42. Say why you think that shot was chosen for that particular moment.*

→ ▲ 121/4

c) *A good film needs a mix of different camera shots. Discuss what would happen if there were **only** close-ups in a film, with no medium or wide shots.*

How to structure film scripts

READING

12 The parts of a film script

Read this extract from a film script based on College Romance. *Then match the names of the script elements (in the box on the right) to their definitions below the box. Write the definitions down in your folder.*

stage directions | location | italics | character names and their dialogue | camera shot information

```
EXT. COLLEGE CAFÉ - DAY

BOY 1 (20), PENNY (20) and ONLOOKERS (all
between 18-22) outside getting coffee.
Boy at front of queue; Penny arrives at
back of queue, gives Boy 1 big smile.
He looks her up and down, likes what he
sees, puts a flirty face on. Walks over
to offer her coffee. Extremely confident.
Penny is nervous.

                  BOY 1
                 Coffee?

                  PENNY
                I'm Penny.

Penny knocks coffee out of his hand when
introducing herself. Boy 1 tries to be
understanding at first. Close-up Boy 1.

                  BOY 1
                 You OK?

Penny cries over spilt coffee, gets more
hysterical. Boy 1 is first surprised,
then very uncomfortable, then he leaves.
Onlookers are all embarrassed, staring.

                  PENNY
                Not again.

Penny now breaks into song.

   Oh no, I did it again. I let myself go.
   And now, everyone's staring at me.
   I feel rather uncomfortable.
   What have I done to deserve this misery?
```

This kind of text tells the film crew and acting team if it's an interior (INT.) or an exterior (EXT.) scene, and what time of day it is.

This kind of text is aligned to the left of the page. The first mention of a new cast member is written in capital letters, incl. age. Any special facial expressions and emotions that are needed are mentioned here, props too (e.g. coffee cups)

This kind of text is always centred.

In a script with both spoken *and* sung lines, this kind of formatting is often used for the sung parts.

Sometimes suggestions for this are made, but often the director likes to decide for him- / herself.

WRITING

13 Practise scriptwriting → WB 22/2

→ △ 121/5

Go back to the scene 01:56–02:29. With a partner, write the script for it. Make sure the stage directions include enough detail to reflect the facial expressions and emotions that this scene shows.

14 Options: Film work from different perspectives

Option A: Write a script for Boy 4
At the end of *College Romance* there was a new boy for Penny ('Boy 4') and a happy ending.

→ S5–6

In groups of 4–6, write the script for ***one*** *new scene with Boy 4. In a typical scene, describe him and his problem before he meets Penny. Points to consider:*

1. **His personality:** Describe what you think Boy 4's personality is, based on his clothing, his looks, and also his problem. (See Point 2.)
2. **Boy 4's problem:** We know that Boy 4 can't help laughing when he sees something funny, even if he doesn't want to laugh and make the person feel bad. Think of an embarrassing 'disaster' that Boy 4 causes in front of a girl.
3. **Musical elements:** Most films need music, so think of whether you want some of your lines / dialogue to be sung. If not, think of where you might want background music.
4. **Camera shots:** What camera shots would be best for your scene?

Option B: Act out your favourite scenes from *College Romance*
For this activity, you could easily involve the whole class! Here are points to think about as you organise your scenes:

- which scenes?
- casting
- costumes and props
- locations
- practise playing with your voice
- practise different facial expressions and body language
- rehearsal time
- who does what?

Option C: Musical film classics
Grease (1978) and *Dirty Dancing* (1987) are two of the biggest-selling musical films ever, and their soundtracks still sell well.

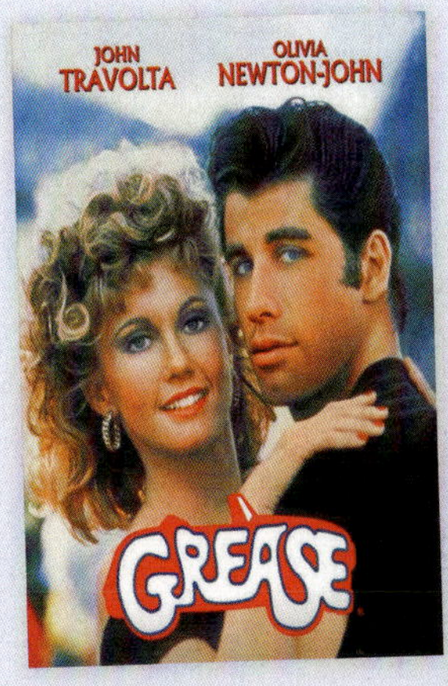

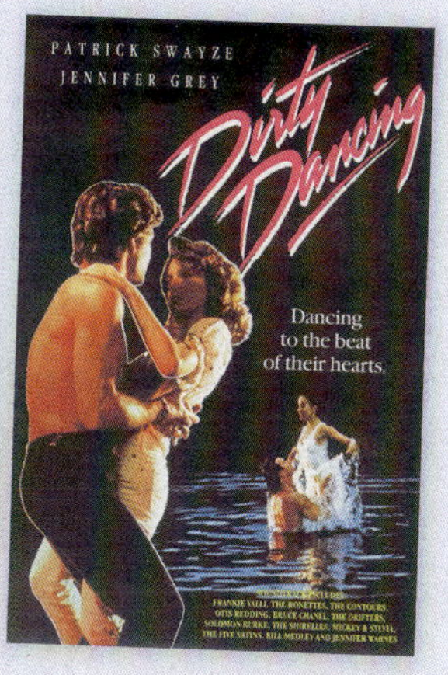

→ S9

In a group, watch ***one*** *of the films. Give a presentation about it in class. Include these points:*

- plot summary
- typical 'teen' elements that are featured
- examples of effective / interesting camera shots
- facial expressions / body language
- use of music and dance

Unit 2

The good life?

Find more online: zs7j6y

SPEAKING

1 Thinking about priorities in life → WB 23/1

→ S1

a) *First, describe what you see in the photo above.*

b) *Now imagine what kind of lives the two people might have, and what their priorities in life might be. Explain what makes you think so.*

c) *Describe the photos on p. 267 at the back of your book. Explain whether the photo above or one of the other two comes closer to your 'good life'.*

Word bank

to (not) make enough money to afford … | to (not) worry … | to (not) have a boring / fulfilling / fun / materialistic / meaningful / an adventurous / … life | to have the right / wrong priorities | to (not) accept other people's priorities / lifestyles / …

LISTENING

2 ⟨The good life in songs⟩ → WB 23/2

L 2/1–2

a) *Listen to the two songs on the next page. Say which one you spontaneously like better, and why.*

b) *Read the lyrics. Point out the references about what makes a 'champagne' or a 'good' life.*

c) 1. Can you see yourself in **both** songs? Explain.
2. Discuss if it's fair to say that one lifestyle is 'better' than the other.

In Unit 2 you learn

… about different aspects of the world of work. You learn:

- how to express your thoughts and dreams about your own future
- how to write important job-related documents (CV; application letter)
- how to make a good impression in an interview situation

Champagne Life (by Ne-Yo, 2010)

Oh got an addiction for life and this living.
Like every day's my birthday, know what I'm getting.
Reserved for top notch, that's where I'm sitting.
Me and my friends and, found six Miss Independents.
And my attitude's so chill and so breezy.
In my designer suit I make this look easy.
Sexy baby, don't you dare act like you don't see me,
Baby I know you see me.

It's all about them fast car nights and them big bold days.
Living this champagne life, everything's OK.
Let's toast it up, oh, let's toast it up, oh.
Said we play all night, and we play all day.
Living this champagne life, everything's OK
Let's toast it up, oh, baby let's toast it up.

The Good Life (by Thirsty Merc, 2015)

Some of us spend all our time
Chasing dreams of dollar signs
But I got riches of a different kind
Love is my fortune.
'Cause all the bucks don't make much sense
If they don't bring you happiness
Love's a picture so immense
It's bigger than Ben Hur.

I'm no billionaire, no VIP, no diamonds on my shoes
But I'm living, living the good life,
  living, living the good life
I got everything I ever need as long as I got you
We'll be living, living the good life,
  living, living the good life …

SPEAKING

3 Thinking about the job world: Statistics on work patterns

→ S2

a) *In groups of 4–5, look at the two charts about work patterns in the UK. Point out the main facts that you learn.*

→ △ 121/1

b) 1. Explain how the following ideas could play a role in the statistics:

job satisfaction | boredom | curiosity

2. Discuss whether it's desirable to stay in a job for more or less than two years.

c) *Your turn: Complete these sentences with ideas about yourself (4–6 lines):*

1. In 10 years' time, I'll have / be / do …
2. My idea of success / a good life is / isn't …,

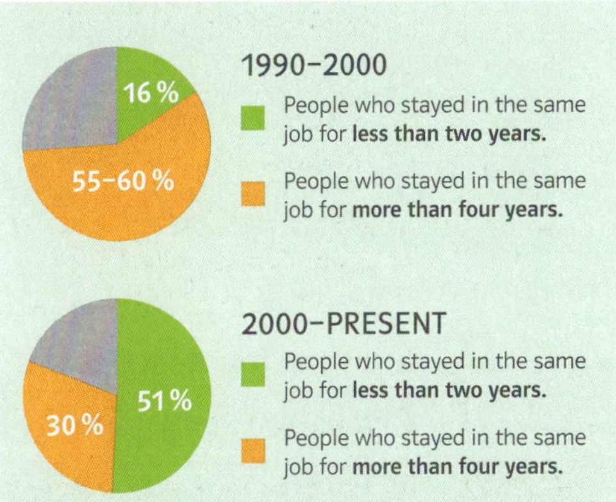

Source: careers.workopolis.com, 2014

Best summer ever!

READING

1 A look at an informal job advert

a) *Read text A, a flyer for a summer job. In your own words, say what job it advertises.*

b) *How successful is the advert in encouraging people to apply? Evaluate it according to these criteria:* raising interest | concrete information | fun
Then exchange your ideas with a partner and say if you would apply for the job or not.

A

Action Summer UK are offering a **FANTASTIC** opportunity to 15–17 year olds just like you! Come and join us as an assistant counsellor in one of our summer camps!

You'll help the senior counsellors to lead children in activities such as sports, arts and outdoor adventures – we have something for everyone, no matter what you're passionate about! You'll become more confident and develop endless new skills.

Experiences as a camp counsellor are some of the BEST a teenager can have – just read our counsellors' testimonials to see what we mean! It's the greatest way to spend a summer. Head for **www.actionsummer.org.uk** now for a complete job description.

B

ACTION SUMMER UK
Position for Assistant Camp Counsellor

Job description: As an assistant camp counsellor, you are supposed to set a good example at all times for the younger children. In your role, you are supposed to support and motivate the children in all their activities, so you should have an outgoing personality. You will also need to be spontaneous in dealing with unexpected situations. And, of course, you are expected to be a team player.

A counsellor's job will/can include all of these areas of responsibility:
1. supporting senior counsellors during sports and other activities
2. preparing and serving food in the cafeteria
3. organising evening entertainment
4. helping with chores (washing clothes, etc.)

You are expected to:
- take part in Orientation Day for counsellors
- be available for at least two weeks in August
- be between 15 and 17 years of age

Please e-mail your CV with an application letter to Martha Ross: **ross@actionsummeruk.ac.uk**

READING

2 A formal job description: The bigger picture

a) *Now read text B, the full job description. Name the main qualifications that are required.*

→ △ 122/2

b) *Point out differences there are between texts A and B.*

c) *What kind of person would be a successful applicant for this job? Consider the following criteria as you justify your ideas:*

specific experience | qualifications and skills | personal characteristics

LISTENING

3 It's such a cliché! → WB 24/3–4

Two friends, Ella and Ryan, are talking about the summer job in the advert.

L 2/3 → S7

a) *Listen and sum up their attitudes towards work in general. Think of the phrases on the right and these two points as you listen:*

- what's useful / enjoyable at the job
- gender

b) *Listen again. Explain why working as a camp counsellor might be a good option for Ella this summer.*

c) *Comment on Ella's and Ryan's views on gender stereotypes.*

Useful phrases

Employers like / don't like:
reliable / responsible / focused applicants | all-rounders | applicants who only think of … | people who stand out / don't stand out from the crowd | applicants with lots of strengths / few weaknesses

It's a cliché / stereotype to think of men / women in jobs that require …

READING

4 What careers do girls and boys prefer?

a) *Read this extract from a news report and sum up the main message. Say if the report surprises you or not, and why.*

Gender stereotyping is still an issue when boys and girls consider career options, research shows. Millions of pounds have been spent trying to persuade more girls to choose science and engineering, and to persuade boys to read more. But a report today says that, in the end, boys and girls choose traditional career paths. The survey of 500 14- to 16-year-olds studying for their GCSEs shows that, when asked about their career ideas, girls listed healthcare (22 percent), education (11 percent) and fashion (10 percent) as their three favourite options. With the boys, a career in IT was the favourite (16 percent) followed by engineering (12 percent) and healthcare (10 percent).

Source: The Independent Online

Female construction workers: still not typical, report shows

b) *Conduct a class survey:*

1. Ask the people in your class what their career ideas and plans are. Put your results on a wall display.
2. Now compare your classroom results with the news report.

→ △ 122/3

c) *Look at the professions below. Discuss which are considered to be typical male or female jobs, or either. Justify your opinions.*

Examples:

A: Any job which involves … is expected to be a female job because women are expected to be good with / at … In my opinion … / If you look more closely …

B: So many people still think men / women are supposed to be … That's why people always associate jobs like a / an … with men / women. When I look around, the reality is …

architect | business executive | dancer | doctor | engineer | fashion designer | firefighter | model | musician | nurse | pilot | reporter | sales assistant | teacher | web designer

VOCABULARY

5 Expressing expectations → Fact page, p. 270

→ △ 122/4, 123/5

Write some sentences about one of the jobs in Ex. 4c), or another job.
*Use **be expected to** and **be supposed to + infinitive**. Take turns to read out your sentences and guess which jobs you're describing.*

Examples:
For this job you'**re supposed to be** good with people and **are** also **expected to have** …
This person **is expected to have** a perfect body and he'**s** / she'**s supposed to be** …

READING

6 The importance of a CV → WB 24/5

a) *For a job application, a CV is a must. Read the one on the right, which Ella has written for the camp counsellor job you read about on p. 48. Say why you think a CV is so important.*

b) *CVs are written for a particular job. Check what Ella has emphasised in her CV. Does she meet the expectations? Give examples and say if you would give her the job.*

Curriculum Vitae

Personal details:

Name:	Ella Lewis
Address:	21 Redhatch Road Brighton BN1 35H
Tel:	06383 8372634
E-mail:	ellal@smail.co.uk
Nationality:	British
Date of birth:	26.04.2002

Education:

2013 – (2018)	Dunstan Comprehensive School Will take GCSEs in 10 subjects
2006 – 2013:	Whiteleaf Primary School

Work experience:

2016 –	Children's party organiser

Personal profile:
I am a hard-working and reliable person. I enjoy meeting new people and have good communication skills. Also, I work well in a team. I like working with children because it gives me the chance to show my people skills. My main hobby is swimming and I have won several local competitions.

References available on request.

WRITING

7 Your turn: A personal profile for your CV → WB 25/6

→ △ 123/6
→ S6

*Go back to text B on p. 48. Choose **one** of the four areas of responsibility for the job. For your own CV, write a personal profile. Emphasise the skills, qualifications and strengths that would be important for your area of responsibility.*

Tip

In more formal texts like CVs or application letters, it's common (but not required) to use **long forms**, not short forms:
~~I'm …~~ → **I am …**
~~I've had …~~ → **I have had …**

Across cultures

In some countries, applicants are expected to include a **photo** with their **CV** – but *not* in the UK or US. And in some countries, you needn't even state your full name, age or gender.

What are the pros and cons of an employer seeing your photo or knowing your name, gender or age?

READING

8 The application letter

→ S5

a) *Read Ella's application letter below. What are the differences between a letter to a friend and a formal letter like this one? Make a grid and fill in the different criteria.*

→ △ 123/7

b) *Say how well Ella 'sells herself' when she emphasises what she could bring to the job.*

Action Summer UK
20–22 Larksdale Rise
Chester CH3 2BD

21 Redhatch Road
Brighton BN1 35H

6th May 2017

Application for position as Assistant Summer Camp Counsellor

Dear Ms Ross,

With reference to your online advertisement, I am writing to apply for a position as an Assistant Summer Camp Counsellor.

As you will see from my CV, I am 15 years old and preparing for my GCSE exams. I enjoy working with children very much; **hopefully**, I will be a teacher one day. **Therefore**, I am very interested in the opportunity you offer. **Moreover**, as I have had a Saturday job for the last year as a children's party organiser, I already have a lot of experience in leading games and activities and in encouraging children of all ages to take part. **Personally**, I enjoy sports activities the most.
At a summer camp with a lake, **surely** a counsellor with good swimming skills could be a useful addition to your team. **Additionally**, I have good canoeing skills.

Thank you for considering my application. I am available for an interview any evening or weekend. I look forward to hearing from you soon.

Yours sincerely,
Ella Lewis
Ella Lewis

Att. CV

Put your **address** and the **date** here.

Put the **address** of the person or company you're writing to here.

Show what the letter is about in an underlined **heading**.

In the 1st paragraph, say **why** you are writing, **where** you saw the ad, **which** job you're applying for.

In the 2nd paragraph, talk about your **background** and **experience** (your age; what you hope to do in the future; description of work experience / skills). Also, refer to your **CV** here.

Use a friendly **ending** and a standard **final sentence**.

Print your **name** under your **signature** and say if there is an **attachment** to your e-mail (or an enclosure to your letter).

LANGUAGE

9 Improve your style: How to sound more formal → G6 → WB 25/7, 26/8–9

a) *Read the letter again. Decide which words in* ***bold*** *are* ***linking adverbs*** *and which are* ***commenting****. Make a grid with those words.*

b) *Now add these adverbs to your grid from a):*

furthermore | however | in fact | luckily | nevertheless | unfortunately

Tip

Sentence adverbs can make a text sound more formal.

They come in two categories: **linking adverbs** and **commenting adverbs**

c) *Link these sentences or begin new sentences with* ***sentence adverbs*** *on this page.*

1. I have well-developed computer skills.
2. I am free in the last week of July.
3. I love music and love to sing.
4. I don't have any cooking experience.
5. My French isn't too bad.
6. I am definitely a team player.

a) I'm able to visit France quite often.
b) I don't play an instrument.
c) I can help with IT issues if you need me.
d) I am very interested in learning!
e) I don't mind working independently.
f) I can be available for all of August.

WRITING **10** **Your turn: Apply for a job of your choice in the UK** → WB 26/10

→ S12

a) *Go online and find an advert for a summer or weekend job in the UK you'd find interesting. Here are some ideas you might like to research, or perhaps you have other ideas:*

lifeguard | assistant at a tourist information centre | waiter

b) *Write a CV and/or an application letter for the job you chose.*

MEDIATION **11** **A male au pair's testimonial**

→ S10

On a camping holiday with your family in Bavaria, you meet some English teenagers. One evening, you're discussing travelling abroad on au pair exchanges. You mention you've heard of male au pairs, but the others don't believe it: "It's a girl's thing." So you find this testimonial below and decide to write about the topic of male au pairs on your social media. You do it in English so your international friends can read it too.

a) *Give your opinion on male au pairs. Then read the testimonial below.*

Mein Name ist Timo und ich werde versuchen, meine Zeit in Neuseeland so gut wie möglich zu beschreiben. Nach meinem Abitur habe ich mich dazu entschlossen, als Au Pair nach Neuseeland zu gehen, da ich nach der langen Zeit des Lernens Lust hatte, ein fernes und exotisches Land kennenzulernen.

Zuerst war ich ein bisschen skeptisch, ob ich als Junge überhaupt eine Chance haben würde, als Au Pair in eine Gastfamilie aufgenommen zu werden. Schon nach einem Monat hat sich aber eine Gastfamilie gemeldet, die mich gerne aufnehmen und mich um ihren 4-jährigen Jungen kümmern lassen wollte.

Ich lebe hier in Waikato ziemlich genau auf halbem Wege zwischen Auckland und Hamilton in der größten Agrarregion. Mit meinem Gastbruder bin ich viel in Spielparks unterwegs oder wir besuchen Freunde, bauen Höhlen, fahren Fahrrad oder springen auf dem Trampolin.

Außerdem habe ich ihm Schreiben beigebracht und sogar Klavierunterricht gegeben, nachdem meine Gasteltern für mich ein kleines Klavier gekauft haben, da ich unheimlich gerne Klavier spiele.

Das ist nur ein Beleg dafür, wie viel Glück ich mit ihnen hatte und wie großzügig sie waren. Der Junge ist wie ein kleiner Bruder für mich geworden und es wird mir schwer fallen, ihn hier zu lassen, wenn ich wieder zurück nach Deutschland muss.

Ich war auch für Hausarbeiten verantwortlich wie „Saubermachen", die Haustiere füttern und pflegen, wobei ich einen Tag in der Woche hatte, an dem ich das ganze Haus geputzt habe, was mir aber keine Probleme bereitet hat. Alles in allem habe ich mich hier sehr wohl gefühlt. Meiner Meinung nach gibt es wirklich keinen Grund, warum man nicht als Au Pair nach Neuseeland gehen sollte. Hier passt einfach alles!

– Timo S.

Mit meinem Gastbruder

Source: AIFS Educational Travel

b) *Write a blog post that sums up Timo's experience and what he had to do as an au pair.*

→ S12 **<c)>** *Internet research: Find out about formal qualifications you need to be an au pair.*

L 2/6

The cocoa controversy

SPEAKING

12 Pre-reading: What do the pictures say?

There's a controversy surrounding cocoa from Africa. Describe the pictures below. What hints do they give you about the controversy? Exchange ideas, and then turn to p. 54.

Chocolate: So sweet, so bitter

by Steve Hartley | Abengourou/Ivory Coast | 26 May 2017

As the main ingredient for the chocolate many Europeans and Americans eat in massive quantities, as well as a main ingredient for many cosmetics, cocoa is one of Ivory Coast's most important exports. The chocolate industry there is worth around £60 billion a year and the country provides about 35% of the world's cocoa. These facts make it difficult to understand why 40% of the population lives below the poverty line and why child labour is such an issue there. In Ivory Coast, about 100,000 children are doing the dangerous and physically difficult work of harvesting cocoa beans. Most of them are sent by their families; they are paid very little and forced to live in terrible conditions on the cocoa plantations. And some children are paid nothing at all; they are slaves. Some farmers claim they have no other way of surviving because they themselves earn less than £2 a day; they can't pay adult workers or provide them with healthcare while keeping their prices low enough to compete. These are the reasons that are given to justify child labour and child slaves.

I came wanting to see for myself what life is like for the young workers at a large cocoa plantation. As I got out of my car about 15 miles outside Abengourou, I felt the sun burning on my skin. I noticed four children walking along a muddy path towards some trees; they could hardly carry all the heavy tools and equipment. They arrived feeling exhausted – and had yet to start their day's work. Slowly, they climbed the largest of the trees and I watched them chop down heavy yellow cocoa pods with their huge machetes, which seemed nearly as big as they were. All of them had scars on their legs from machete injuries.

Then I found Abdoulaye sitting alone. His job was to cut the pods open to get the cocoa beans, again with a machete. "My mother sent me here," he said. "I'm the oldest of five children and I have to work so they can eat. I haven't seen them for two years now and I've never been to school." Abdoulaye said he's heard that children in other countries enjoy chocolate, which he has never tasted, and doesn't understand why his own life is so hard.

As I drove away, I saw three girls carry heavy containers full of cocoa beans and I saw them dump the contents onto a large truck before they walked back for more. I left hoping the cocoa industry would finally wake up and give these children their childhoods back. We've all heard of fair trade products – let's keep buying them and make our message clear.

READING

13 Understanding the issues

→ S3 **a)** *Read the first paragraph of the news report on p. 53. Then:*

1. Sum up the general problem.
2. Explain the importance of these statistics: £60 billion | 35% | 40% | £2 | 100,000

b) *Now read the rest of the report. Sum up its main message. Then describe the different jobs the children do in front of the reporter.*

c) *Your reaction: Point out lines in the text which you feel are emotionally powerful.*

d) *Is this the kind of report that could inspire people to help others? If yes, how? Explain.*

LANGUAGE

14 Present participle or infinitive after verbs of perception + object → G7 → WB 27/11–12

a) *Look at these sentences and find more examples like them in the second half of the text.*

I **felt**	**the sun**	**burning**	on my skin.
I **watched**	**them**	**chop down**	cocoa pods.

b) *Find the rule: When do we use a **participle** or an **infinitive** after **verbs of perception** + **object**?*

→ △ 124/8
→ ▲ 124/9
c) *Look at the picture of a school's fair trade market. Write sentences about the actions. Use a **participle** or **infinitive** after phrases like **I saw / noticed / watched …** | **He felt …***

LANGUAGE

15 Present participle after verbs of rest and motion → G8 → WB 28/13

a) *Look at this phrase and find two more examples on p. 53 (2nd half of text):*

I **came** want**ing** …

→ △ 124/10
b) *Complete the sentences in the text about student protesters who want to help to end child labour.*

Example:
We **arrived** feel**ing** really excited.

We **1** (arrive – feel) ✔ really excited. Sam was late, but when the march started, he **2** (run in – wave) a really cool flag. Then we all **3** (walk along – shout) "Down with child labour!" In the park, we **4** (stay – sing) songs for nearly an hour. At the beginning, we **5** (come – hope) some people would be there. At the end we **6** (leave – know) a lot of people had really listened! I **7** (catch myself – think) how great it feels to try and change things. Everyone can do something!

SPEAKING

16 Social commitment → WB 28/14

For some people, the 'good life' involves helping others, one's community, or maybe the environment. Some make a career out of it; others help as volunteers in their free time.

→ S1

a) *Get together in groups of six. Each group member chooses* ***one*** *of the photos of volunteer activity below. Describe your photo to the others. Take turns.*

b) *In your group, discuss what makes people help other people. Why can it be important for individuals as well as for a community in general?*

c) *Discuss how the following motivations can play a role in actively showing social commitment:*

- having a guilty conscience
- helping for selfish reasons
- really wanting to do something good / helpful

Across cultures

In the UK and the US, job applicants but also applicants to student exchanges and universities are often expected to show examples of **social commitment** on their **CVs**.

SPEAKING

17 Your turn: Your involvement → WB 29/15

a) *In your groups, talk about people you might know who show social commitment. Describe who they are and what they do.*

b) *Are you involved in your local community? If yes, describe what you do and what made you want to get involved. If not, what could you imagine doing: an activity from Ex. 16, or something different? Talk about it briefly in your groups and then write about it (6–8 lines).*

Useful phrases

- I'd like to volunteer my time at a youth / religious / … centre
- Providing services for the elderly / the homeless / the disabled / people who need … is how I'd like to show social commitment.
- I'd like to do volunteer work during a gap year / I'd like to …

L 2/8

I do remember how it feels ...

What's the best way to survive a first job? Read some teenagers' tips for other young people:

The Words-of-Wisdom Wall | "Job stuff you want to know now. NOT later."

Learn from Nathan, Cassie and many other **Words-of-Wisdom** members!

My first job, which I was very happy to get at first, was with a family friend. He's a carpenter and I worked for him on Saturdays. I really jumped at the chance to earn my own money for the first time! The problem was that it was winter when I started. So not only was it super cold, but stacking all the wood outside was exhausting. My friends found much easier jobs in shops that sell cool clothes or computer games, so they still had the energy to have fun after work. Not me! One shouldn't be jealous, I know; but I did feel that way. So my advice is to look around at different job options, don't just take the first easy option. It might not be so easy after all!
– Marlon

@Marlon: I'm one of those kids who works in a cool clothes shop. I know the work day never goes by fast enough for some people, but time does go by quickly when you work in a shop which is full of young people! Another big benefit is that we don't have to pay as much for the clothes we buy for ourselves. It was paradise at first; all the clothes! Never before had I spent so much money on clothes. But before you start to get jealous, listen to this: The result was that I didn't have any money left over for my holiday that year, which was my original reason to earn some money! So no matter what your job is, here are my words of wisdom to everybody: Don't spend all your money on things you don't need, or you'll be very sorry!
– Cassie

@Cassie: Oh, I do remember how it feels to end up with less money than you expected! Hardly had I arrived on my first day at the bike shop when they gave me about a thousand forms to sign. Of course, I signed without reading them because they looked soooooo boring. I thought I knew exactly how much my pay would be – I even knew the exact date I would finally be able to buy the bike that I wanted! But I was wrong. You always get less than you think because they take out money for taxes. I was shocked when I received my first wages. And so I complained. My boss, who could have been very angry, patiently went through all the forms with me. I felt really stupid. But it was a lesson that I had to learn, and I did learn it.
– Nathan

My first Saturday job was at a huge café which was always incredibly busy. I used to work for eight hours, with no break. Exhausting! Nobody ever told me to go outside for some fresh air or something to eat. And stupid 16-year old me: I was too shy to ask! Rarely was the café quiet, so I just kept on working! The boss, who never sat down herself, didn't even notice. Top tip: the law says you're supposed to take breaks, so make sure you do!
– Lucy

READING

18 Understanding the posts → WB 30/16

→ S3 **a)** *Sum up the problem each of the young people experienced in their first job. Then give the reasons for their problems.*

b) *Comment on which 'words of wisdom' you think sound the most helpful.*

LANGUAGE

19 Revision: Defining relative clauses → G9

a) *Look at the sentences from the text. Explain when you use the relative pronouns* ***who, which*** *or* ***that****.*

1. My friends found much easier jobs in shops **that** sell cool clothes.
2. I'm one of those kids **who** works in a cool clothes shop.
3. Time does go by quickly when you work in a shop **which** is full of young people.
4. I would finally be able to buy the bike **that** I wanted.

b) *Read about somebody else's experiences at a first job. Use the phrases to complete the text with* ***defining relative clauses****. Decide where you can leave out the relative pronoun. If you can leave it out, put it in brackets.*

Example: I was part of a student team **who / that** organised social activities.

realised it | organised social activities | I worked in | he showed me | never joined in | they gave me | we like doing | I designed

In my first job, I was part of a student team **1** at a summer school. The office **2** was very noisy and fun, but there was one quiet boy **3**. I decided he was far too serious for me! The first job **4** was to design some posters for a theme party, but, of course, I was so busy joking around that the posters **5** were full of mistakes. The quiet boy, Mark, was the only person **6** and he helped me to correct things before anyone noticed. I liked the friendship **7** and Mark and I are still friends now! There are a lot of things **8** together, especially stuff on our smartphones.

LANGUAGE

20 Find the rule: Non-defining relative clauses → G9

a) *Explain the different function of the relative clause in each sentence:*

1. **Defining relative clause:** That's the boss who patiently went through all the forms with Nathan.
2. **Non-defining relative clause:** Nathan's boss, who could have been very angry, patiently went through all the forms with him.

Tip

In non-defining relative clauses …
- you use **who** for people and **which** for things. You never use **that**.
- you always need a **comma** to separate the main clause from the relative clause.

b) *Find three more* ***non-defining relative clauses*** *in the text on p. 56.*

LANGUAGE

21 Defining or non-defining relative clauses? → WB 30/17

After reading the Words-of-Wisdom Wall, a young boss who employs a lot of young people decided to post a comment herself. Write the text in your exercise book. Decide which sentences have ***defining*** *or* ***non-defining relative clauses****. Put in commas where you need them.*

It was interesting to read your posts which I really enjoyed. Maybe I could add a few memories about young people who have worked for me. I once employed a young man that was a real know-it-all. Dan who was very confident never listened to my advice. He always said he already knew how to do things – and then continued to do things wrong! Then there was Amy. She was the girl who spent several hours a day texting her friends. This was the same girl that complained about how everyone else was so lazy. Hm. Oh, and I'll never forget Sean who worked for me briefly. He was the guy that at his interview had said he was 'passionate' about helping customers but then strangely disappeared every time a customer arrived!
– Emma

LANGUAGE

22 Career Day

Read this information from a leaflet for students at the Career Day. Combine the two sentences. Use ***non-defining relative clauses*** *with extra information.*

Example: Career Day will take place in Hall A, **which** is on the first floor.

1. Career Day will take place in Hall A. It is on the first floor. ✔
2. For a Career Day information leaflet, please go to one of our assistants. They'll be in yellow T-shirts.
3. Local universities will explain how to apply for different courses. They have information desks in the hall.
4. The 'Allegro' café will serve hot food from 12:00 to 2:00. It is near the main entrance.
5. There will be a presentation with useful advice by an interview expert. It will be limited to 25 visitors.
6. Local employers can answer your questions about career options. They will be waiting to meet you.

LANGUAGE

23 Make the text more interesting

Use ***non-defining relative clauses*** *to add the extra information to the text below.*

→ △ 125/11
→ ▲ 125/12

In 2016, a teenage inventor from London became the youngest person ever to win an investment on Dragons' Den. Arminder Singh Dhillon was only eleven when he thought of his idea. He called his product 'Boot Buddy'. Arminder presented his idea with the support of his family. He showed the Dragons his model. The Dragons liked Arminder's invention so much that they offered him £20,000 to start his business.

Arminder: Proud of his idea

1. which is a popular TV show about new business ideas
2. who is still only a teenager
3. which he invented to save time when he cleaned his football boots
4. who appeared with him on the show
5. which was made up of a water bottle, a plastic knife and a toothbrush
6. which does the job in five minutes

LANGUAGE

24 How to: Use inversion for emphasis → G10 → WB 31/18

a) *Look at the example in the tip box below. Then find four examples in the text on p. 56 that also show inversion. Write them down.*

→ △ 125/13, 126/14

b) *Now invert the sentences below in a similar way. Use the word or phrase in **bold** to start with.*

Example: 1. I have **never** felt so nervous. → **Never have I** felt so nervous.

1. I have **never** felt so nervous. ✔
2. He had **hardly** finished lunch when he heard the fire alarm.
3. I **only** realised how much I liked art **when** I went to Italy.
4. She had **no sooner** arrived than the film started.
5. He **not only** got a new office, but he got more money too!
6. We **rarely** have time to just sit and do nothing.

Tip

You can make your language more interesting or dramatic by changing the emphasis of a sentence. With **inversion**, you bring adverbial phrases from the back of a sentence to the front, for more attention.

Example:
He did**n't** smile or greet us **once**!
→ **Not once did he** smile or greet us!

LANGUAGE

25 How to: Use *do / does / did* for emphasis → G11 → WB 31/19, 32/20

Sometimes, **do**, **does** or **did** is added for extra emphasis, especially in conversation.
Often – but not always – somebody has just said something which you see differently.

*Read the dialogue on the right between two colleagues. Then complete Ivy's lines to emphasise that she doesn't agree. Use **do**, **does** or **did** where necessary. Follow the example.*

Example:
A: So you don't like action films?
B: No, I **do** like action films. I just don't like the new one.

Kim: The boss's new assistant never says hello to anyone except to the important people.
Ivy: Oh that's not true. She 1 . She says hello to me and I'm not important.
Kim: And she's got no sense of style. Her skirts are too short and they don't suit her at all.
Ivy: Oh Kim, what are you talking about?! They 2 . I think she looks great in them.
Kim: She gave a presentation yesterday; it didn't go well.
Ivy: Who told you that?! I was there and I can tell you it 3 .
Kim: I hope you don't think I'm jealous of her.
Ivy: Well, really, I 4 that, Kim.

WRITING

26 < Your turn: First day surprise! >

a) *What could happen that would give you a nice surprise on your first day at work?*

→ S5–6

b) *Write a post for an online forum called 'First day surprise!' Remember to add **non-defining relative clauses** with more interesting information. (Also, you could try to use **inversion** or sentences with **do / does / did** to add emphasis.)*

c) *Do a gallery walk and read all the posts. Then, in groups, decide which was the best description. Give reasons for your choices.*

Making a good impression

In an interview situation, you really want to make a good impression. So how do you do that?

1 Criteria for a good impression

a) *Before you watch, exchange ideas on the importance of the following criteria at a job interview:*

knowledge | personality | dress code | body language | register

3 **b)** *Now watch the film. Take notes about each candidate's performance, based on the criteria in a). Then answer these questions:*

1. Describe what the job is for and what kind of skills the person should have.
2. Rate the candidates; explain your ideas.
3. Discuss who you would give the job to.

Saanvi

Phil

Courtney

2 Useful techniques

a) *Think of why, in an interview, you might need to take these actions:*

buy time | change the topic | emphasise positive things

b) *Watch again. What was wrong about how the candidates dealt with these questions?*

1. "What makes you want to work in advertising?"
2. "How would you describe your strengths?"
3. "What's your biggest weakness?"

→ S8
c) *In pairs, take turns asking and answering 'tricky'/difficult/awkward questions like the ones you see in the useful phrases box.*

→ △ 126/15
d) *Role play: Act out scenes from the film. Find ways to improve on the candidates' responses where necessary.*

Useful phrases

What the interviewer can say:
- What is your biggest strength / weakness?
- How would your friends describe you?
- Where do you see yourself 10 years from now?

What the candidate can say:
- That's a good / an interesting question. Let me see … / Let me think for a moment …
- I've been told I'm good at …
- I like to think that … is my biggest strength.

Job interviews for a summer camp

Take part in job interviews for positions at Action Summer UK's camp.

Step 1

Get to know the jobs → WB 33/22

In groups of four, take turns to talk about each of the four counsellor jobs below. Mention what skills you think would be helpful for that job according to the expectations that are listed:

A **sports & activity organiser** is expected to:
- teach sports skills to the children
- organise sports matches
- make sure they have the right equipment

A **cafeteria helper** is expected to:
- help prepare meals for and with the children
- do the food shopping for meals
- organise food for events

An **entertainments organiser** is expected to:
- organise a programme of social activities
- think of fun ideas for competitions
- organise theme parties

A **big sister / brother** is expected to:
- live with a group of children in a tent
- help with chores
- help them with their problems

Step 2

Choose a job → WB 33/23

Go back to the profile you wrote for yourself as part of Ex. 7 on p. 50. Based on what you wrote, decide which of the jobs above would be best for you.

Step 3

Form expert groups → WB 34/24

*Sit in groups with other students who are applying for **the same** job. Decide on how you could answer these interview questions.*

1. What made you decide to apply?
2. What would you bring to the job?
3. How would you describe your strengths?
4. What's your biggest weakness?

→ Vocabulary (pp. 48–51) → Social commitment (p. 55) → Making a good impression (p. 60)

Step 4

Form mixed groups to practise → WB 34/25

*Form new mixed groups of four and take turns being interviewer and applicant. **Interviewers:** Ask questions for the different jobs as in Step 3. **Applicants:** Give answers that focus on your strengths. Give each other feedback on how well you did.*

Step 5

Fish bowl: Conduct interviews with applicants and panels → WB 34/26

1. You need **four** groups of interviewers to form 'interview panels' of 2–3 people. Each panel represents a job from Step 1, so each member of each panel was an expert for the same job in Step 3.
2. Each other student in class will take turns to apply for the job that he / she became an expert on in Step 3.
3. **Inside** the fish bowl: The first interview panel interviews its first applicant, then another, and so on.
4. **Outside** the fish bowl: The rest of the class watches, in a circle, as the panel interviews each applicant one by one.
5. After the first panel is finished, it's the next panel's turn, with new applicants.

S 2/1–6
L 2/11–16

The Giver

In a future world, Jonas is a member of a community whose lives are completely regulated. When young people reach the age of twelve, they go through the special ceremony called 'Assignment': The Elders announce to them the jobs they will do for the rest of their lives. Jonas is now a 'Twelve' and about to find out his destiny at Assignment.

SPEAKING

1 Before you read

The Elders' business is to match professions to young people. Think of criteria you think could play a role in assigning the right job to the right person.

The first speech at the ceremony was made by the Chief Elder, the leader of the community who was elected every ten years. The speech was much the same each year: recollection of the time of childhood and the period of preparation, the coming responsibilities of adult life, the extreme importance of Assignment, the seriousness of training to come.

"This is the time," she began, looking directly at them, "when we acknowledge differences. You have spent all your years till now learning to fit in, to standardize your behavior. But today we honor your differences. They have determined your futures."

She began to describe this year's group and its variety of personalities, though she singled no one out by name. She mentioned that there was one with singular skills at caretaking, another with unusual scientific skills. Jonas shifted in his seat, trying to recognize each reference as one of his groupmates. He heard nothing that he recognized as himself, Jonas.

Eighteen, Fiona, on his left, was called. Jonas knew she must be nervous, but Fiona was a calm female. She had been sitting, serenely, throughout the ceremony.

The photos featured on these pages are stills from the 2014 film adaptation of *The Giver*. (In the film, Jonas is sixteen, not twelve.)

Even the applause, though enthusiastic, seemed serene when Fiona was given the important assignment of Caretaker of the Old. It was perfect for such a sensitive, gentle girl, and her smile was satisfied when she took her seat beside him again.

Jonas prepared himself to walk to the stage when the applause ended and the Chief Elder picked up the next folder and looked down to the group to call forward the next new Twelve. Jonas took a deep breath and smoothed his hair with his hand.

"Twenty," he heard a voice say clearly. "Pierre."

She *skipped* me, Jonas thought. Had he heard wrong? No. There was a sudden stir in the crowd and he knew that the entire community realized that the Chief Elder had moved from Eighteen to Twenty, leaving a gap. On his right, Pierre, with a startled look, rose from his seat and moved to the stage.

A mistake. She had made a mistake. But Jonas knew, even as he had the thought, that she hadn't. The Chief Elder made no mistakes, not at the Ceremony of Twelve.

Much later, after all the other Twelves had been given their Assignments, the Chief Elder finally turned to Jonas.

"Jonas," she said, looking down at him. "I apologize to you in particular. I caused you anguish."

"I accept your apology," Jonas replied in a shaky voice.

"Please come to the stage now."

Earlier that day, alone in his own dwelling, he had practised the kind of self-confident walk that he hoped he could make to the stage when his turn came. All of that was forgotten now. He simply forced himself to stand, to move his feet that felt heavy and clumsy, to go forward, up the steps and across the platform until he stood at her side.

Reassuringly, she placed her arm across his shoulders.

"Jonas has not been assigned," she informed the crowd, and his heart sank. Then she went on, "Jonas has been *selected*."

He blinked. What did that mean? He felt a collective, questioning stir from the audience. They too were puzzled.

In a firm, commanding voice she announced, "Jonas has been selected to be our next Receiver of Memory."

READING

2 The story so far

→ S3

a) *Outline the information given in the text about how the Elders arrive at their decisions.*

b) *Which adjectives can you use to describe how Jonas feels as he realises that he's being treated differently from everyone else?*

Alone in his sleepingroom, prepared for bed, Jonas opened his folder at last. Some of the other Twelves, he had noticed, had been given folders thick with printed pages. He imagined Benjamin, the scientific male in his group, beginning to read pages of rules and instructions with great pleasure. He pictured Fiona smiling her gentle smile as she bent over the lists of duties and methods that she would be required to learn in the coming days. But his own folder was startlingly empty. Inside there was only a single printed sheet. He read it twice.

JONAS
RECEIVER OF MEMORY

1. Go immediately at the end of school hours each day to the Annex behind the House of the Old and present yourself to the attendant.
2. Go immediately to your dwelling at the conclusion of Training Hours each day.
3. From this moment you are exempted from rules governing rudeness. You may ask any question of any citizen and you will receive answers.
4. Do not discuss your training with any other member of the community, including parents and Elders.
5. From this moment you are prohibited from dream-telling.
6. Except for illness or injury unrelated to your training, do not apply for any medication.
7. You are not permitted to apply for release.
8. You may lie.

READING

3 The community

a) *Explain what the rules on Jonas' sheet tell us about the community he lives in.*

b) *Think of more rules which could be important to the community.*

A few days later, Jonas goes for his first training session as the 'Receiver of Memory' and meets The Giver, who will pass on to Jonas his special ability.

In his mind, Jonas had questions. A thousand. A million questions. As many questions as there were books on the walls. But he did not ask one, not yet.

The man sighed, seeming to put his thoughts in order. Then he spoke again. "Simply stated," he said, "although it's not really simple at all, my job is to transmit to you all the memories I have within me. Memories of the past."

"Sir," Jonas started slowy, "I would be very interested to hear the story of your life, and to listen to your memories. I apologize for interrupting," he added quickly.

The man waved his hand impatiently. "No apologies in this room. We haven't time."

"Well," Jonas went on, uncomfortably aware that he might be interrupting again, "I am really interested, I don't mean that I'm not. But I don't exactly understand why it's so important. I could do some adult job in the community, and in my free time I could come and listen to the stories from your childhood. I'd like that. Actually," he added, "I've done that already, in the House of the Old. The Old like to tell about their childhoods, and it's always fun to listen."

The man shook his head. "No, no," he said. "I'm not being clear. It's not my past, not my childhood that I must transmit to you."

He leaned back, resting his head against the back of the chair. "It's the memories of the whole world," he said with a sigh. "Before you, before me, before the previous Receiver, and generations before him."

Jonas frowned. "The whole world?" he asked. "I don't understand. Do you mean not just us? Not just the community? Do you mean Elsewhere too?" he tried, in his mind, to grasp the concept. "I'm sorry, sir. I don't understand exactly. Maybe I'm not smart enough. I don't know what you mean when you say 'the whole world' or 'generations before him'. I thought there was only us. I thought there was only now."

"There's much more. There's all that goes beyond – all that is Elsewhere – and all that goes back. I received all of those when I was selected. And here in this room, all alone, I re-experience them again and again. It is how wisdom comes. And how we shape our future."

He rested for a moment, breathing deeply. "I am so *weighted* with them," he said, finally. "It's as if ..." The man paused, seeming to search his mind for the right words of description. "It's like going downhill through deep snow on a sled," he said, finally. "At first, it's exhilarating: the speed; the sharp, clear air; but then the snow builds upon the runners, and you slow, you have to keep going, and ... –"

He shook his head suddenly, and peered at Jonas. "That meant nothing to you, did it?" he asked.

Jonas was confused. "I didn't understand it, sir."

"Of course you didn't. You don't know what snow is, do you?"

Jonas shook his head.

"Or a sled? Runners?"

"No, sir," Jonas said.

"Downhill? The term means nothing to you?"

"Nothing, sir."

"Well, it's a place to start. I'd been wondering how to begin."

READING

4 The Receiver of Memory

→ S3 **a)** *Sum up the job description of the Receiver of Memory.*

b) *Explain why it's difficult for The Giver to make Jonas understand what he does and how he feels.*

Over the weeks, The Giver passes on many experiences to Jonas, including what it's like on a sled in the snow.

"Why don't we have snow, and sleds, and hills?" he asked. "And when did we, in the past? Did my parents have sleds when they were young? Did you?"

The old man shrugged and gave a short laugh. "No," he told Jonas. "It's a very distant memory. That's why it was so exhausting – I had to pull it forward from many generations back. It was given to me when I was a new Receiver, and the previous Receiver had to pull it through a long time period too."

"But what happened to those things? Snow, and the rest of it?"

"Climate Control. Snow made growing food difficult, limited the agricultural periods. And unpredictable weather made transportation almost impossible at times. It wasn't a practical thing, so it became useless when we went to Sameness.

"And hills too," he added. "They made it difficult, limited the agricultural periods. And they made the transportation of goods difficult: trucks; buses. Slowed them down. So …" He waved his hand, as if a gesture had caused hills to disappear. "Sameness," he concluded.

Jonas frowned. "I wish we had those things, still. Just now and then."

The old man smiled. "So do I," he said. "But that choice is not ours."

Slowly, Jonas starts to realise that he no longer sees the world only in black-and-white, like everybody else in the community.

Days went by, and weeks. Jonas learned, through the memories, the names of colors; and now he began to see them all, in his ordinary life (though he knew it was ordinary no longer, and would never be again). But they didn't last. There would be a flash of green – the landscaped lawn around the Central Plaza; a bush on the riverbank. The bright orange of pumpkins from the agricultural fields beyond the community boundary – seen in an instant, the flash of brilliant color, but gone again, returning to their flat and colorless shade.

The Giver told him that it would be a very long time before he had the colors to keep.

"But I want them!" Jonas said angrily. "It isn't fair that nothing has color!"

"Not fair?" The Giver looked at Jonas curiously. "Explain what you mean."

"Well …" Jonas had to stop and think it through. "If everything's the same, then there aren't any choices! I want to wake up in the morning and *decide* things! A blue tunic or a red one?"

He looked down at himself, at the colorless fabric of his clothing. "But it's all the same, always."

Then he laughed a little. "I know it's not important, what you wear. It doesn't matter. But –

"It's the choosing that's important, isn't it?" The Giver asked him.

Jonas nodded. "My little brother –" he began, and then corrected himself. "No, that's inaccurate. He's not my brother, not really. But this newchild that my family takes care of – his name's Gabriel?"

"Yes, I know about Gabriel."

"Well, he's right at the age where he's learning so much. He grabs toys when we hold them in front of him – my father says he's learning small-muscle control. He's really cute."

The Giver nodded.

"But now that I can see colors, at least sometimes, I was just thinking: What if we could hold up things that were bright red, or bright yellow, and he could choose? Instead of the Sameness."

"He might make wrong choices."

"Oh." Jonas was silent for a minute. "Oh, I see what you mean. It wouldn't matter for a newchild's toy. But later it *does* matter, doesn't it? We don't dare to let people make choices of their own."

"Not safe?" The Giver suggested.

"Definitely not safe," Jonas was sure. "What if they were allowed to choose their own mate? And chose *wrong*?"

"Or what if," he went on, almost laughing at the absurdity, "they chose their own *jobs*?"

"Frightening, isn't it?" The Giver said.

Jonas chuckled. "Very frightening. I can't even imagine it. We really have to protect people from wrong choices."

"It's safer."

"Yes," Jonas agreed. "Much safer."

by Lois Lowry (abridged and adapted)

READING

5 Understanding the key message

In the last of the extracts, Jonas makes the following statement:

"If everything's the same, then there aren't any choices. I want to wake up in the morning and *decide* things!"

a) *Describe how The Giver leads Jonas to change his opinion on choices and Sameness.*

→ ▲ 126/16

b) *Explain how the concept of Sameness is the key idea in the story. Include an explanation of what you think the leaders of the community – the Elders – are so afraid of. The word bank can help you.*

Word bank

- practical / useless | right / wrong | fair / unfair | safe / dangerous
- choice | control | danger
- to control | to make a right / wrong choice

READING

6 A film and literature genre: Dystopia

a) *Read the skills box below. Can you think why dystopian stories are often extremely popular in books and films?*

Reading skills

A **utopia** is an imaginary, ideal society where everybody lives in peace and harmony. In a **dystopia**, society **seems** like a utopia at first, but turns out to be the opposite. The action is often set in a sad, frightening future. Typically, dystopian stories show how totalitarian states do terrible things to their people, e.g. forcing them to live in a certain way, spying on them constantly, and even programming their bodies to function in a desirable way.
Famous examples of dystopian literature are ***1984*** (by George Orwell) and ***The Hunger Games Trilogy*** (by Suzanne Collins).

b) *Point out lines and scenes that show how* The Giver *is a dystopian story.*

<c)> *Your turn: Tell the class about a dystopian book / film that you like.*

SPEAKING

7 Imagine ...

A world like the one Jonas lives in – with no books, no music, no art, no colour – is surely a big contrast to your world.

Make a list of things you do every day. Give your list to your partner, who is a member of Jonas' community. Let him / her comment on these things from the community's perspective. Then switch roles and do the same.

SPEAKING

8 Memories

a) *Comment on the community's decision to allow only one person to hold past memories.*

→ △ 126/17

b) *Explain how memories help countries, communities and individuals to make good decisions about the present and the future.*

c) *Describe one of your own memories which has helped you to make a decision.*

SPEAKING

9 < Role play > → WB 35/27

a) *With your partner, think about some event in the past (on a class trip / at school / at a party). It can be a funny, dangerous, emotional, or sad situation. Now think about pro and con arguments for eliminating these memories. Would it be good or bad not to have those memories any more?*

→ S8

b) *Perform a role play: Partner A agrees to eliminate memories and partner B is against it.*

LISTENING

1 In the bookshop

L 2/18

a) *Listen to a dialogue between two friends, Grace and Bryan. Sum up in 2–3 sentences what they're talking about.*

b) *Take notes about their different personalities. Say what you think might be the right professions for them. Give reasons for your opinion.*

c) *Who can you identify with more – Grace or Bryan? With a partner, talk about your own plans for the future. What's important / not so important for you?*

LANGUAGE

2 Additionally, I'd like to show … → WB 38/1

a) *Decide which* ***linking adverbs*** *fit in these sentences. Sometimes more than one answer is possible.*

additionally | furthermore | however | in fact | moreover | nevertheless | therefore

Example: 1. I have a lot of different skills. **Therefore**, I feel that I should share what I have.

1. I have a lot of different skills. I feel that I should share what I have. ✔
2. I enjoyed working at a kids' summer camp. I think it's the best experience you can have.
3. I'm enthusiastic, reliable and creative. I love challenges and meeting new people.
4. I realise the position doesn't pay anything. I'd like to do it for the experience.
5. I can come in for an interview if that works for you. I can send references.
6. I've done a lot of volunteering. I'd like to work for an NGO[1] later.

b) *Finish these sentences with your own ideas.*

1. I'm waiting for the results of my final exams. In fact, … 2. I've applied for a work and travel programme. Furthermore, … 3. I have to find a room to rent near the university. Therefore, … 4. It's very difficult to get a position there. However, …

LANGUAGE

3 I won't sit waiting for you any longer → WB 38/2

a) *Complete the sentences with a* ***verb of rest or motion*** *and the* ***present participle****.*

Today is the last day of our holidays and what did we do all summer? I **1** (come – hope) for a good time but every morning you **2** (sit – watch) TV. Luckily, you turned it off before lunch, but then you **3** (sit – listen) to the radio. Whenever we met your friends in town, you **4** (stand – chat) to them and you didn't even introduce me. When the weather was good, we went to the beach, but you **5** (lie – stare) into space with earphones on. I **6** (arrive – hope) we'd have a nice time together. And I **7** (stay – think) it could only get better. But now I've had enough. I'm not going to **8** (sit – cry) about it any longer. Goodbye!

b) *Imagine it's the first day at your new job. Make five sentences to describe your day. Use a verb and a present participle from the boxes below.*

arrive | catch myself | come | lay | leave | sit | stand | walk

feeling | looking | reading | smiling | waiting | watching | wondering | worrying

1 **NGO = non-governmental organisation** [ˌnɒngʌvnˈmentl ɔːgnaɪˈzeɪʃn] Nichtregierungsorganisation

LANGUAGE

4 Unfortunately, your application …

a) *In this letter below, the head of Human Resources[1] at a big advertising company writes to an applicant suggesting ways of improving his application. Complete the letter with* ***commenting adverbs****. Sometimes more than one answer is possible.*

certainly | luckily | obviously | personally | surely | unfortunately

Dear Mr Thompson,

1, you weren't paying attention when I explained how to fill out the application so I will explain it again. You 2 know the difference between 'personal details' and 'personal profile'. Please correct these sections accordingly[2]. The profile should 3 tell us why you are suitable[3] for the position. So if you think you are suitable, explain how. 4, I would not include 'watching videos online' and 'hanging out with friends' as your hobbies. 5 for you, we want to give you the chance to improve your application. 6, the deadline[4] is in three days so you must act quickly.

Sincerely,
Anita Fowler
Head of Human Resources

b) *Decide which of these commenting adverbs you could also use for the letter in a).*

clearly | happily | honestly | hopefully | of course | probably

c) *Add a commenting adverb to these sentences.*

Example: 1. Look at her long list of qualifications. **Surely**, she's the best applicant we've had.

1. Look at her long list of qualifications. She's the best applicant we've had. ✔
2. I don't think all the information in your CV is true.
3. All of the candidates we invited are going to come in for interviews.
4. Our pay is comparable to similar companies in the area.
5. She has applied for other jobs and is waiting for the best offer.
6. He accepted a position with our main competitor[5].

VOCABULARY

5 It's all about jobs

a) *For each word write down the first job or profession that comes to your mind.*

adventurous | all-rounder | commitment | exhausted | hard-working | helper | organiser | people skills | physical | responsibility

b) *Compare your list with a partner's. Explain your choices.*

c) *Choose two of the jobs or professions you listed in a) that you could imagine working in. Then add other words that describe them.*

1 **Human Resources** [ˌhjuːmən rɪˈzɔːsɪz] Personalabteilung | 2 **accordingly** [əˈkɔːdɪŋli] entsprechend | 3 **suitable** [ˈsuːtəbl] geeignet | 4 **deadline** [ˈdedlaɪn] Abgabetermin | 5 **competitor** [kəmˈpetɪtə] Konkurrent/-in

LANGUAGE

6 Doesn't he notice me getting desperate? → WB 39/3

a) *Complete the sentences with the* ***present participle*** *or the* ***infinitive*** *of the verb.*

As I was standing outside the gym door, I heard our coach **1** (shout) at the team. Again. Now I knew that this was the day, and I felt my decision **2** (become) even more firm[1]. It was the right thing to do. How many times had I heard him **3** (offend[2]) us and **4** (scream) at us over the years? – Too many times. Did he notice me **5** (get) more and more desperate at every practice? In my head, I listened to my family **6** (cheer) me on and I knew where my priorities were. I'd leave the team although I had good chances of making a career out of basketball. He just wasn't the kind of coach I wanted to play for. When I opened the door, I saw the coach **7** (look) angrily at me and **8** (point) in my direction. This wasn't going to make it any easier.

b) *Complete the sentences with your own ideas.*

1. I felt the pressure … 2. We heard the crowd … 3. The class listened to the teacher … 4. I saw my classmates … 5. My best friend watched me … 6. …

LANGUAGE

7 But I did do everything that was asked for! → WB 39/4

Write a reply to each of these sentences. Use ***do*** *or* ***did*** *for emphasis.*

Example: 1. So they don't have a suitable position available? – Yes, they **do** have one. I just don't know if I want it.

1. So they don't have a suitable position available? ✔
2. If they haven't replied yet, then you probably didn't write a very good application letter.
3. You just don't have the qualifications we're looking for.
4. You mean you didn't name one single weakness when they asked?
5. I don't know why you didn't consider engineering. In my opinion it would be perfect for you.
6. Wait, you don't have any references available?

WRITING

8 What's the good life?

a) *Describe the cartoon, then analyse it. What's the cartoonist making fun of?*

b) *Write a short text about what 'the good life' means to you. You can use one of these sentences or your own to start with:*

Life is too short to … | A good life starts with … | … is the key to a good life.

1 firm [fɜːm] fest; sicher | **2 to offend** [əˈfend] beleidigen

LANGUAGE

9 I'm a woman who …

*Use a **relative pronoun** to combine the two sentences.*

Example: 1. I'm a woman **who** has always had different interests than other women.

1. I'm a woman. I have always had different interests than other women. ✔
2. In Year 6 I had a great teacher. He encouraged me to stand out from the others.
3. Once I met a firefighter. He was very passionate about his job.
4. I chose a profession. It was typically just for men.
5. I joined a new team. It was full of only men.
6. People are meaningful to me. They don't expect me to justify my choices.

LANGUAGE

10 A good life? → WB 40/5

a) *Decide which **relative pronoun** you need to complete the sentences.*

Dave Chappelle, 1 (who / whose) parents were both teachers, is a stand-up comedian and actor. He was born in Washington, D.C., in 1973. His first film appearance was in Mel Brooks' movie *Robin Hood: Men in Tights*[1], 2 (whose / which) was in movie theaters in 1993. Chapelle, 3 (who / whose) mother was a minister[2], converted[3] to Islam in 1998. He continued to act throughout the 1990s, mostly in comedies. In 2003 he started *Chapelle's Show*, 4 (who / which) was a comedy television series. After two seasons[4] of the show, 5 (that / which) was very successful, he suddenly left it. Chapelle, 6 (which / who) said his ego needed to quiet down, went to South Africa to take a much-needed break from the negative sides of being famous. He has since returned to the comedy scene in the US, where he can be seen both on TV and live on stage.

b) *Write a short biography about one of your favourite celebrities. Did they ever give up their celebrity status?*

LANGUAGE

11 Never will you regret[5] working with us!

a) *Here are some guidelines for volunteers working in a refugee camp. Use **inversion** to rewrite the sentences.*

Example: 1. **Never** are you supposed to get involved in an argument between residents.

1. You're **never** supposed to get involved in an argument between residents. ✔
2. You'll only be allowed to work with the children **after** you've received proper training.
3. You should **never** provide medical help. That's a doctor's job.
4. Refugees **not only** need food and a place to sleep, they also need emotional support.
5. You'll **never** have experienced satisfaction like this **before**.
6. The residents will **rarely** be here longer than three months before they move to other refugee homes.

b) *Choose from these adverbs or adverb phrases to write four sentences with inversion.*

hardly | never | never before | no sooner | not for one moment

not only | no way | only then | rarely

1 tights [taɪts] Strumpfhose | **2 minister** ['mɪnɪstə] Pfarrer/-in | **3 to convert** [kən'vɜːt] konvertieren | **4 season** ['siːzn] Staffel | **5 to regret** [rɪ'gret] bedauern

LANGUAGE

12 Let's talk about my boss! → WB 40/6

a) *Have a look at the sentences below and decide if you need a* ***defining*** *or* ***non-defining relative clause****.*

1. My boss is a great guy.
   a) My boss is a great guy who is passionate about his job.
   b) My boss is a great guy, who is passionate about his job.
2. He is married and has one son.
   a) His son who is 20 will be starting university in September.
   b) His son, who is 20, will be starting university in September.
3. He also has two daughters.
   a) The daughter who lives in New York is a model.
   b) The daughter, who lives in New York, is a model.
4. He and his wife have three houses.
   a) They spend most of their time in their house in Florida which is the biggest one.
   b) They spend most of their time in their house in Florida, which is the biggest one.

b) *Write two sentences that go with the sentences below – one with a* ***defining*** *and one with a* ***non-defining relative clause****.*

Example: I'm passionate about shoes.
a) The green shoes I bought yesterday go perfectly with my new green dress.
b) Shoes, which are really a girl's best friend, can be very expensive.

1. My best friend has bought a new tablet.
2. I could talk for hours about my dream jobs.
3. Our favourite holiday destination is Spain.
4. All of her films are really popular.

VOCABULARY

13 Future perspectives

a) *Choose the correct verb in each sentence.*

1. At some schools you're (encouraged / required) to participate in social projects as part of the school curriculum[1].
2. A lot of employers look for people who (were involved in / were never involved in) groups and teams during their time at school.
3. A lot of young people have a hard time (determining / assigning) what they want to do for the rest of their lives.
4. Parents shouldn't (force / regulate) their children's lives too much because young people need to learn to take on responsibilities on their own.
5. Instead, parents should (provide / limit) support and advice.
6. It's also very important that parents (respect / select) their children's choices, no matter what career path they choose.

b) *Write sentences with the verbs you didn't use in a).*

c) *Change these verbs into nouns by adding the suffixes* ***-ment****,* ***-ation*** *or* ***-ion****.*

Example: be involved = involvement

assign | determine | encourage | limit | regulate | require | select

1 school curriculum [ˌskuːl kəˈrɪkjələm] Lehrplan

MEDIATION

14 Can consumer habits[1] change the world?

a) *Which of the aspects below are important to you when you buy a product? Do the same criteria apply to all the different things you buy, e.g. clothes, cosmetics, food? Discuss these questions with your partner.*

price | quality | organic[2] origin | country of production | appearance | brand

b) *One of your friends has joined a volunteer group that wants to inform people about child labour and the advantages of fair trade. He / She asks you to collect information about fair trade chocolate from Ivory Coast. You find this article on the internet and write down the key points for the group's website in English. The annotations below can help you.*

„Kinder"-Schokolade – Ist da drin was draufsteht?

Viele Erwachsene in Deutschland kennen weder die Farbe der Kakaobohne noch wissen sie, wie Kakao eigentlich wächst. Anders ist das bei den Kindern aus der Elfenbeinküste. Sie kennen die Frucht sehr gut. Die Elfenbeinküste ist der größte Kakaoproduzent[3] der Welt. Jeder vierte Einwohner lebt vom Kakaoanbau. Trotzdem liegt die Armutsrate[4] in der Elfenbeinküste laut Statistik bei 43 Prozent. Die Kleinbauern haben ein durchschnittliches Tageseinkommen[5] von gerade einmal 50 US-Cent pro Kopf. Das veranlasst viele Familien, die eigenen Kinder in die harte Arbeit mit einzubinden.

„Wer Kinderarbeit bekämpfen will, muss die Bauern aus der Armut holen", sagt eine ivorische Gewerkschafterin, die als kleines Mädchen oft selbst nicht zur Schule gehen konnte, weil sie ihren Eltern bei der Ernte helfen musste. Offiziell regelt der Staat, wie viel die Bauern beim Verkauf ihrer Bohnen mindestens bezahlt bekommen. Doch in der Region sind Zwischenhändler[6] am Werk, die ihnen weit weniger bezahlen als vorgeschrieben. Da die Bauern mangels Fahrzeugen keine Möglichkeit haben, ihre Ernte selbst an den Hafen zu bringen, sind sie den Machenschaften dieser Händler ausgeliefert.

Ein einzelner Kakaobauer kann das System und die multinationalen Konzerne nicht bezwingen – der Verbraucher jedoch schon! Denn „faire Schokolade" ist längst keine Utopie mehr:

Selbst im Discounter gehört sie längst zum Standardsortiment. Dass der Kauf von Fairtrade-Produkten durchaus Wirkung auf die Menschen in den Anbaugebieten hat, zeigt das Dorf Tiemokokro. Noch vor einigen Jahren passten in die Schlaglöcher der Dorfstraßen ganze Kühe. Das hat sich inzwischen geändert. Besonders stolz sind die Dorfältesten auf ihre neue Schule. In einem Land, in dem laut Schätzungen knapp die Hälfte der Bevölkerung Analphabeten sind, keine Selbstverständlichkeit. Errichtet werden konnte sie aus Geldern der Fairtrade-Kooperative. So sind es oft die kleinen Entscheidungen im Alltag, die das Leben der Bauern und Kinder in anderen Teilen der Erde retten können.

Source: earthlink e.V. (abridged)

c) *In small groups, discuss how consumer habits can change the world.*

1 **consumer habits *(pl)*** [kən'sju:mə ˌhæbɪts] Konsumverhalten | 2 **organic** [ɔ:'gænɪk] biologisch; Bio- | 3 **cocoa producer** ['kəʊkəʊ prəˌdju:sə] | 4 **poverty rate** ['pɒvəti ˌreɪt] | 5 **daily income** [ˌdeɪli 'ɪnkʌm] | 6 **middlemen** ['mɪdlmen]

Find more online: vh5gv9

Text smart 2
Informative texts

In Text smart 2, you're going to look at informative texts from the point of view of two important writing skills: the skills of writing a **text summary** and a **text analysis**.

SPEAKING

1 Warm-up: What information is important?

a) *Look at the scene below. Say what has gone wrong in the situation. What would have been a better answer to the question, and why?*

b) *All of the everyday questions below require you to summarise when you give an answer – some more, some less. In pairs, take turns role-playing the situations with a partner. Before you start, take a moment to think about how you might answer each question:*

How was your day? | What did the news report say about the fire? | How did you celebrate your last birthday? | That book must be good – what's it about? | How did you get to school today? | What happens in the film? | Was it a good football match? | What are your plans for tonight?

SPEAKING

2 Warm-up: Interpreting information

Summarising focuses on the 'what' of a subject, the information. But there's also the aspect of the 'why'; why something is said or written.

a) *Go back to Ex. 1a). What kind of personality does Tom have based on the way he replies?*

b) *Now think of the different text types on the right. Why does an author write texts like these? What would be the same in each; what would be different? Think of these points:*

information | entertainment | writing style | criticism

interview with sports star | news report on earthquake | film review |

How to: Write a text summary

READING

3 The parts of a summary

a) *Look again at the news article about the cocoa controversy on p. 53. With a partner, note down the main points in the article that you'd include in a summary.*

b) *Now read a model summary of the news article. Compare the summary with the key points you both noted in a). The skills and phrases boxes can help you.*

In an online article by Steve Hartley entitled 'Chocolate: So sweet, so bitter', which was published in the Daily News on 26th May 2017, the writer argues that children should not be working on the cocoa plantations in Ivory Coast.

According to the author, around 100,000 children work in terrible conditions there for little or no pay because the farmers can't afford to pay adults to do the dangerous work. The children are often victims of enslavement and unable to leave. They ask why they have to live such difficult lives when children in other countries don't.

The writer illustrates the problem by describing a visit to one cocoa plantation. He sees the children doing a lot of hard physical work, like chopping down heavy cocoa pods with huge machetes. All the children he meets have had machete injuries.

The author concludes by hoping the cocoa industry will finally stop using child labour. He asks his readers to buy fair trade products as a form of protest.

A summary begins with an **umbrella sentence** or paragraph which gives essentials: author, source, publication date / place, and the title and gist of the original text.

Examples of **typical phrases** in a more formal **register** appropriate for a summary

Examples of **key terms** from the original text which help to illustrate its **main points**

Be aware that the **simple present** is usually used.

Writing skills

Important **dos and don'ts** for summaries:
- A summary is always a **reduction**, usually 30–40 % of the original article's length.
- The **order** of the information doesn't have to match the original text.
- Leave out **irrelevant details**. (Example: The reader doesn't need to know that the author got out of his car 15 miles outside of Abengourou.)
- Don't use **direct speech** (i.e. no quotes).
- Don't copy original lines **word for word**.
- Leave out your **feelings** or **views**! A summary only needs to sum up.
- **Register** should be more formal.

Useful phrases

- In an article posted on / published in …, the author states … / mentions … / argues … / points out … / discusses … / explains … / emphasises … / illustrates … / refers to …
- According to the writer, …
- The author's main point is …
- The writer goes on to say …
- The author also believes that …
- The author illustrates … by …
- The writer concludes by stating … / pointing out … / asking … / using … / telling …

c) *Go back to the original report on p. 53. With your partner, point out to each other more examples of information which the summary writer didn't feel was relevant enough to include.*

WRITING

4 Your turn: Your checklist for summary writing

→ △ 127/1

Write a personal checklist of things to do – or ***not*** *to do – when you plan and write a summary. The information on p. 75 gives you the input you need, but you can also include tips of your own. Maybe there's something you feel you need to pay special attention to. Then exchange checklists with a partner for peer-editing.*

Tip

A checklist should be **simple**. It only needs to feature **categories** and **key terms**, not full sentences.

READING

5 Differences in summary quality

a) *Below, a student has written an* ***unsuccessful*** *summary of 'Chocolate: So sweet, so bitter'. As you read it, note down what you find is wrong for a summary. Refer to your checklist.*

In the article, the writer said that cocoa is the main ingredient for the chocolate many Europeans and Americans eat in massive quantities. He also tells us that chocolate is a main ingredient for many cosmetics and that the chocolate industry is worth about £60 billion a year in Ivory Coast. He says that he doesn't understand why 40 % of the population lives below the poverty line or why so many children work on the cocoa plantations. To be honest, I don't understand it either!!! But whatever. Anyway, he suggested that a possible reason is that farmers don't make enough money to employ adult workers or give them healthcare. But he didn't seem to be convinced that this was a good enough reason to employ children. And you know what? I'm not convinced either! Not at all. I mean, would you be? I'm glad that this journalist has got his priorities in life right. He sees what the REAL problems are. Good job!

The writer went to a cocoa plantation 15 miles from the Ivory Coast town of Abengourou to meet the children who worked there. It was a really hot day and the sun was burning on his skin. The children he met were tired and injured. They could hardly carry all the heavy tools and equipment. They arrived feeling exhausted – and had yet to start their day's work. Slowly, they climbed the largest of the trees and the writer watched them chop down heavy yellow cocoa pods with their huge machetes, which seemed nearly as big as they were. All of them had scars on their legs from machete injuries. One boy, Abdoulaye, told him, "I'm the oldest of five children and I have to work so they can eat. I haven't seen them for two years now and I've never been to school." Abdoulaye has never tasted chocolate and doesn't understand why his life is so much harder than that of children in other countries.

The writer wants the cocoa industry to change its ways and so he asked us to support the children by buying fair trade products, which I will definitely do. "Let's keep buying them and make our message clear," he says. Yes, let's do that!

b) *Now look at the points below. With a partner, exchange ideas about the summary's quality for each point. Use your notes from a).*

personal views | irrelevant information | copying original lines word for word | summary length | use of tenses | use of direct speech / quotes | register

READING

6 From oral to written summaries → WB 41/1

→ S3

a) *Before you can do written summary work, you need to understand the content. Read the text below. Then work together to sum up the report's main message, orally.*

Sleep scientists' wake-up call for a later school day

by Jonathan Webb | Science reporter, BBC News, Bradford | 8 September 2015

As they prepare a major study to test the idea, UK scientists have said that starting school at 10:00 could have huge benefits for teenagers. Research suggests that society pays too little attention to our 'body clock' – and teenagers in particular have a late-running biological rhythm. This means an early start can cause sleep deprivation, which can then affect learning and health.

A sleep expert made the argument at the British Science Festival in Bradford. Dr Paul Kelley said that teens lose up to two hours of sleep per day, which is "a huge society issue". He and colleagues from Oxford are leading a project called Teensleep, which is currently recruiting 100 schools from around the UK to take part in a test.

Our body clock is a daily cycle which drives the regular rise and fall of certain genes as well as the ebb and flow of our cognitive performance, our metabolism and so on.

For much of our lives – and especially in our teen years – there is a mismatch between this rhythm and the typical working day. In fact, Dr Kelley said, the body clock of most people between age 10 and 55 is not well-suited to rising early. "Most people wake up to alarms because they don't naturally wake up at the time when they have to get up and go to work. So we've got a sleep deprived society – it's just that this age group of 14- to 24-year-olds is more deprived than any other group."

Dr Kelley and his colleagues, including well-known Oxford sleep researcher Prof Russell Foster, argue that school days should start at 10:00 and university at 11:00, to better match the rhythms of teenagers and young adults. "All the evidence points to the same thing," Dr Kelley told BBC News. "There are no negative outcomes for moving the school day later."

Source: BBC Online (abridged and adapted)

b) *Now each of you writes an umbrella sentence and a first paragraph for a summary. Peer-edit each other's results: What works well? What can be improved, and how?*

c) *Write the rest of the summary. Follow the model on p. 75 and your checklist from Ex. 4.*

d) *Your turn: As a teenager yourself, give your opinion on the report's message about teens and sleep.*

How to: Write a text analysis

READING

7 Text analysis: Comparing two examples

Two students have analysed the report on p. 77 based on how **well-written**, how **convincing** and how **interesting** it is for a general audience of all ages.

Read the students' results below. Exchange ideas with your partner on which analysis is a real modern text based on the criteria mentioned above, and why you think so.

→ △ 127/2

A

Jonathan Webb of the BBC presents an interesting subject: that teenagers need more sleep. I can totally relate to that! But I can't relate to every aspect of how this article was written. The author's style is objective, and he does a good job of presenting basic facts together with quotes from experts. However, he doesn't always do a good job of presenting the topic clearly. For example, he makes the mistake of using pretty language ('ebb and flow') or using terms that are too big and scientific ('cognitive', 'metabolism'). Huh? Who wants to read stuff like that?! I don't! In the end, the writer does his job, but using simpler terms would make the content more interesting and easier to read.

B

The report by Jonathan Webb of the BBC aims to inform the reader about sleep deprivation as a general problem for society.

First, the writer offers plenty of facts without getting lost in detail. Also, the writer quotes experts in the field, and it's interesting for the reader to learn what solutions the experts suggest. This mix of facts and expert views creates an objective impression which is convincing.

From a language point of view, the writer uses scientific terms like 'cognitive performance' or 'metabolism', but he also uses terms like 'body clock' which everybody can understand.

Overall, the writer presents a healthy balance of information that is relevant, objective and easy to follow.

WRITING

8 Building blocks of an analysis → WB 42/2

a) *Read the skills box below. Which points match your ideas from Ex. 7? Which don't?*

Writing skills

For a **successful analysis**, consider these points:
- A text analysis always involves examining **particular aspects** of a text: e.g. why it was written ('author's intention'); how objective he / she is; how interesting the style is; how convincing an argument is; and so on.
- **Structure:** Make sure that you feature an introduction and conclusion, and that you introduce new ideas in new paragraphs.
- **Don't confuse analysing with commenting!** When you analyse, you explain and examine, with examples from the text to justify your assessment. But when you comment, you're expressing your opinion in an open discussion, not always based on particular criteria.
- Like a summary, an analysis needs a more **formal register** with typical **set phrases**.

b) *Work with a partner to make a checklist for a successful text analysis. Include useful phrases.*

c) *Compare your results in class. Edit your checklist to include other classmates' helpful ideas.*

d) *If you analysed the text on p. 53, what would you focus on? Give reasons.*

WRITING

9 Text summary and analysis: Show what you know!

→ △ 127/3
→ S6

Option A: Write a summary

Read the text below and write a summary of it.

Option B: Write an analysis

Read the text below and write an analysis of it. Consider the criteria on the right when deciding what to focus on in your analysis.

level of interest for the reader | objectivity | how well the message is communicated | the writer's intention

Teens and tech: What happens when students give up smartphones?

Erin Cotter | Thursday 23 April 2015

A recent report by Childwise found that children aged five to 16 spend an average of six and a half hours a day in front of a screen, more than twice as much as they did 20 years ago. Debate about the effects of the culture on young people – sexting, bullying, mental health and cyber addiction – has never been livelier. While many young people recognise the problem, they don't question their choices. "Gaming and social media are so much a part of their lives that they haven't really thought about it," says Sally Llewellyn, a teacher at Capital City Academy (CCA) in London.

So what happens when you ask a group of tech-loving teens to switch off for a week? The Disconnect project did that with a group of 15-year-olds from CCA. Over several weeks, we discussed their gaming and social media habits and then challenged them to go offline for a week.

"At first the students were against it," says Llewellyn. "But the more they considered it, the more interesting the idea of disconnecting became. Once we started looking at what they'd done the previous week, and how much time they'd spent on their smartphones and games, they were horrified."

Girls were on their phones from the moment they woke up until they went to bed – they even slept with them by their side. Boys used social media less, but they spent up to six hours a day gaming.

One student, Abdi, was worried about how he would fill his time. "After a week you'd just start repeating what you did the day before. If I wasn't gaming, I'd probably watch a movie or something, and I'd hate to watch the same movie twice."

Was it hard? Yes. But impossible? No. Most who took up the challenge found it less difficult than they expected, which suggests that the relationship they have with their devices is less addictive than compulsive.

More importantly, all of them said they got something out of it. "I watched TV with my friends," says one. "I read a book. I can't remember the last time I did that," adds another. "I got my homework in on time and hung out much more with my family." They also reported going to bed earlier – lack of sleep being a related and growing area of concern.

Source: The Guardian Online (abridged and adapted)

Find more online: ai8h4f

The language of tolerance and respect

SPEAKING

1 Warm-up: Different perspectives

a) *Describe the cartoon about a goat and its targets.*

b) *There are positive and negative sides to the goat's view of the world. Describe both sides. The ideas below might help you:*

differences | similarities | things in common | to look beyond the surface | to see somebody / something from a different perspective

LISTENING

2 Free your mind (En Vogue)

En Vogue, an African-American group from the US, has won various awards for this song.

a) *In groups, find and write down definitions of the three terms below. Then compare your results.*

tolerance | respect | prejudice

L 3/1 **b)** *Listen to the song. Describe who is involved in the action: Who is 'I'? Who is 'you'?*

c) *Use the terms in a) and words / lines from the song to explain its message.*

d) *"Free your mind and the rest will follow". Say what you think 'the rest' means.*

I wear tight clothing, high-heeled shoes
It doesn't mean that I'm a prostitute.
I like rap music, wear hip-hop clothes
That doesn't mean that I'm out sellin' dope.
Oh my, forgive me, for having straight hair
It doesn't mean there's another blood in my heir.
I might date another race or color
It doesn't mean I don't like my strong black brothers.

Why oh why must it be this way?
Before you can read me you gotta learn
How to see me, I say:
Free your mind and the rest will follow
Be color blind, don't be so shallow
Free your mind and the rest will follow
Be color blind, don't be so shallow

SPEAKING

3 Everyday people, everyday situations

*Divide up into groups. Each group works with **one** of the photos below:*

1. Make a list of possible reactions the people in your photo may face in public situations like these.
2. Discuss reasons for those reactions.
3. Explain how you think the people in the photos *themselves* would react to others' reactions and comments. What might they say?
4. Share your ideas with the class.

Word bank

to look different / to behave differently / to have a different lifestyle (from the mainstream) | to be prejudiced against sb (based on race / gender / sexual orientation / religion / differences / stereotypes / clichés) | to provoke others (un)willingly | to (not) accept diversity

Tip

In discussion, everyone is entitled to their opinion, popular or not. Just remember the phrases for arguing a point **politely**. → S8

A

A father, covered in tattoos, and his daughter at a street fair

B

Women in niqabs in a European pedestrian zone

C

A gay couple sharing a kiss in the park

LISTENING

4 Showing respect through language

L 3/2–4

Here and on the following pages, learn more about how to communicate respectfully.

→ S7

a) *Listen. Then sum up the action in each scene.*

b) *Get into groups of three. As you listen again, take notes on **one** of the three points below. Give examples of phrases / dialogue that show how your point is featured. The phrases on the right can help you.*

- judging a book by its cover
- respecting others' privacy
- assuming others share your opinion

Useful phrases

- I don't think it's fair / acceptable / appropriate to …
- Could you please show more respect for …?
- It's hard to judge if you don't know …
- I like to treat others / strangers / people from different … as I like to be treated myself.
- See … from his / her / their point of view.

c) *Your turn: How would you react to the not-so tolerant comments from the scenes you heard?*

d) *With a partner, talk about other possible reactions to the situations.*

e) *Think back to the positive aspects of the cartoon on p. 80. If every person applied it in everyday life, how would there be less prejudice?*

Is that what you really think?

VIEWING

5 Scene 1

a) *Pre-viewing: Describe what you see in stills A and B below. What storyline ideas seem possible?*

A

Mark and two friends

B

Dan and Liam

4 **b)** *Watch the first scene of the film (until 02:00). Then:*

1. Describe the action in stills A and B above. Which of your storyline ideas from a) match what really happens?
2. Identify the different topics the characters bring up.

c) *Sum up Dan's and Liam's opinions on being gay. Mention key statements.*

d) *What do you think could happen next?*

Word bank

- same-sex / gay / lesbian / straight
- to come out
- to have one's coming out
- different ways to live one's life

VIEWING

6 Scene 2

a) *Now watch until 02:28. What has happened to cause Dan's surprise?*

b) *Describe how Dan feels. Use the adjectives below if you think they fit:*

angry | curious | disappointed | disgusted | happy | interested | left out | shocked | surprised

c) *Do you think Dan will want to talk to Liam about what he saw? If yes, what could he say? With a partner, collect phrases you think Dan could use to bring up the subject.*

VIEWING

7 Scene 3

a) *Now watch the film to the end. Say what you think of the ending and why.*

A

B

b) *Look at these key statements from Scene 3. Who says them? Explain why each statement is important. Say which emotions are expressed in each.*

We'll still be hanging out as much as before – if you want. | I thought we were best mates. | I didn't mean it. I wouldn't have said it if I'd known … | But is that what you really think?

c) *Say how much tolerance and respect you feel Liam and Dan have in their friendship.*

‹d)› *How could the story go on? Write an additional scene (or just ideas for it) in script format.*

VOCABULARY

8 Acting and reacting in sensitive situations → WB 43/1

a) *Look at the problematic situations below. For each one, write down how one could / should / shouldn't react to what you hear or see. The phrases in the box can help you. Exchange ideas with a partner.*

1. On the bus, somebody is talking on their phone and using loud, vulgar language.
2. You don't want your friend to embarrass him- / herself at the big party on Saturday with an awful outfit.
3. A classmate likes your new outfit, but is surprised you were able to afford it. "Much nicer than your normal stuff! Didn't think you had that kind of money."
4. A friend is spreading horrible rumours about somebody you like and respect.

Useful phrases

Don't take this the wrong way, but … | I hope it doesn't hurt your feelings when I say … | I wouldn't be a friend if I didn't tell you … | I'm sorry but I need to ask you to … | Do you really think it's appropriate to …?

b) *With your partner, think of how the other side may react to what you say in a). But you must reckon with both positive **and** negative reactions!*

→ S8 **‹c)›** *Role play: Take turns acting out scenes in a) and b). Peer evaluation: Say what worked or didn't work so well.*

Useful phrases

I apologise if it offends you to see / hear … | Well, you've got your opinion / view / …, I've got mine. | Sorry, but do you know the whole situation / story / …? | Maybe I shouldn't have mentioned … | I'm glad you mentioned …

Unit 3
California dreaming

Find more online: s9n8xx

A Hollywood Boulevard

SPEAKING

1 Warm-up: Your ideas about California

a) *What comes to your mind first when you think of California? Collect your ideas in a grid. These categories can help you:*

people | climate | nature | entertainment | lifestyle

→ S1

b) *Now describe the pictures above. When you think of the ideas you collected in a), what pictures would you use to complete your impression of California?*

WRITING

2 Imagine yourself in the scene → WB 44/1

→ △ 128/1

Choose one of the roles below. Then write a short text about what you're doing in the picture and what you feel (see, hear, smell).

a young actor walking along Hollywood Boulevard | a farm worker on the field | a tourist driving across Bixby Bridge | a Google employee at work | a skateboarder at Venice Skatepark

In Unit 3 you learn

... about different aspects of life in California. You learn:

- about the hopes of young actors in Hollywood, California's economy and environmental issues
- different ways of talking about the future
- how to improve your presentation skills

B Bixby Bridge, Big Sur

C At Venice Skatepark

D Farm workers in Salinas

E A lounge at Google headquarters, Silicon Valley

SPEAKING

3 Quotations about California

Think – pair – share: Read the quotations below and think about what they say about California. Share your ideas in small groups and then in class.

Whatever starts in California unfortunately has a tendency to spread.
Jimmy Carter, US President 1977–1981

I live in the Mexican part of L.A.; it's called L.A.
Bobby Slayton, actor

I'm goin' to California / To find my pot of gold
from: Pink, *Gone to California*

There is science, logic, reason; and then there is California.
Edward Abbey, writer

To think that a boy from Austria could grow up to become Governor of California; that's the American Dream.
Arnold Schwarzenegger, actor

As one went to Europe to see the past, so one must visit Southern California to observe the future!
Alison Lurie, writer

L3/5

Hollywood hopes

In his blog Alex, an aspiring young actor, writes about his life in Hollywood:

Have you ever thought of trying your luck out here? It isn't easy. DO NOT expect to just stroll in and get an acting job because it doesn't work that way. By the time you read this, maybe I'll have gotten my first small role in a movie, after years of no glitz and no glamor. – Let me tell you about a typical week in Hollywood.

Okay, so on Monday morning I think, "Wow! You're living in the place where dreams come true! And very soon you'll be living *your* dream!" Then I get ready for work. I entertain tourists while they're waiting for their bus tours. It's just a day job to keep my head above water while I'm waiting for my big break. It's not exactly glamorous work, but it's a good opportunity to showcase my talents. And in L.A. you never know who's watching you, right? Today could just be my lucky day.

Then on Tuesday, maybe there'll be a cattle call. They're open auditions that anyone can go to – and usually 'anyone' does. So they can be a bit of a nightmare. Sometimes you can wait in line for hours with all these other wannabes, then by the time it's your turn, they'll already have filled all the roles! When that happens, you just have to pack up your stuff and wait for the next opportunity. It's best to chalk these interviews up to experience and not give up.

Okay, so now it's Wednesday. There's a movie premiere tonight on Hollywood Boulevard and I'll be going to it. It starts at 8:00 but I'm meeting my buddy there at 6:00 to set up. It isn't much, but I do online movie reviews. I even interview some of the stars – for a couple of minutes anyway. It gets my face out on the internet, maybe causes a small stir.

So that brings me to Thursday – my favorite day. On Thursdays I like to visit my buddy Dave. He owns an RV park just outside L.A. where they often shoot movie scenes. Today they're filming a scene with an exploding trailer for an action movie. Dave is a great guy. He always lets me know when they need 'extras'. Of course, I don't get paid much for the work, but at least I get to meet the stars.

Well, I guess I only made it to Thursday, but that's what my life in L.A. is all about. Making it to the next day. I haven't become a star yet. But I know it's going to happen one day very soon!

READING

1 Living in Hollywood

→ S3

a) *Outline what efforts Alex makes to pursue his dream in Hollywood.*

b) *Analyse Alex's character. Choose three of the character traits below and find examples in the text that show Alex has them.*

confident | determined | hard-working | optimistic | outgoing | passionate | patient | persistent | realistic | relaxed | smart

c) *With a partner talk about character traits you have that would make you (not) suitable for Hollywood. Give reasons.*

VOCABULARY

2 Expressing the same idea differently → WB 45/2

→ △ 128/2

a) *Find words or phrases in the text that go with the definitions below. (They're in the same order as the words / phrases appear in the text.)*

trying to be successful at something | walk in a relaxed way | just be able to survive | show what you're really good at | a person who is trying to become famous, usually without success | learn from something negative that has happened to you | produce a lot of interest or excitement

b) *Choose three of the words / phrases you found in a) and use them to write a short paragraph (4–5 sentences).*

LANGUAGE

3 Simple present and present progressive with future meaning → G12

*Find the rule: Look at these sentences. Think about when you use the **simple present** and the **present progressive** to talk about the future.*

1. The movie premiere **starts** at 8:00, but I'**m interviewing** some of the stars before that.
2. The next bus **leaves** in five minutes. I can't miss it because at 3:00 I'**m meeting** a director who is looking for young talents.
3. Training **ends** at 6:00 tonight, then I'**m picking** up my best friend to go to the movies.

LANGUAGE

4 We're meeting at the premiere tonight → WB 45/3, 46/4

a) *Read the dialogue. Decide if you need the **simple present** or the **present progressive**.*

A: The premiere **1** (start) at 8:00 tonight.
B: But we **2** (meet) at 8:00, aren't we? Then that's too late!
A: No, we **3** (not meet) at 8:00. I **4** (come) to your apartment at 6:30. We talked about it, remember?
B: But my acting lesson **5** (not finish) until 6:00 normally, so I don't know if I'll be home by then.
A: Well, I **6** (pick up) Susan on the way so we'll just wait for you.
B: But Susan **7** (only leave) work at 6:00, so how will that work?
A: It's all arranged. I **8** (pick) her up at the café where she works. Stop worrying!
B: I just want everything to work out. Lots of important people **9** (come) to the premiere!

b) *Compare schedules with a partner. Use the **simple present** and the **present progressive** to talk about the future.*

Example: A: School **ends** at 11:00 on Friday. Let's go downtown together!
B: I'**m** already **doing** something with Tina. But …

LISTENING

5 In line for a cattle call

L3/6
→ S7

a) *Alex, Sarah and Ninja are all standing in line at an open audition when they start a conversation. Listen and sum up in 2–3 sentences what they're talking about.*

b) *Make a grid for the three young actors. Then listen again and take notes about what you learn about their personalities.*

c) *Say who you think might be most successful in Hollywood. Justify your opinion.*

LANGUAGE

6 [Find the rule: Two more future forms] → G13–14

a) *Look at the examples of the **future progressive** and the **future perfect** and explain how they're formed. Then say how you use them differently to talk about the future.*

1. My friends keep telling me that I **won't be going** to any more auditions in five years' time. They say I'**ll be traveling** the world to present my new movie.
2. By the time I get to the premiere, they'**ll** already **have interviewed** all the stars. – Stop worrying! I'm sure they **won't** even **have started**.

b) *Find more examples for the two future forms in the text on p. 86.*

LANGUAGE

7 [What will Alex be doing at different times tomorrow?]

Alex hasn't had his big break yet, but he's found an agent to help him pursue his dream. Tomorrow Alex has a busy day. Look at his planner and say what he'll be doing at the different times.

Start like this: From 9:00 to 10:00 Alex will be entertaining the tourists. At 10:15 …

9:00–10:00 entertain tourists ✔
10:15 meet with agent
11:00–12:30 practice for audition at 2 p.m.
12:45 lunch
1:15 catch train to audition
1:30 arrive at audition; wait backstage
2:00 try luck at audition
3:00–6:30 work in day job again
8:00 interview stars at movie premiere

LANGUAGE

8 [By this time next year …]

→ ▲ 128/3

In order to motivate herself, Sarah imagines what she'll have achieved by this time next year.
*Use the phrases to make sentences with the **future perfect**.*

Example: By this time next year I'**ll have made** my dreams come true. I …

make dreams come true ✔ | stop going to auditions | get first big role | earn enough money to buy own apartment | meet all the stars in Hollywood | change name to something more memorable | be nominated for first award

LANGUAGE

9 [Looking into your future] → WB 46/5

a) *Use the future progressive **(I'll be doing)** and the future perfect **(I'll have done)** to write five sentences about your future. The phrases in the box can help you to get started.*

Examples: When I'm 20 years old, I'**ll be studying** to become an actor. / By 2040, I'**ll have started** my own business.

b) *With a partner, ask each other questions about your future.*

Start like this: **Will** you **have traveled** to Australia in ten years' time? – Yes, I will. / No, I won't. But I'**ll have been** to many other countries. I'**ll** …

Useful phrases

By the time I'm 25 … | In 50 years' time … | By 2040 … | Before I move out … | If you visit me in ten years … | By the time I finish school … | When I'm 20 years old … | At this time next year … | By next September … | …

MEDIATION **10** **A German pioneer in Hollywood: Carl Laemmle** → WB 47/6

→ S10

You told your exchange partner from California that one of the founders of the American film industry was German. He / She is really excited and asks you to write a guest post on his / her 'Hollywood blog'. Read the article and write a post about Carl Laemmle's life.

Carl Laemmle

Es klingt nach einem Drehbuch zu einem echten Hollywood-Blockbuster: Ein Mann aus Baden-Württemberg, der zu einem der Begründer der amerikanischen Filmindustrie wird.

Carl Laemmle wurde am 17. Januar 1867 in der Nähe von Ulm geboren. Er machte eine Ausbildung zum Kaufmann, bevor er mit 17 Jahren nach Amerika auswanderte. In New York verdiente er seinen Lebensunterhalt als Laufbursche, bevor es ihn nach Chicago zog, wo einer seiner Brüder lebte.

Gleich zu Beginn des 20. Jahrhunderts machte sich Laemmle in Chicago selbstständig und erstand ein 5-Cent-Filmtheater, ein sogenanntes Nickelodeon. Nur ein Jahr später gründete er einen Filmverleih und innerhalb kürzester Zeit gehörten ihm 50 Kinos in Chicago. Im Jahr 1908 war Laemmles Firma bereits der größte Filmverleih der USA. Zwei Jahre danach gründete er seine erste eigene Filmproduktion, die „Independent Motion Picture Company". Laemmle setzte dabei als erster Produzent in der amerikanischen Filmindustrie auf Stars, und er nannte die Schauspieler, die in seinen Produktionen mitwirkten, im Vorspann – die Konkurrenz tat dies nicht. Kurze Zeit später zog es ihn an die Westküste.

Im sonnigen Kalifornien waren die Löhne niedriger und das Wetter besser als anderswo. Dadurch konnten mehr Drehtage in kürzerer Zeit bewältigt werden. Laemmle kaufte in einer einsamen Gegend bei Los Angeles eine Hühnerfarm und errichtete die Universal City Studios – heute ist die Gegend unter dem Namen „Hollywood" bekannt. Seine Firma wurde zur größten Filmfirma Amerikas und produzierte Filme wie „Der Glöckner von Notre Dame" und „Das Phantom der Oper". Auch die weltberühmte „Frankenstein"-Verfilmung mit Boris Karloff – die erste Tonfilmversion überhaupt – stammte aus dem Hause Laemmle. Insgesamt produzierte Carl Laemmle mehr als 9.400 Filme. Seine Erfolgsstory endete erst 1936, als er infolge der Weltwirtschaftskrise seine Firma verkaufen musste.

Source: Bremerhaven.de (abridged)

READING **11** **A star on the Walk of Fame** → WB 47/7–8

Read about the Walk of Fame, a popular tourist destination in Hollywood. Can you think of reasons why it might be important for celebrities to have their own star there?

Across cultures

The **Hollywood Walk of Fame** comprises more than 2,500 stars along Hollywood Boulevard and Vine Street. With these stars, actors, musicians, directors, producers, bands, theater groups or others are honored for their contributions to the entertainment business. Anyone, including fans, can nominate a person for a star on the Walk of Fame, as long as the nominee approves the nomination. Each June, about 20 celebrities are selected to receive their stars. Apart from real-life people, fictional characters can be nominated too. In 1978, in honor of his 50th anniversary, Mickey Mouse became the first animated character to receive a star.

L3/8

A golden state?

SPEAKING

12 Before you read

California's official nickname is 'the Golden State'. What do you associate with this term? Collect ideas with a partner.

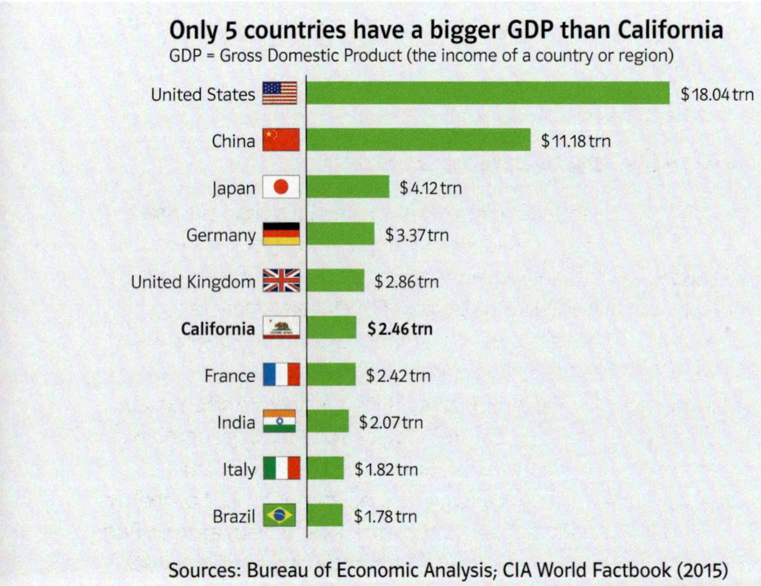

In the 16th and 17th centuries, European explorers on the American continent searched for El Dorado ('the golden one' in Spanish), a city which was said to be made of gold. They never found it (it probably never existed), but the name still refers to any place where great wealth can be found very quickly.

In 1855, the Californian town of Mud Springs changed its name to El Dorado for a very good reason. During the California Gold Rush, it had become a center in the search for the precious yellow metal. Mud Springs boomed and the town decided it needed a more attractive name. And what name could be better than El Dorado? By the 1880s, most of the gold had gone, but the spirit of that rush has remained throughout the Golden State.

Although California's sunny climate is a big attraction for many, the state's strong economy is what really attracts millions of people. Silicon Valley in Northern California, for example, is home to many of the world's largest technology companies: Apple, Facebook, Google, eBay, Netflix and many others. Each of these began as a small start-up company – often just one or two people and a good idea. For example, the first Apple computers were made in a bedroom, and Google began as a student project. In the 1990s, internet start-ups became a kind of 'California Gold Rush 2.0', and millions of dollars were spent on starting new web businesses. People thought this would go on forever, but in 2001 the 'dot-com bubble' burst, and millions of dollars were lost. A new boom, however, has made technology one of the leading industries in California and worldwide.

Agriculture has long been another California success story. The state's climate is ideal for growing fruit and vegetables, and great fortunes have been made from this. However, the good times may not last forever. Growing fruit and vegetables needs a lot of water, and water shortages are one of California's biggest problems. The drought which started in 2011 has caused particularly serious problems for farmers, who are now being urged to use new cultivation techniques to save water.

The success of California's industries also attracts workers from other parts of the US and from Latin America – especially Mexico – who often do jobs such as picking fruit, cleaning homes, working in restaurants, etc. Many of the Hispanic workers cross the border illegally and there are Californians who think the US-Mexican border should be guarded more effectively. In their opinion, it's just one short step from illegal immigration to more serious crimes. Other Californians, however, say that without these illegal immigrants, who often do the hard jobs no Americans want to do, many farms and businesses would have to close down.

READING

13 Understanding the text

→ S2–3

a) *Sum up what you've learned about California's success story from the diagram and the text.*

b) *Think back to the ideas you collected in Ex. 12. Now that you've read the text, would you say that California is a 'golden state'? If so, justify your opinion with examples from the text. If you don't, say what else you'd expect from a 'golden state'.*

c) *The idea of building a wall along the Mexican border is a topic of much controversy in American society. What might the consequences of trying to stop illegal immigration this way be?*

LANGUAGE

14 Revision: Using *the*, *a / an* or no article → G15 → WB 48/9

Read the text about Silicon Valley. Decide if you need **the**, **a / an** *or* **no article (–)**.

Surprisingly enough, Silicon Valley is *not* [1] valley and, of course, it is *not* made of [2] silicon. It's [3] area of around 15,000 km² south of San Francisco in [4] Northern California, and it's famous for having [5] large number of tech companies. The first of these produced [6] microprocessors and 'silicon chips' that were needed for computers, and that's where Silicon Valley got its name from. Although it's famous for [7] companies like Facebook or Google, Silicon Valley is also home to hundreds of other companies which produce [8] components and software for electronic devices that are used by hundreds of millions of [9] people every day. For example, you may never have heard of Cisco Systems or Oracle, but there is probably some of their technology inside [10] devices in your home.

Today, the term 'Silicon Valley' is often used for [11] Californian tech industry in general. A sentence like 'Silicon Valley earns billions of [12] dollars for [13] US economy' would probably refer to tech companies based both around San Francisco as well as in other parts of [14] state.

LANGUAGE

15 Abstract nouns: Article or no article? → G15 → WB 48/10

→ △ 129/4
→ ▲ 129/5

a) *Find the rule: Explain why the definite article* **(the)** *is used in the second sentence but not in the first.*

1. **Industry** plays a major role in California's economy. 2. Technology, agriculture, tourism and entertainment are **the industries** which California is most famous for.

b) *Now use the words in* **bold** *to write new sentences with the definite article.*

1. **Income** is the amount of money you earn from work and other sources. 2. **Success** is what many people look for when they come to California. 3. **Jobs** in Silicon Valley are very popular with young people. 4. **Technology** is important for all kinds of businesses. 5. **Drought** is a big problem for California's agricultural industry. 6. "**Climate** is what we expect, weather is what we get." (Mark Twain)

c) *Explain how the nouns in a) and b) are different from other nouns.*

LISTENING

16 My kind of company!

L3/9

a) *Listen to different people talking about their jobs in Silicon Valley. Take notes about the pros and cons of working in California's tech industry.*

→ S7

b) *Listen again. What is said about prospects for young entrepreneurs in Silicon Valley?*

c) *Can you imagine giving up school and starting a career in Silicon Valley? Discuss with a partner.*

MEDIATION

17 Where is the German Silicon Valley? → WB 49/11–12

→ S10

a) *In an online forum there is a discussion going on about the uniqueness of Silicon Valley. You'd like to offer an example of an innovative entrepreneur from Germany. Read this article and write a short summary in English for the forum.*

Ob Pullover, Hose oder T-Shirt, immer mehr Menschen kaufen ihre Kleidung im Internet. Was nicht gefällt oder nicht passt, wird auf Kosten des Händlers zurückgeschickt. In Deutschland sind das durchschnittlich 40 Prozent der bestellten Waren.

Ob und wie man das ändern könnte, darüber grübelte Sebastian Schulze, Gründer des IT-Unternehmens UPcload, schon während seines Studiums. „Dann sind wir irgendwann darauf gekommen, dass es doch ganz cool wäre, wenn man die Körpermaße einer Person mit einer Webcam erfassen könnte," erzählt Schulze. Sein Unternehmen könne das größte Problem im Onlinehandel lösen, „nämlich dass Menschen, die online Kleidung kaufen möchten, nicht wissen, was ihre passende Größe ist."

Schulze war 22 Jahre alt, als er 2010 mit seinem Partner Asaf Moses in Berlin sein Unternehmen gründete. Sein Studium hatte er gerade beendet, Berufserfahrung hatte er keine. Schulze sagt, er habe während seines Studiums drei Praktika gemacht. „Danach habe ich gedacht, dass ich lieber in der ersten Reihe stehen und Verantwortung tragen will: Wenn ich schon viel arbeite, dann für eine eigene Sache."

Vor allem in Berlin tue sich laut Sebastian Schulze einiges, was IT-Start-ups angeht. Mehr Fördermittel und Kapital kämen in die Stadt, man spüre eine große Euphorie. Die Finanzierung ist neben der brillanten Idee der wichtigste Punkt für ein junges Unternehmen. Was in den USA häufig passiert, dass nämlich ein reicher Nachbar dem Gründer von nebenan Geld leiht, weil ihm dessen Geschäftsidee gefällt, gibt es in Deutschland nicht. In den ersten vier Jahren fließen durchschnittlich 700.000 Euro in ein IT-Start-up.

Source: Deutsche Welle (abridged)

→ △ 129/6

‹b)› *Do you have an idea for your own start-up company? In small groups, collect ideas in a placemat and decide on what kind of company you'd like to start (it needn't have to do with IT!). Prepare a 3-minute talk and present your business idea to the class.*

READING

18 Trendsetting California → Fact page, p. 271

California hasn't only attracted millions of people, it has also exported many trends and innovations. Read the information in the box. Then think about your own lifestyle and say which of these innovations are part of your life.

Across cultures

In 1873, **jeans** were invented by Jacob Davis and Levi Strauss in San Francisco. Originally, they were used as work pants for miners and factory workers. Later they became a symbol of youth rebellion and a fashion statement.

In the 1950s, a group of surfers in Santa Monica attached roller skate wheels to wooden boards to enable them to surf when the waves were flat. This new sport became known as 'landsurfing' or **skateboarding**.

Venice, a well-known Los Angeles beach community, is said to be one of the world's trendsetting hotspots: it was here that **fitness** first became popular with the muscle-packed beach bodybuilders in the 1970s, and it was also here that the **inline skating** craze was born in the 1990s.

LANGUAGE

19 My life as a farm worker

In spite of the state's strong economy, not all the people who come to California find their personal success there. This is how one young farm worker describes her life:

In the 1980s, my father came from Mexico to California to pick strawberries and grapes. He worked hard, learned English and made good money. After four years, he returned to Mexico and he found a good job with a Mexican company that exports agricultural products to the US. My family were very happy when I went to California too, but it's very different today. Most employers only pay the minimum wage, and they make you work as many hours as they like. That's illegal, of course, but nobody really cares. The second problem is that it's seasonal work. In the winter I only work 15 to 20 hours a week. That doesn't even pay my rent. So it's not an easy life. The government doesn't care about people like us and the local community aren't always very friendly to immigrants. I'm not sorry I came. I've found good friends and my English has gotten a lot better. But I don't think I'm going to save any money. Maybe one day I can find a better-paid job.

a) ***Collective nouns*** *are nouns like 'team' or 'company' that refer to groups of people. Look at the text again and write down the sentences with collective nouns from the text.*

b) *Collective nouns can be followed by the singular or plural form of the verb. While in* ***American English*** *collective nouns are usually used with a singular verb, in* ***British English*** *they can be used with either a singular or plural verb. Which form you choose depends on whether you want to talk more about the group as one unit or about individual members of the group. Compare these sentences:*

1. Adriana's family **is** from Mexico. (The sentence refers to the family as one unit.)
2. Adriana's family **are** worried about her. (Individual members of the family are worried.)

SPEAKING

20 Interpreting diagrams: Ethnic diversity in California

Because of constant migration, the make-up of California's population has changed significantly during the last decades.

→ S2 **a)** *Look at the line graph. Point out what it tells you about the state's population today and what it might be like in the future. What can you say about the point on the graph where the blue and red lines cross? Check the skills file at the back of your book (pp. 132–133) if you need help.*

Future population, cultural shift

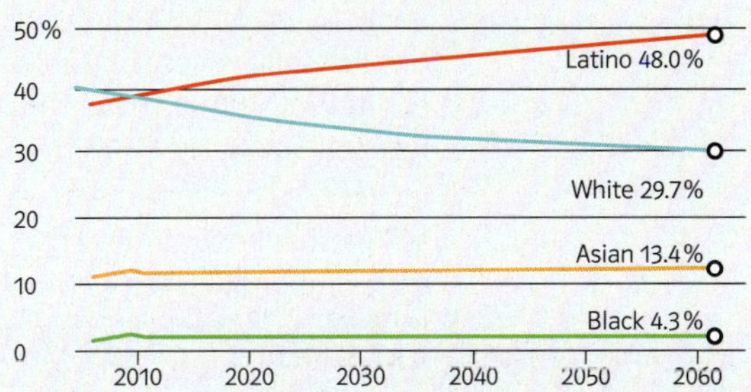

Sources: California Department of Finance; U.S. Census Bureau

→ △ 129/7 **b)** *Comment on what you think will be the consequences of these shifts in California's society.*

L 3/10

Should we be worried?

On its show today, L.A. Talk Radio KABC is speaking to helicopter pilot and firefighter Mario Ramirez about his work.

KABC: Our guest on the show today is CAL FIRE pilot Mario Ramirez. Welcome to the show, Mario, and thanks for taking the time to talk to us. I'm sure you must be busy right now.

Mario: Hi, thanks. Yes, it's wildfire season again, and this is always a very busy time for us. Just this morning, we had to go out to three different incidents.

KABC: Dropping water onto fires from helicopters?

Mario: Yes, that's right. But this morning, we were forced to use tanker planes too. They can carry a lot more water.

KABC: Should we be worried? It sounds like half of California is burning.

Mario: Well, that would be exaggerating. But we're facing some serious problems because of the very hot and dry conditions that we have today. A few years ago, the wildfire season lasted only five months. Today it's seven, thanks to climate change, and the number of larger wildfires has increased dramatically too.

KABC: Sounds as if you're very busy in the dry season, but what happens when it does finally rain?

Mario: Well, that's when we're expected to coordinate with the other emergency services. When you suddenly get a lot of rain after a long dry period, you get floods. Sometimes the only way to rescue people is by helicopter.

KABC: And there are mudslides too. They're said to go hand in hand with wildfires, aren't they?

Mario: Yes, that's another major problem. People love to build nice homes on a beautiful hillside with a view, but then you get a lot of rain followed by a mudslide, followed by collapsed houses half-covered in mud.

KABC: Yes. The fires destroy the trees, so there is nothing to hold the soil in place when the rain comes, is there?

Mario: You know your stuff! Should I get my boss to interview you for a job?

KABC: Ha ha! No, thanks. For that kind of job you need to be willing to risk your life. I'm not that brave.

Mario: You were right about the trees, of course, but it isn't just fire that's causing this problem. People aren't supposed to cut down trees but they do it anyway, especially farmers. They argue that letting them die of dehydration will cause disease and bugs that will then spread to other healthy trees and lead to new problems.

KABC: Mario, I'm going to have to stop you there but many thanks for sharing your experiences with us.

READING

21 Understanding the interview

→ S3

a) *Outline the environmental problems Mario and his colleagues have to deal with.*

b) *Explain how the different environmental problems are connected.*

LANGUAGE

22 Using different English verbs for the same German verb → G16

a) *Look at these two groups of sentences. For each group, find a German verb you could use to translate all the examples.*

Shall / **Should** we go to Yosemite National Park next weekend? Firefighters **are supposed to** / **are expected to** help the public in emergencies. Californians **are supposed to** / **are said to** be laid-back, even in dangerous situations. You **are to** leave your house immediately if there's any risk of a mudslide. I think we **should** / **ought to** leave the house; it's not safe here.
We **had to** / **were forced to** leave the park because there were wildfires. In national parks, tourists **must** / **are required to** / **are obliged to** stay on the marked paths.

b) *Find more sentences with the verbs from a) in the text on p. 94 and translate them into German.*

LANGUAGE

23 What are people supposed to do? → WB 50/13–14

a) *Use the verbs below to complete the text. Sometimes more than one answer is possible.*

be expected to | be to | should | be forced to | be supposed to | be required to | be said to | ought to | have to

Anybody who wants to avoid earthquakes **1** think about moving away from California. On average, there are around ten earthquakes every day. Most of them are very light, but it's not unusual to feel a slight movement and to see small cracks in the walls of buildings.

California's biggest earthquake in recorded history was in San Francisco in 1906. It killed more than 3,000 people and destroyed much of the city. It **2** have been the most important earthquake in modern times because it provided so much information about the causes of earthquakes and about how to make sure buildings survive them. Today architects in California **3** design new buildings which will remain standing in all but the worst earthquakes.

So what **4** you **5** do if there's an earthquake? If you're indoors, stay there. Keep away from the walls and try to get under a desk or table. If you're outdoors, stay away from buildings and trees. If you're driving, you **6** stop immediately but stay in the car until the earthquake stops. If you're

at home and you need help, remember that the emergency services **7** visit the worst affected areas first, so you may **8** wait for hours or even days for help. First check for the smell of gas; then check for damage to your building immediately. If you can smell gas or if there are serious cracks, everybody **9** leave the building. Remember that there may be aftershocks – small earthquakes which follow the main one.

b) *Can you think of any other natural hazards? Collect ideas with a partner. Say what people might be supposed to do when they're affected by these hazards.*

LANGUAGE

24 Brown is said to be the new green!

→ ▲ 130/8

a) *Use the verbs below to rewrite these sentences from a website about California's environment. Sometimes more than one answer is possible.*

be to | be expected to | ought to | be said to | be supposed to | be required to

Example: 1. California **is supposed to / said to** have the best weather in the US.

1. People say that California has the best weather in the US. ✔
2. As a visitor to California, you must respect the environment at all times.
3. You shouldn't have barbecues in dry areas, or waste water.
4. When you visit one of the national parks, you need to be careful with wild animals.
5. When there's a drought, Californians have to stop using water for their gardens and outdoor swimming pools.
6. People in California should follow the water conservation rules, but many of them don't want to give up their lifestyle.

b) *Each of you writes three sentences about California with the verbs in a). Leave a gap where the verb is supposed to be. Then exchange your sentences. Your partner has to guess the right verb.*

SPEAKING

25 ‹ Interpreting diagrams: Cause and effect › → WB 51/15

a) *Los Angeles is said to be a 'multi-hazard city'. Look at the diagram and explain how the different problems are connected with each other. Keep in mind what you've learned from the text on p. 94.*

Word bank

to affect | to cause | to be the consequence / result of | to contribute to | to influence | to lead to | to result in | to show the link (between)

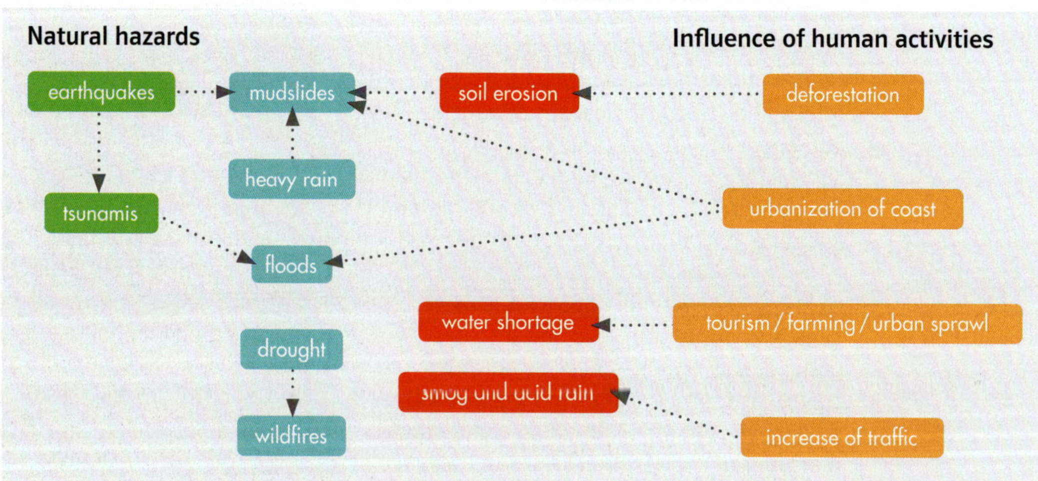

b) *Think back on the interview with Mario Ramirez (p. 94). How could a diagram like this help to support his explanations?*

READING

26 Healthy eating in sports stadiums

a) *Read the information in the box and comment on the idea of healthy eating in sports stadiums.*

<b)> *Role play: You're convinced that this idea should be adopted in your football stadium. There are only food stalls with fast food like burgers, chips, etc. Write and act out a dialogue with the owner of one of these food stalls.*

Across cultures

Healthy eating combined with a better understanding of environmental issues is a worldwide trend that has also found its followers in California. As with many other trends, however, Californians have taken the whole thing a step further by combining healthy eating with a popular American activity – baseball! Just below the scoreboard in the Giants' stadium in San Francisco there is a large garden. The fruits and vegetables grown there – from artichokes to zucchini – are used by two bistros at the stadium to prepare fresh and healthy dishes for the ballgame spectators. In addition, once a week groups of students visit the garden to learn about gardening, nutrition and cooking.

SPEAKING

27 Looking back: Your ideas about California

→ △ 130/9

Think – pair – share: Go back to the Introduction pages and your first impressions of California. Has your picture of California changed after you've looked at it from different perspectives? If so, in what ways? If it hasn't changed, how does the new information fit your first impressions? Share your ideas in small groups and then in class.

SPEAKING

28 How to: Give a group presentation → WB 51–53/16–19

L3/12

a) *Listen to a presentation about Californian symbols, both positive and negative. Take notes about the structure of the presentation.*

b) *Now listen to the presentation again. Write down useful phrases for the following elements:*

introduction | smooth transitions | conclusion

c) *Read the information in the skills box. Then comment on how effective you find the presentation in a). What would you do the same way / differently? Give reasons.*

Speaking skills

These steps can help you with your next **group presentation**:

1. **Research** information about your topic and decide on a clear structure.
2. Decide **who does what** in your group. The speaker who takes on the first part will introduce your topic and give a short conclusion at the end. You can also agree on one person who will take questions from the audience.
3. Each of you makes notes about his / her part. Don't forget to think of a **smooth transition** from your part to the next.
4. **Practise** your presentation. If one of your partners wants to use a **visual** for his / her part, you can help him / her by putting the right slide / showing your group poster. Agree on a **signal** for the right timing.
5. Give your presentation. Remember that **you're 'on'**, even when you aren't speaking! Listen and show interest in what the others are saying. If you look bored, your audience will get bored too.

What's important for a handout?

A handout is a good way of helping listeners to follow the structure of a presentation and to understand the most important points. This page will give you some useful tips to prepare an effective handout for your next presentation.

1 Handout tips

When you make a handout, keep in mind that people who weren't at your presentation should be able to understand the main ideas from your handout. Read the tips on the right. Can you add further tips from your own experience?

Presentation skills

1. Your handout should follow the same **structure** as your presentation. Include a short outline of your main points; keep your sub-points short and simple.
2. Don't use too many different fonts or unnecessary pictures or clip arts; **you don't want to distract** your audience. However, it's a good idea to include a chart, graph or picture that is central to your topic.
3. Make sure you give a **short summary / conclusion**.
4. Give the **sources** you used for your presentation.

2 Example handouts

a) *Look at these example handouts. Use the criteria you collected in Ex. 1 to make notes about what was done well and what could be improved.*

SAN FRANCISCO GIANTS

1. A **great** baseball team
   a) Have won the **most games** of any team in the history of American baseball.
   b) They have played in the World Series **20 times**.
2. History
3. Famous players
   a) Jackie **Robinson** #42
   b) Orlando **Cepeda** #30

Conclusion: One of the **best** teams ever!

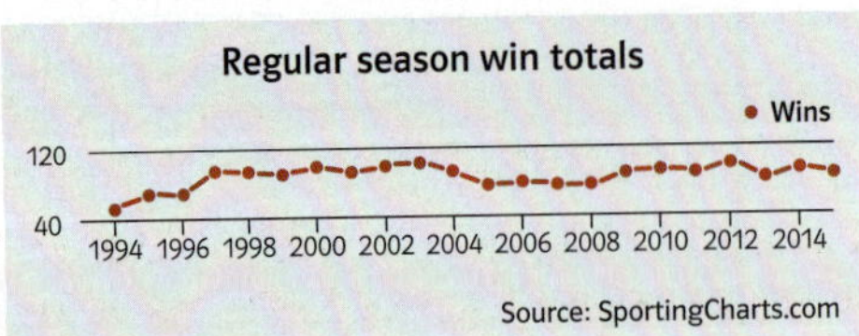

Sources: Wikipedia; San Francisco Giants official website

Chef Brian Malarkey

1. How he became a chef
   A. Family
   B. School
   C. Training
2. How he became a famous celebrity chef
   A. TV (Top Chef, Top Chef Masters, The Real Housewives of Orange County, The Taste)
   B. magazines
3. How he learned from his mistakes
4. How he cooks now
   A. "less pizzazz, more substance"
   B. "back to the craft"
   C. no deep fryer, no freezer

b) *Have a look at your notes about the group presentation on p. 97, Ex. 28 again. Then write a handout for it.*

My star for the Walk of Fame

Your class wants to nominate one person for the Walk of Fame. In order to choose a candidate, you're going to prepare group presentations with which you try to convince your class selection committee that your group's candidate deserves a star.

Step 1

Choose a person to nominate → WB 54/20

In groups of five, each of you chooses one person. This person doesn't need to be an American, and he / she doesn't need to be an entertainer. You can also choose someone from the world of science, politics or sports, for example.

Step 2

Write a short profile → WB 54/21

Collect information for a short profile of your nominee. Think about these questions:

- How did he / she make his / her dream come true?
- What obstacles did he / she have to overcome?
- Why does he / she deserve a star on the Walk of Fame?

Make your profile interesting and enjoyable to listen to since you'll have to convince your group.

Step 3

Present your nominee in your groups → WB 54/22

In your groups, present your nominees to each other. In this same group, agree on one Walk of Fame candidate that you're going to present to the class.

Step 4

Prepare your group presentations → WB 55/23

Before you present your group's nominee to the class, divide up the profile into logical parts and add more information where necessary. Don't forget to make an effective handout.

→ How to: Give a group presentation (p. 97) → What's important for a handout? (p. 98)

Step 5

Your class selection committee → WB 55/24

After the presentations, one member of each group becomes the delegate to your class selection committee. The committee's task is to choose a nominee for the Walk of Fame based on the presentations and handouts. Then, in a fish bowl, the rest of you form a circle around the committee and listen to their arguments for and against each candidate. After they've made their decision, evaluate their decision-making process.

Famous

SPEAKING

1 Before you read

What first comes to your mind when you think about being famous? Share your ideas with a partner.

It started with a camera and a coffee shop.

No, that's not right. Any psychologist will tell you it started way before that. Like, when my brother Alex became seriously ill around the age of three, and five years later when my parents divorced, and all that psychological gobbledygook.

But that camera, a black Nikon P90 with a 24x zoom lens, a fourteenth-birthday present from my father, was the charm that changed everything. It was the bridge I crossed from being a typical, everyday eighth grader to someone completely different.

An atypical eighth grader. A slightly almost-famous eighth grader. Not that it was my plan. It just happened.

The day was gray, wet, and chilly. The coffee shop was called Cafazine, and it provided two of life's greatest pleasures – coffee and gossip. After a quick scan of the headlines, I turned my attention to a tall woman in front of me holding the hand of a little boy. She was wearing a long gray raincoat, wide-brimmed hat, and sunglasses, and suddenly I recognized her – it was Tatiana Frazee, the supermodel! I'd seen enough pictures of her in magazines and on TV to know. Besides, why would anyone *not* famous wear a hat and big sunglasses inside on a cloudy day?

Her son, Connor, was pointing at a large brownie with chocolate chips inside the glass counter.

"I want that, Mommy!" he whined.

"Not before dinner," Tatiana answered.

"But I want it!" Conner persisted.

"I said no," Tatiana repeated.

"Yes!" The boy pulled at the gloved hand.

"No," Tatiana replied icily.

By now they had reached the counter.

"What would you like, ma'am?" the young man by the cash register asked. As the supermodel turned away from her son to answer, Conner suddenly yanked her hand as hard as he could.

Tatiana Frazee lost her balance and toppled forward, banging her perfect chin on a display of CDs, sending them crashing.

To this day I don't know what compelled me to yank the camera from my pocket and slide the shutter into quick-shot mode just in time to catch Tatiana as she wheeled around and slapped Conner on the cheek.

The next shots caught Tatiana glaring at me with a mixture of horror and fury. An instant later she scooped Conner up under her arm and ran out of the shop.

A photo agent friend of my dad's sold the shots to a tabloid and to a website that specialized in celebrities' most embarrassing moments. A few weeks later I received a check for what seemed like a fortune to a fourteen-year-old. Just for taking some pictures.

After more of her photos have been published, there's an article about Jamie in the New York Weekly. *On their way to school one day, Jamie talks about it with her boyfriend, Nasim.*

"You're famous," Nasim said. It was the first time anyone ever told me that, and I had to admit that it felt good. Right up there with "You're pretty" or "You're smart." No, even *better* than "You're smart."

"Thank you," I replied.

"How many people do we know who have been profiled in a major magazine? New York City's youngest paparazzo ever? I believe the correct answer would be one."

I grabbed his arm to stop him and we kissed in the middle of the crowded sidewalk. "Thank you," I said, our faces close. "Only, for the six hundred and seventy-fifth time, I am not a paparazzo. I am a celebrity photographer."

Nasim rolled his eyes, and we started to hurry again, our shoulders now and then bumping. "There is no difference."

"There's a big difference," I insisted. "I may take pictures of celebrities, but I don't stalk or harass them or try to get them to punch me so that I can sue them for assault."

Nasim changed the subject.

Jamie receives an invitation to spend one week hanging out with teen superstar Willow Twine, photographing her and documenting her life. On day seven of her week in L.A., however, she wakes up and realizes that her camera is gone.

I know it sounds like a cliché, but I feel naked without my camera. Or even worse than naked, since these days who cares if you're naked? The camera represents who I am. It's my identity. With it, I'm a sixteen-year-old celebrity photographer. (And maybe something of a celebrity myself?) Without it, who am I?

What am I?

The answers to these questions will have to wait. Right now I just need to find my Nikon. I try to remember last night. Not that it should be difficult; it's just that out here, day and night, and day after day, blend together into a sort of nonstop repetition of the same thing over and over again. Last night was a party. But even on nights when there's no 'official' party there's a loose semiparty atmosphere. People come and go, appear and disappear – Willow's friends, security guard, personal assistant, therapist, masseur, agents, magazine photographer (me!), pool guy, gardeners, cook – in an unending parade.

As best as I can remember, I had my camera with me early this morning when I came upstairs to find a place to sleep. Before that I'd gone out to the guesthouse – where I'd been 'assigned' when I first arrived earlier this week – but the door was locked, so I'd wandered back to the main house and found this room. Normally I would have put the camera on a night table or dresser, but since there is no furniture in the room, I left it on the floor beside the mattress, and close to the wall so I wouldn't accidentally step on it if I got up in the middle of the night, or day, or whatever.

So where is it? I check the bathroom. Not there either. I walk barefoot out into the hallway, then downstairs and out across the grassy lawn. I head toward the pool, where Zach, the house boy, and Daphne, the house techie, are straightening up from last night's frolic.

"Either of you see a camera?" I ask.

"Think I saw one on the kitchen counter," Zach says.

The kitchen counter? That's weird. I don't recall even being in the kitchen last night. I was mostly out around the pool.

Passing through the French doors, the aroma of fresh-brewed coffee is in the air, and there on the marble kitchen counter, where I swear I wouldn't – couldn't – have left it, is my Nikon.

"Buenos dìas, Miss Jamie. You like some breakfast?" Maria, the Mexican cook, hands me the mug of coffee she knows I crave.

The camera rests on the marble counter beside me while I sip my coffee. Now that it's back in my sight, my anxiety has gone. I didn't take many shots at the party last night. Willow asked me not to. Does that sound crazy? After all, I'm here on assignment, right? Document a week in Willow's life, they said.

But 'they' are Willow's management, and 'they' have made it clear that my assignment is to show the world the Willow Twine 'they' want to see – the sweet, girlish pop star (her true age, twenty-one, is a more closely guarded secret than the president's personal cell phone number).

All I'd taken the previous night were a few innocent party shots. I had intentionally not taken the shots that editors everywhere would have paid a lot of money for. As a result, this morning I'm in no rush to review what's in the camera's memory. I wonder if I can really make this idea of staying here in California work. It's not *that* crazy, is it? I've earned the trust of Willow Twine, one of the biggest stars in Hollywood. She's already introduced me to a bunch of her actor friends and has promised to hook me up with even more. If I stay, I have a chance to become the Annie Leibovitz of the L.A. young actor scene. I could grow with them. I could be their favourite go-to photographer for decades to come.

But what about Nasim? My insides clench and my heart beats wildly when I think of him and the fight we had before I left New York. I would so hate to lose him, but I know what my father would say: You're young, you can't let a guy influence the direction of your career.

I pick up the camera, turn the viewer on, and have a look at the previous day's shots. Willow holding the red shoes she bought me for the party. Willow hanging out by the pool with her best friend, Anne-Marie. Willow and Anne-Marie trying on clothes for the party. I get to the last shot I remember taking the night before – Willow in a pink dress by the pool, welcoming guests. But the camera's counter indicates that there are six more shots. How weird is this? I think. First I wake up and my camera isn't where I'm certain I left it. And now I discover I took pictures I don't remember taking.

I flip to the first one … and freeze. I am staring at a shot I definitely don't remember taking. And for good reason. I didn't take it.

But that hardly matters now. I've stopped breathing. My heart is thudding. Goose bumps race up my arms, and it might be imagination, but I think I can feel tiny beads of cold sweat seep out of my pores.

In my camera is a shot that changes everything.

Stop and think:

What do you think the picture on Jamie's camera shows? Collect ideas with a partner.

After finding the mysterious shot on her camera, Jamie hides in a bathroom and has an imaginary conversation with Carla Harris, her photo agent.

I'm sitting in the pink bathroom in Willow's mansion – a digital gold mine in my hands – hearing voices in my head.

Me: "Can I really do this? Destroy Willow's career in order to advance mine?"

Carla: "Darling, are you crazy? This is your ticket. Everything you've dreamed of since day one. People would kill for this kind of opportunity. You think if it was the other way around – if Willow Twine needed to wreck your career to advance her own – she'd hesitate for a second?"

"But Willow and I are friends."

"Oh, please! You've known her for exactly one week."

"You don't know. You haven't been out here with us."

"My dear, they were calling me an old-timer in this business back when you were still in Pampers. I've seen and heard it all. Believe me, I know."

by Todd Strasser (abridged and adapted)

READING

2 Understanding the story

a) *Sum up each part of the story in 2–3 sentences. Then find a heading for each part.*

→ △ 130/10

b) *What adjectives would you use to describe Jamie's character? Give examples from the text to support your ideas.*

READING

3 Two words, same meaning?

→ S3

a) *Jamie insists she is a 'celebrity photographer', not a 'paparazzo'. Explain the difference between these two words from Jamie's point of view.*

b) *Read the first part of the story again when Jamie takes embarrassing photos of Tatiana Frazee. Comment on her definitions of 'celebrity photographer' and 'paparazzo' in a). Would you agree with her that she is* ***not*** *a paparazzo?*

c) *After the incident at the coffee shop, Tatiana Frazee sends a message to her best friend. Think about how she must have felt when she realised that Jamie had taken photos of her embarrassing moment. Then write Tatiana's message to her friend.*

SPEAKING

4 A role play: Jamie's dilemma

a) *While Jamie is sitting in the bathroom in Willow's house, she's talking out loud about her dilemma. In her head Carla, her photo agent, is trying to persuade her to sell the photos, while Nasim, her boyfriend, is trying to talk her out of it. In groups of three, write a short role play. Then act it out in class.*

b) *After what you've heard in your role plays, how would you decide if you were in Jamie's shoes? Write her a message with your advice.*

c) *At the end, Carla's voice in Jamie's head says: "I've seen and heard it all. Believe me, I know." Explain the meaning of this statement.*

SPEAKING

5 At what price fame ...? → WB 56/25

a) *Look at some key lines from the story below. Then compare the lives of Jamie and Willow. In what ways are they different; in what ways are they the same?*

The camera represents who I am. It's my identity. With it, I'm a sixteen-year-old celebrity photographer. (And maybe something of a celebrity myself?) Without it, who am I? What am I? (lines 101–106)

But 'they' are Willow's management, and 'they' have made it clear that my assignment is to show the world the Willow Twine 'they' want to see – the sweet, girlish pop star. (lines 162–165)

b) *Look at the words below. What would or wouldn't you give up to become famous? Explain why.*

anonymity | appearance | family | friends | home | identity | normality | personality | school | security | values

LISTENING

1 From Tinseltown[1] to Techtown

L 3/14

a) *Listen to a journalist interviewing Jack Jonston, who was a Hollywood actor before he started his new career. Sum up what they're talking about in 2–3 sentences.*

b) *Listen again and take notes about the following topics:*

why Jack ended his career in Hollywood |
how he thinks his tech career is continuing his acting career

c) *Write the beginnings of two news articles about Jack's decision to leave Hollywood – one for a tabloid[2] and one for a serious newspaper. In what ways would they be different?*

LANGUAGE

2 A major event

a) *Choose the correct tense to talk about the future:* ***simple present*** *or* ***present progressive****.*

Dear Mom and Dad,
I want to tell you about a very important decision I've made: My new life **1** (start) at 3:30 a.m. tomorrow! That's when my bus to L.A. **2** (leave). I didn't buy a return ticket because I **3** (stay) out there until I've made it. Don't worry – I **4** (plan) on coming home again – but only after I've got my first movie role. Planes to L.A. **5** (fly) every day out of Omaha, but please don't come to visit until I tell you it's OK. Tina **6** (go) with me and our first audition **7** (take place) on Friday at 10:00. We heard that the directors **8** (not arrive) until 11:00 or 12:00, but we **9** (not take) any chances, and our plan is to be there at 6:00. I'm sorry I didn't tell you this in person, but I'm too nervous!
Love, Janey

b) *Write a letter to inform your parents or a friend about a major decision in your life. Use the* ***simple present*** *and the* ***present progressive*** *to talk about the future.*

LANGUAGE

3 Hollywood Dream Factory

a) *Put in* ***relative pronouns*** *only where necessary.*

1. Every year thousands of people ___ have big hopes and dreams move to L.A.
2. Although we think of aspiring actors first, there are also writers, directors, producers, musicians, comedians and others ___ want to chase their dreams in Hollywood.
3. The professions ___ they choose depend on their skills and talents.
4. The age ___ they are when they start their career is also an important factor.
5. People ___ are under 30 have a better chance of becoming famous.
6. And young people ___ parents are already in the business have even better chances.
7. But the competition ___ they face is still hard.
8. There are only about 70,000 people in the US ___ main income is from acting.

b) *Look at the sentences with a relative pronoun in a). Rewrite them in a way you don't need the relative pronoun any more.*

Example: 1. Every year thousands of people with big hopes and dreams move to L.A.

1 Tinseltown ['tɪnsl,taʊn] Hollywood *(umgangssprachlich)* | **2 tabloid** ['tæblɔɪd] Boulevard-/Klatschzeitung

OCABULARY

4 It's the perfect opportunity!

a) *Match the adjectives and the nouns to make suitable **phrases** for the sentences below.*

aspiring | golden | logical | memorable | relaxed | seasonal | southern | worldwide

work | recognition[1] | opportunity | event | solution | border | atmosphere | actor

1. Like millions of others, Kirk Douglas was also once an …
2. Is it really necessary to spend billions of tax dollars to protect the … of the US?
3. Many companies in Silicon Valley emphasize a … in the workplace[2].
4. Getting honored with a star on the Walk of Fame was a …
5. I couldn't miss the chance to work with him. It was a …
6. One of the final steps to real success is when your brand achieves …
7. The … to my family's problems was to risk crossing the border in search of …

b) *In small groups, take turns to act out the verbs from Unit 3 below (you're allowed to use sounds, but you mustn't speak). The others need to guess which verb you chose.*

approve | burst | close down | explode | guard | increase | observe | pack up | photograph | remain | set up | shoot (a film) | showcase (one's talents) | stroll | urge

LANGUAGE

5 Are hamburgers healthy?

a) *Look at these sentences and explain the difference between the nouns in A and B.*

1. A: I'm looking for **a job** and applied at a fast-food place. – B: Did you get **the job**?
2. A: **Food** in California is expensive, isn't it? – B: Yes, but **the food** I buy is also very healthy.

b) *Decide where you need **the**, **a / an** or **no article (–)**.*

Surprisingly enough, 1 hamburgers can be healthy too. 2 hamburgers at In-N-Out Burgers of California are made with 3 freshest ingredients. Usually it's all of 4 extras that people put on them that are unhealthy. Did you know that 5 ketchup has lots of 6 sugar in it? One tablespoon has almost as much as 7 chocolate chip cookie. Some people call 8 sugar the worst ingredient in 9 modern food. However, our bodies do need 10 healthy kind of sugar like 11 sugar you get from fruit, but not added sugar. So next time you go to 12 hamburger stand, think about ordering 13 extra slice of tomato instead of 14 ketchup.

c) *Write two sentences for each of these abstract nouns, one with an article and one without. Then translate the sentences into German. How is the use of the definite article before an abstract noun different in German?*

anonymity | effort | glamor | politics | risk

1 recognition [ˌrekəgˈnɪʃn] Anerkennung | **2 workplace** [ˈwɜːkpleɪs] Arbeitsplatz

LANGUAGE

6 Welcome to the studios!

a) *What did people say to the new employee on his first day on the job? Use the **future progressive** to complete the sentences.*

1. Welcome to the studios! I expect you ▬ (come) to the meeting at 9:00, right?
2. Hi there! In an hour we ▬ (set up) to shoot a new ad. Please be there!
3. I'm from Human Resources[1]. We ▬ (observe) you closely for the next six weeks. Relax!
4. I'm Sue. Next week the boss ▬ (nominate) employees for a workshop. Interested?
5. Hey man! Lots of people ▬ (urge) you to work long hours. Don't listen to them!
6. This is Sheila. She ▬ (take) photos of the new employees for the studio website.

b) *Complete these sentences with your own ideas. Use the **future progressive**.*

Example: 1. While you're still going to school, I'**ll be going** to auditions in Hollywood.

1. While you're still going to school … 2. When you read this letter … 3. This time tomorrow my friends and I … 4. I can't believe her luck. Next month …

LANGUAGE

7 Talking about future plans → WB 59/1

a) *Grant owns a start-up company in Silicon Valley. Look at his schedule. Say what **will be happening** or what **will have happened** at a certain time in the future.*

Start like this: At 8:00 Grant will be … / By 1:00 he'll have …

7:00–8:30	breakfast with Phil
9:00–10:00	Young Inventors – meeting at Hilton Hotel
11:00–1:00	read new applications, choose applicant for new position
1:30	phone interview, reporter will send questions by 10:00
5:30	dinner with Joy, buy flowers on the way to restaurant

b) *Imagine you have your own tech company in Silicon Valley. Make a schedule for new inventions you plan for the future. Then use the **future progressive** and the **future perfect** to talk about these plans.*

Examples: 1. 2028–2030: research use of robots in homes
→ In 2029 we'**ll be researching** the use of robots in homes.
2. 2031: launch[2] new robot onto the market
→ By 2031 we'**ll have launched** a new robot onto the market.

LANGUAGE

8 Planning your business career → WB 60/2

Choose from these words to rewrite the sentences. Sometimes more than one answer is correct.

might | be to | should | must | be said to | need to | have to | be supposed to

1. I was required to pay $400 for the course materials. 2. You ought to look at alternative study programs. 3. He is expected to pay back the student loan[3]. 4. Some of the students may have the chance to receive a scholarship[4]. 5. People say that the company is one of the best in town. 6. If you want to be successful in business, you need to be persistent. 7. We are expected to find our own crowdfunding. 8. You must call her in the morning about your application.

1 **Human Resources** [ˌhjuːmən rɪˈzɔːsɪz] Personalabteilung | 2 **to launch** [lɔːnʃ] einführen | 3 **loan** [ləʊn] Darlehen; Kredit | 4 **scholarship** [ˈskɒləʃɪp] Stipendium

LANGUAGE

9 Tourism in California

a) *Complete the* ***conditional sentences*** *with the correct verb forms.*

If people had to name California's major industries, one of them **1** (definitely – be) tourism, in which national parks play a big role. But if the parks **2** (aim) to preserve[1] nature for future generations, won't it be difficult to remain a multi-billion dollar industry? In 2014 almost four million people visited Yosemite and spent more than $400 million in the park and in surrounding[2] communities. Thousands of people would lose their jobs if the park **3** (not attract) so many tourists. However, the numbers of visitors have left scars on Yosemite and all the other national parks. Many people don't realize it, but if hikers don't stay on the marked paths, they **4** (might destroy) vegetation. If the number of cars in the parks **5** (continue) to rise, air pollution will get worse. Some people believe that if cars **6** (be) banned in the parks, this would greatly improve the situation.

Since they were created, people in the US have been proud of their national parks. If park officials and politicians[3] hadn't worked together at the very beginning, the parks **7** (never succeed). Today they're still working on ways of balancing[4] preservation[5] and protection with enjoyment and education. Other voices remind officials that the parks have always been changing. So, for example, if there weren't forces such as wind and erosion, many of the spectacular sights in the parks **8** (not exist). But how do you find the middle road between loving a park to death and protecting it?

If we just preserve the parks, **9** (the state – still earn) money from tourism?

b) *What do you think about the role of national parks as a multi-billion dollar industry? Write a post for an online forum where there's a discussion between nature lovers and businesspeople.*

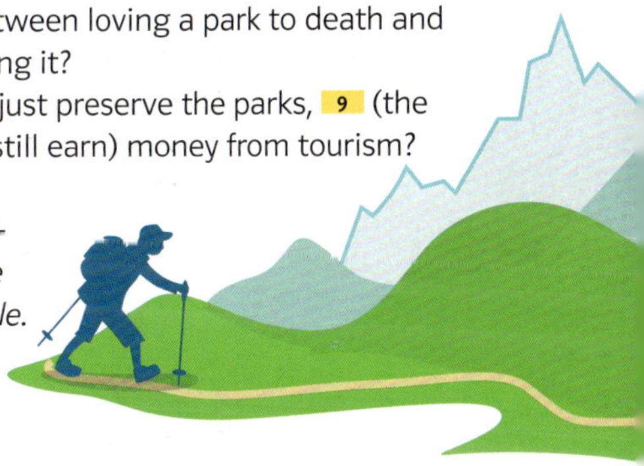

SPEAKING

10 Showcase your talents!

a) *In groups of three, choose one of these reality shows from American TV and find out more about it on the internet.*

b) *Collect arguments to support this statement: "Our show is the best place to showcase your talents."*

c) *Form new groups with one 'expert' for each reality show. Discuss which of the three shows is best to showcase your talents.*

d) *In class, discuss the pros and cons of reality shows for showcasing your talents and achieving success.*

1 **to preserve** [prɪ'zɜːv] schützen | 2 **surrounding** [sə'raʊndɪŋ] umgebend; umliegend | 3 **politician** [ˌpɒlɪ'tɪʃn] Politiker/-in | 4 **to balance** ['bæləns] ausgleichen; ins Gleichgewicht bringen | 5 **preservation** [ˌprezə'veɪʃn] Erhaltung; Bewahrung

Text smart 3
Argumentative texts

Find more online: e8zm94

To argue a point in a serious way, the **letter to the editor** and the **argumentative essay** are frequently-used formats. Both of these formats often play a role in written exams too.

SPEAKING

1 Warm-up: Reasons to speak out

a) *Read the news excerpt below. Say what your first reaction is, and why.*

Harsh media criticism of talent show

by Nisha Kumani | 19 May 2018 | London

The jury of the popular British TV show 'Be The Star You Are' (BTSYA) finds itself under media attack once again. Jury insults and harsh criticism caused contestant Lara Maldini to break down in tears and collapse on stage during last night's show. The audience booed the jury as Maldini had to be …

b) *Stories like the one above can provoke strong reader reactions, whether positive or negative. Look at the criteria below. Say which ones would be the appropriate style for a reaction on* ***social media*** *and for a reaction in* ***letter form*** *to a newspaper. Say why.*

formal | informal | objective | factual | emotional | well-structured | funny | interesting

c) *Your turn: What kind of story or topic could provoke you enough to want to speak out in written form, e.g. in a letter to a news source? Look at the examples on the right for ideas.*

an unfair film or TV review | a provocative advert or report | a negative / one-sided article about your favourite celebrity

READING

2 Responding to a written text in written form

a) *Now read excerpts from two* ***letters to the editor*** *on the news story above. Then:*
1. Sum up the message of each text. 2. Say which point of view you agree with, and why.

One of the most entertaining and popular TV formats is the talent show with a star jury. It's a fact that millions of viewers watch shows like BTSYA each week. Most of these shows, however, are harshly criticised by the media and parent groups. This bashing of a popular form of entertainment must stop. First of all, I'm 17 and I've been enjoying shows like BTSYA since …

I really wonder how many more of these horrible insults people are prepared to tolerate. Young people like myself (I'm 18) are trying to show their talent, but the juries only seem to be interested in bad jokes, insults and how good *they* look on TV. For several reasons, it's time we bring back a certain level of quality to TV. First, it's obvious that the jury has absolutely no …

b) *Discuss in class how each letter could go on, and with which arguments.*

How to: Write a letter to the editor

Letter to the editor:

I would like to address the different letters you have received about your report from 19 May on the Lara Maldini scandal. Basically, I get the feeling that the juries of shows like BTSYA are told to be either extremely positive or extremely negative, but rarely honest. The young contestants need constructive feedback, but they don't get it. Therefore, it is time to do away with juries in order to save the talent shows.

First, I do not want to hear nasty insults like the ones that Peter Dolan threw at Maldini and at so many candidates before her. Although some may find this entertaining, it can really break a young person's spirit and do real damage, as psychologists have often said. My point is that talent – or lack of it – can be described without four-letter words and insults.

Next, if juries are not able to give constructive feedback, then they should not have the job in the first place. In my opinion, all a talent show needs is a host, an audience, and viewers who vote for their favourites. They don't need a jury.

Some might say "It's all just for fun; let it go." But I am convinced that it is not funny when people get hurt. This is why I say that the TV producers need to feel how angry some of us are. If enough people let them know, the message will hopefully get through and cruel, nasty juries may soon be a thing of the past.

Shane Eaton (Radford, Oxfordshire)

READING

3 Understanding the text

→ △ 131/1

Read the letter above which a teenager wrote about the 'Be The Star You Are' show. Then:

1. Sum up the main points the writer makes. 2. Say if you agree or not, and why.

WRITING

4 A model letter to the editor: Structure and language

a) *Read the two boxes and also the text elements below them. In the letter above, find examples of the different elements and write them in your exercise book.*

Writing skills

Points to consider in a **letter to the editor**:
- Show that **your opinion** is the right one.
- **Counter arguments** can help to support your own arguments.
- You can use personal pronouns *(I, my, me)*, but be **serious** and **formal** in tone.
- **Paragraphs** should be clearly structured, e.g. with adverbs like *first, next,* etc.
- Shorter letters are often **reader-friendly**.

Useful phrases

Phrases for your arguments:
In my opinion, … | As far as I know, … | I am convinced that … | Because of … | My point is that … | The fact / truth is that … | It is obvious that …
Introducing counter arguments:
Although … | Some might say that … | Don't let anyone tell you that … | It is a typical mistake to say / think / claim …

argument / counter argument | the main issue | linking words to structure paragraphs / ideas | supporting facts / information | suggestions | conclusion | no short forms

b) *Work with a partner. What other arguments and counter arguments can you think of for Shane's letter?*

WRITING

5 Using the correct register for a more formal context → WB 61/1

→ △ 131/2

Letter to the editor:

Your report about BTSYA yesterday was total crap. Who gave you the right to criticise shows for young people?!?! I'm 17 and I bet if YOU were 17, you'd like BTSYA too! But that's the problem: You're some stupid old idiot who has no idea what young people wanna see! So Lara Maldini cried on TV and collapsed – who the hell cares?! The stupid cow had NO TALENT and she deserved to hear that her voice was crap. Why do you feel so sorry for her after she'd been so nasty to ALL the other contestants on the show?!?! Oh, you didn't know that? Well then, get the FULL STORY next time and stop writing such rubbish!!!

Stella Fox, London

Identify the problems in this short letter to the editor which a newspaper wasn't able to publish. Rewrite it so that the letter would be acceptable for a newspaper context.

Examples:

- You're some stupid old idiot who has no idea what young people …
  → **Better:** I would like to ask if you really know what young people …
- Well then, get the FULL STORY next time …
  → **Better:** I suggest trying to learn the full story next time …

LANGUAGE

6 Sequence adverbs

After the 'BTSYA' show in London, there was an attack on jury member Peter Dolan. An audience member saw it and told the police about it. Read her short written statement for the police. Fill in the missing ***sequence adverbs*** *in a logical way.*

The show had just ended when strange things started to happen in the audience. 1, the man next to me said, "That nasty Peter Dolan can't just insult Lara like that! I'm going to hit him in the face right now!" 2, the woman on the other side of me said, "No, you aren't, because I'm gonna hit YOU first!" 3 the man could say anything, she jumped over me and hit him in the nose. 4, their friends started to hit each other, and 5 almost everybody else in the audience started shouting things like "Lara, we love you!" or "Lara, you loser!" It was chaos, with bloody noses everywhere. I tried and tried to get away, and 6 I was able to. 7 the police arrived, everyone slowly calmed down.

after
after that
before
finally
first
next
then

WRITING

7 How to begin properly

a) *Look at the letter on p. 109 again. What arguments would you offer if you replied to it?*

b) *Write the introduction paragraph of your own reply to the letter on p. 109. Make sure you use the right style and register.*

c) *In pairs, swap introductions. Peer-edit each other's work.*

How to: Write an argumentative essay

Nick Shaw, a writer for the student website at his school in Leeds, has written an essay on an issue he feels strongly about.

The media are failing young people with unrealistic images of the sexes

Everywhere one looks in the media – in adverts, on TV, at the cinema – young men and women are confronted with images of what they are expected to look and be like. Unfortunately, these images are unrealistic and full of clichés. If this does not stop, it may do serious damage to many young people, as the following arguments will show.

First, I would like to begin with body types. Basically, the media present us with only one acceptable body type for each sex: A woman is expected to be skinny and sporty, look like a model, and have a big chest too. A man is also expected to look like a model and be tall, muscular and sporty. On the one hand, one could see this as the media's way of encouraging us to be sportier and healthier. Obviously, there is nothing wrong with that. But on the other hand, it is completely irresponsible to only present perfect images. The fact is that perfect-looking people are the exception, not the rule. As a result, more and more young people are risking their health with steroid use, plastic surgery and extreme diets. I am convinced that if the media presented more normal body types, young people would not risk their health to try to be 'perfect'.

Secondly, I must harshly criticise the image of success in the media. For the most part, we are told that success is an attractive white man in a suit. Although it is true that most high-level businesspeople are men in suits, there are reasons to criticise this one-sided image: One, young people like myself are more likely to look up to the young sweatshirt-and-jeans billionaires of Silicon Valley than to men in suits; times are changing. Two, even if an advert or a film must show someone in a suit, why not a woman? Successful women do exist. Three, success is not just about material things like an expensive suit or car. And four, success is not only for white people; other ethnic groups want – and find – success too. Therefore, it is clear that the media's image of success is outdated, wrong, negative and unrealistic.

To sum up, the media focus too much on unrealistic ideas of perfection and success when they present us with their new films, shows and products. My suggestion would be for the media to present more realism and more variety so that young people have more real role models to choose from.

– Nick Shaw (staff writer, Year 11)

Leave your comments for Nick here.

READING

8 Understanding the text

→ S3 **a)** *Read the essay on the previous page. Summarise the author's main point.*

→ △ 131/3 **b)** *Discuss your attitude to the issue and to this particular essay. Justify your views.*

WRITING

9 How to structure an argumentative essay

a) *There are two main formats for an* ***argumentative essay****:*
- *In a* ***persuasive essay****, the author argues for only* ***one*** *view: his / her own.*
- *In a* ***neutral essay****, the writer presents the reader with a* ***balance*** *of different views to consider.*

Say what essay format has been used on the previous page, and how you know.

b) *Read about the elements of argumentative essays below. Then show that you understand how the essay on p. 111 works by writing an outline for it with a partner. Your outline should name each section of the essay and also* ***briefly*** *summarise what each part is about. Copy your finished outline into your folder.*

Examples: - The intro is from lines xx to xx. It presents … Key words / ideas are …
- Paragraph xx introduces a pro argument. Important facts are …

Writing skills

Both persuasive and neutral essays require a **formal, serious style**. Here are some typical elements of **both** formats:

1. An **introduction** presents your **main point**. It can also include:
   questions you promise to answer | a short explanation of why the topic is relevant.
2. The main body of an essay must include **arguments** and **counter arguments**; the reader must see that the writer has looked at the topic from *different* sides. Arguments are introduced in paragraphs. Two structures are typical:
   a) one side's arguments first, and then counter arguments *(pro-pro-pro; con-con-con)*
   b) argument and counter argument in the *same* paragraph, then a new paragraph for another argument and counter argument, etc. *(pro-con; pro-con; pro-con).*
3. **Quotations** (e.g. from experts) and **facts** which support arguments can also be helpful.
4. A **conclusion** restates the main question, or, shows that you are right.

c) *Go back to the essay and pick out words and phrases that you would use to present arguments and counter arguments. Add these to your folder.*

WRITING

10 More practice: Structuring an argumentative essay → WB 62/2

→ △ 131/4 **a)** *In groups, discuss your opinions on the essay headline below:*

"Our constant use of social media is stopping us from making real friends in real life"

b) *Work together to list arguments for and against the subject. Think of examples and facts that could support different arguments from different points of view.*

c) *Decide on* ***one*** *standpoint for your group and make a list of supporting points. Then write a structured outline of an essay based on the model essay and on the skills box above. For your outline, you must choose between the neutral and the persuasive essay format.*

WRITING

11 Options: What do you think?

→ S6

a) *Select **one** of the controversial topics below. Write a draft for a letter to the editor **or** an argumentative essay with reasons for or against the issue that is being discussed.*

Letter to the editor:
16 year-old-drivers in the UK? No thanks. The UK already has enough problems with its 17-year-old drivers, as the high accident rate reveals. Also, just look at how many traffic accidents all the young drivers in the USA cause, where it is possible to drive at 16 or even younger; the facts speak for themselves. I am quite sure that the UK has enough problems as it is. 16-year-old drivers would be unsafe at *any* speed; keep them away from the wheel until they're 17.
Pippa Lee, York

Angry flight attendants slam airline's decision to force female cabin crew to wear high heels

by Tom Campbell | 7 June 2018 | London

An e-mail sent out to all female flight attendants last week required that heels must be worn by all female crew members at all times, whether on short- or long-distance flights. Angry women have expressed outrage and plan to continue protesting until the decision is done away with and they will be able to get back to their …

Letter to the editor:
In your article 'No shirt, no shoes, no service!', I completely agree with places like Spain or Thailand for issuing fines of $250 or more to tasteless young tourists. If young men think it is fine to walk into a restaurant or a clothing store with no shirt on, far from the beach, then they certainly deserve to pay a big fine. In fact, I would welcome such fines everywhere here in Florida too, where the 'no shirt' tourist crowd is a big problem in our city's streets.
First, it's a fact that not everybody enjoys seeing …

b) *Peer-editing: Once you're finished with your letter or essay, pair up with a classmate who has also finished his/her text on the same topic and in the same format. Peer-edit each other's texts.*

Having a voice

Having a voice is a key aspect of democracy and participation in society. There are many different ways that people can make their voices heard; you're going to look at some of them on these pages, including concrete examples at Thomas Tallis School in Greenwich, London.

READING

1 A questionnaire → WB 63/1

*Do the questionnaire below. Choose the **one** sentence in each set of questions that best describes your attitude towards each point.*

How far would YOU go to have a voice? Take the test and find out!

1
a) If I were on a student council, I'd want to lead it and make change happen!
b) I'd like to be on a student council, but I wouldn't want to lead it.
c) It's enough for me to have a good student council. I don't need to be on it.
d) Who needs a student council? What a waste of time! How boring.

2
a) Why vote in elections? I'm just one person – how can my vote make any difference?
b) I can't believe that some people never vote in elections. What losers!
c) People have fought for our right to vote. It's disrespectful not to vote if you have the opportunity.
d) If you don't understand the issues, it's best to leave it to others to vote.

3
a) I admire political activists who do dangerous protest stunts, like climbing skyscrapers to hang up protest banners.
b) People are crazy and stupid to do dangerous protest stunts. It doesn't change anything – and it's illegal too!
c) Protest is OK, but why be so dramatic with stunts? There are other ways to make your point.
d) I can totally imagine doing a dangerous protest stunt, to draw attention to an issue I really believe in.

4
a) I would sign somebody else's petition, but start one myself? No thanks.
b) Yes, I would volunteer my time to collect signatures on the street for a petition.
c) I can imagine starting my own petition about something I feel strongly about.
d) I would never waste my time on petitions. Don't bother me with stuff like that.

5
a) I respect people who do their bit for the local community. Perhaps I should do more myself.
b) Charity is great, but it should begin with your friends and family, not strangers.
c) I want to get more involved in global issues. The world around me really means something to me.
d) I'm always so busy, a million things to do. I don't have time to 'have a voice'!

6
a) Considering things like child labour and animal protection when we buy clothes is a way to make a statement.
b) I love it when protesters spray-paint people in fur coats. They deserve it! How can people be so cruel to animals?!
c) Clothes are just clothes. They have nothing to do with politics so why waste a thought on them?
d) I wouldn't wear fur myself – but if others do, that's fine. Having a voice doesn't mean you can dictate lifestyles.

SPEAKING

2 Discuss your results → WB 63/2

Now see what results you get below. Say if you agree with yours or not, and why.

Mostly reds: You consider it very important to have a voice! You express your voice and like to persuade others to join you. You would go far – too far perhaps? – to stand up for your beliefs.

Mostly yellows: You see how important it is to get involved. It's just that you prefer other people to take the lead. Maybe you haven't yet found an issue you feel really passionate about?

Mostly greens: You're happy to sit back and let other people do the work. Maybe you don't believe you could make a difference, but don't forget that being involved can bring rewards!

Mostly blues: You live in a bubble and haven't got a political bone in your body! Wider issues don't really interest you. But your voice and your actions are valuable. Don't just run and hide!

VIEWING

3 The Student Council at TTS

Now learn about having a voice at TTS …

5

a) *Watch until 03:25. Sum up what you learn about the Student Council and what they do.*

Word bank

discussion / to discuss | to feel strongly about sth | to nominate sb | participation / to participate | representative / to represent

b) *Watch again and point out the details you found the most interesting. Explain why.*

VIEWING

4 Student Voice at TTS

a) *Watch the rest of the film. Sum up why the members are in Student Voice and how they're making a difference.*

b) *Now compare and contrast the Student Council and the Student Voice.*

SPEAKING

5 Your turn: Having a voice at your school

a) *Compare what you've seen at TTS with your own experiences at school.*

b) *In small groups, try to find agreement on the top three things you'd change / improve at your school. Present your ideas.* → S8

A

B

C

Legende

Diese Symbole und Erklärungen zeigen dir, wie du mit den Hilfen, Aufgaben und Aktivitäten auf den *Diff pool*-Seiten arbeiten kannst.

△ Hilfe zur Unit-Aufgabe | oder eine leichtere Variante der Unit-Aufgabe | oder eine zusätzliche Aufgabe

▲ eine zusätzliche Herausforderung

Unit 1

△ 1 Exciting Australia → Help with Introduction, p. 13/3

These tips for your poster and the presentation can help you turn it into a success:

Designing your poster
- For the title, use interesting adjectives / superlatives to grab your classmates' attention.
- The visuals can be surprising / shocking / unusual to make your listeners interested.
- Keep the text short and concentrate on the most important / interesting information.

Presenting your poster
- Don't read out the poster text.
- Don't describe your visuals in detail, but explain what they say about your topic.
- Add more interesting / exciting / unusual details during the presentation to hold your classmates' attention.
- Use audio elements (sound / song) for your presentation, if possible.

△ 2 Safety advice → After Station 1, p. 15/4

*Use the right **passive forms** to complete the dialogue between Tanya and Mike.*

Mike: Don't worry too much, Tanya. Jim **1** (warn) of the dangers before he left, and he isn't stupid, is he?
Tanya: I'm not so sure about that. When he was in northern Australia, he **2** (tell) that swimming in rock pools can be dangerous. But he still jumped in. You'd think he'd never heard of crocodiles!
Mike: But he **3** (not attack), right?
Tanya: No, but we **4** (tell) so many stories about crocodile attacks that it now seems a wonder he **5** (not hurt).
Mike: Yeah, I heard that more warning signs **6** (put up) soon. Did you hear about the kid who **7** (kill) by a croc just last week? If Jim isn't more careful, he's going to get killed too.
Tanya: If that hasn't already happened. Park rangers are still searching for a guy that's been missing since Thursday. Let's hope he **8** (find) very soon!

▲ 3 Looking for Jim → After Station 1, p. 15/4

*Role play: At the hostel, Tanya and Moshe are questioned by a police officer about Jim. Use the information from the text on p. 14 to write a short dialogue. Make sure you use **passive forms** whenever possible.*

△ 4 The passive infinitive → After Station 1, p. 17/7

Here are some tips on what to do if you see a snake in Australia. Use the ***passive infinitive*** *to complete the sentences.*

1. Snakes can ___ (find) in all parts of Australia. Not all of them are poisonous[1] – but you don't want ___ (bite) by any of them because all snakebites can cause infections.
2. Snakes are shy creatures that like ___ (leave alone). Usually, they'll attack only if they feel threatened[2].
3. If you see a snake, stay calm and don't move. Remember that the snake is probably just as frightened as you are and should ___ (give) a chance to escape.
4. Snakes must ___ (show) respect. They should never ___ (pick up) or ___ (chase).
5. If you're bitten, you'll need ___ (take) to hospital immediately. Snakebites must ___ (treat) as quickly as possible.

△ 5 What's in the news? → Help with Station 1, p. 17/10

Here are some ideas that can help you write a good news story:

floods[3] in northern Australia | farmer | out early one morning | surprised | kangaroo | trapped in the water | remember | large crocodiles in the area | quickly | tell man to watch out for crocs | walk in | grab kangaroo | very frightened | try to free itself | lucky | nobody hurt

△ 6 Down Under → After Station 2, p. 19/13

Complete the text with the correct ***passive forms****.*

In the summer of 1967, when Australia's beaches 1 (visit) by thousands of people, Australia's Prime Minister[4] Harold Holt 2 (report) missing: He'd walked into the sea on Cheviot Beach, south of Melbourne, and 3 (never see) again. This is just one of the fascinating stories that 4 (tell) in Bill Bryson's bestselling book *Down Under*.

In another story, the author describes his first attempt[5] to ride a boogie board. While his friends are having fun on their boards, Bryson 5 (scare) to death by stories of shark attacks and dangerous rip currents.

On his third trip to Australia, Bryson visits Uluru with his friend Allan Sherwin. Both men have heard wonderful things about Uluru before and want to see it for themselves. When they arrive there, they're horrified to see people climbing up the rock in spite of all the signs that 6 (put up). Bryson is shocked that they have no respect for this place, which 7 (see) as sacred by Aboriginal people.

Another story Bryson tells in his book– and one which 8 (almost forget) – is that of Australian pilots Anderson and Hitchcock. When they 9 (tell) that an airplane was missing, they flew out to rescue the pilot Kingsford Smith. However, their plane crashed too and while Anderson and Hitchcock 10 (kill), Smith 11 (can – rescue).

Bryson's book 12 (should – read) by anyone who is thinking of travelling to Australia!

1 poisonous ['pɔɪznəs] giftig | **2 threatened** ['θretnd] bedroht | **3 flood** [flʌd] Überschwemmung | **4 Prime Minister** [ˌpraɪm 'mɪnɪstə] Premierminister/-in | **5 attempt** [ə'temt] Versuch

△ 7 Antonia in Australia → After Station 2, p. 20/15

After she finished school, Antonia from Germany travelled to Australia with InterChange, a work and travel program. Read what she writes about it on her blog. Fill in ***let***, ***allow***, ***make*** *or* ***have***.

My parents didn't want to **1** me go at first and they wouldn't even **2** me to talk about Australia for a while. When that didn't work, they **3** me listen to scary stories about dangerous animals and rip currents. But finally they **4** me pack my bags and even **5** a flight booked for me by a friend at the travel agent's. I'm so lucky to be here! The guys from InterChange gave me a long list of job offers, and they **6** me choose which part of Australia I wanted to see first. They were very helpful, and they even **7** a seat booked for me on the train to Melbourne. The city **8** young artists to turn certain locations into outdoor art galleries – I just had to see that for myself!

△ 8 In Blue Mountains National Park → After Station 2, p. 20/17

Read the text. Then turn the ***active*** *sentences into* ***passive*** *ones, if possible.*

People told me not to miss the beautiful Blue Mountains National Park. You can reach it by car or by train from Sydney. People named the park Blue Mountains because of the blue tinge[1] that the mountains have when you look at them from a distance. Travellers have written a lot about its waterfalls, aboriginal rock paintings and a special rock formation called the Three Sisters. The Katoomba Scenic[2] Railway, which is the world's steepest[3] railway, takes passengers down the Jamison Valley into an ancient rainforest[4]. But there are many more activities that you can do in the park, like rock climbing or mountain biking.

△ 9 The colonisation of Australia → Help with Station 2, p. 21/20

This grid can help you structure your notes:

Captain Phillip and Bennelong	*Hopes for the future*	*What happens later on*
– *Bennelong:* *forced to learn the English language and English manners* – …	– *White people:* … – *Aboriginal people:* …	– *Aboriginal people:* *driven off[5] their land and killed by white settlers* – …

1 tinge [tɪndʒ] Färbung | **2 scenic** ['siːnɪk] landschaftlich schön / reizvoll | **3 steep** [stiːp] steil | **4 rainforest** ['reɪnˌfɒrɪst] Regenwald | **5 to drive sb/sth off** [draɪv‿'ɒf] jmdn./etw. vertreiben

△ 10 If they hadn't found their way … → After Station 3, p. 23/24

The film Rabbit Proof Fence[1] *tells the story of two Aboriginal girls, Molly and Daisy Craig, who escape from an orphanage to find their families. Use the right verb forms to make* ***conditional sentences type 1, 2 or 3****.*

1. If you ___ (want) to learn more about the Stolen Generations, you ___ (should – watch) the film *Rabbit Proof Fence*.
2. The two girls ___ (not see) their mothers again if they ___ (not be) brave enough to escape from the orphanage.
3. If Molly ___ (not be) so good at covering their tracks, the police ___ (find) them.
4. On their journey home, Molly tells Daisy: "It's lucky our village is so close to the fence. If it ___ (be) further away, we ___ (not be able to) find our way back."
5. You ___ (understand) social problems in Australia if you ___ (watch) this film.

▲ 11 Used to do? Used to doing? You decide! → After Station 3, p. 24/26

According to scientists, Australia's famous Great Barrier Reef[2] *is in danger. Complete the text with* ***used to do*** *or* ***used to doing****.*

Not so long ago, people [1] (think) that the Great Barrier Reef on Australia's northeastern coast would always be there because being out in the sea [2] (make) it safe from any kind of environmental problems. But that's no longer true: the reef is in great danger. In the past, tourists were [3] (see) the fantastic colours of the reef, but now higher sea temperatures are destroying the corals[3]. They are losing their colours – what [4] (be) a huge reef of red, blue and orange corals is now turning white. Today, tourists are [5] (travel) out to the reef in glass bottom boats and taking pictures of the reef, but in future they just might have to get [6] (look) at pictures of the reef on the internet instead.

△ 12 Doing an interview → Help with Skills, p. 26/2

An interview is interesting to listen to if the right questions are asked, and if the interviewee has a story to tell. These ideas can help you write a good interview on shark attacks:

Reporter at the scene:
nets – how safe? | swimmers – leave net area? | nets – danger to sharks? | alternative? | how – sharks be taken away from beach? | too expensive? | what else – be done?

Lifeguard:
strong nets – safe | swimmer – must respect net | sharks – killed by nets | catch sharks, take away from beach | airplanes – control area, spot[4] sharks | drones[5] – cheaper | become shark spotter – on land

1 **Rabbit-Proof Fence** [ˌræbɪtpruːf ˈfens] *kaninchensicherer Schutzzaun in Westaustralien* | 2 **reef** [riːf] Riff | 3 **coral** [ˈkɒrəl] Koralle | 4 **to spot** [spɒt] sichten; entdecken | 5 **drone** [drəʊn] Drohne

Text smart 1

△ 1 Before you watch: A first look at Penny → Help with Station 1, p. 39/3

The word bank can give you ideas for describing the two girls' emotions:

Word bank

amused[1] | angry | awkward | disgusted[2] | embarrassed | sad | scared | shocked | sorry | surprised | terrible | unhappy

You can use these phrases to talk about the plot:

Useful phrases

- The girl might have started to cry because …
- The other girl might feel … because …
- The reaction may have been caused by …
- I can imagine that … may have made the girl cry / may have caused the look on the other girl's face.

△ 2 Getting from A to B → Help with Station 1, p. 39/4c)

Here are some ideas and vocabulary for embarrassing situations. Maybe something similar has happened to you, to a friend or to a family member?

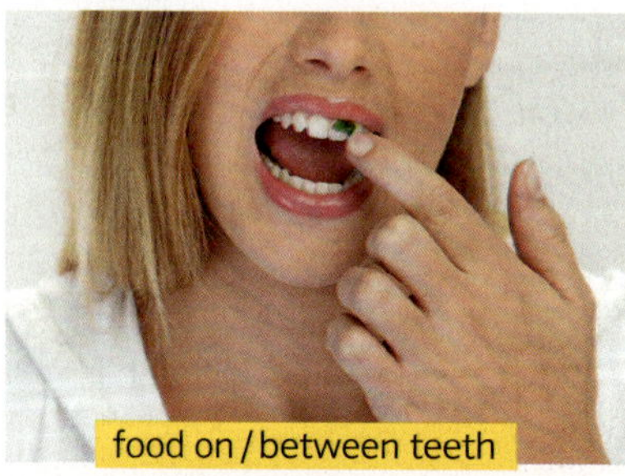

food on / between teeth

didn't know until after school / date / party

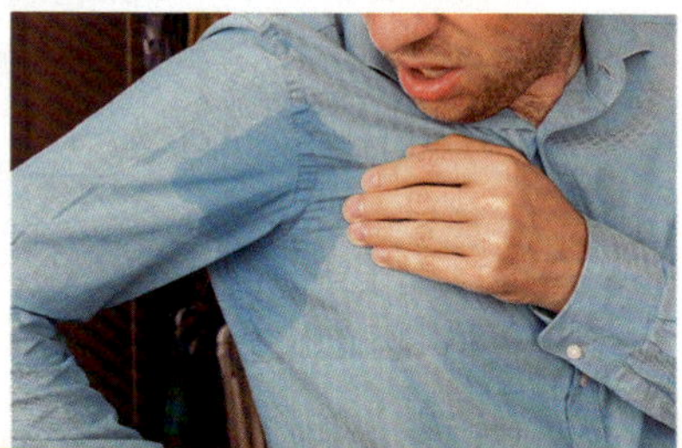

sweat stains[3] | smelled / looked awful

somebody took picture, posted it online

spilt … on shirt / new outfit / …

was on the way to school / a date / a party / …

left home / the toilet / school / … with toilet paper on shoe

everyone laughed!

1 amused [ə'mju:zd] amüsiert | **2 disgusted** [dɪs'gʌstɪd] angewidert | **3 sweat stain** ['swet ˌsteɪn] Schweißfleck

△ 3 Understanding teen comedy → Help with Station 2, p. 41/8b)

Here are some elements of film and their effects:

Elements of teen comedies	Possible effects
humour	makes film more entertaining; shows funny side of problems; shows that some problems maybe aren't so bad
exaggeration	shows how silly some behaviour can be; creates funny scenes; shows that things could be worse
romance and dating	covers a topic that is important for teenagers; makes film genre interesting / relevant for boys *and* for girls

▲ 4 Camera shots and their functions → After Station 2, p. 43/11

Which scenes from your favourite films made a big impression on you? Did interesting camera shots play a role? How? With a partner, discuss the effect of those scenes, and how the effect might have been different if different shots had been used.

△ 5 Practise scriptwriting → Help with Station 3, p. 44/13

These words can help you write about the feelings the two girls in the scene show:

Word bank

angry | arrogant | awkward | bitchy | confused | embarrassed | happy | mean | nervous | self-confident | self-satisfied[1] | unhappy

Unit 2

△ 1 Thinking about the job world → Help with Introduction, p. 47/3b)

This list of reasons for and against changing jobs can help you with Ex. 3b):

- You learn a lot at a new job; you also learn to deal with new situations again and again.
- Having a long-term job[2] means security – that can be important in a person's life.
- Leaving jobs often means you never feel at home at a job – you're always on the move.
- You lose friends; it isn't always easy to stay in touch with colleagues from your old job.
- You meet new people, make new friends.
- Changing jobs often means moving. That's expensive, annoying[3], costs time.
- New people bring new ideas: There's more innovation in a company.
- You satisfy[4] your curiosity.
- The longer you hold a job, the harder it is to get fired[5].

1 **self-satisfied** [ˌselfˈsætɪsfaɪd] selbstgefällig | 2 **long-term job** [ˌlɒŋtɜːm ˈdʒɒb] langfristiger Arbeitsplatz | 3 **annoying** [əˈnɔɪɪŋ] nervig | 4 **to satisfy** [ˈsætɪsfaɪ] befriedigen | 5 **to get fired** [ˌget ˈfaɪəd] entlassen werden

△ 2 A formal job description → Help with Station 1, p. 48/2b)

These words and phrases can help you talk about the differences between the two texts:

Word bank

describes job in detail | mentions tasks | gives a list of responsibilities | says what the person is expected to do | gives information on what the application should contain | gets a lot of people interested in the job | names the benefits | explains what others say about the job

△ 3 What careers do girls and boys prefer? → Instead of Station 1, p. 49/4c)

a) *Look at the different job criteria below. Discuss which ones you think are important for choosing a career.*

- requires more physical[1] / more emotional strength
- can be done full-time / part-time
- is a dream job for little girls / little boys
- matches male / female way of thinking
- is what boys / girls are more interested in
- has lots of male / female role models[2] in real life / in film / on TV
- requires communication / language / organisation / creative skills

b) *What sort of jobs could you describe with these criteria? Describe different jobs and whether you would apply for them or not.*

△ 4 Expressing expectations → Instead of Station 1, p. 50/5

Talk about the jobs in the box with your partner. What do you think is expected of each of them? Does your partner agree? Use ***be expected to / be supposed to + infinitive*** *in your sentences.*

Example:

A: I believe as a doctor you'**re expected to be** good at …

B: I agree, but you'**re** also **supposed to have** … And teachers **are expected to be** …

A: Hm, I think they'**re** …

architect | business executive | dancer | doctor | engineer | fashion designer | firefighter | model | musician | nurse | pilot | reporter | sales assistant | teacher | web designer	be able to work long hours | be attractive | be creative | be good at listening to people | be good at maths / sciences | be great at explaining things | be in good physical shape[3] | enjoy being with children | not get nervous easily | have a good memory | have good communication skills | like working with machines / computers | like being in front of a camera / an audience

1 physical ['fɪzɪkl] körperlich | **2 role model** ['rəʊl ˌmɒdl] Vorbild | **3 shape** [ʃeɪp] *hier:* Verfassung

△ 5 When I was young … → After Station 1, p. 50/5

Tim's great-grandfather grew up a long time ago – and he likes to tell his great-grandchildren how hard everything was back then! Use the information in the box to write down what Great-grandad Arthur tells his family.

Start like this:

When we were young, we **were supposed to** … | My parents were very, very strict. I **was** always **expected to** … | All children **were supposed to** … For example, my sisters …

help on the farm before and after school | walk to school every day | bring wood to school in winter, to stay warm | be very quiet during lessons | respect our teacher | do homework after helping on the farm after school | help with the chores | eat what is on the table even when you don't like it | be thankful for food | do what parents tell us to do | never disagree with parents | go to bed straight after dinner | look after the smaller children | be home before it gets dark

△ 6 A personal profile for your CV → Help with Station 1, p. 50/7

Use the information in the grid below to find ideas for your own profile.

	Sports	Cafeteria	Entertainment	Chores
Qualifications	– coach of a local sports team – member of swim team	– weekend job in a pizza place / cafe	– member of Drama Club / of a band / dancing group	– do garden work for neighbours – wash my own clothes
Strengths	– good with kids / at teaching	– calm – friendly – reliable	– not nervous in front of people – strong nerves[1]	– hard-working – don't mind getting dirty!
Skills	– great at swimming / football	– good at preparing / serving food	– good at singing / dancing / acting / motivating people	– good with my hands

△ 7 The application letter → Help with Station 1, p. 51/8b)

Look at the grid from Ex. 6. Which of the qualifications, strengths and skills does Ella say she has? Copy the grid and complete it with information about Ella.

1 **strong nerves** [ˌstrɒŋ ˈnɜːvz] gute Nerven

△ 8 Verbs of perception: Present participle or infinitive? → After Station 2, p. 54/14

Lisa can't believe all the things that happen in the flats across the street. In the list below you see what happened in just 20 minutes! Use the information to write sentences about her neighbours. Use ***verbs of perception*** *like 'see', 'notice', 'listen to', 'hear'. Which activities need a* ***participle construction****, which need an* ***infinitive****?*

Start like this: I **heard** one man …

1. man – sing non-stop[1] – in an awful voice
2. woman – drop two bags of rubbish out the window!
3. man – clean the flat with no clothes on!
4. woman – hide expensive shopping bags before husband gets home
5. two men – shout at and hit each other non-stop
6. woman – play the piano very nicely
7. man – try to stop a fire in his kitchen
8. two police officers – break down[2] a door to a flat

▲ 9 You're a crime witness → After Station 2, p. 54/14

You came home late at night and saw someone breaking into your neighbour's flat. Then you told the police about it. Write about what you heard, saw, noticed, watched. Did you see all of the action, or just parts of it? Here are some ideas:

stranger | carry big travel bag | walk close to the house | look up at windows | open garden gate[3] | turn round and look up and down street | walk very quietly to back of house | glass – break | someone – switch on torch | walk slowly around house | come out through front door | run down street

△ 10 A winter's dream → After Station 2, p. 54/15

Complete the following sentences with a ***participle*** *or* ***infinitive****. Use the verbs below.*

Lily was walking through the woods when she saw children **1**. She carefully walked across the lake **2**. Suddenly she felt the **3**. She stood still **4**. The children came towards her **5**. Lily could hear the **6**. She turned round and watched the **7**. She felt water **8**. The children stood **9**. Lily heard them **10**, but couldn't understand. She watched them **11** to the side of the lake. Lily felt water **12**. Then she woke up!

skate on the frozen[4] lake | wave her arms | ice – move below her feet | wonder what to do | shout and laugh | ice – break | hole in the ice – get bigger | get into her shoes | stare at her | say something | run back | cover her body

1 non-stop [ˌnɒnˈstɒp] pausenlos; ununterbrochen | **2 to break down** [ˌbreɪk ˈdaʊn] *hier:* einschlagen | **3 gate** [geɪt] Tor | **4 frozen** [ˈfrəʊzn] gefroren

△ 11 A blind date? → After Station 3, p. 58/23

*Rewrite the following text with **defining** and **non-defining relative clauses**.*

Yesterday I saw Jason (he's Sarah's new boyfriend). He walked into the new café in King Street (it sells fair trade coffee and cake). And guess what – he was holding hands with a pretty girl (it wasn't Sarah). So I followed them inside (that was difficult because I didn't want Jason to see me). I pretended to be interested in the chocolate bars (they have them on the counter[1]). I looked into a mirror (it was hanging behind the counter) and saw Jason (he was sitting at a table with the girl). I thought that Sarah (she gets so jealous!) might be really angry. I first thought of taking a photo (I could send it to Sarah). But I realised that I'd left my phone (it was a present for my birthday) at home. So I walked up to them and said hello. Jason (he was surprised) smiled at me and said: "Hi Rebecca! This is Naomi, she goes to the School for the Blind[2]. I work for it on Friday afternoons. She forgot her cane[3] at home, so I said I'd help her to find her way to the café. It belongs to her parents."

▲ 12 Awesome inventions → After Station 3, p. 58/23

*Here are some more inventions that were presented on the show Dragons' Den. What can you do with them? Find out more and then write a short text. Use **defining** and **non-defining relative clauses**. Then 'sell' one or more of the inventions to your classmates!*

One remote control[4] for everything!
Looks like a magic wand[5]: the **Kymera Wand**

A new frozen[6] dessert for people with food allergies: from **Worthenshaws** (name later changed to **Kirsty's**)

An interactive toy for small children: the **iTeddy**

△ 13 How to use inversion for emphasis → Instead of Station 3, p. 59/24b)

*Look at Ex. 24a) on p. 59. Use inversion to rewrite the sentences below in a similar way. Use the word or phrase in **bold** to start with.*

Example: 1. I have **never** felt so nervous. → **Never have I** felt so nervous.

1. I have **never** felt so nervous. → Never have I … ✔
2. He had **hardly** finished lunch when he heard the fire alarm. → Hardly had …
3. I **only** realised how much I liked art **when** I went to Italy. → Only when … did I …
4. She had **no sooner** arrived than the film started. → No sooner had …
5. He **not only** got a new office, but he got more money too! → Not only did he …
6. We **rarely** have time to just sit and do nothing. → Rarely do we …

1 counter ['kaʊntə] Tresen; Theke | **2 for the blind** [blaɪnd] für Sehbehinderte | **3 cane** [keɪn] Stock | **4 remote control** [rɪˌməʊt kən'trəʊl] Fernbedienung | **5 magic wand** [ˌmædʒɪk 'wɒnd] Zauberstab | **6 frozen** ['frəʊzn] gefroren

△ 14 A year in Cameroon[1] → After Station 3, p. 59/24

*Anthony's first job was as a volunteer for a non-profit organisation[2] in Cameroon. Use **inversion** to rewrite what he posted about it on the 'Words-of-Wisdom Wall'.*

1. I did**n't only** work as a volunteer for a non-profit organisation, I also worked for a football club. → Not only …
2. Some of the children had **never** seen a white person **before**. → Never before …
3. I've **rarely** had time to think about my future plans since Cameroon. → Rarely …
4. But I **never** regretted[3] my decision to spend time in Africa. → Never …
5. I did**n't** think **for one moment** about giving up. → Not for one moment …
6. "There's **no way** he'll want to stay there when the rainy season starts!" my friends thought. → No way will …
7. I do**n't only** want to tell people about the hard living conditions in Cameroon, I also want to tell them what a beautiful country it is. → Not only …

△ 15 Acting out a scene from the film → Help with Skills, p. 60/2d)

The following ideas can help you write a different dialogue for Saanvi, Phil and Courtney.

Saanvi: I'm very passionate about advertising; if I wasn't so nervous, it would be more obvious! | Sorry, but I get so nervous at job interviews! | I can be calm under pressure, believe me; if you invite me back, I won't be as nervous.

Phil: I believe it's important to improve yourself, which is why I'm taking extra writing lessons to improve my style. | I might sound a bit too self-confident, but I'll show you I'm the right candidate, just give me a chance. | I've been told I learn quickly.

Courtney: Sorry my bus / underground was late; it won't happen again. | Sorry about my phone; I'm a bit nervous and forgot to turn it off. | I'm interested in new products and how they're sold. | I'm good with people / I've been told I'm a good listener.

▲ 16 How language helps to tell the story → After Story, p. 66/5

On p. 66, line 70, babies are described as 'newchildren'. Find other examples of words used by the community which you find unusual. Explain how their language might affect the way members of the community see the world.

△ 17 Memories → Help with Story, p. 67/8b)

Some memories are very important for the world. Look at these memories and think of where we'd be without them. The useful phrases in the box can help you.

World Wars I & II | the atomic bomb[4] | nuclear disasters like Fukushima in 2011

Useful phrases

The death of … / destruction[5] of … / disaster in … has taught us to: talk to and listen to each other more | be more careful with … | show more respect to … | stop … before it can start | look for different kinds of … / different ways to …

1 Cameroon [ˌkæməˈruːn] Kamerun | **2 non-profit organisation** [ˌnɒnprɒfɪt ɔːgnaɪˈzeɪʃn] gemeinnützige Organisation | **3 to regret** [rɪˈgret] bereuen | **4 atomic bomb** [əˌtɒmɪk ˈbɒm] Atombombe | **5 destruction** [dɪˈstrʌkʃn] Zerstörung

Text smart 2

△ 1 Your checklist for summary writing → Help with Station 1, p. 76/4

Copy the grid and add more information for your own checklist on summary writing.

	Dos	Don'ts
Length	✔ Always remember that a summary is reduction	✘ Don't write too much! 30–40 per cent of original length is enough
Contents	✔ Change order of information if necessary	✘ No direct speech, no quotes ✘ …
Language	✔ …	✘ Don't use the same style you use when you talk to your friends.

△ 2 Compare two examples of an analysis → Help with Station 2, p. 78/7

These aspects of texts can help you judge which analysis is more successful:

A **well-written analysis** …
is easy to understand | doesn't contain too many long / very short sentences | is written in more formal, serious language | is well-structured in paragraphs for different ideas and arguments

A **convincing analysis** …
presents arguments | contains facts and figures | includes quotes to support the arguments | makes sense to the reader | convinces with factual language, information, and sometimes quotes from experts, but not with emotional language and feelings

An **interesting analysis** …
focuses on what would interest the reader, and not just the writer him-/herself! | presents clear examples | contains humour / suspense / surprise to grab / keep the reader's attention | avoids boring style

△ 3 Finding and using key words → Help with Options, p. 79/9

*It's a good idea to think of key words and ideas **before** you write a summary / an analysis:*

Word bank

problems for children / teens: time | bullying | cyber addiction | lack of sleep | relationship with devices / smartphones is addictive / compulsive

switching off is: not impossible | difficult | hard | a challenge

social media: 'Disconnect' project | switch off | go offline | addictive

changes before / after: more time to read / watch TV / do homework / hang out with friends, family

Unit 3

△ 1 Imagine yourself in the scene → Help with Introduction, p. 84/2

Match the sentences below to the photos on pages 84–85. Then choose one of the photos and use the sentence as a starting point for your text about the people and the scene.

1. I can see the waves crashing against the rocks in the distance. 2. I can feel the sun shining on my back. 3. I enjoy walking along the busy streets. 4. The fields in front of me seem to go on forever. 5. I can hear my colleagues chatting and laughing.

△ 2 Expressing the same idea differently → Instead of Station 1, p. 87/2a)

Match the definitions on the left with the words / phrases from the text on p. 86.

cause a stir | stroll | chalk something up to experience | a wannabe | aspiring | keep your head above water | showcase your talents

trying to be successful at something | walk in a relaxed way | just be able to survive | show what you're really good at | a person who is trying to become famous, usually without success | learn from something negative that has happened to you | produce a lot of interest or excitement

▲ 3 Using different future forms → After Station 1, p. 88/8

*Complete the text with **different future forms** – they might be forms you already know or forms you've just learned in Station 1.*

"Hurry now," Jason's mom shouted. "The train **1** (leave) at 10:15, and we **2** (pick up) Cecy on the way, remember?" Jason came running down the stairs. His mom was already in the car, waiting impatiently. "The plane **3** (take off) at 2 p.m. – if Jason doesn't catch the train, he **4** (miss) the plane too. Let's just hope he **5** (be able to) manage without us," she thought. Jason jumped in. "Let's go," he said. "Isn't this just great? At 10 o'clock this evening Cecy and I **6** (sit) in a café and **7** (plan) activities for the summer camp." "Well that sounds fun, but I'm sure that by the time you get back in two months you **8** (do) a lot more work and **9** (spend) less time in a café than you imagine now. Working in a summer camp for kids with special needs isn't easy at all. Did you pack the information the organization sent you?" "Oh no. I forgot. But it doesn't matter. Cecy **10** (remember) to bring it, I'm sure." "And she **11** (think) of

informing the camp team of your arrival time too, right?" "I think so," Jason answered. "I think they **12** (meet) us at the airport. Don't worry, mom. When you hear from me next, I'm sure we **13** (have) the time of our lives, and you **14** (stop) worrying right after my first phone call." "Actually, I've already stopped," his mom thought. "I'm sure Cecy **15** (do) my job for the next few weeks."

4 Some facts about the Academy Awards[1] → After Station 2, p. 91/15

Decide whether you need ***the, a/an*** *or* ***no article (–)****.*

California wouldn't be the same without **1** tech industry, or Hollywood without **2** film industry. Making films has always been **3** big business in L.A.: **4** most people love **5** good movies. That's why so many new films are produced in Hollywood each year. But it's hard to achieve **6** success, and it's not easy to explain **7** success of films like *La La Land* or *Titanic*, which both won **8** number of Academy Awards. A film can win **9** award in many different categories: for best actor or actress, costume design, screenplay[2] or best original score (music). However, most often **10** films are remembered not for **11** money they earned – although **12** money is of course very important – but for **13** fantastic performances of all **14** artists involved. Not all of them are actors: Edith Head won eight Oscars, all for **15** costume design, and Dennis Murren won nine for **16** visual effects in his films.

5 The Golden Raspberry Awards[3] → After Station 2, p. 91/15

Everyone in the film industry wants to win an Oscar – and often nominees have prepared a speech long before Oscar night just in case they win. Nobody wants a Golden Raspberry Award, though, which is the award for particularly bad movies and performances. Choose one of the winners of a 'Razzie Award' below and write a short speech in which you explain why you deserve an Oscar instead.

Halle Berry, for worst actress in *Catwoman* (2011) |
Bill Condon, for worst director in *Breaking Dawn – The Twilight Saga Part 2* (2013) |
Jesse Eisenberg, for worst supporting actor in *Batman versus Superman* (2017)

6 Your own start-up → Help with Station 2, p. 92/17b)

Think about a new business idea that you find interesting and present it to the class. Use these questions as a structure for your presentation:

1. What gets on your (or others') nerves every day that could be improved with a good business idea? Think of your daily routine (school, homework, free time …).
2. What money, talents, equipment or help would you need for your business? Who could you ask for advice? How long will it take to turn the idea into the end product?
3. How would you like to sell your product or idea, to whom and where? At what price?
4. Where do you see your business in one year – five years – ten years? And yourself?

7 California's changing population → Help with Station 2, p. 93/20b)

Here are some possible consequences of California's changing population. Discuss with a partner: Which consequences are likely to happen, which are not? Give reasons.

1. Spanish will become the official language in California. **2.** The Californian government will spend more money on the education of Latino children. **3.** White people will leave California and move to states with a white majority. **4.** There'll be more TV and radio channels[4] in Spanish. **5.** Politicians who are against Mexican immigrants will lose elections in California. **6.** Latinos and whites will mix – there'll be no separate groups by 2060.

1 **Academy Award** [əˌkædəmi əˈwɔːd] Oscar *(Filmpreis der Motion Picture Academy)* | 2 **screenplay** [ˈskriːnpleɪ] Drehbuch | 3 **Golden Raspberry Award** [ˌɡəʊldn ˈrɑːzbri əˌwɔːd] Goldene Himbeere | 4 **channel** [ˈtʃænl] Programm

▲ 8 You're supposed to … → After Station 3, p. 96/24

Read the text. Choose from the verbs below to rewrite the underlined parts. Then think of a suitable translation into German.

should | be expected to | must | be supposed to | ought to | be required to | be said to

If you go to California, do visit its fantastic national parks. Some of them are world-famous, like Yosemite or Redwood – people say that the biggest trees on earth grow there. But make sure you don't leave the trail if you hike in the park because you could easily get lost! If you do get lost, rangers will have to search for you, and they don't like putting in extra time for tourists who have been told to stay on the path. If you decide to camp in the park, put all your food into a plastic bag and hang it on a tree at night. Hungry bears love eating leftovers from your picnic in the park. Some people say that they search for food in the tents too! Although tourists are told to read about all the risks before entering the park, rangers have to go out every day to save those who aren't careful enough.

△ 9 Talking about California → Help with Station 3, p. 97/27

These phrases can help you talk about your ideas about California:

Before we talked about California in class I thought / believed that … | I'd heard a lot about California / I'd seen films that are set in California and thought that … | I knew that California is said to be …, but … | Everything I'd heard about California seemed … | What I found very interesting is … | I didn't know that … | However, after we'd read / learned about … I realized that … | I now think that … | Nevertheless, I still believe …

△ 10 What kind of a person is Jamie? → Instead of Story, p. 103/2b)

From this list of adjectives, choose the ones that you think describe Jamie best. Work with a partner to choose one from each group. Then compare your list of adjectives with a different partner's and again choose five adjectives from your two lists. With a third partner, narrow your choice down to three adjectives. Give reasons for your choice.

1	honest	jealous	optimistic	ambitious[1]	relaxed
2	angry	confident	embarrassed	smart	emotional
3	irresponsible	open	polite	quiet	rude
4	active	lonely	rich	famous	outgoing
5	persistent	generous	friendly	curious	reliable
6	unsure	violent	cold	realistic	clever
7	mean	sensitive	dominant	boastful[2]	passionate
8	open-minded[3]	unfriendly	patient	happy	determined

1 ambitious [æm'bɪʃəs] ehrgeizig | **2 boastful** ['bəʊstfl] angeberisch | **3 open-minded** [ˌəʊpn'maɪndɪd] offen; aufgeschlossen

Text smart 3

△ 1 A model letter to the editor → Help with Station 1, p. 109/3

You can use these phrases to discuss the letter on p. 109 from your point of view:

Useful phrases

- I agree / disagree when the writer says / states / claims that …
- I accept / can't accept the idea that … because I (don't) feel / (don't) believe …
- I share / support the author's view when he says …, but I disagree when he claims …
- Because of this …, / Therefore …, / For this reason, … I agree / disagree with …

△ 2 Phrases for a more formal register → Help with Station 1, p. 110/5

The letter and its phrases below can give you ideas on how to improve the letter on p. 110:

I am writing to complain about how you reported on Peter Dolan and the 'BTSYA' show in yesterday's newspaper. I am sorry to say that there is much to complain about. First, I must point out that your report was totally one-sided. You focused on the negative aspects, but not on what makes the show a success. Additionally, it was clear that the writer was not aware of the complete story: Nobody in the jury likes Lara Maldini, so it was no surprise that they criticised her. I realise that it is not possible to include all the details in stories like this, but I do feel that your readers deserve to read a balanced report. – Ken West, Dover

△ 3 What the media show and don't show → Help with Station 2, p. 112/8b)

The photo on the left was used in an ice cream advert; the one on the right wasn't. Think about reasons why. This could help you with your discussion about the media.

△ 4 Structuring an argumentative essay → Help with Station 2, p. 112/10

Go through the aspects in the box below and sort them. Which ones would help with arguments ***for*** *or* ***against*** *social media? Use the ideas for your essay.*

keep in touch with people | exchange ideas | (not) reliable as a source of information | entertainment | requires (a lot of) time | meet new people | feel less lonely | can't live without it | cyberbullying | real emotions | learn (too much) about the private lives of others | age limits | what is real, what isn't? | dangers of chatting with strangers

Dealing with visuals

S1 Bilder beschreiben und analysieren

Wenn du ein Bild beschreiben und analysieren sollst, kannst du in folgenden Schritten vorgehen:

1. Beschreibe, was in dem Bild zu sehen ist. Dafür verwendest du das *simple present*. Konzentriere dich zunächst auf Personen oder Dinge, die im Vordergrund zu sehen sind, aber vergiss nicht, auch Personen oder Dinge im Hintergrund zu beschreiben. Wenn du ausdrücken willst, was in dem Bild passiert, verwendest du sehr häufig das *present progressive*.
2. Nachdem du das Bild beschrieben hast, kannst du deine Meinung dazu äußern oder erklären, was es deiner Meinung nach ausdrücken möchte. Für die Analyse des Bildes verwendest du das *simple present*.

Useful phrases

Describing pictures:
- At the top / bottom you can see …
- In the foreground / background / middle …
- On the left / right there is / are …
- The people in the picture are talking / having fun / celebrating / fighting / …

Analysing pictures:
- I like / don't like the picture because …
- The picture is interesting / boring / exciting / … because …
- The picture shows … / represents …
- The picture tries to show … but I think a picture with … instead of … would work better because …

Etwas anders sieht es aus, wenn du aufgefordert wirst, einen Cartoon zu beschreiben und zu analysieren. Hier ist es wichtig, dass du besonders auf die Kombination von Bild und Text achtest. Karikaturisten verwenden häufig die Stilmittel der Ironie und der Übertreibung, um ihre Aussage deutlich zu machen.

S2 Statistiken auswerten

Mit Diagrammen lässt sich eine Vielzahl von Informationen auf sehr kleinem Raum zusammenfassen. Häufig findest du die folgenden Diagramme, die jeweils einen anderen Schwerpunkt in der Darstellung haben:

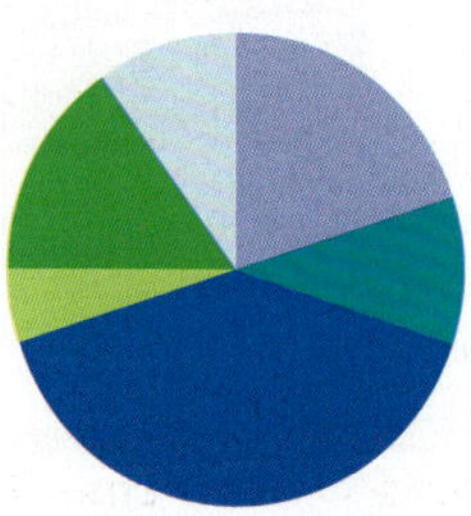

Mit einem Kuchendiagramm *(pie chart)* lassen sich Prozentzahlen darstellen, ausgehend vom gesamten Kreis (= 100 %).

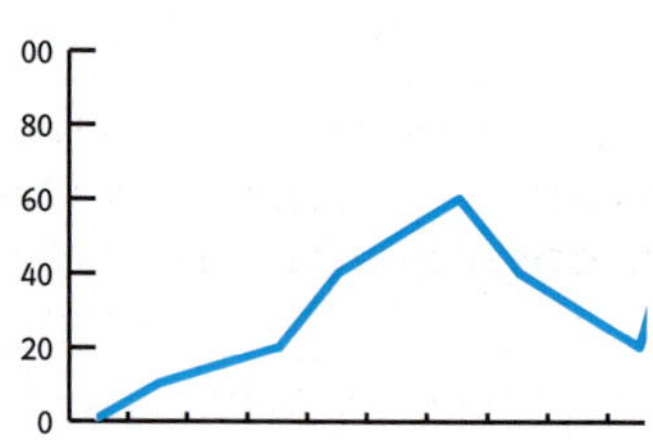

Ein Kurvendiagramm *(line graph)* eignet sich am besten, um eine Entwicklung über einen längeren Zeitraum hinweg darzustellen.

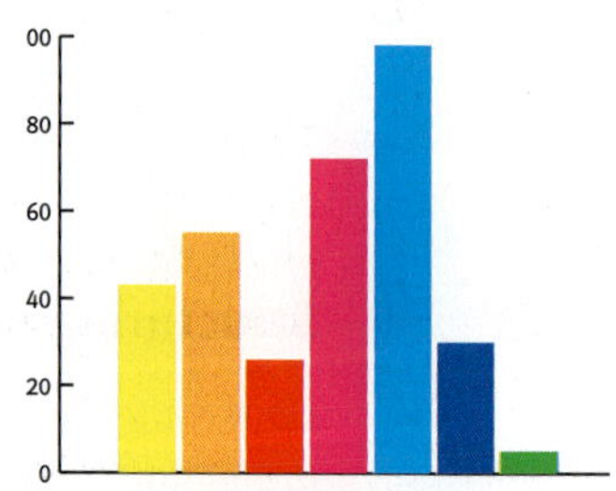

Ein Säulen- oder Balkendiagramm *(bar graph)* verwendest du, um Zahlen direkt miteinander zu vergleichen.

Wenn du die Auswertung eines Diagramms präsentieren sollst, hilft es dir, schrittweise vorzugehen:

1. Sage zunächst, um welche Art von Diagramm es sich handelt und was es darstellt. Vergiss nicht, die Quelle und das Jahr der Veröffentlichung zu nennen.
2. Beschreibe, was du aus dem Diagramm ablesen kannst.
3. Fasse die wichtigsten Aussagen des Diagramms in 1–2 Sätzen zusammen.

Useful phrases

- The table / bar graph / line graph / pie chart / … was published by … in …
- It's about … / deals with … / …
- The (next) largest group of … | The majority / minority of … | Half of … | Most of … | 30 percent of the people …
- The number of … goes up / grows by … / drops / goes down / doesn't change.
- The numbers / figures show / suggest that …
- We can draw the conclusion that …

Text skills

S3 Schnelllesetechniken

Skimming („den Rahm abschöpfen“)	Scanning („maschinell durchsuchen“)
Wenn du danach gefragt wirst, worum es in einem Text geht, solltest du nur das Wichtigste *(gist)* zusammenfassen. Hierzu überfliegst du den Text und achtest darauf, ob bestimmte Wörter *(key words)* oder Personen häufiger vorkommen. Auch die Überschrift oder Bilder können dir helfen einzuschätzen, was wichtig ist und was nicht. Diese Art des Schnelllesens nennt man auch *skimming*.	Wenn du nach bestimmten Einzelheiten *(details)* gefragt wirst, solltest du den Text überfliegen, um die Stellen mit den wichtigen Informationen zu finden. Dabei suchst du gezielt nach passenden Stichwörtern *(key words)*. Sie zeigen dir an, welche Teile du genauer lesen solltest, um die gesuchten Informationen zu erhalten. Diese Art des Überfliegens nennt man auch *scanning*.

S4 Wichtige Merkmale von Texten erkennen

Story

Wenn du eine Geschichte genauer liest oder analysierst, solltest du nicht nur über die Handlung *(plot)* selbst nachdenken, sondern auch darüber, wie die Geschichte erzählt wird. Zu den wichtigsten Erzähltechniken *(narrative techniques)* gehören:

Atmosphere / Mood	Bestimmte Wörter und Beschreibungen schaffen in einer Geschichte eine gewisse Stimmung *(atmosphere* oder *mood)*. Stimmung entsteht z. B. dadurch, dass die fünf Sinne *(five senses)* angesprochen werden: Wenn man liest, was die Figuren sehen, hören, riechen, schmecken oder fühlen, ist es leichter, sich in sie hineinzuversetzen.

Climax	Der Höhepunkt *(climax)* ist der Hauptwendepunkt in einer Geschichte, an dem die Spannung am höchsten ist. Die Hauptfigur befindet sich oft in einer schwierigen Situation und macht Veränderungen durch, sie wird z. B. stärker oder selbstbewusster. Siehe auch *turning point.*
Flashback	Eine Rückblende *(flashback)* erzählt Ereignisse, die vor einem bestimmten Zeitpunkt in der Geschichte stattgefunden haben. So wird z. B. die Erinnerung einer Figur an etwas Vergangenes beschrieben.
Narrative perspective	Die Wirkung, die eine Geschichte auf den Leser hat, wird stark von der Erzählperspektive *(narrative perspective)* beeinflusst. Die häufigsten Erzählperspektiven sind: **Ich-Erzähler *(first-person narrator)*** Der Ich-Erzähler erzählt aus seiner eigenen Perspektive und oft (aber nicht immer) ist er die Hauptfigur der Geschichte. Der Leser und der Ich-Erzähler erleben die Geschichte sozusagen „gemeinsam". **Er- / Sie-Erzähler *(third-person narrator)*** Dieser Erzähler erzählt die Geschichte „von außen". Die Perspektive ist nicht die der Hauptfigur.
Suspense	Spannung *(suspense)* ist eine wichtige Erzähltechnik, um den Leser in die Geschichte hineinzuziehen. Spannung kann direkt in den ersten Zeilen oder aber langsam im Verlauf der Geschichte aufgebaut werden. Sie wird z. B. durch starke, dramatische Sprache oder durch das Zurückhalten von Informationen erzeugt.
Turning point	Ein Wendepunkt *(turning point)* ist der Teil einer Geschichte, in dem eine Figur eine wichtige Entscheidung treffen muss. Diese Entscheidung beeinflusst den weiteren Verlauf der Geschichte. Siehe auch *climax.*

Graphic novel

In einem Comicroman *(graphic novel)* wird eine Geschichte nicht nur mit Worten, sondern vor allem mit Bildern erzählt. Es ist deshalb wichtig, dass du nicht nur auf die Sprechblasen *(speech bubbles)* und die Bildtexte *(captions)* achtest, sondern auch auf die Gestaltung und Anordnung der einzelnen Bilder *(panels)*.

Poetry

Beim Verständnis von Gedichten geht es nicht darum, die „richtige" Bedeutung zu finden – dasselbe Gedicht kann von verschiedenen Menschen ganz unterschiedlich verstanden werden. Wichtig ist aber, dass du deine Interpretation am Text belegen kannst. Dazu ist es hilfreich, auch formale Merkmale zu untersuchen und mit dem Inhalt in Verbindung zu bringen.

Rhyme scheme	Gedichte, die sich reimen, folgen immer einem bestimmten Reimschema *(rhyme scheme)*. Typische Reimschemata sind: **AABB** und **ABAB** sowie **ABCB**. Es gibt aber auch Gedichte, die sich nicht reimen, sogenannte *free verse poems*.

Rhythm / Stress	Ein Gedicht funktioniert nur mit dem richtigen Rhythmus *(rhythm)*. Er bestimmt, welche Stelle in jeder Zeile betont wird. Die Betonung *(stress)* liegt dann immer an der gleichen Stelle. Bei Gedichten, die sich nicht reimen, ist es wichtig, dass du selbst entscheidest, wo die Betonung liegt oder wo eine Pause gemacht werden sollte.
Symbol / Simile / Metaphor	In Gedichten spielen Symbole eine wichtige Rolle. Ein **Symbol** *(symbol)* steht stellvertretend für etwas anderes, z. B. für ein Gefühl, eine Idee oder eine Handlung. So ist das Herz ein Symbol für die Liebe. Bei einem **Vergleich** *(simile)* werden Dinge oder Personen mit etwas anderem verglichen, um auszudrücken, dass sie die gleichen Eigenschaften besitzen. Dabei wird *like* oder *as* verwendet, z. B. *happy as a rainbow*. Eine **Metapher** *(metaphor)* ist ein verkürzter Vergleich ohne *like* oder *as*, z. B. *I'll be the light to guide you*.

Drama

Theaterstücke sind in Akte *(acts)* und Szenen *(scenes)* unterteilt. Es gibt in der Regel keinen Erzähler, der die Figuren genauer beschreibt. Stattdessen wird die Handlung direkt durch die gesprochene Sprache und durch die Darstellung der Figuren vermittelt. Deshalb ist es bei der Interpretation von Theaterstücken besonders wichtig, neben dem Text auch auf die Sprechweise, Gestik und Mimik zu achten. So kannst du Rückschlüsse auf Charaktereigenschaften, Gedanken und Gefühle der Figuren ziehen.

Characters	Die Figuren *(characters)* stellen oft klassische Typen oder Rollen dar. Auf der einen Seite gibt es einen Helden *(good guy)*, dem ein Bösewicht *(bad guy)* gegenübersteht.
Language	In Theaterstücken wird die Handlung durch gesprochene Sprache vermittelt. Die Figuren sprechen in Dialogen miteinander.
Stage directions	Alles, was nicht durch gesprochene Sprache vermittelt werden kann, wird in Regieanweisungen *(stage directions)* vorgegeben. Hier werden auch Angaben zu Requisiten *(props)*, Bühnenbild und Licht gemacht. Wenn man ein Theaterstück liest, können die Regieanweisungen wichtige Hinweise z. B. auf die Stimmung der Szene und die Gefühle der Figuren geben. Sieht man das Theaterstück auf der Bühne, wird die Handlung und Stimmung des Stückes durch Körpersprache, Bewegungen, Bühnenbild, Licht, usw. getragen.

Film

Wenn du einen Film beschreibst, kommt es darauf an, wo und zu welcher Zeit er spielt *(setting)*, sowie auf die Besetzung der Rollen *(cast)*, den Schauplatz *(location)* und die Handlung *(plot)*. Ein Film erzählt eine Geschichte mit Worten, aber auch mit Bildern, Geräuschen, Licht, Farben und Musik. Diese audiovisuellen Effekte *(audio-visual effects)* schaffen eine ganz bestimmte Atmosphäre und verstärken damit die Wirkung des Gesehenen. So wird z. B. eine Actionszene meist mit schneller, lauter Musik unterlegt, eine romantische Szene eher mit ruhiger, leiser Musik. Die Kameraeinstellungen *(shots)* beeinflussen, wie wir Szenen wahrnehmen. Sie sind nicht zufällig gewählt, sondern werden gezielt eingesetzt, um die Wirkung einer Szene zu unterstreichen.

Writing skills

S5 Textsorten und ihre Besonderheiten

Hier sind einige der wichtigsten Textsorten, die dir im Unterricht immer wieder begegnen werden:

Print ads	Werbeanzeigen sprechen den Leser direkt an und verwenden eine emotionale Sprache, um ihn vom Kauf eines Produkts zu überzeugen. Wichtige Elemente sind der *eye-catcher* (ein Bild und / oder ein Text), ein ansprechender Slogan, weitere Textelemente *(ad copy)*, 1–2 Fotos des Produkts sowie Kontaktinformationen bzw. Angaben, wo das Geschäft oder die Firma zu finden ist.
Argumentative texts	Bei argumentativen Texten wird zwischen zwei wesentlichen Textsorten unterschieden, dem *letter to the editor* und dem *argumentative essay*. In einem *letter to the editor* äußerst du deine Meinung zu einem Thema und unterstreichst diese mithilfe von Fakten und Beispielen. Bei einem *argumentative essay* kommt es darauf an, ein kontroverses Thema aus verschiedenen Blickwinkeln zu beleuchten, d. h. du bist aufgefordert, Argumente und Gegenargumente zu präsentieren.
Blog post	Ein Blog ist eine Art Online-Tagebuch, in dem regelmäßig Beiträge veröffentlicht werden. Meist sind Blog-Einträge aus der Ich-Perspektive geschrieben und drücken den persönlichen Standpunkt des Bloggers aus.
Dialogue / Film script	Wenn du einen Dialog schreibst, z. B. für eine Filmszene, denke daran, dass du ihn kurz hältst und echte mündliche Sprache verwendest, also z. B. *short forms*, *question tags*, verstärkende Ausdrücke, usw. Achte bei den *stage directions* für ein Film- oder Theaterskript darauf, dass du nur das angibst, was man auch sehen oder darstellen kann. Gedanken kann man nicht sehen, aber du kannst in den *stage directions* Hinweise auf die Gefühle einer Person geben, z. B. durch Anweisungen für Mimik und Gestik.
Diary entry	Ein Tagebucheintrag erzählt und kommentiert Ereignisse aus der ganz persönlichen Sicht einer Person und ist normalerweise nicht für andere Leser bestimmt. Verwende ausdrucksstarke Adjektive und Adverbien, um die Gedanken und Gefühle dieser Person zu beschreiben.
E-mail / Letter	Achte auf die richtige Anrede für den Adressaten, z. B. *Dear …*, Grußformeln am Schluss, z. B. *Yours / Love / Best wishes*, und beachte die Höflichkeitsregeln. Bei formellen E-Mails oder Briefen verwendet man eher die Langformen, z. B. *I am* statt *I'm*. Denke bei einem Brief an die Angabe der Empfänger- und Absenderadresse und an das Datum.

News report	Konzentriere dich bei einem Tatsachenbericht auf die Fakten und spare deine persönliche Meinung aus. Achte außerdem auf eine sachliche Sprache und vermeide emotionale Ausdrücke. Die Schlagzeile *(headline)* sollte direkt auf das Thema des Artikels hinweisen und außerdem das Interesse des Lesers wecken. Beachte, dass in Zeitungsberichten häufig Passivformen verwendet werden.
Review / Online rating	Eine Rezension hilft dem Leser zu entscheiden, ob es sich lohnt, einen bestimmten Film anzuschauen oder ein bestimmtes Buch zu lesen. Zuerst beschreibst du kurz die wichtigsten Details, dann folgt deine Bewertung, die du mit guten Argumenten belegen solltest. Achte darauf, dass du bei deiner Bewertung fair bleibst.
Story	Wenn du deine eigene Geschichte schreibst, schmücke sie aus und gestalte sie sprachlich abwechslungsreich. Meistens sind Geschichten im *simple past* geschrieben. Wenn du eine Geschichte vervollständigen sollst, muss dein Teil zum vorgegebenen Text passen. Vermeide also inhaltliche Widersprüche. Außerdem sollten sich Erzählperspektive und Erzählzeit im Verlauf der Geschichte nicht ändern.
Summary	Bei einer *summary* kommt es darauf an, die wichtigsten Informationen aus einem Ausgangstext zusammenzufassen. Achte darauf, dass deine *summary* nicht länger ist als 30–40 % des Ausgangstextes.
Text analysis	In einer Textanalyse beurteilst du die Qualität eines Ausgangstextes. Dabei solltest du verschiedene Aspekte beleuchten: Warum hat der Autor den Text geschrieben? Wie objektiv ist er? Wie gut oder schlecht bringt er dem Leser seine Ideen nahe? Wie interessant ist der Text geschrieben? usw.

S6 Einen eigenen Text schreiben

1. Die Planung deines Textes

Nimm dir für diese Phase ausreichend Zeit. Lies die Aufgabenstellung genau durch und überlege, für wen dein Text bestimmt ist (Adressat) und welche Textsorte verlangt wird (Bericht, Zusammenfassung, Kommentar, usw.). Vor dem Schreiben erstellst du am besten eine Gliederung, indem du kurz notierst, wie dein Text aufgebaut sein soll.

Ein guter Text besteht normalerweise aus den folgenden drei Teilen:

Einleitung *(introduction)*: Hier erfährt der Leser, worum es in deinem Text geht. Du kannst auch eine Fragestellung einführen, die in deinem Text erörtert werden soll.

Hauptteil *(main part)*: Der Hauptteil ist in mehrere Abschnitte gegliedert und beinhaltet die Details (Fakten, Argumente, Beispiele, usw.) zu deinem Thema.

Schluss *(conclusion)*: Deinen Text solltest du mit einem geeigneten Schlussteil beenden. Dies kann eine Zusammenfassung von dem sein, was du im Hauptteil geschrieben hast, oder eine persönliche Äußerung.

2. Der erste Entwurf

Auf der Grundlage deiner Planung kannst du einen ersten Entwurf schreiben. Denke daran, dass du für jede neue Idee einen eigenen Abschnitt beginnst.

3. Die Überarbeitung

Nachdem du den ersten Entwurf erstellt hast, ist es wichtig, dass du oder einer deiner Mitschüler den Text noch einmal kritisch durchliest. Am hilfreichsten ist es, wenn du den Text mehrmals liest, jedes Mal mit einem anderen Schwerpunkt. Dabei kann dir eine Checkliste helfen (siehe rechts).

Überarbeite anschließend die kritischen Stellen. Wenn du Feedback von einem Mitschüler bekommen hast *(peer-editing)*, sieh es dir genau an und entscheide, was davon du für deinen Text übernehmen möchtest. Wenn du von einem Mitschüler gebeten wirst, seinen Text zu lesen, achte darauf, dass du bei deiner Kritik fair bleibst.

Inhalt:
- Sind alle wesentlichen Punkte enthalten?
- Gibt es keine inhaltlichen Fehler?
- Ist der Text logisch aufgebaut und hat eine klare Struktur?
- Passt die Sprachebene *(register)* zur Textsorte?

Rechtschreibung:
- Sind die Wörter richtig geschrieben?
- Stimmt die Zeichensetzung?
- Ist der Text einheitlich im *British* oder *American English* geschrieben?

Grammatik:
- Stimmen die Zeitformen?
- Ist die Formenbildung richtig (z. B. Adjektive, Adverbien, usw.)?

Listening skills

S7 Hörverstehen üben

Beim Englisch lernen hilft es, möglichst viele authentische Texte anzuhören, z. B. Nachrichten in Radio und Fernsehen, Podcasts oder Hörbücher. Dabei ist es nicht schlimm, wenn du nicht jedes Wort verstehst. Dir wird außerdem auffallen, wie unterschiedlich die Aussprache des Englischen je nach Herkunft des Sprechers sein kann. So gibt es neben den Unterschieden zwischen dem britischen, amerikanischen oder australischen Englisch z. B. auch innerhalb Großbritanniens verschiedene Dialekte oder regionale Akzente. Aber auch hier ist es nicht schlimm, wenn du nicht alles verstehst. Selbst ein Engländer aus London könnte Schwierigkeiten haben, einen Schotten aus Glasgow auf Anhieb zu verstehen.

Analog zum Leseverstehen (→ S3) können dir beim Hörverstehen die beiden folgenden Techniken helfen:

Listening for gist	Listening for detail
Versuche, das Wichtigste *(gist)* in einem Hörtext zu erkennen und kurz zusammenzufassen. Achte dabei besonders auf Wörter *(key words)* und Themen, die mehrmals vorkommen und vermutlich eine wichtige Rolle spielen.	Versuche gezielt, dem Text bestimmte Einzelinformationen *(details)* zu entnehmen. Achte dabei besonders auf Wörter, die du bei der Beantwortung der Fragestellung erwartest, und die passenden Informationen dazu.

Speaking skills

S8 Gespräche führen

Die folgenden Schritte können dir helfen, ein erfolgreiches Gespräch zu führen:

1. Beginne das Gespräch freundlich, z. B. mit etwas, was euch beide verbindet (der Ort, die Situation, usw.).
2. Halte das Gespräch am Laufen. Es ist wichtig, deinem Gesprächspartner das Gefühl zu geben, dass er einbezogen wird. Dazu dienen *feedback phrases*, Nachfragen und *question tags*, wie du anhand des folgenden Beispiels sehen kannst:

   Then we went to the new shoe shop in town, you know. And there were these amazing trainers – I showed you a photo, didn't I? Guess what Linda said when she saw them!

   Wenn du etwas nicht verstehst, frage höflich nach *(What was that you mentioned about …?/Sorry, I didn't catch what you just said about …)*. Wenn du etwas nicht sagen kannst, weil dir der nötige Wortschatz fehlt, versuche es zu umschreiben oder bitte deinen Gesprächspartner um Hilfe.
3. Beende das Gespräch so freundlich, wie du es angefangen hast, und verabschiede dich. Vergiss nicht, dich zu bedanken, wenn du um Hilfe gebeten hast.

In vielen Situationen des täglichen Lebens – im Klassenzimmer, mit Freunden, in der Familie – hast du es in Diskussionen mit unterschiedlichen Meinungen zu tun. Umso wichtiger ist es, bei Meinungsverschiedenheiten höflich zu bleiben und Kompromisse zu finden. Die *useful phrases* können dir helfen, typische Diskussionssituationen zu meistern.

Tip

Lass dich nicht verunsichern, wenn du beim Sprechen ins Stocken gerätst. In der gesprochenen Sprache ist es normal, dass Pausen, unvollständige Sätze, Wiederholungen oder Füllwörter vorkommen: *Well, I – I really don't know. It's – er, maybe you want to …?*

Useful phrases

I agree with you but … | It's true that …, but … | I admit that …, but … | But don't forget … | I'm afraid I don't agree with … | In my opinion … | Surely you have to admit that … | You might think differently if … | I think it's wrong to say … because … | I can relate to both sides but …

S9 Eine Präsentation vorbereiten und halten

Ob in der Schule oder später im Beruf, die Fähigkeit, eine gut vorbereitete und klar strukturierte Präsentation zu halten, spielt eine wichtige Rolle. Die folgenden Schritte können dir bei der Vorbereitung und Durchführung deiner Präsentation helfen:

1. Recherchiere Informationen zu deinem Thema und strukturiere sie, indem du z. B. eine Gliederung anlegst.
2. Überlege dir, mit welchem Material du deine Präsentation unterstützen willst. Gestalte dein Poster / deine Folie / dein Handout.
3. Bereite deine Präsentation vor, indem du nummerierte Karteikarten *(prompt cards)* anlegst, auf denen du dir die wichtigsten Punkte in Stichworten notierst.
4. Übe deine Präsentation zu Hause vor dem Spiegel oder vor einem kleinen Publikum (Eltern, Großeltern, Freunde). Stoppe die Zeit, die du brauchst, damit du bei deiner Präsentation nicht in Zeitnot gerätst.
5. Wenn du deine Präsentation hältst, achte darauf, dass du die Aufmerksamkeit aller Zuhörer hast. Dann erkläre kurz, worüber du sprechen wirst und wie deine Präsentation aufgebaut ist. Sprich langsam und möglichst frei. Verwende deine *prompt cards* nur als Hilfestellung. Beende deine Präsentation mit einer kurzen Zusammenfassung der wichtigsten Punkte. Bedanke dich fürs Zuhören und frage nach, ob deine Zuhörer Fragen haben.

Useful phrases

- My presentation is about … | Today I'll talk about … | First I'd like to talk about … Then …
- Here's a new word. It's … in German.
- On my poster you can see … | The mind map shows … | I've prepared a handout for you.
- That's the end of my presentation. Do you have any questions?
- Thanks for listening.

Mediation skills

S10 Bearbeitung von *Mediation*-Aufgaben

Mediation ist die Übertragung wichtiger Informationen aus einem gesprochenen oder geschriebenen Text in eine andere Sprache, z. B. aus dem Englischen ins Deutsche oder umgekehrt. Das machst du, wenn du einen Text für jemanden zusammenfassen sollst, der die Sprache des Ausgangstextes nicht versteht. Gelegentlich kann es auch sein, dass du dolmetschen musst, also zwischen Gesprächspartnern vermittelst, die nicht dieselbe Sprache sprechen. Ganz wichtig: Es geht bei der *mediation* niemals um eine wörtliche Übersetzung *(translation)*!

Lies dir die Mediation-Aufgabe gut durch und beachte besonders folgende Punkte:

Adressat:
Für wen ist die Information bestimmt?
--→ Je nachdem, wer die Person ist und wie viel sie schon weiß, sprichst du sie unterschiedlich an.

Zweck:
Wozu benötigt die Person die Information?
--→ Du musst nur die Informationen wiedergeben, die für den Adressaten in der jeweiligen Situation wichtig sind. Alles andere kannst du weglassen. Es kann aber auch vorkommen, dass du Dinge zusätzlich erklären musst.

Einen schriftlichen Ausgangstext kannst du in Ruhe durchlesen und die wichtigsten Informationen auswählen. Dabei helfen dir die Lesetechniken, die unter *Text skills* beschrieben werden (→ S3). Formuliere die entsprechenden Inhalte so, dass der Adressat sie gut verstehen kann.

Tip

Achte bei einer schriftlichen *mediation* darauf, dass dein Text nicht länger als ca. 30–40 % des Ausgangstextes ist, ähnlich wie bei einer *summary*.

Bei einer Dolmetschaufgabe wird eine echte mündliche Gesprächssituation simuliert. Deshalb musst du schneller reagieren, um möglichst viel von dem sinngemäß wiederzugeben, was die Gesprächspartner zueinander sagen. Nicht ganz einfach ist es, wenn du Durchsagen am Flughafen oder am Bahnhof aus dem Englischen ins Deutsche übertragen sollst, da sie oft unbekannte Wörter enthalten und durch die Hintergrundgeräusche schwer zu verstehen sind. Hier kann es dir helfen, dich auf die Namen von Personen oder Orten, Zahlen, Zeitangaben oder auf andere wichtige Schlüsselwörter *(key words)* zu konzentrieren.

S11 Paraphrasieren

Wenn du wichtige Informationen aus einer Sprache in die andere übertragen willst, kann es vorkommen, dass dir ein Wort nicht einfällt, vor allem in Gesprächssituationen, wenn alles sehr schnell gehen muss. Bleibe ganz ruhig und versuche, das Wort zu umschreiben *(paraphrasing)*.

Useful phrases

- It's somebody / a person who …
- It's something that you use to …
- It's a place that / where …
- It's the same as … / the opposite of …

Wenn du Zeit brauchst, um das richtige Wort oder eine Umschreibung dafür zu finden, kannst du dir mit folgenden *phrases* behelfen: *Just a second … / Let me think …*

Study skills

S12 Im Internet recherchieren

Das Internet bietet eine Fülle von Informationen, die in der Regel frei zugänglich sind. Die folgenden Tipps können dir dabei helfen, genau die Informationen zu finden, die du für eine Präsentation oder für die Erstellung eines Textes brauchst:

1. Überlege dir gute Stichwörter, die du in eine Suchmaschine eingeben kannst. Wenn du z. B. eine Übersicht über das amerikanische Schulsystem suchst, kannst du als Stichwort *US school system* eingeben. Je mehr Stichwörter du eingibst, desto genauer sind deine Ergebnisse.
2. Wenn du eine Webseite mit interessanten Informationen gefunden hast, achte darauf, wer die Webseite erstellt hat. Sind die Informationen zuverlässig (Online-Lexikon, seriöse Zeitung, usw.) oder handelt es sich eher um persönliche Meinungen (Forum, Blog, usw.)?
3. Kopiere nicht einfach ganze Artikel aus dem Internet. Mache dir Notizen zu den wichtigsten Informationen und gebe sie anschließend in deinen eigenen Worten wieder.
4. Ordne dein Material und suche gezielt weiter, falls du zusätzliche Informationen brauchst.

S13 Umgang mit neuen Wörtern

Die folgenden Tipps können dir dabei helfen, unbekannte Wörter in einem Text zu verstehen:

Ähnlichkeit mit Wörtern, die du schon kennst

Oft haben verwandte Wörter den gleichen Stamm, aber andere Präfixe oder Suffixe. Wenn du z. B. *usual* schon kennst, wirst du *unusual* sicher verstehen. Englische Wörter haben oft keine Suffixe, aber es gibt sie in verschiedenen Wortarten. Wenn du das Wort *guide* als Nomen kennst, kannst du dir bestimmt denken, was das Verb *to guide* oder die Zusammensetzung *travel guide bedeutet*.

Ähnlichkeit mit Wörtern, die du aus einer anderen Sprache kennst

Viele englische Wörter gibt es genauso oder ähnlich auch im Deutschen, z. B. *computer* oder *hobby*. Manchmal hilft dir auch ein Wort, das du aus einer anderen Sprache kennst, ein englisches Wort zu verstehen, z. B. weil es ähnlich geschrieben wird oder ähnlich klingt.

Tip

Nicht alle Wörter, die im Deutschen und Englischen ähnlich sind, haben dieselbe Bedeutung. Achte daher auf ***false friends***, z. B. *to become* = „werden" (nicht „bekommen"); *brand* = „Marke" (nicht „Feuer").

Verstehen der Wörter im Zusammenhang

Manchmal kannst du dir anhand eines Bildes oder einer Überschrift denken, was ein Wort in einem Text bedeutet. Und wenn du alle Wörter in einem Satz verstehst außer einem, kann dieses oft nur eine bestimmte Bedeutung haben. Was bedeutet z. B. *ridiculous* in folgendem Satz: *That's the silliest thing I've ever heard. It's **ridiculous**!*

S14 Mit dem Wörterbuch arbeiten

Wenn du die Bedeutung eines Wortes nachschlagen willst, dann benutzt du am besten ein zweisprachiges Wörterbuch (Englisch-Deutsch bzw. Deutsch-Englisch beim Erstellen von eigenen Texten oder *Mediation*-Aufgaben). Wenn du zusätzliche Informationen zu einem englischen Wort brauchst, z. B. einen Beispielsatz oder eine Definition, dann bietet sich ein einsprachiges Wörterbuch an.

Zweisprachige Wörterbücher

Die Leitwörter *(running heads)* oben auf der Seite helfen dir, schnell zu finden, was du suchst. Links steht das erste Stichwort, rechts das letzte Stichwort auf der Seite.

Hier findest du das Stichwort *(headword)*. Die Stichwörter sind alphabetisch geordnet.

Diese Ziffern zeigen an, dass ein Stichwort unterschiedliche Bedeutungen hat.

Einem Stichwort sind häufig Redewendungen und typische *phrases* zugeordnet.

Unregelmäßige Verb-, Plural- und Steigerungsformen stehen oft in Klammern.

pay [peɪ] **I.** *n no pl* (*wages*) Lohn *m;* (*salary*) Gehalt *nt; of a civil servant* Bezüge *pl; of a soldier* Sold *m* **II.** *vt* <paid, paid> ❶ (*give*) [be]zahlen; ■ ~ **out** etw [aus]zahlen; **to ~ cash/dollars/money** [in] bar/in Dollar/Geld [be]zahlen; **to ~ dividends** *investment* Dividenden ausschütten; *firm* Dividenden ausbezahlen; (*fig*) sich auszahlen ❷ (*give money for/to, settle*) bezahlen; **to ~ one's dues** (*debts*) seine Schulden bezahlen; (*fig: obligations*) seine Schuldigkeit tun; *into account* einzahlen (auf +*akk*) ❸ (*fig: suffer the consequences*) **to ~ the price [for sth]** [für etw *akk*] bezahlen ❹ (*bestow*) **to ~ attention** Acht geben *akk*; **to ~ [sb] a compliment** [jdm] ein Kompliment machen ▶ PHRASES: **to ~ one's way** finanziell unabhängig sein **III.** *vi* <paid, paid> ❶ (*give money*) [be]zahlen ❷ (*be worthwhile*) sich auszahlen; (*be profitable*) rentabel sein; ■ **it ~s to do sth** es lohnt sich, etw zu tun ❸ (*fig: suffer*) ■ **to ~ [for sth]** [für etw *akk*] bezahlen; **to ~ with one's life** mit dem Leben bezahlen ◆ **pay back** *vt* ❶ (*give back*) zurückzahlen; *debts* bezahlen; *money* zurückgeben ❷ (*fig: for revenge*) ■ **to ~ sb back for sth** jdm etw heimzahlen ◆ **pay down** *vt* an-

Die Lautschrift zeigt dir, wie das Wort ausgesprochen und betont wird.

Die kursiv gedruckten Hinweise helfen dir, die für deinen Text passende Bedeutung zu finden.

Die römischen Ziffern machen deutlich, dass ein Stichwort unterschiedlichen Wortarten angehört.

Einsprachige Wörterbücher

Ein einsprachiges Wörterbuch erklärt die Bedeutung eines englischen Wortes auf Englisch. Da manche Wörter mehrere Bedeutungen haben, ist es wichtig, alle Einträge und Beispielsätze zu einem Wort zu lesen und mit deinem englischen Text zu vergleichen, um die richtige Bedeutung herauszufinden.

Das Wörterbuch hilft dir auch, die passende Verbindung mit anderen Wörtern zu finden. Das ist nützlich, wenn du selbst einen englischen Text schreiben willst und nach passenden Formulierungen suchst.

pay
verb [peɪ] PAST TENSE AND PAST PARTICIPLE **paid**

BUY
to give money to someone because you are buying something from them, or because you owe them money:
*Helen **paid** for the tickets.*
*Did you **pay** the telephone bill?*
*You can **pay** by cash or credit card.*

WORK
to give someone money for the work that they do:
*She gets **paid** twice a month.*
*People work for them because they **pay** well.*

→ **pay attention**
to look at or listen to someone or something carefully:
*I missed what she was saying because I **wasn't paying attention**.*

In diesem Grammatik-Anhang findest du ausführliche Erklärungen zu allen grammatischen Themen, die in *Green Line 5* behandelt werden. Die Grammatikkapitel (G) helfen dir, die Grammatik zu verstehen, einzelne Punkte nachzuholen oder bestimmte Regeln für Hausaufgaben und die Vorbereitung von Tests und Klassenarbeiten nachzuschlagen.

Regeln sind mit einem blauen Punkt (◎) gekennzeichnet. Ein Ausrufezeichen (!) bedeutet, dass du hier besonders aufpassen musst. Die englische Zusammenfassung der wichtigsten Regeln findest du in der **English summary**. Mit **Test yourself** überprüfst du, ob du alles verstanden hast.
Die Lösungen hierzu findest du ab Seite 264.

Grammatical terms

	English term	*Deutsche Bezeichnung*
G1	The different tenses of the passive voice	*Das Passiv in den verschiedenen Zeitformen*
G2	English equivalents for the German verb *lassen*	*Englische Entsprechungen für das deutsche Verb „lassen"*
G3	From active to passive	*Vom Aktiv ins Passiv*
G4	Conditional sentences types 1, 2 and 3	*Bedingungssätze Typ 1, 2 und 3*
G5	Used to	*Früher, damals (immer)*
G6	Sentence adverbs	*Satzadverbien*
G7	Present participle or infinitive after verbs of perception + object	*Das Partizip Präsens oder der Infinitiv nach Verben der Wahrnehmung + Objekt*
G8	Present participle after verbs of rest and motion	*Das Partizip Präsens nach Verben der Ruhe und der Bewegung*
G9	Defining and non-defining relative clauses	*Notwendige und nicht-notwendige Relativsätze*
G10	Inversion of the verb for emphasis after certain adverbs	*Hervorhebung durch Inversion des Verbs nach bestimmten Adverbien*
G11	Emphatic do / does / did	*Hervorhebung mit do / does / did*
G12	The simple present and present progressive with future meaning	*Das Präsens mit Futurbedeutung*
G13	The future progressive	*Die Verlaufsform des Futurs*
G14	The future perfect	*Das Futur II*
G15	The definite and the indefinite article	*Der bestimmte und der unbestimmte Artikel*
G16	English equivalents for the German verbs *sollen* and *müssen*	*Englische Entsprechungen für die deutschen Verben „sollen" und „müssen"*

Unit 1

G1 Has he been found yet?

→ Seiten 14–19

Das Passiv in den verschiedenen Zeitformen
The different tenses of the passive voice

Missing Brit found alive

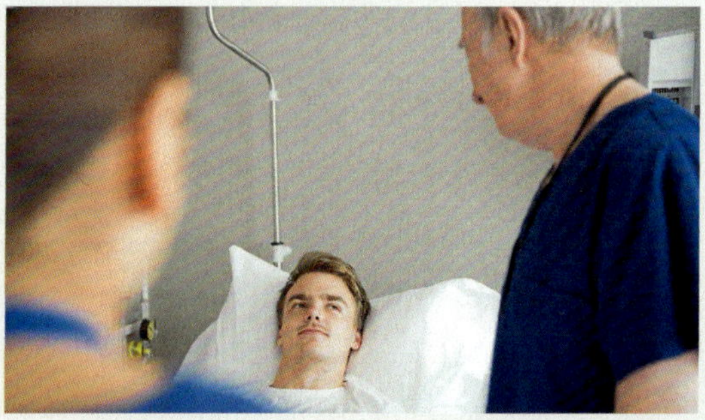

James Furness, the British backpacker who went missing in Purnululu National Park, **has been found** alive after almost two weeks in the Australian outback. The 19-year-old, who **hadn't been seen** since he left a youth hostel near the park on January 20th, **was found** by an emergency rescue team early yesterday evening. James **was taken** to hospital, where he **is being treated** for shock.

Passivsätze stellen Handlungen aus einer anderen Sicht dar als Aktivsätze. Aktivsätze betonen, ***wer*** *die Handlung ausführt; Passivsätze betonen,* ***was*** *mit einer Person oder mit einer Sache ohne eigenes Zutun geschieht. Damit rückt die Handlung selbst in den Vordergrund. Das Passiv wird häufig in Sachtexten, Regeln und vor allem in Zeitungsberichten verwendet. Bei Zeitungsüberschriften wird allerdings meistens die verkürzte Form (ohne* be*) verwendet, z. B.* Missing Brit found alive.

a) ***Die Zeitformen des Passivs (Wiederholung)***
Das Passiv bildest du mit einer Form von **be** *in der jeweiligen Zeitform und dem* **past participle** *des Vollverbs (*infinitive + -ed *oder unregelmäßige Form).*

Zeitform	*Form von* be + past participle	*Beispiel*
simple present	am / is / are + past participle	Bondi Beach **is visited** by millions of tourists every year. *… wird … besucht.*
simple past	was / were + past participle	We **were taken** there as part of our Sydney tour. *… wurden … gebracht.*
present perfect simple	have / has been + past participle	It **has been described** as one of the world's most popular beaches. *… ist … beschrieben worden.*

! *Im Passivsatz liegt die Betonung auf der Handlung. Das Subjekt des Aktivsatzes wird entweder nicht genannt oder mit Hilfe der Präposition* **by** *(auf Deutsch: von) angefügt, z. B. …* **by** millions of tourists.

b) *Weitere Zeitformen des Passivs*

Zeitform	*Form von* be + past participle	*Beispiel*
past perfect	had been + past participle	We didn't swim at Bondi Beach because we **had been warned** about strong rip currents. *… waren … gewarnt worden.*
going-to future	am / is / are going to be + past participle	Some visitors to Bondi Beach are worried that they **are going to be bitten** by a shark. *… gebissen werden.*
will future	will be + past participle	But it's more likely that they **will be swept** out to sea by a strong rip current. *… hinausgetrieben werden.*

- *Für die Verwendung der Zeitformen in Passivsätzen gelten dieselben Regeln wie für die Zeitformen in Aktivsätzen.*

c) *Der* passive infinitive *nach bestimmten Verben*

1. *Die Form* **to be + past participle** *verwendest du nach Vollverben wie* want, would like, expect *und* hope.

Vollverb + to be + past participle	
Tanya doesn't want **to be stung** by a box jellyfish.	*… will nicht … gestochen werden.*
Moshe wouldn't like **to be attacked** by a shark.	*… würde nicht gerne … angegriffen werden.*
The guests expected **to be given** a room with a spectacular view.	*… erwarteten … zu bekommen.*
The girls hope **to be invited** to a barbie on the beach.	*… hoffen darauf … eingeladen zu werden.*

2. *Die Form* **be + past participle** *verwendest du nach Modalverben und deren Ersatzformen.*

Modalverb / Ersatzform + be + past participle	
All visits to the outback should **be planned** very carefully.	*… sollten sehr sorgfältig geplant werden.*
Anything can happen, so you must / have to **be prepared** for problems.	*… deshalb musst du auf Probleme vorbereitet sein.*
Always make sure that you can **be contacted** at all times.	*… dass du immer erreicht werden kannst.*

- *Nach folgenden Modalverben wird der* **passive infinitive** *ebenfalls mit* be + past participle *gebildet:* may, mustn't, ought to, might, could.

d) *Die Verlaufsformen des Passivs*

Neben den einfachen Formen des Passivs gibt es zwei Verlaufsformen: das **present progressive passive** *und das* **past progressive passive**. *Diese bildest du mit* be + being + past participle.

Zeitform	*Form von* be + being + past participle	*Beispiel*
present progressive	am / is / are being + past participle	Moshe feels that he **is being pulled** in two different directions. *… dass er … gezogen wird.*
past progressive	was / were being + past participle	When we saw the man, he **was being chased** by a policeman. *… wurde er von einem Polizisten verfolgt.*

- *Für die Verwendung der Verlaufsformen in Passivsätzen gelten die gleichen Regeln wie für die Verlaufsformen in Aktivsätzen:*
  1. *Mit dem* **present progressive passive** *beschreibst du Vorgänge, die im Moment gerade ablaufen und noch nicht abgeschlossen sind.*
  2. *Mit dem* **past progressive passive** *beschreibst du Vorgänge, die in der Vergangenheit abliefen und noch nicht abgeschlossen waren.*

English summary

You form the passive voice with a form of **be** and the **past participle**.

You use the passive voice to say what happens to a person or thing. The person who causes the action is often not known or is not important. If it's necessary to mention the person who causes the action, you use **by**.	The missing Brit **has been found**. He'**s being treated** for shock. He's been visited **by** his family.

Test yourself *Read this newspaper report about a family that was rescued at sea. Put the verbs in brackets into the correct form of the* **passive**.

Family of four rescued at sea

Two adults and two young children had to (rescue) by a lifeboat on Saturday after their boat (catch) by a rip current and (pull) out to sea.

They weren't very far from the shore when they suddenly noticed that they (carry) further and further away from the beach. Although there were four people on the boat, they had only one lifejacket and no other safety equipment with them. A lifeboat (send out) and the family (find) about two kilometres down the coast, close to some dangerous rocks from where they (bring) safely back to shore.

Coastguard Tom Walsh said that people often didn't realise how easily these small boats can (sweep) out to sea and that this family had had a lucky escape. Nobody (hurt) this time. But if their boat had crashed into the rocks, it would have been a very different story.

G2 They let her go to Australia

→ Seiten 19–20

Englische Entsprechungen für das deutsche Verb „lassen"
English equivalents for the German verb *lassen*

Tanya's parents **let** her **go** / **allowed** her **to go** to Australia on her own.	But they **made** her **promise** to chat every week and to tell them if she has a problem.	While Tanya is away, her parents are going to **have** her room **renovated.**

*Das deutsche Verb **„lassen"** hat unterschiedliche Bedeutungen, die im Englischen **mit verschiedenen Verben** wiedergegeben werden.*

a) ***jemandem erlauben, etwas zu tun*** = **let somebody do something** *oder* **allow somebody to do something**

let + object + infinitive without *to*	
My parents **let** me **have** a party.	*… ließen mich … haben.*
allow + object + infinitive with *to*	
But they **didn't allow** us **to use** the pool.	*… ließen uns … nicht benutzen.*

b) ***jemanden dazu bringen, etwas zu tun*** = **make somebody do something**

Aktiv: make + object + infinitive without *to*	
They **made** us **clear up** after the party.	*… ließen uns … aufräumen.*
Passiv: make + infinitive with *to*	
And I **was made to pay** for the broken glasses.	*… musste … bezahlen.*

c) ***etwas machen lassen*** = **have something done**

have + object + past participle	
Last week we **had** the roof **repaired**.	*… ließen … reparieren.*
This week we **are having** the house **painted**.	*… lassen … streichen.*

English summary

If you **let somebody do something**, you allow them to do it.	Mum **let** us **have** a party. Mum **allowed** us **to have** a party.
If you **make somebody do something**, you force them to do it	But she **made** us **clean up** the mess.
If you **have something done**, you arrange for somebody to do something for you.	We didn't clean the carpets ourselves. We **had** them **cleaned**.

Test yourself *Mike is talking to his best friend about a barbie he wants to have. Put in* ***let***, ***allow***, ***make*** *or* ***have*** *in the correct form.*

Good news. Mum and Dad are going to 1 me have the barbie at their house and they're going to 2 us to use the pool too. But I can't 3 anybody sleep at the house and they're going to 4 me tidy up after the party. They're even going to 5 me cut the grass. Oh yeah, and we haven't 6 the pool cleaned this year yet. So guess who has to do that? I think they're getting a really good deal. I'm being 7 to do everything!

G3 I've been sent some brochures

→ Seite 20

Vom Aktiv ins Passiv
From active to passive

Active:
Between 1788 and 1868, the British government **sent** around 162,000 convicts to Australia.

Passive:
Between 1788 and 1868, around 162,000 convicts **were sent** to Australia by the British government.

Im Aktivsatz ist das Subjekt die Person oder Sache, die die Handlung auslöst.
Im Passivsatz ist das Subjekt die Person oder Sache, mit der etwas geschieht.

a) *Vom Aktiv ins Passiv bei Verben mit einem Objekt (Wiederholung)*

Wenn du einen Aktivsatz in einen Passivsatz umwandelst, musst du Folgendes beachten:

1. *Das Objekt des Aktivsatzes wird zum Subjekt im Passivsatz. Aus Objektpronomen* (me, you, him / her / it …) *werden Subjektpronomen* (I, you, he / she / it …).
2. *Die Aktivform des Verbs wird zur Passivform* (take → am / is / are taken). *Die Zeitform bleibt in beiden Sätzen gleich.*
3. *Das Subjekt des Aktivsatzes wird nicht genannt oder mit der Präposition* **by** *angehängt.*

Aktiv	*Passiv*
Somebody stole my new bike yesterday. *… stahl …*	My new bike **was stolen** yesterday. *… wurde … gestohlen.*
A man in a red jacket took it. *… nahm …*	It **was taken** by a man in a red jacket. *… wurde von … mitgenommen.*
Somebody saw him in my garden. *… sah …*	He **was seen** in my garden. *… wurde … gesehen.*

b) ***Vom Aktiv ins Passiv bei Verben mit zwei Objekten***

Einige Verben im Englischen können (ähnlich wie ihre deutschen Entsprechungen) zwei Objekte haben: ein Personenobjekt und ein Sachobjekt. Zu ihnen gehören: give, tell, offer, pay, promise, lend, show *und* send. *Bei diesen Verben wird im Englischen meistens das Personenobjekt zum Subjekt im Passivsatz.*

Aktiv	*Passiv*
They showed **us a photo**. *Sie zeigten uns ein Foto.*	**We were shown a photo**. *Uns wurde ein Foto gezeigt.*

c) ***Vom Aktiv ins Passiv bei Verben mit Präposition***

Wenn Verb und Präposition eine Einheit bilden, steht im Passivsatz die Präposition immer hinter dem Vollverb. Beispiele sind die Verben: look after, break into, deal with, run over, take care of.

Aktiv	*Passiv*
The police are dealing **with** the matter. *Die Polizei kümmert sich …*	The matter **is being dealt with** by the police. *Um die Sache wird sich von … gekümmert.*

English summary

1. If an active sentence has two objects, you usually begin the passive sentence with the person. — Somebody has given **the police** the man's name. → **The police** have been given the man's name.
2. If a preposition belongs to the verb, it must remain with that verb when you form the passive sentence. — They'll deal with the matter. → The matter **will be dealt with** by them.

Test yourself *Change the active verbs in these sentences into the* ***passive****, where possible.*

1. We were in a jewellery shop and the assistant was showing us some expensive rings when a woman in the street started to scream.
2. A car had run over her dog.
3. Somebody called the police.
4. When they arrived, somebody gave them a photo of the car.
5. The owner of the dog hopes that they'll find the driver of the car soon.
6. They're asking anyone with any information to contact the police.

G4 If I hadn't seen it for myself

→ Seiten 22–23

Bedingungssätze Typ 1, 2 und 3
Conditional sentences types 1, 2 and 3

If you **study** Aboriginal art, you **will learn** a lot about the culture of Indigenous Australians.	If I **went** to Sydney for a holiday, I **would visit** the Australian Museum, which is the oldest museum in Australia.	If Aboriginal people **hadn't had** their art, they **wouldn't have been** able to communicate with other tribes.

*Mit einem **Bedingungssatz** (Konditionalsatz) beschreibst du die Folge, wenn eine bestimmte Bedingung erfüllt ist.*

*Bedingungssätze bestehen aus einem **if-Satz** und einem **Hauptsatz**. Im **if-Satz** drückst du die Bedingung aus, im **Hauptsatz** die Folge. Es gibt drei Grundtypen von Bedingungssätzen:*

a) *Bedingungssätze Typ 1*

Bedingung	*Folge*
If I **go** to Sydney,	I **will visit** the Australian Museum.

- *Bei Bedingungssätzen vom Typ 1 hält der Sprecher es für **möglich**, dass sich die Bedingung erfüllt. Die Bedingung steht im **simple present**, die Folge im **will future**.*
- *Im Hauptsatz kann statt des* will future *auch ein Modalverb + Infinitiv oder der Imperativ stehen, z. B.* If you want to find out more about Indigenous Australians, you **should visit** the Australian Museum / **visit** the Australian Museum.

b) *Bedingungssätze Typ 2*

Bedingung	*Folge*
If I **went** to Sydney,	I **would visit** the Australian Museum.

- *Bei Bedingungssätzen vom **Typ 2** hält der Sprecher es für **unwahrscheinlich**, dass sich die Bedingung erfüllt. Die Bedingung steht im* **simple past**, *die Folge im* **conditional** (would + infinitive).
- *Im Hauptsatz können statt* would *auch die Modalverben* could, should *oder* might + *Infinitiv stehen, z. B.* If you want to find out more about Indigenous Australians, you **could / should visit / might want to visit** the Australian Museum.

c) ***Bedingungssätze Typ 3***

Bedingung	*Folge*
If I **had gone** to Sydney,	I **would have visited** the Australian Museum.

- *Bei Bedingungssätzen vom **Typ 3** weiß der Sprecher, dass die Bedingung **nicht mehr erfüllbar** ist. Er bringt zum Ausdruck, was passiert wäre (oder hätte passieren können), wenn die Vergangenheit anders verlaufen wäre. Die Bedingung steht im* **past perfect**, *die Folge im* **conditional perfect** (would + have + past participle).

English summary

There are three main types of conditional sentences.

You use **type 1** when the action in the if-clause is **possible**.	If Charlie **doesn't pass on** his art to the young, they **won't learn** the Dreaming.
You use **type 2** when the action in the if-clause is **not possible or not probable**.	If Cindy **wanted** to, she **could use** the information in the emu Dreaming to hunt emus.
You use **type 3** when the action in the if-clause refers to a time in the past and is **impossible to change**.	If her ancestors **hadn't had** their art, they **wouldn't have been** able to survive in the harsh landscape.

Test yourself *Mike and Jim are out walking in the bush. Use the information in brackets to write **conditional sentences**.*

Mike: Most snakes aren't aggressive. Normally, (only / bite you – if / feel threatened).
Jim: I know. So it was really lucky that I saw that snake in time. (If / step on it – bite me).
Mike: Yes. And (if / bite you – we / be in real trouble). The nearest hospital is miles away. Yesterday I heard that a tourist was attacked by a crocodile.
Jim: Yes, some people are really stupid. (probably / not attack him – if / not throw a stone at it).
Mike: Oh look! There's a baby kangaroo over there. Be quiet. (If / make a noise – frighten it / and jump away).

G5 I used to

→ Seite 24

Früher, damals (immer)
Used to

Mit **used to + *Infinitiv*** *drückst du Gewohnheiten oder Tatsachen aus, die in der Vergangenheit liegen und heute nicht mehr zutreffen. Im Deutschen kannst du* used to *mit „früher" oder „damals" wiedergeben.*

Australia **used to consist of** six British colonies. Today it is one nation which is independent from Britain.

Von **used to** *gibt es nur die* simple past-*Form:*

Aussage:	Aboriginals **used to communicate** with people from other tribes through their artwork.
Verneinung:	They **didn't use to speak / never used to speak** a common language like English.
Frage:	How **did** they **use to pass** on their culture?

English summary

You use **used to + infinitive** when you want to say that:

1. something that happened regularly in the past no longer happens now.
2. a situation which existed in the past is no longer true now.

Aboriginals **used to move** from one location to the next.
They **didn't use to settle** in one place.

Test yourself *Angela is an Indigenous Australian who grew up in rural Australia. Now she lives in Sydney. Complete her sentences about how life used to be. Use* ***used to / didn't use to / never used to*** *and a suitable verb.*

1. I ___ in rural Australia, but now I live in Sydney.
2. At home we usually spoke our own language; we ___ English very often.
3. I ___ a room with my three sisters, but now I have my own room.
4. I ___ coffee, but now I drink it all the time.
5. I ___ interested in sport, but now I love surfing.

Unit 2

G6 How to sound more formal

→ Seite 51

Satzadverbien
Sentence adverbs

Position for Assistant Camp Counsellor

Job description
As an assistant camp counsellor, you must have good communication skills and you must enjoy working with children. **Furthermore**, you must be hard-working, fit and healthy. As assistant camp counsellor, **of course** you are also expected to be friendly and outgoing. **However**, you are also expected to set a good example at all times.

Training
We think it is important that all camp counsellors receive good training. **Therefore**, all successful applicants will be required to go to an Orientation Day when we will **happily** answer all your questions.

Satzadverbien sind Adverbien, die sich auf die Aussage des ganzen Satzes beziehen. Zu ihnen gehören sowohl **linking adverbs** *(satzverknüpfende Adverbien) als auch* **commenting adverbs** *(kommentierende Adverbien).*

- **Linking adverbs** *verbinden die Gedanken zweier Sätze und stellen eine logische Beziehung her. Sie können u.a. eine* ***zusätzliche Information*** (moreover, furthermore, additionally), *einen* ***gegensätzlichen Gedanken*** (however, nevertheless), *eine* ***Erläuterung*** (in fact) *oder eine* ***Schlussfolgerung*** (therefore) *einleiten.*
  Adverbien dieser Art stehen meist ***am Satzanfang****.*
- **Commenting adverbs** *leiten den folgenden Gedanken ein und kommentieren diesen zugleich. Sie drücken aus, was der Sprecher über den Inhalt des Satzes denkt. Zu diesen Adverbien gehören u.a.* of course, happily, hopefully, luckily, fortunately, unfortunately, surely, certainly, probably, personally.
  Adverbien dieser Art stehen meistens ***am Satzanfang****, treten aber mitunter auch als Nachgedanke am* ***Satzende*** *oder auch in der* ***Binnenstellung*** *auf, z.B.:*
  - **Hopefully**, they'll offer me the job.
  - They'll offer me the job, **hopefully**.
  - I'll **certainly** be disappointed if they don't offer me the job.

English summary

Linking adverbs connect sentences logically. They usually appear in front position. They can be used to add on information, make a contrast, give an explanation or draw a conclusion.	Camp counselling is a fun and flexible job. **Moreover**, it's a great experience.
Commenting adverbs add information about the speaker's opinion of events. They can often be found in front position, sometimes in mid-position, and sometimes in end position.	Being a camp counsellor is **probably** one of the most challenging jobs you can have.

Test yourself *After working as assistant camp counsellors, this is what some of the teenagers posted online. Complete their testimonials with these* ***sentence adverbs****:* personally, in fact, hopefully, moreover, nevertheless, probably.

1. Being a camp counsellor gives you an opportunity to lead groups, take on responsibility and to build your self-confidence. ___, it looks great on your CV. - Tom
2. ___, I think that working as an assistant camp counsellor at a summer camp is the best experience any teenager can have. - Jane
3. It was really hard work. ___, it was ___ the hardest job I've ever had to do! - Brian
4. Spending 24 hours a day with a group of active young kids can be exhausting. ___, I wouldn't have missed the experience for the world. - Sarah
5. You don't have to be crazy to work as a camp counsellor, but it helps! It was the most amazing job I've ever had and I had a fantastic time. ___ I can go back for more next year! - Marco

G7 I watched the kids ...

→ Seiten 53–54

Das Partizip Präsens oder der Infinitiv nach Verben der Wahrnehmung + Objekt
Present participle or infinitive after verbs of perception + object

I **watched** the kids **harvesting** the cocoa pods. = I watched the kids while they were doing it.	I **watched** the kids **harvest** the cocoa pods. = I watched the complete action

Nach einem ***Verb der Wahrnehmung*** *(z. B.* feel, hear, notice, see, smell *und* watch*)* ***und einem direkten Objekt*** *kann a) das* **present participle** *oder b) der* **Infinitiv** *(ohne* to*) stehen. Ob man ein* present participle *oder einen* infinitive *verwendet, hängt davon ab, wie viel von einer Tätigkeit man wahrgenommen hat. Im Deutschen wird diese Konstruktion meist mit einem Nebensatz mit „wie" wiedergegeben.*

a) ***Das present participle nach einem Verb der Wahrnehmung + Objekt***

	Verb der Wahrnehmung	*Direktes Objekt*	Present participle	
I	**watched**	**them**	**harvesting**	the cocoa pods.
Ich sah zu, wie sie gerade die Kakaoschoten ernteten.				

- *Das* **present participle** *nach einem Verb der Wahrnehmung und einem direkten Objekt drückt aus, dass ein Geschehen gerade abläuft oder ablief. Es wird besonders dann verwendet, wenn nur* ***ein Teil des gesamten Geschehens*** *wahrgenommen wird.*

b) ***Der infinitive nach einem Verb der Wahrnehmung + Objekt***

	Verb der Wahrnehmung	*Direktes Objekt*	*Infinitiv ohne* to	
I	**watched**	**them**	**harvest**	the cocoa pods.
Ich sah zu, wie sie die Kakaoschoten ernteten.				

- *Der* **infinitive** *nach einem Verb der Wahrnehmung und einem direkten Objekt drückt aus, dass ein Geschehen* ***von Anfang bis Ende*** *wahrgenommen wurde. Diese Konstruktion steht besonders dann, wenn zwei oder mehrere Handlungen aufeinander folgen, z. B.* I watched the kids climb the tree and chop down the pods.

English summary

After verbs of perception (hear, see, watch, feel etc.) and a direct object it is possible to use a present participle or an infinitive (without *to*).

You use the **present participle** when you see, feel or hear only part of the action.	I **felt** the sun **burning** on my skin.
You use the **infinitive** when you see the complete action from beginning to end.	I **watched** three girls **carry** heavy containers full of beans to a lorry, **dump** the contents, then **walk** back for more.

Test yourself *A girl is talking about a lazy colleague. Complete what she says with the* ***present participle*** *or the* ***infinitive*** *form of the verbs in brackets.*

1. He always arrives really late for work and then he leaves early. Yesterday I saw him (arrive) at 9:30, (hang) his jacket on the chair, then (leave) again.
2. He prefers magazines to company reports. Today I noticed him (read) a car magazine.
3. And he makes a lot of personal phone calls. This morning I was walking past his office when I heard him (tell) somebody all about his last holiday.
4. He also takes other people's equipment without asking. Yesterday I watched him (pick up) a pen from his colleague's desk, quickly (put) it into his pocket and then (walk away).
5. Our boss isn't happy with him. As I was walking past her office today, I could hear her (shout) at him.

G8 They arrived feeling exhausted

→ Seiten 53–54

Das Partizip Präsens nach Verben der Ruhe und der Bewegung
Present participle after verbs of rest and motion

The children **arrived carrying** heavy tools and equipment.

I **stood watching** them.

Nach ***Verben der Bewegung*** *wie* arrive, leave, come, go, run, walk *und* ***Verben der Ruhe*** *wie* sit, stand, lie, stay, remain *sowie nach anderen Verben wie* find *und* catch *(erwischen) + Objekt wird im Englischen häufig das* **present participle** *gebraucht.*

- *Das* **present participle** *steht nach einem* ***Verb der Bewegung oder der Ruhe****, wenn zwei Handlungen mit dem gleichen Subjekt zur gleichen Zeit ablieten, z.B.:*
  - The children **arrived** **feeling** exhausted. *(= Die Kinder fühlten sich erschöpft, als sie ankamen.)*
  - I **stood** **watching** them for a while. *(= Ich stand da und schaute ihnen eine Weile zu.)*
- *Das* **present participle** *steht auch nach* ***Verben wie* find *oder* catch** *+ Objekt, z.B.:*
  - Later I **found** Abdoulaye **sitting** alone.
  - I **caught** him **crying**.

English summary

The **present participle** is often used after verbs of rest and motion and after verbs such as find / catch + object.

The man **came hoping** to see what life was like for the children.
He **found** himself **wishing** he could do something to help them.

Test yourself *Read what happened to Julia at the beach yesterday and complete her blog.*

After a busy morning at work yesterday, I decided to spend my lunch break relaxing on the beach. But as I (lie – read) quietly, I soon (find – myself – wonder) if I had made the right choice. There weren't many people on the beach, just a few dog-walkers and two girls who were chatting quietly nearby as they (sit – eat) ice creams. Then suddenly a large dog (come – run) towards the two girls. He was barking loudly and the girls were scared.
So they began to scream. When that didn't help, they threw stones. A moment later, the dog's owner (arrive – shout) angrily at the two girls. Then he (catch – me – watch) the drama, so he started shouting at me too! I (come – hope) for some peace on the beach. I (leave – think) the world had gone crazy!

G9 The Words-of-Wisdom Wall

→ Seiten 56–58

Notwendige und nicht-notwendige Relativsätze
Defining and non-defining relative clauses

My first job was at a café **which was always incredibly busy**. Unfortunately, my boss was the kind of person **who never sat down herself**, so it was often difficult to take a break.	My first job, **which I was very happy to get at first**, was with a family friend. My boss, **who has his own business as a carpenter**, thought he was helping me out, but the work was really hard.

Relativsätze sind Nebensätze, die ihr **Bezugswort** *im Hauptsatz a) näher bestimmen* (… a café which was always incredibly busy) *oder b) zusätzlich beschreiben* (My first job, which I was very happy to get at first, …). *Im Englischen nennt man diese zwei Arten von Relativsätzen* **defining** *und* **non-defining relative clauses**.

a) Defining relative clauses

Cassie has a job in **a shop which / that sells cool clothes**.
She is **one of those kids who / that loves to wear the latest fashion trends**.
The problem is she keeps buying **things which / that she doesn't need**.

- **Defining relative clauses** *bestimmen oder beschreiben ihr vorangestelltes* ***Bezugswort*** *näher. Sie legen fest, wer oder was gemeint ist. Welcher Laden? Welche Jugendliche? Welche Dinge? Ohne den Relativsatz wäre der Sinn des Hauptsatzes unvollständig, unklar oder sinnlos.*
- *Relativsätze, die ihr Bezugswort näher bestimmen, stehen* ***ohne Komma****. Beim Sprechen macht man keine Pause.*
- **Defining relative clauses** *werden durch Relativpronomen wie* **who** *oder* **that** *(bei Personen) und* **which** *oder* **that** *(bei Sachen) eingeleitet, wenn sie Subjekt im Relativsatz sind. Hat der Relativsatz ein eigenes Subjekt, können* who / which / that *auch weggelassen werden, z.B.* things (**which / that**) she doesn't need. *Diese Relativsätze nennt man* **contact clauses**.

b) Non-defining relative clauses

Marlon, **who found his first job exhausting**, wished he'd looked around for an easier job in a shop.
Cassie, **who works in a cool clothes shop**, wishes she'd saved a bit more of her money for a holiday.
Lucy, **whose first job was at a huge café**, wishes she had spoken to her boss about a break. **The café**, **which was open all day**, was always full, so she had to work non-stop.

- *Bei* **non-defining relative clauses** *ist das vorangestellte* ***Bezugswort bereits definiert****. Auch ohne den Relativsatz bleibt klar, wer oder was gemeint ist: Marlon, Cassie, Lucy und das Café, in dem Lucy arbeitet. Zu einer Verwechslung mit einer anderen Person oder mit einem anderen Café kann es nicht kommen. Die Relativsätze bestimmen daher ihr Bezugswort* ***nicht*** *näher. Sie enthalten lediglich eine zusätzliche oder ergänzende Information, die im Gegensatz zu den* defining relative clauses *ebenso gut in Klammern stehen oder gar entfallen könnte, ohne dass die Aussage im Hauptsatz verändert wird.*
- *Relativsätze, die nur Zusatzinformationen enthalten, werden vom Hauptsatz immer* ***durch Kommas abgetrennt****. Beim Sprechen wird eine Pause gemacht.*
- *Im Gegensatz zu* defining relative clauses *beginnen* **non-defining relative clauses** ***immer mit einem Relativpronomen****: Für Personen verwendet man* **who**; *für Dinge verwendet man* **which**; *und* **whose** *verwendet man für Personen oder Dinge. Das Relativpronomen* **that** *ist in einem* **non-defining relative clause** ***nicht möglich.***
- *Das Relativpronomen* **which** *verwendet man außerdem, wenn der Relativsatz sich auf den ganzen Satz bezieht. Solche Relativsätze werden im Deutschen mit dem Pronomen* ***was*** *eingeleitet. Beim Sprechen wird eine Pause gemacht:*
  Marlon found a job with a family friend, **which** wasn't a good idea.
  Marlon hat einen Job bei einem Freund der Familie gefunden, ***was*** *keine gute Idee war.*

English summary

There are two types of relative clause: **defining** and **non-defining**.

1. **Defining relative clauses** tell you which person or thing the speaker is talking about. **No comma** is used between the noun and the relative clause.

   Nathan is the guy **who / that** stupidly signed all the forms without reading them first.

2. **Non-defining relative clauses** are used after nouns that are definite already. They give extra information about a person or thing or about the main clause.
   You always need a **comma** to separate the main clause from the relative clause.

   Nathan, **who** stupidly signed all the forms without reading them, was shocked when he got his first wages. But his boss sat down with him and patiently explained everything, **which** was really nice of him.

Test yourself *Read Dan's comments about his Saturday job at a pet shop. Write the text in your exercise book. Decide if the sentences have* ***defining*** *or* ***non-defining relative clauses****. If you can leave the relative pronoun out, put it in brackets. Put in commas where necessary.*

I was walking past the pet shop **which** I often do on my way into town when I noticed a job advert in the window. They were looking for a student **who** could help them on Saturdays. It seemed the perfect job for me, so I went in. The shop manager **who** was really busy quickly explained everything **that** I needed to know and then offered me the position. I liked the other people **who** worked there and I liked the job. But it was *hard*. When the shop was full of people **which** it usually was it was difficult to find time to take a break. And the money **that** I earned wasn't enough for the hours **which** I had to put in. - Dan

G10 Not only was it super cold, but ...

→ Seiten 56, 59

Hervorhebung durch Inversion des Verbs nach bestimmten Adverbien
Inversion of the verb for emphasis after certain adverbs

Negative (never, not only, ...) *und einschränkende* (hardly, rarely, ...) *Adverbialbestimmungen treten meist im Inneren eines Satzes auf. Zur besonderen Betonung einer Aussage können sie jedoch auch am Satzanfang stehen. Tritt dieser Fall ein, wird eine* ***Inversion*** *von Subjekt und Verb ausgelöst (hier:* it was → was it*). Aus der Aussageform wird die* ***Frageform****.*

It was not only super cold, but the work was exhausting too.
Not only **was it** super cold, but the work was exhausting too.

- *Negative und einschränkende Adverbialbestimmungen mit und ohne Inversion*

Adverbiale Bestimmung	*Gewöhnlicher Aussagesatz* *Aussagesatz mit Inversion (Frageform) des Verbs*
not only ... but	He **not only** works hard, **but** he enjoys his life too. **Not only** does he work hard, **but** he enjoys his life too.
rarely / never	I have **rarely / never** heard anything so stupid. **Rarely / Never** have I heard anything so stupid.
hardly	She had **hardly** put the phone down when it rang again. **Hardly** had she put the phone down when it rang again.
not for one moment	I didn't imagine **for one moment** that they would ever apologise. **Not for one moment** did I imagine that they would ever apologise.

- *Wenn eine negative oder einschränkende Adverbialbestimmung zur besonderen Hervorhebung am Satzanfang steht, ändert sich die übliche Wortstellung. Subjekt und Verb stehen nicht mehr in der Aussageform, sondern in der* ***Frageform*** *umgesetzt, z. B.:*
  he works → does he work; I have heard → have I heard; I imagined → did I imagine

❗ *Beachte auch die Besonderheiten bei den Adverbialbestimmungen in den folgenden Beispielen:*

Adverbiale Bestimmung	*Gewöhnlicher Aussagesatz* *Aussagesatz mit Inversion des Verbs*
never … before → Never before …	I **had never spent** so much money on clothes **before**. **Never before had** I **spent** so much money on clothes.
There's no way … → No way …	**There's no way that** we'**ll get** there on time. **No way will** we **get** there on time.
no sooner … than → No sooner … than	We had **no sooner left** the house **than** it started to rain. **No sooner had** we **left** the house **than** it started to rain.
only … when (she …) → Only when (she …)	She **only realised** that she'd lost her key **when she got home**. **Only when she got home did** she **realise** that she'd lost her key.
It was only then that … → Only then …	**It was only then that** she **realised** she had lost her key. **Only then did** she **realise** she had lost her key.

English summary

If an adverb or adverb phrase with a negative or restrictive sense is placed at the beginning of the sentence for emphasis or dramatic effect, it must be followed by the inverted question form of the verb.

Never before **have I felt** so jealous.

Only then **did I realise** my mistake.

Test yourself *Read one person's view on the use of mobile phones in public places. Rewrite the text using* ***inversion*** *for emphasis.*

There is no way that people should be allowed to use mobile phones in public places. They not only make lots of noise, but they also force others to listen to their private conversations. Yesterday a woman on my bus talked non-stop. She had hardly finished one call when she started again. I have never heard such silly, unnecessary conversations! I was glad when she got off the bus. It was only then that I was able to read my book in peace.

G11 I do remember how it feels ...

→ Seiten 56, 59

Hervorhebung mit do / does / did
Emphatic *do / does / did*

In der Regel verwendest du **do / does** *und* **did** *und den* ***Infinitiv*** *in Fragen und Verneinungen.* **Do / does / did** *können aber auch in bejahten Sätzen verwendet werden, wenn sie stärker betont werden sollen. Im Deutschen verwendest du hierfür oft Wörter wie „tatsächlich", „wirklich", „sehr" und „doch".*

- **do / does / did** + ***Infinitiv*** *wird in einem bejahten Aussagesatz verwendet:*

  a) ***zur Betonung einer Meinung oder eines Gefühls***

genau	I **do** **understand** what you're trying to say.
tatsächlich	You're right. That sentence **does** **sound** strange.
wirklich	Oh yeah, I **did** **enjoy** the film. It was fantastic.
so sehr	I **do** **hope** that you'll be able to visit me next year.

Im Deutschen kannst du mit Wörtern wie „genau", „tatsächlich", „wirklich" und „so sehr" deine Meinung / Empfindung stärker zum Ausdruck bringen. Im Englischen verwendest du hierfür **do / does / did** *und den Infinitiv des Vollverbs.*

b) ***zur Betonung eines Gegensatzes (im Sinne von „doch")***

Tom never takes the dog for a walk. – That isn't true. He **does take** him. Just not very often.
You didn't do your homework yesterday. – That isn't true, Mum. I **did do** it.
I know I said I didn't want to go to the party, but in the end I **did go**.

c) ***um eine Aufforderung oder Bitte höflicher oder formeller auszudrücken***

Please **do come** in, Mrs Delacruz. Nice to see you again.
Do have a seat, I'll be right with you.

English summary

Do, does and **did** are sometimes used with the infinitive in positive sentences to emphasise a feeling, agreement or disagreement. They can also be used in polite requests.

Your hair **does** look good today; nice!
You're right; Tom **did** mention plans for a party next weekend.
That's rubbish! She **does** love him.
Do tell me if you need anything, Mr Tate.

Test yourself *Translate these sentences into English. Use **do / does / did** for emphasis.*

1. Das überrascht mich. Ich sehe doch ganz gut aus in Grau!
2. Ich hoffe so sehr, dass du den Job bekommst.
3. Also, du hast Tom gestern doch getroffen!
4. Du hast Recht. Die Milch schmeckt tatsächlich komisch.
5. Ich weiß genau, was du meinst, aber das stimmt nicht.
6. Sagen Sie doch Bescheid, wenn ich Ihnen mehr Kaffee bringen kann.
7. Sie hat so viel Gutes von dir gehört und möchte dich so gerne kennenlernen!
8. Guten Abend, schön, dass Sie kommen konnten! Kommen Sie doch bitte herein, die anderen sind schon da.

9. Mr Braxton, Sie wissen sehr wohl, dass man nie zu spät zu einem Vorstellungsgespräch kommen sollte, und trotzdem sind Sie zu spät gekommen.
10. Du hast dich auf der Party nicht wirklich amüsiert. – Doch, ich habe mich amüsiert. Ich musste nur früh weg.

Unit 3

G12 It starts at 8:00 but we're meeting at 6:00

→ Seiten 86–87

Das Präsens mit Futurbedeutung
The simple present and present progressive with future meaning

Neben dem will future *und dem* going-to future *werden im Englischen häufig auch das* **simple present** (I do) *und das* **present progressive** (I'm doing) *verwendet, um über zukünftige Handlungen zu sprechen.*

- *Das* **simple present** *verwendest du für zukünftige Handlungen, die durch* ***Fahrpläne***, ***Programme*** *oder andere* ***offizielle Vorgaben*** *festgelegt sind. Solche Handlungen werden häufig mit Verben wie* arrive, leave, start, finish, open, close etc. *gebraucht, z. B.* The premiere starts at 8:00.
- *Das* **present progressive** *verwendest du für zukünftige Handlungen, wenn es sich um* ***Pläne*** *oder* ***Vereinbarungen*** *handelt, die persönlich vereinbart wurden. Solche Handlungen werden häufig mit Verben wie* meet, come *und* go *gebraucht, z. B.* Alex is meeting his buddy at 6:00.

! *Das* **present progressive** *mit Futurbedeutung bietet eine Alternative zum* going-to future, *die von englischen Muttersprachlern häufig verwendet wird, z. B.* I'm meeting my friend at the premiere tonight. *statt* I'm going to meet my friend at the premiere tonight.

English summary

You use the **simple present** to talk about timetables, programmes, etc.	When **does** the train **leave**? – It **leaves** at 6:10.
You use the **present progressive** to talk about something that you've arranged to do in the future.	What **are** you **doing** this weekend? – I'**m working** on Saturday. On Sunday I'**m going** to the beach with some friends.

Test yourself *Choose the **simple present** or the **present progressive** to complete the dialogue.*

Ella: What **1** (you – do) tomorrow?
Mia: I **2** (meet) my cousin at the new shopping mall. It **3** (open) tomorrow at 10:00. Why don't you come with us?
Ella: That sounds like a great idea. How **4** (you – get) there?
Mia: By bus or by subway. I haven't decided yet. The bus is cheaper but it **5** (leave) earlier and it **6** (take) a lot longer.
Ella: I've got a better idea. My brother **7** (drive) into town tomorrow morning. I'm sure he won't mind taking us with him. But let me ask him first what time he **8** (go).

G13 What will Alex be doing by the time he's 30?

→ Seiten 86, 88

Die Verlaufsform des Futurs
The future progressive

*Das **future progressive** ist die Verlaufsform des Futurs. Mit dieser Zeitform beschreibst du:*

1. *Handlungen, die zu einem bestimmten Zeitpunkt **in der Zukunft gerade stattfinden** und **noch nicht beendet** sind (Bild A). Der Zeitpunkt wird häufig durch eine Zeitangabe wie* at 9:30 tomorrow morning, by the time (+ simple present), in two weeks' time *etc. festgelegt.*
2. *Handlungen, die **für die Zukunft fest vereinbart** worden sind (Bild B).*

- *Das* **future progressive** *bildest du aus* **will / won't be + present participle**.

Aussage:	Very soon Alex **will be living** his dream.
Verneinung:	He **won't be working** for the tour bus company any more.
Entscheidungsfrage mit Kurzantwort:	**Will** he still **be going** to cattle calls? – No, he **won't**.

❗ *Wenn du Handlungen beschreiben willst, die für die Zukunft fest vereinbart worden sind, kannst du das* future progressive *als Alternative zum* present progressive *mit Futurbedeutung oder zum* going-to future *verwenden, z.B.* I'll be seeing Tom at the premiere. / I'm seeing Tom at the premiere. / I'm going to see Tom at the premiere.

English summary

You use the **future progressive** to describe an unfinished action that will be taking place at a given time in the future.	Don't call me between 9 and 10 a.m. I'**ll be working**.
It is also used to describe or ask about an action which has been planned for the future.	I'**ll be going** to a cattle call on Tuesday. **Will** you **be going** too?

Test yourself *Next week Alex has another busy week. Look at his plans and say what he'll be doing each day.*

On Monday morning I'm meeting my agent. In the afternoon I've got a movie review to write for the internet. On Tuesday I'm going to an audition. On Wednesday I'll interview stars at a movie premiere on Hollywood Boulevard. On Thursday I'm going to visit my buddy Dave. And on Friday my parents are coming for the weekend so I'm picking them up from the airport.

Start like this: On Monday morning Alex will be meeting …

G14 What will Alex have done by the time he's 30?

→ Seiten 86, 88

Das Futur II
The future perfect

By the time I'm 30, I'**ll have hit** the big time.

Mit dem **future perfect** *drückst du aus, dass eine Handlung oder ein Vorgang zu einem bestimmten Zeitpunkt in der Zukunft abgeschlossen sein wird. Dieser Zeitpunkt wird häufig durch eine Zeitangabe wie* by this time next year, by the time (+ simple present), in two weeks' time etc. *festgelegt.*

- *Das* future perfect *bildest du aus* **will / won't have + past participle** *(3. Verbform).*

Aussage:	By the time people read his blog, Alex **will have gotten** his first part in a movie, hopefully.
Verneinung:	The producers **won't have given** him a big part, surely.
Entscheidungsfrage mit Kurzantwort:	**Will** he **have given up** his day job by then? – No, he **won't**.

Wie du bestimmt bemerkt hast, gelten für das future progressive *und das* future perfect *dieselben* signal phrases *(z. B.* by this time next week, by Friday etc.*). Es ist wichtig, dass du auf den Kontext achtest, um zu entscheiden, welche Form des Futurs du verwenden musst.*

English summary

You use the **future perfect** for an action that will have been completed at a given time in the future.

By this time next year Alex hopes that he **will have gotten** his big break.

Test yourself *Alex tells his buddy Dave about his hopes for the future. Decide if you need the* ***future perfect*** *or the* ***future progressive*** *for the verbs in brackets.*

I really hope that by the time people read my blog I 1 (get) my big break and that I 2 (live) my dream. In six months' time, I'm sure I 3 (become) a star and the reporters 4 (want) to interview me. Then of course I'll be friendly and polite, but I'll tell them never to call me before 11:00 because I 5 (not get up) by then. I 6 (still – sleep).

G15 California in the world

→ Seite 91

Wiederholung: Der bestimmte und der unbestimmte Artikel
Revision: The definite and the indefinite article

Every year people arrive in Hollywood looking for **fame**. But very few people actually achieve **the fame** they're looking for.

Für den Gebrauch und das Weglassen des bestimmten Artikels **the** *und des unbestimmten Artikels* **a / an** *gibt es im Englischen feste Regeln. Diese unterscheiden sich in einigen Fällen von der Verwendung des bestimmten und unbestimmten Artikels im Deutschen.*

1. ***Der bestimmte Artikel*** **the**

- ***Mit*** *dem bestimmten Artikel stehen:*

Gebirge, Flüsse, Meere	**the** Sierra Nevadas, **the** Colorado River, **the** Pacific Ocean
Ländernamen im Plural	**the** US, **the** UK, **the** Netherlands
Adjektive im Superlativ	**the** most famous, **the** most popular, **the** best (sights)
Musikinstrumente	I don't play **the** piano but I play **the** guitar.

- ***Ohne*** *den bestimmten Artikel stehen:*

Eigennamen von Bergen und Seen	Mount Whitney, Lake Tahoe
Namen von Straßen, Städten und Ländernamen im Singular	Hollywood Boulevard, Los Angeles, San Francisco, England, Germany
„die meisten" (ohne Einschränkung)	Most people like chocolate. *(= fast alle Leute)*
„die meisten" (mit Einschränkung)	Most of the people I know like chocolate. *(= fast alle Leute, die ich kenne)*

- ***Mit und ohne*** den bestimmten Artikel stehen:

Konkrete Begriffe (Dinge, die du sehen, berühren und fühlen kannst) sowie abstrakte Begriffe (Dinge wie fun, success, fame, life, happiness, etc.*)*

Wenn die genannten Begriffe im allgemeinen Sinne verwendet werden, stehen sie ohne den bestimmten Artikel:	*Wenn die genannten Begriffe durch eine Ergänzung (oft einen Relativsatz oder* of-phrase*) näher bestimmt werden, stehen sie mit dem bestimmten Artikel:*
During the 1850s many people came to California looking for gold.	By the 1880s most of **the** gold had gone.
Immigrants are important for California's economy.	It's **the** immigrants who often do the hard jobs no Americans want to do.
Each year thousands of people arrive in L.A. hoping for success.	But only very few people ever find **the** success they're looking for.
What does happiness mean to you?	There are no words to describe **the** happiness Alex felt when he got his first movie role.

Mahlzeiten (breakfast, lunch, dinner) *und Stoffbezeichnungen* (milk, water, air)

Ohne den bestimmten Artikel:	*Mit dem bestimmten Artikel:*
Let's have lunch at Arnie's.	**The** lunch I had there last week was delicious.
Water is a problem in California.	About 80 % of **the** water used in California is needed for agriculture.

Institutionen (school, work, college, church, prison, hospital) *und Verkehrsmittel* (bus, train, plane)

Ohne den bestimmten Artikel:	*Mit dem bestimmten Artikel:*
Alex didn't like school much.	He wasn't very happy at **the** school he went to.
We usually go into town by bus.	**The** bus into town leaves in five minutes.

2. ***Der unbestimmte Artikel* a / an**

- *Der unbestimmte Artikel steht* ***vor****:*

Berufsbezeichnungen	Jack is **a** vet.	*Jack ist Tierarzt.*
Maßeinheiten (= pro / je)	two euros **a** kilo	*zwei Euro* ***das*** *Kilo*
Zeiteinheiten (= pro / je)	three times **a** day / year	*dreimal* ***am*** *Tag /* ***im*** *Jahr*
100 und 1000	**a** hundred, **a** thousand	*hundert / tausend*

- *sowie* ***nach****:*

half	half **an** hour	***eine*** *halbe Stunde*
quite, kind of	quite **a** / kind of **a** long way	***ein*** *ziemlich langer Weg*
such	such **a** nice day	*so* ***ein*** *schöner Tag*

- *und in* phrases *wie:* in **a** hurry *(in Eile)*; for **a** long time *(lange Zeit)*; have **a** headache *(Kopfschmerzen haben).*

English summary

You use the definite article *(the)* before:
1. nouns that refer to specific people or things;
2. names of rivers, seas, mountain chains, plural names of countries and musical instruments.

The sun is shining.
the Rhine, **the** Pacific Ocean, **the** Rockies, **the** US, **the** guitar

You do **not** use the definite article before:
1. an abstract noun;
2. names of mountains, lakes, towns, roads, countries and *most* when it means *almost all.*

Life is never boring in Hollywood.
Mt Whitney, Lake Ontario, Park Road
Most people like ice cream.

You use the indefinite article *(a / an)* before:
1. jobs, units of measurement, time, 100, 1000;
2. after *half, quite, kind of, such;*
3. and in certain expressions.

Mr. Summer is **a** pilot.
I've been waiting for half **an** hour.
I'm in **a** hurry.

Test yourself *Complete Alex's e-mail to his mother. Put in the* ***definite*** *or* ***indefinite article****. If* ***no article*** *is needed, write (–).*

Sorry I didn't send you an e-mail earlier, but I was tired after all **1** fun we had at **2** movie premiere last night. When I got up, it was already 10:30. Then after **3** breakfast, I had to learn all about **4** history of California for **5** test on Wednesday. That took about **6** hour and **7** half. And I haven't even started to learn about **8** economy or **9** different landscapes yet. No, I haven't gone back to **10** college. **11** test is for **12** job with **13** Tourist Office. If I pass, I'll soon be able to work as **14** tour guide two or three times **15** week in-between my auditions. But I've already heard it's pretty difficult and **16** most people have to take it at least twice, so I'm not very hopeful. I haven't found **17** fame as **18** actor yet. But I can honestly say that I've found **19** happiness. L.A. is such **20** fantastic city and I just love **21** excitement of living here. For me, it's simply **22** most exciting city in **23** US.

G16 Should we be worried?

→ Seiten 94–96

Englische Entsprechungen für die Verben „sollen" und „müssen"
English equivalents for the German verbs *sollen* and *müssen*

Die deutschen Verben „sollen" und „müssen" werden im Englischen durch verschiedene Verben und Verbphrasen wiedergegeben.

a) ***Das Verb „sollen"***

shall / should / ought to / be to

Bitte um Anweisung / Rat	shall (I / we) should	**Shall** I open the window? What **shall** we do? What **should** he / she / they do?
Verpflichtung	should	If you made a mistake, you **should** apologise.
Meinung / Ratschlag	should / ought to	I think we **should / ought to** care more about our environment.
Anweisung / Befehl	be to	If we hear the fire alarm, we **are to** leave the building immediately.

❗ *Das Verb* shall *klingt sehr formal und wird von jungen Sprechern kaum noch verwendet (in den USA auch nur noch selten von erwachsenen Sprechern).*

be supposed to / be expected to / be said to

Regel	be supposed to	You**'re supposed to** call 911 only in an emergency. You **aren't supposed to** use it for general advice.
Erwartung	be supposed to / be expected to	Firefighters **are supposed to / are expected to** prevent fires, as well as put them out.
Erwartung, die sich nicht erfüllt	be supposed to	The Emergency Services **are supposed to** be on their way. But they haven't arrived yet.
Gerücht / Behauptung	be supposed to / be said to	Some fires **are supposed to / are said to** be good for the environment.

b) ***Das Verb „müssen"***

must / have to / need to

Notwendigkeit	must / have to / need to	Firefighting is a dangerous job. You **must / have to / need to** be very brave to do that kind of work.
keine Notwendigkeit	needn't / don't have to / don't need to	But you **needn't / don't have to / don't need to** worry because you'll be given good training.
schriftliche Anweisungen (Schilder; Vorschriften)	must	Fire doors **must** be kept closed. Firefighters **must** wear protective clothing.

! Must *und* have to *sind häufig austauschbar, aber es gibt einen wichtigen Unterschied:*
Must *weist auf ein persönliches Gefühl hin;* have to *auf eine auferlegte Pflicht oder eine Tatsache.*
I must tidy my room today. *(= Der Sprecher selbst hält es für wichtig.)*
I have to tidy my room every Saturday. *(= Es ist eine auferlegte Pflicht oder eine Tatsache.)*

be required to / be forced to / be obliged to

Zwang	be forced to	Firefighters **are** often **forced to** work long hours.
Verpflichtung	be required to / be obliged to	They**'re** also **required to / are obliged to** work on holidays and on weekends.

English summary

The German verbs *sollen* and *müssen* can be expressed in English in different ways.

Equivalents for *sollen*: shall, should, ought to, be to, be supposed to, be expected to, be said to

Where **shall / should** we go for lunch?
If the door is locked, we **are to** wait outside.
You **were supposed to** be here half an hour ago.

Equivalents for *müssen*: must, have to, need to, be forced to, be required to, be obliged to, be supposed to, be to

I **must / need to / have to** water the plants today.
Are you **required to / obliged to** wear a school uniform?

Test yourself a) *Complete these sentences with the correct verb for the German 'sollen'.*

1. If Mrs. Kent is late today, we ___ wait for her in the hall. 2. Have you been to the new restaurant in West Street? It ___ be very good. 3. The plane landed early. It ___ land at 8:30. 4. If Lisa isn't feeling better soon, I think she ___ see a doctor. 5. Are you hungry? ___ I make us a sandwich? 6. We can take cell phones to school but we ___ use them in class.

b) *Use a different verb for 'have to' in these sentences. Sometimes more than one answer is correct.*

1. We've got plenty of time. We **don't have to** hurry. 2. It's not going to rain today, so we **won't have to** take an umbrella. 3. There were no trains or buses to the village, so I **had to** take a taxi. 4. There's no food in the cupboard. I'**ll have to** go shopping today. 5. Sometimes we **have to** make difficult decisions. We have no choice. 6. **Do** firefighters **have to** rescue animals?

Im ***Vocabulary*** findest du alle wichtigen englischen Wörter und Redewendungen aus *Green Line* 5. Sie stehen in der Reihenfolge, in der sie im Buch vorkommen. Diese Wörter solltest du lernen und anwenden können. Andere nützliche Wörter (*Vocabulary for instructions and activities*), die du **nicht** auswendig lernen musst, findest du auf S. 260–261.
Auf das *Vocabulary* folgt das ***Dictionary (English – German)***. Falls du ein Wort vergessen hast, kannst du in dieser alphabetischen Wortliste nachsehen.

Englische Begriffe wie *e-mail*, *cool* oder *cornflakes*, die du auch im Deutschen verwendest, stehen nicht im *Vocabulary*. Du kannst ihre Aussprache und Übersetzung aber im *Dictionary* nachschlagen. Das Gleiche gilt für Wörter, die auf Englisch und Deutsch fast gleich geschrieben und ausgesprochen werden, wie z. B. *park* oder *partner*.

In den drei Teilen von ***Text smart*** musst du nicht alle neuen Vokabeln auswendig lernen. Die Wörter und Ausdrücke, die im *Vocabulary* aufgelistet sind, sind die wichtigsten und sie solltest du lernen und anwenden können. Alle anderen neuen Wörter aus *Text smart* kannst du ebenfalls im *Dictionary* ab S. 208 nachschlagen.

Abkürzungen und Zeichen

pl	Mehrzahl (Plural)	!	Achtung!
sg	Einzahl (Singular)	↔	ist das Gegenteil von
AE	amerikanisch-englisches Wort	→	ist verwandt mit
coll/ugs	umgangssprachlich	=	entspricht
liter	literarisch	≠	entspricht nicht
5	In dieser Übung kommen die Wörter vor.	*Fr./Lat.*	verwandte Wörter in anderen Fremdsprachen

Englische Laute

Konsonanten

[b]	**b**ed	[p]	**p**icture
[d]	**d**ay	[r]	**r**ed
[ð]	**th**e	[s]	**s**ix
[f]	**f**amily	[ʃ]	**sh**e
[g]	**g**o	[t]	**t**en
[ŋ]	morni**ng**	[tʃ]	**ch**air
[h]	**h**ouse	[v]	**v**ideo
[j]	**y**ou	[w]	**w**e, **o**ne
[k]	**c**an, mil**k**	[z]	ea**s**y
[l]	**l**etter	[ʒ]	revi**s**ion
[m]	**m**an	[dʒ]	pa**ge**
[n]	**n**o	[θ]	**th**ank you

Vokale

[ɑː]	c**ar**	[i]	happ**y**
[æ]	**a**pple	[iː]	t**ea**cher
[e]	p**e**n	[ɒ]	d**o**g
[ə]	**a**gain	[ɔː]	b**a**ll
[ɜː]	g**ir**l	[ʊ]	b**oo**k
[ʌ]	b**u**t	[u]	Jan**u**ary
[ɪ]	**i**t	[uː]	t**oo**, tw**o**

Doppellaute

[aɪ]	**I**, m**y**
[aʊ]	n**ow**, m**ou**se
[eɪ]	n**a**me, th**ey**
[eə]	th**ere**, p**air**
[ɪə]	h**ere**, id**ea**
[əʊ]	hell**o**
[ɔɪ]	b**oy**
[ʊə]	s**ure**

[ː] der vorangehende Laut ist lang, z. B. *you* [juː]
[‿] der Bindebogen zeigt, dass zwei Wörter in der Aussprache verbunden werden
[ˈ] die folgende Silbe trägt den Hauptakzent
[ˌ] die folgende Silbe trägt den Nebenakzent

Der Aussprachestandard in *Green Line* ist *British English*. Auch Wörter, die den Zusatz *AE* haben, werden entsprechend lautschriftlich dargestellt. Bei den Tonträgern und Filmsequenzen wird die jeweils passende Aussprache verwendet.

Across cultures 1 The world speaks English

1	**square** [skweə]	Quadrat; Quadrat-	Areas are often given in *square* miles or *square* kilometres.
	including [ɪn'klu:dɪŋ]	einschließlich; inklusive	In South Africa there are eleven official languages, *incl.* English.
	parliament ['pɑ:ləmənt]	Parlament	! Be careful with the spelling.
	court [kɔ:t]	Hof; Gericht; Gerichtshof	Before people are sent to prison, they appear in *court*.
	racial ['reɪʃl]	Rassen-	
	segregation [ˌsegrɪ'geɪʃn]	Segregation; Trennung; Rassentrennung	Apartheid meant racial *segregation*.
	bitterness *(no pl)* ['bɪtənəs]	Bitterkeit; Verbitterung	After apartheid had ended, it was hard for the people to forget their *bitterness*.
	racism ['reɪsɪzm]	Rassismus	*racism* → racist *Fr.* racisme *(m)*
	icon ['aɪkɒn]	Ikone; Symbol	Nelson Mandela was an *icon* for the black population.
	civil rights *(pl)* [ˌsɪvl 'raɪts]	Bürgerrechte	Nelson Mandela was South Africa's most important *civil rights* leader.
	election [ɪ'lekʃn]	Wahl	The first free *elections* in South Africa were in 1994.
	back [bæk]	damals	*Back* in 1994, South Africa became a free country.
	middle class [ˌmɪdl 'klɑ:s]	Mittelschicht	During apartheid, there was no black *middle class* in South Africa.
	Hindu ['hɪndu:]	Hindu; hinduistisch	
	Muslim ['mʊzlɪm]	Muslim/-in; muslimisch	She's Hindu and her husband is *Muslim* and they're happy together. *Fr.* musulman/-e *(m,f)*
	plastic surgery *(no pl)* [ˌplæstɪk 'sɜ:dʒəri]	Schönheitschirurgie	*Plastic surgery* is very expensive.
	ancient ['eɪnʃnt]	alt; altertümlich; antik	= very, very old *Fr.* ancien/-ne
	spirituality [ˌspɪrɪtʃu'æləti]	Spiritualität	Tourists often come to India to look for *spirituality*.
	Buddhist ['bʊdɪst]	buddhistisch	
	romantic [rə'mæntɪk]	romantisch	If I ever get married, I don't want any of that *romantic* stuff.
	mixed [mɪkst]	gemischt	*mixed* → to mix
	reality [ri'æləti]	Realität; Wirklichkeit	Some people imagine certain countries to be much nicer than they are in *reality*. *reality* → real *Fr.* réalité *(f)*
	democracy [dɪ'mɒkrəsi]	Demokratie	Germany, Great Britain and the USA are *democracies*.
	discrimination [dɪˌskrɪmɪ'neɪʃn]	Diskriminierung	We must stop *discrimination* against ethnic minorities.
	widespread ['waɪdspred]	weit verbreitet	

sexual ['sekʃʊəl]	sexuell	
harassment [hə'ræsmənt]	Belästigung; Schikane	In India, sexual *harassment* is widespread.
democratic [ˌdemə'krætɪk]	demokratisch	*democratic* → democracy
human rights [ˌhju:mən 'raɪts]	Menschenrechte	= the basic rights and freedoms which everyone should have
intense [ɪn'tens]	intensiv; heftig	an *intense* feeling
I can't help *(+ -ing)* [aɪ ˌkɑ:nt 'help]	Ich kann nicht anders (als zu) …	*I couldn't help* laughing, it was so funny.
to **turn on** [ˌtɜ:n‿'ɒn]	einschalten	*Turn on* the lights, please.
chaotic [keɪ'ɒtɪk]	chaotisch	*chaotic* → chaos
Latin ['lætɪn]	Latein; lateinisch	The Italian, Spanish and French languages all come from *Latin*.
southern ['sʌðən]	südlich; Süd-	! Be careful with the pronunciation. *southern* → south
Italian [ɪ'tæliən]	Italiener/-in; italienisch; Italienisch; aus Italien	*Italian* → Italy
Chinese [tʃaɪ'ni:z]	Chinese/Chinesin; chinesisch; Chinesisch; aus China	Many Australians have an Italian or *Chinese* background. *Chinese* → China
Aboriginal [ˌæbə'rɪdʒnl]	von australischen Ureinwohnern abstammend	*Aboriginal* culture/history
crocodile ['krɒkədaɪl]	Krokodil	
saltie *(coll)* ['sɔ:lti]	Salzwasserkrokodil	*Saltie* is an informal word used in Australia for a crocodile that lives in saltwater.
length [leŋθ]	Länge	*length* → long
Aussie *(coll)* ['ɒzi]	Australier/-in; australisch *(ugs.)*	*Aussie* = Australian
surf instructor [ˌsɜ:f‿ɪn'strʌktə]	Surflehrer/-in	A *surf instructor* shows you how to surf. **Lat.** instructor *(m)*
to **envy** ['envi]	beneiden	Paul *envied* his brother. He wanted to be as successful as he was, but he simply wasn't good enough.
to **apply (to)** [ə'plaɪ tə]	gelten (für); zutreffen (auf)	This method of working *applies to* other tasks or situations too.
to **respect** [rɪ'spekt]	respektieren	If you *respect* sb's rights, you accept them and agree that they're important.
resident ['rezɪdnt]	Bewohner/-in; Einwohner/-in	He's a *resident* of South Africa; he's lived there for two years now.
gay [geɪ]	schwul; homosexuell; Schwuler; Homosexueller	If a guy says another guy is good-looking, he must be *gay*. – Oh please, who told you that rubbish? What a joke.
mate [meɪt]	Kumpel	In Australia or Britain (but not the US), boys and men often call their friends their *mates*.
to **head out** [ˌhed‿'aʊt]	hinausgehen	
the outback [ði 'aʊtbæk]	Outback *(australisches Hinterland)*	*The outback* is the wild, empty country far away from Australia's towns and cities.
bushfire ['bʊʃfaɪə]	Buschfeuer	

Unit 1 G'day Australia!

G'day! *(= Good day!)* [gə'daɪ]	Guten Tag.; Hallo.; Hi. *(Begrüßung in Australien)*	This is how Australians say hello.

Station 1: Just me and my backpack

youth hostel ['ju:θ ˌhɒstl]	Jugendherberge	= a cheap place where young people can stay
to **gleam** [gli:m]	glänzen; schimmern	The surface of the lake *gleams* in the sun.
cluster ['klʌstə]	Bündel; Anhäufung	
giant [dʒaɪənt]	Riesen-; riesig	= very, very, very big *Fr.* géant/-e
seashell ['si:ʃel]	Muschel	The roof of the Sydney Opera House looks like a cluster of *seashells*.
to **overhear** [ˌəʊvə'hɪə], **overheard** [ˌəʊvə'hɜ:d], **overheard** [ˌəʊvə'hɜ:d]	belauschen; zufällig mit anhören	! False friend: *to overhear* ≠ überhören
owner ['əʊnə]	Besitzer/-in	*owner* → to own
terrace ['terɪs]	Terrasse	The hostel had a roof *terrace*.
snake [sneɪk]	Schlange	
air ambulance ['eər‿æmbjələns]	Rettungshubschrauber	! Be careful with the word stress.
satellite ['sætlaɪt]	Satellit	! Be careful with the pronunciation.
to **go off** [gəʊ‿'ɒf]	weggehen	
on one's own [ˌɒn wʌnz‿'əʊn]	allein; für sich	Never go off into the outback *on your own*.
bushwalking ['bʊʃˌwɔ:kɪŋ]	Buschwandern	
box jellyfish ['bɒks ˌdʒelifɪʃ]	Würfelqualle	
marine stinger [məˌri:n 'stɪŋə]	Seewespe *(Würfelquallen-Art)*	
to **net off** [net‿'ɒf]	durch ein Netz abtrennen	Some beaches in Australia are *netted off* so that people can swim there.
to **be likely** [bi 'laɪkli]	wahrscheinlich sein	Look at the sun; it *isn't likely* to rain today.
rip current ['rɪp ˌkʌrnt]	Brandungsrückströmung	
to **be swept out to sea** [bi ˌswept‿aʊt tə 'si:]	aufs offene Meer getrieben werden	This place is dangerous. You may be *swept out to sea* by a rip current.
comforting ['kʌmfətɪŋ]	tröstlich; ermutigend	She's sad and needs some *comforting* words.
1 **safety** ['seɪfti]	Sicherheit	*safety* → safe
2 to **call off** [ˌkɔ:l‿'ɒf]	abbrechen; absagen	The search for the missing boy was *called off* when it got dark.
risk [rɪsk]	Gefahr; Risiko	Be careful! Don't take too many *risks*.
spokesperson ['spəʊksˌpɜ:sn]	Sprecher/-in; PR-Sprecher/-in	

	association [əˌsəʊʃiˈeɪʃn]	Verband; Organisation	The Bushwalking *Association* organises trips into the outback. *Fr.* association
	survival [səˈvaɪvl]	Überleben	*survival* → to survive
5	**climatic** [klaɪˈmætɪk]	klimatisch	*climatic* → climate
	mostly [ˈməʊstli]	meistens; größtenteils; hauptsächlich	
	interior [ɪnˈtɪəriə]	Inneres; Landesinneres	A big part of Australia's *interior* is uninhabitable.
6	to **show sb around (a place)** [ˌʃəʊ‿əˈraʊnd]	jmdn. (an einem Ort) herumführen	A guide's job is to *show* tourists *around*.
	barbie *(infml)* (= **barbecue**) [ˈbɑ:bi]	Grillparty	Let's have a *barbie* on the beach.
	to **serve** [sɜ:v]	servieren; dienen; bedienen	In a restaurant or café, customers *are served* by a waiter. *to serve* → service *Fr.* servir
7	to **pick** [pɪk]	pflücken	Fruit tastes best when it's freshly *picked*.
	litter [ˈlɪtə]	Müll; Abfall	*litter* = garbage, rubbish
	track [træk]	Weg; Pfad	
	to **disturb** [dɪˈstɜ:b]	stören	Don't *disturb* Grandpa. He's sleeping.
	site [saɪt]	Ort; Gelände; Schauplatz	You mustn't walk on Aboriginal *sites*.
	to **damage** [ˈdæmɪdʒ]	schaden; beschädigen	Be careful: Don't *damage* the plants.
8	**lizard** [ˈlɪzəd]	Echse; Eidechse	
9	**deadly** [ˈdedli]	tödlich	

Station 2: When did your folks get here?

folks *(infml) (pl)* [fəʊks]	Leute	Hi *folks*, what's going on?
No worries. [ˌnəʊ ˈwʌriz]	Kein Problem.; Gern geschehen.	
How are you doing? [ˌhaʊ‿ɑ: jə ˈdu:ɪŋ]	Wie geht es dir/euch/Ihnen?	*How are you doing?* – OK, thanks. What about you?
Nice to meet you. [ˌnaɪs tə ˈmi:t ju:]	Nett, dich/euch/Sie kennenzulernen.	You can only say this when you meet a person for the first time, but not after that.
Kiwi *(infml)* [ˈki:wi:]	Neuseeländer/-in	= an informal word for a person from New Zealand
to **trace back** [ˌtreɪs ˈbæk]	zurückverfolgen	I can *trace* my family *back* to the 16th century.
ancestor [ˈænsestə]	Vorfahr/-in; Ahn/-in	My *ancestors* came from Scotland long ago. = family members that lived in the past, usually a long time ago
convict [ˈkɒnvɪkt]	Sträfling	= sb who has been sent to prison
to **bump into sb** [ˌbʌmp‿ˈɪntə]	jmdn. anrempeln	I was walking down the street when somebody *bumped into me* and I fell over.
sentence [ˈsentəns]	Verurteilung; Strafmaß	The convict's *sentence* was five years in prison.
victim [ˈvɪktɪm]	Opfer	Bill wasn't the criminal. He was the *victim* of the crime.

	used to *(+ infinitive)* ['ju:st tə]	pflegte(n) zu; tat(en) früher	! *Used to + infinitive* can only be used in the past tense: We *used to* live in Munich. = Wir wohnten früher in München.
	to **oppress** [ə'pres]	unterdrücken	The government *oppressed* the people.
	indigenous *(fml)* [ɪn'dɪdʒɪnəs]	einheimisch; heimisch	*indigenous* peoples, *indigenous* languages *indigenous* = native *Fr.* indigène
	to **have sth done** [hæv]	etw. machen lassen	You'*ve had* your hair cut, haven't you?
	to **renovate** ['renəveɪt]	renovieren	My parents *are renovating* our new house.
13	**leftovers** *(pl)* ['leftəʊvəz]	Überbleibsel; Überreste	
14	to **allow** [ə'laʊ]	erlauben; gestatten	My parents don't *allow* me to stay out late.
	to **make** [meɪk]	*hier:* lassen	My parents *made* me read an article about the dangers in Australia.
15	**farewell** [ˌfeə'wel]	Abschied; Abschieds-	When our teacher moved to another town, we gave her a *farewell* present.
	to **deliver** [dɪ'lɪvə]	liefern	My brother *delivers* pizzas as a student job. *Fr.* délivrer
16	**overseas** [ˌəʊvə'si:z]	in Übersee; im Ausland	Would you like to do an *overseas* job?
	to **host** [həʊst]	ausrichten *(Veranstaltung)*	South Africa *hosted* the Football World Championship in 2010.
	variety (of) [və'raɪəti ˌəv]	Vielzahl (an); Vielfalt (von)	The local vegetable market often has more *variety* than the supermarkets.
	celebration [ˌselə'breɪʃn]	Feier	*celebration* → to celebrate
	to **apply (for)** [ə'plaɪ fə]	sich bewerben (um); beantragen	to *apply* for a job/a visa, to *apply* online
	occupation [ˌɒkjə'peɪʃn]	Beruf; Beschäftigung	What's your parents' *occupation*?
	policy ['pɒləsi]	Politik; politische Linie	The government's *policies* have made the gap between rich and poor even larger.
	restrictive [rɪ'strɪktɪv]	beschränkend; einengend	When a country is *restrictive* about immigration, it wants to keep immigration numbers low. *Lat.* restrictus

Station 3: The land owns us

value ['vælju:]	Wert	You and Tom aren't friends any more? – No, our *values* were just too different, we couldn't agree on anything. *Fr.* valeur *(f)*
Dreaming ['dri:mɪŋ]	Traumzeit	
knowledge *(no pl)* ['nɒlɪdʒ]	Wissen; Kenntnisse	a piece of *knowledge* *knowledge* → to know
underground ['ʌndəgraʊnd]	unterirdisch	
soil [sɔɪl]	Erde; Boden	= the (brown) earth that plants grow in
track [træk]	Spur; Fährte	This morning we found the *tracks* of a large animal in our garden. But what animal exactly?

	common ['kɒmən]	gemeinsam	to have a *common* language to communicate; to have sth in *common* *common* ↔ separate; different
23	**foster** ['fɒstə]	Pflege-	A lot of Aboriginal children were placed with white *foster* families.
24	to **place** [pleɪs]	unterbringen	
	senior ['si:niə]	älter	At our school *senior* students help the younger ones.
	permission [pə'mɪʃn]	Erlaubnis; Genehmigung	There are many things a child needs his/her parents' *permission* for.
	disrespectful [ˌdɪsrɪ'spektfl]	respektlos	It's *disrespectful* to take something without asking first. *disrespectful* → respect → to respect
	elder ['eldə]	Älteste/-r	= old people in a community
	guardian ['gɑ:diən]	Hüter/-in; Wächter/-in	*guardian* → guard
	territory ['terɪtri]	Gebiet; Revier; Territorium	*Fr.* territoire
	childhood ['tʃaɪldhʊd]	Kindheit	When I was young, I was a happy child. I had a very happy *childhood*.
25	**anniversary** [ˌænɪ'vɜ:sri]	Jubiläum; Jahrestag	An *anniversary* is a day when you remember or celebrate sth that happened on the same date in the past.
	to **protest** [prə'test]	protestieren	! Be careful with the word stress. *to protest* → protest
26	**nomad** ['nəʊmæd]	Nomade/Nomadin	
	no longer [ˌnəʊ 'lɒŋgə]	nicht länger; nicht mehr	We can *no longer* go to that park. It's closed. = not any more

Skills: How to structure a radio news report

1	**attack** [ə'tæk]	Angriff; Überfall	*attack* → to attack
	full [fʊl]	ganz	Answer the questions. Write *full* sentences.
	to **be involved (in)** [bi‿ɪn'vɒlvd‿ɪn]	beteiligt sein (an); involviert sein (in); engagiert sein (in)	There was a terrible accident, but we don't yet know who *was involved*.
	newsreader ['nju:sˌri:də]	Nachrichtensprecher/-in	*newspaper* → news
2	**at the scene** [ˌət ðə 'si:n]	vor Ort	John is live *at the scene*.
	lifeguard ['laɪfgɑ:d]	Rettungsschwimmer/-in	
	to **prevent** [prɪ'vent]	verhindern; abhalten	The government has done everything it could to *prevent* new attacks.
	over to ... ['əʊvə tə]	weiter zu ...	That's all we know about the bushfires today. Now *over to* John Johnson for a look at sports.

Australia collocations

The outback
Aboriginal culture
bushwalking tours
great scenery
helpful survival training
huge distances
outback trails
partly uninhabitable
remote places

Sydney
beautiful beaches
cool hostels
interesting history
international visitors / travellers
multicultural festivals
spectacular scenery / sights
urban lifestyle

Aboriginal people
Aboriginal art
ancient traditions
Dreaming stories
Indigenous Australians
many different languages / tribes
sacred nature
Stolen Generations

Positive and negative aspects
(+) exotic animals
(+) multicultural society / festivals
(+) sparsely populated

(–) dangerous bushfires / rip currents
(–) deadly animals
(–) extreme climatic conditions

Write five sentences with five of the collocations.

Story: Nona and me

1	**guilty conscience** [ˌɡɪlti ˈkɒnʃns]	Schuldbewusstsein; schlechtes Gewissen	When I took my sister's smartphone to look at all her texts, I really had a *guilty conscience* afterwards.
	to **stand up for sb/sth** [ˌstænd‿ˈʌp fə]	jmdn./etw. verteidigen; für jmdn./etw. einstehen	Good friends *stand up for* each other.

glimpse [glɪms]	(kurzer/flüchtiger) Blick	Staying with a host family in a foreign country offers *glimpses* into family life that tourists normally don't get.
determined [dɪ'tɜ:mɪnd]	(fest) entschlossen; entschieden; zielstrebig	She's *determined* to be a big success in life.
upright ['ʌpraɪt]	aufrecht	
walk [wɔ:k]	Gang	You need to have an upright *walk* to be a model in a fashion show. *walk* → to walk
strength [streŋθ]	Stärke; Kraft	Are you sure you have the *strength* to play American football? Those guys are huge! *strength* → strong
rib [rɪb]	Rippe	When he fell down the stairs, he broke two *ribs*.
desperate ['desprət]	verzweifelt; hoffnungslos; ausweglos	*Fr.* désespéré/-e
to **sigh** [saɪ]	seufzen	People often *sigh* if they feel disappointed or tired.
to **get ready** [ˌget 'redi]	sich vorbereiten; sich fertig machen	Kids, *get ready* for school now!
to **grin** [grɪn]	grinsen	= to smile (with a big smile)
reluctant [rɪ'lʌktnt]	widerstrebend; widerwillig	He was *reluctant* to do what his dad told him, but he knew it would mean trouble if he didn't.
to **face** [feɪs]	anblicken; sich zuwenden	The teacher turned round to *face* the class.
federation [ˌfedr'eɪʃn]	Bundesstaat; Föderation	The US is a *federation* of 50 states.
to **raise one's eyes** [ˌreɪz wʌnz‿'aɪz]	den Blick heben; aufblicken; hochblicken	He *raised his eyes* just as the most beautiful girl he'd ever seen walked into the café.
scar [skɑ:]	Narbe	Careful, that's hot! If you burn your skin badly, it could leave a *scar*.
desk [desk]	Schreibtisch	In the classroom there are 20 *desks* for 20 students.
nod [nɒd]	Nicken	
to **nod** [nɒd]	nicken	= to say 'yes' with your head
enthusiastic [ɪnˌθju:zi'æstɪk]	enthusiastisch; begeistert	She wasn't *enthusiastic* about our plans for the weekend, but she'll join us, she said. *enthusiastic* ↔ bored
university [ˌju:nɪ'vɜ:səti]	Universität	Harvard is a very famous American *university*.
beat [bi:t]	Takt; Rhythmus	They clapped their hands to the *beat* of the music.
to **be related to** [bi rɪ'leɪtɪd tə]	verwandt sein mit	*Are* you *related to* the famous musician of the same name?
laughter ['lɑ:ftə]	Gelächter; Lachen	*laughter* → to laugh
soft [sɒft]	weich; sanft	*soft* ↔ hard
harmless ['hɑ:mləs]	harmlos; ungefährlich	Kangaroos aren't as *harmless* as they might look; they can kill with a hard kick to the head.
to **lean forward** [ˌli:n 'fɔ:wəd]	sich nach vorn lehnen	

	previous ['pri:viəs]	früher; vorherig; vorhergehend	the *previous* night = the night before *Lat.* praevius
	fingernail ['fɪŋgəneɪl]	Fingernagel	
	pale [peɪl]	blass	= light in colour, almost white *pale* ↔ dark
	to **shake** [ʃeɪk], **shook** [ʃʊk], **shaken** ['ʃeɪkn]	schütteln	to *shake* your head, to *shake* hands
	to **frown** [fraʊn]	die Stirn runzeln	His parents *frowned* when he told them about his plans.
	abrupt [ə'brʌpt]	abrupt	She turned round *abruptly* and left.
	ceiling ['si:lɪŋ]	Zimmerdecke; Decke	A room has four walls, a floor and a *ceiling*.
	fan [fæn]	Ventilator	
	armchair ['ɑ:mtʃeə]	Sessel	*armchair* → chair
	to **glance at** ['glɑ:ns‿ət]	einen Blick werfen auf; blicken auf	*to glance at* = to look at
	grateful ['greɪtfl]	dankbar	"Dear Sir or Madam, I would be *grateful* if you could send me …" *Lat.* gratus
3	**awkward** ['ɔ:kwəd]	peinlich; ungünstig; ungeschickt; unbeholfen	I often feel *awkward* in a group if I don't know anybody.

Text smart 1 A short film

Introduction

	key feature [ˌki: 'fi:tʃə]	Hauptmerkmal	= the most important aspect of sth
1	**clip** [klɪp]	Clip; Ausschnitt	I haven't watched the whole film, just a *clip*.
	visual ['vɪʒuəl]	visuell; optisch	*Visual* elements in a presentation are things like pictures or charts that help to illustrate your points.
2	**crew** [kru:]	Crew; Besatzung; Mannschaft; Team	The film *crew* was big, with more than 100 people.
	appearance [ə'pɪərns]	Erscheinung; Aussehen; Auftritt	*Appearance* is important for actors and models. *appearance* → to appear
	cast [kɑ:st]	Besetzung; Ensemble	What a great *cast*! There were a lot of famous actors in the film.
	supporting role [sə'pɔ:tɪŋ ˌrəʊl]	Nebenrolle	
	wide shot ['waɪd ʃɒt]	Totale *(Kameraeinstellung)*	Let's use a *wide shot* for this scene so we can see everything that's going on.

Station 1: A first look

3	**emotion** [ɪ'məʊʃn]	Gefühl; Emotion	If you can't show *emotion*, then being an actor is the wrong occupation.
5	**misery** *(no pl)* ['mɪzri]	Elend; Jammer; Not	We often see photos of people in *misery* in the news. *Lat.* miser, miserabilis
	uncomfortable [ʌn'kʌmftəbl]	unwohl; unbehaglich; unbe-quem	This café has the most *uncomfortable* chairs, don't you think? ! Be careful with the pronunciation. *uncomfortable* ↔ comfortable
	tear [tɪə]	Träne	When she heard the bad news, she couldn't hold back her *tears*.
6	**master** ['mɑːstə]	Herr/-in; Meister/-in	
	fate [feɪt]	Schicksal; Fügung; Vorsehung	= the things you can't control that will happen to you

Station 2: Key elements of films

9	**movement** ['muːvmənt]	Bewegung	*movement* → to move *Fr.* mouvement *(m)*
10	**flirty** ['flɜːti]	zum Flirten aufgelegt; kokett	I can't believe how *flirty* Emma is with MY boyfriend! Who does she think she is?!
	extremely [ɪk'striːmli]	sehr; äußerst	*extremely* = very
	annoyed [ə'nɔɪd]	verärgert	First I was just a bit *annoyed*, but then I got really angry.
	bitchy ['bɪtʃi]	gehässig; gemein	I can understand that you're annoyed, but it doesn't mean you have to be so *bitchy* to everyone!
	disgusted [dɪs'gʌstɪd]	angeekelt; angewidert	He was telling all these dirty jokes at the dinner table and everyone was totally *disgusted*.
	turned off [ˌtɜːnd‿'ɒf]	abgetörnt	She was really *turned off* when the boy she liked started talking about how all the girls want him.
11	**entire** [ɪn'taɪə]	gesamt; ganz; komplett	It wasn't just a bad day; it was the worst day in my *entire* life! *entire* = whole *Fr.* entier/entière
	context ['kɒntekst]	Kontext; Zusammenhang	If a quote is used out of *context*, it can cause misunderstandings.
	surroundings *(pl)* [sə'raʊndɪŋz]	Umgebung	*surroundings* = environment *surroundings* → to surround *(v)*
	to **establish** [ɪ'stæblɪʃ]	einführen	In a film or book, the main characters are usually *established* early in the storyline. *Fr.* établir

Station 3: How to structure film scripts

12	**onlooker** ['ɒnˌlʊkə]	Zuschauer/-in	= the people standing around and watching
	front [frʌnt]	Spitze; vorderer Bereich	The man is standing at the *front* of the queue.
	back [bæk]	Ende; hinterer Bereich	*back* ↔ front
	to **knock** [nɒk]	stoßen; schlagen	Penny *knocked* the boy's coffee out of his hand.

	to **introduce** [ˌɪntrəˈdju:s]	vorstellen	"Let me *introduce* you to my friend Peter: Peter, this is Sarah." ***Lat.*** introducere
	understanding [ˌʌndəˈstændɪŋ]	verständnisvoll	*understanding* → to understand
	hysterical [hɪˈsterɪkl]	hysterisch	He always laughs *hysterically* when he's nervous, he can't control it.
	rather [ˈrɑ:ðə]	ziemlich	It was *rather* embarrassing when the student told his teacher that the dog had eaten his homework. I mean, who would believe it?

Unit 2 The good life?

Introduction

1	**fulfilling** [fʊlˈfɪlɪŋ]	erfüllend; befriedigend	! Be careful with the spelling: full + fill = *fulfilling*
	materialistic [məˌtɪəriəˈlɪstɪk]	materialistisch	I'm not into owning too many things. I guess I'm not very *materialistic*.
	meaningful [ˈmi:nɪŋfl]	bedeutsam; wichtig	Whether something is *meaningful* or not depends on one's perspective; people see things differently.
	adventurous [ədˈventʃrəs]	abenteuerlich; unternehmungslustig; wagemutig; experimentierfreudig	My older sister has an *adventurous* lifestyle: She flies all over the world for her job. *adventurous* → adventure
3	**satisfaction** [ˌsætɪsˈfækʃn]	Zufriedenheit	For my job *satisfaction*, money isn't the most important thing. = feeling of happiness about sth sb has done
	boredom [ˈbɔ:dəm]	Langeweile	*boredom* → boring → bored
	curiosity [ˌkjʊəriˈɒsəti]	Neugier	*Curiosity* definitely plays a role in my life: I always want to try something new. ***Fr.*** curiosité *(f)*; ***Lat.*** curiositas *(f)*
	desirable [dɪˈzaɪərəbl]	wünschenswert; erstrebenswert	Good manners are *desirable* if you want to make a good impression on a first date.

Station 1: Best summer ever!

1	to **encourage** [ɪnˈkʌrɪdʒ]	unterstützen; ermutigen	My dad *encouraged* me to apply for this job. ***Fr.*** encourager
	to **raise** [reɪz]	(er)wecken *(Interesse)*; aufwerfen *(Fragen)*	to *raise* interest, to *raise* a problem/question
	opportunity [ˌɒpəˈtju:nəti]	Chance; Gelegenheit; Möglichkeit	= a great chance to do sth
	assistant counsellor [əˌsɪstnt ˈkaʊnslə]	Hilfsbetreuer/-in	

	senior counsellor [ˌsi:niə 'kaʊnslə]	leitender Betreuer/leitende Betreuerin; ranghohe/-r Minister/-in	*senior counsellor* ↔ assistant counsellor
	to **be passionate about sth** [bi 'pæʃnət əˌbaʊt]	etw. leidenschaftlich gern tun; eine Leidenschaft für etw. haben; für etw. brennen	If you*'re passionate about* sth, then you don't just like it, you love it!
	testimonial [ˌtestɪ'məʊniəl]	Erfahrungsbericht	Go online and read some of the people's *testimonials* about that company. ***Lat.*** testimonium *(nt)*
2	**qualification** [ˌkwɒlɪfɪ'keɪʃn]	Qualifikation; Befähigung; Abschluss; Schulabschluss	What *qualifications* do you need for a job as a sales assistant?
	to **require** [rɪ'kwaɪə]	benötigen; erfordern	If you *require* sth, it's necessary for you to have it. *to require* = to need
	applicant ['æplɪkənt]	Bewerber/-in	In a letter of application, the *applicant* applies for a job. *applicant* → to apply → application
	position [pə'zɪʃn]	Stelle; Position	*position* = job
	to **be supposed to** *(+ inf)* [bi sə'pəʊzd tə]	sollen	If you *are supposed to do sth*, you are expected to do it.
	to **set a good example** [set‿ə ˌgʊd‿ɪg'zɑ:mpl]	ein Vorbild sein	Parents are supposed to *set a good example* for their children.
	at all times [ˌət‿ɔ:l 'taɪmz]	immer; jederzeit; stets	*at all times* = always
	to **be expected to** *(+ inf)* [bi ɪk'spektɪd tə]	sollen	When there's an accident, you*'re expected to* call the police.
	to **be a team player** [ˌbi‿ə 'ti:m ˌpleɪə]	gern im Team arbeiten	Some jobs can only be done by people who *are team players*.
	responsibility [rɪˌspɒnsə'bɪləti]	Verantwortung; Aufgabe	That job includes a lot of interesting areas of *responsibility*. *responsibility* → responsible
	CV *(Curriculum Vitae)* [ˌsi:'vi: (kəˌrɪkjələm 'vi:taɪ)]	Lebenslauf	A *CV* describes what jobs and activities you've done in your life so far, what exams you've passed, etc. *CV (BE)* = résumé *(AE)*
	application letter [ˌæplɪ'keɪʃn ˌletə]	Bewerbungsschreiben	If you want a job, you first have to send in an *application letter* and a CV.
3	**gender** ['dʒendə]	Geschlecht	*gender* differences/roles
	employer [ɪm'plɔɪə]	Arbeitgeber/-in	The company my mum works for is one of the region's biggest *employers*. *employer* → to employ sb → employee
	focused ['fəʊkəst]	zielgerichtet	Turning off your phone may help you to stay *focused* on your work. *focused* → focus → to focus (on)
	all-rounder [ɔ:l'raʊndə]	Alleskönner/-in; Multitalent	An *all-rounder* doesn't focus on just one special talent.
	to **stand out (from)** [ˌstænd‿'aʊt]	sich abheben (von); herausragen (aus)	If you don't *stand out from* the hundreds of applicants, you won't get the job.
	weakness ['wi:knəs]	Schwäche	*weakness* ↔ strength *weakness* → weak

	stereotype ['steriəʊtaɪp]	Klischee; Stereotyp	A *stereotype* is an (often wrong) idea about what you expect a person to be like before you even know him/her.
4	**gender stereotyping** ['dʒendə ˌsteriəʊtaɪpɪŋ]	geschlechtsspezifische Klischees	It's *gender stereotyping* to expect all women to be good in the kitchen and all men to love fast cars.
	to **consider** [kən'sɪdə]	betrachten; erwägen	In Britain people *consider* it bad manners to take sth without saying 'thank you'. = to regard sth as *Fr.* considérer
	engineering [ˌendʒɪ'nɪərɪŋ]	Technik; Maschinenbau	*engineering* → engineer
	GCSE *(= General Certificate of Secondary Education)* [ˌdʒiːsiːes'iː (ˌdʒenrl səˌtɪfɪkət‿əv ˌsekəndri‿edʒʊ'keɪʃn)]	*allg. Abschluss der weiterführenden Schulen in GB*	
	to **list** [lɪst]	auflisten; nennen	Please *list* all your strengths and weaknesses.
	healthcare ['helθkeə]	Gesundheitsversorgung	I work in the *healthcare* industry. I'm a nurse. – Oh, me too!
	female ['fiːmeɪl]	weiblich	
	construction worker [kən'strʌkʃn ˌwɜːkə]	Bauarbeiter/-in	*Construction workers* build roads, buildings, bridges, etc.
	profession [prə'feʃn]	Beruf	What *professions* pay the most?
	male [meɪl]	männlich	*male* ↔ female
	to **associate** [ə'səʊʃieɪt]	assoziieren; verbinden	What do you *associate* with healthcare professions?
	(business) executive ['bɪznɪs ɪgˌzekjətɪv]	Geschäftsführer/-in; Manager/-in; gehobene Führungskraft	The *executives* all have their offices on the top floor of our building.
	firefighter ['faɪəˌfaɪtə]	Feuerwehrmann/-frau	A lot of young boys say they want to become *firefighters* one day.
	sales assistant ['seɪlz‿əˌsɪstnt]	Verkäufer/-in	
6	**nationality** [ˌnæʃn'æləti]	Nationalität; Staatsangehörigkeit	He was born in Pakistan, but he grew up in Britain; his *nationality* is British. *nationality* → nation → national
	comprehensive school [kɒmprɪ'hensɪv ˌskuːl]	Gesamtschule	
	organiser ['ɔːgənaɪzə]	Organisator/-in	*organiser* → to organise → organisation
	hard-working [ˌhɑːd'wɜːkɪŋ]	fleißig	*hard-working* ↔ lazy
	people skills *(pl)* ['piːpl ˌskɪlz]	soziale Kompetenz	If you have good *people skills*, you communicate well and make people feel comfortable.
	reference ['refrns]	Referenz; Referenzschreiben	A *reference* is a letter written by sb who knows you and thinks you'd be able to do a job well.
	request [rɪ'kwest]	Anfrage; Nachfrage	I'll send the company more information on *request*.
7	**common** ['kɒmən]	üblich; verbreitet; gängig	
8	**with reference to** [wɪð 'refrns tə]	bezugnehmend auf	! = a phrase typical only for formal letters *with reference to* → to refer to sth
	hopefully ['həʊpfli]	hoffentlich	I really want this job, so *hopefully* I'll get it!

therefore ['ðeəfɔ:]	deshalb; deswegen; daher; somit	Miss Ellis, I'm sorry, but the quality of your work has been a problem, again. *Therefore*, I'm going to give your project to somebody else.
moreover [mɔ:r'əʊvə]	überdies; außerdem	
addition [ə'dɪʃn]	Zusatz; Ergänzung	Let's give her the job. – Yeah, she'd be a great *addition* to our team. *addition* → to add
(job) interview ['dʒɒb ˌɪntəvju:]	Vorstellungsgespräch	I applied for a job and now I've been invited for an *interview* on Thursday.
Yours sincerely [ˌjɔ:z sɪn'sɪəli]	Mit freundlichen Grüßen	This can be used at the end of a formal letter.
signature ['sɪgnətʃə]	Unterschrift	Is THAT your *signature*?! Nobody can read it. Practise a bit before you sign your application! *signature* → to sign *Fr.* signature *(f)*
enclosure [ɪn'kləʊʒə]	Anlage; Beilage	= sth you include with a letter
attachment [ə'tætʃmənt]	Anhang	= sth you attach to an e-mail
9 **furthermore** [ˌfɜ:ðə'mɔ:]	überdies; außerdem	= a formal word you can use to introduce another point that helps your argument
nevertheless [ˌnevəðə'les]	trotzdem; dennoch; nichtsdestoweniger	
unfortunately [ʌn'fɔ:tʃnətli]	leider; unglücklicherweise	*Unfortunately*, I can't come to your birthday party. Sorry!

Frequently-used sentence adverbs

Remember that commenting adverbs have to do with one's personal view; one uses them to comment. Linking adverbs, on the other hand, are for factual statements.

commenting		**linking**	
actually	really	additionally	in general
definitely	seriously	after all	in the end
hopefully	surely	finally	moreover
luckily	typically	furthermore	nevertheless
normally	unfortunately	however	otherwise
originally	usually	in addition to	overall
personally		in fact	therefore

Write four sentences using two commenting and two linking adverbs.

Station 2: The cocoa controversy

cocoa ['kəʊkəʊ]	Kakao	There would be no chocolate without *cocoa*.
controversy ['kɒntrəvɜ:si]	Kontroverse; Auseinandersetzung	to create/to cause *controversy* = a public discussion that features very different and often emotional opinions
12 **quantity** ['kwɒntɪti]	Menge; Quantität	Chocolate is sold in large *quantities* in Europe.
cosmetics *(pl)* [kɒz'metɪks]	Kosmetik	! You can't use this noun in the singular.

	to **provide** [prə'vaɪd]	liefern; bereit stellen	They *provided* us with plenty of food every day. 1. to give sth that is needed; 2. to make available ***Lat.*** providēre
	poverty line ['pɒvəti ˌlaɪn]	Armutsgrenze	There are more and more people who live below the *poverty line*.
	poverty ['pɒvəti]	Armut	*poverty* → poor
	physical ['fɪzɪkl]	physisch; körperlich	Construction workers do hard *physical* work.
	to **harvest** ['hɑ:vɪst]	ernten	
	bean [bi:n]	Bohne	Harvesting cocoa *beans* is a difficult and dangerous job.
	to **force** [fɔ:s]	zwingen	If you *force* sb to do sth, you make them do it.
	plantation [plæn'teɪʃn]	Plantage	In the southern states of the US, there used to be a lot of *plantations* which required the work of many, many slaves.
	to **justify** ['dʒʌstɪfaɪ]	rechtfertigen	Can anything *justify* child labour?
	exhausted [ɪg'zɔ:stɪd]	erschöpft	After running a marathon, they were *exhausted*.
	to **chop** [tʃɒp]	hacken; klein schneiden	Please *chop* the vegetables for the soup.
	pod [pɒd]	Hülse; Schote	
	machete [mə'ʃeti]	Machete; Buschmesser	= a very big knife ! Be careful with the pronunciation.
	to **dump** [dʌmp]	abladen	
	onto ['ɒntə]	auf … hinauf	They dumped the containers *onto* a large truck.
	trade [treɪd]	Handel	Are these cocoa beans from fair *trade*?
15	**march** [mɑ:tʃ]	Marsch; Kundgebung	We're organising a protest *march* against child labour.
	to **catch oneself doing sth** [kætʃ]	sich (selbst) dabei ertappen, wie …	During lessons I *caught myself dreaming* of our next holiday.
16	**commitment** [kə'mɪtmənt]	Bindung; Verpflichtung; Engagement	Showing social *commitment* helps others, but it's meaningful for your own life as well. = a plan to do sth or to support sb
	volunteer [ˌvɒlən'tɪə]	Freiwillige/-r; Ehrenamtliche/-r	She works as a *volunteer* at a hospital.
	selfish ['selfɪʃ]	selbstsüchtig; egoistisch	Some people say it's *selfish* to do charity work only to make your CV look better. What do you think?
17	**involvement** [ɪn'vɒlvmənt]	Engagement; Beteiligung	How much *involvement* do you have time for: once or twice a week? *involvement* → to be involved (in)
	to **volunteer** [ˌvɒlən'tɪə]	eine ehrenamtliche Tätigkeit übernehmen	I *volunteered* to help with our school's clothing drive. *to volunteer* → volunteer *(n)*
	religious [rɪ'lɪdʒəs]	religiös; gläubig	***Fr.*** religieux/religieuse; ***Lat.*** religiosus
	the elderly [ði 'eldəli]	ältere Menschen; Senioren	= a more polite word for 'old' (when you speak about people)
	the homeless [ðə 'həʊmləs]	Obdachlose	*the homeless* → home
	the disabled [ðə dɪ'seɪbld]	Behinderte	I can't decide if I want to volunteer my time for the homeless or *the disabled*; they all need help.
	volunteer [ˌvɒlən'tɪə]	freiwillig; ehrenamtlich	*volunteer* → to volunteer → volunteer *(n)*

gap year ['gæp ˌjɪə]	*ein Jahr Auszeit (zwischen Schule und Ausbildung/ Studium), das oft für einen freiwilligen ökologischen oder sozialen Dienst genutzt wird*	In many European countries it's now common to spend a *gap year* abroad.

Adjectives as nouns

You can use some adjectives as nouns by adding the definite article 'the'.

One way to show social commitment is offering services for **the disabled**.
What does your community do for **the elderly**?
My aunt is member of a volunteer group that offers hot meals to **the homeless**.

Eine Möglichkeit, soziales Engagement zu zeigen, ist, Dienste für **Behinderte** anzubieten.
Was tut deine Gemeinde für **ältere Menschen**?
Meine Tante ist Mitglied einer Gruppe von Freiwilligen, die **Obdachlosen** warmes Essen anbietet.

the poor | the rich | the young

Write sentences for the three other nouns.

Station 3: I do remember how it feels ...

wisdom *(no pl)* ['wɪzdəm]	Weisheit; Klugheit	*Wisdom* comes with age and experience.
carpenter ['kɑːpntə]	Schreiner/-in; Zimmermann	Being a *carpenter* is great for me because I'm able to work with my hands.
not only ... but (also) [nɒt‿əʊnli bʌt‿'ɔːlsəʊ]	nicht nur ... sondern (auch)	*Not only* did I lose my passport in Australia, *but* I *also* lost my phone! Great holiday.
to **stack** [stæk]	stapeln	*Stacking* wood all day isn't my idea of job satisfaction!
to **go by** [ˌgəʊ‿'baɪ]	vorbeigehen	School days never *go by* fast enough.
left over [left‿'əʊvə]	übrig	At the end of a month I never have any pocket money *left over*.
pay [peɪ]	Lohn; Gehalt	= the money a person receives for doing their job *pay* → to pay
tax [tæks]	Steuer; Abgabe	Without *taxes* there would be no public schools, police or firefighters, for example.
wage [weɪdʒ]	Lohn	*wage* = pay
patient ['peɪʃnt]	geduldig	*Fr.* patient/-e
rarely ['reəli]	selten	= not often
top [tɒp]	Spitzen-; oberster; bester	A *top* restaurant is a very good restaurant.

	law [lɔː]	Gesetz; Recht	If you break the *law*, you may get into serious trouble. *Fr.* loi *(f)*
21	**know-it-all** ['nəʊɪtɔːl]	Besserwisser/-in	I can't believe you don't know what the capital of Australia is! Everyone knows it's Canberra. – Don't be such a *know-it-all*!
	brief [briːf]	kurz	Has Mrs Chen told you about the new project yet? – No, I only saw her *briefly* this morning, there was no time.
22	to **limit to** ['lɪmɪt tə]	limitieren auf; begrenzen auf, beschränken auf	The guided tour *is limited to* 15 people. *to limit* → limit
23	**investment** [ɪn'vesmənt]	Einlage; Beteiligung; Investition	She's got a great business idea but needs an *investment* of £30.000 to get started.
	buddy *(infml)* ['bʌdi]	Kumpel	*buddy* = mate
	to **be made up of/from** [bi meɪd‿'ʌp‿əv/frəm]	zusammengesetzt sein aus; bestehen aus	What *is* this device *made up of*?
	toothbrush ['tuːθbrʌʃ]	Zahnbürste	
24	**no sooner** [nəʊ 'suːnə]	kaum	*No sooner* had I told him my secret than the whole school knew! What a friend.
25	**colleague** ['kɒliːg]	Kollege/Kollegin	I share my office with three *colleagues*.
	to **suit sb** [suːt]	(zu) jmdm. passen; jmdm. stehen	Which colour *suits me* better: black or grey?

Skills: Making a good impression

1	**candidate** ['kændɪdət]	Bewerber/-in; Kandidat/-in	The ideal *candidate* should be able to take on responsibility, but also be a team player. *Fr.* candidat/-e *(m, f)*
2	to **emphasise** ['emfəsaɪz]	betonen	At job interviews, it's important to *emphasise* what you do well.
	tricky ['trɪki]	schwierig; kompliziert	Be prepared for *tricky* questions at job interviews. *tricky* → trick

Unit task: Job interviews for a summer camp

	helper ['helpə]	Helfer/-in	*helper* → to help → help

Story: The Giver

	giver ['gɪvə]	Geber/-in; Spender/-in	*giver* → to give
	to **regulate** ['regjəleɪt]	regeln; regulieren	= to control sth by introducing rules
	assignment [ə'saɪnmənt]	Aufgabe; Auftrag; Mission	Her boss is going to give her a tricky new *assignment*. = a piece of work that you must do for school or for a job
	destiny ['destɪni]	Schicksal; Fügung; Vorsehung	*destiny* = fate *Fr.* destin *(m)*
1	to **assign** [ə'saɪn]	zuordnen; übertragen	We're going to do group work, but don't divide up into groups yourselves: I'll *assign* you to your groups. *to assign* → assignment
	to **acknowledge** [ək'nɒlɪdʒ]	anerkennen; einräumen	= to admit or accept that sth is true or that a situation exists

	to **fit in** [ˌfɪt‿ˈɪn]	hineinpassen; sich einfügen	We've got a new neighbour who I think will really *fit in* well.
	to **standardize** *(AE)* [ˈstændədaɪz]	standardisieren; vereinheitlichen	How boring would it be if everyone's behavior *was standardized*?
	to **honor** *(AE)* [ˈɒnə]	ehren; würdigen; auszeichnen	In some cultures, it is very important to *honor* the elderly. ***Fr.*** honorer; ***Lat.*** honorare
	to **determine** [dɪˈtɜːmɪn]	bestimmen; ermitteln	How well one performs at work will *determine* how far one will go at that company. *to determine* = to influence strongly = to find out ***Fr.*** déterminer
	throughout [θruˈaʊt]	während; überall in	! Be careful with the spelling.
	satisfied [ˈsætɪsfaɪd]	zufrieden; befriedigt	He just got a text message and now he's got a very *satisfied* look on his face. Hm … *satisfied* → satisfaction
	apology [əˈpɒlədʒi]	Entschuldigung	After the argument she accepted her friend's *apology*. *apology* → to apologise
	to **select** [sɪˈlekt]	auswählen; aussuchen	= a more formal word for 'to choose' ***Lat.*** seligere: selectum
	receiver [rɪˈsiːvə]	Empfänger/-in; *hier:* Hüter/-in	*receiver* → to receive
2	**sheet** [ʃiːt]	Blatt	Write the facts on a *sheet* of paper.
3	**session** [ˈseʃn]	Sitzung; Stunde	
	ability [əˈbɪləti]	Fähigkeit	At the camp he showed his *abilities* as a leader. *ability* → to be able
	to **transmit** [trænzˈmɪt]	übertragen	
	sir [sɜː]	mein Herr *(Anrede)*	
	impatient [ɪmˈpeɪʃnt]	ungeduldig	= not being able to wait *impatient* ↔ patient ***Fr.*** impatient/-e
4	**laugh** [lɑːf]	Lachen	*laugh* → to laugh
	distant [ˈdɪstnt]	entfernt; distanziert	Most of my memories from childhood are very *distant*, but some feel like it was yesterday. *distant* → distance
	sameness [ˈseɪmnəs]	Gleichheit; Gleichförmigkeit	*sameness* → the same
	to **slow down** [ˌsləʊ ˈdaʊn]	langsamer werden; bremsen	*Slow down*, please, there are children in the street.
	ordinary [ˈɔːdnri]	gewöhnlich; normal	I thought he was just an *ordinary* boy from school. I had no idea he was a famous actor. ! False friend: *ordinary* ≠ ordinär ***Fr.*** ordinaire
	curious [ˈkjʊəriəs]	neugierig	My little brother always tries to listen to my private conversations. He's very *curious*. *curious* → curiosity ***Fr.*** curieux/curieuse; ***Lat.*** curiosus
	to **make a choice** [ˌmeɪk‿ə ˈtʃɔɪs]	eine Wahl treffen	*to make a choice* = to choose

to **matter** ['mætə]	von Bedeutung sein; etw. ausmachen	Some people say it doesn't *matter* how rich you are, it's what you do with your life that really *matters*.
to **dare** [deə]	wagen	Nobody *dares* to go there. = Everybody is too frightened to go there.
mate [meɪt]	Partner/-in	! '*Mate*' is used as a biological term here.
6 **literature** ['lɪtrətʃə]	Literatur	

Jobs

... in business / economy
auditor
(business) executive
spokesperson

... in education
principal; head teacher
professor
teacher

... in sales
assistant
sales assistant
travel agent

... in service
attendant
(camp) counsellor
detective
firefighter
flight attendant
guard
guide
lifeguard
pilot
police officer
postman
private detective
waiter

... in film / entertainment / media
actor
advertiser
agent
director
DJ
extra
filmmaker
journalist; reporter
model
producer
publisher

... in healthcare / care
au pair
doctor
nurse

... in farming / with animals
farmer
vet

... in official functions
governor
historian
official
politician
president

... in construction
architect
construction worker
electrician
engineer
mechanic
miner
plumber

... in science / technology / IT areas
astronaut
IT manager
scientist
web designer

... in creative areas
artist
dancer
entertainer
(fashion/web) designer
musician
photographer
scriptwriter

Students getting job information at a Job Fair

general terms
businessman
employee
employer
entrepreneur
founder
worker

What job would you like to do in the future? Write a short text.

Collocations: Jobs and life

hard / difficult / exhausting / well-paid / traditional	job / profession
fulfilling / adventurous / fun / boring	lifestyle / job / career
materialistic / meaningful / desirable	life / lifestyle
(un)qualified / (ir)responsible / (un)reliable / (un)focused	applicant / worker / candidate
passionate / confident / hard-working / (im)patient / interested / independent	person / character
outgoing / spontaneous / creative	personality
specific / practical / useless	qualifications
well-developed / good	skills

Text smart 2 Informative texts

Introduction

2	**earthquake** ['ɜ:θkweɪk]	Erdbeben	*earthquake* → earth
	review [rɪ'vju:]	Kritik	After the first night of a new play, there are *reviews* in the newspapers.
	criticism ['krɪtɪsɪzm]	Kritik	*criticism* → critical

Station 1: How to: Write a text summary

3	**entitled** [ɪn'taɪtld]	mit dem Titel	He read a novel *entitled* ***Room***. *entitled* → title
	around [ə'raʊnd]	ungefähr; etwa	Only *around* 200 people were at the concert.
	enslavement [ɪn'sleɪvmənt]	Versklavung	*enslavement* → slave
	to **be unable to do sth** [bi‿ʌn'eɪbl tə]	unfähig sein, etw. zu tun; nicht in der Lage sein, etw. zu tun	On nice sunny days I'*m unable to focus* on my homework. *to be unable to* ↔ to be able to
	to **conclude** [kən'klu:d]	enden; schließen; schlussfolgern	*to conclude* → conclusion
5	**journalist** ['dʒɜ:nlɪst]	Journalist/-in	A *journalist* writes for a newspaper.
	injured ['ɪndʒəd]	verletzt	*injured* → injury
	irrelevant [ɪ'reləvnt]	irrelevant; nicht von Bedeutung	= not important
6	**study** ['stʌdi]	Studie; Untersuchung	Is there a *study* about how sleep influences your health?
	in particular [ˌɪn pə'tɪkjələ]	im besonderen	We should all pay more attention to our 'body clock', *in particular* teenagers.
	biological [ˌbaɪə'lɒdʒɪkl]	biologisch	*biological* → biology
	deprivation [ˌdeprɪ'veɪʃn]	Entbehrung; Entzug	Sleep *deprivation* is bad enough, but chocolate *deprivation*? To me, that's much worse!

currently ['kʌrntli]	momentan	= now; at this moment in time
to **recruit** [rɪ'kru:t]	rekrutieren; anwerben; einstellen	Soldiers *are recruited* to the army.
cycle ['saɪkl]	Zyklus; Kreislauf	There are four seasons in the *cycle* of a year.
rise [raɪz]	Anstieg; Zunahme	There's a *rise* in the world's population every year.
fall [fɔ:l]	Abnahme	*fall* ↔ rise
gene [dʒi:n]	Gen	Our *genes* determine our lives in many ways.
cognitive ['kɒgnətɪv]	kognitiv	= referring to the mind
performance [pə'fɔ:məns]	Leistung	Most people's cognitive *performance* is better in the morning than in the afternoon.
metabolism [mə'tæblɪzm]	Stoffwechsel	
and so on [ənd 'səʊ‿ɒn]	und so weiter	I love animals like dogs, cats, horses, rabbits, guinea pigs, *and so on*.
mismatch ['mɪsmætʃ]	Missverhältnis	I'm sorry, Ryan, but there's a *mismatch* between what you say and what you do.
well-suited (to doing sth) [ˌwel'su:tɪd]	geeignet (für/um zu); passend (für)	I hate the sight of blood. I'm not *well-suited* to being a doctor.
to **rise** [raɪz]	aufstehen	= a more formal way to say 'to get up'
deprived [dɪ'praɪvd]	beraubt; entzogen	*deprived* → deprivation
well-known [ˌwel'nəʊn]	(wohl) bekannt	My uncle is a *well-known* scientist.
researcher [rɪ'sɜ:tʃə]	Forscher/-in	*researcher* → to research → research
evidence *(no pl)* ['evɪdns]	Beweis; Beleg; Beweismaterial	Is there any *evidence* he's a criminal? *Fr.* évidence *(f)*
to **point to** ['pɔɪnt tə]	deuten auf; hindeuten auf; zeigen auf	Everything we know *points to* that result.
outcome ['aʊtkʌm]	Ergebnis; Resultat	*outcome* = result

Station 2: How to: Write a text analysis

7 to **relate to** [rɪ'leɪt tə]	nachvollziehen; sich identifizieren mit; verstehen	I can't *relate to* the arguments in the text. I see it differently.
objective [əb'dʒektɪv]	objektiv	= not influenced by any personal opinion
scientific [ˌsaɪən'tɪfɪk]	wissenschaftlich; naturwissenschaftlich	*scientific* → science → scientist *Fr.* scientifique
to **aim to do sth** [eɪm]	anstreben; abzielen auf	What do you *aim to do* in life?
plenty of ['plenti‿əv]	eine Menge	*plenty of* food = lots of food
to **quote** [kwəʊt]	zitieren	The journalist *quoted* an expert from the police. *to quote* → quote
balance ['bæləns]	Gleichgewicht	In the article he finds a good *balance* between scientific and normal language. *Fr.* balance *(f)*
relevant ['reləvnt]	relevant; von Bedeutung	*relevant* ↔ irrelevant

Across cultures 2 The language of tolerance and respect

	tolerance ['tɒlrns]	Toleranz	*Fr.* tolérance *(f)*
1	**goat** [gəʊt]	Ziege	
	beyond [bi'ɒnd]	jenseits; über … hinaus	If you look just *beyond* the lake, you'll see our house.
2	to **free** [fri:]	befreien	I wish I could *free* those poor kids who have to work on cocoa plantations. *to free* → free → freedom
	various ['veəriəs]	verschieden; verschiedenartig	There are *various* options of how to do this task.
	prejudice ['predʒədɪs]	Vorurteil	= a negative opinion or feeling
3	**mainstream** ['meɪnstrɪ:m]	Masse; Durchschnitt; Massen-; Durchschnitts-	I don't like what everybody else likes, that's boring. I'm not into the *mainstream*.
	to **be prejudiced against sb/sth** [bi 'predʒədɪst əˌgenst]	voreingenommen sein gegenüber jmdm./etw.	*to be prejudiced against* → prejudice
	race [reɪs]	Rasse	
	to **provoke** [prə'vəʊk]	provozieren; hervorrufen	The president's speech *provoked* a lot of protest. *Lat.* provocare
	willingly ['wɪlɪŋli]	gern; freiwillig	
	unwillingly [ʌn'wɪlɪŋli]	ungern; widerwillig	
	diversity [daɪ'vɜ:səti]	Vielfalt; Verschiedenheit	We speak of cultural *diversity* when people of different races, nationalities, languages, sexual orientations and religions live in the same community.
	street fair ['stri:t feə]	Straßenfest	I love all the different kinds of food and music at *street fairs*.
	pedestrian [pɪ'destriən]	Fußgänger/-in; Fußgänger-	You won't find as many *pedestrian* zones in America as you can find in Europe.
	kiss [kɪs]	Kuss	When they said goodbye, she gave him a *kiss*.
4	**respectful** [rɪ'spektfl]	respektvoll	*respectful* → respect *(n)* → to respect *(v)*
	privacy ['prɪvəsi]	Privatsphäre	You want people to respect your *privacy*, so it's only fair to respect theirs.
	to **assume** [ə'sju:m]	annehmen	You can't *assume* everybody shares your likes and dislikes.
	acceptable [ək'septəbl]	akzeptabel; annehmbar	*acceptable* → to accept *Fr.* acceptable
5	to **bring up** [ˌbrɪŋ_'ʌp]	zur Sprache bringen	During the class discussion their teacher *brought up* all the problems there were among the students.
	same-sex [ˌseɪm'seks]	gleichgeschlechtlich	Many countries, including quite a few in Europe, do a lot for *same-sex* rights. Some do very little.
	lesbian ['lezbiən]	lesbisch; Lesbe	
	straight [streɪt]	heterosexuell	*straight* ↔ gay/lesbian
	to **come out** [ˌkʌm_'aʊt]	sich outen	Her parents never really knew much about gays or lesbians, but when Lisa *came out* they had no problem with it at all.

8 **sensitive** ['sensɪtɪv]	sensibel; empfindsam; heikel	1. If you're *sensitive*, you're aware of other people's feelings. 2. A *sensitive* person can get annoyed very easily if sb says the wrong thing.
problematic [ˌprɒblə'mætɪk]	problematisch; schwierig	*problematic* → problem *Fr.* problématique
vulgar ['vʌlgə]	vulgär; gewöhnlich	He always tells really dirty jokes; he's so *vulgar*. *vulgar* = rude
to **embarrass** [ɪm'bærəs]	in Verlegenheit bringen	*to embarrass* → embarrassing → embarrassed
to **spread** [spred], **spread** [spred], **spread** [spred]	(sich) verbreiten	If sth *spreads*, it reaches a larger and larger area or more and more people.
horrible ['hɒrəbl]	schrecklich; furchtbar	*horrible* = terrible = awful *horrible* → horror
rumour ['ru:mə]	Gerücht	There are *rumours* that she's left him. – Well, don't believe everything you hear. = sth people say about sb that might not be true *Fr.* rumeur *(f)*
to **take sth the wrong way** [ˌteɪk‿ðə rɒŋ 'weɪ]	etw. falsch auffassen; etw. in den falschen Hals bekommen	He *took* my joke *the wrong way*.
to **offend** [ə'fend]	beleidigen; verletzen	It really *offends* me when you make jokes about black people. My best friend is black, and anyway, it just isn't acceptable to talk like that, in my opinion.

Word families

noun	adjective(s)	verb(s)	noun with prefix	adjective with prefix
tolerance	tolerant	to tolerate; to be tolerant; to show tolerance	intolerance	intolerant
respect	respectful	to respect; to show respect	disrespect	disrespectful
fairness	fair	to be fair	unfairness	unfair
embarrassment	embarrassed / embarrassing	to embarrass		
offence	offensive	to offend		
prejudice		to show prejudice		
	acceptable	to accept; to be acceptable		
	appropriate	to be appropriate		
racism	racist	to be racist		

Unit 3 California dreaming

Introduction

	skatepark ['skeɪtpɑ:k]	Skateboardanlage	*skatepark* → to skate → skates
	lounge [laʊndʒ]	Lounge; Aufenthaltsraum	
	headquarters *(pl)* [ˌhed'kwɔ:təz]	Zentrale; Hauptsitz	Google *headquarters* are in Silicon Valley. ! Only used in the plural form.
2	**skateboarder** ['skeɪtbɔ:də]	Skateboardfahrer/-in	*skateboarder* → skateboard → skateboarding
3	**tendency** ['tendənsi]	Tendenz	For years, trends from California have had a *tendency* to spread quickly. *Fr.* tendance *(f)*
	Mexican ['meksɪkn]	mexikanisch; Mexikanisch; aus Mexiko; Mexikaner/-in	*Mexicans* speak Spanish.
	pot [pɒt]	Topf	We need new *pots* for our plants.
	reason ['ri:zn]	Vernunft; Verstand	*reason* ↔ emotion *Fr.* raison *(f)*
	governor ['gʌvnə]	Gouverneur/-in	In the US each state has its own *governor*. *governor* → government
	to **observe** [əb'zɜ:v]	beobachten; beachten; befolgen	Dolphins were *observed* near the coast yesterday. *Fr.* observer

Station 1: Hollywood hopes

aspiring [ə'spaɪrɪŋ]	aufstrebend	= working hard to be successful
luck [lʌk]	Glück	He's going to try his *luck* in Hollywood.
to **stroll** [strəʊl]	schlendern; bummeln; spazieren	= to walk in a relaxed way
that way [ˌðæt 'weɪ]	so; auf diese Weise	Sorry, but it doesn't work *that way* in the entertainment business.
glitz and glamor *(AE) (no pl)* [ˌglɪts‿n‿'glæmə]	Glanz und Glamour	Many young actors in Hollywood hope for a life of *glitz and glamor*, but reality is often very different. *glamor* → glamorous
to **keep one's head above water** [ˌki:p wʌnz ˌhed‿əbʌv 'wɔ:tə]	sich über Wasser halten	Entertaining tourists is just a job to *keep my head above water*.
to **showcase one's talent** [ˌʃəʊkeɪs wʌnz 'tælənt]	sein Talent unter Beweis stellen	The video *showcased their talent* as entertainers, but not as singers. *to showcase* = to present
lucky day [ˌlʌki 'deɪ]	Glückstag	This is my *lucky day*: I've just found 100 dollars.
cattle call *(AE)* ['kætl ˌkɔ:l]	Vorspielen; Vorsingen	*cattle call* = audition
wannabe *(infml)* ['wɒnəbi]	Möchtegern; Möchtegern-	You can find *wannabe* stars everywhere in Hollywood.
to **pack up** ['pæk‿ʌp]	zusammenpacken	= to put your things in a bag before you go away

	to **chalk sth up to experience** [ˌtʃɔ:kˍʌp tə ɪk'spɪəriəns]	etw. als Erfahrung verbuchen	She's gone to at least 100 auditions so far and still hasn't gotten a role. She just *chalks it up to experience*.
	premiere ['premieə]	Premiere; Uraufführung	! Be careful with the pronunciation.
	to **cause a stir** [ˌkɔ:zˍə 'stɜ:]	für Aufsehen sorgen	She *caused a stir* when she fell down on the red carpet.
	RV park *(AE)* [ˌɑ:'vi: ˌpɑ:k]	Campingplatz	
	to **shoot** [ʃu:t]	drehen *(Film)*	At the school's Film Club we *shot* a film last year.
	to **explode** [ɪk'spləʊd]	explodieren	In action films cars *explode* all the time.
	trailer *(AE)* ['treɪlə]	Wohnwagen	In the US some people don't live in houses, they live in big *trailers*.
	extra ['ekstrə]	Statist/-in; Komparse/Komparsin	As an *extra*, you can get a feeling for what life as an actor is like. = a character in a film that doesn't speak *extra* ↔ protagonist
	what it's all about [ˌwɒtˍɪtsˍ ɔ:lˍə'baʊt]	worum es geht	My grandpa always tells us *what life is all about*.
1	**effort** ['efət]	Bemühung; Mühe	*Fr.* effort *(m)*
	to **pursue** [pə'sju:]	verfolgen	to *pursue* a dream/a goal *to pursue sb/sth* = to follow sb/sth
	persistent [pə'sɪstnt]	hartnäckig; ausdauernd; beharrlich	You have to be *persistent* in Hollywood, you can't give up too quickly.
	relaxed [rɪ'lækst]	entspannt; locker; gelassen	'*Relaxed*' is an adjective many people associate with California. *relaxed* → to relax
	suitable ['su:təbl]	geeignet; passend	Why do you think you're *suitable* for the job?
7	**agent** ['eɪdʒnt]	Agent/-in	Every actor or singer needs an *agent*.
	to **catch** [kætʃ], **caught** [kɔ:t], **caught** [kɔ:t]	nehmen *(Zug, Bus)*	I need to *catch* the train at 1:15.
	backstage [ˌbæk'steɪdʒ]	backstage; hinter der Bühne	If you have *backstage* tickets, there's a chance for you to meet the star personally.
8	**memorable** ['memrəbl] Max, Luca	denkwürdig; unvergesslich	What a *memorable* moment it was when I took a selfie with my favorite star!
	to **nominate** ['nɒmɪneɪt]	nominieren; ernennen	= to suggest that sb should be chosen for an award
10	**founder** ['faʊndə]	Gründer/-in	*founder* → to found
11	to **comprise** [kəm'praɪz]	umfassen; beinhalten; einschließen	The USA *comprises* 50 states. *to comprise* = to include = to contain
	producer [prə'dju:sə]	Produzent/-in	To make a film, you need a director, actors, a *producer*, and lots of other people.
	contribution [ˌkɒntrɪ'bju:ʃn]	Beitrag; Beteiligung	What's your *contribution* to the party? Food, music?
	as long as [əz 'lɒŋˍəz]	solange	I'll lend you my car for your trip *as long as* you promise to drive carefully.
	nominee [ˌnɒmɪ'ni:]	vorgeschlagener Kandidat/vorgeschlagene Kandidatin	There are five *nominees* for the award.

to **approve** [ə'pru:v]	anerkennen; gutheißen; genehmigen	My university application *has been approved*!
nomination [ˌnɒmɪ'neɪʃn]	Nominierung; Ernennung	*nomination* → to nominate → nominee
in honor of *(AE)* [ɪn‿'ɒnər‿əv]	zu Ehren	
animated ['ænɪmeɪtɪd]	Zeichentrick-	*Animated* films are popular with people of all ages, not just with children.

Station 2: A golden state?

golden ['gəʊldn]	golden; Gold-	*golden* → gold
GDP [ˌdʒi:di:'pi:]	BIP *(= Bruttoinlandsprodukt)*	The *GDP (= Gross Domestic Product)* refers to the total value of things and services produced in a country within a year.
income ['ɪnkʌm]	Einkommen	= the money you earn either from work or investments
explorer [ɪk'splɔ:rə]	Forscher/-in; Forschungsreisende/-r; Entdecker/-in	In the 16th century there were many Spanish *explorers* in North and South America. *explorer* → to explore
to **be said to** *(+ inf)* [bi 'sed tə]	sollen; gelten als	French cooking *is said to* be the world's best, though many people would disagree.
to **exist** [ɪg'zɪst]	existieren; bestehen	Do you think life after death *exists*? ***Fr.*** exister
wealth [welθ]	Reichtum; Vermögen	*wealth* ↔ poverty *wealth* → wealthy
Californian [ˌkælɪ'fɔ:niən]	kalifornisch; Kalifornier/-in	
Gold Rush ['gəʊld ˌrʌʃ]	Goldrausch	The California *Gold Rush* took place in the 19th century.
precious ['preʃəs]	wertvoll; kostbar	These old family photos are more *precious* to me than all the gold and silver in the world.
metal ['metl]	Metall	***Fr.*** métal *(m)*; ***Lat.*** metallum *(nt)*
to **boom** [bu:m]	florieren; boomen	In 1855 Mud Springs *boomed* and changed its name to El Dorado.
to **remain** [rɪ'meɪn]	bleiben	*to remain* = to stay
sunny ['sʌni]	sonnig	*sunny* → sun
attraction [ə'trækʃn]	Anziehung; Anziehungskraft	California's climate is a big part of its *attraction* as a tourist destination.
northern ['nɔ:ðən]	nördlich; Nord-	*northern* – eastern – southern – western
start-up company ['stɑ:tʌp ˌkʌmpəni]	Start-up (-Unternehmen); Unternehmensgründung	No place in the world is more famous for innovative *start-up companies* than California. = a company that has been created based on a new idea
dot-com bubble [ˌdɒtkɒm 'bʌbl]	Internetblase; Dotcom-Blase	
to **burst** [bɜ:st], **burst** [bɜ:st], **burst** [bɜ:st]	bersten; platzen	The dot-com bubble *burst* in 2001.
boom [bu:m]	wirtschaftlicher Aufschwung; Boom; Hochkonjunktur	California isn't the only US region to experience an IT *boom* over the years; the Seattle area is another. *boom* → to boom

	leading ['li:dɪŋ]	führend	*leading* → to lead → leader
	worldwide [ˌwɜ:ld'waɪd]	weltweit	Technology is one of the leading industries *worldwide*.
	agriculture ['ægrɪkʌltʃə]	Landwirtschaft; Agrikultur	*agriculture* ↔ industry *Lat.* ager *(m)* + cultura *(f)*
	fortune ['fɔ:tʃu:n]	Vermögen; Reichtum	My uncle made a *fortune* with buying and selling cars.
	to **last** [lɑ:st]	dauern; andauern; anhalten	Hot weather doesn't usually *last* very long.
	shortage ['ʃɔ:tɪdʒ]	Knappheit; Mangel	If there's a *shortage* of sth, there isn't enough of it. *shortage* → short
	drought [draʊt]	Dürre; Trockenheit	! '*Drought*' rhymes with 'out'.
	to **urge sb to do sth** [ɜ:dʒ]	jmdn. zu etw. drängen	= to encourage sb very strongly to do sth
	cultivation [ˌkʌltɪ'veɪʃn]	Anbau	The *cultivation* of fruit and vegetables needs a lot of water.
	Hispanic [hɪ'spænɪk]	lateinamerikanisch; Latino/ Latina; Hispano-Amerikaner/-in	He comes from Mexico, so he's *Hispanic*.
	border ['bɔ:də]	Grenze	A large number of people cross the US-Mexican *border* illegally each year to try to start a better life in the US.
	to **guard** [gɑ:d]	bewachen	Many Americans feel the US-Mexican border isn't *guarded* well enough.
	to **close down** [ˌkləʊz 'daʊn]	den Betrieb einstellen; schließen	A lot of mining companies have had to *close down* over the last several years.
14	**silicon** ['sɪlɪkən]	Silizium	
	component [kəm'pəʊnənt]	Bestandteil; Komponente	Almost all companies in our town produce *components* for the car industry.
	device [dɪ'vaɪs]	Gerät; Vorrichtung	A smartphone is an electronic *device*.
	to **be based** [bi 'beɪst]	ansässig sein	Hundreds of companies *are based* in Silicon Valley.
15	**agricultural** [ˌægrɪ'kʌltʃrl]	landwirtschaftlich	*agricultural* → agriculture
16	**entrepreneur** [ˌɒntrəprə'nɜ:]	Unternehmer/-in	
19	**strawberry** ['strɔ:bri]	Erdbeere	
	grape [greɪp]	Traube	
	to **export** [ɪk'spɔ:t]	exportieren; ausführen	*to export* → export *Fr.* exporter
	minimum wage [ˌmɪnɪməm 'weɪdʒ]	Mindestlohn	Waiters in the US often only earn the *minimum wage*, which is why they depend on good tips to improve their income.
	seasonal ['si:znl]	saisonal; jahreszeitlich bedingt	Picking fruit is *seasonal* work.
	That doesn't pay my rent. [ˌðət dʌznt ˌpeɪ maɪ 'rent]	Davon kann ich meine Miete nicht bezahlen.	My dad's seasonal work *doesn't pay our rent*.
20	**decade** ['dekeɪd]	Jahrzehnt	= period of ten years *Fr.* décade *(f)*
	Latino [lə'ti:nəʊ]	lateinamerikanisch	In the US, there is a strong *Latino* influence in states like California, Arizona or Florida.

Collocations

California

agricultural / tech / entertainment industries
destroyed / protected nature / environment
healthy eating / food
illegal immigrants
immigration problems
sports / fitness craze
sporty / relaxed people
strong economy
sunny / hot / dry climate
technology / start-up companies
trendsetting hotspot / lifestyle / business

Entertainment phrases

aspiring actor; wannabe actor
glitz and glamor
to chalk sth up to experience
to find your pot of gold
to get a (big) role / a big break
to keep one's head above water
to live your dream; to make your dream come true
to shoot / film a scene
to showcase your talent
to try your luck
to wait for one's break / for a cattle call

Write a dialogue between two friends: One sees only the positive aspects of California; the other sees the negative ones.

Station 3: Should we be worried?

wildfire ['waɪldfaɪə]	Flächenbrand	OMG, that rumor about Ben is spreading like *wildfire*!
incident ['ɪnsɪdnt]	Vorfall; Ereignis	Tell me about that horrible *incident* at school last week.
tanker plane ['tæŋkə ˌpleɪn]	Tankflugzeug	
thanks to ['θæŋks tə]	dank; wegen	Thank you for your help. *Thanks to* you we can go home earlier.
climate change ['klaɪmət ˌtʃeɪndʒ]	Klimawandel	A lot of people still don't believe in *climate change*.
to **increase** [ɪn'kriːs]	zunehmen; wachsen	= to grow in size or number
to **coordinate** [kəʊ'ɔːdɪneɪt]	koordinieren	
emergency [ɪ'mɜːdʒnsi]	Notfall; Notlage; Notfall-	That plane can't land, something's wrong with it – it's an *emergency*!
flood [flʌd]	Flut; Hochwasser; Überschwemmung	Too much rain can cause *floods*. = a large amount of water (e.g. covering an area that is usually dry)
mudslide ['mʌdslaɪd]	Schlammlawine	*Mudslides* often come with floods. *mudslide* → mud → muddy

hillside ['hɪlsaɪd]	Hang	Houses on a *hillside* with a nice view can be very expensive.
to **collapse** [kə'læps]	kollabieren; zusammenbrechen; einstürzen	= to fall down, to fall to the ground
to **be willing to do sth** [bi 'wɪlɪŋ tə]	gewillt sein, etw. zu tun; bereit sein, etw. zu tun	How much *are* they *willing to* pay for the bike? *to be willing to do sth* = to be prepared to do sth
to **cut down** [ˌkʌt 'daʊn]	fällen	To build the new neighborhood, they had to *cut down* a lot of trees.
dehydration [ˌdi:haɪ'dreɪʃn]	Austrocknung	
disease [dɪ'zi:z]	Krankheit	In refugee camps *diseases* spread quickly.
bugs *(pl)* [bʌgz]	Ungeziefer	We had to leave our holiday flat because there were *bugs* everywhere.
22 **shall** [ʃæl]	sollen	! *'Shall'* is used in formal conversations.
to **be to** *(+ inf)* ['bi tə]	sollen	*to be to* = should
ought to *(+ inf)* ['ɔ:t tə]	sollen	*ought to* = should
to **be required to** *(+ inf)* [bi rɪ'kwaɪəd tə]	müssen	We're *required to* clean the street in front of the house every week.
to **be obliged to** *(+ inf)* [bi‿ə'blaɪdʒd tə]	verpflichtet sein, etw. zu tun; müssen	Nurses *are obliged to* work on weekends.
23 **on average** [ɒn‿'ævrɪdʒ]	durchschnittlich; im Durchschnitt	*On average* around 10,000 people visit the shopping center every day.
unusual [ʌn'ju:ʒl]	ungewöhnlich	*unusual* ↔ usual
slight [slaɪt]	gering; leicht	A *slight* difference between two things is a very small one.
crack [kræk]	Riss; Spalt	Look, there's a new *crack* in that wall. How did that happen?
recorded history [rɪˌkɔ:dɪd 'hɪstri]	*hier:* Aufzeichnung	*Recorded history* shows that there haven't been any earthquakes here for the past 50 years.
all but ['ɔ:l bʌt]	alle bis auf	*All but* two of the students passed the exam.
indoors [ˌɪn'dɔ:z]	im Inneren	= inside, in a building
outdoors [ˌaʊt'dɔ:z]	im Freien	*outdoors* ↔ indoors
smell [smel]	Geruch; Duft; Gestank	Oh, what a terrible *smell*! *smell* → to smell
damage ['dæmɪdʒ]	Schaden; Beschädigung	Natural disasters like earthquakes can cause a lot of *damage*.
aftershock ['ɑ:ftəʃɒk]	Nachbeben	After the earthquake there were at least ten *aftershocks*.
24 **conservation** [ˌkɒnsə'veɪʃn]	Schutz; Erhaltung	The *conservation* of nature is one of our most important tasks.
26 **eating** ['i:tɪŋ]	Essen; Ess-	A lot of people don't know what healthy *eating* means because they've never had healthy food.
28 **smooth** [smu:ð]	glatt; weich; geschmeidig	Feel this wood – it's really *smooth*.
transition [træn'zɪʃn]	Übergang	*Transitions* in a presentation should be smooth.

Skills: What's important for a handout?

handout ['hændaʊt]	Informationsblatt; Arbeitsblatt	= a piece of paper that gives important information (e.g. from a talk)
2 **chef** [ʃef]	Koch; Küchenchef	! False friend: der Chef = the boss der Koch = the *chef*

True and false friends

Many English words look like German words. But you have to be careful; there are different categories you need to be aware of:

1. ***True friends:*** *These are words that look the same (often with very small differences in spelling) and have the same meaning, for example 'address', 'camera', 'camel', etc.*
2. ***False friends:*** *These are words that look the same but have a completely* ***different*** *meaning:*

to become = werden (≠ bekommen)
brave = mutig (≠ brav)
chef = Koch (≠ Chef)
chips = Pommes frites (≠ Chips)
director = Regisseur (≠ Direktor)
fabric = Stoff (≠ Fabrik)
familiar = vertraut (≠ familiär)
gift = Geschenk (≠ Gift)
to grab = greifen (≠ graben)
gym(nasium) = Turnhalle (≠ Gymnasium)
handy = handlich (≠ Handy)
map = Karte (≠ Mappe)
murder = Mord (≠ Mörder)
photograph = Foto (≠ Fotograf)
plate = Teller (≠ Platte)
receipt = Quittung, Beleg (≠ Rezept)
sea = Meer (≠ See)
sensible = vernünftig (≠ sensibel)
to spend = ausgeben (≠ spenden)
while = während (≠ weil)
where = wo (≠ wer)
to wink = zwinkern (≠ winken)
who = wer (≠ wo)
to wonder = sich fragen (≠ sich wundern)

3. *Another category to be aware of: English words which have been taken into German, but used in ways that English speakers wouldn't understand:*
   Handy → mobile (phone) / cell (phone) → In English, 'handy' is an adjective which means *handlich, geschickt.* It isn't a noun.)
   Smoking → tuxedo → In English, 'smoking' refers only to *Rauchen*, not to clothing.

4. *Be careful! There are also German words which look like English ones but which don't exist in English at all!*
   Fitnessstudio → gym
   Mobbing → bullying
   Showmaster → TV host

training ['treɪnɪŋ]	Ausbildung	The restaurant's chef received his *training* in different hotels.
substance ['sʌbstns]	Substanz; Gehalt	
craft [krɑːft]	Handwerk; Gewerbe	= traditional skill of making things by hand
deep fryer [ˌdiːp 'fraɪə]	Fritteuse	You can make chips in a *deep fryer*.
freezer ['friːzə]	Tiefkühlschrank	If you keep food in the *freezer*, it stays fresh.

Unit task: My star for the Walk of Fame

selection [sɪ'lekʃn]	Auswahl; Auswahl-	*selection* → to select
politics *(pl only)* ['pɒlətɪks]	Politik	! *'Politics'* is usually used with the singular form of the verb: I think *politics* **is** important.

	obstacle ['ɒbstəkl]	Hindernis	
	to **overcome** [ˌəʊvə'kʌm]	überwinden	Sad experiences can be very difficult to *overcome*.

Story: Famous

1	**tabloid** ['tæblɔɪd]	Boulevardzeitung	*Bild* is a German *tabloid*.
	to **specialize in** *(AE)* ['speʃlaɪzˌɪn]	sich spezialisieren auf	My dad is a doctor, he *specializes in* heart diseases.
	to **insist (on)** [ɪn'sɪstˌɒn]	insistieren; bestehen auf	Are you sure it's OK for us to stay in your apartment in New York? – Absolutely. I *insist*! *Fr.* insister
	to **stalk sb** [stɔːk]	jmdn. stalken; jmdm. nachstellen	Why do people *stalk* other people? That's so weird.
	to **harass** ['hærəs; hə'ræs]	belästigen; drangsalieren	A lot of stars are *harassed* by their fans.
	to **photograph** ['fəʊtəgrɑːf]	fotografieren	= to take a photo *to photograph* → photographer
5	**fame** [feɪm]	Ruhm	*fame* → famous
	anonymity [ænə'nɪməti]	Anonymität	*Anonymity* is something famous people often miss most of all.
	normality [nɔː'mæləti]	Normalität	*normality* → normal

Important differences

	AE	BE
Different spelling	glam**or**, hum**or**, neighb**or** cent**er**, met**er** to organ**ize**, to real**ize**, to recogn**ize** special**ty**, jewe**lry** to practi**ce** trave**l**ing	glam**our**, hum**our**, neighb**our** cent**re**, met**re** to organi**se**, to reali**se**, to recogni**se** special**ity**, jewe**llery** to practi**se** trave**ll**ing
Different words	apartment grade have/has gotten highway, freeway movie period RV park soccer store subway trailer vacation	flat class have/has got motorway film lesson camping area football shop underground camper holiday(s)

Text smart 3 Argumentative texts

Introduction

	letter to the editor [ˌletə tʊ ðiˌˈedɪtə]	Leserbrief	*Letters to the editor* are reader reactions to news reports.
	editor [ˈedɪtə]	Herausgeber/-in; Redakteur/-in	= 1. sb who works as the head of a newspaper or magazine; = 2. sb who writes articles or checks other writers' articles
	argumentative essay [ɑ:gjəˌmentətɪvˌˈeseɪ]	Erörterung	An *argumentative essay* needs to be convincing, but sorry, this essay isn't.
	frequent [ˈfri:kwənt]	häufig	FAQs are *frequently*-asked questions.
1	to **speak out (about sth)** [ˌspi:kˌˈaʊt]	seine Meinung (über etw.) deutlich vertreten; sich (zu etw.) äußern	Paul is always the first to *speak out about* things he thinks are wrong or unfair.
	insult [ˈɪnsʌlt]	Beleidigung	Fair criticism is one thing, but there's nothing fair about a nasty *insult*.
	contestant [kənˈtestnt]	Kandidat/-in	= sb who takes part in a competition, quiz, show, etc. ! Be careful with the word stress.
	to **break down** [ˌbreɪk ˈdaʊn]	zusammenbrechen	I've never seen dad so emotional, but he really *broke down* and cried after he heard about the accident.
	one-sided [ˌwʌnˈsaɪdɪd]	einseitig	If an article features *one-sided* arguments, it isn't objective.
2	to **criticise** [ˈkrɪtɪsaɪz]	kritisieren	= to point out what is negative or bad about sth or sb *to criticise* → criticism *Fr.* critiquer
	to **tolerate** [ˈtɒlreɪt]	tolerieren; dulden	I can *tolerate* a lot, but I've really had enough of his insults. *Fr.* tolérer

Station 1: How to: Write a letter to the editor

3	**basically** [ˈbeɪsɪkli]	eigentlich; grundsätzlich; im Grunde genommen	You're *basically* right, but please consider my arguments too.
	psychologist [saɪˈkɒlədʒɪst]	Psychologe/Psychologin	*Psychologists* help people with their problems. ! Be careful with the pronunciation.
	My point is … [ˌmaɪ ˈpɔɪntˌɪz]	Was ich sagen will ist, …	*My point is* that talent shows don't need a jury.
	host [həʊst]	Gastgeber/-in; Talkmaster	In the US, many TV show *hosts* are bigger stars than their guests.
4	**as far as** [əz ˈfɑ:rˌəz]	soweit	*As far as* I know, talent shows are still very popular, aren't they?
5	to **bet** [bet], **bet** [bet], **bet** [bet]	wetten	I *bet* you £10 that our team will win!
6	to **insult** [ɪnˈsʌlt]	beleidigen	= to say rude things about sb or to treat sb unfairly *to insult* → insult *Fr.* insulter

Station 2: How to: Write an argumentative essay

	to **fail sb** [feɪl]	jmdn. hängenlassen; jmdn. im Stich lassen	
	sex [seks]	Geschlecht; Sexualität	
	to **be confronted with** [bi kən'frʌntɪd wɪð]	konfrontiert werden mit	On TV, we're often *confronted with* images which are difficult to look at. – to face something that you have to deal with or react to
	to **present sb with sth** [prɪ'zent wɪð]	jmdm. etw. bieten	Adverts *present us with* a lot of things we don't need, but which we often want.
	sporty ['spɔ:ti]	sportlich	*sporty* → sport
	chest [tʃest]	Busen	
	muscular ['mʌskjələ]	muskulös	Football players often have very *muscular* legs.
	irresponsible [ˌɪrɪ'spɒnsəbl]	unverantwortlich; leichtsinning	He acted *irresponsibly* when he left the kids on their own. *irresponsible* ↔ responsible
	exception [ɪk'sepʃn]	Ausnahme	People with a perfect body are the *exception* and not the rule.
	secondly ['sekndli]	zweitens	First, I have to say that … And *secondly*, …
	high-level [ˌhaɪ'levl]	Spitzen-; auf höchster Ebene	Wow, what a difference: In that suit, you look like a *high-level* businessman!
	to **look up to sb** [ˌlʊk‿'ʌp tə]	zu jmdm. aufschauen; jmdn. bewundern	Teenagers often *look up to* rock or film stars.
	material [mə'tɪəriəl]	materiell	How many *material* things do we really need, and how many do we simply want?
	outdated [ˌaʊt'deɪtɪd]	veraltet; überholt	I say his views are *outdated*, but he insists they're just traditional. *outdated* = old-fashioned *outdated* ↔ modern
	perfection [pə'fekʃn]	Perfektion; Vollkommenheit	*perfection* → perfect
	realism ['rɪəlɪzm]	Realismus; Realitätssinn	*realism* → real → realistic
	role model ['rəʊl ˌmɒdl]	Vorbild	My *role model* is my older sister.
10	to **stop sb from doing sth** ['stɒp frəm]	jmdn. davon abhalten, etw. zu tun	You can't *stop me from doing* what I want, so don't even try.

Across cultures 3 Having a voice

to **have a voice** [ˌhæv‿ə 'vɔɪs]	ein Mitspracherecht haben	
participation [pɑ:ˌtɪsɪ'peɪʃn]	Mitwirkung; Beteiligung	*participation* → to participate
to **make one's voice heard** [ˌmeɪk wʌnz ˌvɔɪs 'hɜ:d]	sich Gehör verschaffen	How can we *make our voices heard*?

1	**student council** [ˌstjuːdnt ˈkaʊnsl]	Schülerrat	The *Student Council* meets every Monday after school.
	vote [vəʊt]	Abstimmung; Stimme; Wahl	A candidate has to earn my *vote*; then I might vote for him/her. *vote* → to vote
	to **make a difference (to sth)** [ˌmeɪk‿ə ˈdɪfrəns]	etw. verändern	A lot of votes can *make a difference*.
	to **admire** [ədˈmaɪə]	bewundern	Everyone *admires* a hero. ***Fr.*** admirer; ***Lat.*** admirari
	activist [ˈæktɪvɪst]	Aktivist/-in *(jmd. der sich für etw. engagiert)*	*activist* → active → activity
	banner [ˈbænə]	Banner; Spruchband; Transparent	
	to **make one's point** [ˌmeɪk wʌnz ˈpɔɪnt]	seinen Standpunkt deutlich machen	You needn't shout to *make your point*.
	to **believe in sb/sth** [bɪˈliːv‿ɪn]	an jmdn./etw. glauben	Betty *believes in* God.
	petition [pəˈtɪʃn]	Petition; Unterschriftenliste	Most students signed the *petition* for a new gym.
	to **do one's bit** [ˌduː‿wʌnz ˈbɪt]	seinen Teil beitragen	We all should *do our bit* to protect the environment.
	global [ˈgləʊbl]	global; weltweit	A *global* problem is one that the whole world is confronted with.
	protection [prəˈtekʃn]	Schutz	*protection* → to protect
	to **spray-paint** [ˈspreɪpeɪnt]	mit Farbe besprühen	The students were allowed to *spray-paint* the school's walls.
	fur [fɜː]	Fell; Pelz	*Fur* is the thick hair that covers the skin of many animals.
	coat [kəʊt]	Mantel	
	to **dictate** [dɪkˈteɪt]	diktieren; vorschreiben	Emma, you can't say you're tolerant and respectful of others' views when you always *dictate* YOUR views to everyone else.
2	**belief** [bɪˈliːf]	Glaube; Überzeugung	*belief* → to believe (in)
	reward [rɪˈwɔːd]	Belohnung; Preis	A *reward* of $100 has been offered to anybody who finds the stolen car.
	to **take the lead** [ˌteɪk ðə ˈliːd]	die Führung übernehmen	My mum always *takes the lead* when we go hiking.
	bubble [ˈbʌbl]	Blase	Can you make *bubbles* with chewing gum?
	bone [bəʊn]	Knochen	Dogs love *bones*.
	valuable [ˈvæljuəbl]	wertvoll	= sth that could be sold for a lot of money *valuable* → value
3	**representative** [ˌreprɪˈzentətɪv]	Repräsentant/-in; Stellvertreter/-in	*representative* → to represent

How words can start or end

You already know a lot of words which can have prefixes and suffixes. Here is a new collection.

Adjectives

dis-	honest, respectful, abled	desir(e), memor(y), suit, valu(e)	**-able**
im-	possible, patient	agricultur(e), glob(e), logic, season	**-al**
in-	direct, convenient, secure	grate, meaning, respect	**-ful**
ir-	regular, relevant, responsible	democrat, enthusiast	**-ic**
un-	able, comfortable, expected	biolog(y), hyster(y)	**-ical**
		real, material	**-istic**
		harm, home	**-less**
		adventur(e), glamour	**-ous**
		flirt, sport, trick	**-y**

Verbs

dis-	appear, agree, obey	standard, symbol	**-ise/ize**
en-	courage		
over-	come, hear		
re-	build, read, tell, write		
un-	wrap, pack		

Find at least four more examples for adjectives and verbs with suffixes.

In dieser alphabetischen Wortliste findest du das gesamte Vokabular von *Green Line* 1 bis 5.
Namen stehen in einer extra Liste am Ende des *Dictionary*.
Einträge, die aus mehreren Wörtern bestehen, kannst du meist unter verschiedenen Stichwörtern nachschlagen. So ist z.B. *after all* unter *after* und unter *all* eingetragen.
Die Fundstellen stehen immer hinter dem jeweiligen Wort und zeigen dir an, wo es zum ersten Mal vorkommt, z. B.:
addition [ə'dɪʃn] Zusatz; Ergänzung **V U2**, 51 kommt zum ersten Mal vor in Band 5, Unit 2, Seite 51
to **aim** to do sth [eɪm] anstreben; abzielen auf **V TS2**, 78 kommt zum ersten Mal vor in Band 5, Text smart 2, Seite 78
U = Unit, AC = Across cultures, TS = Text smart
Die mit * gekennzeichneten Verben sind unregelmäßig.
Die mit ° gekennzeichneten Vokabeln sind rezeptiv.
Die mit ⟨ ⟩ gekennzeichneten Vokabeln sind fakultativ.

A

a [ə] ein/-e **I**
 a bit [ə 'bɪt] ein bisschen; ein wenig **II**
 a couple of [ə 'kʌpl‿əv] ein paar **I**
 a few [ə 'fju:] ein paar; wenige; einige **I**
 a little [ə 'lɪtl] ein wenig; etwas **I**
 a lot [ə 'lɒt] viel **I**
 a lot of [ə 'lɒt‿əv] viel/-e; eine Menge **I**
 a total of [ə 'təʊtl‿əv] insgesamt **IV**
 a (day/week/year) [ə 'deɪ/wi:k/jɪə] pro (Tag/Woche/Jahr) **IV**
 a lot to learn [ə ˌlɒt tə 'lɜ:n] viel zu lernen **I**
a.m. [ˌeɪ'em] vormittags *(Uhrzeit)* **I**
to **abandon** [ə'bændən] aufgeben; zurücklassen **IV**
ability [ə'bɪləti] Fähigkeit **V U2**, 64
*to be **able** to (do sth) [bi‿'eɪbl tə] fähig sein zu; können; dürfen **II**
aboard [ə'bɔ:d] an Bord **I**
Aboriginal [ˌæbə'rɪdʒnl] von australischen Ureinwohnern abstammend **V AC1**, 10
about [ə'baʊt] ungefähr; circa; etwa **I**
about [ə'baʊt] über; von **I**
 *to be **about** to do sth [bi‿ə'baʊt tə] im Begriff sein, etw. zu tun **IV**
 out and **about** [ˌaʊt‿ən‿ə'baʊt] unterwegs **II**
 What **about** ...? ['wɒt‿əbaʊt] Wie wär's mit ...?; Was ist mit ...? **I**
 What is ... **about**? [ˌwɒt‿ɪz ...‿ə'baʊt] Worum geht es in/im ...? **I**
 what it's all **about** [ˌwɒt‿ɪts‿ɔ:l‿ə'baʊt] worum es geht **V U3**, 86
above [ə'bʌv] oben **II**
abridged [ə'brɪdʒd] gekürzt °**V U2**, 66
abroad [ə'brɔ:d] im Ausland; ins Ausland **III**
abrupt [ə'brʌpt] abrupt **V U1**, 30
absolutely [ˌæbsə'lu:tli] absolut; völlig **II**
abstract ['æbstrækt] abstrakt **IV**
absurdity [əb'zɜ:dəti] Absurdität ⟨**V U2**, 66⟩
accent ['æksnt] Akzent **II**
to **accept** [ək'sept] akzeptieren; hinnehmen; annehmen **III**
acceptable [ək'septəbl] akzeptabel; annehmbar **V AC2**, 81
access permit ['ækses ˌpɜ:mɪt] Zugangsberechtigung ⟨**V U1**, 30⟩
accident ['æksɪdnt] Unfall **II**
accidentally [ˌæksɪ'dentli] versehentlich; aus Versehen ⟨**V U3**, 101⟩
according to [ə'kɔ:dɪŋ tə] laut; gemäß **IV**
account settings [ə'kaʊnt ˌsetɪŋz] Profileinstellungen **III**
to **achieve** [ə'tʃi:v] erreichen; erlangen **IV**
acid rain [ˌæsɪd 'reɪn] saurer Regen ⟨**V U3**, 96⟩
to **acknowledge** [ək'nɒlɪdʒ] anerkennen; einräumen **V U2**, 62
across [ə'krɒs] auf der anderen Seite von; über; hinüber; herüber; quer durch **I**
 Across cultures [əˌkrɒs 'kʌltʃəz] Interkulturelles **I**
to **act** [ækt] spielen *(Theater)* **I**; sich verhalten; handeln **IV**
 to **act** like ['ækt laɪk] tun als ob **II**
 to **act** out [ækt 'aʊt] nachspielen **II**
 acting a scene [ˌæktɪŋ‿ə 'si:n] eine Theaterszene spielen **I**
acting ['æktɪŋ] Schauspielen **II**
action ['ækʃn] Handlung; Action; Aktion **I**
active ['æktɪv] aktiv **III**
activist ['æktɪvɪst] Aktivist/-in *(jmd. der sich für etw. engagiert)* **V AC3**, 114
activity [æk'tɪvəti] Aktivität **I**
actor ['æktə] Schauspieler **II**
actual ['æktʃuəl] tatsächlich; wirklich; eigentlich **IV**
ad [əd'vɜ:tɪsmənt] Anzeige; Werbespot **IV**
 ad copy ['æd ˌkɒpi] Werbetext **IV**
AD (= Anno Domini) [ˌeɪ'di:] nach Christus **III**
film **adaptation** [ˌfɪlm‿ædæp'teɪʃn] Verfilmung °**V U2**, 62
adapted [ə'dæptɪd] adaptiert; angepasst **IV**
to **add** [æd] hinzufügen; ergänzen **I**
addict ['ædɪkt] Süchtige/-r; Abhängige/-r **III**
addiction [ə'dɪkʃn] Sucht; Abhängigkeit ⟨**V U2**, 47⟩
 cyber **addiction** ['saɪbər‿əˌdɪkʃn] Internetsucht; Internetabhängigkeit ⟨**V TS2**, 79⟩
*to be **addictive** [bi‿ə'dɪktɪv] süchtig machen ⟨**V TS2**, 79⟩
addition [ə'dɪʃn] Zusatz; Ergänzung **V U2**, 51
 in **addition** to [ɪn‿ə'dɪʃn tə] neben; daneben; darüber hinaus **IV**
additional [ə'dɪʃnl] zusätzlich **II**
address [ə'dres] Adresse **I**
to **address** [ə'dres] ansprechen; sich wenden an **IV**
adjective ['ædʒɪktɪv] Adjektiv; Eigenschaftswort **II**
to **admire** [əd'maɪə] bewundern **V AC3**, 114
to **admit** [əd'mɪt] zugeben ⟨**V U3**, 101⟩
to **adopt** [ə'dɒpt] übernehmen; annehmen; adoptieren ⟨**V U3**, 97⟩
adult ['ædʌlt] Erwachsene/-r **II**
advance [əd'vɑ:ns] Fortschritt ⟨**V AC1**, 11⟩
to **advance** [əd'vɑ:ns] vorantreiben ⟨**V U3**, 102⟩
advantage [əd'vɑ:ntɪdʒ] Vorteil **IV**
adventure [əd'ventʃə] Abenteuer **II**
adventurous [əd'ventʃrəs] abenteuerlich; unternehmungslustig; wagemutig; experimentierfreudig **V U2**, 46
adverb ['ædvɜ:b] Adverb **II**
adverbial clause [ədˌvɜ:biəl 'klɔ:z] Adverbialsatz **IV**
advert ['ædvɜ:t] Anzeige; Werbespot **III**
to **advertise** ['ædvətaɪz] Werbung machen; werben; anpreisen; inserieren **IV**
advertisement [əd'vɜ:tɪsmənt] Anzeige; Werbespot **IV**
advertiser ['ædvətaɪzə] Werbefachmann/-frau **IV**
advertising *(no pl)* ['ædvətaɪzɪŋ] Werbung; Reklame **IV**
advice [əd'vaɪs] Rat; Ratschlag **II**
to **affect** [ə'fekt] beeinflussen; beeinträchtigen; betreffen **IV**
to **afford** [ə'fɔ:d] sich leisten **III**
*to be **afraid** (of) [bi‿ə'freɪd‿əv] (sich) fürchten; Angst haben (vor) **III**
 I'm **afraid** ... [ˌaɪm‿ə'freɪd] Leider ... **IV**
Afrikaans [ˌæfrɪ'kɑ:ns] Afrikaans *(Sprache in Südafrika)* ⟨**V AC1**, 8⟩
after ['ɑ:ftə] nach *(zeitlich)* **I**; nachdem **IV**
 after all [ˌɑ:ftər‿'ɔ:l] doch; schließlich; immerhin **I**
 after that [ˌɑ:ftə 'ðæt] danach **I**
afternoon [ˌɑ:ftə'nu:n] Nachmittag **I**
 this **afternoon** [ðɪs 'ɑ:ftənu:n] heute Nachmittag **II**
aftershock ['ɑ:ftəʃɒk] Nachbeben **V U3**, 95
afterwards ['ɑ:ftəwədz] danach; hinterher **IV**

again [ə'gen] wieder; noch einmal; noch mal **I**
over and over **again** [ˌəʊvər‿ən‿ˌəʊvər‿ə'gen] immer wieder **III**
against [ə'genst] gegen **II**
against all odds [əˌgenst‿ɔ:l‿'ɒdz] entgegen allen Erwartungen **III**
age [eɪdʒ] Alter **III**
Bronze **Age** ['brɒnz eɪdʒ] Bronzezeit *(ca. 2200–800 v. Chr.)* **II**
golden **age** [ˌgəʊldn 'eɪdʒ] goldenes Zeitalter **III**
aged [eɪdʒd] im Alter von ⟨**VTS2**, 79⟩
travel **agency** ['trævl‿ˌeɪdʒnsi] Reisebüro **III**
agent ['eɪdʒnt] Agent/-in **VU3**, 88
travel **agent**'s ['trævl‿ˌeɪdʒnts] Reisebüro **II**
aggressive [ə'gresɪv] aggressiv **II**
ago [ə'gəʊ] vor *(zeitlich)* **II**
agony aunt ['ægəni‿ˌɑ:nt] Kummerkastentante **II**
to **agree** (on) [ə'gri:] sich einigen (auf) **II**
to **agree** (with) [ə'gri:] einer Meinung sein (mit); zustimmen **II**
agreement [ə'gri:mənt] Übereinstimmung; Einigkeit °**V AC3**, 115
agricultural [ˌægrɪ'kʌltʃrl] landwirtschaftlich **VU3**, 91
agriculture ['ægrɪkʌltʃə] Landwirtschaft; Agrikultur **VU3**, 90
to **aim** to do sth [eɪm] anstreben; abzielen auf **VTS2**, 78
ain't (= isn't/aren't) [eɪnt] ist nicht; sind nicht **IV**
air [eə] Luft **III**
air ambulance ['eər‿ˌæmbjələns] Rettungshubschrauber **VU1**, 14
air-conditioned [ˌeəkən'dɪʃnd] klimatisiert ⟨**VU1**, 30⟩
air-conditioning [ˌeəkən'dɪʃnɪŋ] Klimaanlage **III**
airline ['eəlaɪn] Fluggesellschaft ⟨**VTS3**, 113⟩
airplane ['eəpleɪn] Flugzeug **IV**
airport ['eəpɔ:t] Flughafen **II**
aka [ˌeɪkeɪ'eɪ] alias **IV**
alarm [ə'lɑ:m] Alarm **VU2**, 59
alarm clock [ə'lɑ:m ˌklɒk] Wecker **II**
alcohol *(no pl)* ['ælkəhɒl] Alkohol **VU1**, 28
alien ['eɪliən] Außerirdische/-r; außerirdisches Wesen **I**
aligned [ə'laɪnd] ausgerichtet °**VTS1**, 44
alive [ə'laɪv] lebend; am Leben; lebendig **IV**
all [ɔ:l] alle/-s; ganz **I**
after **all** [ˌɑ:ftər‿'ɔ:l] doch; schließlich; immerhin **I**
all day [ˌɔ:l 'deɪ] den ganzen Tag **II**
all night [ˌɔ:l 'naɪt] die ganze Nacht **I**
all over [ˌɔ:l‿'əʊvə] überall (in) **I**
all the time [ˌɔ:l ðə 'taɪm] die ganze Zeit **II**
at **all** [ət‿'ɔ:l] überhaupt **I**
to start **all** over again [ˌstɑ:t‿ɔ:l‿'əʊvər‿əˌgen] ganz von vorn beginnen **IV**
all but ['ɔ:l bʌt] alle bis auf **VU3**, 95
all of them ['ɔ:l‿əv ˌðem] alle **I**
all of us ['ɔ:l‿əv ˌʌs] wir alle **II**
bowling **alley** ['bəʊlɪŋ‿ˌæli] Bowlingbahn **I**
to **allow** [ə'laʊ] erlauben; gestatten **VU1**, 19
*to be **allowed** to (do sth) [bi‿ə'laʊd tə] dürfen **II**
allowance *(AE)* [ə'laʊəns] Taschengeld **IV**
all-rounder [ɔ:l'raʊndə] Alleskönner/-in; Multitalent **VU2**, 49
almost ['ɔ:lməʊst] fast; beinahe **II**
alone [ə'ləʊn] allein; ohne fremde Hilfe **I**
*to leave sb **alone** [ˌli:v‿ə'ləʊn] jmdn. in Ruhe lassen **IV**
let **alone** [ˌlet‿ə'ləʊn] geschweige denn ⟨**VU1**, 28⟩
along [ə'lɒŋ] entlang **I**
*to sing **along** [ˌsɪŋ‿ə'lɒŋ] mitsingen **III**
along for the ride [əˌlɒŋ fə ðə 'raɪd] mit dabei **IV**
aloud [ə'laʊd] laut °**VTS1**, 41
alphabet ['ælfəbet] Alphabet **I**
alphabetical [ˌælfə'betɪkl] alphabetisch **II**
already [ɔ:l'redi] schon; bereits **I**
also ['ɔ:lsəʊ] auch **II**
although [ɔ:l'ðəʊ] obwohl **III**
always ['ɔ:lweɪz] immer; ständig **I**
amazed [ə'meɪzd] erstaunt; verblüfft **IV**
amazing [ə'meɪzɪŋ] unglaublich; toll; erstaunlich **II**
ambulance ['æmbjələns] Krankenwagen **III**
air **ambulance** ['eər‿ˌæmbjələns] Rettungshubschrauber **VU1**, 14
American [ə'merɪkən] Amerikanisch; amerikanisch; aus Amerika; Amerikaner/-in **II**
Native **American** [ˌneɪtɪv‿ə'merɪkən] Ureinwohner/-in Amerikas; Indianer/-in; indianisch **IV**
among [ə'mʌŋ] unter; inmitten **III**
amount (of) [ə'maʊnt] Menge **IV**
an [ən] ein/-e **I**
to **analyse** ['ænlaɪz] analysieren **VTS1**, 39
analysis [ə'næləsɪs] Analyse; Untersuchung °**VU1**, 31
to **analyze** *(AE)* ['ænlaɪz] analysieren **IV**
ancestor ['ænsestə] Vorfahr/-in; Ahn/-in **VU1**, 18
ancient ['eɪnʃnt] alt; altertümlich; antik **VAC1**, 9
and [ænd; ənd] und **I**
and so on [ənd 'səʊ‿ɒn] und so weiter **VTS2**, 77
angel ['eɪndʒl] Engel **III**
anger *(no pl)* ['æŋgə] Zorn; Wut **III**
angry ['æŋgri] wütend; zornig; verärgert; böse **I**
*to make sb **angry** [meɪk 'æŋgri] jmdn. wütend machen; jmdn. verärgern **III**
anguish ['æŋgwɪʃ] Qual; Leid ⟨**VU2**, 63⟩
animal ['ænɪməl] Tier **I**
animal shelter ['ænɪml ˌʃeltə] Tierheim **III**
animated ['ænɪmeɪtɪd] Zeichentrick- **VU3**, 89
ankle ['æŋkl] Fußgelenk; Fußknöchel **II**
to twist your **ankle** [ˌtwɪst jɔ:r‿'æŋkl] sich den Knöchel verrenken **II**
annex [ə'neks] Nebengebäude; Anbau ⟨**VU2**, 63⟩
anniversary [ˌænɪ'vɜ:sri] Jubiläum; Jahrestag **VU1**, 24
to **announce** [ə'naʊns] ankündigen; durchsagen **IV**
announcement [ə'naʊnsmənt] Ankündigung; Durchsage **II**
annoyed [ə'nɔɪd] verärgert **VTS1**, 42
anonymity [ænə'nɪməti] Anonymität **VU3**, 103
anonymous [ən'ɒnɪməs] anonym **II**
another [ə'nʌðə] ein/-e andere/-r/-s; noch ein/-e; ein/-e andere/-r/-s **I**
answer ['ɑ:nsə] Antwort **I**
short **answer** [ˌʃɔ:t‿'ɑ:nsə] Kurzantwort **I**
to **answer** ['ɑ:nsə] antworten; beantworten **I**
to **answer** the phone [ˌɑ:nsə ðə 'fəʊn] einen Anruf entgegennehmen **I**
answering machine ['ɑ:nsrɪŋ məˌʃi:n] Anrufbeantworter **I**
anthem ['ænθəm] Hymne **III**
anxiety [æŋ'zaɪəti] Angst; Sorge; Besorgnis ⟨**VU3**, 101⟩
any ['eni] irgendein/-e/-er; irgendwelche **I**
not **any** more [ˌnɒt‿eni 'mɔ:] nicht mehr **I**
not … **any** [nɒt … eni] kein/-e/-en **I**
not **anymore** *(AE)* [ˌnɒt‿eni'mɔ:] nicht mehr **IV**
anyone else [ˌeniwʌn 'els] jemand anderes **II**
not … **anything** [ˌnɒt 'eniθɪŋ] nichts **I**
Anything else? [ˌeniθɪŋ‿'els] Sonst noch etwas? **I**
anyway ['eniweɪ] trotzdem; jedenfalls; sowieso **II**
anywhere ['eniweə] irgendwo; überall (egal, wo) **II**
just about **anywhere** [ˌdʒʌst‿əˌbaʊt 'eniweə] praktisch überall **IV**
apart [ə'pɑ:t] auseinander; getrennt **IV**
apart from [ə'pɑ:t frəm] abgesehen von; außer **III**
apartheid [ə'pɑ:taɪt] Apartheid **VAC1**, 8
apartment *(AE)* [ə'pɑ:tmənt] Apartment; Wohnung **IV**
to **apologise** [ə'pɒlədʒaɪz] sich entschuldigen **III**
apology [ə'pɒlədʒi] Entschuldigung **VU2**, 63
app [æp] App **II**
to **appear** [ə'pɪə] auftauchen; erscheinen **IV**
appearance [ə'pɪərns] Erscheinung; Aussehen; Auftritt **VTS1**, 38
applause [ə'plɔ:z] Applaus; Beifall ⟨**VU2**, 62⟩
apple ['æpl] Apfel **I**
applicant ['æplɪkənt] Bewerber/-in **VU2**, 48
application [ˌæplɪ'keɪʃn] Bewerbung; Antrag **VU2**, 48; Bewerbungs- °**VU2**, 47

application letter [ˌæplɪ'keɪʃn ˌletə] Bewerbungsschreiben **V U2**, 48
to **apply** (to) [ə'plaɪ tə] gelten (für); zutreffen (auf) **V AC1**, 10; anwenden (auf) °**V AC2**, 81
to **apply** (for) [ə'plaɪ fə] sich bewerben (um); beantragen **V U1**, 20
to **apply** for [ə'plaɪ fə] fragen nach ⟨**V U2**, 63⟩
approach [ə'prəʊtʃ] Herangehensweise; Vorgehensweise; Ansatz; Annäherung **IV**
appropriate [ə'prəʊpriət] angemessen **III**
to **approve** [ə'pru:v] anerkennen; gutheißen; genehmigen **V U3**, 89
April ['eɪprəl] April **I**
Arab ['ærəb] arabisch **III**
Arabic ['ærəbɪk] Arabisch ⟨**V AC1**, 11⟩
architect ['ɑ:kɪtekt] Architekt/-in **II**
architecture ['ɑ:kɪtektʃə] Architektur **IV**
area ['eəriə] Areal; Gebiet; Fläche **II**
run **area** ['rʌn ˌeəriə] Gehege; Auslauf **III**
to **argue** ['ɑ:gju:] argumentieren; streiten; erörtern **IV**
argument ['ɑ:gjəmənt] Auseinandersetzung; Streit; Argument **III**
argumentative [ˌɑ:gjə'mentətɪv] erörternd **IV**
argumentative essay [ɑ:gjəˌmentətɪv‿'eseɪ] Erörterung **VTS3**, 108
arm [ɑ:m] Arm **II**
armchair ['ɑ:mtʃeə] Sessel **V U1**, 30
army ['ɑ:mi] Armee **IV**
aroma [ə'rəʊmə] Duft ⟨**V U3**, 101⟩
around [ə'raʊnd] um … herum; umher **I**
*to be **around** [bi‿ə'raʊnd] da sein; zusammen sein mit **IV**
*to find one's way **around** [ˌfaɪnd wʌnz ˌweɪ‿ə'raʊnd] sich zurechtfinden **IV**
*to show sb **around** (a place) [ˌʃəʊ‿ə'raʊnd] jmdn. (an einem Ort) herumführen **V U1**, 16
to turn **around** [ˌtɜ:n‿(ə)'raʊnd] (sich) umdrehen; wenden **II**
around [ə'raʊnd] ungefähr; etwa **VTS2**, 75
to **arrange** [ə'reɪndʒ] arrangieren; anordnen **III**
to **arrest** [ə'rest] festnehmen; verhaften **II**
arrival [ə'raɪvl] Ankunft **III**; Ankommende/-r; Neuzugang **IV**
arrivals hall [ə'raɪvlz ˌhɔ:l] Ankunftshalle **III**
to **arrive** [ə'raɪv] ankommen **II**
arrow ['ærəʊ] Pfeil **III**
Art [ɑ:t] Kunstunterricht **I**
art [ɑ:t] Kunst **II**
clip **art** ['klɪp‿ɑ:t] Clipart; Grafik °**V U3**, 98
artichoke ['ɑ:tɪtʃəʊk] Artischocke ⟨**V U3**, 97⟩
article ['ɑ:tɪkl] Artikel; Bericht *(in einer Zeitschrift, Zeitung)* **II**
definite **article** [ˌdefɪnət 'ɑ:tɪkl] bestimmter Artikel °**V U3**, 91
reference **article** ['refrns ˌɑ:tɪkl] Referenzartikel **III**
to **articulate** [ɑ:'tɪkjəleɪt] artikulieren; aussprechen ⟨**V U1**, 29⟩
artist ['ɑ:tɪst] Künstler/-in **IV**
artwork ['ɑ:twɜ:k] Illustrationen; Bebilderung **IV**
as [æz; əz] als **II**
as if [əz‿'ɪf] als ob **III**
as [æz] während; indem **I**; wie **II**
as … **as** [əz … əz] so … wie **I**
as far **as** [əz 'fɑ:r‿əz] soweit **VTS3**, 109
as long **as** [əz 'lɒŋ‿əz] solange **V U3**, 89
as soon **as** [əz 'su:n‿əz] sobald **II**
as with ['æz wɪð] wie (auch) bei ⟨**V U3**, 97⟩
… **as** well **as** … [əz 'wel‿əz] sowie; und (auch) **IV**
as best **as** I can remember [əz ˌbest əz‿aɪ kæn rɪ'membə] soweit ich mich erinnern kann ⟨**V U3**, 101⟩
as [æz; əz] da; weil **IV**
to **ask** [ɑ:sk] fragen; bitten **I**
Ask about … ['ɑ:sk‿əˌbaʊt] Frage/Fragt nach … **I**
to **ask** for ['ɑ:sk fə] fragen nach; bitten um **I**
*to be **asleep** [bi‿ə'sli:p] schlafen **II**
*to fall **asleep** [ˌfɔ:l‿ə'sli:p] einschlafen **I**
aspect ['æspekt] Aspekt; Gesichtspunkt **IV**
aspiring [ə'spaɪrɪŋ] aufstrebend **V U3**, 86
assault [ə'sɔ:lt] Übergriff; Angriff; Tätlichkeit ⟨**V U3**, 101⟩
assembly [ə'sembli] Versammlung; Morgenappell **II**
assessment [ə'sesmənt] Bewertung; Einschätzung; Beurteilung °**VTS2**, 78
to **assign** [ə'saɪn] zuordnen; übertragen **V U2**, 62
assignment [ə'saɪnmənt] Aufgabe; Auftrag; Mission **V U2**, 62
to **assist** [ə'sɪst] helfen ⟨**V AC1**, 11⟩
assistant [ə'sɪstnt] Assistent/-in; Verkäufer/-in **II**
assistant counsellor [əˌsɪstnt 'kaʊnslə] Hilfsbetreuer/-in **V U2**, 48
sales **assistant** ['seɪlz‿əˌsɪstnt] Verkäufer/-in **V U2**, 49
to **associate** [ə'səʊʃieɪt] assoziieren; verbinden **V U2**, 49
*to be **associated** with [bi‿ə'səʊʃieɪtɪd wɪð] verbunden werden mit; stehen für ⟨**V AC1**, 11⟩
association [əˌsəʊʃi'eɪʃn] Verband; Organisation **V U1**, 15
to **assume** [ə'sju:m] annehmen **V AC2**, 81
astronaut ['æstrənɔ:t] Astronaut/-in **IV**
at [æt; ət] in; auf; bei; an; um *(bei Uhrzeitangaben)* **I**
at 7:30 [ət ˌsevn‿'θɜ:ti] um halb acht **I**
at all [ət‿'ɔ:l] überhaupt **I**
at all times [ˌət‿ɔ:l 'taɪmz] immer; jederzeit; stets **V U2**, 48
at first [ət 'fɜ:st] zuerst; zunächst **II**
at home [ət 'həʊm] zu Hause **I**
at last [ət 'lɑ:st] endlich; schließlich **I**
at least [ət 'li:st] mindestens; wenigstens **II**
at present [ət 'preznt] derzeitig; momentan ⟨**V AC1**, 11⟩
at the back of [ət ðə 'bæk‿əv] hinten; am Ende; im hinteren Teil **II**
at the moment [ət ðə 'məʊmənt] im Moment; gerade **I**
at the same time [ət ðə ˌseɪm 'taɪm] zur selben Zeit; gleichzeitig **I**
at the scene [ˌət ðə 'si:n] vor Ort **V U1**, 26
at the time [ˌət ðə 'taɪm] damals **IV**
at the weekend [ət ðə ˌwi:k'end] am Wochenende **I**
athletics *(no pl)* [æθ'letɪks] Leichtathletik **III**
atlas ['ætləs] Atlas **II**
atmosphere ['ætməsfɪə] Atmosphäre; Stimmung **II**
to **attach** [ə'tætʃ] anfügen; anhängen ⟨**V U3**, 92⟩
attachment [ə'tætʃmənt] Anhang **V U2**, 51
attack [ə'tæk] Angriff; Überfall **V U1**, 26
to **attack** [ə'tæk] angreifen **III**
attendant [ə'tendnt] Aufseher/-in; Wärter/-in ⟨**V U2**, 63⟩
flight **attendant** ['flaɪt‿əˌtendnt] Flugbegleiter/-in **III**
attention [ə'tenʃn] Aufmerksamkeit; Beachtung **II**
to grab **attention** [ˌgræb‿ə'tenʃn] Aufmerksamkeit erregen °**V U1**, 17
*to pay **attention** to sb/sth [ˌpeɪ‿ə'tenʃn tʊ] jmdn./etw. beachten **III**
attic ['ætɪk] Dachboden **II**
attitude ['ætɪtju:d] Haltung; Einstellung **IV**
to **attract** [ə'trækt] anziehen **IV**
attraction [ə'trækʃn] Attraktion; Sehenswürdigkeit **II**; Anziehung; Anziehungskraft **V U3**, 90
attractive [ə'træktɪv] attraktiv **IV**
atypical [ˌeɪ'tɪpɪkl] atypisch ⟨**V U3**, 100⟩
au pair [ˌəʊ'peə] Au-pair **V U2**, 52
audience ['ɔ:diəns] Publikum **II**
audio ['ɔ:diəʊ] Audio-; Hör- **I**
audio tour ['ɔ:diəʊ ˌtʊə] Audioführung **II**
audio-visual effect [ˌɔ:diəʊvɪʒuəl ɪ'fekt] audiovisueller Effekt **II**
audition [ɔ:'dɪʃn] Vorsprechen; Vorsingen; Vortanzen **III**
August ['ɔ:gəst] August **I**
aunt [ɑ:nt] Tante **I**
agony **aunt** ['ægəni‿ɑ:nt] Kummerkastentante **II**
auntie ['ɑ:nti] Tantchen **IV**
Aussie *(coll)* ['ɒzi] Australier/-in; australisch *(ugs.)* **V AC1**, 10
Australian [ɒs'treɪliən] australisch; Australier/-in **III**
author ['ɔ:θə] Autor/-in **III**

available [ə'veɪləbl] erhältlich; verfügbar **IV**
to be **available** [bi ə'veɪləbl] zur Verfügung stehen; abkömmlich sein **V U2**, 48
average ['ævrɪdʒ] Durchschnitt; Durchschnitts- ⟨**VTS2**, 79⟩
on **average** [ɒn‿'ævrɪdʒ] durchschnittlich; im Durchschnitt **V U3**, 95
to **avoid** [ə'vɔɪd] vermeiden, meiden; aus dem Weg gehen **III**
award [ə'wɔ:d] Auszeichnung; Preis **II**
to be **aware** of sth [bi‿ə'weər‿əv] sich etw. bewusst sein **IV**
away [ə'weɪ] weg **I**
*to do **away** with sth [ˌdu:‿ə'weɪ wɪð] etw. abschaffen; etw. loswerden ⟨**VTS3**, 109⟩
*to give **away** [ˌgɪv‿ə'weɪ] verteilen; verschenken; verraten; preisgeben **IV**
right **away** [ˌraɪt‿ə'weɪ] sofort; gleich **I**
*to run **away** [ˌrʌn‿ə'weɪ] wegrennen **I**
straight **away** [ˌstreɪt‿ə'weɪ] sofort; gleich **III**
*to throw **away** [ˌθrəʊ‿ə'weɪ] wegwerfen **I**
to turn **away** from sb/sth [ˌtɜ:n‿ə'weɪ frəm] sich von jmdm./etw. abwenden ⟨**V U3**, 100⟩
awesome ['ɔ:səm] super; spitze **IV**
awful ['ɔ:fl] schrecklich; furchtbar **I**
awkward ['ɔ:kwəd] peinlich; ungünstig; ungeschickt; unbeholfen **V U1**, 31
axe [æks] Axt **III**

B

baby ['beɪbi] Baby; Säugling **I**
babysitting ['beɪbɪsɪtɪŋ] Babysitting **IV**
back [bæk] Rückseite; Rücken **II**; Ende; hinterer Bereich **VTS1**, 44
at the **back** of [ət ðə 'bæk‿əv] hinten, am Ende; im hinteren Teil **II**
back to **back** [ˌbæk tʊ 'bæk] Rücken an Rücken **I**
back [bæk] zurück **I**; damals **V AC1**, 8
back then [bæk 'ðen] damals **III**
*to go right **back** to [ˌgəʊ raɪt 'bæk tə] zurückgehen auf **II**
*to lean **back** [ˌli:n 'bæk] sich zurücklehnen ⟨**V U2**, 64⟩
to turn **back** [tɜ:n 'bæk] umkehren; zurückgehen **II**
backache ['bækeɪk] Rückenschmerzen; Rückenweh **II**
background ['bækgraʊnd] Hintergrund **I**
backing ['bækɪŋ] Hintergrund-; Background- **III**
backing dancer ['bækɪŋ ˌdɑ:nsə] Backgroundtänzer/-in **III**
backpack ['bækpæk] Rucksack **III**
backseat ['bæksi:t] Rücksitz **IV**
backstage [ˌbæk'steɪdʒ] backstage; hinter der Bühne **V U3**, 88
backyard [ˌbæk'jɑ:d] Garten; Hinterhof **III**
bacon ['beɪkn] Schinkenspeck; Speck **I**
bad [bæd] schlecht; böse; schlimm *(ugs.)* **I**
*to go **bad** [ˌgəʊ 'bæd] schiefgehen; schlecht werden; verderben **IV**
Too **bad**! [ˌtu: 'bæd] Zu dumm!; Schade! **I**
badly-written [ˌbædli'rɪtn] schlecht geschrieben **IV**
badminton ['bædmɪntən] Badminton **I**
bag [bæg] Tasche; Tüte **I**
tea **bag** ['ti: bæg] Teebeutel **III**
bagpipes *(pl)* ['bægpaɪps] Dudelsack **III**
baked beans *(pl)* [ˌbeɪkt 'bi:nz] weiße Bohnen in Tomatensoße **I**
balance ['bæləns] Gleichgewicht **VTS2**, 78
ball [bɔ:l] Ball **I**
*to keep the **ball** bouncing [ˌki:p ðə bɔ:l 'baʊntsɪŋ] *hier:* das Gespräch am Laufen halten **III**
ballgame ['bɔ:lgeɪm] Baseballspiel ⟨**V U3**, 97⟩
to **ban** [bæn] bannen; verbieten; sperren **III**
banana [bə'nɑ:nə] Banane **I**
band [bænd] Band; Musikgruppe **III**
to **bang** [bæŋ] schlagen; knallen ⟨**V U3**, 100⟩
to **bang** shut [ˌbæŋ 'ʃʌt] zuknallen ⟨**V U1**, 30⟩
Bang! [bæŋ] Peng! **II**
bank [bæŋk] Ufer **II**; Bank **IV**
word **bank** ['wɜ:d ˌbæŋk] Wortsammlung **III**
banner ['bænə] Banner; Spruchband; Transparent **V AC3**, 114
bar [bɑ:] Bar **IV**
bar graph ['bɑ: grɑ:f] Säulendiagramm; Balkendiagramm **IV**
chocolate **bar** ['tʃɒklət ˌbɑ:] Schokoriegel **IV**
snack **bar** ['snæk ˌbɑ:] Café; Imbissstube **I**
barbecue ['bɑ:bɪkju:] Grillparty **IV**
barbie *(infml)* (= barbecue) ['bɑ:bi] Grillparty **V U1**, 16
bare [beə] nackt; bloß **III**
barefoot [beə'fʊt] barfuß ⟨**V U3**, 101⟩
bargain ['bɑ:gɪn] Schnäppchen **I**
to **bark** [bɑ:k] bellen **I**
to **base** on ['beɪs‿ɒn] stützen auf **IV**
baseball ['beɪsbɔ:l] Baseball **IV**
based on ['beɪst‿ɒn] basierend auf; beruhend auf **IV**
*to be **based** [bi 'beɪst] ansässig sein **V U3**, 91
bashing ['bæʃɪŋ] Prügel; Schelte ⟨**VTS3**, 108⟩
basic ['beɪsɪk] grundlegend; Grund- **II**
basically ['beɪsɪkli] eigentlich; grundsätzlich; im Grunde genommen **VTS3**, 109
basics *(pl)* ['beɪsɪks] Grundlagen **III**
basketball ['bɑ:skɪtbɔ:l] Basketball **I**
bat [bæt] Schläger *(Tischtennis; Baseball)* **IV**
bath [bɑ:θ] Bad; Badewanne **I**
baths *(pl)* [bɑ:θs] Badehaus; Therme **III**
bathroom ['bɑ:θrʊm] Bad; Badezimmer **I**
battery ['bætri] Batterie; Akku **II**
battle ['bætl] Schlacht; Kampf **III**
BC (= before Christ) [ˌbi:'si:] vor Christus **III**
*to **be** [bi:] sein **I**
*to **be** a team player [ˌbi‿ə 'ti:m ˌpleɪə] gern im Team arbeiten **V U2**, 48
*to **be** able to (do sth) [bi‿'eɪbl tə] fähig sein zu; können; dürfen **II**
*to **be** about [bi‿ə'baʊt] sich handeln um **I**
*to **be** about to do sth [bi‿ə'baʊt tə] im Begriff sein, etw. zu tun **IV**
*to **be** addictive [bi‿ə'dɪktɪv] süchtig machen ⟨**VTS2**, 79⟩
*to **be** afraid (of) [bi‿ə'freɪd‿əv] (sich) fürchten; Angst haben (vor) **III**
*to **be** allowed to (do sth) [bi‿ə'laʊd tə] dürfen **II**
*to **be** around [bi‿ə'raʊnd] da sein; zusammen sein mit **IV**
*to **be** asleep [bi‿ə'sli:p] schlafen **II**
*to **be** associated with [bi‿ə'səʊʃieɪtɪd wɪð] verbunden werden mit; stehen für ⟨**V AC1**, 11⟩
to **be** available [bi ə'veɪləbl] zur Verfügung stehen; abkömmlich sein **V U2**, 48
to **be** aware of sth [bi‿ə'weər‿əv] sich etw. bewusst sein **IV**
*to **be** based [bi 'beɪst] ansässig sein **V U3**, 91
*to **be** born [bi 'bɔ:n] geboren werden **III**
*to **be** called [bi 'kɔ:ld] heißen; genannt werden **III**
*to **be** called to do sth [bi 'kɔ:ld tə du:] auserwählt sein, etw. zu tun **III**
*to **be** confronted with [bi kən'frʌntɪd wɪð] konfrontiert werden mit **VTS3**, 111
*to **be** connected [bi kə'nektɪd] zusammenhängen; in Zusammenhang stehen **II**
*to **be** considered (to be) sth [bi kən'sɪdəd tə] als etw. gelten **IV**
*to **be** crazy about [bi 'kreɪzi‿əbaʊt] verrückt sein nach; abfahren auf **IV**
*to **be** done with [bi 'dʌn wɪð] fertig sein mit **IV**
to **be** entitled to sth [bi‿ɪn'taɪtld tə] berechtigt sein; ein Anrecht haben auf; Anspruch haben auf °**V AC2**, 81
*to **be** etched with [bi 'etʃt wɪð] geprägt sein von ⟨**V U1**, 30⟩
*to **be** expected to *(+ inf)* [bi ɪk'spektɪd tə] sollen **V U2**, 48
*to **be** fed up (with) [bi fed‿'ʌp wɪð] sauer sein (auf); die Nase voll haben (von) **III**
*to **be** gone [bi 'gɒn] verschwunden sein; weg sein **II**
*to **be** good at [bi 'gʊd‿ət] gut sein in **I**
*to **be** grounded [bi 'graʊndɪd] Hausarrest haben **III**
*to **be** hard on sb [bi 'hɑ:d‿ɒn] streng mit jmdm. sein **III**
*to **be** homesick [bi 'həʊmsɪk] Heimweh haben **III**
*to **be** in [bi‿'ɪn] dabei sein; mitmachen **II**
*to **be** in a hurry [ˌbi‿ɪn‿ə 'hʌri] es eilig haben; in Eile sein **IV**

*to **be** in charge (of) [bi‿ɪn 'tʃɑ:dʒ‿əv] die Verantwortung tragen (für); zuständig sein (für) **III**
*to **be** in sb's shoes [ˌbi: ɪn sʌmbɒdɪz 'ʃu:z] an jmds. Stelle sein; in jmds. Haut stecken **III**
*to **be** in the way [ˌbi‿ɪn ðə 'weɪ] im Weg sein/stehen **I**
*to **be** interested in [bi‿'ɪntrəstɪd‿ɪn] interessiert sein an; sich interessieren für **II**
*to **be** into [bi‿'ɪntə] mögen; stehen auf **I**
*to **be** involved (in) [bi‿ɪn'vɒlvd‿ɪn] involviert sein (in); engagiert sein (in); beteiligt sein (an) **V U1**, 26
*to **be** jealous (of) [bi 'dʒeləs] eifersüchtig sein (auf); neidisch sein (auf) **I**
*to **be** known as [bi 'nəʊn‿əz] bekannt sein als **IV**
*to **be** late [bi 'leɪt] zu spät dran sein; zu spät kommen **I**
*to **be** like [bi 'laɪk] sein **III**
*to **be** likely [bi 'laɪkli] wahrscheinlich sein **V U1**, 14
*to **be** located [bi ləʊ'keɪtɪd] gelegen sein; liegen **IV**
*to **be** lucky [bi 'lʌki] Glück haben **II**
*to **be** made of [bi 'meɪd‿əv] bestehen aus **III**
*to **be** made up of/from [bi meɪd‿'ʌp‿əv/frəm] zusammengesetzt sein aus; bestehen aus **V U2**, 58
*to **be** obliged to *(+ inf)* [bi:‿ə'blaɪdʒd tə] verpflichtet sein, etw. zu tun; müssen **V U3**, 95
*to **be** on [bi‿'ɒn] an sein; laufen **II**; auf Sendung sein °**V U3**, 97
*to **be** on fire [ˌbi:‿ɒn 'faɪə] brennen **III**
*to **be** passionate about sth [bi 'pæʃnət əˌbaʊt] etw. leidenschaftlich gern tun; eine Leidenschaft für etw. haben; für etw. brennen **V U2**, 48
*to **be** prejudiced against sb/sth [bi 'predʒədɪst əˌgenst] voreingenommen sein gegenüber jmdm./etw. **V AC2**, 81
*to **be** regarded as [bi rɪ'gɑ:dɪd‿əz] angesehen werden als; gelten als ⟨**V AC1**, 11⟩
*to **be** related to [bi rɪ'leɪtɪd tə] verwandt sein mit **V U1**, 29
*to **be** required to *(+ inf)* [bi rɪ'kwaɪəd tə] müssen **V U3**, 95
*to **be** right [bi 'raɪt] recht haben **I**
*to **be** said to *(+ inf)* [bi 'sed tə] sollen; gelten als **V U3**, 90
*to **be** scared (of) [bi 'skeəd‿əv] Angst haben (vor) **I**
*to **be** set (in) [bi 'set ɪn] spielen (in); seinen Schauplatz haben (in) **III**
*to **be** sick [bi 'sɪk] sich übergeben **III**
*to **be** sorry [bi 'sɒri] leid tun **I**
*to **be** stressed out [bi ˌstrest‿'aʊt] völlig gestresst sein **III**
*to **be** stuck [bi 'stʌk] festsitzen; feststecken; hängen bleiben **IV**
*to **be** supposed to *(+ inf)* [bi sə'pəʊzd tə] sollen **V U2**, 48
*to **be** surprised [bi sə'praɪzd] überrascht sein **II**
*to **be** suspended [bi sə'spendɪd] suspendiert werden; zeitweilig vom Unterricht ausgeschlossen werden **IV**
*to **be** swept out to sea [bi ˌswept‿aʊt tə 'si:] aufs offene Meer getrieben werden **V U1**, 14
*to **be** tired of [bi 'taɪəd‿əv] es müde sein (zu); es leid sein (zu); es satt haben (zu) **IV**
*to **be** to *(+ inf)* ['bi tə] sollen **V U3**, 95
*to **be** trapped [bi 'træpt] eingeschlossen sein; in der Falle sitzen **III**
*to **be** true to oneself [bi 'tru: tu wʌnˌself] sich selbst treu bleiben **IV**
*to **be** unable to do sth [bi‿ʌn'eɪbl tə] unfähig sein, etw. zu tun; nicht in der Lage sein, etw. zu tun **VTS2**, 75
*to **be** unlucky [bi‿ʌn'lʌki] Pech haben **I**
*to **be** up to [bi‿'ʌp tə] vorhaben **II**
*to **be** used to [bi 'ju:s‿tə] gewöhnt sein an; gewohnt sein **III**
*to **be** willing to do sth [bi 'wɪlɪŋ tə] gewillt sein, etw. zu tun; bereit sein, etw. zu tun **V U3**, 94
*to **be** worried [bi 'wʌrid] beunruhigt sein; besorgt sein **II**
*to **be** worth [bi 'wɜ:θ] wert sein **I**
*to **be** worth the wait [bi ˌwɜ:θ ðə 'weɪt] das Warten wert sein ⟨**VTS1**, 41⟩
*to **be** wrong [bi 'rɒŋ] unrecht haben; sich irren **I**
Be careful! [bi: 'keəfl] Vorsicht!; Pass/Passt auf! **I**
Here you **are**. [ˌhɪə ju‿'ɑ:] Bitte schön. **I**
Is this how you (do) ...? [ɪz 'ðɪs haʊ jʊ ˌdu:] Machst du so ...? **I**
I'**m** from ... [ˌaɪm frɒm] Ich bin aus ... **I**
beach [bi:tʃ] Strand **II**
bead of sweat [ˌbi:d‿əv 'swet] Schweißperle ⟨**V U3**, 102⟩
bean [bi:n] Bohne **V U2**, 53
baked **beans** *(pl)* [ˌbeɪkt 'bi:nz] weiße Bohnen in Tomatensoße **I**
bear [beə] Bär **II**
grizzly **bear** ['grɪzli ˌbeə] Grizzlybär **IV**
beat [bi:t] Takt; Rhythmus **V U1**, 29
*to **beat** [bi:t] schlagen; besiegen **II**
beautiful ['bju:tɪfl] schön; hübsch; wunderbar **II**
because [bɪ'kɒz] weil; da **I**
because of [bɪ'kɒz‿əv] wegen **II**
*to **become** [bɪ'kʌm] werden **II**
*to **become** extinct [bɪˌkʌm‿ɪk'stɪŋkt] aussterben **III**
*to **become** friends [bɪˌkʌm‿'frendz] sich anfreunden; Freundschaft schließen **IV**
bed [bed] Bett **I**
*to go to **bed** [ˌgəʊ tə 'bed] ins Bett gehen **I**
bedroom ['bedrʊm] Schlafzimmer **I**
bee [bi:] Biene **II**
Beefeater ['bi:fˌi:tə] königlicher Leibgardist **II**
before [bɪ'fɔ:] vor *(zeitlich)*; bevor **I**; schon einmal; vorher; zuvor **II**
*to **begin** [bɪ'gɪn] beginnen; anfangen **II**
beginning [bɪ'gɪnɪŋ] Anfang; Beginn **II**
to **behave** [bɪ'heɪv] sich benehmen; sich verhalten **III**
behavior *(no pl) (AE)* [bɪ'heɪvjə] Verhalten; Benehmen; Betragen **IV**
behaviour *(no pl)* [bɪ'heɪvjə] Verhalten; Benehmen; Betragen **III**
behind [bɪ'haɪnd] hinter **I**
*to leave **behind** [ˌli:v‿bɪ'haɪnd] zurücklassen **III**
belief [bɪ'li:f] Glaube; Überzeugung **V AC3**, 115
believable [bɪ'li:vəbl] glaubwürdig **IV**
to **believe** [bɪ'li:v] glauben **I**
to **believe** in sb/sth [bɪ'li:v‿ɪn] an jmdn./etw. glauben **V AC3**, 114
He couldn't **believe** his eyes. [hi ˌkʊdnt bɪˌli:v hɪz‿'aɪz] Er traute seinen Augen nicht. **II**
bell [bel] Glocke **II**
saved by the **bell** [ˌseɪvd baɪ ðə 'bel] noch mal Glück gehabt **III**
belongings *(pl)* [bɪ'lɒŋɪŋz] Habseligkeiten; Hab und Gut **IV**
to **belong** (to) [bɪ'lɒŋ (tə)] gehören (zu) **II**
below [bɪ'ləʊ] unterhalb; unten **I**
belt [belt] Gürtel **III**
seat **belt** ['si:t belt] Sicherheitsgurt **IV**
bench [benʃ] Bank; Sitzbank **III**
*to **bend** over [ˌbend‿'əʊvə] sich vorbeugen; sich beugen über ⟨**V U2**, 63⟩
benefit ['benɪfɪt] Vorteil; Nutzen; Unterstützung **IV**
beside [bɪ'saɪd] neben ⟨**V U2**, 62⟩
besides [bɪ'saɪdz] neben **II**; außerdem; überdies ⟨**V U3**, 100⟩
(the) **best** [best] (der/die/das) Beste **II**
to save the **best** for last [ˌseɪv ðə ˌbest fə 'lɑ:st] sich das Beste bis zum Schluss aufheben **IV**
best [best] beste/-r/-s; am besten **I**
as **best** as I can remember [əz ˌbest əz‿aɪ kæn rɪ'membə] soweit ich mich erinnern kann ⟨**V U3**, 101⟩
Best wishes [ˌbest 'wɪʃɪz] Viele Grüße; Herzliche Grüße **II**
the **best** ... ever ['best ... ˌevə] der/die/das beste ... überhaupt **III**
*to **bet** [bet] wetten **VTS3**, 110
better ['betə] besser; lieber **I**
You'd **better** ... *(= You had better)* ['ju:d ˌbetə] Du solltest lieber ... **IV**

between [bɪ'twi:n] zwischen **I**
in **between** [ˌɪn bɪ'twi:n] dazwischen **III**
beyond [bi'ɒnd] jenseits; über … hinaus **V AC2**, 80
bicycle motocross [ˌbaɪsɪkl 'məʊtəʊkrɒs] Fahrradmotocross **II**
big [bɪg] groß **I**
big deal [bɪg 'di:l] große Sache **III**
bighorn sheep [ˌbɪghɔ:n 'ʃi:p] Dickhornschaf **IV**
bike [baɪk] Fahrrad **I**
mountain **biking** ['maʊntɪn ˌbaɪkɪŋ] Mountainbikefahren **II**
bilingual [baɪ'lɪŋgwl] zweisprachig **II**
bill *(AE)* [bɪl] Geldschein; Rechnung **IV**
billboard ['bɪlbɔ:d] Plakatwand **IV**
billion ['bɪliən] Milliarde **III**
billionaire ['bɪliəneə] Milliardär/-in **IV**
biographical [ˌbaɪəʊ'græfɪkl] biografisch **III**
biological [ˌbaɪə'lɒdʒɪkl] biologisch **VTS2**, 77
bird [bɜ:d] Vogel **II**
birdwatching ['bɜ:dˌwɒtʃɪŋ] Vogelbeobachtung **II**
date of **birth** [ˌdeɪt‿əv 'bɜ:θ] Geburtsdatum **III**
birthday ['bɜ:θdeɪ] Geburtstag **I**
Happy **Birthday**! [ˌhæpi 'bɜ:θdeɪ] Alles Gute zum Geburtstag!; Herzlichen Glückwunsch zum Geburtstag! **I**
biscuit ['bɪskɪt] Keks **I**
bison ['baɪsn], **bison** ['baɪsn] *(pl)* Bison; Büffel **IV**
bistro ['bi:strəʊ] Bistro ⟨**V U3**, 97⟩
a **bit** [ə 'bɪt] ein bisschen; ein wenig **II**
bit by **bit** [ˌbɪt baɪ 'bɪt] Stück für Stück **III**
*to do one's **bit** [ˌdu:‿wʌnz 'bɪt] seinen Teil beitragen **V AC3**, 114
bitchy ['bɪtʃi] gehässig; gemein **VTS1**, 42
*to **bite** [baɪt] beißen **II**
bitter ['bɪtə] bitter **V U2**, 53
bitterness *(no pl)* ['bɪtənəs] Bitterkeit; Verbitterung **V AC1**, 8
black [blæk] schwarz **I**
black eye [blæk‿'aɪ] blaues Auge **IV**
*to go **black** [ˌgəʊ 'blæk] schwarz werden **II**
to **blend** together [ˌblend tə'geðə] ineinander verschmelzen ⟨**V U3**, 101⟩
blind [blaɪnd] blind ⟨**V AC2**, 80⟩
to **blink** [blɪŋk] blinzeln; zwinkern ⟨**V U2**, 63⟩
block [blɒk] Block; Häuserblock **IV**
building **block** ['bɪldɪŋ blɒk] Baustein **II**
to **block** [blɒk] blockieren; abblocken **II**
blog [blɒg] Blog; Internettagebuch **III**
blogger ['blɒgə] Blogger/-in **IV**
bloke *(fam)* [bləʊk] Typ *(ugs.)* **III**
blond [blɒnd] blond **III**
blood [blʌd] Blut **III**
bloody ['blʌdi] blutig ⟨**VTS3**, 110⟩
*to **blow out** [ˌbləʊ‿'aʊt] ausblasen; auspusten **I**
blue [blu:] blau **I**
blurred [blɜ:d] verschwommen; verwischt **III**
BMX [ˌbi:em'eks] BMX **II**
board [bɔ:d] Brett; Tafel **III**
tourist **board** ['tʊərɪst bɔ:d] Touristeninformation **II**
boarding ['bɔ:dɪŋ] Boarding **III**
boarding card ['bɔ:dɪŋ ˌkɑ:d] Bordkarte **III**
boat [bəʊt] Boot **I**
boating lake ['bəʊtɪŋ ˌleɪk] See zum Rudern **I**
body ['bɒdi] Körper **III**
human **body** [ˌhju:mən 'bɒdi] menschlicher Körper **II**
bodybuilder ['bɒdiˌbɪldə] Bodybuilder/-in **V U3**, 92
bodyguard ['bɒdigɑ:d] Bodyguard **IV**
bold [bəʊld] fett gedruckt **III**; fett ⟨**V U2**, 47⟩
bone [bəʊn] Knochen **V AC3**, 115
bonfire ['bɒnfaɪə] Lagerfeuer; Freudenfeuer **I**
to **boo** sb [bu:] jmdn. ausbuhen ⟨**VTS3**, 108⟩
booboo ['bu:bu:] Aua ⟨**VTS1**, 40⟩
book [bʊk] Buch **I**
exercise **book** ['eksəsaɪz ˌbʊk] Übungsheft **I**
to **book** [bʊk] buchen; reservieren **II**
boom [bu:m] wirtschaftlicher Aufschwung; Boom; Hochkonjunktur **V U3**, 90
to **boom** [bu:m] dröhnen **II**; florieren; boomen **V U3**, 90
boomtown ['bu:mtaʊn] schnell wachsende Stadt **IV**
boot [bu:t] Stiefel; Kofferraum **III**
border ['bɔ:də] Grenze **V U3**, 90
bored [bɔ:d] gelangweilt **I**
boredom ['bɔ:dəm] Langeweile **V U2**, 47
boring ['bɔ:rɪŋ] langweilig **I**
*to be **born** [bi 'bɔ:n] geboren werden **III**
to **borrow** ['bɒrəʊ] (sich) ausleihen **II**
boss [bɒs] Boss; Chef **III**
bossy ['bɒsi] herrisch; rechthaberisch **III**
both [bəʊθ] beide **II**
both … and … ['bəʊθ … ənd] sowohl … als auch … °**V AC2**, 83
to **bother** ['bɒðə] stören; belästigen **III**
bottle ['bɒtl] Flasche **I**
bottom ['bɒtəm] Boden; unterer Teil; Grund **IV**
to **bounce** [baʊnts] springen; hüpfen **III**
*to keep the ball **bouncing** [ˌki:p ðə bɔ:l 'baʊntsɪŋ] *hier:* das Gespräch am Laufen halten **III**
boundary ['baʊndri] Grenze; Abgrenzung ⟨**V U2**, 65⟩
bowl [bəʊl] Schale; Schälchen; Schüssel **I**
to play **bowls** [ˌpleɪ 'bəʊlz] Bowling spielen **III**
bowling alley ['bəʊlɪŋ‿æli] Bowlingbahn **I**
box [bɒks] Box; Kasten; Schachtel; Kiste **I**
box jellyfish ['bɒks ˌdʒelifɪʃ] Würfelqualle **V U1**, 14
phone **box** ['fəʊn ˌbɒks] Telefonzelle **III**
boxing ['bɒksɪŋ] Boxen **II**
round of **boxing** [ˌraʊnd‿əv 'bɒksɪŋ] Boxrunde **II**
boy [bɔɪ] Junge **I**
cabin **boy** ['kæbɪn ˌbɔɪ] Schiffsjunge **I**
boyfriend ['bɔɪfrend] Freund *(in einer Paarbeziehung)* **IV**
bracelet ['breɪslət] Armband **I**
bracket ['brækɪt] Klammer **II**
brain(s) [breɪn(z)] Gehirn; Verstand **IV**
brain-dead ['breɪnˌded] hirntot **IV**
to **brainstorm** ['breɪnstɔ:m] Ideen sammeln **IV**
brand [brænd] Marke **IV**
brand-new [ˌbrænd'nju:] brandneu **IV**
brave [breɪv] mutig; tapfer **I**
bread [bred] Brot **I**
bread roll ['bred rəʊl] Brötchen **III**
break [breɪk] Pause **II**; Durchbruch **IV**
half-term **break** [ˌhɑ:ftɜ:m 'breɪk] Halbjahresferien **I**
lunch **break** ['lʌnʃbreɪk] Mittagspause **I**
*to **break** [breɪk] brechen; zerbrechen **I**
*to **break** down [ˌbreɪk 'daʊn] zusammenbrechen **VTS3**, 108
*to **break** into a song [ˌbreɪk‿ɪntʊ‿ə 'sɒŋ] plötzlich anfangen zu singen °**VTS1**, 44
*to **break** sb's spirit [ˌbreɪk sʌmbədiz 'spɪrɪt] jmdn. entmutigen ⟨**VTS3**, 109⟩
broken ['brəʊkn] gebrochen; kaputt **I**
breakfast ['brekfəst] Frühstück **I**
*to have **breakfast** [ˌhæv 'brekfəst] frühstücken **I**
breath [breθ] Atem; Atemzug **III**
*to take a **breath** [ˌteɪk‿ə 'breθ] Luft holen; Atem holen **III**
Take a deep **breath**. [ˌteɪk‿ə ˌdi:p 'breθ] Atme(t) tief ein. **II**
to **breathe** [bri:ð] atmen **II**
breathtaking ['breθˌteɪkɪŋ] atemberaubend **IV**
breezy ['bri:zi] unbeschwert; heiter ⟨**V U2**, 47⟩
bridge [brɪdʒ] Brücke **II**
brief [bri:f] kurz **V U2**, 58
bright [braɪt] hell; leuchtend; strahlend **IV**
brilliant ['brɪliənt] leuchtend ⟨**V U2**, 65⟩
*to **bring** [brɪŋ] bringen; mitbringen **I**
*to **bring** up [ˌbrɪŋ‿'ʌp] großziehen ⟨**V U1**, 23⟩; zur Sprache bringen **V AC2**, 82
on the **brink** of [ˌɒn ðə 'brɪŋk‿əv] am Rande von; kurz vor **III**
Brit [brɪt] Brite/Britin *(ugs.)* **IV**
British ['brɪtɪʃ] britisch; Brite/Britin **I**
brochure ['brəʊʃə] Broschüre; Prospekt **I**
broken ['brəʊkn] gebrochen; kaputt **I**
Bronze Age ['brɒnz eɪdʒ] Bronzezeit *(ca. 2200–800 v. Chr.)* **II**
brother ['brʌðə] Bruder **I**
brown [braʊn] braun **I**
brownie ['braʊni] Brownie ⟨**V U3**, 100⟩

bubble ['bʌbl] Blase **VAC3**, 115
dot-com **bubble** [ˌdɒtkɒm 'bʌbl] Internetblase; Dotcom-Blase **VU3**, 90
buck *(AE) (coll)* [bʌk] Dollar ⟨**VU2**, 47⟩
bucket ['bʌkɪt] Eimer **II**
Buddhist ['bʊdɪst] buddhistisch **VAC1**, 9
buddy *(infml)* ['bʌdi] Kumpel **VU2**, 58
bugs *(pl)* [bʌgz] Ungeziefer **VU3**, 94
*to **build** [bɪld] bauen **II**; aufbauen **III**
*to **build** upon [ˌbɪld‿ə'pɒn] sich türmen auf ⟨**VU2**, 64⟩
building ['bɪldɪŋ] Gebäude **I**
building block ['bɪldɪŋ blɒk] Baustein **II**
cyber **bully** [ˌsaɪbə 'bʊli] *jemand, der andere in sozialen Netzwerken belästigt oder mobbt* **II**
bullying ['bʊliɪŋ] Mobbing ⟨**VTS2**, 79⟩
*to give the **bumps** [ˌgɪv ðə 'bʌmps] hochleben lassen **I**
goose **bumps** ['guːs ˌbʌmps] Gänsehaut ⟨**VU3**, 102⟩
to **bump** [bʌmp] anstoßen; stoßen ⟨**VU3**, 101⟩
to **bump** into sb [bʌmp‿'ɪntə] jmdn. zufällig treffen; *hier:* jmdn. anrempeln **VU1**, 18
a **bunch** of [ə‿'bʌnʃ‿əv] ein Haufen ⟨**VU3**, 102⟩
burger ['bɜːgə] Hamburger **I**
*to **burn** [bɜːn] brennen; verbrennen **III**
*to **burn** down [ˌbɜːn 'daʊn] abbrennen; niederbrennen **III**
*to **burst** [bɜːst] bersten; platzen **VU3**, 90
bus [bʌs] Bus **I**
bus station ['bʌs ˌsteɪʃn] Busbahnhof **I**
bush [bʊʃ] Busch *(Buschlandschaft)*; Wildnis **III**; Busch; Strauch ⟨**VU2**, 65⟩
bushfire ['bʊʃfaɪə] Buschfeuer **VAC1**, 10
bushwalking ['bʊʃˌwɔːkɪŋ] Buschwandern **VU1**, 14
business ['bɪznɪs] Geschäft; Business **III**
business executive ['bɪznɪs ɪgˌzekjətɪv] Geschäftsführer/-in; Manager/-in; gehobene Führungskraft **VU2**, 49
businessman ['bɪznɪsmæn] Geschäftsmann **IV**
busker ['bʌskə] Straßenmusikant/-in **IV**
busy ['bɪzi] belebt; beschäftigt **I**
but [bʌt] aber **I**
not only … **but** (also) [nɒt‿əʊnli … bʌt‿'ɔːlsəʊ] nicht nur … sondern (auch) **VU2**, 56
all **but** ['ɔːl bʌt] alle bis auf **VU3**, 95
butter ['bʌtə] Butter **III**
button ['bʌtn] Knopf **III**
*to **buy** [baɪ] kaufen **I**
*to **buy** time [ˌbaɪ 'taɪm] Zeit gewinnen **IV**
buyer ['baɪə] Käufer/-in **I**
by [baɪ] bei; neben; an **II**; von **III**
by the river [baɪ ðə 'rɪvə] am Fluss **II**
by the time [ˌbaɪ ðə 'taɪm] bis *(zu dem Zeitpunkt)* **IV**
*to go **by** [ˌgəʊ‿'baɪ] vorbeigehen **VU2**, 56
by any means [baɪ‿enɪ 'miːnz] mit allen Mitteln **IV**
by *(+ gerund)* [baɪ] indem **IV**
by *(bike)* [baɪ] mit *(dem Fahrrad)* **I**
Bye! [baɪ] Tschüss! **II**

C

cabin ['kæbɪn] Kabine ⟨**VTS3**, 113⟩
cabin boy ['kæbɪn ˌbɔɪ] Schiffsjunge **I**
cache [kæʃ] Cache **II**
cactus ['kæktəs] Kaktus **IV**
café ['kæfeɪ] Café **I**
cafeteria [ˌkæfə'tɪəriə] Cafeteria **I**
cake [keɪk] Kuchen; Torte **I**
calendar ['kæləndə] Kalender **III**
Californian [ˌkælɪ'fɔːniən] kalifornisch; Kalifornier/-in **VU3**, 90
(phone) **call** ['fəʊn ˌkɔːl] Anruf; Telefonanruf **I**
cattle **call** *(AE)* ['kætl ˌkɔːl] Vorspielen; Vorsingen **VU3**, 86
to **call** [kɔːl] nennen; anrufen; rufen **I**
*to be **called** [bi 'kɔːld] heißen; genannt werden **III**
*to be **called** to do sth [bi 'kɔːld tə duː] auserwählt sein, etw. zu tun **III**
to **call** forward [ˌkɔːl 'fɔːwəd] nach vorn rufen ⟨**VU2**, 62⟩
to **call** off [ˌkɔːl‿'ɒf] abbrechen; absagen **VU1**, 15
caller ['kɔːlə] Anrufer/-in **I**
call-in ['kɔːlɪn] *Sendung, bei der sich das Publikum telefonisch beteiligen kann* **III**
calm [kɑːm] Ruhe **IV**
to **calm** down [ˌkɑːm 'daʊn] sich beruhigen **II**
calm [kɑːm] ruhig; friedlich **IV**
camel ['kæml] Kamel **VU1**, 17
camel racing ['kæml ˌreɪsɪŋ] Kamelrennen **II**
camera ['kæmrə] Fotoapparat; Kamera **II**
caught on **camera** [ˌkɔːt‿ɒn 'kæmrə] ertappt; mit der Kamera festgehalten **II**
camp [kæmp] Camp; Lager **VU1**, 18
summer **camp** ['sʌmə kæmp] Sommerferienlager **II**
to **camp** [kæmp] campen; zelten **II**
to **campaign** (for) [kæm'peɪn fɔː] demonstrieren (für); aufmerksam machen (auf); sich engagieren (für) **III**
camping ['kæmpɪŋ] Camping; Zelten **II**
can [kæn] Dose; Büchse **I**
tin **can** ['tɪn kæn] Blechdose **III**
can [kæn; kən] können; dürfen **I**
can't [kɑːnt] kann nicht; können nicht **I**
Canadian [kə'neɪdiən] kanadisch; Kanadier/-in **IV**
candidate ['kændɪdət] Bewerber/-in; Kandidat/-in **VU2**, 60
candle ['kændl] Kerze **I**
candlelight *(no pl)* ['kændlaɪt] Kerzenlicht **II**
cannot ['kænɒt] kann nicht; können nicht **II**
canoe [kə'nuː] Kanu **IV**
capital ['kæpɪtl] Hauptstadt **II**
capital letter [ˌkæpɪtl 'letə] Großbuchstabe **I**
captain ['kæptɪn] Kapitän/-in; Mannschaftsführer/-in **I**
caption ['kæpʃn] Bildunterschrift; Untertitel **III**
to **capture** ['kæptʃə] ergreifen; einfangen **III**
car [kɑː] Auto **I**
motor **car** ['məʊtə ˌkɑː] Automobil **IV**
card [kɑːd] Karte; Spielkarte **I**
boarding **card** ['bɔːdɪŋ ˌkɑːd] Bordkarte **III**
prompt **card** ['prɒmpt kɑːd] Stichwortkarte; Rollenkarte **II**
cardboard ['kɑːdbɔːd] Pappe; Karton **IV**
*to take **care** of sb/sth [ˌteɪk‿'keər‿əv] sich um jmdn./etw. kümmern; für jmdn. sorgen **III**
to **care** (about) ['keər‿əˌbaʊt] wichtig nehmen; sich kümmern (um); sich interessieren (für) **II**
career [kə'rɪə] Beruf; Laufbahn; Karriere **III**
careful ['keəfl] vorsichtig; sorgfältig **II**
Be **careful**! [biː 'keəfl] Vorsicht!; Pass/Passt auf! **I**
caretaker *(AE)* ['keəˌteɪkə] Pfleger/-in ⟨**VU2**, 62⟩
caretaking ['keəˌteɪkɪŋ] Pflege ⟨**VU2**, 62⟩
carnival ['kɑːnɪvl] Karneval **II**
carpenter ['kɑːpntə] Schreiner/-in; Zimmermann **VU2**, 56
carpet ['kɑːpɪt] Teppich **II**
carrot ['kærət] Karotte; Möhre **I**
to **carry** ['kæri] tragen **II**
cart [kɑːt] Karren **IV**
cartoon [kɑː'tuːn] Cartoon; Zeichentrickfilm **III**
to **carve** [kɑːv] *hier:* prägen ⟨**VU1**, 24⟩
case [keɪs] Fall ⟨**VU1**, 20⟩
to clear a **case** [ˌklɪər‿ə 'keɪs] einen Fall klären ⟨**VU1**, 20⟩
cash register ['kæʃ ˌredʒɪstə] Kasse ⟨**VU3**, 100⟩
cast [kɑːst] Besetzung; Ensemble **VTS1**, 38
plaster **cast** ['plɑːstə kɑːst] Gipsverband **III**
casting ['kɑːstɪŋ] Casting; Rollenbesetzung **III**
castle ['kɑːsl] Schloss; Burg **II**
cat [kæt] Katze **I**
*to **catch** [kætʃ] fangen **II**; mitbekommen *(ugs.)*; mitkriegen *(ugs.)* **III**; erwischen ⟨**VU1**, 29⟩; nehmen *(Zug, Bus)* **VU3**, 88
*to **catch** an infection [ɪn'fekʃn] sich eine Infektion holen; sich einen Infekt holen **IV**
*to **catch** oneself doing sth [kætʃ] sich (selbst) dabei ertappen, wie … **VU2**, 54
catchy ['kætʃi] eingängig; einprägsam **III**
category ['kætəgri] Kategorie; Klasse **II**
cattle call *(AE)* ['kætl ˌkɔːl] Vorspielen; Vorsingen **VU3**, 86

*to get **caught** [get 'kɔ:t] erwischt werden; ertappt werden **IV**
caught on camera [ˌkɔ:t‿ɒn 'kæmrə] ertappt; mit der Kamera festgehalten **II**
cause [kɔ:z] Grund; Ursache **IV**
to **cause** [kɔ:z] verursachen **II**
to **cause** a stir [ˌkɔ:z‿ə 'stɜ:] für Aufsehen sorgen **V U3**, 86
cave [keɪv] Höhle **II**
ceiling ['si:lɪŋ] Zimmerdecke; Decke **V U1**, 30
to **celebrate** ['seləbreɪt] feiern **I**
celebration [ˌselə'breɪʃn] Feier **V U1**, 20
celebrity [sə'lebrəti] Prominente/-r; berühmte Person **III**
cell phone *(AE)* ['selfəʊn] Mobiltelefon; Handy **IV**
Celt [kelt] Kelte/Keltin **III**
Celtic ['keltɪk; 'seltɪk] keltisch **II**
cent [sent] Cent *(Währung)* **I**
center *(AE)* ['sentə] Zentrum; Center **IV**
central ['sentrl] zentral; Zentral- **II**
centre ['sentə] Zentrum; Center **I**
community **centre** [kə'mju:nəti ˌsentə] Gemeindezentrum **I**
leisure **centre** ['leʒə ˌsentə] Freizeitzentrum **I**
tourist information **centre** [ˌtʊərɪst ɪnfə'meɪʃn ˌsentə] Touristeninformation **I**
centred ['sentəd] zentriert °**VTS1**, 44
century ['senʃrl] Jahrhundert **II**
cereal *(no pl)* ['sɪəriəl] Frühstückszerealie; Getreideprodukt *(z. B. Cornflakes oder Müsli)* **I**
ceremony ['serɪməni] Zeremonie **IV**
certain ['sɜ:tn] bestimmt; sicher; gewiss **IV**
certainly ['sɜ:tnli] sicherlich ⟨**VTS3**, 113⟩
chain [tʃeɪn] Kette **IV**
chair [tʃeə] Stuhl; Sessel **I**
to **chalk** sth up to experience [ˌtʃɔ:k‿ʌp tə ɪk'spɪəriəns] etw. als Erfahrung verbuchen **V U3**, 86
challenge ['tʃælɪndʒ] Herausforderung **II**
to **challenge** ['tʃælɪndʒ] herausfordern **IV**
champagne [ʃæm'peɪn] Champagner ⟨**V U2**, 46⟩
champion ['tʃæmpiən] Gewinner/-in; Sieger/-in; Champion **III**
championship ['tʃæmpiənʃɪp] Meisterschaft **IV**
chance [tʃɑ:ns] Chance; Gelegenheit; Möglichkeit **II**
change [tʃeɪndʒ] Änderung; Veränderung; Wechsel **II**; Münzgeld; Wechselgeld **IV**
climate **change** ['klaɪmət ˌtʃeɪndʒ] Klimawandel **V U3**, 94
to **change** [tʃeɪndʒ] wechseln; (sich) ändern **II**
to **change** (onto) [tʃeɪndʒ ('ɒntʊ)] umsteigen (in) **II**
to **change** one's mind [ˌtʃeɪndʒ wʌnz 'maɪnd] seine Meinung ändern **III**
chant [tʃɑ:nt] Sprechgesang **II**
chaos ['keɪɒs] Chaos; Durcheinander **III**
chaotic [keɪ'ɒtɪk] chaotisch **V AC1**, 9
chapter ['tʃæptə] Kapitel **III**
character ['kærəktə] Charakter; Figur **I**
character trait [ˌkærəktə 'treɪt] Charaktereigenschaft °**V U3**, 86
characterisation [ˌkærəktraɪ'zeɪʃn] Beschreibung; Personenbeschreibung; Charakterisierung °**V U1**, 31
characteristic [ˌkærəktə'rɪstɪk] typisches Merkmal **IV**
*to be in **charge** (of) [bi‿ɪn 'tʃɑ:dʒ‿əv] die Verantwortung tragen (für); zuständig sein (für) **III**
charity ['tʃærɪti] Wohltätigkeitsverein; wohltätige Zwecke; Wohlfahrt **I**
charity shop ['tʃærɪti ʃɒp] Second-Hand-Laden **I**
charm [tʃɑ:m] Zauberspruch ⟨**V U3**, 100⟩
lucky **charm** [ˌlʌki 'tʃɑ:m] Glücksbringer; Talisman **I**
chart [tʃɑ:t] Diagramm; Tabelle **IV**
pie **chart** ['paɪ ˌtʃɑ:t] Kuchendiagramm; Tortendiagramm **IV**
to **chase** [tʃeɪs] jagen; nachjagen **I**
chat [ˌtʃæt] Chat **III**
video **chat** ['vɪdiəʊ ˌtʃæt] Videochat **II**
to **chat** [tʃæt] plaudern; chatten *(sich online unterhalten)* **I**
chatroom ['tʃætrʊm] Chatroom *(Internet-forum, wo man sich online unterhalten kann)* **III**
cheap [tʃi:p] billig; preiswert **I**
to **cheat** [tʃi:t] mogeln; betrügen **IV**
cheat sheet ['tʃi:t ʃi:t] Spickzettel **IV**
check [tʃek] Scheck ⟨**V U3**, 100⟩
to **check** [tʃek] überprüfen; prüfen; kontrollieren **I**
to **check** out *(coll)* [ˌtʃek‿'aʊt] prüfen; abchecken; auschecken **III**
checklist ['tʃeklɪst] Checkliste **II**
checkpoint ['tʃekpɔɪnt] Kontrollpunkt **III**
cheek [tʃi:k] Wange ⟨**V U3**, 100⟩
cheer [tʃɪə] Jubel; Hurraruf **IV**
to **cheer** [tʃɪə] anfeuern; jubeln; zujubeln **II**
to **cheer** sb up [ˌtʃɪər‿'ʌp] jmdn. aufheitern **III**
Cheers! [tʃɪəz] Danke! **III**
cheese [tʃi:z] Käse **I**
chef [ʃef] Koch; Küchenchef **V U3**, 98
chess [tʃes] Schach **II**
chest [tʃest] Brust; Brustkorb **IV**; Busen **VTS3**, 111
chewing gum ['tʃu:ɪŋ ˌgʌm] Kaugummi **III**
chicken ['tʃɪkɪn] Huhn; Hähnchen **I**
chicken-shit ['tʃɪkɪnʃɪt] Hühnerkacke ⟨**V U1**, 30⟩
Chief Elder [ˌtʃi:f 'eldə] Ratschef/-in; Ratsvorsitzende/-r ⟨**V U2**, 62⟩
child [tʃaɪld], **children** ['tʃɪldrən] *(pl)* Kind **I**
child labor *(AE)* [ˌtʃaɪld 'leɪbə] Kinderarbeit **IV**
child labour [ˌtʃaɪld 'leɪbə] Kinderarbeit **V AC1**, 9
only **child** ['əʊnli ˌtʃaɪld] Einzelkind **I**
childhood ['tʃaɪldhʊd] Kindheit **V U1**, 23
to **chill** out [tʃɪl‿'aʊt] chillen **III**
chill [tʃɪl] kalt ⟨**V U2**, 47⟩
chilly ['tʃɪli] kühl; frisch ⟨**V U3**, 100⟩
to **chime** in [tʃaɪm‿'ɪn] sich einschalten; einstimmen ⟨**V U1**, 28⟩
chimney ['tʃɪmni] Kamin; Schornstein **II**
chin [tʃɪn] Kinn ⟨**V U3**, 100⟩
Chinese [tʃaɪ'ni:z] Chinese/Chinesin; chinesisch; Chinesisch; aus China **V AC1**, 10
Mandarin **Chinese** [ˌmændrɪn tʃaɪ'ni:z] Mandarin *(chinesische Hochsprache)* ⟨**V AC1**, 11⟩
chip [tʃɪp] Chip **V U3**, 91; Stückchen ⟨**V U3**, 100⟩
chips *(pl)* [tʃɪps] Pommes frites **I**
chocolate ['tʃɒklət] Schokolade **I**
chocolate bar ['tʃɒklət ˌbɑ:] Schokoriegel **IV**
choice [tʃɔɪs] Wahl; Auswahl **II**
*to make a **choice** [ˌmeɪk‿ə 'tʃɔɪs] eine Wahl treffen **V U2**, 66
*to **choose** [tʃu:z] auswählen; wählen **II**
to **chop** [tʃɒp] hacken; klein schneiden **V U2**, 53
chore [tʃɔ:] (lästige) Pflicht; Bürde **IV**
chorus ['kɔ:rəs] Refrain **III**
in **chorus** [ɪn 'kɔ:rəs] im Chor **III**
clam **chowder** [ˌklæm 'tʃaʊdə] Muschelsuppe **IV**
Christmas ['krɪsməs] Weihnachten **I**
to **chuckle** ['tʃʌkl] in sich hineinlachen ⟨**V U2**, 66⟩
church [tʃɜ:tʃ] Kirche **I**
my stomach **churns** [maɪ ˌstʌmək 'tʃɜ:nz] mir dreht sich der Magen um ⟨**V U1**, 28⟩
cinema ['sɪnəmə] Kino **I**
circle ['sɜ:kl] Kreis; Ring **I**
*to go round in **circles** [gəʊ ˌraʊnd ɪn 'sɜ:klz] sich im Kreis drehen **III**
citizen ['sɪtɪzn] Bürger/-in ⟨**V U2**, 63⟩
city ['sɪti] Stadt; Großstadt **I**
civil rights *(pl)* [ˌsɪvl 'raɪts] Bürgerrechte **V AC1**, 8
to **claim** [kleɪm] behaupten **IV**
clam chowder [ˌklæm 'tʃaʊdə] Muschelsuppe **IV**
clan [klæn] Clan; Sippe; Stamm ⟨**V U1**, 24⟩
to **clap** [klæp] klatschen **I**
Clap your hands. [ˌklæp jɔ: 'hændz] Klatsch/Klatscht in die Hände. **I**
clarification [ˌklærɪfɪ'keɪʃn] Klärung; Klarstellung **III**
class [klɑ:s] Klasse; Schulklasse **I**; *hier:* Unterricht **II**
class display ['klɑ:s dɪˌspleɪ] Ausstellung in der Klasse **I**
class poster ['klɑ:s ˌpəʊstə] Klassenposter **I**

middle **class** [ˌmɪdl ˈklɑːs] Mittelschicht **V AC1**, 8
classic [ˈklæsɪk] Klassiker °**VTS1**, 43
classical [ˈklæsɪkl] klassisch **IV**
classmate [ˈklɑːsmeɪt] Klassenkamerad/-in; Mitschüler/-in **I**
classroom [ˈklɑːsrʊm] Klassenzimmer **I**
adverbial clause [ədˌvɜːbiəl ˈklɔːz] Adverbialsatz **IV**
contact **clause** [ˈkɒntækt ˌklɔːz] *Relativsatz ohne Relativpronomen* **II**
defining relative **clause** [dɪˌfaɪnɪŋ ˈrelətɪv ˌklɔːz] notwendiger Relativsatz **II**
if-**clause** [ˈɪfˌklɔːz] if-Satz **II**
main **clause** [ˈmeɪn ˌklɔːz] Hauptsatz **II**
non-defining relative **clause** [ˌnɒndɪfaɪnɪŋ ˈrelətɪv ˌklɔːz] nicht notwendiger Relativsatz **IV**
clay [kleɪ] Ton ⟨**V U1**, 30⟩
clay pipe [ˈkleɪ paɪp] Tonpfeife **II**
to clean [kliːn] säubern; reinigen **I**
to **clean** out [ˌkliːn‿ˈaʊt] ausräumen; entrümpeln **IV**
to **clean** up [ˌkliːn‿ˈʌp] aufräumen; sauber machen **IV**
clean [kliːn] sauber **III**
to clear a case [ˌklɪər‿ə ˈkeɪs] einen Fall klären ⟨**V U1**, 20⟩
to **clear** out [ˌklɪər‿ˈaʊt] ausräumen; entrümpeln **I**
clear [klɪə] klar; deutlich **I**
to clench [klenʃ] sich zusammenziehen ⟨**V U3**, 102⟩
clever [ˈklevə] schlau; klug **II**
cliché [ˈkliːʃeɪ] Klischee **V AC1**, 9
click [klɪk] Klicken; Klick **II**
to click on [ˈklɪk‿ɒn] anklicken **II**
cliff [klɪf] Klippe; Kliff **III**
climate [ˈklaɪmət] Klima **III**
climate change [ˈklaɪmət ˌtʃeɪndʒ] Klimawandel **V U3**, 94
climatic [klaɪˈmætɪk] klimatisch **V U1**, 16
climax [ˈklaɪmæks] Höhepunkt **III**
to climb [klaɪm] klettern; besteigen; steigen **I**
climbing [ˈklaɪmɪŋ] Klettern **II**
*to cling [klɪŋ] (to sb/sth) sich an jmdm./etw. festhalten; sich an jmdm./etw. festklammern ⟨**V U1**, 30⟩
clip [klɪp] Clip; Ausschnitt **VTS1**, 38
clip art [ˈklɪp‿ɑːt] Clipart; Grafik °**V U3**, 98
clique [kliːk] Clique **IV**
clock [klɒk] Uhr **I**
alarm **clock** [əˈlɑːm ˌklɒk] Wecker **II**
o'**clock** [əˈklɒk] Uhr *(Zeitangabe bei vollen Stunden)* **I**
to clone [kləʊn] klonen **III**
close [kləʊs] schmaler Durchgang **III**
to close [kləʊz] schließen; zumachen **I**
to **close** down [ˌkləʊz ˈdaʊn] den Betrieb einstellen; schließen **V U3**, 90
to **close** oneself away from [ˌkləʊz əˈweɪ frəm] sich abschotten von **III**
close [kləʊs] eng; knapp **I**; nahe **II**
Look **closely** … [ˌlʊk ˈkləʊsli] Schau(t) genau … **II**
That was **close**! [ˌðæt wəz ˈkləʊs] Das war knapp! **I**
closed [kləʊzd] geschlossen; zu **III**
closet [ˈklɒzɪt] Schrank; Wandschrank **IV**
walk-in **closet** [ˌwɔːkɪn ˈklɒzɪt] begehbarer Kleiderschrank **IV**
close-up [ˈkləʊsʌp] Nahaufnahme **II**
clothes *(pl)* [kləʊðz] Kleider; Kleidung **I**
clothing [ˈkləʊðɪŋ] Kleidung **IV**
clothing drive [ˈkləʊðɪŋ ˌdraɪv] Kleidersammlung **IV**
cloud [klaʊd] Wolke **II**
word **cloud** [ˈwɜːd ˌklaʊd] Wörterwolke **II**
cloudy [ˈklaʊdi] bedeckt; bewölkt **II**
clown [klaʊn] Clown **II**
club [klʌb] Klub; Verein; AG **I**
Cooking **Club** [ˈkʊkɪŋ ˌklʌb] Koch-AG **I**
clue [kluː] Hinweis; Spur **II**
*to have no **clue** [ˌhæv nəʊ ˈkluː] keine Ahnung haben **IV**
clumsy [ˈklʌmzi] ungeschickt; unbeholfen ⟨**V U2**, 63⟩
cluster [ˈklʌstə] Bündel; Anhäufung **V U1**, 14
coach [kəʊtʃ] Trainer/-in **I**; Reisebus **II**
coast [kəʊst] Küste **III**
coastal path [ˌkəʊstl ˈpɑːθ] Küstenweg **II**
coastline [ˈkəʊstlaɪn] Küste; Küstenverlauf **II**
coat [kəʊt] Mantel **V AC3**, 114
cocoa [ˈkəʊkəʊ] Kakao **V U2**, 53
coconut [ˈkəʊkənʌt] Kokosnuss **II**
code [kəʊd] Code; Verschlüsselung **IV**
dress **code** [ˈdres ˌkəʊd] Kleiderordnung; Bekleidungsvorschriften **IV**
coffee [ˈkɒfi] Kaffee **I**
cognitive [ˈkɒgnətɪv] kognitiv **VTS2**, 77
coin [kɔɪn] Münze **I**
coincidence [kəʊˈɪnsɪdns] Zufall **IV**
coke [ˈkəʊk] Cola **I**
cold [kəʊld] Erkältung **II**
cold [kəʊld] kalt **II**
collage [kɒlˈɑːʒ] Collage **IV**
to collapse [kəˈlæps] kollabieren; zusammenbrechen; einstürzen **V U3**, 94
colleague [ˈkɒliːg] Kollege/Kollegin **V U2**, 59
to collect [kəˈlekt] sammeln **I**
collection [kəˈlekʃn] Kollektion; Sammlung **II**
collective [kəˈlektɪv] gemeinsam; kollektiv ⟨**V U2**, 63⟩
collective noun [kəˈlektɪv] Sammelbegriff °**V U3**, 93
college [ˈkɒlɪdʒ] Universität *(in den USA)* **IV**
collocation [ˌkɒləˈkeɪʃn] Wortverbindung **II**
colonial [kəˈləʊniəl] kolonial; Kolonial- **IV**
colonialism [kəˈləʊniəlɪzm] Kolonialismus ⟨**V AC1**, 11⟩
colonisation [ˌkɒlənaɪˈzeɪʃn] Kolonisierung; Kolonisation °**V U1**, 21
colonist [ˈkɒlənɪst] Siedler/-in; Kolonist/-in **IV**
to colonize *(AE)* [ˈkɒlənaɪz] kolonisieren **IV**
colony [ˈkɒləni] Kolonie **II**
penal **colony** [ˈpiːnl ˌkɒləni] Strafkolonie ⟨**V U1**, 20⟩
color *(AE)* [ˈkʌlə] Farbe ⟨**V AC2**, 80⟩
colorful *(AE)* [ˈkʌləfl] farbenfroh; bunt **IV**
colorless *(AE)* [ˈkʌlələs] farblos ⟨**V U2**, 65⟩
colour [ˈkʌlə] Farbe **I**
What **colour** is …? [ˌwɒt ˈkʌlər‿ɪz] Welche Farbe hat …? **I**
to colour in [ˌkʌlər‿ˈɪn] ausmalen ⟨**V U1**, 29⟩
coloured-in [ˌkʌlərd‿ˈɪn] ausgemalt ⟨**V U1**, 30⟩
colourful [ˈkʌləfl] farbenfroh; bunt **I**
column [ˈkɒləm] Spalte **III**
combination [ˌkɒmbɪˈneɪʃn] Kombination; Verbindung **IV**
to combine [kəmˈbaɪn] kombinieren; verbinden **IV**
*to come [kʌm] kommen **I**
*to **come** down [ˌkʌm ˈdaʊn] herunterkommen **I**
*to **come** in [ˌkʌm‿ˈɪn] hereinkommen **II**
*to **come** out [ˌkʌm‿ˈaʊt] sich outen **V AC2**, 82
*to **come** to one's mind [ˌkʌm tə wʌnz ˈmaɪnd] jmdm. in den Sinn kommen; jmdm. einfallen **IV**
*to **come** true [ˌkʌm ˈtruː] wahr werden; in Erfüllung gehen **IV**
*to **come** up [ˌkʌm‿ˈʌp] vorkommen **III**
*to **come** up to [ˌkʌm‿ˈʌp tə] zukommen auf **IV**
Come on! [ˌkʌm‿ˈɒn] Komm schon!; Komm jetzt! **I**
comedian [kəˈmiːdiən] Komiker/-in; Comedian **II**
comedy [ˈkɒmədi] Komödie **III**
comedy show [ˈkɒmədi ˌʃəʊ] Comedy Show **II**
to comfort [ˈkʌmfət] trösten; ermutigen **IV**
comfortable [ˈkʌmftəbl] komfortabel; bequem **II**
comforting [ˈkʌmfətɪŋ] tröstlich; ermutigend **V U1**, 14
comic [ˈkɒmɪk] Comicheft **II**
coming out [ˌkʌmɪŋ‿ˈaʊt] Coming-out **V AC2**, 82
comma [ˈkɒmə] Komma **IV**
command [kəˈmɑːnd] Befehl **III**; Beherrschen ⟨**V AC1**, 11⟩
commanding [kəˈmɑːndɪŋ] gebieterisch; befehlend ⟨**V U2**, 63⟩
comment [ˈkɒment] Kommentar **II**
to comment (on) [ˈkɒment‿(ɒn)] kommentieren **II**
commenting [ˈkɒmentɪŋ] kommentierend °**V U2**, 51
commerce [ˈkɒmɜːs] Handel ⟨**V AC1**, 11⟩
commitment [kəˈmɪtmənt] Bindung; Verpflichtung; Engagement **V U2**, 55

committee [kə'mɪti] Komitee; Ausschuss **IV**
common ['kɒmən] gemeinsam **V U1**, 22; üblich; verbreitet; gängig **V U2**, 50
*to have in **common** [ˌhæv‿ɪn 'kɒmən] gemeinsam haben **III**
to **communicate** [kə'mju:nɪkeɪt] kommunizieren; sich verständigen **II**
communication [kəˌmju:nɪ'keɪʃn] Kommunikation **II**
communications network [kəˌmju:nɪ'keɪʃnz ˌnetwɜ:k] Kommunikationsnetz; Nachrichtennetz **IV**
community [kə'mju:nəti] Gemeinde; Gemeinschaft **IV**
community centre [kə'mju:nəti ˌsentə] Gemeindezentrum **I**
company ['kʌmpəni] Gesellschaft; Firma; Unternehmen **III**
start-up **company** ['stɑ:tʌp ˌkʌmpəni] Start-up(-Unternehmen); Unternehmensgründung **V U3**, 90
tour **company** ['tʊə ˌkʌmpəni] Reiseanbieter **IV**
comparative [kəm'pærətɪv] Komparativ **II**
to **compare** (with/to) [kəm'peə] vergleichen (mit) **I**
comparison [kəm'pærɪsn] Vergleich **II**
to **compel** [kəm'pel] zwingen; veranlassen ⟨**V U3**, 100⟩
to **compete** (with) [kəm'pi:t] konkurrieren (mit); sich messen (mit); in Wettbewerb treten (mit) **III**
competition [ˌkɒmpə'tɪʃn] Wettbewerb; Turnier **II**
*to hold a **competition** [ˌhəʊld‿ə ˌkɒmpə'tɪʃn] einen Wettbewerb durchführen **IV**
competitive [kəm'petɪtɪv] leistungsorientiert; konkurrierend **III**; konkurrenzfähig; wettbewerbsfähig ⟨**V AC1**, 11⟩
to **complain** [kəm'pleɪn] sich beschweren; sich beklagen **IV**
to **complete** [kəm'pli:t] fertigstellen; vervollständigen; vollenden **IV**
complete [kəm'pli:t] vollständig; komplett; völlig **IV**
completely [kəm'pli:tli] völlig **II**
complicated ['kɒmplɪkeɪtɪd] kompliziert **IV**
compliment ['kɒmplɪmənt] Kompliment **V AC1**, 9
component [kəm'pəʊnənt] Bestandteil; Komponente **V U3**, 91
compound word ['kɒmpaʊnd wɜ:d] Kompositum *(zusammengesetztes Wort)* **II**
comprehension [ˌkɒmprɪ'henʃn] Verständnis; Verstehen °**VTS1**, 39
comprehension sheet [ˌkɒmprɪ'henʃn ˌʃi:t] Blatt mit Verständnisaufgaben ⟨**V U1**, 29⟩
comprehensive school [kɒmprɪ'hensɪv ˌsku:l] Gesamtschule **V U2**, 50
to **comprise** [kəm'praɪz] umfassen; beinhalten; einschließen **V U3**, 89

compromise ['kɒmprəmaɪz] Kompromiss **II**
to **compromise** ['kɒmprəmaɪz] Kompromisse eingehen **III**
compulsive [kəm'pʌlsɪv] zwanghaft ⟨**VTS2**, 79⟩
computer [ˌkəm'pju:tə] Computer **I**
computing [ˌkəm'pju:tɪŋ] EDV ⟨**V AC1**, 11⟩
con [kɒn] Argument dagegen **II**
pros and **cons** *(pl)* [ˌprəʊz‿ən 'kɒnz] Argumente für und gegen etw.; Pro und Kontra °**V U3**, 91
to **concentrate** ['kɒnsntreɪt] (sich) konzentrieren **III**
concept ['kɒnsept] Vorstellung; Idee; Konzept **IV**
concern [kən'sɜ:n] Sorge ⟨**VTS2**, 79⟩
concert ['kɒnsət] Konzert **IV**
concise [kən'saɪs] präzise; kurz; prägnant °**V U1**, 26
to **conclude** [kən'klu:d] enden; schließen; schlussfolgern **VTS2**, 75
conclusion [kən'klu:ʒn] Schluss; Schlussfolgerung **IV**
concrete ['kɒŋkri:t] Beton **III**
concrete ['kɒŋkri:t] konkret **IV**
condition [kən'dɪʃn] Kondition; Bedingung **II**
conditional sentence [kənˌdɪʃnl 'sentəns] Bedingungssatz **II**
to **conduct** [kən'dʌkt] durchführen; ausführen **IV**
conference ['kɒnfrns] Konferenz; Tagung **IV**
confident ['kɒnfɪdnt] selbstsicher; selbstbewusst **II**
conflict ['kɒnflɪkt] Konflikt; Auseinandersetzung °**V U1**, 31
*to be **confronted** with [bi kən'frʌntɪd wɪð] konfrontiert werden mit **VTS3**, 111
to **confuse** sb/sth with sb/sth [kən'fju:z] jmdn./etw. mit jmdm./etw. verwechseln °**VTS2**, 78
confused [kən'fju:zd] verwirrt; wirr; konfus **III**
confusion [kən'fju:ʒn] Verwirrung ⟨**V U1**, 30⟩
to **connect** (to) [kə'nekt tə] verbinden (mit); vermitteln; anschließen **IV**
*to be **connected** [bi kə'nektɪd] zusammenhängen; in Zusammenhang stehen **II**
connection [kə'nekʃn] Verbindung **II**
conscience ['kɒnʃns] Gewissen **III**
guilty **conscience** [ˌgɪlti 'kɒnʃns] Schuldbewusstsein; schlechtes Gewissen **V U1**, 28
consecutive [kən'sekjʊtɪv] aufeinanderfolgend; fortlaufend **IV**
consequence ['kɒnsɪkwəns] Konsequenz; Folge **IV**
conservation [ˌkɒnsə'veɪʃn] Schutz; Erhaltung **V U3**, 96
to **consider** [kən'sɪdə] betrachten; erwägen **V U2**, 49
*to be **considered** (to be) sth [bi kən'sɪdəd tə] als etw. gelten **IV**
to **consist** of [kən'sɪst‿əv] bestehen aus **IV**

conspiracy [kən'spɪrəsi] Verschwörung **IV**
conspiratorial [kənˌspɪrə'tɔ:rɪəl] verschwörerisch ⟨**V U1**, 28⟩
constant ['kɒnstənt] ständig; konstant; stetig; gleichmäßig **IV**
construction [kən'strʌkʃn] Konstruktion **IV**
construction worker [kən'strʌkʃn ˌwɜ:kə] Bauarbeiter/-in **V U2**, 49
constructive [kən'strʌktɪv] konstruktiv **VTS3**, 109
contact ['kɒntækt] Kontakt **II**
contact clause ['kɒntækt ˌklɔ:z] *Relativsatz ohne Relativpronomen* **II**
to **contain** [kən'teɪn] enthalten **III**
container [kən'teɪnə] Container; Behälter; Behältnis **V U2**, 53
content ['kɒntent] Inhalt **IV**
contest ['kɒntest] Wettkampf; Wettbewerb **I**
contestant [kən'testnt] Kandidat/-in **VTS3**, 108
context ['kɒntekst] Kontext; Zusammenhang **VTS1**, 43
continent ['kɒntɪnənt] Kontinent; Erdteil **IV**
to **continue** [kən'tɪnju:] fortfahren; andauern; weitermachen; weitergehen **III**
contrast ['kɒntrɑ:st] Kontrast; Unterschied; Gegensatz **IV**
to **contrast** [kən'trɑ:st] kontrastieren; gegenüberstellen **IV**
to **contribute** to [kən'trɪbju:t tə] beitragen zu ⟨**V U3**, 96⟩
contribution [ˌkɒntrɪ'bju:ʃn] Beitrag; Beteiligung **V U3**, 89
control [kən'trəʊl] Kontrolle **III**
to **control** [kən'trəʊl] kontrollieren; steuern **IV**
controversial [ˌkɒntrə'vɜ:ʃl] umstritten; kontrovers ⟨**VTS3**, 113⟩
controversy ['kɒntrəvɜ:si] Kontroverse; Auseinandersetzung **V U2**, 53
conversation [ˌkɒnvə'seɪʃn] Konversation; Gespräch; Unterhaltung **I**
to hog a **conversation** [ˌhɒg‿ə kənvə'seɪʃn] ein Gespräch für sich in Beschlag nehmen; ein Gespräch dominieren **III**
convict ['kɒnvɪkt] Sträfling **V U1**, 18
to **convince** [kən'vɪns] überzeugen **II**
convinced [kən'vɪnst] überzeugt **III**
convincing [kən'vɪnsɪŋ] überzeugend **III**
cook [kʊk] Koch/Köchin ⟨**V U3**, 101⟩
to **cook** [kʊk] kochen **II**
cooker ['kʊkə] Herd **I**
cooking ['kʊkɪŋ] Kochen **I**
Cooking Club ['kʊkɪŋ ˌklʌb] Koch-AG **I**
*to leave it to **cool** [ˌli:v‿ɪt tə 'ku:l] kalt stellen **I**
cool [ku:l] cool; super **I**; kühl **IV**
to **coordinate** [kəʊ'ɔ:dɪneɪt] koordinieren **V U3**, 94
copper ['kɒpə] Kupfer **IV**
copper-mining ['kɒpəˌmaɪnɪŋ] Kupferbergbau **IV**

ad **copy** ['æd ˌkɒpi] Werbetext **IV**
to **copy** ['kɒpi] abschreiben; kopieren **I**
corn [kɔ:n] Korn; Mais; Getreide **IV**
corner ['kɔ:nə] Ecke **II**
Cornish ['kɔ:nɪʃ] in Cornwall **II**
corporation [ˌkɔ:pr'eɪʃn] Konzern; Unternehmen **IV**
correct [kə'rekt] korrigieren **I**; verbessern; berichtigen ⟨**V U2**, 66⟩
correct [kə'rekt] richtig; korrekt **I**
corridor ['kɒrɪdɔ:] Gang; Flur; Korridor **IV**
cosmetics *(pl)* [kɒz'metɪks] Kosmetik **V U2**, 53
*to **cost** [kɒst] kosten **I**
costume ['kɒstju:m] Kostüm **I**
cougar ['ku:gə] Puma; Berglöwe **IV**
cough [kɒf] Husten **II**
could [kʊd] könnte/-n **II**; konnte/-n **III**
student **council** [ˌstju:dnt 'kaʊnsl] Schülerrat **V AC3**, 114
counsellor ['kaʊnslə] Betreuer/-in **V U2**, 48
assistant **counsellor** [əˌsɪstnt 'kaʊnslə] Hilfsbetreuer/-in **V U2**, 48
senior **counsellor** [ˌsi:niə 'kaʊnslə] leitender Betreuer/leitende Betreuerin; ranghohe/-r Minister/-in **V U2**, 48
to **count** (on) ['kaʊnt‿ɒn] zählen (auf) **I**
counter ['kaʊntə] Theke ⟨**V U3**, 100⟩; Zähler ⟨**V U3**, 102⟩
counter ['kaʊntə] Gegen- °**VTS3**, 109
country ['kʌntri], **countries** ['kʌntriz] *(pl)* Land **I**
in the **country** [ˌɪn ðə 'kʌntri] auf dem Land **IV**
countryside ['kʌntrisaɪd] Land **II**
couple ['kʌpl] Paar **II**
a **couple** of [ə 'kʌpl‿əv] ein paar **I**
course [kɔ:s] Kurs **II**
of **course** [əv 'kɔ:s] natürlich; selbstverständlich **I**
court [kɔ:t] Spielfeld **II**; Hof; Gericht; Gerichtshof **V AC1**, 8
cousin ['kʌzn] Cousin/Cousine **I**
cover ['kʌvə] Cover; Titelblatt **III**
cover version ['kʌvə ˌvɜ:ʃn] Coverversion **III**
to **cover** ['kʌvə] abdecken; bedecken; zudecken **III**
covered wagon [ˌkʌvəd 'wægən] Planwagen **IV**
cover-up ['kʌvərʌp] Vertuschung **IV**
cow [kaʊ] Kuh **II**
cowboy ['kaʊbɔɪ] Cowboy; Rinderhirte **IV**
crack [kræk] Knacken; Krachen **III**; Riss; Spalt **V U3**, 95
cracking ['krækɪŋ] knackend; brechend **III**
craft [krɑ:ft] Handwerk; Gewerbe **V U3**, 98
cramp [kræmp] Krampf **II**
crane [kreɪn] Kran **III**
total **crap** [ˌtəʊtl 'kræp] völliger Quatsch ⟨**VTS3**, 110⟩
to **crash** [kræʃ] abstürzen **II**; zusammenstoßen **III**; krachend herunterfallen ⟨**V U3**, 100⟩
to **crave** [kreɪv] sich sehnen nach ⟨**V U3**, 101⟩
craze [kreɪz] Manie; Fimmel; fixe Idee ⟨**V U3**, 92⟩
crazy ['kreɪzi] verrückt **I**
*to be **crazy** about [bi 'kreɪzi‿əbaʊt] verrückt sein nach; abfahren auf **IV**
*to go **crazy** [ˌgəʊ 'kreɪzi] ausflippen; durchdrehen; verrückt werden **II**
cream [kri:m] Creme; Sahne **I**
ice **cream** [ˌaɪs 'kri:m] Eis; Eiscreme **I**
to **create** [kri'eɪt] schaffen; erschaffen; erfinden **I**
creative [kri'eɪtɪv] kreativ **I**
creature ['kri:tʃə] Kreatur; Lebewesen; Geschöpf **IV**
credit ['kredɪt] Guthaben **II**
crest [krest] Kuppe ⟨**V U1**, 30⟩
crew [kru:] Crew; Besatzung; Mannschaft; Team **VTS1**, 38
cricket ['krɪkɪt] Cricket **II**
crime [kraɪm] Verbrechen; Kriminalität **II**
criminal ['krɪmɪnəl] Kriminelle/-r; Verbrecher/-in **II**
to **cringe** [krɪndʒ] schaudern; sich ducken **IV**
crisp [krɪsp] Kartoffelchip **I**
criterion [kraɪ'tɪəriən], **criteria** [kraɪ'tɪəriə] *(pl)* Kriterium; Argument **III**
critical ['krɪtɪkl] kritisch **IV**
to **criticise** ['krɪtɪsaɪz] kritisieren **VTS3**, 108
criticism ['krɪtɪsɪzm] Kritik **VTS2**, 74
crocodile ['krɒkədaɪl] Krokodil **V AC1**, 10
to **crop** (a photo) [krɒp] (ein Foto) zurechtschneiden **III**
cross [krɒs] Kreuz **II**
to **cross** [krɒs] überqueren; kreuzen **II**; sich kreuzen °**V U3**, 93
*to keep your fingers **crossed** [ˌki:p jɔ: ˌfɪŋgəz 'krɒst] die Daumen drücken **I**
crowd [kraʊd] Menschenmenge **II**
crowded ['kraʊdɪd] überfüllt **III**
crown [kraʊn] Krone **III**
crown jewels [ˌkraʊn 'dʒu:əlz] Kronjuwelen **II**
cruel ['kru:əl] grausam **II**
crumple ['krʌmpl] Häufchen ⟨**V U1**, 30⟩
crushed [krʌʃt] eingequetscht; eingeklemmt **III**
to **cry** [kraɪ] schreien; rufen **II**; weinen **III**
CU *(= See you)* ['si: ju] Bis dann!; Bis … **I**
cultivation [ˌkʌltɪ'veɪʃn] Anbau **V U3**, 90
cultural ['kʌltʃrl] kulturell **IV**
culture ['kʌltʃə] Kultur **I**
Across **cultures** [əˌkrɒs 'kʌltʃəz] Interkulturelles **I**
cup [kʌp] Tasse **III**
cupboard ['kʌbəd] Küchenschrank; Schrank **I**
curfew ['kɜ:fju:] Sperrstunde; Ausgangssperre **IV**
curiosity [ˌkjʊəri'ɒsəti] Neugier **V U2**, 47
curious ['kjʊəriəs] neugierig **V U2**, 65
currency ['kʌrnsi] Währung **III**
rip **current** ['rɪp ˌkʌrnt] Brandungsrückströmung **V U1**, 14
currently ['kʌrntli] momentan **VTS2**, 77
curry ['kʌri] Curry *(Gewürz oder Gericht)* **I**
custard ['kʌstəd] Vanillesoße; Vanillepudding **I**
custom ['kʌstəm] Gewohnheit; Brauch; Sitte **III**
customer ['kʌstəmə] Kunde/Kundin **II**
customs *(sg)* ['kʌstəmz] Zoll **III**
*to **cut** (off) [kʌt (ɒf)] schneiden; abschneiden **II**
*to **cut** down [ˌkʌt 'daʊn] fällen **V U3**, 94
*to **cut** up [kʌt‿'ʌp] zerschneiden **IV**
cute [kju:t] niedlich; süß **I**
CV *(Curriculum Vitae)* [ˌsi:'vi: (kəˌrɪkjələm 'vi:taɪ)] Lebenslauf **V U2**, 48
cyber addiction ['saɪbər‿əˌdɪkʃn] Internetsucht; Internetabhängigkeit ⟨**VTS2**, 79⟩
cyber bully [ˌsaɪbə 'bʊli] *jemand, der andere in sozialen Netzwerken belästigt oder mobbt* **II**
cycle ['saɪkl] Zyklus; Kreislauf **VTS2**, 77
to **cycle** ['saɪkl] Fahrrad fahren **IV**
cycling ['saɪklɪŋ] Radfahren **I**

D

dad [dæd] Papa **I**
dam [dæm] Damm; Staumauer **IV**
damage ['dæmɪdʒ] Schaden; Beschädigung **V U3**, 95
to **damage** ['dæmɪdʒ] schaden; beschädigen **V U1**, 17
dance [dɑ:ns] Tanz; Tanzveranstaltung **III**
to **dance** [dɑ:ns] tanzen **I**
to **dance** to ['dɑ:ns tə] tanzen zu **III**
dancer ['dɑ:nsə] Tänzer/-in **II**
backing **dancer** ['bækɪŋ ˌdɑ:nsə] Backgroundtänzer/-in **III**
danger ['deɪndʒə] Gefahr **III**
dangerous ['deɪndʒrəs] gefährlich **I**
to **dare** [deə] wagen **V U2**, 66
the **dark** [ðə 'dɑ:k] Dunkelheit **II**
dark [dɑ:k] dunkel **II**
darkness ['dɑ:knəs] Dunkelheit **II**
darling ['dɑ:lɪŋ] Liebling ⟨**V U1**, 30⟩
date [deɪt] Datum **I**; Verabredung; Date **IV**
date of birth [ˌdeɪt‿əv 'bɜ:θ] Geburtsdatum **III**
to **date** [deɪt] ausgehen mit ⟨**V AC2**, 80⟩
dating ['deɪtɪŋ] Partnersuche; Daten °**VTS1**, 41
daughter ['dɔ:tə] Tochter **III**
day [deɪ] Tag **I**
all **day** [ˌɔ:l 'deɪ] den ganzen Tag **II**
G'**day**! *(= Good day!)* [gə'daɪ] Guten Tag.; Hallo.; Hi. *(Begrüßung in Australien)* **V U1**, 12
lucky **day** [ˌlʌki 'deɪ] Glückstag **V U3**, 86

one **day** [wʌn 'deɪ] eines Tages **II**
*to take the **day** off [ˌteɪk ðə ˌdeɪ‿'ɒf] sich den Tag freinehmen **IV**
the other **day** [ði‿ʌðə 'deɪ] neulich **III**
these **days** [ˌði:z 'deɪz] zurzeit **III**; heutzutage ⟨**V U3**, 101⟩
a (**day**/week/year) [ə 'deɪ/wi:k/jɪə] pro (Tag/Woche/Jahr) **IV**
a **day** out in … [ə ˌdeɪ‿'aʊt ɪn] ein Tag in … **II**
the next **day** [ðə ˌnekst 'deɪ] am nächsten Tag **II**
daydream ['deɪdri:m] Tagtraum ⟨**V U1**, 28⟩
dead [ded] tot **II**
deadly ['dedli] tödlich **V U1**, 17
deal [di:l] Abmachung; Übereinkunft; Handel; Geschäft **IV**
big **deal** [bɪg 'di:l] große Sache **III**
*to **deal** (with) [di:l] sich befassen mit; umgehen mit **II**
dear [dɪə] Schatz ⟨**V U3**, 102⟩
Oh **dear**! [ˌəʊ 'dɪə] Oje! **II**
Dear … [dɪə] Lieber …; Liebe … *(Anrede in Briefen)* **I**
Dear Sir or Madam [dɪə ˌsɜ:r‿ɔ: 'mædəm] Sehr geehrte Dame, sehr geehrter Herr **II**
death [deθ] Tod **III**
to scare sb to **death** [ˌskeə tə 'deθ] jmdn. zu Tode erschrecken **IV**
debate [dɪ'beɪt] Debatte **IV**
decade ['dekeɪd] Jahrzehnt **V U3**, 93
December [dɪ'sembə] Dezember **I**
to **decide** [dɪ'saɪd] (sich) entscheiden **I**
decision [dɪ'sɪʒn] Entscheidung **II**
*to make a **decision** [ˌmeɪk‿ə dɪ'sɪʒn] eine Entscheidung treffen **II**
deck [dek] Deck **I**
to **declare** [dɪ'kleə] erklären **IV**
to **decorate** ['dekəreɪt] dekorieren; verzieren; schmücken **I**
decorations *(pl)* [ˌdekə'reɪʃnz] Dekoration; Schmuck **I**
deep [di:p] tief **II**
deep fryer [ˌdi:p 'fraɪə] Fritteuse **V U3**, 98
to **defeat** [dɪ'fi:t] besiegen **III**
defining relative clause [dɪˌfaɪnɪŋ 'relətɪv ˌklɔ:z] notwendiger Relativsatz **II**
definite article [ˌdefɪnət 'ɑ:tɪkl] bestimmter Artikel °**V U3**, 91
definitely ['defɪnətli] bestimmt; definitiv; eindeutig **III**
definition [ˌdefɪ'nɪʃn] Definition **II**
deforestation *(no pl)* [di:ˌfɒrɪ'steɪʃn] Abholzung; Entwaldung ⟨**V U3**, 96⟩
degree Fahrenheit (°F) ['færnhaɪt] Grad Fahrenheit **IV**
dehydration [ˌdi:haɪ'dreɪʃn] Austrocknung **V U3**, 94
delay [dɪ'leɪ] Verzögerung; Verspätung **III**
delegate ['delɪgət] Vertreter/-in; Delegierte/-r °**V U3**, 99
to **delete** [dɪ'li:t] löschen **III**
delicious [dɪ'lɪʃəs] köstlich **IV**
to **deliver** [dɪ'lɪvə] liefern **V U1**, 20
democracy [dɪ'mɒkrəsi] Demokratie **V AC1**, 9
democratic [ˌdemə'krætɪk] demokratisch **V AC1**, 9
to **demonstrate** ['demənstreɪt] demonstrieren **IV**
dense [dens] dicht **IV**
to **depart** [dɪ'pɑ:t] abfahren **II**
departure [dɪ'pɑ:tʃə] Abflug; Abreise **III**
departure lounge [dɪ'pɑ:tʃə ˌlaʊndʒ] Abflughalle **III**
to **depend** (on) [dɪ'pend‿(ɒn)] abhängen von **II**
depressing [dɪ'presɪŋ] deprimierend; bedrückend **III**
deprivation [ˌdeprɪ'veɪʃn] Entbehrung; Entzug **V TS2**, 77
deprived [dɪ'praɪvd] beraubt; entzogen **V TS2**, 77
to **descend** from [dɪ'send frəm] abstammen von; herstammen von **IV**
descent [dɪ'sent] Abstammung ⟨**V U1**, 23⟩
to **describe** [dɪ'skraɪb] beschreiben **I**
description [dɪ'skrɪpʃn] Beschreibung **II**
descriptive [dɪ'skrɪptɪv] beschreibend **IV**
desert ['dezət] Wüste **IV**
to **deserve** [dɪ'zɜ:v] verdienen **II**
design [dɪ'zaɪn] Design; Gestaltung; Entwurf **II**
to **design** [dɪ'zaɪn] entwerfen; gestalten **II**
designer [dɪ'zaɪnə] Designer/-in **III**
web **designer** ['web dɪˌzaɪnə] Webdesigner **III**
desirable [dɪ'zaɪərəbl] wünschenswert; erstrebenswert **V U2**, 47
desk [desk] Schalter **III**; Schreibtisch **V U1**, 29
desperate ['desprət] verzweifelt; hoffnungslos; ausweglos **V U1**, 28
destination [ˌdestɪ'neɪʃn] Ziel; Reiseziel **III**
destiny ['destɪni] Schicksal; Fügung; Vorsehung **V U2**, 62
to **destroy** [dɪ'strɔɪ] zerstören **IV**
detail ['di:teɪl] Detail; Einzelheit **II**
detective [dɪ'tektɪv] Detektiv/-in; Detektivgeschichte; Kriminalroman; Kriminalfilm; Krimi **III**
private **detective** [ˌpraɪvət dɪ'tektɪv] Privatdetektiv/-in **II**
detention [dɪ'tenʃn] Nachsitzen; Haft; Verhaftung **IV**
to **determine** [dɪ'tɜ:mɪn] bestimmen; ermitteln **V U2**, 62
determined [dɪ'tɜ:mɪnd] (fest) entschlossen; entschieden; zielstrebig **V U1**, 28
to **develop** [dɪ'veləp] (sich) entwickeln **IV**
development [dɪ'veləpmənt] Entwicklung ⟨**V AC1**, 11⟩
device [dɪ'vaɪs] Gerät; Vorrichtung **V U3**, 91
devil ['devl] Teufel **III**
diagram ['daɪəgræm] Diagramm **I**
dialect ['daɪəlekt] Dialekt **II**
dialogue ['daɪəlɒg] Dialog; Gespräch **I**
diamond ['daɪəmənd] Diamant ⟨**V U2**, 47⟩
diary ['daɪəri] Tagebuch **II**
diary entry ['daɪəri entri] Tagebucheintrag **II**
*to keep a **diary** [ˌki:p‿ə 'daɪəri] ein Tagebuch führen **IV**
dice [daɪs] Würfel **II**
Roll two **dice**. [ˌrəʊl ˌtu: 'daɪs] Würfle/Würfelt mit zwei Würfeln. **I**
throw the **dice** twice [ˌθrəʊ ðə daɪs 'twaɪs] würfle zweimal **II**
to **dictate** [dɪk'teɪt] diktieren; vorschreiben **V AC3**, 114
dictionary ['dɪkʃnri] Wörterbuch **I**
to **die** [daɪ] sterben **III**
It's to **die** for! [ˌɪts tə 'daɪ fɔ:] Dafür könnte ich sterben!; Das ist unwiderstehlich! **IV**
diet [daɪət] Diät ⟨**V TS3**, 111⟩
difference ['dɪfrəns] Unterschied **I**
*to make a **difference** (to sth) [ˌmeɪk‿ə 'dɪfrəns] etw. verändern **V AC3**, 114
different ['dɪfrnt] anders; unterschiedlich; verschieden **I**
difficult ['dɪfɪklt] schwierig **II**
difficulty ['dɪfɪklti] Schwierigkeit **IV**
*to **dig** [dɪg] graben **II**
digital ['dɪdʒɪtl] digital ⟨**V U3**, 102⟩
dilemma [daɪ'lemə] Dilemma; Zwickmühle **III**
diner *(AE)* ['daɪnə] einfaches Restaurant mit Theke und Tischen **IV**
dinner ['dɪnə] Abendessen **I**
dinosaur ['daɪnəsɔ:] Dinosaurier **II**
diplomacy [dɪ'pləʊməsi] Diplomatie ⟨**V AC1**, 11⟩
direct [dɪ'rekt] direkt **III**
direct speech [ˌdɪrekt 'spi:tʃ] direkte Rede **III**
direction [dɪ'rekʃn] Richtung **I**
stage **direction** ['steɪdʒ dɪˌrekʃn] Regieanweisung **III**
director [dɪ'rektə] Regisseur/-in **III**
dirt [dɜ:t] Schmutz; Dreck **III**
dirty ['dɜ:ti] dreckig; schmutzig **II**
the **disabled** [ðə dɪ'seɪbld] Behinderte **V U2**, 55
disadvantage [ˌdɪsəd'vɑ:ntɪdʒ] Nachteil **IV**
to **disagree** [ˌdɪsə'gri:] anderer Meinung sein; nicht einverstanden sein **III**
to **disappear** [ˌdɪsə'pɪə] verschwinden **IV**
disappointed [ˌdɪsə'pɔɪntɪd] enttäuscht **I**
disappointing [ˌdɪsə'pɔɪntɪŋ] enttäuschend **IV**
disaster [dɪ'zɑ:stə] Desaster; Katastrophe; Unglück **II**
disbelieving [ˌdɪsbɪ'li:vɪŋ] ungläubig ⟨**V U1**, 28⟩
to **disconnect** [ˌdɪskə'nekt] trennen; abschalten ⟨**V TS2**, 79⟩
to **discover** [dɪ'skʌvə] entdecken **II**

discovery [dɪ'skʌvri] Entdeckung **III**
discrimination [dɪˌskrɪmɪ'neɪʃn] Diskriminierung **V AC1**, 9
to **discuss** [dɪ'skʌs] diskutieren **I**
discussion [dɪ'skʌʃn] Diskussion **II**
disease [dɪ'zi:z] Krankheit **V U3**, 94
disgusted [dɪs'gʌstɪd] angeekelt; angewidert **VTS1**, 42
dish [dɪʃ] Gericht; Speise **IV**
dishes *(pl)* ['dɪʃɪz] Geschirr **IV**
*to do the **dishes** [ˌdu: ðə 'dɪʃɪz] den Abwasch machen **IV**
dishonest [dɪ'sɒnɪst] unehrlich **III**
dishwasher ['dɪʃˌwɒʃə] Spülmaschine **IV**
to **dislike** [dɪs'laɪk] nicht mögen **IV**
dislikes *(pl)* [dɪs'laɪks] Abneigungen **IV**
to **disobey** [ˌdɪsə'beɪ] nicht gehorchen; ungehorsam sein **III**
display [dɪ'spleɪ] Ausstellung **II**; Ständer ⟨**V U3**, 100⟩
class **display** ['klɑ:s dɪˌspleɪ] Ausstellung in der Klasse **I**
disrespectful [ˌdɪsrɪ'spektfl] respektlos **V U1**, 23
distance ['dɪstns] Distanz; Entfernung **II**
distant ['dɪstnt] entfernt; distanziert **V U2**, 65
to **distract** [dɪ'strækt] ablenken °**V U3**, 98
district ['dɪstrɪkt] Distrikt; Bezirk **IV**
to **disturb** [dɪ'stɜ:b] stören **V U1**, 17
diversity [daɪ'vɜ:səti] Vielfalt; Verschiedenheit **V AC2**, 81
to **divide** (up) [dɪ'vaɪd] aufteilen **III**
to **divorce** [dɪ'vɔ:s] sich scheiden lassen ⟨**V U3**, 100⟩
dizzy ['dɪzi] schwindelig **IV**
DJ [ˌdi:'dʒeɪ] DJ; Discjockey **III**
*to **do** [du:] machen; tun **I**
*to be **done** with [bi 'dʌn wɪð] fertig sein mit **IV**
*to **do** about ['du:‿əˌbaʊt] unternehmen wegen **II**
*to **do** away with sth [ˌdu:‿ə'weɪ wɪð] etw. abschaffen; etw. loswerden ⟨**VTS3**, 109⟩
*to **do** one's bit [ˌdu:‿wʌnz 'bɪt] seinen Teil beitragen **V AC3**, 114
*to **do** our hair [ˌdu:‿aʊə 'heə] uns frisieren; unsere Haare machen **I**
*to **do** the dishes [ˌdu: ðə 'dɪʃɪz] den Abwasch machen **IV**
*to **do** the shopping [ˌdu: ðə 'ʃɒpɪŋ] Einkäufe machen; Besorgungen machen **III**
*to **do** well [ˌdu: 'wel] gute Leistungen erbringen **III**
Don't worry! [ˌdəʊnt 'wʌri] Keine Sorge! **I**
dos and **don'ts** [ˌdu:z‿ənd 'dəʊnts] Ge- und Verbote; was man tun und was man nicht tun sollte **III**
We **did** it! [ˌwi: 'dɪd‿ɪt] Wir haben es geschafft! **II**
You can **do** it! [ˌju: kən 'du: ɪt] Du schaffst es! **III**
doctor ['dɒktə] Arzt/Ärztin **II**
document ['dɒkjəmənt] Dokument °**V U2**, 47
to **document** ['dɒkjəment] dokumentieren; festhalten ⟨**V U3**, 101⟩
dog [dɒg] Hund **I**
to walk the **dog** [ˌwɔ:k ðə 'dɒg] den Hund ausführen; mit dem Hund spazieren gehen **I**
I'm **dog-tired**. [ˌaɪm ˌdɒg'taɪəd] Ich bin hundemüde. **I**
dollar ['dɒlə] Dollar *(Währung)* **III**
dolphin ['dɒlfɪn] Delfin **III**
dominance ['dɒmɪnəns] Dominanz ⟨**V AC1**, 11⟩
dominant ['dɒmɪnənt] dominant; dominierend ⟨**V AC1**, 11⟩
dominoes ['dɒmɪnəʊz] Domino **III**
to **donate** [də'neɪt] spenden; stiften **IV**
door [dɔ:] Tür **I**
French **doors** [ˌfrenʃ 'dɔ:z] Terrassentür ⟨**V U3**, 101⟩
front **door** [ˌfrʌnt 'dɔ:] Haustür **II**
next **door** [ˌnekst 'dɔ:] (von) nebenan **III**
screen **door** [skri:n] Eingangstür mit Fliegengitter ⟨**V U1**, 30⟩
doorbell ['dɔ:bel] Türklingel **III**
dope [dəʊp] Rauschgift; Stoff ⟨**V AC2**, 80⟩
dot-com bubble [ˌdɒtkɒm 'bʌbl] Internetblase; Dotcom-Blase **V U3**, 90
double ['dʌbl] Doppel-; zweimal **IV**
doubt [daʊt] Zweifel **III**
down [daʊn] nach unten; herunter; hinunter **II**; nieder **IV**
*to break **down** [ˌbreɪk 'daʊn] zusammenbrechen **VTS3**, 108
to close **down** [ˌkləʊz 'daʊn] den Betrieb einstellen; schließen **V U3**, 90
*to come **down** [ˌkʌm 'daʊn] herunterkommen **I**
*to go **down** [ˌgəʊ 'daʊn] hinuntergehen; nach unten gehen; entlanggehen **I**
to note **down** [ˌnəʊt 'daʊn] notieren; aufschreiben **II**
to pull **down** [ˌpʊl‿'daʊn] abreißen **III**
*to sit **down** [ˌsɪt 'daʊn] sich hinsetzen; sich setzen **I**
to slow **down** [ˌsləʊ 'daʊn] langsamer werden; bremsen **V U2**, 65
to touch **down** [tʌtʃ 'daʊn] landen **IV**
*to write **down** [ˌraɪt 'daʊn] aufschreiben **I**
downhill ['daʊnhɪl] bergab; abwärts ⟨**V U2**, 64⟩
to **download** [ˌdaʊn'ləʊd] herunterladen *(aus dem Internet)* **II**
downriver [ˌdaʊn'rɪvə] flussabwärts; stromabwärts **IV**
downstairs [ˌdaʊn'steəz] nach unten; im Untergeschoss; unten **II**
downtown *(AE)* [ˌdaʊn'taʊn] im Stadtzentrum **IV**
draft [drɑ:ft] Entwurf; Konzept **I**
drama ['drɑ:mə] Theater; Drama **II**
dramatic [drə'mætɪk] dramatisch **II**
*to **draw** [drɔ:] zeichnen **I**; ziehen **II**
*to **draw** the reader into the story/action [ˌdrɔ: ðə ˌri:də ɪntə ðə 'stɔ:ri/'ækʃn] den Leser/die Leserin in die Geschichte/Handlung hineinziehen **III**
drawing ['drɔ:ɪŋ] Zeichnung **I**
dream [dri:m] Traum **II**
*to **dream** [dri:m] träumen **IV**
Dreaming ['dri:mɪŋ] Traumzeit **V U1**, 22
dress [dres] Kleid **III**
dress code ['dres ˌkəʊd] Kleiderordnung; Bekleidungsvorschriften **IV**
fancy **dress** ['fænsi dres] Verkleidung; Kostüm **II**
dresser ['dresə] Kommode ⟨**V U3**, 101⟩
drink [drɪŋk] Getränk **I**
*to **drink** [drɪŋk] trinken **I**
drinking water ['drɪŋkɪŋ ˌwɔ:tə] Trinkwasser **IV**
drive [draɪv] Fahrt; Anfahrt; Autofahrt **IV**
clothing **drive** ['kləʊðɪŋ ˌdraɪv] Kleidersammlung **IV**
*to **drive** [draɪv] fahren **III**
*to **drive** off [draɪv‿'ɒf] wegfahren **III**
driver ['draɪvə] Fahrer/-in **II**
drizzle ['drɪzl] Nieselregen **III**
to **drop** [drɒp] fallen (lassen) **II**
to **drop** out (of) [ˌdrɒp 'aʊt‿əv] abbrechen **III**
to **drop** sb off [ˌdrɒp‿'ɒf] jmdn. absetzen; jmdn. aussteigen lassen **IV**
drop-off ['drɒpɒf] Abgabe **IV**
drought [draʊt] Dürre; Trockenheit **V U3**, 90
to **drown** [draʊn] ertrinken; ertränken **III**
drum [drʌm] Trommel **IV**
drums *(pl)* [drʌmz] Schlagzeug **III**
dry [draɪ] trocken **III**
to **duck** [dʌk] (sich) ducken ⟨**V U1**, 30⟩
dude *(coll)* [du:d] Mann; Alter *(ugs.)* **IV**
to **dump** [dʌmp] abladen **V U2**, 53
during *(+ noun)* ['djʊərɪŋ] während *(+ Nomen)* **II**
dusty ['dʌsti] staubig **IV**
duty ['dju:ti] Pflicht ⟨**V U2**, 63⟩
duty-free [ˌdju:ti'fri:] zollfrei **III**
DVD [ˌdi:vi:'di:] DVD **I**
dwelling ['dwelɪŋ] Behausung; Wohnstätte ⟨**V U2**, 63⟩
dystopia [dɪs'təʊpiə] Dystopie °**V U2**, 67
dystopian [dɪs'təʊpiən] dystopisch °**V U2**, 67

E

e.g. *(= for example)* [ˌi:'dʒi:] z.B. *(= zum Beispiel)* **I**
each [i:tʃ] jede/-r/-s **I**
each other [ˌi:tʃ‿'ʌðə] einander; sich; sich gegenseitig **I**
each [i:tʃ] pro Person; pro Stück **I**

ear [ɪə] Ohr **III**
early ['ɜ:li] früh **I**
this **early** ['ðɪs ˌɜ:li] so früh **III**
to **earn** [ɜ:n] verdienen **I**
earth [ɜ:θ] Erdboden; Erde; die Erde **II**
What on **earth** …? [ˌwɒt‿ɒn‿'ɜ:θ] Was um alles in der Welt …? **II**
earthquake ['ɜ:θkweɪk] Erdbeben **VTS2**, 74
east [i:st] Osten; Ost- **I**
Easter ['i:stə] Ostern **I**
eastern ['i:stn] östlich; Ost- **IV**
easy ['i:zi] einfach; leicht **I**
easy-going [ˌi:zi'gəʊɪŋ] locker; unkompliziert **III**
*to **eat** [i:t] essen; fressen **I**
eating ['i:tɪŋ] Essen; Ess- **V U3**, 97
the **ebb** and **flow** [ði‿ˌeb‿ənd 'fləʊ] das Auf und Ab; die Höhen und Tiefen ⟨**VTS2**, 77⟩
Eco ['i:kəʊ] Öko- **II**
economic [ˌi:kə'nɒmɪk] ökonomisch; wirtschaftlich ⟨**V AC1**, 11⟩
economy [ɪ'kɒnəmi] Ökonomie; Wirtschaft **IV**
edge of town [ˌedʒ‿əv 'taʊn] Stadtrand **IV**
to **edit** ['edɪt] bearbeiten; überarbeiten °**VTS2**, 78
to **edit** out [ˌedɪt‿'aʊt] herausschneiden **III**
editor ['edɪtə] Herausgeber/-in; Redakteur/-in **VTS3**, 108
letter to the **editor** [ˌletə tʊ ði‿'edɪtə] Leserbrief **VTS3**, 108
to **educate** ['edʒʊkeɪt] erziehen; bilden **IV**
education *(no pl)* [ˌedʒʊ'keɪʃn] Erziehung; Bildung **III**
effect [ɪ'fekt] Effekt; Wirkung **IV**
audio-visual **effect** [ˌɔ:diəʊvɪʒuəl ɪ'fekt] audiovisueller Effekt **II**
special **effect** [ˌspeʃl‿ɪ'fekt] Spezialeffekt **IV**
effective [ɪ'fektɪv] effektiv; wirkungsvoll **IV**
effectiveness [ɪ'fektɪvnəs] Effektivität; Wirksamkeit **IV**
effort ['efət] Bemühung; Mühe **V U3**, 86
egg [eg] Ei **I**
Egyptian [ɪ'dʒɪpʃn] Ägypter/-in; ägyptisch **III**
eight [eɪt] acht **I**
either ['aɪðə; 'i:ðə] beide(s) °**V U2**, 49
not … **either** [nɒt … 'aɪðə; nɒt … 'i:ðə] auch nicht **IV**
either … or … ['aɪðə/'i:ðə … ɔ:] entweder … oder … **IV**
either of you ['aɪðər‿əv ˌju:] einer von euch ⟨**V U3**, 101⟩
elder ['eldə] Älteste/-r **V U1**, 23
Chief **Elder** [ˌtʃi:f 'eldə] Ratschef/-in; Ratsvorsitzende/-r ⟨**V U2**, 62⟩
the **elderly** [ði 'eldəli] ältere Menschen; Senioren **V U2**, 55
elderly ['eldəli] älter **III**
to **elect** [ɪ'lekt] wählen ⟨**V U2**, 62⟩
election [ɪ'lekʃn] Wahl **V AC1**, 8
electric [ɪ'lektrɪk] elektrisch **III**
electrician [ˌelɪk'trɪʃn] Elektriker/-in **II**
electricity [ˌelɪk'trɪsəti] Elektrizität; Strom **II**
electrics [ɪ'lektrɪks] Elektrik **II**
electronic [ˌelek'trɒnɪk] elektronisch **II**
elegant ['elɪgnt] elegant **IV**
element ['elɪmənt] Element **II**
elephant ['elɪfənt] Elefant **III**
elevator *(AE)* ['elɪveɪtə] Aufzug; Lift **IV**
eleven [ɪ'levn] elf **I**
to **eliminate** [ɪ'lɪmɪneɪt] eliminieren; beseitigen ⟨**V U2**, 67⟩
elk [elk] Elch **IV**
else [els] andere/-r/-s; sonst noch **III**
nobody **else** ['nəʊbədi els] niemand anderes **II**
what **else** [ˌwɒt‿'els] was sonst; was noch **I**
elsewhere ['elsweə] anderswo; woanders ⟨**V U2**, 64⟩
e-mail ['i:meɪl] E-Mail **I**
to **e-mail** ['i:meɪl] mailen; per E-Mail schicken **II**
to **embarrass** [ɪm'bærəs] in Verlegenheit bringen **V AC2**, 83
embarrassed [ɪm'bærəst] verlegen **II**
embarrassing [ɪm'bærəsɪŋ] peinlich **II**
emergency [ɪ'mɜ:dʒnsi] Notfall; Notlage; Notfall- **V U3**, 94
emotion [ɪ'məʊʃn] Gefühl; Emotion **VTS1**, 39
emotional [ɪ'məʊʃnl] emotional; Gefühls- **III**
emperor ['emprə] Kaiser **III**
emphasis ['emfəsɪs] Betonung °**V U2**, 59
to **emphasise** ['emfəsaɪz] betonen **V U2**, 60
empire ['empaɪə] Reich; Kaiserreich **III**
to **employ** [ɪm'plɔɪ] einstellen; anstellen; beschäftigen **IV**
employee [ɪm'plɔɪi:] Angestellte/-r; Mitarbeiter/-in; Arbeitnehmer/-in **IV**
employer [ɪm'plɔɪə] Arbeitgeber/-in **V U2**, 49
to **empty** ['emti] leeren; ausräumen **IV**
empty ['emti] leer **III**
emu ['i:mju:] Emu **V U1**, 22
to **enable** [ɪ'neɪbl] befähigen; ermöglichen ⟨**V U3**, 92⟩
enclosure [ɪn'kləʊʒə] Anlage; Beilage **V U2**, 51
to **encourage** [ɪn'kʌrɪdʒ] unterstützen; ermutigen **V U2**, 48
encyclopaedia [ɪnˌsaɪklə'pi:diə] Enzyklopädie; Lexikon **IV**
end [end] Ende; Schluss **I**
in the **end** [ˌɪn ði‿'end] schließlich; zum Schluss **II**
to **end** [end] enden; beenden **II**
to **end** up [ˌend‿'ʌp] enden; landen **II**
ending ['endɪŋ] Ende; Schluss *(einer Geschichte)* **I**
happy **ending** [ˌhæpi 'endɪŋ] Happy End **III**
endless ['endləs] endlos; unendlich; unzählig **IV**
enemy ['enəmi] Feind/-in **III**
energy ['enədʒi] Energie; Kraft **III**
search **engine** ['sɜ:tʃ‿ˌendʒɪn] Suchmaschine **IV**
steam **engine** ['sti:m‿ˌendʒɪn] Dampfmaschine **III**
engineer [ˌendʒɪ'nɪə] Ingenieur/-in; Techniker/-in **IV**
engineering [ˌendʒɪ'nɪərɪŋ] Technik; Maschinenbau **V U2**, 49
English ['ɪŋglɪʃ] englisch; Englisch; aus England; Engländer/-in **I**
English-speaking ['ɪŋglɪʃˌspi:kɪŋ] englischsprachig **I**
I'm **English**. [aɪm‿'ɪŋglɪʃ] Ich bin Engländer/-in. **I**
to **engulf** [ɪn'gʌlf] umringen; verschlingen ⟨**V U1**, 30⟩
to **enjoy** [ɪn'dʒɔɪ] genießen; sich freuen an **II**
to **enjoy** oneself [ɪn'dʒɔɪ] Spaß haben; sich amüsieren **III**
enjoyable [ɪn'dʒɔɪəbl] angenehm; unterhaltsam **IV**
enlightenment [ɪn'laɪtnmənt] Aufklärung; Erleuchtung **IV**
enough [ɪ'nʌf] genug; genügend **I**
enslavement [ɪn'sleɪvmənt] Versklavung **VTS2**, 75
to **enter** ['entə] hineingehen; betreten; eintreten; *hier:* mitmachen **II**
to **entertain** [ˌentə'teɪn] unterhalten **III**
entertainer [ˌentə'teɪnə] Entertainer/-in; Unterhaltungskünstler/-in **IV**
entertaining [ˌentə'teɪnɪŋ] unterhaltsam **IV**
entertainment *(no pl)* [ˌentə'teɪnmənt] Unterhaltung **III**
enthusiasm [ɪn'θju:ziæzm] Enthusiasmus; Begeisterung **IV**
enthusiastic [ɪnˌθju:zi'æstɪk] enthusiastisch; begeistert **V U1**, 29
entire [ɪn'taɪə] gesamt; ganz; komplett **VTS1**, 43
entitled [ɪn'taɪtld] mit dem Titel **VTS2**, 75
to be **entitled** to sth [bi‿ɪn'taɪtld tə] berechtigt sein; ein Anrecht haben auf; Anspruch haben auf °**V AC2**, 81
entrance ['entrəns] Eingang; Eintritt **III**
entrepreneur [ˌɒntrəprə'nɜ:] Unternehmer/-in **V U3**, 91
entry ['entri] Eintrag **III**; Beitrag; Einsendung **IV**
diary **entry** ['daɪəri entri] Tagebucheintrag **II**
envelope ['envələʊp] Umschlag; Briefumschlag °**V U1**, 28
environment [ɪn'vaɪrnmənt] Umwelt; Umgebung **II**
environmental [ɪnˌvaɪrn'mentl] Umwelt-; umweltbedingt °**V U3**, 85
to **envy** ['envi] beneiden **V AC1**, 10
epic ['epɪk] episch; *hier:* geil **IV**
equal ['i:kwəl] gleich; gleichwertig **IV**

equipment [ɪ'kwɪpmənt] Ausstattung; Ausrüstung **II**
equivalent [ɪ'kwɪvlənt] Entsprechung; Äquivalent ⟨**V U1**, 21⟩
er [ɜ:] äh **I**
era ['ɪərə] Ära; Zeitalter **III**
erosion [ɪ'rəʊʒn] Erosion; Abtragung ⟨**V U3**, 96⟩
eruption [ɪ'rʌpʃn] Ausbruch *(Vulkan)* **IV**
escalator ['eskəleɪtə] Rolltreppe **I**
escape [ɪ'skeɪp] Flucht **III**
to **escape** (from) [ɪ'skeɪp frəm] fliehen; entfliehen; flüchten; entkommen **IV**
especially [ɪ'speʃli] besonders; vor allem **IV**
essay ['eseɪ] Essay **VTS3**, 108
argumentative **essay** [ɑ:gjəˌmentətɪv‿'eseɪ] Erörterung **VTS3**, 108
the **essentials** *(pl)* [ði‿ɪ'senʃlz] das Wesentliche; die wichtigsten Punkte °**VTS2**, 75
to **establish** [ɪ'stæblɪʃ] einrichten; gründen; herstellen ⟨**V U1**, 21⟩ø einführen **VTS1**, 43
to **estimate** ['estɪmeɪt] schätzen **IV**
etc. *(= et cetera)* [ɪt'setrə] usw. *(= und so weiter)* **II**
*to be **etched** with [bi 'etʃt wɪð] geprägt sein von ⟨**V U1**, 30⟩
ethnic ['eθnɪk] ethnisch; Volks-; *hier:* exotisch **IV**
euro ['jʊərəʊ] Euro *(Währung)* **I**
European [ˌjʊərə'pi:ən] Europäer/-in; europäisch; aus Europa **IV**
to **evaluate** [ɪ'væljueɪt] evaluieren; auswerten; bewerten °**V U2**, 48
peer **evaluation** [ˌpɪər‿ɪˌvælju'eɪʃn] gegenseitige Beurteilung ⟨**V AC2**, 83⟩
even ['i:vn] sogar; selbst **I**
even though [ˌi:vn 'ðəʊ] auch wenn; obwohl **IV**
evening ['i:vnɪŋ] Abend **I**
in the **evenings** [ɪn ði‿'i:vnɪŋz] abends **I**
event [ɪ'vent] Ereignis; Veranstaltung **I**
ever ['evə] jemals **II**
the best … **ever** ['best … ˌevə] der/die/das beste … überhaupt **III**
every ['evri] jede/-r/-s **I**
everybody ['evribɒdi] jeder; alle **II**
everyday ['evrideɪ] alltäglich **III**
everyone ['evriwʌn] jeder; alle **I**
everything ['evriθɪŋ] alles **I**
everywhere ['evriweə] überall **I**
evidence *(no pl)* ['evɪdns] Beweis; Beleg; Beweismaterial **VTS2**, 77
exact [ɪg'zækt] exakt; genau **V U2**, 56
to **exaggerate** [ɪg'zædʒəreɪt] übertreiben **III**
exaggerated [ɪg'zædʒəreɪtɪd] übertrieben **IV**
exaggeration [ɪgˌzædʒr'eɪʃn] Übertreibung °**VTS1**, 40
exam [ɪg'zæm] Examen; Prüfung **II**
examination [ɪgˌzæmɪ'neɪʃn] Untersuchung; Prüfung **IV**
to **examine** [ɪg'zæmɪn] untersuchen; kontrollieren °**VTS2**, 78
example [ɪg'zɑ:mpl] Beispiel **I**
*to set a good **example** [set‿ə ˌgʊd‿ɪg'zɑ:mpl] ein Vorbild sein **V U2**, 48
for **example** [fər‿ɪg'zɑ:mpl] zum Beispiel **II**
except [ɪk'sept] außer; bis auf **III**
exception [ɪk'sepʃn] Ausnahme **VTS3**, 111
excerpt ['eksɜ:pt] Auszug **IV**
exchange [ɪks'tʃeɪndʒ] Austausch; Austausch- **III**
exchange student [ɪks'tʃeɪndʒ ˌstju:dnt] Austauschschüler/-in **III**
student **exchange** ['stju:dnt ɪksˌtʃeɪndʒ] Schüleraustausch **III**
to **exchange** [ɪks'tʃeɪndʒ] austauschen **II**
excited [ɪk'saɪtɪd] aufgeregt; begeistert **I**
excitement *(no pl)* [ɪk'saɪtmənt] Aufregung **III**
exciting [ɪk'saɪtɪŋ] spannend; aufregend **I**
Excuse me … [ɪk'skju:z mi] Entschuldigung!; Entschuldigen Sie! **I**
(business) **executive** ['bɪznɪs ɪgˌzekjətɪv] Geschäftsführer/-in; Manager/-in; gehobene Führungskraft **V U2**, 49
to **exempt** from [ɪg'zempt frəm] befreien von ⟨**V U2**, 63⟩
exercise ['eksəsaɪz] Übung; Aufgabe **I**
exercise book ['eksəsaɪz ˌbʊk] Übungsheft **I**
exhausted [ɪg'zɔ:stɪd] erschöpft **V U2**, 53
exhausting [ɪg'zɔ:stɪŋ] anstrengend **IV**
exhilarating [ɪg'zɪlreɪtɪŋ] berauschend; aufregend ⟨**V U2**, 64⟩
to **exist** [ɪg'zɪst] existieren; bestehen **V U3**, 90
to **expand** [ɪk'spænd] (sich) ausdehnen; erweitern **IV**
to **expect** [ɪk'spekt] erwarten **III**
*to be **expected** to *(+ inf)* [bi ɪk'spektɪd tə] sollen **V U2**, 48
expectation [ˌekspek'teɪʃn] Erwartung **IV**
*to meet sb's **expectations** [ˌmi:t sʌmbədiz‿ekspek'teɪʃnz] jmds. Erwartungen erfüllen **IV**
expensive [ɪk'spensɪv] teuer **I**
experience [ɪk'spɪəriəns] Erfahrung **II**
to chalk sth up to **experience** [ˌtʃɔ:k‿ʌp tə ɪk'spɪəriəns] etw. als Erfahrung verbuchen **V U3**, 86
to **experience** [ɪk'spɪəriəns] erfahren; erleben **III**
expert ['ekspɜ:t] Experte/Expertin **II**
to **explain** [ɪk'spleɪn] erklären **I**
explanation [ˌeksplə'neɪʃn] Erklärung; Erläuterung **IV**
to **explode** [ɪk'spləʊd] explodieren **V U3**, 86
to **explore** [ɪk'splɔ:] auf Entdeckungsreise gehen; sich umschauen; erkunden; erforschen **I**
explorer [ɪk'splɔ:rə] Forscher/-in; Forschungsreisende/-r; Entdecker/-in **V U3**, 90
export ['ekspɔ:t] Export; Ausfuhr **V U2**, 53
to **export** [ɪk'spɔ:t] exportieren; ausführen **V U3**, 93
exportation [ˌekspɔ:'teɪʃn] Export; Ausfuhr ⟨**V AC1**, 11⟩
to **express** [ɪk'spres] ausdrücken **II**
expression [ɪk'spreʃn] Ausdruck; Wendung; Äußerung **II**
facial **expression** [ˌfeɪʃl ɪk'spreʃn] Gesichtsausdruck **III**
exterior [ɪk'stɪəriə] Außen- °**VTS1**, 44
*to become **extinct** [bɪˌkʌm‿ɪk'stɪŋkt] aussterben **III**
extinction *(no pl)* [ɪks'tɪŋkʃn] Aussterben **III**
extra ['ekstrə] Statist/-in; Komparse/Komparsin **V U3**, 86
extra ['ekstrə] extra; zusätzlich **I**
extract ['ekstrækt] Extrakt; Auszug; Exzerpt °**VTS1**, 44
extreme [ɪk'stri:m] extrem; radikal **IV**
extremely [ɪk'stri:mli] sehr; äußerst **VTS1**, 42
eye [aɪ] Auge **II**
black **eye** [blæk‿'aɪ] blaues Auge **IV**
to raise one's **eyes** [ˌreɪz wʌnz‿'aɪz] den Blick heben; aufblicken; hochblicken **V U1**, 28
to roll one's **eyes** [ˌrəʊl wʌnz‿'aɪz] die Augen verdrehen **III**
He couldn't believe his **eyes**. [hi ˌkʊdnt bɪˌli:v hɪz‿'aɪz] Er traute seinen Augen nicht. **II**
eye-catcher ['aɪkætʃə] Blickfang; Hingucker **IV**
eyewitness ['aɪwɪtnəs] Augenzeuge/Augenzeugin **II**

F

fabric *(no pl)* ['fæbrɪk] Stoff ⟨**V U2**, 65⟩
fabulous ['fæbjələs] sagenhaft; fantastisch **IV**
face [feɪs] Gesicht **I**
Put … **face** down. [pʊt ˌfeɪs 'daʊn] Lege/Legt … umgedreht hin. **I**
to **face** [feɪs] gegenüber stehen; konfrontiert werden mit **III**; anblicken; sich zuwenden **V U1**, 28
Let's **face** it. [lets 'feɪs‿ɪt] Machen wir uns doch nichts vor. **III**
face-to-face [ˌfeɪstə'feɪs] von Angesicht zu Angesicht; Auge in Auge **IV**
facial expression [ˌfeɪʃl ɪk'spreʃn] Gesichtsausdruck **III**
fact [fækt] Fakt; Tatsache **II**
in **fact** [ɪn 'fækt] tatsächlich; eigentlich; genau genommen **IV**
factory ['fæktri] Fabrik; Werk **III**
factual ['fæktʃʊəl] sachlich **III**
factual text [ˌfæktʃʊəl 'tekst] Sachtext **III**
degree **Fahrenheit** (°F) ['færnhaɪt] Grad Fahrenheit **IV**

to **fail** sb [feɪl] jmdn. hängenlassen; jmdn. im Stich lassen **VTS3**, 111
to **fail** to do sth ['feɪl tə] versäumen, etw. zu tun; es nicht schaffen, etw. zu tun **IV**
street **fair** ['stri:t feə] Straßenfest **V AC2**, 81
fair [feə] gerecht; fair **I**
fair play [feə 'pleɪ] Fairplay **III**
to **fake** [feɪk] vortäuschen; fälschen **II**
fake [feɪk] falsch; gefälscht **III**
fall [fɔ:l] Abnahme **VTS2**, 77
*to **fall** [fɔ:l] fallen; hinfallen **I**
*to **fall** asleep [ˌfɔ:l‿ə'sli:p] einschlafen **I**
*to **fall** down [ˌfɔ:l‿'daʊn] stürzen; hinunterfallen **III**
*to **fall** for ['fɔ:l fə] hereinfallen auf **IV**
*to **fall** off [ˌfɔ:l‿'ɒf] herunterfallen; hinunterfallen **II**
*to **fall** over [ˌfɔ:l‿'əʊvə] hinfallen; umkippen **I**
fame [feɪm] Ruhm **V U3**, 103
*to get **familiar** [ˌget fə'mɪliə] sich vertraut machen **IV**
family ['fæmli] Familie **I**
family tree ['fæmli ˌtri:] Stammbaum **I**
host **family** ['həʊst ˌfæmli] Gastfamilie **III**
famous ['feɪməs] berühmt **I**
fan [fæn] Fan; Anhänger/-in **II**; Ventilator **V U1**, 30
fancy dress ['fænsi dres] Verkleidung; Kostüm **II**
fantastic [fæn'tæstɪk] fantastisch; großartig **II**
fantasy ['fæntəsi] Fantasie; Traum- **I**; Fantasy **III**
fanzine [fæn'zi:n] Fanzeitschrift **II**
FAQ [ˌefeɪ'kju:] Liste mit häufig gestellten Fragen **III**
far [fɑ:] weit **II**
as **far** as [əz 'fɑ:r‿əz] soweit **VTS3**, 109
so **far** [ˌsəʊ 'fɑ:] bis jetzt **II**
in the **far** west [ɪn ðə fɑ: 'west] im äußersten Westen **II**
fare [feə] Fahrpreis **II**
farewell [ˌfeə'wel] Abschied; Abschieds- **V U1**, 20
farm [fɑ:m] Farm; Bauernhof **I**
to **farm** [fɑ:m] Landwirtschaft betreiben **IV**
farmer ['fɑ:mə] Farmer/-in; Landwirt/-in **II**
fascinating ['fæsɪneɪtɪŋ] faszinierend **III**
fashion ['fæʃn] Mode **II**
fast [fɑ:st] schnell **I**
fast food [ˌfɑ:st'fu:d] Fastfood ⟨**V U3**, 97⟩
fate [feɪt] Schicksal; Fügung; Vorsehung **VTS1**, 40
father ['fɑ:ðə] Vater **I**
in **favor** (of) *(AE)* [ɪn 'feɪvər‿əv] dafür; zugunsten (von) **IV**
favourite ['feɪvrɪt] Favorit/-in; Günstling **III**
favourite ['feɪvrɪt] Lieblings- **I**
fear [fɪə] Angst; Furcht; Befürchtung **II**
to **fear** [fɪə] (sich) fürchten **IV**
fearful ['fɪəfl] ängstlich **III**
feather ['feðə] Feder **III**
feature ['fi:tʃə] Eigenschaft; Merkmal **III**; Gesichtszug ⟨**V U1**, 30⟩
key **feature** [ˌki: 'fi:tʃə] Hauptmerkmal **VTS1**, 38
to **feature** ['fi:tʃə] zeigen; aufweisen **III**
February ['februri] Februar **I**
*to be **fed** up (with) [bi fed‿'ʌp wɪð] sauer sein (auf); die Nase voll haben (von) **III**
federation [ˌfedr'eɪʃn] Bundesstaat; Föderation **V U1**, 28
fee [fi:] Gebühr **II**
school **fees** *(pl)* ['sku:l fi:z] Schulgeld; Schulgebühren **III**
*to **feed** [fi:d] füttern; ernähren **II**
feedback ['fi:dbæk] Feedback; Rückmeldung **II**
*to **feel** [fi:l] fühlen; sich fühlen **I**
*to **feel** left out [ˌfi:l left‿'aʊt] sich ausgeschlossen fühlen **II**
*to **feel** sick [ˌfi:l 'sɪk] Übelkeit verspüren; sich schlecht fühlen **II**
*to **feel** sorry for [ˌfi:l 'sɒri fɔ:] Mitleid haben mit; bedauern **III**
feeling ['fi:lɪŋ] Gefühl **II**
fellow ['feləʊ] Bursche; Kerl **IV**
female ['fi:meɪl] weiblich **V U2**, 49
ferry ['feri] Fähre **III**
festival ['festɪvl] Festival; Fest **I**
to **fetch** [fetʃ] holen; abholen **III**
fever ['fi:və] Fieber **II**
few [fju:] wenige **II**
a **few** [ə 'fju:] ein paar; wenige; einige **I**
fiction *(no pl)* ['fɪkʃn] Erzählliteratur; Erfindung; Prosa; Fiktion **III**
science **fiction** [ˌsaɪəns 'fɪkʃn] Science-Fiction *(Zukunftsdichtung)* **II**
fictional ['fɪkʃnl] fiktional; fiktiv; erdichtet **III**
field [fi:ld] Feld; Spielfeld; Wiese; Weide; Acker **II**
fifteen [ˌfɪf'ti:n] fünfzehn **I**
fight [faɪt] Kampf; Streit **II**
*to **fight** [faɪt] kämpfen; (sich) streiten **II**
figure ['fɪgə] Figur; Gestalt **II**; Ziffer; Zahl **III**
wax **figure** ['wæks ˌfɪgə] Wachsfigur **II**
file [faɪl] Mappe; Datei; Sammlung °**V U3**, 93
to **fill** [fɪl] (sich) füllen **III**
to **fill** in [ˌfɪl‿'ɪn] ausfüllen **II**
filling ['fɪlɪŋ] Füllung **IV**
film [fɪlm] Film **I**
film adaptation [ˌfɪlm‿ædæp'teɪʃn] Verfilmung °**V U2**, 62
to **film** [fɪlm] filmen; drehen **II**
filmmaker ['fɪlmˌmeɪkə] Filmemacher/-in **II**
final ['faɪnl] endgültig **II**; letzte/-r/-s **III**
finally ['faɪnli] schließlich; endlich; zum Schluss; letztlich **II**
*to **find** [faɪnd] finden; herausfinden **I**
*to **find** one's way around [ˌfaɪnd wʌnz ˌweɪ‿ə'raʊnd] sich zurechtfinden **IV**
*to **find** out [ˌfaɪnd‿'aʊt] herausfinden **I**
fine [faɪn] Geldstrafe; Bußgeld ⟨**VTS3**, 113⟩
fine [faɪn] gut; in Ordnung; schön **I**
I'm **fine**. [ˌaɪm 'faɪn] Mir geht's gut. **I**
finger ['fɪŋgə] Finger **I**
*to keep your **fingers** crossed [ˌki:p jɔ: ˌfɪŋgəz 'krɒst] die Daumen drücken **I**
fingernail ['fɪŋgəneɪl] Fingernagel **V U1**, 29
finish line ['fɪnɪʃ ˌlaɪn] Ziellinie **II**
to **finish** ['fɪnɪʃ] beenden; enden; fertigstellen; aufhören **I**
finished ['fɪnɪʃt] fertig **II**
fire [faɪə] Feuer **III**
*to be on **fire** [ˌbi:‿ɒn 'faɪə] brennen **III**
firefighter ['faɪəˌfaɪtə] Feuerwehrmann/-frau **V U2**, 49
fireworks *(pl)* ['faɪəwɜ:ks] Feuerwerk **I**
firm [fɜ:m] fest ⟨**V U2**, 63⟩
first [fɜ:st] zuerst; als Erstes; erste/-r/-s **I**
at **first** [ət 'fɜ:st] zuerst; zunächst **II**
first language [ˌfɜ:st 'læŋgwɪdʒ] Muttersprache **II**
first person narrator [ˌfɜ:st ˌpɜ:sn nə'reɪtə] Ich-Erzähler/-in **III**
in the **first** place [ɪn ðə 'fɜ:st ˌpleɪs] überhaupt erst; von vornherein ⟨**VTS3**, 109⟩
fish [fɪʃ], **fish** [fɪʃ] *(pl)* Fisch **I**
fishing ['fɪʃɪŋ] Angeln; Fischen; Fischerei **II**
to **fit** [fɪt] passen **II**
to **fit** in [ˌfɪt‿'ɪn] hineinpassen; sich einfügen **V U2**, 62
*to get **fit** [ˌget 'fɪt] in Form kommen; fit werden **I**
fitness ['fɪtnəs] Fitness **V U3**, 92
five [faɪv] fünf **I**
to **fix** [fɪks] reparieren; befestigen **II**
flag [flæg] Flagge; Fahne **III**
flair [fleə] Flair; Atmosphäre **II**
flame [fleɪm] Flamme **III**
flash [flæʃ] Blitz; Lichtblitz **III**
flashback ['flæʃbæk] Rückblende; Flashback **III**
flat [flæt] Wohnung **I**
flat [flæt] flach; platt **IV**
flavor *(AE)* ['fleɪvə] Geschmack; Aroma **IV**
flea market ['fli: ˌmɑ:kɪt] Flohmarkt **I**
to **flick** open [flɪk‿'əʊpn] schnell öffnen; schnell aufmachen ⟨**V U1**, 30⟩
flight [flaɪt] Flug **III**
flight attendant ['flaɪt‿əˌtendnt] Flugbegleiter/-in **III**
to **flip** [flɪp] blättern ⟨**V U3**, 102⟩
flip-flops ['flɪpflɒps] Flip-Flops ⟨**V U1**, 21⟩
flirty ['flɜ:ti] zum Flirten aufgelegt; kokett **VTS1**, 42
flood [flʌd] Flut; Hochwasser; Überschwemmung **V U3**, 94
floor [flɔ:] Fußboden **I**; Stockwerk **IV**
flour [flaʊə] Mehl **IV**
the ebb and **flow** [ði‿eb‿ənd 'fləʊ] das Auf und Ab; die Höhen und Tiefen ⟨**VTS2**, 77⟩
to **flow** out [fləʊ‿'aʊt] hinausfließen **II**
flower ['flaʊə] Blume **II**
*to **fly** [flaɪ] fliegen **III**; hissen **IV**

flyer ['flaɪə] Flyer **I**
focus ['fəʊkəs] Blickpunkt; Schwerpunkt; Fokus **III**
out of **focus** [ˌaʊt‿əv 'fəʊkəs] unscharf **III**
to **focus** (on) ['fəʊkəs‿ɒn] sich konzentrieren (auf) **II**
focused ['fəʊkəst] zielgerichtet **V U2**, 49
folder ['fəʊldə] Ordner; Mappe **I**
folks *(infml) (pl)* [fəʊks] Leute **V U1**, 18
to **follow** ['fɒləʊ] folgen; hinterhergehen; befolgen **II**
follower ['fɒləʊə] Anhänger/-in; Follower/-in ⟨**V U3**, 97⟩
the **following** [ðə 'fɒləʊɪŋ] folgende/-r/-s **II**
follow-up ['fɒləʊʌp] Fortsetzung; Folge- **IV**
font [fɒnt] Schriftart °**V U3**, 98
food [fu:d] Essen; Lebensmittel **I**; Futter **III**
fast **food** [ˌfɑ:st'fu:d] Fastfood ⟨**V U3**, 97⟩
food stall ['fu:d stɔ:l] Essensstand; Fressbude ⟨**V U3**, 97⟩
foot [fʊt], **feet** [fi:t] *(pl)* Fuß **I**; Fuß *(Längenmaß: 30,48 cm)* **IV**
on **foot** [ɒn 'fʊt] zu Fuß **II**
football ['fʊtbɔ:l] Fußball **I**
footprint ['fʊtprɪnt] Fußabdruck ⟨**V U1**, 24⟩
for [fɔ:; fə] wegen **II**
for example [fər‿ɪg'zɑ:mpl] zum Beispiel **II**
for free [fə 'fri:] umsonst; kostenlos **IV**
for *(+ Zeitraum)* [fɔ:; fə] seit **III**
for … [fɔ:; fə] … lang **II**
*to **forbid** [fə'bɪd] verbieten ⟨**V U1**, 23⟩
force [fɔ:s] Kraft; Macht **III**
to **force** [fɔ:s] zwingen **V U2**, 53
to **force** a smile [ˌfɔ:s‿ə 'smaɪl] sich zu einem Lächeln zwingen ⟨**V U1**, 29⟩
weather **forecast** ['weðə ˌfɔ:kɑ:st] Wettervorhersage **II**
foreground ['fɔ:graʊnd] Vordergrund **IV**
foreign ['fɒrɪn] ausländisch; fremd **III**
foreign language [ˌfɒrɪn 'læŋgwɪdʒ] Fremdsprache **II**
forest ['fɒrɪst] Wald **II**
forever [fə'revə] für immer; ewig **II**
*to **forget** [fə'get] vergessen **I**
*to **forgive** [fə'gɪv] vergeben; verzeihen **II**
fork [fɔ:k] Gabel **III**
form [fɔ:m] Form **I**; Formular **II**
negative **form** ['negətɪv ˌfɔ:m] verneinte Form **I**
past **form** ['pɑ:st fɔ:m] Vergangenheitsform **II**
possessive **form** [pəˌsesɪv 'fɔ:m] Possessivform **I**
short **form** ['ʃɔ:t fɔ:m] Kurzform **I**
to **form** [fɔ:m] formen; bilden **II**
formal ['fɔ:ml] formal; formell; förmlich **II**
format ['fɔ:mæt] Format **VTS3**, 108
formatting ['fɔ:mætɪŋ] Formatierung °**VTS1**, 44
fortune ['fɔ:tʃu:n] Vermögen; Reichtum **V U3**, 90
forum ['fɔ:rəm] Forum **II**
forward ['fɔ:wəd] vorwärts **III**
to call **forward** [ˌkɔ:l 'fɔ:wəd] nach vorn rufen ⟨**V U2**, 62⟩
*to lean **forward** [ˌli:n 'fɔ:wəd] sich nach vorn lehnen **V U1**, 29
to look **forward** to [ˌlʊk 'fɔ:wəd tə] sich freuen auf **II**
foster ['fɒstə] Pflege- **V U1**, 23
to **found** [faʊnd] gründen **III**
foundation [faʊn'deɪʃn] Stiftung; Gründung **IV**
founder ['faʊndə] Gründer/-in **V U3**, 89
water **fountain** ['wɔ:tə ˌfaʊntɪn] Wasserspender **IV**
four [fɔ:] vier **I**
four-letter word [ˌfɔ:letə 'wɜ:d] Schimpfwort ⟨**VTS3**, 109⟩
fox [fɒks] Fuchs **II**
freeze **frame** ['fri:z ˌfreɪm] Standbild **III**
lingua **franca** [ˌlɪŋgwə 'fræŋkə] Verkehrssprache ⟨**V AC1**, 11⟩
to **free** [fri:] befreien **V AC2**, 80
free [fri:] frei; kostenlos **I**
free time [ˌfri: 'taɪm] Freizeit **I**
for **free** [fə 'fri:] umsonst; kostenlos **IV**
freedom *(no pl)* ['fri:dəm] Freiheit; Unabhängigkeit **III**
freeway *(AE)* ['fri:weɪ] Autobahn **IV**
*to **freeze** [fri:z] erstarren ⟨**V U3**, 102⟩
freeze frame ['fri:z ˌfreɪm] Standbild **III**
freezer ['fri:zə] Tiefkühlschrank **V U3**, 98
French [frenʃ] französisch; Französisch **II**
French doors [ˌfrenʃ 'dɔ:z] Terrassentür ⟨**V U3**, 101⟩
frequent ['fri:kwənt] häufig **VTS3**, 108
frequently asked [ˌfri:kwəntli‿'ɑ:skt] häufig gefragt **I**
fresh [freʃ] frisch **I**
fresh-brewed ['freʃbru:d] frisch aufgebrüht ⟨**V U3**, 101⟩
Friday ['fraɪdeɪ] Freitag **I**
fridge [frɪdʒ] Kühlschrank **I**
to **fridge** [frɪdʒ] einen Kühlschrank plündern ⟨**V U1**, 28⟩
fried [fraɪd] gebraten *(in der Pfanne)* **IV**
friend [frend] Freund/-in **I**
*to become **friends** [bɪˌkʌm‿'frendz] sich anfreunden; Freundschaft schließen **IV**
*to make **friends** [ˌmeɪk 'frendz] Freundschaft schließen **II**
That's what **friends** are for. [ˌðæts wɒt 'frendz‿ɑ: ˌfɔ:] Dafür sind Freunde da. **I**
friendly ['frendli] freundlich; nett **II**
friendship ['frendʃɪp] Freundschaft **II**
frightened ['fraɪtnd] verängstigt **IV**
frightening ['fraɪtnɪŋ] furchterregend **IV**
fringe [frɪndʒ] Rand-; Alternativ- **III**
frolic ['frɒlɪk] Spaß ⟨**V U3**, 101⟩
from [frɒm; frəm] aus; von **I**
from the outside [ˌfrəm ði‿aʊt'saɪd] von außen **IV**
from … to [frəm … tə] von … bis **I**
Where … **from**? [ˌweə … 'frɒm] Woher …? **I**
from around the world [frɒm əˌraʊnd ðə 'wɜ:ld] aus aller Welt **II**
front [frʌnt] Vorderseite; Front-; Vorder- **II**; Spitze; vorderer Bereich **VTS1**, 44
front door [ˌfrʌnt 'dɔ:] Haustür **II**
front office [ˌfrʌnt 'ɒfɪs] *hier:* Büro ⟨**V U1**, 28⟩
front yard *(AE)* [ˌfrʌnt 'jɑ:d] Vorgarten **IV**
in **front** of [ɪn 'frʌnt‿əv] vor **I**
up the **front** [ˌʌp ðə 'frʌnt] ganz vorn ⟨**V U1**, 29⟩
to **frown** [fraʊn] die Stirn runzeln **V U1**, 30
fruit [fru:t] Frucht; Obst **I**
deep **fryer** [ˌdi:p 'fraɪə] Fritteuse **V U3**, 98
fulfilling [fʊl'fɪlɪŋ] erfüllend; befriedigend **V U2**, 46
full [fʊl] ganz **V U1**, 26
to talk with your mouth **full** [ˌtɔ:k wɪð jɔ: 'maʊθ fʊl] mit vollem Mund sprechen **III**
full (of) [fʊl‿əv] voll (von) **I**
fun [fʌn] Freude; Spaß **I**
*to have **fun** [ˌhæv 'fʌn] Spaß haben; sich amüsieren **I**
*to make **fun** of [ˌmeɪk 'fʌn‿əv] sich lustig machen über **IV**
It's **fun**. [ɪts 'fʌn] Es macht Spaß. **I**
No risk, no **fun**! [nəʊ ˌrɪsk nəʊ 'fʌn] Wer nicht wagt, der nicht gewinnt. **IV**
fun [fʌn] lustig; witzig; fröhlich **I**
function ['fʌŋkʃn] Funktion **IV**
to **function** ['fʌŋkʃn] funktionieren °**V U2**, 67
funny ['fʌni] lustig; witzig **I**; merkwürdig; komisch **III**
fur [fɜ:] Fell; Pelz **V AC3**, 114
furniture *(singular noun with plural meaning)* ['fɜ:nɪtʃə] Möbel **IV**
further ['fɜ:ðə] weiter (weg) **III**; weitere ⟨**V AC1**, 11⟩ø °**V U2**, 54
furthermore [ˌfɜ:ðə'mɔ:] überdies; außerdem **V U2**, 51
fury ['fjʊəri] Wut ⟨**V U3**, 100⟩
future ['fju:tʃə] Zukunft **II**
future perfect [ˌfju:tʃə 'pɜ:fɪkt] vollendetes Futur; Futur II °**V U3**, 88
future progressive [ˌfju:tʃə prə'gresɪv] Verlaufsform der Zukunft °**V U3**, 88
future ['fju:tʃə] zukünftig **III**

G

gadget ['gædʒɪt] Gerät; technische Spielerei **III**
Gaelic ['geɪlɪk] gälisch; Gälisch **II**
gallery **walk** ['gælri ˌwɔ:k] Museumsrundgang; Vernissage **I**
game [geɪm] Spiel **I**
guessing **game** ['gesɪŋ ˌgeɪm] Ratespiel **II**
gaming ['geɪmɪŋ] Spielen; Zocken ⟨**VTS2**, 79⟩

gap [gæp] Lücke; Spalt; Abstand **I**
gap year ['gæp ˌjɪə] *ein Jahr Auszeit (zwischen Schule und Ausbildung/Studium), das oft für einen freiwilligen ökologischen oder sozialen Dienst genutzt wird* **V U2**, 55
gapan ['gʌpʌn] Lehm *(australisch)* ⟨**V U1**, 30⟩
garage ['gærɑ:ʒ] Garage **I**
garbage *(AE)* ['gɑ:bɪdʒ] Müll; Abfall **IV**
garden ['gɑ:dn] Garten **I**
gardener ['gɑ:dnə] Gärtner/-in ⟨**V U3**, 101⟩
gardening ['gɑ:dnɪŋ] Gärtnern; Gartenarbeit ⟨**V U3**, 97⟩
garlic ['gɑ:lɪk] Knoblauch **III**
gas [gæs] Gas **V U3**, 95
gas(oline) *(AE)* ['gæsli:n] Benzin **IV**
to **gasp** [gɑ:sp] tief Luft holen; keuchen **IV**
gate [geɪt] Gate; Flugsteig; Ausgang **III**
gay [geɪ] schwul; homosexuell; Schwuler; Homosexueller **V AC1**, 10
GCSE *(= General Certificate of Secondary Education)* [ˌdʒi:si:es'i: (ˌdʒenrl səˌtɪfɪkət‿əv ˌsekəndri‿edʒʊ'keɪʃn)] *allg. Abschluss der weiterführenden Schulen in GB* **V U2**, 49
GDP [ˌdʒi:di:'pi:] BIP *(= Bruttoinlandsprodukt)* **V U3**, 90
geek [gi:k] Außenseiter/-in **IV**
gender ['dʒendə] Geschlecht **V U2**, 49
gender stereotyping ['dʒendə ˌsterɪəʊtaɪpɪŋ] geschlechtsspezifische Klischees **V U2**, 49
gene [dʒi:n] Gen **V TS2**, 77
general ['dʒenrl] General **IV**
general ['dʒenrl] allgemein **IV**
in **general** [ɪn 'dʒenrl] im allgemeinen **IV**
generation [ˌdʒenə'reɪʃn] Generation **III**
generous ['dʒenrəs] großzügig **III**
genius ['dʒi:niəs] Genie **II**
genre ['ʒɑ̃:nrə] Gattung **III**
gentle ['dʒentl] sanft; behutsam ⟨**V U2**, 62⟩
gentleman ['dʒentlmən], **gentlemen** ['dʒentlmen] *(pl)* Gentleman; feiner Herr **III**
geocaching ['dʒi:əʊkæʃɪŋ] Geocaching **II**
geography [dʒi'ɒgrəfi] Geografie; Erdkunde **II**
German ['dʒɜ:mən] deutsch; Deutsch; aus Deutschland; Deutsche/-r **I**
gerund ['dʒernd] Gerundium **IV**
gesture ['dʒestʃə] Geste; Gebärde **III**
*to **get** [get] holen; bringen; bekommen; besorgen; kaufen **I**; werden **II**
*to **get** a ride [ˌget‿ə 'raɪd] eine Mitfahrgelegenheit bekommen **IV**
*to **get** around [ˌget‿ə'raʊnd] *hier:* sich fortbewegen **II**
*to **get** away with [ˌget‿ə'weɪ wɪð] davonkommen mit **II**
*to **get** caught [ˌget 'kɔ:t] erwischt werden; ertappt werden **IV**
*to **get** familiar [ˌget fə'mɪliə] sich vertraut machen **IV**
*to **get** fit [ˌget 'fɪt] in Form kommen; fit werden **I**
*to **get** in [ˌget‿'ɪn] einsteigen **IV**
*to **get** in the way [ˌget‿ɪn ðə 'weɪ] stören; im Weg stehen **II**
*to **get** into [ˌget‿'ɪntə] einsteigen; hineingelangen **I**
*to **get** into trouble [ˌget‿ɪntə 'trʌbl] in Schwierigkeiten geraten **IV**
*to **get** lost [ˌget 'lɒst] verloren gehen; sich verirren **II**
*to **get** off (a bus/train) [ˌget‿'ɒf] aussteigen (aus einem Bus/Zug) **II**
*to **get** on (the bus) [ˌget‿'ɒn] einsteigen (in den Bus) **II**
*to **get** on people's nerves [ˌget‿ɒn sʌmbɒdiz 'nɜ:vz] jemandem auf die Nerven gehen **I**
*to **get** organised [get 'ɔ:gənaɪzd] sich organisieren **II**
*to **get** out of [get ˌaʊt‿əv] aussteigen; herauskommen aus **II**
*to **get** ready [ˌget 'redi] sich vorbereiten; sich fertig machen **V U1**, 28
*to **get** right [get 'raɪt] richtig beantworten **II**
*to **get** started [ˌget 'stɑ:tɪd] anfangen **II**
*to **get** sth out of one's head [get ˌaʊt‿əv wʌnz 'hed] etw. aus dem Kopf bekommen **III**
*to **get** there ['get ðeə] hinkommen **I**
*to **get** to ['get tə] kommen zu; kommen nach; erreichen **I**
*to **get** to know [ˌget tə 'nəʊ] kennenlernen **II**
*to **get** up [ˌget‿'ʌp] aufstehen *(aus dem Bett)* **I**
*to **get** used to sth [ˌget 'ju:zd tə] sich an etw. gewöhnen **IV**
*to **get** well [ˌget 'wel] gesund werden **IV**
Time to **get** up! [ˌtaɪm tə ˌget‿'ʌp] Es ist Zeit aufzustehen! **I**
ghost [gəʊst] Geist **II**
giant [dʒaɪənt] Riesen-; riesig **V U1**, 14
gift [gɪft] Geschenk; Gabe **IV**
gig [gɪg] Auftritt; Gig **III**
gigantic [dʒaɪ'gæntɪk] gigantisch; riesig **IV**
girl [gɜ:l] Mädchen **I**
girlfriend ['gɜ:lfrend] Freundin *(in einer Paarbeziehung)* **II**
girlish ['gɜ:lɪʃ] mädchenhaft ⟨**V U3**, 102⟩
gist [dʒɪst] das Wesentliche **II**
*to **give** [gɪv] geben; schenken **I**
*to **give** a talk [ˌgɪv‿ə 'tɔ:k] einen Vortrag halten **IV**
*to **give** away [ˌgɪv‿ə'weɪ] verteilen; verschenken; verraten; preisgeben **IV**
*to **give** sb a piggyback [gɪv‿ə 'pɪgibæk] jmdn. Huckepack nehmen **III**
*to **give** sb funny looks [ˌgɪv fʌni 'lʊks] jmdn. schief anschauen **III**
*to **give** thanks [ˌgɪv 'θæŋks] danken **IV**
*to **give** the bumps [ˌgɪv ðə 'bʌmps] hochleben lassen **I**
*to **give** up [ˌgɪv‿'ʌp] aufgeben **III**
giver ['gɪvə] Geber/-in; Spender/-in **V U2**, 62
glacial ['gleɪsiəl; 'gleɪʃl] eisig; Gletscher- **IV**
glad [glæd] froh **III**
glitz and **glamor** *(AE)* *(no pl)* [ˌglɪts‿n‿'glæmə] Glanz und Glamour **V U3**, 86
glamorous ['glæmrəs] glamourös **IV**
to **glance** at ['glɑ:ns‿ət] einen Blick werfen auf; blicken auf **V U1**, 30
to **glare** at sb [gleə] jmdn. (zornig) anstarren ⟨**V U3**, 100⟩
glass [glɑ:s] Glas **I**
glasses *(pl)* ['glɑ:sɪz] Brille **II**
to **gleam** [gli:m] glänzen; schimmern **V U1**, 14
glimpse [glɪms] (kurzer/flüchtiger) Blick **V U1**, 28
glitz and glamor *(AE)* *(no pl)* [ˌglɪts‿n‿'glæmə] Glanz und Glamour **V U3**, 86
global ['gləʊbl] global; weltweit **V AC3**, 114
glossary ['glɒsri] Glossar; Stichwortverzeichnis **III**
glove [glʌv] Handschuh **I**
gloved [glʌvd] behandschuht ⟨**V U3**, 100⟩
to **glow** [gləʊ] leuchten; glühen ⟨**V U1**, 28⟩
to **glue** [glu:] kleben ⟨**V U1**, 28⟩
*to **go** [gəʊ] gehen; fahren **I**
*to **go** *(+ adj)* [gəʊ] werden **IV**
*to **go** bad [ˌgəʊ 'bæd] schiefgehen; schlecht werden; verderben **IV**
*to **go** black [ˌgəʊ 'blæk] schwarz werden **II**
*to **go** by [ˌgəʊ‿'baɪ] vorbeigehen **V U2**, 56
*to **go** crazy [ˌgəʊ 'kreɪzi] ausflippen; durchdrehen; verrückt werden **II**
*to **go** down [ˌgəʊ 'daʊn] hinuntergehen; nach unten gehen; entlanggehen **I**
*to **go** for a walk [ˌgəʊ fər‿ə 'wɔ:k] spazieren gehen **II**
*to **go** off [gəʊ‿'ɒf] weggehen **V U1**, 14
*to **go** on [ˌgəʊ‿'ɒn] weitergehen; weitermachen; weiterführen; fortfahren **I**
*to **go** out [ˌgəʊ‿'aʊt] ausgehen; hinausgehen **II**
*to **go** over to [ˌgəʊ 'əʊvə tə] hinübergehen zu; zu jmdm. nach Hause gehen **II**
*to **go** right back to [ˌgəʊ raɪt 'bæk tə] zurückgehen auf **II**
*to **go** round in circles [gəʊ ˌraʊnd ɪn 'sɜ:klz] sich im Kreis drehen **III**
*to **go** shopping [ˌgəʊ 'ʃɒpɪŋ] einkaufen gehen **I**
*to **go** swimming [ˌgəʊ 'swɪmɪŋ] Schwimmen gehen **I**
*to **go** to bed [ˌgəʊ tə 'bed] ins Bett gehen **I**
*to **go** together [ˌgəʊ tə'geðə] zueinander passen; zueinander gehören **I**
*to **go** with ['gəʊ wɪð] passen zu; gehören zu **I**

*to **go** wrong [ˌgəʊ ˈrɒŋ] schiefgehen **I**
*to let **go** (of) [ˌlet ˈgəʊ (əv)] loslassen **II**
Go on! [ˌgəʊ‿ˈɒn] Los! **IV**
How ya **going**? [ˌhaʊ‿jə ˈgəʊɪŋ] Wie geht es dir/euch/Ihnen? ⟨**V U1**, 21⟩
It's **gone**. [ɪts ˈgɒn] Es ist weg. **II**
What's **going** on? [wɒts ˌgəʊɪŋ‿ˈɒn] Was ist los?; Was geht ab? **III**
goal [gəʊl] Tor; Ziel **I**
goat [gəʊt] Ziege **V AC2**, 80
gobbledygook [ˈgɒbldiˌgu:k] Kauderwelsch ⟨**V U3**, 100⟩
the **gods** *(liter)* [ðə ˈgɒdz] die Götter *(literarisch)* **IV**
goddess [ˈgɒdes] Göttin **IV**
gold [gəʊld] Gold **III**
Gold Rush [ˈgəʊld ˌrʌʃ] Goldrausch **V U3**, 90
golden [ˈgəʊldn] golden; Gold- **V U3**, 90
golden age [ˌgəʊldn ˈeɪdʒ] goldenes Zeitalter **III**
golf [gɒlf] Golf **II**
*to be **gone** [bi ˈgɒn] verschwunden sein; weg sein **II**
gonna (= going to) *(coll)* [ˈgɒnə] wird/werden **IV**
good [gʊd] gut **I**
*to be **good** at [bi ˈgʊd‿ət] gut sein in **I**
*to set a **good** example [set‿ə ˌgʊd‿ɪgˈzɑ:mpl] ein Vorbild sein **V U2**, 48
good luck [ˌgʊd ˈlʌk] viel Glück **IV**
Good morning. [ˌgʊd ˈmɔ:nɪŋ] Guten Morgen. **I**
Good on ya! [ˈgʊd ɒn jə] Gut gemacht! ⟨**V U1**, 21⟩
G'day! *(= Good day!)* [gəˈdaɪ] Guten Tag.; Hallo.; Hi. *(Begrüßung in Australien)* **V U1**, 12
goodbye [gʊdˈbaɪ] auf Wiedersehen **I**
goods *(pl)* [gʊdz] Güter; Waren ⟨**V U2**, 65⟩
goose bumps [ˈgu:s ˌbʌmps] Gänsehaut ⟨**V U3**, 102⟩
gorge scrambling [ˈgɔ:dʒ ˌskræmblɪŋ] Schluchtenklettern **II**
gossip [ˈgɒsɪp] Klatsch; Tratsch; Gerede ⟨**V U3**, 100⟩
gotta (= got to) *(coll)* [ˈgɒtə] muss/müssen ⟨**V AC2**, 80⟩
gotten *(AE)* [ˈgɒtn] bekommen *(past participle von 'to get' in AE)*; geworden *(past participle von 'to get' in AE)* °**V U3**, 86
to **govern** [ˈgʌvn] regeln; verwalten ⟨**V U2**, 63⟩
government [ˈgʌvnmənt] Regierung **IV**
governor [ˈgʌvnə] Gouverneur/-in **V U3**, 85
to **grab** [græb] greifen; ergreifen; schnappen **II**
to **grab** attention [ˌgræb‿əˈtenʃn] Aufmerksamkeit erregen °**V U1**, 17
grade *(AE)* [greɪd] Note **IV**
8th-**grader** *(AE)* [ˈeɪtθˌgreɪdə] Achtklässler/-in **IV**
grammar [ˈgræmə] Grammatik **II**
grammar school [ˈgræmə ˌsku:l] Gymnasium **II**
grandad [ˈgrændæd] Opa **I**
great-great-**grandfather** [ˌgreɪtgreɪtˈgrænˌfɑ:ðə] Urururgroßvater **IV**
grandma [ˈgrænmɑ:] Oma **I**
grandmother [ˈgrænˌmʌðə] Großmutter **IV**
grandparents *(pl)* [ˈgrænˌpeərənts] Großeltern **I**
granny [ˈgræni] Oma **I**
grape [greɪp] Traube **V U3**, 93
graph [grɑ:f] Diagramm; Schaubild **IV**
bar **graph** [ˈbɑ: grɑ:f] Säulendiagramm; Balkendiagramm **IV**
line **graph** [ˈlaɪn grɑ:f] Kurvendiagramm **IV**
graphic novel [ˌgræfɪk ˈnɒvl] Bildergeschichte; Comic **III**
to **grasp** [grɑ:sp] erfassen; begreifen ⟨**V U2**, 64⟩
grass [grɑ:s] Gras **IV**
grassy [ˈgrɑ:si] grasbewachsen ⟨**V U3**, 101⟩
grateful [ˈgreɪtfl] dankbar **V U1**, 30
gratitude [ˈgrætɪtju:d] Dankbarkeit **III**
gray [greɪ] grau ⟨**V U3**, 100⟩
great [greɪt] großartig; toll; super **I**
great wheel [ˌgreɪt ˈwi:l] Riesenrad **IV**
great-great-grandfather [ˌgreɪtgreɪtˈgrænˌfɑ:ðə] Urururgroßvater **IV**
It's **great** for … [ɪts ˈgreɪt fə] Es ist super zum/für … **I**
green [gri:n] grün **I**
Greenwich Mean Time *(= GMT)* [ˌgrenɪdʒ ˈmi:n ˌtaɪm] westeuropäische Zeit **I**
to **greet** [gri:t] begrüßen; grüßen °**V U2**, 59
greeting [ˈgri:tɪŋ] Gruß **I**
grey [greɪ] grau **I**
grid [grɪd] Gitter; Tabelle; Raster **I**
to **grin** [grɪn] grinsen **V U1**, 28
grizzly bear [ˈgrɪzli ˌbeə] Grizzlybär **IV**
groan [grəʊn] Stöhnen **III**
to **groan** [grəʊn] stöhnen **IV**
ground [graʊnd] Boden; Erdboden **III**
*to be **grounded** [bi ˈgraʊndɪd] Hausarrest haben **III**
group [gru:p] Gruppe; Klasse **I**
tutor **group** [ˈtju:tə ˌgru:p] Klasse *(in einer englischen Schule)* **I**
to **group** (around) [gru:p (əˈraʊnd)] gruppieren (um) **III**
groupmate [ˈgru:pmeɪt] Kamerad/Kameradin ⟨**V U2**, 62⟩
*to **grow** [grəʊ] wachsen **II**; anbauen; züchten **III**
*to **grow** by [ˈgrəʊ baɪ] steigen um **IV**
*to **grow** up [ˌgrəʊ‿ˈʌp] aufwachsen; erwachsen werden **III**
growth [grəʊθ] Wachstum **IV**
guard [gɑ:d] Wache; Wächter/-in **II**
to **guard** [gɑ:d] bewachen **V U3**, 90
guardian [ˈgɑ:diən] Hüter/-in; Wächter/-in **V U1**, 23
to **guess** [ges] raten; erraten; vermuten **I**; annehmen **III**
guessing game [ˈgesɪŋ ˌgeɪm] Ratespiel **II**
guest [gest] Gast **III**
guesthouse [ˈgesthaʊs] Gästehaus ⟨**V U3**, 101⟩
guide [gaɪd] Führer/-in; Reiseführer **II**
to **guide** [gaɪd] führen; leiten **III**
guidebook [ˈgaɪdbʊk] Reiseführer **IV**
guilty [ˈgɪlti] schuldig **III**
guilty conscience [ˌgɪlti ˈkɒnʃns] Schuldbewusstsein; schlechtes Gewissen **V U1**, 28
guinea pig [ˈgɪni: ˌpɪg] Meerschweinchen **I**
guitar [gɪˈtɑ:] Gitarre **III**
guku [ˈgu:ku:] Buschhonig *(australisch)* ⟨**V U1**, 30⟩
chewing **gum** [ˈtʃu:ɪŋ ˌgʌm] Kaugummi **III**
guy [gaɪ] Typ; Kerl; *(Pl.)* Leute **II**
gym(nasium) [dʒɪm; dʒɪmˈneɪziəm] Turnhalle **IV**

H

habit [ˈhæbɪt] Gewohnheit ⟨**V TS2**, 79⟩
haggis [ˈhægɪs] Haggis *(schottisches Gericht aus in einem Schafsmagen gekochten Schafsinnereien und Haferschrot)* **III**
hair [heə] Haar; Haare **IV**
*to do our **hair** [ˌdu:‿aʊə ˈheə] uns frisieren; unsere Haare machen **I**
hairbrush [ˈheəbrʌʃ] Haarbürste **III**
half [hɑ:f], **halves** [hɑ:vz] *(pl)* (of) die Hälfte **I**
half [hɑ:f] halb **I**
half an hour [ˌhɑ:f‿ən‿ˈaʊər] eine halbe Stunde **III**
half past [ˌhɑ:f ˈpɑ:st] halb *(bei Uhrzeitangaben)* **I**
half-sister [ˈhɑ:fˌsɪstə] Halbschwester **I**
half-term break [ˌhɑ:ftɜ:m ˈbreɪk] Halbjahresferien **I**
*to meet **halfway** [ˌmi:t hɑ:fˈweɪ] sich auf halbem Weg treffen **III**
hall [hɔ:l] Halle; Saal; Flur; Diele; Korridor **II**
arrivals **hall** [əˈraɪvlz ˌhɔ:l] Ankunftshalle **III**
hall pass [ˈhɔ:l pɑ:s] *Erlaubnis, sich während des Unterrichts auf dem Flur aufzuhalten* **IV**
hallway [ˈhɔ:lweɪ] Flur; Diele; Korridor **IV**
ham [hæm] Schinken **III**
hammer [ˈhæmə] Hammer **II**
hand [hænd] Hand **I**
Clap your **hands**. [ˌklæp jɔ: ˈhændz] Klatsch/Klatscht in die Hände. **I**
On the one **hand** …, (but) on the other **hand** … [ɒn ðə‿ˈwʌn ˌhænd … (bʌt) ɒn ði‿ˈʌðə ˌhænd …] Einerseits …, (aber) andererseits … **II**
to **hand** [hænd] reichen ⟨**V U3**, 101⟩

to **hand** out [ˌhænd‿ˈaʊt] austeilen ⟨**V U1**, 29⟩
handout ['hændaʊt] Informationsblatt; Arbeitsblatt **V U3**, 98
*to **hang** on [ˌhæŋ‿ˈɒn] (einen Augenblick) warten **III**
*to **hang** out (with) *(infml)* [ˌhæŋ‿ˈaʊt wɪð] sich herumtreiben (mit); rumhängen (mit); sich treffen (mit) **III**
*to **hang** up [ˌhæŋ‿ˈʌp] aufhängen **II**
to **happen** ['hæpn] geschehen; passieren **I**
happiness ['hæpɪnəs] Glück; Zufriedenheit; Fröhlichkeit **IV**
happy ['hæpi] glücklich; froh; fröhlich **I**
happy ending [ˌhæpi ˈendɪŋ] Happy End **III**
Happy Birthday! [ˌhæpi ˈbɜ:θdeɪ] Alles Gute zum Geburtstag!; Herzlichen Glückwunsch zum Geburtstag! **I**
to **harass** ['hærəs; həˈræs] belästigen; drangsalieren **V U3**, 101
harassment [həˈræsmənt] Belästigung; Schikane **V AC1**, 9
harbour ['hɑ:bə] Hafen **II**
hard [hɑ:d] hart; schwer; schwierig; *hier:* stark **II**
*to be **hard** on sb [bi ˈhɑ:d‿ɒn] streng mit jmdm. sein **III**
hardly ['hɑ:dli] kaum **III**
hard-working [ˌhɑ:dˈwɜ:kɪŋ] fleißig **V U2**, 50
harmless ['hɑ:mləs] harmlos; ungefährlich **V U1**, 29
harmony ['hɑ:məni] Harmonie °**V U2**, 67
harsh [hɑ:ʃ] rau; hart **IV**
harvest ['hɑ:vɪst] Ernte **IV**
to **harvest** ['hɑ:vɪst] ernten **V U2**, 53
hat [hæt] Hut **I**
to **hate** [heɪt] hassen; nicht mögen **II**
*to **have** [hæv] haben **I**
*to **have** *(a sweet)* [hæv] *(ein Bonbon)* nehmen; *(ein Bonbon)* essen **I**
*to **have** a look (at) [ˌhæv‿ə ˈlʊk] anschauen **II**
*to **have** a point [ˌhæv‿ə ˈpɔɪnt] nicht ganz Unrecht haben **III**
*to **have** a voice [ˌhæv‿ə ˈvɔɪs] ein Mitspracherecht haben **V AC3**, 114
*to **have** breakfast [ˌhæv ˈbrekfəst] frühstücken **I**
*to **have** fun [ˌhæv ˈfʌn] Spaß haben; sich amüsieren **I**
*to **have** got [hæv ˈgɒt] besitzen; haben **I**
*to **have** in common [ˌhæv‿ɪn ˈkɒmən] gemeinsam haben **III**
*to **have** no clue [ˌhæv nəʊ ˈklu:] keine Ahnung haben **IV**
*to **have** sth done [hæv] etw. machen lassen **V U1**, 18
*to **have** to ['hæv tə] müssen **II**
hazard ['hæzəd] Gefahr; Risiko °**V U3**, 95
he [hi:] er **I**
head [hed] Kopf **I**
*to get sth out of one's **head** [get ˌaʊt‿əv wʌnz ˈhed] etw. aus dem Kopf bekommen **III**
head of state [ˌhed‿əv ˈsteɪt] Staatsoberhaupt **II**
*to **keep one's head above water** [ˌki:p wʌnz ˌhed‿əbʌv ˈwɔ:tə] sich über Wasser halten **V U3**, 86
With a very big **head**! [ˌwɪð ə ˌveri bɪg ˈhed] Und ein Angeber! **II**
to **head** (for) ['hed fə] zusteuern auf **IV**
to **head** out [ˌhed‿ˈaʊt] hinausgehen **V AC1**, 10
headache *(no pl)* ['hedeɪk] Kopfschmerzen; Kopfweh **II**
heading ['hedɪŋ] Überschrift; Titel **I**
headline ['hedlaɪn] Schlagzeile **III**
headphones *(pl)* ['hedfəʊnz] Kopfhörer **II**
headquarters *(pl)* [ˌhedˈkwɔ:təz] Zentrale; Hauptsitz **V U3**, 85
health [helθ] Gesundheit **II**
healthcare ['helθkeə] Gesundheitsversorgung **V U2**, 49
healthy ['helθi] gesund **I**
*to **hear** [hɪə] hören **I**
I **hear** … [aɪ ˈhɪə] Ich habe gehört, dass … **I**
heart [hɑ:t] Herz; *hier:* Zentrum **II**
*to learn … by **heart** [ˌlɜ:n baɪ ˈhɑ:t] auswendig lernen **I**
heat *(no pl)* [hi:t] Hitze; Wärme **IV**
heating ['hi:tɪŋ] Heizung **III**
underfloor **heating** *(no pl)* [ˌʌndəflɔ: ˈhi:tɪŋ] Fußbodenheizung **III**
heatwave ['hi:tweɪv] Hitzewelle ⟨**V U1**, 17⟩
heavy ['hevi] schwer; stark **III**
hedgehog ['hedʒhɒg] Igel **III**
high **heels** ['haɪ hi:lz] Stöckelschuhe ⟨**VTS3**, 113⟩
heir [eə] *hier:* Erbgut ⟨**V AC2**, 80⟩
helicopter ['helɪkɒptə] Helikopter; Hubschrauber **V U3**, 94
Who the **hell** cares? [ˌhu: ðə hel ˈkeəz] Wen zum Teufel interessiert's? ⟨**VTS3**, 110⟩
Hello. [helˈəʊ] Hallo. **I**
*to say **hello** (to) [ˌseɪ helˈəʊ tə] grüßen; Grüße ausrichten (an) **I**
help [help] Hilfe **I**
to **help** [help] helfen **I**
to **help** out [ˌhelp‿ˈaʊt] aushelfen **III**
I can't **help** *(+ -ing)* [aɪ ˌkɑ:nt ˈhelp] Ich kann nicht anders (als zu) … **V AC1**, 9
helper ['helpə] Helfer/-in **V U2**, 61
helpful ['helpfl] hilfsbereit; hilfreich **I**
helpless ['helpləs] hilflos **I**
her [hɜ:] ihr/-e; sie **I**
herb [hɜ:b] Kraut **III**
herd [hɜ:d] Herde; Rudel **IV**
here [hɪə] hier **I**
right **here** [ˌraɪt ˈhɪə] genau hier **II**
Here you are. [ˌhɪə ju‿ˈɑ:] Bitte schön. **I**
heritage ['herɪtɪdʒ] Erbe ⟨**V U1**, 24⟩
hero ['hɪərəʊ], **heroes** ['hɪərəʊz] *(pl)* Held **II**
heroine ['herəʊɪn] Heldin **II**
to **hesitate** ['hezɪteɪt] zögern **III**
Hey! [heɪ] Hi.; He!; Hallo. **I**
Hi. [haɪ] Hi.; Hallo. **I**
hibernation [ˌhaɪbəˈneɪʃn] Winterschlaf **III**
*to **hide** [haɪd] (sich) verstecken **II**
high [haɪ] hoch; groß **II**
high heels ['haɪ hi:lz] Stöckelschuhe ⟨**VTS3**, 113⟩
high school *(AE)* ['haɪ ˌsku:l] High School *(weiterführende Schule in den USA, Oberstufe)* **IV**
high tide ['haɪ ˌtaɪd] Flut **II**
the **high** street [ðə ˈhaɪ ˌstri:t] die Haupteinkaufsstraße **III**
high-heeled shoes [ˌhaɪ‿hi:ld ˈʃu:z] Stöckelschuhe ⟨**V AC2**, 80⟩
high-level [ˌhaɪˈlevl] Spitzen-; auf höchster Ebene **VTS3**, 111
highlight ['haɪlaɪt] Highlight; Höhepunkt **II**
highly ['haɪli] höchst- **IV**
highway *(AE)* ['haɪweɪ] Landstraße; Bundesautobahn *(amerik.)*; Highway **IV**
hiking ['haɪkɪŋ] Wandern **II**
hill [hɪl] Berg; Hügel **II**
hillside ['hɪlsaɪd] Hang **V U3**, 94
him [hɪm] ihn; ihm **I**
himself [hɪmˈself] er/sich (selbst); selber **II**
Hindu ['hɪndu:] Hindu; hinduistisch **V AC1**, 9
hint [hɪnt] Hinweis; Andeutung; Tipp **III**
hip [hɪp] hip; total in **IV**
hip-hop ['hɪphɒp] Hip-Hop ⟨**V AC2**, 80⟩
his [hɪz] sein/-e **I**
Hispanic [hɪˈspænɪk] lateinamerikanisch; Latino/Latina; Hispano-Amerikaner/-in **V U3**, 90
historian [hɪˈstɔ:riən] Historiker/-in **IV**
historic [hɪˈstɒrɪk] historisch **III**
historical [hɪˈstɒrɪkl] historisch; geschichtlich **I**
history ['hɪstri] Geschichte **II**
living **history** show [ˌlɪvɪŋ ˈhɪstəri ˌʃəʊ] *Show, in der historischer Alltag nachgespielt wird* **II**
recorded **history** [rɪˌkɔ:dɪd ˈhɪstri] *hier:* Aufzeichnung **V U3**, 95
*to **hit** [hɪt] schlagen; treffen **I**
to **hitchhike** ['hɪtʃhaɪk] trampen; per Anhalter fahren **IV**
hitchhiker ['hɪtʃˌhaɪkə] Tramper/-in **IV**
hitchhiking ['hɪtʃˌhaɪkɪŋ] Trampen **IV**
hoax [həʊks] Täuschung; Trick **IV**
hobby ['hɒbi], **hobbies** ['hɒbiz] *(pl)* Hobby **I**
hockey [hɒki] Hockey **II**
to **hog** a conversation [ˌhɒg‿ə kɒnvəˈseɪʃn] ein Gespräch für sich in Beschlag nehmen; ein Gespräch dominieren **III**
*to **hold** [həʊld] halten; festhalten **I**
*to **hold** a competition [ˌhəʊld‿ə ˌkɒmpəˈtɪʃn] einen Wettbewerb durchführen **IV**

*to **hold** onto [ˌhəʊld_ˈɒntə] (sich) festhalten an **III**
*to **hold** open [ˌhəʊld_ˈəʊpn] aufhalten **III**
hole [həʊl] Loch **II**
holiday [ˈhɒlədeɪ] Urlaub; Feiertag **I**
holidays *(pl)* [ˈhɒlədeɪz] Ferien **I**
home [həʊm] Zuhause; Heim; nach Hause **I**
at **home** [ət ˈhəʊm] zu Hause **I**
to pop **home** [ˌpɒp_ˈhəʊm] schnell zu Hause vorbeigehen ⟨**V U1**, 30⟩
homeless [ˈhəʊmləs] obdachlos **IV**
homeless shelter [ˈhəʊmləs ˌʃeltə] Obdachlosenunterkunft **IV**
the **homeless** [ðə ˈhəʊmləs] Obdachlose **V U2**, 55
homepage [ˈhəʊmpeɪdʒ] Homepage **I**
*to be **homesick** [bi ˈhəʊmsɪk] Heimweh haben **III**
hometown [ˈhəʊmtaʊn] Heimatstadt **IV**
homework [ˈhəʊmwɜːk] Hausaufgabe(n) **I**
honest [ˈɒnɪst] ehrlich **III**
honey [ˈhʌni] Honig **III**
honor *(AE)* [ˈɒnə] Ehre **IV**
in **honor** of *(AE)* [ɪn_ˈɒnər_əv] zu Ehren **V U3**, 89
to **honor** *(AE)* [ˈɒnə] ehren; würdigen; auszeichnen **V U2**, 62
to **hook** [hʊk] *hier:* fesseln **III**
to **hook** sb up with sb [hʊk_ˈʌp wɪð] jmdn. mit jmdm. bekannt machen ⟨**V U3**, 102⟩
hope [həʊp] Hoffnung **II**
to **hope** [həʊp] hoffen **I**
hopeful [ˈhəʊpfl] hoffnungsvoll **I**
hopefully [ˈhəʊpfli] hoffentlich **V U2**, 51
horn [hɔːn] Horn **III**
horrible [ˈhɒrəbl] schrecklich; furchtbar **V AC2**, 83
horrified [ˈhɒrɪfaɪd] entsetzt **I**
horror [ˈhɒrə] Horrorgeschichte; Horrorfilm; Horror **III**
horse [hɔːs] Pferd **I**
hospital [ˈhɒspɪtl] Hospital; Krankenhaus **II**
host [həʊst] Gastgeber/-in; Talkmaster **V TS3**, 109
host family [ˈhəʊst ˌfæmli] Gastfamilie **III**
to **host** [həʊst] ausrichten *(Veranstaltung)* **V U1**, 20
hostel [ˈhɒstl] Herberge **III**
youth **hostel** [ˈjuːθ ˌhɒstl] Jugendherberge **V U1**, 14
hot [hɒt] heiß **III**
hotel [həʊˈtel] Hotel **II**
hotspot [ˈhɒtspɒt] Hotspot; gefragter Ort **V U3**, 92
hour [aʊə] Stunde **II**
half an **hour** [ˌhɑːf_ən_ˈaʊər] eine halbe Stunde **III**
house [haʊs] Haus **I**
to move (**house**) [muːv (haʊs)] umziehen **II**
household [ˈhaʊshəʊld] Haushalt **IV**
how [haʊ] wie **I**
How many …? [ˌhaʊ ˈmeni] Wie viele …? **I**
How are you doing? [ˌhaʊ_ɑː jə ˈduːɪŋ] Wie geht es dir/euch/Ihnen? **V U1**, 18
How are you? [ˌhaʊ_ˈɑː jə] Wie geht es dir/euch/Ihnen?; Wie geht es euch?; Wie geht es Ihnen? **I**
How much (is/are) …? [ˌhaʊ ˈmʌtʃ_ɪz/ɑː] Wie viel (kostet/kosten) …? **I**
How old are you? [haʊ_ˈəʊld_ə ˌjuː] Wie alt bist du?; Wie alt sind Sie? **I**
How to … [ˈhaʊ tə] Wie man … **I**
How ya going? [ˌhaʊ_jə ˈɡəʊɪŋ] Wie geht es dir/euch/Ihnen? ⟨**V U1**, 21⟩
Is this **how** you (do) …? [ɪz ˈðɪs haʊ jʊ ˌduː] Machst du so …? **I**
that's **how** [ðæts ˈhaʊ] so **II**
however [haʊˈevə] jedoch **IV**
to **hug** [hʌɡ] umarmen **I**
huge [hjuːdʒ] riesig; riesengroß; gewaltig **II**
to **hum** [hʌm] summen **II**
human [ˈhjuːmən] Mensch **IV**
human body [ˌhjuːmən ˈbɒdi] menschlicher Körper **II**
human rights [ˌhjuːmən ˈraɪts] Menschenrechte **V AC1**, 9
Humanities *(pl)* [hjuːˈmænətiz] Sozialwissenschaften **II**
humor *(no pl) (AE)* [ˈhjuːmə] Humor; Stimmung **IV**
humour *(no pl)* [ˈhjuːmə] Humor; Stimmung **III**
sense of **humour** *(no pl)* [ˌsens_əv ˈhjuːmə] Sinn für Humor **III**
hundreds of [ˈhʌndrədz_əv] Hunderte (von) **III**
hungry [ˈhʌŋɡri] hungrig **I**
to **hunt** [hʌnt] jagen **IV**
*to be in a **hurry** [ˌbi_ɪn_ə ˈhʌri] es eilig haben; in Eile sein **IV**
to **hurry** [ˈhʌri] eilen; sich beeilen **I**
hurt [hɜːt] Schmerz ⟨**V U1**, 30⟩
*to **hurt** [hɜːt] verletzen; weh tun **II**
hurt [hɜːt] verletzt **II**
husband [ˈhʌzbənd] Ehemann **II**
hydroplane [ˈhaɪdrəpleɪn] Gleitboot **IV**
hysterical [hɪˈsterɪkl] hysterisch **V TS1**, 44

I

I [aɪ] ich **I**
I can't help *(+ -ing)* [aɪ ˌkɑːnt ˈhelp] Ich kann nicht anders (als zu) … **V AC1**, 9
I don't know! [ˌaɪ ˌdəʊnt ˈnəʊ] Ich weiß (es) nicht! **I**
I don't like … [aɪ ˈdəʊnt laɪk] Ich mag … nicht.; Ich mache … nicht gern. **I**
I hear … [aɪ ˈhɪə] Ich habe gehört, dass … **I**
I like … [aɪ ˈlaɪk] Mir gefällt …; Ich mag … **I**
I love you. [aɪ ˈlʌv ju] Ich liebe dich.; Ich mag dich. **I**
I love … [aɪ ˈlʌv] Ich liebe …; Ich mag … total gern. **I**
I'd like to … *(= I would like to)* [aɪd ˈlaɪk tə] Ich möchte …; Ich würde gern … **I**
I'd rather [aɪd ˈrɑːðə] ich würde lieber **III**
I'm (not) scared of … [ˌaɪm (nɒt) ˈskeəd_əv] Ich habe (keine) Angst vor … **I**
I'm afraid … [ˌaɪm_əˈfreɪd] Leider … **IV**
I'm dog-tired. [ˌaɪm ˌdɒɡˈtaɪəd] Ich bin hundemüde. **I**
I'm English. [aɪm_ˈɪŋɡlɪʃ] Ich bin Engländer/-in. **I**
I'm fine. [ˌaɪm ˈfaɪn] Mir geht's gut. **I**
I'm from … [ˌaɪm frɒm] Ich bin aus … **I**
I'm sorry! [ˌaɪm ˈsɒri] Tut mir leid! **I**
ice [aɪs] Eis **I**
ice cream [ˌaɪs ˈkriːm] Eis; Eiscreme **I**
ice rink [ˈaɪs ˌrɪŋk] Eisbahn; Schlittschuhbahn **I**
icebreaker [ˈaɪsˌbreɪkə] Eisbrecher *(Sätze, um mit jmdm. ins Gespräch zu kommen)* **III**
icon [ˈaɪkɒn] Ikone; Symbol **V AC1**, 8
icy [ˈaɪsi] eisig ⟨**V U3**, 100⟩
idea [aɪˈdɪə] Idee; Einfall **I**
no **idea** [ˌnəʊ_aɪˈdɪə] keine Ahnung **II**
ideal [aɪˈdɪəl] ideal **V U3**, 90
to **identify** [aɪˈdentɪfaɪ] aufzeigen; identifizieren °**V AC2**, 82
to **identify** with [aɪˈdentɪfaɪ wɪð] sich identifizieren mit **III**
identity [aɪˈdentəti] Identität **II**
idiot [ˈɪdiət] Idiot/-in **II**
i.e. [aɪˈiː] d.h. °**V TS2**, 75
if [ɪf] wenn; falls; ob **I**
as **if** [əz_ˈɪf] als ob **III**
if-clause [ˈɪfˌklɔːz] if-Satz **II**
If I were you … [ˌɪf aɪ wɜː ˈjuː] Wenn ich du wäre … **IV**
to **ignore** [ɪɡˈnɔː] ignorieren; außer Acht lassen **III**
ill [ɪl] krank **III**
illegal [ɪˈliːɡl] illegal; unrechtmäßig; rechtswidrig **III**
illness [ˈɪlnəs] Krankheit **IV**
to **illustrate** [ˈɪləstreɪt] veranschaulichen; darstellen; illustrieren **IV**
image [ˈɪmɪdʒ] Bild; Abbildung **IV**
imaginary [ɪˈmædʒɪnri] erfunden; eingebildet **IV**
imagination [ɪˌmædʒɪˈneɪʃn] Fantasie; Vorstellungskraft **III**; Einbildung ⟨**V U3**, 102⟩
imaginative [ɪˈmædʒɪnətɪv] einfallsreich; fantasievoll **III**
to **imagine** [ɪˈmædʒɪn] sich (etwas) vorstellen **I**
immediately [ɪˈmiːdiətli] sofort; gleich **IV**
immense [ɪˈmens] riesig ⟨**V U2**, 47⟩
immigrant [ˈɪmɪɡrənt] Immigrant/-in; Einwanderer/-in **IV**
immigration [ˌɪmɪˈɡreɪʃn] Immigration; Einwanderung; Einreise **III**

immigration office [ˌɪmɪ'greɪʃn ˌɒfɪs] Einwanderungsbehörde **III**
impatient [ɪm'peɪʃnt] ungeduldig **V U2**, 64
imperative [ɪm'perətɪv] Imperativ; Befehlsform **III**
impolite [ˌɪmp'laɪt] unhöflich **III**
importance [ɪm'pɔ:tns] Bedeutung; Wichtigkeit **IV**
important [ɪm'pɔ:tnt] wichtig **I**
impossible [ɪm'pɒsəbl] unmöglich **IV**
impressed [ɪm'prest] beeindruckt **II**
impression [ɪm'preʃn] Impression; Eindruck **IV**
to **improve** [ɪm'pru:v] sich verbessern; verbessern **I**
improvement [ɪm'pru:vmənt] Verbesserung **IV**
in [ɪn] in; im; rein; herein **I**
in addition to [ɪn‿ə'dɪʃn tə] neben; daneben; darüber hinaus **IV**
in between [ˌɪn bɪ'twi:n] dazwischen **III**
in chorus [ɪn 'kɔ:rəs] im Chor **III**
in fact [ɪn 'fækt] tatsächlich; eigentlich; genau genommen **IV**
in favor (of) *(AE)* [ɪn 'feɪvər‿əv] dafür; zugunsten (von) **IV**
in front of [ɪn 'frʌnt‿əv] vor **I**
in general [ɪn 'dʒenrl] im allgemeinen **IV**
in need [ɪn 'ni:d] bedürftig; in Not **II**
in order to [ɪn‿'ɔ:də tə] um … zu; mit der Absicht **IV**
in particular [ˌɪn pə'tɪkjələ] im besonderen **VTS2**, 77
in secret [ɪn 'si:krət] heimlich **II**
in spite of [ɪn 'spaɪt‿əv] trotz **IV**
in the country [ˌɪn ðə 'kʌntri] auf dem Land **IV**
in the end [ˌɪn ði‿'end] schließlich; zum Schluss **II**
in the evenings [ɪn ði‿'i:vnɪŋz] abends **I**
in the mornings [ˌɪn ðə 'mɔ:nɪŋz] morgens; vormittags **I**
in the photo(s) [ˌɪn ðə 'fəʊtəʊ(z)] auf dem Foto/den Fotos **I**
in the street [ˌɪn ðə 'stri:t] in der Straße; auf der Straße **I**
in honor of *(AE)* [ɪn‿'ɒnər‿əv] zu Ehren **V U3**, 89
in the first place [ɪn ðə 'fɜ:st ˌpleɪs] überhaupt erst; von vornherein ⟨**VTS3**, 109⟩
inaccurate [ɪn'ækjərət] ungenau ⟨**V U2**, 66⟩
incident ['ɪnsɪdnt] Vorfall; Ereignis **V U3**, 94
to **include** [ɪn'klu:d] einschließen; beinhalten **II**; aufnehmen; einbeziehen **III**
including [ɪn'klu:dɪŋ] einschließlich; inklusive **V AC1**, 8
income ['ɪnkʌm] Einkommen **V U3**, 90
incomplete [ˌɪnkəm'pli:t] unvollständig **IV**
inconvenient [ˌɪnkən'vi:niənt] unbequem; lästig **IV**
increase ['ɪnkri:s] Zunahme; Wachstum; Anstieg ⟨**V U3**, 96⟩
to **increase** [ɪn'kri:s] zunehmen; wachsen **V U3**, 94
increasingly [ɪn'kri:siŋli] zunehmend ⟨**V AC1**, 11⟩
incredible [ɪn'kredəbl] unglaublich **IV**
in-crowd ['ɪnkraʊd] Szene; die Angesagten; die Beliebten **III**
independence *(no pl)* [ˌɪndɪ'pendəns] Unabhängigkeit **III**
independent [ˌɪndɪ'pendənt] unabhängig **III**
Indian ['ɪndiən] Inder/-in; indisch **I**; Indianer/-in; indianisch **IV**
to **indicate** ['ɪndɪkeɪt] anzeigen; angeben ⟨**V U3**, 102⟩
indigenous *(fml)* [ɪn'dɪdʒɪnəs] einheimisch; heimisch **V U1**, 18
indirect ['ɪndɪrekt] indirekt **III**
indirect speech [ˌɪndɪrekt 'spi:tʃ] indirekte Rede **III**
individual [ˌɪndɪ'vɪdʒuəl] Einzelperson; Einzelne/-r; Individuum **IV**
individual [ˌɪndɪ'vɪdʒuəl] individuell; einzeln **II**
indoors [ˌɪn'dɔ:z] im Inneren **V U3**, 95
industry ['ɪndəstri] Industrie; Branche; Gewerbe **III**
infection [ɪn'fekʃn] Infektion; Infekt; Ansteckung **IV**
*to catch an **infection** [ɪn'fekʃn] sich eine Infektion holen; sich einen Infekt holen **IV**
infinitive [ɪn'fɪnətɪv] Infinitiv **I**
influence ['ɪnfluəns] Einfluss **IV**
to **influence** ['ɪnfluəns] beeinflussen **II**
to **inform** [ɪn'fɔ:m] informieren **IV**
informal [ɪn'fɔ:ml] informell; zwanglos **IV**
information *(no pl)* [ˌɪnfə'meɪʃn] Information; Informationen **I**
informative [ɪn'fɔ:mətɪv] informativ **IV**
ingredient [ɪn'gri:diənt] Zutat **II**
injured ['ɪndʒəd] verletzt **VTS2**, 76
injury ['ɪndʒəri] Verletzung **II**
inline skating ['ɪnlaɪn ˌskeɪtɪŋ] Inlineskatefahren **I**
inner ['ɪnə] innere/-r/-s; Innen- **IV**
innocent ['ɪnəsnt] unschuldig ⟨**V U3**, 102⟩
innovation [ˌɪnə'veɪʃn] Innovation; Neuerung **IV**
innovative [ɪ'nəʊvətɪv; 'ɪnəvətɪv] innovativ; kreativ **IV**
input ['ɪnpʊt] Beitrag; Input °**VTS2**, 76
insecure [ˌɪnsɪ'kjʊə] unsicher **IV**
on the **inside** [ˌɒn ði‿'ɪnsaɪd] innen **IV**
inside [ˌɪn'saɪd] innen; im Innern; hinein; nach drinnen; in; drin **I**
insides *(pl)* [ˌɪn'saɪdz] Innereien ⟨**V U1**, 29⟩
to **insist** (on) [ɪn'sɪst‿ɒn] insistieren; bestehen auf **V U3**, 101
to **inspire** [ɪn'spaɪə] inspirieren; anregen **IV**
instant ['ɪnstənt] Augenblick; Moment ⟨**V U2**, 65⟩
instantly ['ɪnstəntli] sofort **IV**
instead [ɪn'sted] stattdessen **III**
instead of [ɪn'sted‿əv] statt; anstatt; an Stelle von **IV**
to **instruct** [ɪn'strʌkt] anweisen; beauftragen ⟨**V U1**, 21⟩
instruction [ɪn'strʌkʃn] Instruktion; Anweisung **I**
instructor [ɪn'strʌktə] Lehrer/-in; Betreuer/-in **II**
surf **instructor** [ˌsɜ:f‿ɪn'strʌktə] Surflehrer/-in **V AC1**, 10
instrument ['ɪnstrəmənt] Instrument **IV**
insult ['ɪnsʌlt] Beleidigung **VTS3**, 108
to **insult** [ɪn'sʌlt] beleidigen **VTS3**, 110
insurance [ɪn'ʃʊərns] Versicherung **IV**
intense [ɪn'tens] intensiv; heftig **V AC1**, 9
intention [ɪn'tenʃn] Absicht; Intention °**VTS2**, 78
intentionally [ɪn'tenʃnli] absichtlich ⟨**V U3**, 102⟩
interest ['ɪntrəst] Interesse **II**
to **interest** ['ɪntrəst] (sich) interessieren **II**
*to be **interested** in [bi‿'ɪntrəstɪd‿ɪn] interessiert sein an; sich interessieren für **II**
interesting ['ɪntrəstɪŋ] interessant **I**
interior [ɪn'tɪəriə] Inneres; Landesinneres **V U1**, 16
interior [ɪn'tɪəriə] Innen- °**VTS1**, 44
international [ˌɪntə'næʃnl] international **I**
internet ['ɪntənet] Internet **I**
to **interpret** [ɪn'tɜ:prɪt] interpretieren °**VTS2**, 74
to **interrupt** [ˌɪntə'rʌpt] unterbrechen ⟨**V U2**, 64⟩
intersection [ˌɪntə'sekʃn] Kreuzung **IV**
interview ['ɪntəvju:] Interview; Befragung **I**
(job) **interview** ['dʒɒb ˌɪntəvju:] Vorstellungsgespräch **V U2**, 51
to **interview** ['ɪntəvju:] interviewen; befragen **I**
interviewee [ˌɪntəvju'i:] Befragte/-r; Interviewte/-r **IV**
interviewer ['ɪntəvju:ə] Interviewer/-in; Befrager/-in **IV**
into ['ɪntə] in; in … hinein **I**
*to be **into** [bi‿'ɪntə] mögen; stehen auf **I**
intransitive [ɪn'trænsətɪv] intransitiv **IV**
to **introduce** [ˌɪntrə'dju:s] einführen; einleiten **III**; vorstellen **VTS1**, 44
introduction [ˌɪntrə'dʌkʃn] Einführung; Einleitung; Vorstellung **II**
to **invade** [ɪn'veɪd] einmarschieren (in); eindringen (in); überfallen **III**
to **invent** [ɪn'vent] erfinden **III**
invention [ɪn'venʃn] Erfindung **III**
inventor [ɪn'ventə] Erfinder/-in **III**
inversion [ɪn'vɜ:ʃn] Inversion °**V U2**, 59
to **invert** [ɪn'vɜ:t] umdrehen °**V U2**, 59
investment [ɪn'vesmənt] Einlage; Beteiligung; Investition **V U2**, 58
invisible [ɪn'vɪzəbl] unsichtbar **III**
invitation [ˌɪnvɪ'teɪʃn] Einladung **I**
to **invite** [ɪn'vaɪt] einladen **I**

to **involve** [ɪn'vɒlv] involvieren; einbeziehen; beteiligen **IV**
*to be **involved** [bi ɪn'vɒlvd] involviert sein; engagiert sein **V U2**, 55
*to be **involved** (in) [bi ɪn'vɒlvd ɪn] beteiligt sein (an) **V U1**, 26
involvement [ɪn'vɒlvmənt] Engagement; Beteiligung **V U2**, 55
inward ['ɪnwəd] ankommend **II**
Irish ['aɪrɪʃ] irisch; Irisch **II**
ironic [ˌaɪ'rɒnɪk] ironisch **IV**
irregular [ɪ'regjələ] unregelmäßig **I**
irrelevant [ɪ'reləvnt] irrelevant; nicht von Bedeutung **VTS2**, 76
irresponsible [ˌɪrɪ'spɒnsəbl] unverantwortlich; leichtsinning **VTS3**, 111
to **irritate** ['ɪrɪteɪt] verärgern; reizen °**V U1**, 18
island ['aɪlənd] Insel **II**
issue ['ɪʃu:; 'ɪsju:] Abneigung; Problem; Thema **IV**
to **issue** ['ɪʃu:; 'ɪsju:] ausstellen; verhängen ⟨**VTS3**, 113⟩
it [ɪt] es **I**
*to make **it** ['meɪk ɪt] es schaffen **IV**
It's fun. [ɪts 'fʌn] Es macht Spaß. **I**
It's great for … [ɪts 'greɪt fə] Es ist super zum/für … **I**
It's to die for! [ˌɪts tə 'daɪ fɔ:] Dafür könnte ich sterben!; Das ist unwiderstehlich! **IV**
It's your turn. [ˌɪts 'jɔ: tɜ:n] Du bist dran. **I**
It's …/They're … [ɪts/ðeə] Es kostet …/ Sie kosten … **I**
IT *(= Information Technology)* [ˌaɪ'ti:] Informatik; Informationstechnik **III**
Italian [ɪ'tæliən] italienisch; Italienisch; aus Italien **IV**; Italiener/-in **V AC1**, 10
italics [ɪ'tælɪks] Kursivschrift °**VTS1**, 44
item ['aɪtəm] Gegenstand; Objekt **IV**
its [ɪts] sein/-e; ihr/-e **I**
ivory *(no pl)* ['aɪvri] Elfenbein **III**

J

to **jab** [dʒæb] piksen; tippen ⟨**V U1**, 28⟩
jacket ['dʒækɪt] Jacke **III**
jam [dʒæm] Marmelade; Konfitüre **III**
January ['dʒænjuri] Januar **I**
*to be **jealous** (of) [bi 'dʒeləs] eifersüchtig sein (auf); neidisch sein (auf) **I**
jeans *(pl)* [dʒi:nz] Jeans **V U3**, 92
jelly ['dʒeli] Tortenguss; Götterspeise; Wackelpudding; Gelee **I**
jellyfish ['dʒelifɪʃ] Qualle **V U1**, 14
box **jellyfish** ['bɒks ˌdʒelifɪʃ] Würfelqualle **V U1**, 14
jewel ['dʒu:əl] Juwel; Edelstein **III**
crown **jewels** [ˌkraʊn 'dʒu:əlz] Kronjuwelen **II**
jewellery ['dʒu:əlri] Schmuck **I**
jewelry *(AE)* ['dʒu:əlri] Schmuck **IV**
Jewish ['dʒu:ɪʃ] jüdisch **IV**
job [dʒɒb] Arbeit; Aufgabe; Job **I**
(**job**) interview ['dʒɒb ˌɪntəvju:] Vorstellungsgespräch **V U2**, 51
job-related ['dʒɒbrɪˌleɪtɪd] berufsbezogen °**V U2**, 47
mouth **jogging** ['maʊθ ˌdʒɒgɪŋ] Training für den Mund **I**
to **join** [dʒɔɪn] beitreten; sich anschließen; verbinden **II**
to **join** in [ˌdʒɔɪn 'ɪn] teilnehmen; mitmachen **IV**
joke [dʒəʊk] Witz **I**
to **joke** [dʒəʊk] scherzen **II**
journalist ['dʒɜ:nlɪst] Journalist/-in **VTS2**, 76
journey ['dʒɜ:ni] Reise; Fahrt **II**
to **judge** [dʒʌdʒ] beurteilen; bewerten **III**
juggling ['dʒʌglɪŋ] Jonglieren **II**
juice [dʒu:s] Saft **I**
July [dʒʊ'laɪ] Juli **I**
to **jump** [dʒʌmp] springen **I**
to **jump** back [dʒʌmp 'bæk] zurückspringen; *hier:* zurückschrecken **II**
to **jump** the queue [ˌdʒʌmp ðə 'kju:] sich vordrängeln **I**
June [dʒu:n] Juni **I**
jungle ['dʒʌŋgl] Dschungel **IV**
junior ['dʒu:niə] Junior; der/die Jüngere **IV**
piece of **junk** [ˌpi:s əv 'dʒʌŋk] Stück Schrott **III**
jury ['dʒʊəri] Jury; Preisgericht **VTS3**, 108
just [dʒʌst] gerade; nur; einfach **I**
Just a second … [ˌdʒʌst ə 'seknd] Einen Augenblick … **IV**
just about anywhere [ˌdʒʌst əˌbaʊt 'eniweə] praktisch überall **IV**
just in time [ˌdʒʌst ɪn 'taɪm] gerade rechtzeitig **IV**
justice ['dʒʌstɪs] Gerechtigkeit **IV**
to **justify** ['dʒʌstɪfaɪ] rechtfertigen **V U2**, 53

K

kangaroo [ˌkæŋgr'u:] Känguru **V U1**, 17
*to **keep** [ki:p] behalten; aufbewahren; halten **I**; weiter tun; immer wieder tun **IV**
*to **keep** a diary [ˌki:p ə 'daɪəri] ein Tagebuch führen **IV**
*to **keep** away from [ˌki:p ə'weɪ frəm] (sich) fernhalten von **II**
*to **keep** going [ˌki:p 'gəʊɪŋ] aufrechterhalten **II**
*to **keep** in mind [ˌki:p ɪn 'maɪnd] beachten; im Gedächtnis behalten **IV**
*to **keep** in touch [ˌki:p ɪn 'tʌtʃ] in Kontakt bleiben **IV**
*to **keep** one's head above water [ˌki:p wʌnz ˌhed əbʌv 'wɔ:tə] sich über Wasser halten **V U3**, 86
*to **keep** out (of) [ˌki:p 'aʊt əv] draußen bleiben; draußen halten **III**
*to **keep** the ball bouncing [ˌki:p ðə bɔ:l 'baʊntsɪŋ] *hier:* das Gespräch am Laufen halten **III**
*to **keep** up (with) [ˌki:p 'ʌp (wɪð)] mithalten (mit); Schritt halten (mit) **II**
*to **keep** your fingers crossed [ˌki:p jɔ: ˌfɪŋgəz 'krɒst] die Daumen drücken **I**
key [ki:] Schlüssel **II**
key feature [ˌki: 'fi:tʃə] Hauptmerkmal **VTS1**, 38
key ring ['ki: ˌrɪŋ] Schlüsselbund; Schlüsselanhänger **III**
key word ['ki: wɜ:d] Stichwort; Schlüsselbegriff **I**
to **kick** [kɪk] schießen; treten **II**
kid [kɪd] Jugendliche/-r; Kind **IV**
to **kidnap** ['kɪdnæp] kidnappen; entführen ⟨**V U1**, 21⟩
to **kill** [kɪl] töten; umbringen **III**
killer ['kɪlə] Killer/-in **IV**
kilometre (km) ['kɪləˌmi:tə; kɪ'lɒmɪtə] Kilometer **III**
kilt [kɪlt] Kilt; Schottenrock **III**
kind [kaɪnd] Art; Sorte **I**
kind of ['kaɪnd əv] ziemlich **IV**
king [kɪŋ] König **I**
kiss [kɪs] Kuss **V AC2**, 81
to **kiss** [kɪs] (sich) küssen ⟨**V U3**, 101⟩
kitchen ['kɪtʃɪn] Küche **I**
kitty litter ['kɪti ˌlɪtə] Katzenstreu **IV**
Kiwi *(infml)* ['ki:wi:] Neuseeländer/-in **V U1**, 18
knife [naɪf], **knives** [naɪvz] *(pl)* Messer **III**
knight [naɪt] Ritter **II**
knob [nɒb] Griff **II**
knock [nɒk] Klopfen; Schlag; Stoß ⟨**V U1**, 28⟩
to **knock** [nɒk] stoßen; schlagen **VTS1**, 44
*to **know** [nəʊ] kennen; wissen **I**
*to be **known** as [bi 'nəʊn əz] bekannt sein als **IV**
*to get to **know** [ˌget tə 'nəʊ] kennenlernen **II**
I don't **know**! [ˌaɪ ˌdəʊnt 'nəʊ] Ich weiß (es) nicht! **I**
You **know** how to … [ju: 'nəʊ ˌhaʊ tə] Du weißt, wie man …; Ihr wisst, wie man … **I**
know-it-all ['nəʊɪtɔ:l] Besserwisser/-in **V U2**, 58
knowledge *(no pl)* ['nɒlɪdʒ] Wissen; Kenntnisse **V U1**, 22
koala [kəʊ'ɑ:lə] Koala **III**
Korean [kə'ri:ən] koreanisch; Koreanisch; Koreaner/-in **II**
South **Korean** [ˌsaʊθ kə'ri:ən] Südkoreaner/-in; südkoreanisch; Südkoreanisch **II**

L

lab(oratory) [læb; lə'bɒrətri] Labor **IV**
child **labor** *(AE)* [ˌtʃaɪld 'leɪbə] Kinderarbeit **IV**
laboratory [læb; lə'bɒrətri] Labor **IV**
child **labour** [ˌtʃaɪld 'leɪbə] Kinderarbeit **V AC1**, 9

a **lack** of ['læk‿əv] Mangel an ⟨**VAC1**, 11⟩
ladder ['lædə] Leiter **II**
lady ['leɪdi] Lady; Dame **III**
lady-in-waiting [ˌleɪdiɪn'weɪtɪŋ] Hofdame **III**
laid-back [leɪd'bæk] entspannt; locker **III**
lake [leɪk] See **I**
boating **lake** ['bəʊtɪŋ ˌleɪk] See zum Rudern **I**
lamb [læm] Lamm; Lämmchen **I**
lame [leɪm] lahm; langweilig **IV**
land [lænd] Land **I**
to **land** [lænd] landen **II**
landing ['lændɪŋ] Landung **III**
moon **landing** ['mu:n ˌlændɪŋ] Mondlandung **IV**
landscape ['lændskeɪp] Landschaft **II**
landscaped ['lændskeɪpt] gepflegt ⟨**VU2**, 65⟩
landsurfing ['lændsɜ:fɪŋ] Landsurfen ⟨**VU3**, 92⟩
language ['læŋgwɪdʒ] Sprache **I**
first **language** [ˌfɜ:st 'læŋgwɪdʒ] Muttersprache **II**
foreign **language** [ˌfɒrɪn 'læŋgwɪdʒ] Fremdsprache **II**
official **language** [əˌfɪʃl 'læŋgwɪdʒ] Amtssprache **II**
laptop ['læptɒp] Laptop **II**
large [lɑ:dʒ] groß; riesig **II**
lassi ['lʌsi] Lassi **I**
to **last** [lɑ:st] dauern; andauern; anhalten **VU3**, 90
last [lɑ:st] letzte/-r/-s **I**
at **last** [ət 'lɑ:st] endlich; schließlich **I**
last name *(AE)* ['lɑ:st neɪm] Nachname; Familienname **IV**
to save the best for **last** [ˌseɪv ðə ˌbest fə 'lɑ:st] sich das Beste bis zum Schluss aufheben **IV**
late [leɪt] spät; zu spät **I**
*to be **late** [bi 'leɪt] zu spät dran sein; zu spät kommen **I**
later ['leɪtə] später **I**
latest ['leɪtɪst] neueste/-r/-s **III**
Latin ['lætɪn] Latein; lateinisch **VAC1**, 10
Latino [lə'ti:nəʊ] lateinamerikanisch **VU3**, 93
laugh [lɑ:f] Lachen **VU2**, 65
to **laugh** [lɑ:f] lachen **I**
laughter ['lɑ:ftə] Gelächter; Lachen **VU1**, 29
lavish ['lævɪʃ] üppig; verschwenderisch **III**
law [lɔ:] Gesetz; Recht **VU2**, 56
lawn [lɔ:n] Rasen ⟨**VU2**, 65⟩
*to **lay** [leɪ] legen **IV**
layer (of) ['leɪər‿əv] Schicht (aus); Lage (aus) **III**
layout ['leɪaʊt] Layout; Anordnung **III**
lazy ['leɪzi] faul **III**
*to take the **lead** [ˌteɪk ðə 'li:d] die Führung übernehmen **VAC3**, 115
*to **lead** [li:d] führen; anführen **III**
*to **lead** off [li:d‿'ɒf] wegführen **III**
lead [li:d] Haupt- **III**
lead part [ˌli:d 'pɑ:t] Hauptrolle **III**
leader ['li:də] Führer/-in; Anführer/-in **IV**
lead-in ['li:dɪn] Einführung; Einleitung **IV**
leading ['li:dɪŋ] führend **VU3**, 90
leaflet ['li:flət] Broschüre; Informationsblatt; Prospekt **III**
*to **lean** back [ˌli:n 'bæk] sich zurücklehnen ⟨**VU2**, 64⟩
*to **lean** forward [ˌli:n 'fɔ:wəd] sich nach vorn lehnen **VU1**, 29
*to **learn** [lɜ:n] lernen **I**
*to **learn** about ['lɜ:n‿əˌbaʊt] erfahren über **III**
*to **learn** … by heart [ˌlɜ:n baɪ 'hɑ:t] auswendig lernen **I**
at **least** [ət 'li:st] mindestens; wenigstens **II**
*to **leave** [li:v] verlassen; lassen; abfahren; losgehen **II**
*to **leave** a message [ˌli:v‿ə 'mesɪdʒ] eine Nachricht hinterlassen **I**
*to **leave** behind [ˌli:v‿bɪ'haɪnd] zurücklassen **III**
*to **leave** it to cool [ˌli:v‿ɪt tə 'ku:l] kalt stellen **I**
*to **leave** out [ˌli:v‿'aʊt] auslassen; weglassen **IV**
*to **leave** sb alone [ˌli:v‿ə'ləʊn] jmdn. in Ruhe lassen **IV**
*to **leave** space [li:v 'speɪs] Platz lassen **I**
Leave that to me. [ˌli:v ðæt tə 'mi:] Überlass das mir. **IV**
left [left] linke/-r/-s; links **I**
on the **left** [ɒn ðə 'left] auf der linken Seite; links **I**
left [left] übrig **I**
left over [left‿'əʊvə] übrig **VU2**, 56
left-hand ['lefthænd] linke/-r/-s **IV**
leftovers *(pl)* ['leftəʊvəz] Überbleibsel; Überreste **VU1**, 19
leg [leg] Bein **II**
legend ['ledʒənd] Legende; Sage **II**
legendary ['ledʒəndri] legendär °**VTS1**, 43
leisure ['leʒə] Freizeit; Freizeit- **I**
leisure centre ['leʒə ˌsentə] Freizeitzentrum **I**
lemon ['lemən] Zitrone **II**
lemonade [ˌlemə'neɪd] Limonade **I**
*to **lend** ['lend tə] leihen; verleihen **III**
length [leŋθ] Länge **VAC1**, 10
zoom **lens** ['zu:m ˌlenz] Zoomobjektiv ⟨**VU3**, 100⟩
lesbian ['lezbiən] lesbisch; Lesbe **VAC2**, 82
less [les] weniger **III**
to settle for **less** [ˌsetl fə 'les] sich mit weniger zufrieden geben **IV**
lesson ['lesn] Unterrichtsstunde; Schulstunde; Unterricht **I**
*to **let** [let] lassen **I**
*to **let** go (of) [ˌlet 'gəʊ (əv)] loslassen **II**
let alone [ˌlet‿ə'ləʊn] geschweige denn ⟨**VU1**, 28⟩
Let's face it. [lets 'feɪs‿ɪt] Machen wir uns doch nichts vor. **III**
letter ['letə] Buchstabe **I**; Brief **II**
application **letter** [ˌæplɪ'keɪʃn ˌletə] Bewerbungsschreiben **VU2**, 48
capital **letter** [ˌkæpɪtl 'letə] Großbuchstabe **I**
letter to the editor [ˌletə tʊ ði‿'edɪtə] Leserbrief **VTS3**, 108
level ['levl] Niveau; Level **VTS3**, 108
liberty ['lɪbəti] Freiheit **IV**
library ['laɪbri] Bibliothek; Bücherei **III**
lie [laɪ] Lüge **III**
white **lie** [ˌwaɪt 'laɪ] Notlüge **III**
to **lie** [laɪ] lügen **II**
*to **lie** [laɪ] liegen **II**
life [laɪf], **lives** [laɪvz] *(pl)* Leben **II**
lifeboat ['laɪfbəʊt] Rettungsboot **I**
lifebuoy ['laɪfbɔɪ] Rettungsring **I**
lifeguard ['laɪfgɑ:d] Rettungsschwimmer/-in **VU1**, 26
lifestyle ['laɪfstaɪl] Lebensstil; Lifestyle **III**
to **lift** [lɪft] heben; hochheben; anheben **IV**
light [laɪt] Licht; Lampe **II**
light [laɪt] leicht **III**
to **lighten** ['laɪtn] aufhellen **III**
lightning *(no pl)* ['laɪtnɪŋ] Blitz **II**
to **like** [laɪk] mögen; gern haben **I**
would **like** [wʊd 'laɪk] würde/-st/-n/-t gern; hätte/-st/-n/-t gern **I**
I don't **like** … [aɪ 'dəʊnt laɪk] Ich mag … nicht.; Ich mache … nicht gern. **I**
I **like** singing and dancing. [ˌaɪ laɪk ˌsɪŋɪŋ‿ənd 'dɑ:nsɪŋ] Ich singe und tanze gern. **I**
I **like** … [aɪ 'laɪk] Mir gefällt …; Ich mag … **I**
I'd **like** to … *(= I would like to)* [aɪd 'laɪk tə] Ich möchte …; Ich würde gern … **I**
Would you **like** …? [ˌwʊd jʊ 'laɪk] Möchtest du …?; Möchten Sie …?; Möchtet ihr …? **II**
like [laɪk] wie; als ob **I**
*to be **like** [bi 'laɪk] sein **III**
like that [laɪk 'ðæt] so **I**
like this [laɪk 'ðɪs] so **I**
What was it **like**? [ˌwɒt wɒz‿ɪt 'laɪk] Wie war es? **III**
*to be **likely** [bi 'laɪkli] wahrscheinlich sein **VU1**, 14
likes *(pl)* [laɪks] Vorlieben **IV**
limit ['lɪmɪt] Limit; Grenze **III**
to **limit** to ['lɪmɪt tə] limitieren auf; begrenzen auf; beschränken auf **VU2**, 58
line [laɪn] Zeile; Linie **I**
finish **line** ['fɪnɪʃ ˌlaɪn] Ziellinie **II**
line graph ['laɪn grɑ:f] Kurvendiagramm **IV**
opening **line** ['əʊpnɪŋ‿laɪn] der erste Satz **III**
poverty **line** ['pɒvəti ˌlaɪn] Armutsgrenze **VU2**, 53

*to stand in **line** *(AE)* [ˌstænd‿ɪn 'laɪn] anstehen; Schlange stehen; (sich) anstellen **IV**
time **line** ['taɪm ˌlaɪn] Zeitstrahl **I**
lines *(pl)* [laɪnz] Text **III**
to **line** up [laɪn‿'ʌp] (sich) aufstellen **III**
lingua franca [ˌlɪŋgwə 'fræŋkə] Verkehrssprache ⟨**V AC1**, 11⟩
link [lɪŋk] Link; Verbindung **II**
to **link** [lɪŋk] verbinden **II**
linking ['lɪŋkɪŋ] verbindend °**V U2**, 51
linking word ['lɪŋkɪŋ ˌwɜːd] Bindewort **I**
lion [laɪən] Löwe **II**
list [lɪst] Liste **I**
to **list** [lɪst] auflisten; nennen **V U2**, 49
to **listen** (to) ['lɪsn] zuhören; anhören **I**
to **listen** for ['lɪsn fə] horchen auf **I**
listener ['lɪsənə] Zuhörer/-in **II**
listening ['lɪsnɪŋ] Hören **I**
literature ['lɪtrətʃə] Literatur **V U2**, 67
litre (l) ['liːtə] Liter **III**
litter ['lɪtə] Müll; Abfall **V U1**, 17
kitty **litter** ['kɪti ˌlɪtə] Katzenstreu **IV**
to **litter** ['lɪtə] verschmutzen; verunreinigen; Müll herumliegen lassen **III**
little ['lɪtl] klein **I**
little ['lɪtl] wenig **IV**
a **little** [ə 'lɪtl] ein wenig; etwas **I**
to **live** [lɪv] wohnen; leben **I**
standard of **living** [ˌstændəd‿əv 'lɪvɪŋ] Lebensstandard **IV**
live [laɪv] live **III**
lively ['laɪvli] lebendig **II**
*to make a **living** (from) [ˌmeɪk‿ə 'lɪvɪŋ frəm] seinen Lebensunterhalt bestreiten (mit) **IV**
living history show [ˌlɪvɪŋ 'hɪstəri ˌʃəʊ] *Show, in der historischer Alltag nachgespielt wird* **II**
living room ['lɪvɪŋ rʊm] Wohnzimmer **I**
lizard ['lɪzəd] Echse; Eidechse **V U1**, 17
to **load** [ləʊd] einräumen; laden **IV**
local ['ləʊkl] örtlich; lokal **II**
to **locate** sb/sth [lə'keɪt] jmdn./etw. ausfindig machen; lokalisieren ⟨**V U1**, 28⟩
*to be **located** [bi ləʊ'keɪtɪd] gelegen sein; liegen **IV**
location [ləʊ'keɪʃn] Handlungsort; Lage; Standort **II**
loch [lɒx; lɒk] See *(in Schottland)* **III**
locked [lɒkt] abgeschlossen **II**
locker ['lɒkə] Schließfach; Spind **I**
loft [lɒft] Dachboden **I**
logbook ['lɒgbʊk] Logbuch **IV**
logic ['lɒdʒɪk] Logik **III**
logical ['lɒdʒɪkl] logisch °**V U3**, 99
LOL (= laughing out loud) [lɒl] LOL **II**
lollies *(pl)* ['lɒliz] Süßigkeiten *(Pl.)* ⟨**V U1**, 21⟩
Londoner ['lʌndənə] Londoner/-in **I**
lonely ['ləʊnli] einsam **I**
loner ['ləʊnə] Einzelgänger/-in ⟨**V U1**, 30⟩
long [lɒŋ] lang **I**
as **long** as [əz 'lɒŋ‿əz] solange **V U3**, 89
long shot ['lɒŋ ʃɒt] Totale *(Kameraeinstellung)* **IV**
no **longer** [ˌnəʊ 'lɒŋgə] nicht länger; nicht mehr **V U1**, 24
(not) any **longer** [nɒt‿eni 'lɒŋgə] (nicht) mehr; (nicht) länger **II**
longhouse ['lɒŋhaʊs] Langhaus **IV**
long-lasting ['lɒŋlɑːstɪŋ] lang anhaltend **IV**
look [lʊk] Blick **I**
*to give sb funny **looks** [ˌgɪv fʌni 'lʊks] jmdn. schief anschauen **III**
*to have a **look** (at) [ˌhæv‿ə 'lʊk] anschauen **II**
*to take a **look** at [ˌteɪk‿ə 'lʊk‿æt] einen Blick werfen auf **II**
to **look** [lʊk] schauen; sehen; aussehen **I**
to **look** after [ˌlʊk‿'ɑːftə] aufpassen auf; hüten; sich kümmern um **I**
to **look** at ['lʊk‿ət] anschauen; ansehen **I**
to **look** for ['lʊk fɔː] suchen nach **I**
to **look** forward to [ˌlʊk 'fɔːwəd tə] sich freuen auf **II**
to **look** out [ˌlʊk‿'aʊt] aufpassen **II**
to **look** up [ˌlʊk‿'ʌp] nachschlagen; nachschauen **I**
to **look** up to sb [ˌlʊk‿'ʌp tə] zu jmdm. aufschauen; jmdn. bewundern **V TS3**, 111
Look closely … [ˌlʊk 'kləʊsli] Schau(t) genau … **II**
looks *(pl)* [lʊks] Aussehen **III**
loose [luːs] locker; frei ⟨**V U3**, 101⟩
lord [lɔːd] Lord; Herr **III**
lore *(no pl)* [lɔː] (überliefertes) Wissen ⟨**V U1**, 24⟩
lorry ['lɒri] Lastwagen **IV**
*to **lose** [luːz] verlieren **II**
loser ['luːzə] Verlierer/-in; Loser/-in **IV**
*to get **lost** [ˌget 'lɒst] verloren gehen; sich verirren **II**
a **lot** [ə 'lɒt] viel **I**
a **lot** of [ə 'lɒt‿əv] viel/-e; eine Menge **I**
lots (of) ['lɒts‿əv] viel/-e; jede Menge **I**
parking **lot** ['pɑːkɪŋ ˌlɒt] Parkplatz **IV**
loud [laʊd] laut **I**
*to read out **loud** [ˌriːd‿aʊt 'laʊd] laut vorlesen **III**
*to sing out **loud** [ˌsɪŋ‿aʊt 'laʊd] laut vorsingen **III**
lounge [laʊndʒ] Lounge; Aufenthaltsraum **V U3**, 85
departure **lounge** [dɪ'pɑːtʃə ˌlaʊndʒ] Abflughalle **III**
lounge room ['laʊndʒ rʊm] Wohnzimmer ⟨**V U1**, 30⟩
love [lʌv] Liebe **II**
Love … [lʌv] Liebe Grüße; Herzliche Grüße *(am Briefende)* **I**
to **love** [lʌv] lieben; gern mögen **I**
would **love** [wʊd 'lʌv] würde/-st/-n/-t sehr gern; hätte/-st-/-n/-t sehr gern **I**
I **love** you. [aɪ 'lʌv ju] Ich liebe dich.; Ich mag dich. **I**
I **love** … [aɪ 'lʌv] Ich liebe …; Ich mag … total gern. **I**
lovebirds *(pl)* ['lʌvˌbɜːdz] Turteltauben **II**
lovely ['lʌvli] schön; hübsch **IV**
lover ['lʌvə] Freund/-in; Liebhaber/-in **IV**
nature **lover** ['neɪtʃə ˌlʌvə] Naturfreund/-in **IV**
low [ləʊ] niedrig **II**
low tide ['ləʊ ˌtaɪd] Ebbe **II**
to **lower** one's voice [ˌləʊə wʌnz 'vɔɪs] die Stimme senken ⟨**V U1**, 29⟩
luck [lʌk] Glück **V U3**, 86
good **luck** [ˌgʊd 'lʌk] viel Glück **IV**
What **luck**! [wɒt 'lʌk] Was für ein Glück! **III**
luckily ['lʌkɪli] glücklicherweise **IV**
lucky … ['lʌki] … der/die Glückliche **I**
*to be **lucky** [bi 'lʌki] Glück haben **II**
lucky charm [ˌlʌki 'tʃɑːm] Glücksbringer; Talisman **I**
lucky day [ˌlʌki 'deɪ] Glückstag **V U3**, 86
luggage *(no pl)* ['lʌgɪdʒ] Gepäck **III**
lunch [lʌnʃ] Mittagessen **I**
lunch break ['lʌnʃbreɪk] Mittagspause **I**
lunchtime ['lʌnʃtaɪm] Mittagszeit; Mittagspause **IV**
lung [lʌŋ] Lunge **IV**
the **lungs** *(pl)* [ðə 'lʌŋz] die Lunge **III**
luxury ['lʌkʃri] Luxus **IV**
(song) **lyrics** *(pl)* [sɒŋ 'lɪrɪks] Liedtext **III**

M

Ma [mɑː] Mama **IV**
ma'am [mæm] gnädige Frau *(Anrede)* ⟨**V U3**, 100⟩
machete [mə'ʃeti] Machete; Buschmesser **V U2**, 53
machine [mə'ʃiːn] Automat; Maschine; Apparat; Gerät **I**
answering **machine** ['ɑːnsrɪŋ məˌʃiːn] Anrufbeantworter **I**
vending **machine** ['vendɪŋ məˌʃiːn] Automat **III**
washing **machine** ['wɒʃɪŋ məˌʃiːn] Waschmaschine **II**
mad [mæd] verrückt **II**; wütend **IV**
Dear Sir or **Madam** [dɪə ˌsɜːr‿ɔː 'mædəm] Sehr geehrte Dame, sehr geehrter Herr **II**
made up from [ˌmeɪd‿'ʌp frəm] zusammengesetzt aus **IV**
made-up ['meɪdʌp] erfunden ⟨**V U1**, 30⟩
magazine [ˌmægə'ziːn] Zeitschrift **I**
magic ['mædʒɪk] Magie; Zauberei **III**
magical ['mædʒɪkəl] magisch; Zauber- **II**
mail [meɪl] Post **IV**
to **mail** ['iːmeɪl] mailen; per E-Mail schicken **II**
main [meɪn] Haupt- **I**
main clause ['meɪn ˌklɔːz] Hauptsatz **II**

mainstream ['meɪnstriːm] Masse; Durchschnitt; Massen-; Durchschnitts- **V AC2**, 81
major ['meɪdʒə] wichtig; bedeutend; Haupt- **IV**
majority [mə'dʒɒrəti] Mehrheit; Mehrzahl **IV**
*to **make** [meɪk] machen; tun; bilden; ergeben **I**; *hier:* lassen **V U1**, 19
*to be **made** of [bi 'meɪd_əv] bestehen aus **III**
*to be **made** up of/from [bi meɪd_'ʌp_əv/frəm] zusammengesetzt sein aus; bestehen aus **V U2**, 58
*to **make** a choice [ˌmeɪk_ə 'tʃɔɪs] eine Wahl treffen **V U2**, 66
*to **make** a decision [ˌmeɪk_ə dɪ'sɪʒn] eine Entscheidung treffen **II**
*to **make** a difference (to sth) [ˌmeɪk_ə 'dɪfrəns] etw. verändern **V AC3**, 114
*to **make** a living (from) [ˌmeɪk_ə 'lɪvɪŋ frəm] seinen Lebensunterhalt bestreiten (mit) **IV**
*to **make** a wish [ˌmeɪk_ə 'wɪʃ] sich etwas wünschen **I**
*to **make** friends [ˌmeɪk 'frendz] Freundschaft schließen **II**
*to **make** fun of [ˌmeɪk 'fʌn_əv] sich lustig machen über **IV**
*to **make** it ['meɪk_ɪt] es schaffen **IV**
*to **make** money [ˌmeɪk 'mʌni] Geld verdienen **I**
*to **make** notes [ˌmeɪk 'nəʊts] Notizen machen **I**
*to **make** one's point [ˌmeɪk wʌnz 'pɔɪnt] seinen Standpunkt deutlich machen **V AC3**, 114
*to **make** one's voice heard [ˌmeɪk wʌnz ˌvɔɪs 'hɜːd] sich Gehör verschaffen **V AC3**, 114
*to **make** sb angry [meɪk 'æŋgri] jmdn. wütend machen; jmdn. verärgern **III**
*to **make** sb do sth [meɪk] jmdn. dazu bringen, etw. zu tun **II**
*to **make** sense [ˌmeɪk 'sens] Sinn ergeben; einleuchten **IV**
*to **make** sure [ˌmeɪk 'ʃɔː] sich versichern **I**
*to **make** trouble [ˌmeɪk 'trʌbl] Ärger machen; in Schwierigkeiten bringen **I**
*to **make** use of [meɪk 'juːz_əv] benutzen; verwenden **IV**
make-up ['meɪkʌp] Make-up **VTS1**, 38; Zusammensetzung °**V U3**, 93
male [meɪl] männlich **V U2**, 49
shopping **mall** ['ʃɒpɪŋ ˌmɔːl] Einkaufszentrum **IV**
man [mæn], **men** [men] *(pl)* Mann **I**
to **manage** (to do sth) ['mænɪdʒ tə] schaffen (etw. zu tun) **IV**
management ['mænɪdʒmənt] Management ⟨**V U3**, 101⟩
manager ['mænɪdʒə] Manager/-in **V AC1**, 9

Mandarin Chinese [ˌmændrɪn tʃaɪ'niːz] Mandarin *(chinesische Hochsprache)* ⟨**V AC1**, 11⟩
manga ['mæŋgə] Manga *(japanischer Comic)* **II**
mango ['mæŋgəʊ] Mango **I**
manners *(pl)* ['mænəz] Manieren; Benehmen **III**
mansion ['mænʃn] Herrenhaus; Villa ⟨**V U3**, 102⟩
software **manual** ['sɒftweə ˌmænjuəl] Softwarehandbuch **III**
many ['meni] viele **I**
How **many** …? [ˌhaʊ 'meni] Wie viele …? **I**
map [mæp] Stadtplan; Landkarte **I**
mind **map** ['maɪnd mæp] Wörternetz *(eine Art Schaubild)* **I**
marathon ['mærəθn] Marathon **II**
marble ['mɑːbl] Marmor ⟨**V U3**, 101⟩
March [mɑːtʃ] März **I**
march [mɑːtʃ] Marsch; Kundgebung **V U2**, 54
to **march** [mɑːtʃ] marschieren **III**
margin ['mɑːdʒɪn] Rand ⟨**V U1**, 29⟩
marine stinger [məˌriːn 'stɪŋə] Seewespe *(Würfelquallen-Art)* **V U1**, 14
mark [mɑːk] Note **III**
to **mark** [mɑːk] markieren; kennzeichnen **II**
marked [mɑːkt] markiert **IV**
market ['mɑːkɪt] Markt **I**
flea **market** ['fliː ˌmɑːkɪt] Flohmarkt **I**
marmalade ['mɑːməleɪd] Marmelade aus Zitrusfrüchten **III**
to **marry** ['mæri] heiraten **III**
mashed potatoes *(pl)* [ˌmæʃt pə'teɪtəʊz] Kartoffelpüree **III**
mask [mɑːsk] Maske **III**
mass [mæs] Masse; Massen- **IV**
mass migration [ˌmæs maɪ'greɪʃn] Massenwanderung **IV**
masseur [mæs'ɜː] Masseur ⟨**V U3**, 101⟩
massive ['mæsɪv] riesig; massiv; *hier:* super **IV**
master ['mɑːstə] Herr/-in; Meister/-in **VTS1**, 40
raven **master** ['reɪvn ˌmɑːstə] Herr der Raben **II**
match [mætʃ] Spiel; Match **II**
to **match** [mætʃ] zuordnen; passen zu; entsprechen **I**
mate [meɪt] Schiffsoffizier; Maat **I**; Kumpel **V AC1**, 10; Partner/-in **V U2**, 66
material [mə'tɪəriəl] Material **II**
material [mə'tɪəriəl] materiell **VTS3**, 111
materialistic [məˌtɪəriə'lɪstɪk] materialistisch **V U2**, 46
Maths [mæθs] Mathematik; Mathe **II**
no **matter** [nəʊ 'mætə] egal; ganz gleich **IV**
What's the **matter**? [ˌwɒts ðə 'mætə] Was ist los?; Was hast du? **II**
to **matter** ['mætə] von Bedeutung sein; etw. ausmachen **V U2**, 66

It doesn't **matter**. [ɪt ˌdʌznt 'mætə] Es ist egal. **III**
mattress ['mætrəs] Matratze ⟨**V U3**, 101⟩
May [meɪ] Mai **I**
may [meɪ] (vielleicht) können; dürfen **II**
maybe ['meɪbi] vielleicht **I**
me [miː] ich; mich; mir **I**
meal [miːl] Mahlzeit; Essen **II**
ready **meal** [ˌredi 'miːl] Fertiggericht **I**
*to **mean** [miːn] bedeuten; meinen **II**
(I) didn't **mean** to … [aɪ ˌdɪdnt 'miːn tə] Ich wollte nicht … **IV**
mean [miːn] gemein **III**
meaning ['miːnɪŋ] Bedeutung; Sinn **II**
meaningful ['miːnɪŋfl] bedeutsam; wichtig **V U2**, 46
by any **means** [baɪ_enɪ 'miːnz] mit allen Mitteln **IV**
meat *(no pl)* [miːt] Fleisch **III**
mechanic [mə'kænɪk] Mechaniker/-in; Mechatroniker/-in **II**
media ['miːdiə] Medien **II**
social **media** [ˌsəʊʃl 'miːdiə] soziale Netzwerke **IV**
mediation [ˌmiːdi'eɪʃn] Sprachmittlung **I**
medical ['medɪkl] medizinisch; ärztlich; Medizin- **IV**
medication [ˌmedɪ'keɪʃn] medizinische Behandlung; Medikamente ⟨**V U2**, 63⟩
medicine *(no pl)* ['medsn] Medizin, Medikamente **III**
medicine people ['medsn ˌpiːpl] Medizinmänner **IV**
medieval [ˌmedi'iːvl] mittelalterlich **II**
medium ['miːdiəm] mittel; mittelgroß **IV**
medium shot ['miːdiəm ʃɒt] Halbtotale *(Kameraeinstellung)* **IV**
*to **meet** [miːt] treffen; sich treffen **I**
*to **meet** halfway [ˌmiːt hɑːf'weɪ] sich auf halbem Weg treffen **III**
*to **meet** sb's expectations [ˌmiːt sʌmbədiz_ekspek'teɪʃnz] jmds. Erwartungen erfüllen **IV**
*to **meet** up [ˌmiːt_'ʌp] sich treffen **IV**
Nice to **meet** you. [ˌnaɪs tə 'miːt juː] Nett, dich/euch/Sie kennenzulernen. **V U1**, 18
melody ['melədi] Melodie **III**
melting pot ['meltɪŋ ˌpɒt] Schmelztiegel **IV**
member ['membə] Mitglied **II**
memorable ['memrəbl] denkwürdig; unvergesslich **V U3**, 88
memory ['memri] Erinnerung; Gedächtnis **II**; Speicher ⟨**V U3**, 102⟩
mental ['mentl] geistig ⟨**VTS2**, 79⟩
mention ['menʃn] Erwähnung °**VTS1**, 44
to **mention** ['menʃn] erwähnen **II**
menu ['menjuː] Speisekarte **IV**
merchant ['mɜːtʃənt] Kaufmann; Händler **II**
mess [mes] Unordnung; Durcheinander; Schweinerei **IV**
to **mess** sth up [ˌmes_'ʌp] etw. durcheinanderbringen; etw. vergeigen **III**

message ['mesɪdʒ] Botschaft; Nachricht **I**
*to leave a **message** [ˌli:v‿ə 'mesɪdʒ] eine Nachricht hinterlassen **I**
*to take a **message** [ˌteɪk‿ə 'mesɪdʒ] eine Nachricht entgegennehmen; jmdm. etw. ausrichten **I**
text (**message**) ['tekst ˌmesɪdʒ] SMS; Kurznachricht **I**
messy ['mesi] unordentlich **III**
metabolism [mə'tæblɪzm] Stoffwechsel **VTS2**, 77
metal ['metl] Metall **V U3**, 90
method ['meθəd] Methode ⟨**V U2**, 63⟩
metre ['mi:tə] Meter **II**
Mexican ['meksɪkn] mexikanisch; Mexikanisch; aus Mexiko; Mexikaner/-in **V U3**, 85
microprocessor ['maɪkrəprəʊsesə] Mikroprozessor **V U3**, 91
middle ['mɪdl] Mitte **I**
middle class [ˌmɪdl 'klɑ:s] Mittelschicht **V AC1**, 8
middle school *(AE)* ['mɪdl ˌsku:l] Mittelschule *(weiterführende Schule in den USA, Mittelstufe)* **IV**
in the **middle** of nowhere [ɪn ðə ˌmɪdl‿əv 'nəʊweə] mitten im Nirgendwo **IV**
midnight ['mɪdnaɪt] Mitternacht **III**
might [maɪt] könnte/-n (vielleicht) **IV**
It **might** as well be … [ˌɪt maɪt əs 'wel bi: …] Es könnte/-n auch … sein. **III**
to **migrate** [maɪ'greɪt] wandern; umherziehen **IV**
migration [maɪ'greɪʃn] Migration; Wanderung **IV**
mass **migration** [ˌmæs maɪ'greɪʃn] Massenwanderung **IV**
mile [maɪl] Meile *(Längenmaß)* **II**
milk [mɪlk] Milch **I**
to **milk** [mɪlk] melken **II**
million ['mɪljən] Million **II**
I've done this a **million** times before. [ˌaɪv dʌn ðɪs ə ˌmɪljən taɪmz bɪ'fɔ:] Ich habe das schon eine Million Mal gemacht. **II**
millionaire [ˌmɪljə'neə] Millionär/-in **III**
mind [maɪnd] Geist; Verstand; Kopf **III**
to change one's **mind** [ˌtʃeɪndʒ wʌnz 'maɪnd] seine Meinung ändern **III**
*to come to one's **mind** [ˌkʌm tə wʌnz 'maɪnd] jmdm. in den Sinn kommen; jmdm. einfallen **IV**
*to keep in **mind** [ˌki:p‿ɪn 'maɪnd] beachten; im Gedächtnis behalten **IV**
mind map ['maɪnd mæp] Wörternetz *(eine Art Schaubild)* **I**
*to rise up in one's **mind** [raɪz‿ʌp ɪn wʌnz 'maɪnd] jmdm. in den Sinn kommen **III**
to **mind** [maɪnd] etwas dagegen haben; einem etwas ausmachen **IV**
to **mind** sth [maɪnd] auf etw. aufpassen **IV**
mine [maɪn] Mine **II**
mine [maɪn] mein/-er/-e/-es **II**
miner ['maɪnə] Bergarbeiter/-in ⟨**V U3**, 92⟩
mini [mɪni] Mini- **II**
minimum wage [ˌmɪnɪməm 'weɪdʒ] Mindestlohn **V U3**, 93
mining ['maɪnɪŋ] Bergbau **II**
Prime **Minister** [ˌpraɪm 'mɪnɪstə] Premierminister/-in ⟨**V U1**, 23⟩
minority [maɪ'nɒrəti] Minderheit **IV**
minute ['mɪnɪt] Minute **I**
mirror ['mɪrə] Spiegel **III**
misery *(no pl)* ['mɪzri] Elend; Jammer; Not **VTS1**, 40
mismatch ['mɪsmætʃ] Missverhältnis **VTS2**, 77
Miss [mɪs] Fräulein *(Anrede)* **III**
to **miss** [mɪs] verpassen; versäumen; vermissen **II**
to **miss** out on sth [ˌmɪs‿'aʊt‿ɒn] etw. verpassen ⟨**V AC1**, 11⟩
missing ['mɪsɪŋ] fehlend; verschwunden **II**
What is **missing**? [ˌwɒt‿ɪz 'mɪsɪŋ] Was fehlt? **I**
mission ['mɪʃn] Mission; Auftrag **IV**
mistake [mɪ'steɪk] Fehler **I**
misunderstanding [ˌmɪsʌndə'stændɪŋ] Missverständnis **IV**
misunderstood [ˌmɪsʌndə'stʊd] missverstanden **III**
mix [mɪks] Mix **III**
to **mix** [mɪks] zusammenpassen **IV**
to **mix** (up) [mɪks‿'ʌp] mischen; vermischen **III**
mixed [mɪkst] gemischt **V AC1**, 9
mixture ['mɪkstʃə] Mischung ⟨**V U3**, 100⟩
mobile ['məʊbaɪl] Handy; Mobiltelefon **II**
modal ['məʊdl] Modalverb **II**
modal ['məʊdl] Modal- °**V U1**, 16
quick-shot **mode** ['kwɪkʃɒt ˌməʊd] Serienaufnahmemodus ⟨**V U3**, 100⟩
model ['mɒdl] Modell; Tonmodell; Model **I**
role **model** ['rəʊl ˌmɒdl] Vorbild **VTS3**, 111
modelling ['mɒdəlɪŋ] Modeln **III**
modern ['mɒdn] modern **II**
modernity [mɒd'ɜ:nəti] Modernität ⟨**V AC1**, 11⟩
mom *(AE)* [mɒm] Mama **IV**
moment ['məʊmənt] Moment; Augenblick **II**
at the **moment** [ət ðə 'məʊmənt] im Moment; gerade **I**
mommy *(AE)* ['mɒmi] Mami ⟨**V U3**, 100⟩
monarch ['mɒnək] Monarch/-in **III**
Monday ['mʌndeɪ] Montag **I**
on **Mondays** [ɒn 'mʌndeɪz] montags **I**
money ['mʌni] Geld **I**
*to make **money** [ˌmeɪk 'mʌni] Geld verdienen **I**
pocket **money** ['pɒkɪt ˌmʌni] Taschengeld **I**
to raise **money** [ˌreɪz 'mʌni] Geld sammeln **II**
monster ['mɒnstə] Monster; Ungeheuer **I**
montage [mɒn'tɑ:ʒ] Montage **IV**
month [mʌnθ] Monat **II**
monument ['mɒnjəmənt] Monument; Denkmal **II**
mood [mu:d] Stimmung; Laune **II**
moon [mu:n] Mond **IV**
moon landing ['mu:n ˌlændɪŋ] Mondlandung **IV**
moonlight ['mu:nlaɪt] Mondlicht **III**
more [mɔ:] mehr; weitere **I**
no **more** [ˌnəʊ 'mɔ:] nicht mehr **IV**
not any **more** [ˌnɒt‿eni 'mɔ:] nicht mehr **I**
more … than ['mɔ: ðən] mehr … als **I**
moreover [mɔ:r'əʊvə] überdies; außerdem **V U2**, 51
morning ['mɔ:nɪŋ] Morgen; Vormittag **I**
in the **mornings** [ˌɪn ðə 'mɔ:nɪŋz] morgens; vormittags **I**
Good **morning**. [ˌgʊd 'mɔ:nɪŋ] Guten Morgen. **I**
(the) **most** [ðə 'məʊst] der/die/das meiste; die meisten **I**
mostly ['məʊstli] meistens; größtenteils; hauptsächlich **V U1**, 16
mother ['mʌðə] Mutter **I**
motion ['məʊʃn] Bewegung °**V U2**, 54
motion picture [ˌməʊʃn 'pɪktʃə] Film; Spielfilm **IV**
to **motivate** ['məʊtɪveɪt] motivieren **I**
motivation [ˌməʊtɪ'veɪʃn] Motivation; Beweggründe **III**
motive ['məʊtɪv] Motiv; Beweggrund **III**
bicycle **motocross** [ˌbaɪsɪkl 'məʊtəʊkrɒs] Fahrradmotocross **II**
motor car ['məʊtə ˌkɑ:] Automobil **IV**
mountain ['maʊntɪn] Berg **II**
mountain biking ['maʊntɪn ˌbaɪkɪŋ] Mountainbikefahren **II**
mountainous ['maʊntɪnəs] bergig **IV**
mouse [maʊs], **mice** [maɪs] *(pl)* Maus/Mäuse **I**
mouth [maʊθ] Mund **I**; Mündung **IV**
mouth jogging ['maʊθ ˌdʒɒgɪŋ] Training für den Mund **I**
to talk with your **mouth** full [ˌtɔ:k wɪð jɔ: 'maʊθ fʊl] mit vollem Mund sprechen **III**
move [mu:v] Bewegung **I**; Umzug **IV**
on the **move** [ˌɒn‿ðə 'mu:v] unterwegs **III**
to **move** [mu:v] (sich) bewegen **I**
to **move** (house) [mu:v (haʊs)] umziehen **II**
to **move** in/into [ˌmu:v‿'ɪn/'ɪntə] einziehen in **II**
movement ['mu:vmənt] Bewegung **VTS1**, 41
movie *(AE)* ['mu:vi] Film **IV**
movie theater *(AE)* ['mu:vi ˌθɪətə] Kino **IV**
Mr ['mɪstə] Herr *(Anrede)* **I**
Mrs ['mɪsɪz] Frau *(Anrede)* **I**
much [mʌtʃ] viel **I**
that **much** [ðæt 'mʌtʃ] so viel **III**
mud [mʌd] Schlamm **II**
muddy ['mʌdi] schlammig **II**

mudlark ['mʌdlɑ:k] *jemand, der im Schlamm nach Sachen sucht, die er dann verkaufen kann* **II**
mudslide ['mʌdslaɪd] Schlammlawine **V U3**, 94
muesli ['mju:zli] Müsli **III**
mug [mʌg] Becher **III**
multi- [ˌmʌlti] viel-; multi- ⟨**V U3**, 96⟩
multicultural [ˌmʌlti'kʌltʃrl] multikulturell °**V U1**, 18
multi-ethnic [ˌmʌlti'eθnɪk] Vielvölker-; international **II**
mum [mʌm] Mama **I**
mummy ['mʌmi] Mama; Mami; Mutti **III**
murder ['mɜ:də] Mord **III**
to **murder** ['mɜ:də] ermorden; umbringen **IV**
muscle ['mʌsl] Muskel ⟨**V U2**, 66⟩
muscle-packed ['mʌslˌpækt] muskelbepackt ⟨**V U3**, 92⟩
muscular ['mʌskjələ] muskulös **V TS3**, 111
museum [mju:'zi:əm] Museum **I**
music ['mju:zɪk] Musik **I**
musical ['mju:zɪkl] Musical **V TS1**, 39
musical ['mju:zɪkl] musikalisch; Musik- **III**
musician [mju:'zɪʃn] Musiker/-in **II**
Muslim ['mʊzlɪm] Muslim/-in; muslimisch **V AC1**, 9
must [mʌst] müssen **I**
  mustn't ['mʌsnt] nicht dürfen **I**
  a **must** [ə 'mʌst] ein Muss °**V U2**, 50
to **mutter** ['mʌtə] murmeln **III**
my [maɪ] mein/-e **I**
  My favourite ... [maɪ 'feɪvrɪt] Mein/e Lieblings ... **I**
  My name is ... [maɪ 'neɪm‿ɪz] Ich heiße ... **I**
myself [maɪ'self] ich/mir/mich (selbst); selber **II**
mysterious [mɪ'stɪəriəs] mysteriös; geheimnisvoll **II**
mystery ['mɪstri] Mysterium; Rätsel; Geheimnis **III**
mythical ['mɪθɪkl] sagenhaft; sagenumwoben **III**

N

naked ['neɪkɪd] nackt **IV**
name [neɪm] Name **I**
  last **name** *(AE)* ['lɑ:st neɪm] Nachname; Familienname **IV**
  name day ['neɪm ˌdeɪ] Namenstag **I**
  My **name** is ... [maɪ 'neɪm‿ɪz] Ich heiße ... **I**
  What's your **name**? [ˌwɒts jə 'neɪm] Wie heißt du?; Wie heißen Sie? **I**
to **name** [neɪm] nennen; benennen **I**
narrative perspective [ˌnærətɪv pə'spektɪv] Erzählperspektive **III**
  narrative technique [ˌnærətɪv tek'ni:k] Erzähltechnik **IV**
narrator [nə'reɪtə] Erzähler/-in **III**
  first person **narrator** [ˌfɜ:st ˌpɜ:sn nə'reɪtə] Ich-Erzähler/-in **III**
  third person **narrator** [ˌθɜ:d ˌpɜ:sn nə'reɪtə] Er/Sie-Erzähler/-in **III**
narrow ['nærəʊ] eng; schmal **III**
NASA *(= National Aeronautics and Space Administration)* ['næsə] NASA **IV**
nasty ['nɑ:sti] garstig; gemein **II**
nation ['neɪʃn] Nation **IV**
national ['næʃnl] national; landesweit **I**
  national park [ˌnæʃnl 'pɑ:k] Nationalpark; Naturpark **IV**
nationality [ˌnæʃn'æləti] Nationalität; Staatsangehörigkeit **V U2**, 50
native ['neɪtɪv] einheimisch; eingeboren **IV**
  Native American [ˌneɪtɪv‿ə'merɪkən] Ureinwohner/-in Amerikas; Indianer/-in; indianisch **IV**
  native speaker [ˌneɪtɪv 'spi:kə] Muttersprachler/-in ⟨**V AC1**, 11⟩
natural ['nætʃrl] natürlich; Natur- **IV**
nature ['neɪtʃə] Natur **II**
  nature lover ['neɪtʃə ˌlʌvə] Naturfreund/-in **IV**
near [nɪə] nahe; in der Nähe von **I**
nearby [ˌnɪə'baɪ] in der Nähe **IV**
nearly ['nɪəli] fast; annähernd **II**
not **necessarily** [ˌnɒt nesə'serəli] nicht notwendigerweise; nicht unbedingt **IV**
necessary ['nesəsri] nötig; notwendig; erforderlich **IV**
necessity [nə'sesəti] Notwendigkeit **IV**
necklace ['nekləs] Halskette **III**
in **need** [ɪn 'ni:d] bedürftig; in Not **II**
  There's no **need** to ... [ˌðeəz nəʊ 'ni:d tə] Es gibt keinen Grund zu ... **III**
  with special **needs** [wɪð ˌspeʃl 'ni:dz] behindert **II**
to **need** (to) [ni:d] brauchen; benötigen **I**
  to **need** (to do) [ni:d] (tun) müssen **I**
  needn't ['ni:dnt] nicht brauchen; nicht müssen **I**
needless to say [ˌni:dləs tə 'seɪ] natürlich; selbstverständlich **IV**
negative ['negətɪv] negativ; verneint **II**
  negative form ['negətɪv ˌfɔ:m] verneinte Form **I**
neighborhood *(AE)* ['neɪbəhʊd] Nachbarschaft **IV**
neighbour ['neɪbə] Nachbar/-in **I**
neighbourhood ['neɪbəhʊd] Nachbarschaft **III**
neither ['naɪðə; 'ni:ðə] keine/-r/-s (von beiden) ⟨**V AC1**, 11⟩
nephew ['nefju:] Neffe **III**
nerd [nɜ:d] Nerd *(Person, die intelligent, aber sozial unbeholfen ist)* **IV**
*to get on people's **nerves** [ˌget‿ɒn sʌmbɒdiz 'nɜ:vz] jemandem auf die Nerven gehen **I**
nervous ['nɜ:vəs] nervös; aufgeregt **II**
net [net] Netz **II**
to **net** off [net‿'ɒf] durch ein Netz abtrennen **V U1**, 14
netball ['netbɔ:l] Korbball **I**
network ['netwɜ:k] Netzwerk **IV**
  communications **network** [kəˌmju:nɪ'keɪʃnz ˌnetwɜ:k] Kommunikationsnetz; Nachrichtennetz **IV**
  social **network** [ˌsəʊʃl 'netwɜ:k] soziales Netzwerk **II**
neutral ['nju:trl] neutral °**V TS3**, 112
never ['nevə] nie; niemals **I**
nevertheless [ˌnevəðə'les] trotzdem; dennoch; nichtsdestoweniger **V U2**, 51
new [nju:] neu **I**
New Yorker [ˌnju: 'jɔ:kə] New Yorker/-in **IV**
newchild ['nju:tʃaɪld], **newchildren** ['nju:ˌtʃɪldrən] *(pl) hier:* Baby ⟨**V U2**, 66⟩
newcomer ['nju:ˌkʌmə] Neuling; Neuankömmling ⟨**V U1**, 21⟩
newly-arrived [ˌnju:li‿ə'raɪvd] frisch angekommen **IV**
news *(sg)* [nju:z] Nachrichten; Neuigkeiten **II**
  news report ['nju:z rɪˌpɔ:t] Tatsachenbericht; Nachrichtenbeitrag; Meldung **III**
newspaper ['nju:sˌpeɪpə] Zeitung **III**
newsreader ['nju:sˌri:də] Nachrichtensprecher/-in **V U1**, 26
next [nekst] nächste/-r/-s **I**
  next door [ˌnekst 'dɔ:] (von) nebenan **III**
  next to ['nekst tə] neben **I**
  the **next** day [ðə ˌnekst 'deɪ] am nächsten Tag **II**
next [nekst] der/ die Nächste(n); als Nächstes **I**
nice [naɪs] nett; schön; lieb **I**
  Nice to meet you. [ˌnaɪs tə 'mi:t ju:] Nett, dich/euch/Sie kennenzulernen. **V U1**, 18
nickname ['nɪkneɪm] Spitzname **IV**
night [naɪt] Nacht **I**
  all **night** [ˌɔ:l 'naɪt] die ganze Nacht **I**
  night walk ['naɪt wɔ:k] Nachtwanderung **II**
nightmare ['naɪtmeə] Alptraum **IV**
nine [naɪn] neun **I**
niqab [ni:'kɒb] Niqab *(Gesichtsschleier)* **V AC2**, 81
2nite *(= tonight)* [tə'naɪt] heute Abend **I**
no [nəʊ] kein/-e **I**
  no longer [ˌnəʊ 'lɒŋgə] nicht länger; nicht mehr **V U1**, 24
  no matter [nəʊ 'mætə] egal; ganz gleich **IV**
  no more [ˌnəʊ 'mɔ:] nicht mehr **IV**
  no one ['nəʊ wʌn] niemand ⟨**V U2**, 62⟩
  no idea [ˌnəʊ‿aɪ'dɪə] keine Ahnung **II**
  no sooner [nəʊ 'su:nə] kaum **V U2**, 59
  no wonder [ˌnəʊ 'wʌndə] kein Wunder **IV**
  No worries. [ˌnəʊ 'wʌriz] Kein Problem.; Gern geschehen. **V U1**, 18
no [nəʊ] nein **I**
nobody ['nəʊbədi] niemand **II**

nobody else ['nəʊbədi els] niemand anderes **II**
nod [nɒd] Nicken **V U1**, 29
to **nod** [nɒd] nicken **V U1**, 29
noise [nɔɪz] Lärm; Geräusch **II**
noisy ['nɔɪzi] laut **III**
nomad ['nəʊmæd] Nomade/Nomadin **V U1**, 24
to **nominate** ['nɒmɪneɪt] nominieren; ernennen **V U3**, 88
nomination [ˌnɒmɪ'neɪʃn] Nominierung; Ernennung **V U3**, 89
nominee [ˌnɒmɪ'niː] vorgeschlagener Kandidat/vorgeschlagene Kandidatin **V U3**, 89
non- [nɒn] nicht- **II**
non-defining relative clause [ˌnɒndɪfaɪnɪŋ 'relətɪv ˌklɔːz] nicht notwendiger Relativsatz **IV**
none [nʌn] keine/-r/-s **IV**
a sort of **nonstop** repetition [ə ˌsɔːt‿əv ˌnɒnstɒp ˌrepɪ'tɪʃn] eine Art Dauerschleife ⟨**V U3**, 101⟩
nope *(infml)* [nəʊp] nee; nö **IV**
normal ['nɔːml] normal **II**
normality [nɔː'mæləti] Normalität **V U3**, 103
normally ['nɔːmli] normalerweise **III**
Norman ['nɔːmən] Normanne/Normannin; normannisch **III**
north [nɔːθ] Norden; Nord- **II**; nördlich; im Norden **III**
northern ['nɔːðən] nördlich; Nord- **V U3**, 90
nose [nəʊz] Nase **II**
not [nɒt] nicht **I**
not any more [ˌnɒt‿eni 'mɔː] nicht mehr **I**
not anymore *(AE)* [ˌnɒt‿eni'mɔː] nicht mehr **IV**
not necessarily [ˌnɒt nesə'serəli] nicht notwendigerweise; nicht unbedingt **IV**
not only … but (also) [ˌnɒt‿əʊnli … bʌt‿'ɔːlsəʊ] nicht nur … sondern (auch) **V U2**, 56
not until [ˌnɒt‿ən'tɪl] nicht vor; erst um/im **IV**
not … any [nɒt … eni] kein/-e/-en **I**
not … anything [ˌnɒt 'eniθɪŋ] nichts **I**
not … either [nɒt … 'aɪðə; nɒt … 'iːðə] auch nicht **IV**
not … yet [nɒt 'jet] noch nicht **II**
notch [nɒtʃ] *hier:* Klasse ⟨**V U2**, 47⟩
note [nəʊt] Notiz; Anmerkung **I**
*to make **notes** [ˌmeɪk 'nəʊts] Notizen machen **I**
*to take **notes** [ˌteɪk 'nəʊts] sich Notizen machen **I**
to **note** down [ˌnəʊt 'daʊn] notieren; aufschreiben **II**
nothing ['nʌθɪŋ] nichts **I**
to **notice** ['nəʊtɪs] bemerken; wahrnehmen **II**
noticeboard ['nəʊtɪsbɔːd] schwarzes Brett **II**
noun [naʊn] Nomen; Hauptwort **I**
collective **noun** [kə'lektɪv] Sammelbegriff °**V U3**, 93
novel ['nɒvl] Roman **III**
graphic **novel** [ˌgræfɪk 'nɒvl] Bildergeschichte; Comic **III**
November [nə'vembə] November **I**
now [naʊ] jetzt; nun **I**
right **now** [ˌraɪt 'naʊ] jetzt gleich; sofort; gerade **II**
nowhere ['nəʊweə] nirgendwo; nirgendwohin **II**
in the middle of **nowhere** [ɪn ðə ˌmɪdl‿əv 'nəʊweə] mitten im Nirgendwo **IV**
to **nudge** [nʌdʒ] schubsen; stupsen ⟨**V U1**, 29⟩
number ['nʌmbə] Zahl; Nummer **I**
nurse [nɜːs] Krankenschwester; Krankenpfleger **III**
nut [nʌt] Nuss **I**
nutrition [njuː'trɪʃn] Ernährung ⟨**V U3**, 97⟩

O

o'clock [ə'klɒk] Uhr *(Zeitangabe bei vollen Stunden)* **I**
oak [əʊk] Eiche **III**
to **obey** [ə'beɪ] gehorchen **IV**
object ['ɒbdʒɪkt] Objekt **II**; Gegenstand **III**
object pronoun [ˌɒbdʒɪkt 'prəʊnaʊn] Objektpronomen **III**
objective [əb'dʒektɪv] objektiv **VTS2**, 78
objectivity [ˌɒbdʒek'tɪvəti] Objektivität ⟨**VTS2**, 79⟩
to be **obliged** to *(+ inf)* [biː‿ə'blaɪdʒd tə] verpflichtet sein, etw. zu tun; müssen **V U3**, 95
to **observe** [əb'zɜːv] beobachten; beachten; befolgen **V U3**, 85
obstacle ['ɒbstəkl] Hindernis **V U3**, 99
obvious ['ɒbviəs] offensichtlich **IV**
occupation [ˌɒkjə'peɪʃn] Beruf; Beschäftigung **V U1**, 20
October [ɒk'təʊbə] Oktober **I**
against all **odds** [əˌgenst‿ɔːl‿'ɒdz] entgegen allen Erwartungen **III**
odd [ɒd] seltsam; komisch **III**
of [ɒv; əv] von **I**
of course [əv 'kɔːs] natürlich; selbstverständlich **I**
of one's own [ˌəv wʌnz‿'əʊn] eigen **III**
to drop sb **off** [ˌdrɒp‿'ɒf] jmdn. absetzen; jmdn. aussteigen lassen **IV**
*to take **off** [ˌteɪk‿'ɒf] abnehmen; herunternehmen; ausziehen **I**
*to take the day **off** [ˌteɪk ðə ˌdeɪ‿'ɒf] sich den Tag freinehmen **IV**
to turn **off** [ˌtɜːn‿'ɒf] abschalten; ausschalten **II**
to **offend** [ə'fend] beleidigen; verletzen **V AC2**, 83
special **offer** [ˌspeʃl‿'ɒfə] Sonderangebot **I**
to **offer** ['ɒfə] anbieten **II**
office ['ɒfɪs] Büro **I**
front **office** [ˌfrʌnt 'ɒfɪs] *hier:* Büro ⟨**V U1**, 28⟩
immigration **office** [ˌɪmɪ'greɪʃn ˌɒfɪs] Einwanderungsbehörde **III**
ticket **office** ['tɪkɪt ˌɒfɪs] Kartenschalter **III**
police **officer** [pə'liːs‿ɒfɪsə] Polizeibeamter; Polizist/-in **II**
official [ə'fɪʃl] Schiedsrichter/-in **II**; Beamter/Beamtin **III**
official [ə'fɪʃl] offiziell **III**
official language [əˌfɪʃl 'læŋgwɪdʒ] Amtssprache **II**
offline ['ɒflaɪn] offline **II**
often ['ɒfn] oft; häufig **I**
oh [əʊ] null *(bei Telefonnummern und Uhrzeitangaben)* **I**
Oh! [əʊ] O! **I**
Oh dear! [ˌəʊ 'dɪə] Oje! **II**
ointment ['ɔɪntmənt] Salbe **II**
OK [əʊ'keɪ] o.k.; in Ordnung **I**
okay [ə'keɪ] okay **III**
old [əʊld] alt **I**
the **old** [ðiˌ'əʊld] die Alten ⟨**V U2**, 62⟩
How **old** are you? [haʊ‿'əʊld‿ə ˌjuː] Wie alt bist du?; Wie alt sind Sie? **I**
11-year-**old** [ɪˌlevn'jɪərəʊld] 11-Jährige/-r **II**
old-timer [ˌəʊld'taɪmə] alter Hase ⟨**V U3**, 102⟩
OMG! (Oh my god!) [ˌəʊ maɪ 'gɒd] OMG! (Oh mein Gott!) **IV**
on [ɒn] auf; an; am; in; im **I**
*to be **on** [bi‿'ɒn] an sein; laufen **II**; auf Sendung sein °**V U3**, 97
on a shoestring [ˌɒn‿ə 'ʃuːstrɪŋ] für/mit wenig Geld **IV**
on average [ɒn‿'ævrɪdʒ] durchschnittlich; im Durchschnitt **V U3**, 95
on Mondays [ɒn 'mʌndeɪz] montags **I**
on one's own [ˌɒn wʌnz‿'əʊn] allein; für sich **V U1**, 14
on the brink of [ˌɒn ðə 'brɪŋk‿əv] am Rande von; kurz vor **III**
on the inside [ˌɒn ði‿'ɪnsaɪd] innen **IV**
on the left [ɒn ðə 'left] auf der linken Seite; links **I**
on the move [ˌɒn‿ðə 'muːv] unterwegs **III**
on the outside [ˌɒn ði‿'aʊtsaɪd] außen **IV**
on the right [ɒn ðə 'raɪt] auf der rechten Seite; rechts **I**
on time [ɒn 'taɪm] pünktlich **II**
on top [ɒn 'tɒp] oben; obendrauf **I**
Come **on**! [ˌkʌm‿'ɒn] Komm schon!; Komm jetzt! **I**
once [wʌns] einmal; einst **I**
one [wʌn] eins **I**
no **one** ['nəʊ wʌn] niemand ⟨**V U2**, 62⟩
one day [wʌn 'deɪ] eines Tages **II**
one-way ticket ['wʌnweɪ ˌtɪkɪt] einfache Fahrkarte **II**
one [wʌn], **ones** [wʌnz] *(pl)* eine/-r/-s **II**
one-sided [ˌwʌn'saɪdɪd] einseitig **VTS3**, 108
online [ˌɒn'laɪn] online **II**

onlooker ['ɒnˌlʊkə] Zuschauer/-in **VTS1**, 44
only ['əʊnli] einzige/-r/-s **II**
only ['əʊnli] erst; bloß; nur **I**
not **only** … but (also) [nɒtˌəʊnli … bʌtˈɔ:lsəʊ] nicht nur … sondern (auch) **V U2**, 56
only child ['əʊnli ˌtʃaɪld] Einzelkind **I**
onto ['ɒntə] auf … hinauf **V U2**, 53
Oops! [u:ps] Hoppla!; Huch! **I**
to **open** ['əʊpn] öffnen; aufmachen **I**; *hier:* beginnen **III**; eröffnen **IV**
open ['əʊpn] offen; geöffnet; aufgeschlagen **I**
to flick **open** [flɪkˈəʊpn] schnell öffnen; schnell aufmachen ⟨**V U1**, 30⟩
*to hold **open** [ˌhəʊldˈəʊpn] aufhalten **III**
opening ['əʊpnɪŋ] Öffnung; Beginn **III**
opening line ['əʊpnɪŋˌlaɪn] der erste Satz **III**
opinion [ə'pɪnjən] Meinung **II**
opportunity [ˌɒpə'tju:nəti] Chance; Gelegenheit; Möglichkeit **V U2**, 48
opposite ['ɒpəzɪt] Gegenteil °**V U2**, 67
opposite ['ɒpəzɪt] gegenüber; auf der anderen Seite von **I**
to **oppress** [ə'pres] unterdrücken **V U1**, 18
optimistic [ˌɒptɪ'mɪstɪk] optimistisch **III**
option ['ɒpʃn] Möglichkeit; Wahl; Option **III**
or [ɔ:] oder **I**
either … **or** … ['aɪðə/'i:ðə … ɔ:] entweder … oder … **IV**
oral ['ɔ:rl] mündlich **IV**
orange ['ɒrɪndʒ] Orange **I**
orange ['ɒrɪndʒ] orange **I**
orca ['ɔ:kə] Schwertwal **IV**
order ['ɔ:də] Reihenfolge; Ordnung **I**; Befehl **III**
in **order** to [ɪnˈɔ:də tə] um … zu; mit der Absicht **IV**
out of **order** [ˌaʊtˌəv 'ɔ:də] kaputt; außer Betrieb **III**
word **order** ['wɜ:dˌɔ:də] Wortstellung; Satzstellung **I**
to **order** ['ɔ:də] bestellen **III**
ordinary ['ɔ:dnri] gewöhnlich; normal **V U2**, 65
organisation [ˌɔ:gnaɪ'zeɪʃn] Organisation **II**
to **organise** ['ɔ:gənaɪz] organisieren **I**
*to get **organised** [get 'ɔ:gənaɪzd] sich organisieren **II**
organiser ['ɔ:gənaɪzə] Organisator/-in **V U2**, 50
to **organize** *(AE)* ['ɔ:gənaɪz] organisieren **IV**
orientation [ˌɔ:riən'teɪʃn] Orientierung; Orientierungs- **IV**
origin ['ɒrɪdʒɪn] Ursprung; Herkunft; Abstammung **III**
original [ə'rɪdʒnl] Original **III**
original [ə'rɪdʒnl] original; ursprünglich **III**
orphanage ['ɔ:fnɪdʒ] Waisenhaus ⟨**V U1**, 23⟩
other ['ʌðə] anders; andere/-r/-s; weitere **I**
each **other** [ˌi:tʃˈʌðə] einander; sich; sich gegenseitig **I**
the **others** [ðiˈʌðəz] die anderen **I**
the **other** way around [ðiˌʌðə weɪ 'raʊnd] andersrum; umgekehrt ⟨**V U3**, 102⟩
otherwise ['ʌðəwaɪz] sonst **IV**
Ouch! [aʊtʃ] Aua! **II**
ouchie ['aʊtʃi] aua ⟨**VTS1**, 40⟩
ought to *(+ inf)* ['ɔ:t tə] sollen **V U3**, 95
our [aʊə; ɑ:] unser/-e **I**
out [aʊt] außerhalb; heraus; hinaus; nach draußen **I**
to clean **out** [ˌkli:nˈaʊt] ausräumen; entrümpeln **IV**
to clear **out** [ˌklɪərˈaʊt] ausräumen; entrümpeln **I**
*to come **out** [ˌkʌmˈaʊt] sich outen **V AC2**, 82
to drop **out** (of) [ˌdrɒp 'aʊtˌəv] abbrechen **III**
*to hang **out** (with) *(infml)* [ˌhæŋˈaʊt wɪð] sich herumtreiben (mit); rumhängen (mit); sich treffen (mit) **III**
*to leave **out** [ˌli:vˈaʊt] auslassen; weglassen **IV**
to miss **out** on sth [ˌmɪsˈaʊtˌɒn] etw. verpassen ⟨**V AC1**, 11⟩
out and about [ˌaʊtˌənˌə'baʊt] unterwegs **II**
out of ['aʊtˌəv] aus … heraus **III**
out of focus [ˌaʊtˌəv 'fəʊkəs] unscharf **III**
out of order [ˌaʊtˌəv 'ɔ:də] kaputt; außer Betrieb **III**
to pick **out** [ˌpɪkˈaʊt] aussuchen; auswählen; heraushören; herausfiltern; herauslesen °**VTS3**, 112
to toss **out** [ˌtɒsˈaʊt] ausstoßen; hinauswerfen **IV**
to turn **out** to be [ˌtɜ:nˈaʊt tə] sich herausstellen als ⟨**V U1**, 21⟩Ø °**V U2**, 67
a day **out** in … [ə ˌdeɪˈaʊt ɪn] ein Tag in … **II**
the **outback** [ði 'aʊtbæk] Outback *(australisches Hinterland)* **V AC1**, 10
outcome ['aʊtkʌm] Ergebnis; Resultat **VTS2**, 77
outdated [ˌaʊt'deɪtɪd] veraltet; überholt **VTS3**, 111
outdoor [ˌaʊt'dɔ:] Freiluft-; Outdoor- **II**
outdoors [ˌaʊt'dɔ:z] im Freien **V U3**, 95
the **outdoors** [ði ˌaʊt'dɔ:z] die Natur **IV**
outfit ['aʊtfɪt] Outfit; Kleidung **II**
outgoing [aʊt'gəʊɪŋ] kontaktfreudig **III**
outlaw ['aʊtlɔ:] Geächtete/-r; Gesetzlose/-r **II**
outline ['aʊtlaɪn] Skizze; Umriss **II**
to **outline** ['aʊtlaɪn] skizzieren; umreißen °**V U2**, 63
out-of-character [ˌaʊtəv'kærəktə] ungewöhnlich **IV**
outrage ['aʊtreɪdʒ] Empörung ⟨**VTS3**, 113⟩
outside [aʊt'saɪd] nach draußen; draußen; außerhalb **I**
from the **outside** [ˌfrəm ðiˌaʊt'saɪd] von außen **IV**
on the **outside** [ˌɒn ðiˈaʊtsaɪd] außen **IV**
outside world ['aʊtsaɪd ˌwɜ:ld] Außenwelt **IV**
outward ['aʊtwəd] abfahrend **II**
over ['əʊvə] hinüber; über **I**; vorüber; vorbei **II**
*to bend **over** [ˌbendˈəʊvə] sich vorbeugen; sich beugen über ⟨**V U2**, 63⟩
*to go **over** to [ˌgəʊ 'əʊvə tə] hinübergehen zu; zu jmdm. nach Hause gehen **II**
over and **over** again [ˌəʊvərˌənˌəʊvərˌə'gen] immer wieder **III**
over to … ['əʊvə tə] weiter zu … **V U1**, 26
*to run **over** [ˌrʌnˈəʊvə] überfahren **IV**
*to win sb **over** [ˌwɪnˈəʊvə] jmdn. für sich gewinnen; jmdn. überzeugen **IV**
overall [ˌəʊvr'ɔ:l] allgemein; Gesamt-; insgesamt **IV**
overall [ˌəʊvr'ɔ:l] insgesamt **IV**
*to **overcome** [ˌəʊvə'kʌm] überwinden **V U3**, 99
*to **overdo** [əʊvə'du:] übertreiben; zu weit gehen **IV**
to **over-exaggerate** [ˌəʊvərɪg'zædʒreɪt] völlig übertreiben **IV**
*to **overhear** [ˌəʊvə'hɪə] belauschen, zufällig mit anhören **V U1**, 14
to **overlap** [ˌəʊvə'læp] (sich) überlappen **IV**
overloaded [ˌəʊvə'ləʊdɪd] überladen **III**
overnight [ˌəʊvə'naɪt] über Nacht **III**
to **overreact** [ˌəʊvəri'ækt] überreagieren **II**
overseas [ˌəʊvə'si:z] in Übersee; im Ausland **V U1**, 20
to **own** [əʊn] besitzen **IV**
own [əʊn] eigene/-r/-s **I**
of one's **own** [ˌəv wʌnzˈəʊn] eigen **III**
on one's **own** [ˌɒn wʌnzˈəʊn] allein; für sich **V U1**, 14
owner ['əʊnə] Besitzer/-in **V U1**, 14

P

p.m. [ˌpi:'em] nachmittags *(Uhrzeit)*; abends *(Uhrzeit)* **I**
Pa [pɑ:] Papa **IV**
to **pack** [pæk] packen; einpacken **IV**
to **pack** up ['pækˌʌp] zusammenpacken **V U3**, 86
to **package** ['pækɪdʒ] verpacken °**VTS1**, 41
muscle-**packed** ['mʌslˌpækt] muskelbepackt ⟨**V U3**, 92⟩
packet ['pækɪt] Päckchen; Paket; Packung **I**
to **paddle** ['pædl] paddeln **IV**
paddleboard ['pædlbɔ:d] Paddling Board *(eine Art Surfbrett, auf dem man aufrecht stehend paddelt)* **IV**
page [peɪdʒ] Seite **I**
pain [peɪn] Schmerz **II**

to paint [peɪnt] anmalen; malen **I**
painting ['peɪntɪŋ] Malerei; Gemälde **II**
pair [peə] Paar **I**
pair work ['peə wɜ:k] Partnerarbeit **II**
to pair [peə] Paare bilden **III**
to **pair** up [peər‿'ʌp] Paare bilden ⟨**V TS3**, 113⟩
pale [peɪl] blass **V U1**, 29
palm [pɑ:m] Handfläche ⟨**V U1**, 29⟩
palm tree ['pɑ:m ˌtri:] Palme **II**
Pampers ['pæmpəz] Windeln ⟨**V U3**, 102⟩
panel ['pænl] Bild *(eines Comics)* **IV**; Gruppe; Team °**V U2**, 61
to panic ['pænɪk] panisch werden **II**
pants *(pl)* [pænts] Hose ⟨**V U3**, 92⟩
paparazzo [ˌpæpr'ætsəʊ] Paparazzo ⟨**V U3**, 101⟩
paper ['peɪpə] Papier **I**
piece of **paper** [ˌpi:s‿əv 'peɪpə] Stück Papier **I**
papers *(pl)* ['peɪpəz] Unterlagen; Papiere **IV**
parade [pə'reɪd] Parade ⟨**V U1**, 30⟩
paradise ['pærədaɪs] Paradies **II**
paragraph ['pærəgrɑ:f] Paragraf; Absatz **IV**
parallel ['pærəlel] Parallele °**V U1**, 31
to paraphrase ['pærəfreɪz] paraphrasieren; umschreiben **IV**
parcel ['pɑ:sl] Paket; Päckchen **I**
parents *(pl)* ['peərənts] Eltern **I**
park [pɑ:k] Park **I**
national **park** [ˌnæʃnl 'pɑ:k] Nationalpark; Naturpark **IV**
RV **park** *(AE)* [ˌɑ:'vi: ˌpɑ:k] Campingplatz **V U3**, 86
parking lot ['pɑ:kɪŋ ˌlɒt] Parkplatz **IV**
parliament ['pɑ:ləmənt] Parlament **V AC1**, 8
part [pɑ:t] Teil; Stadtteil **I**; Rolle **III**
lead **part** [ˌli:d 'pɑ:t] Hauptrolle **III**
*to take **part** (in) [ˌteɪk 'pɑ:t (ɪn)] teilnehmen (an) **II**
partially sighted [ˌpɑ:ʃəli 'saɪtɪd] sehbehindert **II**
to participate [pɑ:'tɪsɪpeɪt] teilnehmen **II**
participation [pɑ:ˌtɪsɪ'peɪʃn] Mitwirkung; Beteiligung **V AC3**, 114
participle [pɑ:'tɪsɪpl] Partizip **IV**
past **participle** [ˌpɑ:st pɑ:'tɪsɪpl] Partizip **II**
present **participle** [ˌpreznt pɑ:'tɪsɪpl] Partizip Präsens **IV**
particular [pə'tɪkjələ] bestimmte/-r/-s **III**
in **particular** [ˌɪn pə'tɪkjələ] im besonderen **V TS2**, 77
particularly [pə'tɪkjələli] besonders **IV**
partner ['pɑ:tnə] Partner/-in **I**
part-time [ˌpɑ:t'taɪm] Teilzeit-; Halbtags- **IV**
party ['pɑ:ti] Party; Feier **I**; Partei **III**
hall pass ['hɔ:l pɑ:s] *Erlaubnis, sich während des Unterrichts auf dem Flur aufzuhalten* **IV**
to pass [pɑ:s] zupassen; zuspielen **II**; durchgehen; vorbeigehen (an); passieren; bestehen **IV**
to **pass** (on) [ˌpɑ:s‿'ɒn] weitergeben **I**
passenger ['pæsndʒə] Passagier/-in; Fahrgast **III**
passenger seat ['pæsndʒə ˌsi:t] Beifahrersitz **IV**
***to be passionate about sth** [bi 'pæʃnət əˌbaʊt] etw. leidenschaftlich gern tun; eine Leidenschaft für etw. haben; für etw. brennen **V U2**, 48
passive ['pæsɪv] Passiv **III**
passive progressive [ˌpæsɪv prə'gresɪv] Verlaufsform des Passivs °**V U1**, 19
passive ['pæsɪv] passiv **III**
passport ['pɑ:spɔ:t] Pass; Reisepass **III**
past [pɑ:st] Vergangenheit **II**
past form ['pɑ:st fɔ:m] Vergangenheitsform **II**
past participle [ˌpɑ:st pɑ:'tɪsɪpl] Partizip **II**
past perfect [ˌpɑ:st 'pɜ:fɪkt] Plusquamperfekt **III**
past perfect progressive [ˌpɑ:st ˌpɜ:fɪkt prə'gresɪv] Verlaufsform des Plusquamperfekts **IV**
past progressive [ˌpɑ:st prə'gresɪv] Verlaufsform der Vergangenheit **II**
simple **past** [ˌsɪmpl 'pɑ:st] Vergangenheitsform **II**
past [pɑ:st] letzte/-r/-s; vergangen °**V U2**, 67
past [pɑ:st] nach *(bei Uhrzeitangaben)*; vorbei (an); vorüber (an) **I**
half **past** [ˌhɑ:f 'pɑ:st] halb *(bei Uhrzeitangaben)* **I**
quarter **past**/to ['kwɔ:tə pɑ:st/tə] Viertel nach/vor **I**
pasta ['pæstə] Pasta; Nudeln **I**
pastry ['peɪstri] Teig; Teigtasche **IV**
patch [pætʃ] Fleck; Stelle ⟨**V U1**, 30⟩
path [pɑ:θ] Pfad; Weg **IV**
coastal **path** [ˌkəʊstl 'pɑ:θ] Küstenweg **II**
patient ['peɪʃnt] geduldig **V U2**, 56
pattern ['pætn] Muster **II**
pause [pɔ:z] Pause **III**
to pause [pɔ:z] (eine kurze) Pause machen; innehalten ⟨**V U2**, 64⟩
pawn shop ['pɔ:n ʃɒp] Pfandhaus; Pfandleihe **III**
pay [peɪ] Lohn; Gehalt **V U2**, 56
***to pay (for)** [peɪ] bezahlen **I**
*to **pay** attention to sb/sth [ˌpeɪ‿ə'tenʃn tʊ] jmdn./etw. beachten **III**
That doesn't **pay** my rent. [ˌdət dʌznt ˌpeɪ maɪ 'rent] Davon kann ich meine Miete nicht bezahlen. **V U3**, 93
PC *(= Personal Computer)* [pi:'si:] PC **II**
PE *(= Physical Education)* [ˌpi:'i:; ˌfɪzɪkl‿edʒʊ'keɪʃn] Sportunterricht **II**
peace [pi:s] Frieden **IV**
peaceful ['pi:sfl] friedlich **IV**
peach [pi:tʃ] Pfirsich **III**
peak [pi:k] Haupt-; Spitzen- **IV**
pedestrian [pɪ'destriən] Fußgänger/-in; Fußgänger- **V AC2**, 81
peer evaluation [ˌpɪər‿ɪˌvælju'eɪʃn] gegenseitige Beurteilung ⟨**V AC2**, 83⟩
peer pressure ['pɪə ˌpreʃə] Gruppenzwang **III**
to peer at ['pɪər‿ət] anschauen ⟨**V U2**, 64⟩
to peer-edit ['pɪər‿ˌedɪt] gegenseitig kontrollieren **II**
peer-editing ['pɪər‿ˌedɪtɪŋ] gegenseitige Kontrolle °**V TS2**, 76
pen [pen] Füller **I**
penal colony ['pi:nl ˌkɒləni] Strafkolonie ⟨**V U1**, 20⟩
pencil ['pensl] Bleistift; Buntstift **I**
pencil-case ['pensl ˌkeɪs] Federmäppchen; Mäppchen **I**
penicillin [ˌpenɪ'sɪlɪn] Penicillin **III**
penny ['peni], **pence** [pens] *(pl)* Penny; Pence *(brit. Währungseinheit)* **I**
penthouse ['penthaʊs] Penthouse; Wohnung mit Dachterrasse **IV**
people ['pi:pl] Volk **IV**
people *(pl)* ['pi:pl] Leute; Menschen **I**
medicine **people** ['medsn ˌpi:pl] Medizinmänner **IV**
people skills *(pl)* ['pi:pl ˌskɪlz] soziale Kompetenz **V U2**, 50
per [pɜ:; pə] pro **II**
percent [pə'sent], **percent** [pə'sent] *(pl)* Prozent **IV**
perception [pə'sepʃn] Wahrnehmung °**V U2**, 54
future perfect [ˌfju:tʃə 'pɜ:fɪkt] vollendetes Futur; Futur II °**V U3**, 88
past **perfect** [ˌpɑ:st 'pɜ:fɪkt] Plusquamperfekt **III**
past **perfect** progressive [ˌpɑ:st ˌpɜ:fɪkt prə'gresɪv] Verlaufsform des Plusquamperfekts **IV**
present **perfect** [ˌpreznt 'pɜ:fɪkt] das Perfekt **II**
present **perfect** progressive [ˌpreznt ˌpɜ:fɪkt prə'gresɪv] Verlaufsform des Perfekts **III**
perfect ['pɜ:fɪkt] perfekt; vollkommen **I**
perfection [pə'fekʃn] Perfektion; Vollkommenheit **V TS3**, 111
to perform [pə'fɔ:m] aufführen; auftreten **IV**
performance [pə'fɔ:məns] Aufführung; Vorstellung **III**; Leistung **V TS2**, 77
perhaps [pə'hæps] vielleicht **III**
period ['pɪəriəd] Periode; Zeitspanne **III**
period *(AE)* ['pɪəriəd] Stunde; Unterrichtsstunde **IV**
periphery [pə'rɪfri] Rand; Peripherie ⟨**V U1**, 30⟩
permanent ['pɜ:mnənt] permanent; dauerhaft **IV**
permission [pə'mɪʃn] Erlaubnis; Genehmigung **V U1**, 23
access permit ['ækses ˌpɜ:mɪt] Zugangsberechtigung ⟨**V U1**, 30⟩

to **permit** [pə'mɪt] erlauben; genehmigen ⟨**V U2**, 63⟩
to **persist** [pə'sɪst] beharren ⟨**V U3**, 100⟩
persistent [pə'sɪstnt] hartnäckig; ausdauernd; beharrlich **V U3**, 86
person ['pɜːsn], **people** ['piːpl] *(pl)* Person; Mensch **I**
first **person** narrator [ˌfɜːst ˌpɜːsn nə'reɪtə] Ich-Erzähler/-in **III**
third **person** narrator [ˌθɜːd ˌpɜːsn nə'reɪtə] Er/Sie-Erzähler/-in **III**
personal ['pɜːsnl] persönlich **I**
personal prounoun [ˌpɜːsnl 'prəʊnaʊn] Personalpronomen °**VTS3**, 109
personality [ˌpɜːsn'æləti] Persönlichkeit **III**
perspective [pə'spektɪv] Perspektive; Blickwinkel **II**
narrative **perspective** [ˌnærətɪv pə'spektɪv] Erzählperspektive **III**
to **persuade** [pə'sweɪd] überreden **II**
persuasive [pə'sweɪsɪv] überzeugend **III**
pet [pet] Haustier **I**
petition [pə'tɪʃn] Petition; Unterschriftenliste **V AC3**, 114
phone [fəʊn] Telefon; Handy **I**
to answer the **phone** [ˌɑːnsə ðə 'fəʊn] einen Anruf entgegennehmen **I**
cell **phone** *(AE)* ['selfəʊn] Mobiltelefon; Handy **IV**
phone box ['fəʊn ˌbɒks] Telefonzelle **III**
phone call ['fəʊn ˌkɔːl] Anruf; Telefonanruf **I**
rotary **phone** ['rəʊtri fəʊn] Telefon mit Wählscheibe **III**
to **phone** [fəʊn] anrufen; telefonieren **III**
photo ['fəʊtəʊ] Foto; Fotografie **I**
in the **photo**(s) [ˌɪn ðə 'fəʊtəʊ(z)] auf dem Foto/den Fotos **I**
photo shoot ['fəʊtəʊ ˌʃuːt] Fotoshooting; Fotoaufnahmen **III**
photo story ['fəʊtəʊ ˌstɔːri] Fotostory; Bildgeschichte **I**
*to take **photos** [ˌteɪk 'fəʊtəʊz] fotografieren; Fotos machen **I**
to **photobomb** ['fəʊtəʊbɒm] ins Foto laufen **III**
to **photograph** ['fəʊtəgrɑːf] fotografieren **V U3**, 101
photographer [fə'tɒgrəfə] Fotograf/-in **III**
phrase [freɪz] Redewendung; Ausdruck; Satz **I**
set **phrase** [set 'freɪs] Floskel; feststehender Ausdruck °**VTS2**, 78
Useful **phrases** [ˌjuːsfl 'freɪsɪz] nützliche Ausdrücke **I**
physical ['fɪzɪkl] physisch; körperlich **V U2**, 53
piano [pi'ænəʊ] Klavier; Piano **IV**
to **pick** [pɪk] auswählen; aussuchen **II**; pflücken **V U1**, 17
to **pick** out [ˌpɪk‿'aʊt] aussuchen; auswählen; heraushören; herausfiltern; herauslesen °**VTS3**, 112
to **pick** up [ˌpɪk‿'ʌp] aufheben; mitnehmen; abholen **III**
pick-up ['pɪkʌp] Pick-up; Wiederaufnehmen **I**
picnic ['pɪknɪk] Picknick **I**
picture ['pɪktʃə] Bild; Foto **I**
motion **picture** [ˌməʊʃn 'pɪktʃə] Film; Spielfilm **IV**
*to see the bigger **picture** [ˌsiː ðə ˌbɪgə 'pɪktʃə] über den Tellerrand hinausschauen **IV**
to **picture** ['pɪktʃə] sich vorstellen ⟨**V U2**, 63⟩
pie [paɪ] Kuchen; Pastete **I**
pie chart ['paɪ ˌtʃɑːt] Kuchendiagramm; Tortendiagramm **IV**
piece [piːs] Stück **I**
piece of junk [ˌpiːs‿əv 'dʒʌŋk] Stück Schrott **III**
piece of paper [ˌpiːs‿əv 'peɪpə] Stück Papier **I**
pier [pɪə] Pier; Hafendamm **I**
pig [pɪg] Schwein **I**
guinea **pig** ['gɪniː ˌpɪg] Meerschweinchen **I**
*to give sb a **piggyback** [gɪv‿ə 'pɪgibæk] jmdn. Huckepack nehmen **III**
Pilgrim ['pɪlgrɪm] Pilger/-in **IV**
pill [pɪl] Pille; Tablette **II**
pilot ['paɪlət] Pilot/-in **II**
pineapple ['paɪnæpl] Ananas **III**
pink [pɪŋk] pink; rosa **I**
pioneer [ˌpaɪə'nɪə] Pionier/-in **IV**
pipe [paɪp] Rohr; Rohrleitung; Pfeife **II**
clay **pipe** ['kleɪ paɪp] Tonpfeife **II**
pitch [pɪtʃ] Spielfeld; Platz **II**
pizza ['piːtsə] Pizza **I**
place [pleɪs] Ort; Stelle; Platz **I**
starting **place** ['stɑːtɪŋ pleɪs] Startpunkt **II**
*to take **place** [ˌteɪk 'pleɪs] stattfinden **I**
in the first **place** [ɪn ðə 'fɜːst ˌpleɪs] überhaupt erst; von vornherein ⟨**VTS3**, 109⟩
to **place** [pleɪs] legen **II**; unterbringen **V U1**, 23
placemat ['pleɪsmæt] Placemat; Platzdeckchen **I**
plan [plæn] Plan; Entwurf **I**
to **plan** [plæn] planen **I**
plane [pleɪn] Flugzeug **III**
tanker **plane** ['tæŋkə ˌpleɪn] Tankflugzeug **V U3**, 94
planet ['plænɪt] Planet **II**
planner ['plænə] Handbuch; Kalender **I**
route **planner** ['ruːt ˌplænə] Routenplaner **IV**
plant [plɑːnt] Pflanze **II**
to **plant** [plɑːnt] pflanzen; anpflanzen **II**
plantation [plæn'teɪʃn] Plantage **V U2**, 53
plaster cast ['plɑːstə kɑːst] Gipsverband **III**
plastic ['plæstɪk] Plastik; Kunststoff; Plastik- **V U2**, 58
plastic surgery *(no pl)* [ˌplæstɪk 'sɜːdʒəri] Schönheitschirurgie **V AC1**, 9
plate [pleɪt] Teller **III**
platform ['plætfɔːm] Plattform; Bahnsteig **II**
platinum *(no pl)* ['plætɪnəm] Platin ⟨**V AC1**, 8⟩
play [pleɪ] Theaterstück **III**
fair **play** [feə 'pleɪ] Fairplay **III**
play on words [ˌpleɪ‿ɒn 'wɜːdz] Wortspiel **III**
role **play** ['rəʊl ˌpleɪ] Rollenspiel **I**
to **play** [pleɪ] spielen **I**
to **play** a trick (on) [ˌpleɪ‿ə 'trɪk‿ɒn] einen Streich spielen **I**
to **play** bowls [ˌpleɪ 'bəʊlz] Bowling spielen **III**
player ['pleɪə] Spieler/-in; Mitspieler/-in **II**
*to be a team **player** [ˌbi‿ə 'tiːm ˌpleɪə] gern im Team arbeiten **V U2**, 48
Please. [pliːz] Bitte. **I**
pleasure ['pleʒə] Freude; Vergnügen ⟨**V U2**, 63⟩
plenty of ['plenti‿əv] eine Menge **VTS2**, 78
plot [plɒt] Handlung **III**
plumber ['plʌmə] Installateur/-in; Klempner/-in **II**
plumbing ['plʌmɪŋ] Sanitärarbeit **II**
plural ['plʊərəl] Plural; Mehrzahl **I**
poaching *(no pl)* ['pəʊtʃɪŋ] Wilderei **III**
pocket ['pɒkɪt] Tasche; Hosentasche **III**
pocket money ['pɒkɪt ˌmʌni] Taschengeld **I**
a **pocketful** of [ə 'pɒkɪtfl‿əv] Unmengen von/an **IV**
pod [pɒd] Hülse; Schote **V U2**, 53
podcast ['pɒdkɑːst] Podcast **IV**
poem ['pəʊɪm] Gedicht **I**
point [pɔɪnt] Punkt; Zeitpunkt **II**
*to have a **point** [ˌhæv‿ə 'pɔɪnt] nicht ganz Unrecht haben **III**
*to make one's **point** [ˌmeɪk wʌnz 'pɔɪnt] seinen Standpunkt deutlich machen **V AC3**, 114
point of view [ˌpɔɪnt‿əv 'vjuː] Standpunkt; Ansicht; Perspektive **II**
to the **point** [tə ðə 'pɔɪnt] prägnant; treffend **III**
turning **point** ['tɜːnɪŋ ˌpɔɪnt] Wendepunkt **III**
I can't see the **point** of … [aɪ ˌkɑːnt siː ðə 'pɔɪnt‿əv] Ich sehe keinen Sinn darin … **IV**
My **point** is … [ˌmaɪ 'pɔɪnt‿ɪz] Was ich sagen will ist, … **VTS3**, 109
to **point** at sb/sth ['pɔɪnt æt] mit dem Finger auf jmdn./etw. zeigen **III**
to **point** out sth [ˌpɔɪnt‿'aʊt] hinweisen auf etw. **IV**
to **point** to ['pɔɪnt tə] deuten auf; hindeuten auf; zeigen auf **VTS2**, 77
totem **pole** ['təʊtəm ˌpəʊl] Totempfahl **IV**

police [pə'li:s] Polizei **II**
police officer [pə'li:s‿ɒfɪsə] Polizeibeamter; Polizist/-in **II**
policy ['pɒləsi] Politik; politische Linie **V U1**, 20
polite [pə'laɪt] höflich **I**
political [pə'lɪtɪkl] politisch **IV**
politics *(pl only)* ['pɒlətɪks] Politik **V U3**, 99
pollution [pə'lu:ʃn] Verschmutzung **II**
pond [pɒnd] Teich **II**
pony ['pəʊni] Pony **I**
pony trekking ['pəʊni ˌtrekɪŋ] Ponyreiten im Gelände **II**
ponytail ['pəʊniteɪl] Pferdeschwanz ⟨**V U1**, 28⟩
swimming **pool** ['swɪmɪŋ ˌpu:l] Swimmingpool; Schwimmbecken **III**
poor [pɔ:; pʊə] arm **III**
the **poor** [ðə pʊə] die Armen **II**
soda **pop** *(AE)* ['səʊdə ˌpɒp] Limo **IV**
to **pop** home [ˌpɒp‿'həʊm] schnell zu Hause vorbeigehen ⟨**V U1**, 30⟩
popular ['pɒpjələ] beliebt; populär **I**; Pop- ⟨**V AC1**, 11⟩
populated ['pɒpjəleɪtɪd] bevölkert; besiedelt **IV**
population [ˌpɒpjə'leɪʃn] Bevölkerung; Population **IV**
populous ['pɒpjələs] bevölkerungsreich ⟨**V AC1**, 11⟩
pore [pɔ:] Pore ⟨**V U3**, 102⟩
pose [pəʊz] Pose; Haltung **IV**
position [pə'zɪʃn] Stelle; Position **V U2**, 48
positive ['pɒzətɪv] positiv **II**
possessive form [pəˌsesɪv 'fɔ:m] Possessivform **I**
possibility [ˌpɒsə'bɪləti] Möglichkeit **II**
possible ['pɒsəbl] möglich **I**
post [pəʊst] Post *(Eintrag im Internet)* **I**
to **post** [pəʊst] online stellen; posten **II**
postcard ['pəʊstkɑ:d] Postkarte **II**
poster ['pəʊstə] Poster **I**
class **poster** ['klɑ:s ˌpəʊstə] Klassenposter **I**
postman ['pəʊstmən] Briefträger **II**
pot [pɒt] Topf **V U3**, 85
melting **pot** ['meltɪŋ ˌpɒt] Schmelztiegel **IV**
potato [pə'teɪtəʊ], **potatoes** [pə'teɪtəʊz] *(pl)* Kartoffel **III**
mashed **potatoes** *(pl)* [ˌmæʃt pə'teɪtəʊz] Kartoffelpüree **III**
pound [paʊnd] Pfund *(Maßeinheit)* **IV**
pound (£) [paʊnd] Pfund *(brit. Währungseinheit)* **I**
to **pour** [pɔ:] einschenken; eingießen; schütten **I**
poverty ['pɒvəti] Armut **V U2**, 53
poverty line ['pɒvəti ˌlaɪn] Armutsgrenze **V U2**, 53
power [paʊə] Kraft; Macht; Stärke **II**
those in **power** [ˌðəʊz ɪn 'paʊə] die Regierenden; die Herrschenden **III**
power [paʊə] Strom; Elektrizität; Energie **IV**
power cut ['paʊə ˌkʌt] Stromausfall **II**
powerful ['paʊəfl] stark; mächtig **II**
practical ['præktɪkl] praktisch **II**
practice ['præktɪs] Training; Übung **III**; Praktik; Gewohnheit; Sitte ⟨**V U1**, 20⟩
to **practice** *(AE)* ['præktɪs] üben; ausüben; praktizieren; trainieren **IV**
to **practice** a religion [ˌpræktɪs‿ə rɪ'lɪdʒn] eine Religion ausüben **IV**
to **practise** ['præktɪs] üben; trainieren **I**
practising ['præktɪsɪŋ] Üben **I**
prairie ['preəri] Prärie **IV**
to **pray** [preɪ] beten **III**
precious ['preʃəs] wertvoll; kostbar **V U3**, 90
prediction [prɪ'dɪkʃn] Vorhersage; Voraussage **II**
to **prefer** [prɪ'fɜ:] vorziehen **IV**
preference ['prefrns] Vorliebe **IV**
prehistoric [ˌpri:hɪ'stɒrɪk] vorgeschichtlich **II**
prejudice ['predʒədɪs] Vorurteil **V AC2**, 80
*to be **prejudiced** against sb/sth [bi 'predʒədɪst əˌgenst] voreingenommen sein gegenüber jmdm./etw. **V AC2**, 81
premiere ['premieə] Premiere; Uraufführung **V U3**, 86
preparation [ˌprepr'eɪʃn] Vorbereitung **IV**
to **prepare** [prɪ'peə] vorbereiten; zubereiten **I**
preposition [ˌprepə'zɪʃn] Präposition **I**
pre-reading [ˌpri:'ri:dɪŋ] vor dem Lesen **I**
prescription [prɪ'skrɪpʃn] Rezept *(für Arzneimittel)* **II**
present ['preznt] Geschenk **I**
present ['preznt] Gegenwart; Präsens **II**
at **present** [ət 'preznt] derzeitig; momentan ⟨**V AC1**, 11⟩
present participle [ˌpreznt pɑ:'tɪsɪpl] Partizip Präsens **IV**
present perfect [ˌpreznt 'pɜ:fɪkt] das Perfekt **II**
present perfect progressive [ˌpreznt ˌpɜ:fɪkt prə'gresɪv] Verlaufsform des Perfekts **III**
present progressive [ˌpreznt prə'gresɪv] Verlaufsform des Präsens/der Gegenwart **I**
simple **present** [ˌsɪmpl 'preznt] Gegenwart; Präsens **I**
to **present** [prɪ'zent] präsentieren; vorstellen **I**
to **present** sb with sth [prɪ'zent wɪð] jmdm. etw. bieten **VTS3**, 111
present ['preznt] heutig; Gegenwarts- **III**
presentation [ˌprezn'teɪʃn] Präsentation; Vortrag **I**
presenter [prɪ'zentə] Moderator/-in **I**
president ['prezɪdnt] Präsident/-in **IV**
to **press** [pres] drücken; pressen **II**
peer **pressure** ['pɪə ˌpreʃə] Gruppenzwang **III**
to **pretend** [prɪ'tend] vortäuschen; tun als ob **III**
pretty ['prɪti] hübsch **III**
to **prevent** [prɪ'vent] verhindern; abhalten **V U1**, 26
pre-viewing [ˌpri:'vju:ɪŋ] vor dem Ansehen °**V AC2**, 82
previous ['pri:viəs] früher; vorherig; vorhergehend **V U1**, 29
price [praɪs] Preis **I**
primary school ['praɪmri ˌsku:l] Grundschule **I**
Prime Minister [ˌpraɪm 'mɪnɪstə] Premierminister/-in ⟨**V U1**, 23⟩
principal *(AE)* ['prɪnsɪpl] Schulleiter/-in **IV**
print [prɪnt] Druck ⟨**V U1**, 30⟩
to **print** [prɪnt] drucken °**V U2**, 51
print [prɪnt] gedruckt; Druck- **II**
printed ['prɪntɪd] gedruckt ⟨**V U2**, 63⟩
priority [praɪ'ɒrəti] Priorität; Vorrang **IV**
prison ['prɪzn] Gefängnis **II**
privacy ['prɪvəsi] Privatsphäre **V AC2**, 81
private detective [ˌpraɪvət dɪ'tektɪv] Privatdetektiv/-in **II**
prize [praɪz] Preis; Gewinn **I**
pro [prəʊ] Argument dafür **II**
pros and cons *(pl)* [ˌprəʊz‿ən 'kɒnz] Argumente für und gegen etw.; Pro und Kontra °**V U3**, 91
probably ['prɒbəbli] möglicherweise; wahrscheinlich **II**
problem ['prɒbləm] Problem; Schwierigkeit **I**
problematic [ˌprɒblə'mætɪk] problematisch; schwierig **V AC2**, 83
process ['prəʊsəs] Prozess °**V U3**, 99
to **produce** [prə'dju:s] herstellen; produzieren **III**
producer [prə'dju:sə] Produzent/-in **V U3**, 89
product ['prɒdʌkt] Produkt; Erzeugnis **IV**
production [prə'dʌkʃn] Produktion; Inszenierung **III**
profession [prə'feʃn] Beruf **V U2**, 49
professor [prə'fesə] Professor/-in **VTS2**, 77
profile ['prəʊfaɪl] Profil; Porträt **I**
to **profile** ['prəʊfaɪl] porträtieren ⟨**V U3**, 101⟩
program *(AE)* ['prəʊgræm] Programm; Sendung **IV**
space **program** ['speɪs ˌprəʊgræm] Raumfahrtprogramm **IV**
programme ['prəʊgræm] Programm; Sendung **II**
to **programme** ['prəʊgræm] programmieren °**V U2**, 67
progress ['prəʊgres] Fortschritt **II**
future **progressive** [ˌfju:tʃə prə'gresɪv] Verlaufsform der Zukunft °**V U3**, 88
passive **progressive** [ˌpæsɪv prə'gresɪv] Verlaufsform des Passivs °**V U1**, 19
past perfect **progressive** [ˌpɑ:st ˌpɜ:fɪkt prə'gresɪv] Verlaufsform des Plusquamperfekts **IV**

past **progressive** [ˌpɑːst prəˈgresɪv] Verlaufsform der Vergangenheit **II**
present perfect **progressive** [ˌpreznt ˌpɜːfɪkt prəˈgresɪv] Verlaufsform des Perfekts **III**
present **progressive** [ˌpreznt prəˈgresɪv] Verlaufsform des Präsens/der Gegenwart **I**
to **prohibit** [prəˈhɪbɪt] untersagen; verbieten ⟨**V U2**, 63⟩
project [ˈprɒdʒekt] Projekt **I**
to **promise** [ˈprɒmɪs] versprechen **II**
prompt [prɒmpt] Stichwort **III**
prompt card [ˈprɒmpt kɑːd] Stichwortkarte; Rollenkarte **II**
pronoun [ˈprəʊnaʊn] Pronomen; Fürwort **IV**
object **pronoun** [ˌɒbdʒɪkt ˈprəʊnaʊn] Objektpronomen **III**
reflexive **pronoun** [rɪˌfleksɪv ˈprəʊnaʊn] Reflexivpronomen **III**
relative **pronoun** [ˌrelətɪv ˈprəʊnaʊn] Relativpronomen **II**
to **pronounce** [prəˈnaʊns] aussprechen **IV**
pronunciation [prəˌnʌnsiˈeɪʃn] Aussprache **I**
prop [prɒp] Requisite **II**
proper [ˈprɒpə] richtig; ordentlich; angemessen **IV**
prospect [ˈprɒspekt] Aussicht °**V U3**, 91
prostitute [ˈprɒstɪtjuːt] Prostituierte ⟨**V AC2**, 80⟩
protagonist [prəʊˈtægnɪst] Protagonist/-in; Hauptfigur **III**
to **protect** sb/sth (from) [prəˈtekt frəm] jmdn./etw. beschützen (vor) **IV**
protection [prəˈtekʃn] Schutz **V AC3**, 114
protest [ˈprəʊtest] Protest **III**
to **protest** [prəˈtest] protestieren **V U1**, 24
protester [ˈprəʊtestə] Protestierende/-r; Demonstrant/-in **IV**
proud (of) [ˈpraʊd‿ əv] stolz (auf) **II**
personal **prounoun** [ˌpɜːsnl ˈprəʊnaʊn] Personalpronomen °**V TS3**, 109
to **prove** [pruːv] sich erweisen als ⟨**V AC1**, 11⟩
to **provide** [prəˈvaɪd] liefern; bereit stellen **V U2**, 53
provocative [prəˈvɒkətɪv] provokativ; provozierend **V TS3**, 108
to **provoke** [prəˈvəʊk] provozieren; hervorrufen **V AC2**, 81
psychological [ˌsaɪklˈɒdʒɪkl] psychologisch; psychisch ⟨**V U3**, 100⟩
psychologist [saɪˈkɒlədʒɪst] Psychologe/Psychologin **V TS3**, 109
the **public** [ðə ˈpʌblɪk] die Öffentlichkeit **IV**
public [ˈpʌblɪk] öffentlich **II**
public transport *(no pl)* [ˌpʌblɪk ˈtrænspɔːt] öffentliche Verkehrsmittel **II**
publication [ˌpʌblɪˈkeɪʃn] Veröffentlichung **IV**
to **publish** [ˈpʌblɪʃ] veröffentlichen; publizieren; verlegen **IV**
pudding [ˈpʊdɪŋ] Pudding; Nachtisch **I**
to **pull** [pʊl] ziehen **I**
to **pull** down [ˌpʊl‿ˈdaʊn] abreißen **III**
pumpkin [ˈpʌmpkɪn] Kürbis ⟨**V U2**, 65⟩
punch [pʌnʃ] Faustschlag; Boxhieb **IV**
to **punch** [pʌnʃ] mit der Faust schlagen; boxen **IV**
purple [ˈpɜːpl] violett; lila **I**
purpose [ˈpɜːpəs] Ziel; Absicht; Zweck **III**
to **pursue** [pəˈsjuː] verfolgen **V U3**, 86
to **push** [pʊʃ] stoßen; schieben; schubsen **II**
to **push** oneself [ˈpʊʃ wʌnˌself] sich alles abverlangen; sich Mühe geben **III**
pushy [ˈpʊʃi] aufdringlich; penetrant; aggressiv **III**
*to **put** [pʊt] setzen; stellen; legen **I**
Put in … [pʊt‿ˈɪn] Setze/Setzt ein … **I**
Put it in … [ˌpʊt‿ɪt‿ˈɪn] Lege/Legt es in …; Stelle/Stellt es in … **I**
*to **put** on [ˌpʊt‿ˈɒn] anziehen **III**
*to **put** through [ˌpʊt‿ˈθruː] verbinden **I**
*to **put** up [ˌpʊt‿ˈʌp] aufstellen; errichten; aufhängen **II**
Put … face down. [pʊt ˌfeɪs ˈdaʊn] Lege/Legt … umgedreht hin. **I**
puzzle [ˈpʌzl] Rätsel; Puzzle **I**
puzzled [ˈpʌzld] verwirrt; verdutzt ⟨**V U2**, 63⟩
pyjamas *(pl)* [pɪˈdʒɑːməz] Schlafanzug; Pyjama **II**

Q

qualification [ˌkwɒlɪfɪˈkeɪʃn] Qualifikation; Befähigung; Abschluss; Schulabschluss **V U2**, 48
quality [ˈkwɒləti] Qualität **I**
quantity [ˈkwɒntɪti] Menge; Quantität **V U2**, 53
quarter past/to [ˈkwɔːtə pɑːst/tə] Viertel nach/vor **I**
queen [kwiːn] Königin **II**
question [ˈkwestʃən] Frage **I**
question tag [ˈkwestʃən ˌtæg] Frageanhängsel; Bestätigungsfrage **II**
to **question** [ˈkwestʃən] fragen; hinterfragen **IV**
questioning [ˈkwestʃənɪŋ] fragend ⟨**V U2**, 63⟩
questionnaire [ˌkwestʃəˈneə] Fragebogen **III**
queue [kjuː] Schlange; Warteschlange **I**
to jump the **queue** [ˌdʒʌmp ðə ˈkjuː] sich vordrängeln **I**
quick [kwɪk] schnell **I**
quickly [ˈkwɪkli] schnell **II**
quick-shot mode [ˈkwɪkʃɒt ˌməʊd] Serienaufnahmemodus ⟨**V U3**, 100⟩
quiet [kwaɪət] still; ruhig; leise **I**
quill [kwɪl] Federkiel **III**
quite [kwaɪt] ziemlich; ganz; völlig **III**
quiz [kwɪz] Quiz; Rätsel **I**
quotation [kwəˈtəɪʃn] Zitat; Belegstelle **IV**
quote [kwəʊt] Zitat **II**
to **quote** [kwəʊt] zitieren **V TS2**, 78

R

rabbit [ˈræbɪt] Kaninchen **I**
race [reɪs] Wettlauf; Rennen **II**; Rasse **V AC2**, 81
to **race** [reɪs] laufen ⟨**V U3**, 102⟩
racial [ˈreɪʃl] Rassen- **V AC1**, 8
camel **racing** [ˈkæml ˌreɪsɪŋ] Kamelrennen **II**
racism [ˈreɪsɪzm] Rassismus **V AC1**, 8
racist [ˈreɪsɪst] rassistisch; Rassist/-in **IV**
racquet [ˈrækɪt] Schläger **II**
radio [ˈreɪdiəʊ] Radio **II**
raffle [ˈræfl] Tombola **I**
raft [rɑːft] Floß **IV**
rubber **raft** [ˌrʌbə ˈrɑːft] Schlauchboot **IV**
rags to riches [ˌrægz tə‿ˈrɪtʃɪz] vom Tellerwäscher zum Millionär **IV**
rain [reɪn] Regen **III**
acid **rain** [ˌæsɪd ˈreɪn] saurer Regen ⟨**V U3**, 96⟩
to **rain** [reɪn] regnen **II**
rainbow [ˈreɪnbəʊ] Regenbogen **III**
raincoat [ˈreɪnkəʊt] Regenmantel **III**
to **raise** [reɪz] wecken *(Interesse)*; aufwerfen *(Fragen)* **V U2**, 48
to **raise** money [ˌreɪz ˈmʌni] Geld sammeln **II**
to **raise** one's eyes [ˌreɪz wʌnz‿ˈaɪz] den Blick heben; aufblicken; hochblicken **V U1**, 28
ranch [rɑːntʃ; ræntʃ] Ranch **IV**
rap [ræp] Rap **I**
to **rap** [ræp] rappen **I**
rarely [ˈreəli] selten **V U2**, 56
rat [ræt] Ratte **I**
rate [reɪt] Rate ⟨**V TS3**, 113⟩
to **rate** [reɪt] bewerten; einstufen **IV**
rather [ˈrɑːðə] ziemlich **V TS1**, 44
I'd **rather** [aɪd ˈrɑːðə] ich würde lieber **III**
rating [ˈreɪtɪŋ] Kritik **III**
raven [ˈreɪvn] Rabe **II**
raven master [ˈreɪvn ˌmɑːstə] Herr der Raben **II**
RE *(= Religious Education)* [ˌɑːrˈiː; rɪˌlɪdʒəs‿ edʒʊˈkeɪʃn] Religion *(Schulfach)* **II**
to **reach** [riːtʃ] erreichen; dran kommen **II**
to **reach** (for) [ˈriːtʃ fə] greifen (nach) **IV**
to **react** [riˈækt] reagieren **III**
reaction [riˈækʃn] Reaktion **II**
*to **read** [riːd] lesen **I**
*to **read** out loud [ˌriːd‿aʊt ˈlaʊd] laut vorlesen **III**
reader [ˈriːdə] Leser/-in **I**
*to draw the **reader** into the story/action [ˌdrɔː ðə ˌriːdə ɪntə ðə ˈstɔːri/ˈækʃn] den Leser/die Leserin in die Geschichte/Handlung hineinziehen **III**
reading [ˈriːdɪŋ] Lesen **I**
ready [ˈredi] fertig; bereit **II**
*to get **ready** [ˌget ˈredi] sich vorbereiten; sich fertig machen **V U1**, 28
ready meal [ˌredi ˈmiːl] Fertiggericht **I**
real [rɪəl] echt; richtig; wirklich **II**

to realise ['rɪəlaɪz] erkennen; realisieren **III**
realism ['rɪəlɪzm] Realismus; Realitätssinn **VTS3**, 111
realistic [ˌrɪə'lɪstɪk] realistisch **II**
reality [ri'æləti] Realität; Wirklichkeit **VAC1**, 9
to realize *(AE)* ['rɪəlaɪz] erkennen; realisieren **IV**
really ['rɪəli] wirklich **I**
reason ['ri:zn] Grund **II**; Vernunft; Verstand **VU3**, 85
reassuring [ˌri:ə'ʃʊərɪŋ] beruhigend; beschwichtigend ⟨**VU1**, 29⟩
rebellion [rɪ'beliən] Rebellion ⟨**VU3**, 92⟩
*to **rebuild** [ˌri:'bɪld] wieder aufbauen **III**
to recall [rɪ'kɔ:l] sich erinnern ⟨**VU3**, 101⟩
to receive [rɪ'si:v] empfangen; erhalten; bekommen **II**
receiver [rɪ'si:və] Empfänger/-in; *hier:* Hüter/-in **VU2**, 63
recent ['ri:snt] kürzlich; neueste/-r/-s; letzte/-r/-s **IV**
recently ['ri:sntli] kürzlich; neulich **IV**
reception [rɪ'sepʃn] Empfang **IV**
receptive [rɪ'septɪv] empfänglich **IV**
recipe ['resɪpi] Rezept **III**
to recite [rɪ'saɪt] vortragen; rezitieren **III**
to reckon with ['rekn wɪð] rechnen mit °**VAC2**, 83
to recognise ['rekəgnaɪz] erkennen; anerkennen **VTS2**, 79
to recognize *(AE)* ['rekəgnaɪz] erkennen; anerkennen **IV**
recollection [rekə'lekʃn] Erinnerung ⟨**VU2**, 62⟩
record ['rekɔ:d] Rekord; Rekord- ⟨**VU1**, 17⟩
to record [rɪ'kɔ:d] aufnehmen; aufzeichnen **II**
recorded history [rɪˌkɔ:dɪd 'hɪstri] *hier:* Aufzeichnung **VU3**, 95
recorder [rɪ'kɔ:də] Flöte **III**
recording [rɪ'kɔ:dɪŋ] Aufnahme; Aufzeichnung **I**
recording studio [rɪ'kɔ:dɪŋ ˌstju:diəʊ] Aufnahmestudio; Tonstudio **I**
to recruit [rɪ'kru:t] rekrutieren; anwerben; einstellen **VTS2**, 77
recycling [ˌri:'saɪklɪŋ] Recycling; Wiederaufbereitung **II**
red [red] rot **I**
reduction [rɪ'dʌkʃn] Reduzierung; Verminderung °**VTS2**, 75
redwood (tree) ['redwʊd ˌtri:] Mammutbaum **IV**
to reef the sails [ˌri:f ðə 'seɪlz] die Segel einholen **I**
re-enactment [ˌri:ɪ'næktmənt] Nachspielen eines Ereignisses ⟨**VU1**, 21⟩
to re-experience [ˌri:ɪk'spɪəriəns] noch einmal erleben ⟨**VU2**, 64⟩
to refer to [rɪ'fɜ: tə] sich beziehen auf **IV**
reference ['refrns] Referenz; Referenzschreiben **VU2**, 50
reference (to sth) ['refrns tə] Anspielung (auf etw.); Erwähnung (von etw.); Bezugnahme (auf etw.) ⟨**VU2**, 46⟩
reference article ['refrns ˌɑ:tɪkl] Referenzartikel **III**
with **reference** to [wɪð 'refrns tə] bezugnehmend auf **VU2**, 51
referendum [ˌrefr'endəm] Referendum; Volksentscheid **III**
to reflect [rɪ'flekt] wiederspiegeln; reflektieren °**VTS1**, 41
reflexive [rɪ'fleksɪv] reflexiv; Reflexiv- **III**
reflexive pronoun [rɪˌfleksɪv 'prəʊnaʊn] Reflexivpronomen **III**
refugee [ˌrefjʊ'dʒi:] Flüchtling **III**
*to be **regarded** as [bi rɪ'gɑ:dɪd‿əz] angesehen werden als; gelten als ⟨**VAC1**, 11⟩
region ['ri:dʒn] Region; Gegend **II**
register ['redʒɪstə] Sprachebene; Register **IV**
cash **register** ['kæʃ ˌredʒɪstə] Kasse ⟨**VU3**, 100⟩
registration [ˌredʒɪs'treɪʃn] Anwesenheitskontrolle **II**
regular ['regjələ] regelmäßig; gleichmäßig **I**; normal; üblich °**VU3**, 98
to regulate ['regjəleɪt] regeln; regulieren **VU2**, 62
regulator ['regjəleɪtə] Regulator/-in; Aufsicht führende Person **IV**
rehearsal [rɪ'hɜ:sl] Probe °**VTS1**, 45
to rehearse [rɪ'hɜ:s] proben **III**
reign [reɪn] Herrschaft; Regierungszeit **III**
to reign [reɪn] herrschen; regieren **III**
rejection [rɪ'dʒekʃn] Ablehnung; Absage **IV**
*to be **related** to [bi rɪ'leɪtɪd tə] verwandt sein mit **VU1**, 29
to relate to [rɪ'leɪt tə] Zugang finden zu **III**; nachvollziehen; sich identifizieren mit; verstehen **VTS2**, 78
relationship [rɪ'leɪʃnʃɪp] Beziehung **II**
defining **relative** clause [dɪˌfaɪnɪŋ 'relətɪv ˌklɔ:z] notwendiger Relativsatz **II**
non-defining **relative** clause [ˌnɒndɪfaɪnɪŋ 'relətɪv ˌklɔ:z] nicht notwendiger Relativsatz **IV**
relative pronoun [ˌrelətɪv 'prəʊnaʊn] Relativpronomen **II**
to relax [rɪ'læks] sich entspannen; sich ausruhen; sich beruhigen **II**
relaxed [rɪ'lækst] entspannt; locker; gelassen **VU3**, 86
release [rɪ'li:s] Freistellung; Entlassung ⟨**VU2**, 63⟩
relevant ['reləvnt] relevant; von Bedeutung **VTS2**, 78
reliable [rɪ'laɪəbl] verlässlich; zuverlässig; vertrauenswürdig **IV**
relieved [rɪ'li:vd] erleichtert **IV**
religion [rɪ'lɪdʒn] Religion **IV**
to practice a **religion** [ˌpræktɪs‿ə rɪ'lɪdʒn] eine Religion ausüben **IV**
religious [rɪ'lɪdʒəs] religiös; gläubig **I**
reluctant [rɪ'lʌktnt] widerstrebend; widerwillig **VU1**, 28
to rely (on) [rɪ'laɪ‿ɒn] sich verlassen (auf); vertrauen (auf) **III**
to remain [rɪ'meɪn] bleiben **VU3**, 90
to remember [rɪ'membə] sich erinnern (an); sich merken; denken an **I**
Remember? [rɪ'membə] Erinnerst du dich?; Erinnert ihr euch? **I**
as best as I can **remember** [əz ˌbest əz‿aɪ kæn rɪ'membə] soweit ich mich erinnern kann ⟨**VU3**, 101⟩
to remind (sb of sth/sb) [rɪ'maɪnd əv] (jmdn. an etw./jmdn.) erinnern **III**
remote [rɪ'məʊt] abgelegen; fern ⟨**VU1**, 13⟩
to remove [rɪ'mu:v] entfernen; abreißen **IV**
to renovate ['renəveɪt] renovieren **VU1**, 18
rent [rent] Miete **VU3**, 93
That doesn't pay my **rent**. [ˌdət dʌznt ˌpeɪ maɪ 'rent] Davon kann ich meine Miete nicht bezahlen. **VU3**, 93
to rent (out) [ˌrent‿'aʊt] mieten **III**
to repeat [rɪ'pi:t] wiederholen **II**
repetition [ˌrepɪ'tɪʃn] Wiederholung **III**
a sort of nonstop **repetition** [ə ˌsɔ:t‿əv ˌnɒnstɒp ˌrepɪ'tɪʃn] eine Art Dauerschleife ⟨**VU3**, 101⟩
to replace (by/with) [rɪ'pleɪs] ersetzen (durch) **IV**
to replay [ˌri:'pleɪ] in Gedanken nochmals durchspielen ⟨**VU1**, 28⟩
reply [rɪ'plaɪ] Antwort; Erwiderung; Entgegnung **I**
to reply [rɪ'plaɪ] antworten; erwidern; entgegnen **I**
report [rɪ'pɔ:t] Bericht; Meldung **II**
news **report** ['nju:z rɪˌpɔ:t] Tatsachenbericht; Nachrichtenbeitrag; Meldung **III**
travel **report** [ˌtrævl rɪ'pɔ:t] Reisebericht **II**
to report [rɪ'pɔ:t] berichten; wiedergeben **III**
reporter [rɪ'pɔ:tə] Reporter/-in **II**
to represent [ˌreprɪ'zent] repräsentieren; darstellen; stehen für **IV**
representative [ˌreprɪ'zentətɪv] Repräsentant/-in; Stellvertreter/-in **VAC3**, 115
request [rɪ'kwest] Bitte **III**; Anfrage; Nachfrage **VU2**, 50
to require [rɪ'kwaɪə] benötigen; erfordern **VU2**, 48
*to be **required** to *(+ inf)* [bi rɪ'kwaɪəd tə] müssen **VU3**, 95
*to **reread** ['ri:ri:d] noch einmal lesen **III**
rescue ['reskju:] Rettung **II**
to rescue ['reskju:] retten **III**
research *(no pl)* [rɪ'sɜ:tʃ] Recherche; Forschung; Untersuchung **III**
to research [rɪ'sɜ:tʃ] recherchieren; erforschen; untersuchen **IV**
researcher [rɪ'sɜ:tʃə] Forscher/-in **VTS2**, 77

to **resent** sb/sth [rɪ'zent] sich ärgern über jmdn./etw. ⟨**V U1**, 23⟩
reservation [ˌrezə'veɪʃn] Reservat **IV**
reserved [rɪ'zɜːvd] reserviert; vorbehalten ⟨**V U2**, 47⟩
resident ['rezɪdnt] Bewohner/-in; Einwohner/-in **V AC1**, 10
respect [rɪ'spekt] Respekt **IV**
to **respect** [rɪ'spekt] respektieren **V AC1**, 10
respectful [rɪ'spektfl] respektvoll **V AC2**, 81
to **respond** to [rɪ'spɒnd tə] reagieren auf; erwidern auf; antworten auf °**VTS3**, 108
response [rɪ'spɒns] Antwort; Erwiderung; Rückmeldung **IV**
responsibility [rɪˌspɒnsə'bɪləti] Verantwortung; Aufgabe **V U2**, 48
responsible [rɪs'pɒnsəbl] verantwortlich; verantwortungsvoll **III**
rest [rest] Rast; Ruhe °**V U2**, 54
the **rest** [rest] der Rest **I**
to **rest** [rest] ausruhen; liegen ⟨**V U2**, 64⟩
to **restate** [ˌriː'steɪt] noch einmal (mit anderen Worten) sagen °**VTS3**, 112
restaurant ['restrɒnt] Restaurant; Gaststätte **I**
to **restrict** [rɪ'strɪkt] begrenzen; beschränken °**V U1**, 20
restrictive [rɪ'strɪktɪv] beschränkend; einengend **V U1**, 20
restroom *(AE)* ['restrʊm] Toilette **IV**
result [rɪ'zʌlt] Ergebnis; Resultat **II**
to **result** in sth [rɪ'zʌlt‿ɪn] etw. ergeben; in etw. resultieren ⟨**V U3**, 96⟩
retail ['riːteɪl] Einzelhandel **IV**
*to **retell** [ˌriː'tel] nacherzählen; nochmals erzählen **I**
return ticket [rɪ'tɜːn ˌtɪkɪt] Hin- und Rückfahrkarte **II**
to **return** [rɪ'tɜːn] zurückkehren; zurückfahren **II**
to **reveal** [rɪ'viːl] offenbaren; aufdecken ⟨**VTS3**, 113⟩
review [rɪ'vjuː] Kritik **VTS2**, 74
to **review** [rɪ'vjuː] prüfen; durchsehen ⟨**V U3**, 102⟩
to **revise** [rɪ'vaɪz] wiederholen °**VTS1**, 38
revision [rɪ'vɪʒn] Wiederholung **II**
reward [rɪ'wɔːd] Belohnung; Preis **V AC3**, 115
*to **rewrite** [ˌriː'raɪt] umschreiben; neu schreiben **III**
rhino ['raɪnəʊ] Rhinozeros; Nashorn **III**
rhyme [raɪm] Reim **I**
rhyme scheme ['raɪm skiːm] Reimschema **III**
to **rhyme** [raɪm] (sich) reimen **III**
rhyming ['raɪmɪŋ] sich reimend **III**
rhythm ['rɪðm] Rhythmus **I**
rib [rɪb] Rippe **V U1**, 28
rich [rɪtʃ] reich **III**
the **rich** [ðə rɪtʃ] die Reichen **II**
riches *(pl)* ['rɪtʃɪz] Reichtümer ⟨**V U2**, 47⟩
rags to **riches** [ˌræɡz tə‿'rɪtʃɪz] vom Tellerwäscher zum Millionär **IV**
ride [raɪd] Fahrt; Ritt **IV**
*to get a **ride** [ˌɡet‿ə 'raɪd] eine Mitfahrgelegenheit bekommen **IV**
along for the **ride** [əˌlɒŋ fə ðə 'raɪd] mit dabei **IV**
*to **ride** [raɪd] fahren; reiten **IV**
rider ['raɪdə] Reiter/-in; Fahrer/-in **IV**
rigging ['rɪɡɪŋ] Takelage **I**
right [raɪt] Recht **IV**
civil **rights** *(pl)* [ˌsɪvl 'raɪts] Bürgerrechte **V AC1**, 8
human **rights** [ˌhjuːmən 'raɪts] Menschenrechte **V AC1**, 9
right [raɪt] richtig; korrekt; rechts; rechte/-r/-s **I**
*to be **right** [bi 'raɪt] recht haben **I**
*to get **right** [ɡet 'raɪt] richtig beantworten **II**
on the **right** [ɒn ðə 'raɪt] auf der rechten Seite; rechts **I**
right [raɪt] direkt **IV**; genau ⟨**V U2**, 66⟩
right away [ˌraɪt‿ə'weɪ] sofort; gleich **I**
right here [ˌraɪt 'hɪə] genau hier **II**
right now [ˌraɪt 'naʊ] jetzt gleich; sofort; gerade **II**
right into [ˌraɪt‿'ɪntʊ] bis hinein in ⟨**V U1**, 23⟩
ring [rɪŋ] Ring **III**
key **ring** ['kiː ˌrɪŋ] Schlüsselbund; Schlüsselanhänger **III**
*to **ring** [rɪŋ] klingeln; läuten **I**; anrufen **III**
ice **rink** ['aɪs ˌrɪŋk] Eisbahn; Schlittschuhbahn **I**
rip current ['rɪp ˌkʌrnt] Brandungsrückströmung **V U1**, 14
rise [raɪz] Anstieg; Zunahme **VTS2**, 77
*to **rise** [raɪz] steigen; sich erheben **III**; aufgehen *(Sonne)* **IV**; aufstehen **VTS2**, 77
*to **rise** up in one's mind [raɪz‿ˌʌp ɪn wʌnz 'maɪnd] jmdm. in den Sinn kommen **III**
risk [rɪsk] Gefahr; Risiko **V U1**, 15
*to take a **risk** [ˌteɪk‿ə 'rɪsk] ein Risiko eingehen **III**
No **risk**, no fun! [nəʊ ˌrɪsk nəʊ 'fʌn] Wer nicht wagt, der nicht gewinnt. **IV**
to **risk** [rɪsk] riskieren **IV**
river ['rɪvə] Fluss **I**
by the **river** [baɪ ðə 'rɪvə] am Fluss **II**
riverbank ['rɪvəbæŋk] Flussufer ⟨**V U2**, 65⟩
road [rəʊd] Straße **II**
to **roar** [rɔː] dröhnen; brüllen; rauschen **III**
roaring ['rɔːrɪŋ] dröhnend; tosend; donnernd **III**
to **rob** [rɒb] ausrauben; rauben; berauben **IV**
robber ['rɒbə] Räuber/-in **II**
rock [rɒk] Rock *(Musik)* **III**
rock 'n' roll [ˌrɒk‿ən 'rəʊl] Rock 'n' Roll **II**
to **rock** [rɒk] schaukeln **III**
rocky ['rɒki] felsig; steinig **II**
role [rəʊl] Rolle **I**
role model ['rəʊl ˌmɒdl] Vorbild **VTS3**, 111
role play ['rəʊl ˌpleɪ] Rollenspiel **I**
supporting **role** [sə'pɔːtɪŋ ˌrəʊl] Nebenrolle **VTS1**, 38
to swap **roles** [ˌswɒp 'rəʊlz] Rollen tauschen **I**
to **role-play** ['rəʊlˌpleɪ] ein Rollenspiel machen °**VTS2**, 74
bread **roll** ['bred rəʊl] Brötchen **III**
rock 'n' **roll** [ˌrɒk‿ən 'rəʊl] Rock 'n' Roll **II**
to **roll** off [rəʊl] hinunterrollen; herunterrollen **II**
to **roll** one's eyes [ˌrəʊl wʌnz‿'aɪz] die Augen verdrehen **III**
Roll two dice. [ˌrəʊl ˌtuː 'daɪs] Würfle/Würfelt mit zwei Würfeln. **I**
roller skate ['rəʊlə ˌskeɪt] Rollschuh; Rollschuh- ⟨**V U3**, 92⟩
Roman ['rəʊmən] Römer/-in; römisch **II**
romance [rə'mæns] Liebesgeschichte; Liebesfilm **III**
Romanian [rʊ'meɪniən] Rumäne/Rumänin; rumänisch; Rumänisch **II**
romantic [rə'mæntɪk] romantisch **V AC1**, 9
roof [ruːf] Dach **II**
room [ruːm; rʊm] Zimmer; Raum **I**
living **room** ['lɪvɪŋ rʊm] Wohnzimmer **I**
lounge **room** ['laʊndʒ rʊm] Wohnzimmer ⟨**V U1**, 30⟩
side **room** ['saɪd ˌrʊm] Nebenraum **III**
roommate ['ruːmmeɪt] Zimmergenosse/Zimmergenossin **I**
rope [rəʊp] Seil **III**
rotary phone ['rəʊtri fəʊn] Telefon mit Wählscheibe **III**
rough [rʌf] rau; grob; uneben; holprig **IV**
round [raʊnd] Runde **II**
round of boxing [ˌraʊnd‿əv 'bɒksɪŋ] Boxrunde **II**
the **Round** Table [ðə ˌraʊnd 'teɪbl] die Tafelrunde **II**
round [raʊnd] um … herum **II**
*to go **round** in circles [ɡəʊ ˌraʊnd ɪn 'sɜːklz] sich im Kreis drehen **III**
to turn **round** [ˌtɜːn‿(ə)'raʊnd] (sich) umdrehen; wenden **II**
route [ruːt] Strecke; Route **II**
route planner ['ruːt ˌplænə] Routenplaner **IV**
routine [ruː'tiːn] Routine **III**
royal ['rɔɪəl] königlich **I**
rubber ['rʌbə] Radiergummi **I**
rubber raft [ˌrʌbə 'rɑːft] Schlauchboot **IV**
rubbish ['rʌbɪʃ] Müll; Gerümpel **I**
rude [ruːd] unhöflich; unverschämt **I**
rudeness ['ruːdnəs] Unhöflichkeit; Unverschämtheit ⟨**V U2**, 63⟩
rug [rʌɡ] Vorleger; Teppich **IV**
rugby ['rʌɡbi] Rugby **II**
to **ruin** ['ruːɪn] ruinieren; zerstören **II**
rule [ruːl] Regel **I**

What's the **rule** for …? [ˌwɒts ðə 'ru:l fə] Was ist die Regel für …? **I**
to **rule** [ru:l] herrschen; regieren **II**
ruler ['ru:lə] Lineal **I**
rumour ['ru:mə] Gerücht **V AC2**, 83
run [rʌn] Rennen; Lauf **II**
run area ['rʌn ˌeəriə] Gehege; Auslauf **III**
salmon **run** ['sæmən ˌrʌn] Lachswanderung **IV**
*to **run** [rʌn] rennen; laufen **I**; betreiben; leiten; führen **IV**
*to **run** away [ˌrʌn‿ə'weɪ] wegrennen **I**
*to **run** over [ˌrʌn‿'əʊvə] überfahren **IV**
runner ['rʌnə] Läufer/-in **II**
running ['rʌnɪŋ] Laufen; Rennen **II**
rural ['rʊərl] ländlich **IV**
rush [rʌʃ] Rausch **V U3**, 90; Eile ⟨**V U3**, 102⟩
Gold **Rush** ['gəʊld ˌrʌʃ] Goldrausch **V U3**, 90
Russian ['rʌʃn] Russe/Russin; russisch; Russisch **IV**
RV **park** *(AE)* [ˌɑ:'vi: ˌpɑ:k] Campingplatz **V U3**, 86

S

sacred ['seɪkrɪd] heilig **IV**
sad [sæd] traurig **I**
safari [sə'fɑ:ri] Safari **V AC1**, 8
safe [seɪf] sicher; ungefährlich **II**
safety ['seɪfti] Sicherheit **V U1**, 14
to reef the **sails** [ˌri:f ðə 'seɪlz] die Segel einholen **I**
to **sail** [seɪl] segeln; umsegeln **III**
sailboat ['seɪlbəʊt] Segelboot **II**
sailor ['seɪlə] Seemann; Matrose **I**
salad ['sæləd] Salat **I**
sale [seɪl] Verkauf **II**
sales assistant ['seɪlz‿əˌsɪstnt] Verkäufer/-in **V U2**, 49
salmon ['sæmən], **salmon** ['sæmən] *(pl)* Lachs **IV**
salmon run ['sæmən ˌrʌn] Lachswanderung **IV**
saltie *(coll)* ['sɔ:lti] Salzwasserkrokodil **V AC1**, 10
saltwater ['sɔ:ltˌwɔ:tə] Salzwasser- ⟨**V U1**, 21⟩
same-sex [ˌseɪm'seks] gleichgeschlechtlich **V AC2**, 82
the **same** [ðə 'seɪm] der-/die-/dasselbe; der/die/das gleiche **I**
the **same** way as [ˌðə seɪm 'weɪ æz] genauso wie **II**
sameness ['seɪmnəs] Gleichheit; Gleichförmigkeit **V U2**, 65
sample ['sɑ:mpl] Probe; Muster **IV**
sand [sænd] Sand **V U1**, 19
sandal ['sændl] Sandale **III**
sandwich ['sænwɪdʒ] Sandwich; belegtes Brot **I**
sandy ['sændi] sandig; Sand- **II**
satellite ['sætlaɪt] Satellit **V U1**, 14
satisfaction [ˌsætɪs'fækʃn] Zufriedenheit **V U2**, 47
satisfied ['sætɪsfaɪd] zufrieden; befriedigt **V U2**, 62
Saturday ['sætədeɪ] Samstag **I**
sauce [sɔ:s] Soße **III**
sausage ['sɒsɪdʒ] Wurst; Bratwurst **III**
to **save** [seɪv] retten; bergen **I**; sparen **III**
to **save** the best for last [ˌseɪv ðə ˌbest fə 'lɑ:st] sich das Beste bis zum Schluss aufheben **IV**
saved by the bell [ˌseɪvd baɪ ðə 'bel] noch mal Glück gehabt **III**
sax ['sæks] Saxofon **I**
saxophone ['sæksəfəʊn] Saxofon **I**
*to **say** [seɪ] sagen; aufsagen; sprechen **I**
*to be **said** to *(+ inf)* [bi 'sed tə] sollen; gelten als **V U3**, 90
needless to **say** [ˌni:dləs tə 'seɪ] natürlich; selbstverständlich **IV**
*to **say** hello (to) [ˌseɪ hel'əʊ tə] grüßen; Grüße ausrichten (an) **I**
saying ['seɪɪŋ] Redensart; Sprichwort **III**
scan [skæn] Überfliegen ⟨**V U3**, 100⟩
to **scan** [skæn] scannen; nach Details durchsuchen **II**
scandal ['skændl] Skandal **VTS3**, 109
scar [skɑ:] Narbe **V U1**, 28
to **scare** sb [skeə] jmdm. Angst machen; jmdn. erschrecken **IV**
to **scare** sb to death [ˌskeə tə 'deθ] jmdn. zu Tode erschrecken **IV**
scared [skeəd] verängstigt; ängstlich **IV**
*to be **scared** (of) [bi 'skeəd‿əv] Angst haben (vor) **I**
I'm (not) **scared** of … [ˌaɪm (nɒt) 'skeəd‿əv] Ich habe (keine) Angst vor … **I**
scary ['skeəri] unheimlich; gruselig; beängstigend **II**
scene [si:n] Szene **I**; Schauplatz **II**
acting a **scene** [ˌæktɪŋ‿ə 'si:n] eine Theaterszene spielen **I**
at the **scene** [ˌət ðə 'si:n] vor Ort **V U1**, 26
scenery ['si:nri] Landschaft **IV**
sceptical ['skeptɪkl] skeptisch **IV**
schedule *(AE)* ['ʃedju:l; 'skedʒu:l] Stundenplan; Fahrplan; Terminkalender **IV**
rhyme **scheme** ['raɪm ski:m] Reimschema **III**
school [sku:l] Schule **I**
comprehensive **school** [kɒmprɪ'hensɪv ˌsku:l] Gesamtschule **V U2**, 50
grammar **school** ['græmə ˌsku:l] Gymnasium **II**
high **school** *(AE)* ['haɪ ˌsku:l] High School *(weiterführende Schule in den USA, Oberstufe)* **IV**
middle **school** *(AE)* ['mɪdl ˌsku:l] Mittelschule *(weiterführende Schule in den USA, Mittelstufe)* **IV**
primary **school** ['praɪmri ˌsku:l] Grundschule **I**
school fees *(pl)* ['sku:l fi:z] Schulgeld; Schulgebühren **III**
schoolbag ['sku:lbæg] Schultasche **I**
schoolwork ['sku:lwɜ:k] Schularbeiten **III**
Science [saɪəns] Naturwissenschaften **II**
science [saɪəns] Wissenschaft; Naturwissenschaft **IV**
science fiction [ˌsaɪəns 'fɪkʃn] Science-Fiction *(Zukunftsdichtung)* **II**
scientific [ˌsaɪən'tɪfɪk] wissenschaftlich; naturwissenschaftlich **VTS2**, 78
scientist ['saɪəntɪst] Wissenschaftler/-in **III**
to **scoop** [sku:p] *hier:* fließen ⟨**V U1**, 30⟩
to **scoop** up [ˌsku:p‿'ʌp] hochheben ⟨**V U3**, 100⟩
score [skɔ:] Punktestand; Spielstand **II**
scoreboard ['skɔ:bɔ:d] Anzeigetafel ⟨**V U3**, 97⟩
Scot [skɒt] Schotte/Schottin **III**
Scottish ['skɒtɪʃ] schottisch **II**
gorge **scrambling** ['gɔ:dʒ ˌskræmblɪŋ] Schluchtenklettern **II**
to **scream** [skri:m] schreien; kreischen **II**
screen [skri:n] Bildschirm ⟨**VTS2**, 79⟩
screen door [skri:n] Eingangstür mit Fliegengitter ⟨**V U1**, 30⟩
script [skrɪpt] Drehbuch; Skript **III**
scriptwriting ['skrɪptˌraɪtɪŋ] Drehbuchschreiben °**VTS1**, 44
scrub *(no pl)* [skrʌb] Gestrüpp; Busch ⟨**V U1**, 30⟩
sculpture ['skʌlptʃə] Skulptur **IV**
sea [si:] Meer **I**
*to be swept out to **sea** [bi ˌswept‿aʊt tə 'si:] aufs offene Meer getrieben werden **V U1**, 14
seal [si:l] Siegel **IV**
search [sɜ:tʃ] Suche; Such- **II**
search engine ['sɜ:tʃ‿ˌendʒɪn] Suchmaschine **IV**
to **search** [sɜ:tʃ] durchsuchen ⟨**V U2**, 64⟩
to **search** for ['sɜ:tʃ fə] suchen (nach) **III**
seashell ['si:ʃel] Muschel **V U1**, 14
seasick ['si:sɪk] seekrank **III**
season ['si:zn] Saison; Jahreszeit **IV**
seasonal ['si:znl] saisonal; jahreszeitlich bedingt **V U3**, 93
seat [si:t] Sitz; Sitzplatz **III**
passenger **seat** ['pæsndʒə ˌsi:t] Beifahrersitz **IV**
seat belt ['si:t belt] Sicherheitsgurt **IV**
second ['seknd] Sekunde **IV**
Just a **second** … [ˌdʒʌst‿ə 'seknd] Einen Augenblick … **IV**
second ['seknd] zweite/-r/-s **I**; zweitens ⟨**V AC1**, 11⟩
secondly ['sekndli] zweitens **VTS3**, 111
secret ['si:krət] Geheimnis **II**
in **secret** [ɪn 'si:krət] heimlich **II**
secret ['si:krət] geheim **III**
section ['sekʃn] Abschnitt; Paragraf **II**

security [sɪ'kjʊərəti] Sicherheit; Schutz; Wachdienst; Wach-; Sicherheits- **III**
*to **see** [si:] sehen **I**
*to **see** the bigger picture [ˌsi: ðə ˌbɪgə 'pɪktʃə] über den Tellerrand hinausschauen **IV**
See you! ['si: jə] Bis dann!; Bis … **I**
I can't **see** the point of … [aɪ ˌkɑ:nt si: ðə 'pɔɪnt‿əv] Ich sehe keinen Sinn darin … **IV**
Wait and **see**! [ˌweɪt‿ənd 'si:] Warte ab! **I**
to **seem** [si:m] scheinen **III**
to **seep** [si:p] sickern ⟨**V U3**, 102⟩
segregation [ˌsegrɪ'geɪʃn] Segregation; Trennung; Rassentrennung **V AC1**, 8
to **select** [sɪ'lekt] auswählen; aussuchen **V U2**, 63
selection [sɪ'lekʃn] Auswahl; Auswahl- **V U3**, 99
self [self], **selves** [selvz] *(pl)* das Selbst **III**
self-confident [self'kɒnfɪdnt] selbstsicher; selbstbewusst ⟨**V U2**, 63⟩
self-critical ['selfˌkrɪtɪkl] selbstkritisch **II**
self-evaluation [ˌselfɪˌvælju'eɪʃn] Selbsteinschätzung **I**
selfie ['selfi] Selfie **II**
selfish ['selfɪʃ] selbstsüchtig; egoistisch **V U2**, 55
*to **sell** [sel] verkaufen **I**
seller ['selə] Verkäufer/-in *(auf einem Flohmarkt)* **I**
semi- ['semɪ] Halb- ⟨**V U3**, 101⟩
*to **send** [send] schicken; senden **I**
*to **send** off [send‿'ɒf] abschicken **II**
senior ['si:niə] älter **V U1**, 23
senior counsellor [ˌsi:niə 'kaʊnslə] leitender Betreuer/leitende Betreuerin; ranghohe/-r Minister/-in **V U2**, 48
sense [sens] Sinn **III**
*to make **sense** [ˌmeɪk 'sens] Sinn ergeben; einleuchten **IV**
sense of humour *(no pl)* [ˌsens‿əv 'hju:mə] Sinn für Humor **III**
sensible ['sensɪbl] vernünftig **III**
sensitive ['sensɪtɪv] sensibel; empfindsam; heikel **V AC2**, 83
sentence ['sentəns] Satz **I**; Verurteilung; Strafmaß **V U1**, 18
conditional **sentence** [kənˌdɪʃnl 'sentəns] Bedingungssatz **II**
to **separate** ['sepreɪt] (sich) trennen **IV**
separate ['seprət] separat; getrennt; verschieden **II**
September [sep'tembə] September **I**
sequence ['si:kwəns] Sequenz; Szene **III**; Abfolge; Reihenfolge **IV**
serene [sə'ri:n] ruhig; gelassen ⟨**V U2**, 62⟩
series ['sɪəri:z], **series** ['sɪəri:z] *(pl)* Serie **III**
serious ['sɪəriəs] ernsthaft; ernst **I**
seriousness *(no pl)* ['sɪəriəsnəs] Ernst; Ernsthaftigkeit ⟨**V U2**, 62⟩
to **serve** [sɜ:v] servieren; dienen; bedienen **V U1**, 16
service ['sɜ:vɪs] Service; Dienstleistung; Dienst **IV**
session ['seʃn] Sitzung; Stunde **V U2**, 64
set [set] Umgebung; Rahmen **II**; Aufnahmeort; Drehort **III**
a **set** of [ə 'set‿əv] eine Liste von **III**
set phrase [set 'freɪs] Floskel; feststehender Ausdruck °**VTS2**, 78
*to be **set** (in) [bi 'set ɪn] spielen (in); seinen Schauplatz haben (in) **III**
*to **set** a good example [set‿ə ˌgʊd‿ɪg'zɑ:mpl] ein Vorbild sein **V U2**, 48
*to **set** off [ˌset‿'ɒf] *hier:* ein Feuerwerk zünden **III**
*to **set** the table [ˌset ðə 'teɪbl] den Tisch decken **IV**
*to **set** up [ˌset‿'ʌp] einrichten; aufbauen **I**
setting ['setɪŋ] Schauplatz; Rahmen **II**
account **settings** [ə'kaʊnt ˌsetɪŋz] Profileinstellungen **III**
to **settle** for less [ˌsetl fə 'les] sich mit weniger zufrieden geben **IV**
settlement ['setlmənt] Siedlung **IV**
settler ['setlə] Siedler/-in **IV**
seven ['sevn] sieben **I**
several ['sevrl] einige; mehrere; verschiedene **II**
sex [seks] Geschlecht; Sexualität **VTS3**, 111
same-**sex** [ˌseɪm'seks] gleichgeschlechtlich **V AC2**, 82
sexting ['sekstɪŋ] *Versenden von Nacktfotos per Handy* ⟨**VTS2**, 79⟩
sexual ['sekʃʊəl] sexuell **V AC1**, 9
sexy ['seksi] sexy **VTS1**, 42
shade [ʃeɪd] Schattierung; Schatten ⟨**V U2**, 65⟩
shadow ['ʃædəʊ] Schatten **III**
*to **shake** [ʃeɪk] schütteln **V U1**, 29
shaky ['ʃeɪki] zitternd; bebend ⟨**V U2**, 63⟩
shall [ʃæl] sollen **V U3**, 95
shallow ['ʃæləʊ] seicht; flach; oberflächlich ⟨**V AC2**, 80⟩
shampoo [ʃæm'pu:] Shampoo **IV**
shape [ʃeɪp] Form **IV**
to **shape** [ʃeɪp] formen **IV**
to **share** [ʃeə] teilen **II**
shark [ʃɑ:k] Hai **III**
sharp [ʃɑ:p] scharf; schneidend **III**
she [ʃi:] sie **I**
sheep [ʃi:p], **sheep** [ʃi:p] *(pl)* Schaf **II**
bighorn **sheep** [ˌbɪghɔ:n 'ʃi:p] Dickhornschaf **IV**
sheet [ʃi:t] Blatt **V U2**, 63
cheat **sheet** ['tʃi:t ʃi:t] Spickzettel **IV**
comprehension **sheet** [ˌkɒmprɪ'henʃn ˌʃi:t] Blatt mit Verständnisaufgaben ⟨**V U1**, 29⟩
animal **shelter** ['ænɪml ˌʃeltə] Tierheim **III**
homeless **shelter** ['həʊmləs ˌʃeltə] Obdachlosenunterkunft **IV**
shift [ʃɪft] Verschiebung; Wechsel °**V U3**, 93
to **shift** [ʃɪft] hin- und herrutschen ⟨**V U2**, 62⟩
*to **shine** [ʃaɪn] scheinen; glänzen **II**
shinty ['ʃɪnti] Shinty *(eine Art Hockey)* **III**
ship [ʃɪp] Schiff **I**
shipbuilding ['ʃɪpbɪldɪŋ] Schiffsbau **III**
shipping ['ʃɪpɪŋ] Versand; Transport *(von Gütern)* ⟨**V AC1**, 11⟩
shirt [ʃɜ:t] Hemd; Shirt ⟨**VTS3**, 113⟩
shock [ʃɒk] Schock **II**
shocked [ʃɒkt] schockiert; geschockt **III**
shoe [ʃu:] Schuh **I**
*to be in sb's **shoes** [ˌbi: ɪn sʌmbɒdɪz 'ʃu:z] an jmds. Stelle sein; in jmds. Haut stecken **III**
high-heeled **shoes** [ˌhaɪ‿hi:ld 'ʃu:z] Stöckelschuhe ⟨**V AC2**, 80⟩
in Jay's **shoes** [ɪn dʒeɪz 'ʃu:z] an Jays Stelle **III**
on a **shoestring** [ˌɒn‿ə 'ʃu:strɪŋ] für/mit wenig Geld **IV**
photo **shoot** ['fəʊtəʊ ˌʃu:t] Fotoshooting; Fotoaufnahmen **III**
*to **shoot** [ʃu:t] drehen *(Film)* **V U3**, 86
*to **shoot** (at) [ʃu:t‿ət] schießen (auf) **III**
shop [ʃɒp] Geschäft; Laden **I**
charity **shop** ['tʃærɪti ʃɒp] Second-Hand-Laden **I**
pawn **shop** ['pɔ:n ʃɒp] Pfandhaus; Pfandleihe **III**
to **shop** [ʃɒp] einkaufen; shoppen **IV**
shopper ['ʃɒpə] Käufer/-in **IV**
shopping ['ʃɒpɪŋ] Einkaufen; Einkäufe **I**
*to do the **shopping** [ˌdu: ðə 'ʃɒpɪŋ] Einkäufe machen; Besorgungen machen **III**
*to go **shopping** [ˌgəʊ 'ʃɒpɪŋ] einkaufen gehen **I**
shopping mall ['ʃɒpɪŋ ˌmɔ:l] Einkaufszentrum **IV**
shore [ʃɔ:] Ufer; Küste **II**
short [ʃɔ:t] kurz **I**
short answer [ˌʃɔ:t‿'ɑ:nsə] Kurzantwort **I**
short form ['ʃɔ:t fɔ:m] Kurzform **I**
shortage ['ʃɔ:tɪdʒ] Knappheit; Mangel **V U3**, 90
shorts *(pl)* [ʃɔ:ts] Shorts; kurze Hose **II**
shot [ʃɒt] Einstellung; Kameraeinstellung **II**; Aufnahme **III**
long **shot** ['lɒŋ ʃɒt] Totale *(Kameraeinstellung)* **IV**
medium **shot** ['mi:diəm ʃɒt] Halbtotale *(Kameraeinstellung)* **IV**
wide **shot** ['waɪd ʃɒt] Totale *(Kameraeinstellung)* **VTS1**, 38
should [ʃʊd] sollte; solltest; sollten; solltet **II**
shouldn't ['ʃʊdnt] sollte(n) nicht **II**
shoulder ['ʃəʊldə] Schulter **II**
to **shout** [ʃaʊt] schreien; rufen **I**
show [ʃəʊ] Show; Schau; Aufführung **II**
comedy **show** ['kɒmədi ˌʃəʊ] Comedy Show **II**

living history **show** [ˌlɪvɪŋ 'hɪstəri ˌʃəʊ] *Show, in der historischer Alltag nachgespielt wird* **II**
talent **show** ['tælənt ˌʃəʊ] Talentwettbewerb **I**
*to **show** [ʃəʊ] zeigen **I**
*to **show** off [ʃəʊ‿'ɒf] angeben **II**
*to **show** sb around (a place) [ˌʃəʊ‿ə'raʊnd] jmdn. (an einem Ort) herumführen **V U1**, 16
*to **show** sb in [ˌʃəʊ‿'ɪn] jmdn. hereinführen; jmdn. hineinführen ⟨**V U1**, 28⟩
to **showcase** one's talent [ˌʃəʊkeɪs wʌnz 'tælənt] sein Talent unter Beweis stellen **V U3**, 86
shower ['ʃaʊə] Dusche **I**
show-off ['ʃəʊ‿ɒf] Angeber/-in **III**
to **shrug** (one's shoulders) [ʃrʌg] mit den Schultern zucken ⟨**V U2**, 65⟩
to **shuffle** ['ʃʌfl] mischen **II**
to bang **shut** [ˌbæŋ 'ʃʌt] zuknallen ⟨**V U1**, 30⟩
shutter ['ʃʌtə] Fensterladen **III**
*to slide the **shutter** [ˌslaɪd ðə 'ʃʌtə] die Blende einstellen ⟨**V U3**, 100⟩
shy [ʃaɪ] schüchtern **II**
sick [sɪk] krank; unwohl **II**
*to be **sick** [bi 'sɪk] sich übergeben **III**
*to feel **sick** [ˌfi:l 'sɪk] Übelkeit verspüren; sich schlecht fühlen **II**
side [saɪd] Seite **II**
side room ['saɪd ˌrʊm] Nebenraum **III**
sidewalk *(AE)* ['saɪdwɔ:k] Gehweg; Gehsteig **IV**
sigh [saɪ] Seufzer ⟨**V U2**, 64⟩
to **sigh** [saɪ] seufzen **V U1**, 28
sight [saɪt] Sehenswürdigkeit; Anblick **II**; *hier:* Blick **III**
sighting ['saɪtɪŋ] Sichten **IV**
sightseeing ['saɪtsi:ɪŋ] Sightseeing-; Besichtigungs- **II**
sign [saɪn] Zeichen; Schild **II**
to **sign** [saɪn] unterschreiben; unterzeichnen **IV**
signal ['sɪgnl] Signal; Empfang **III**
signal word ['sɪgnəl ˌwɜ:d] Signalwort **I**
signature ['sɪgnətʃə] Unterschrift **V U2**, 51
significantly [sɪg'nɪfɪkəntli] auffallend; signifikant °**V U3**, 93
silence *(no pl)* ['saɪləns] Stille; Schweigen; Ruhe **III**
silent ['saɪlənt] still; ruhig; schweigsam; stumm **III**
silicon ['sɪlɪkən] Silizium **V U3**, 91
silly ['sɪli] Dummkopf **II**
silly ['sɪli] dumm; doof; albern **I**
silver ['sɪlvə] Silber **II**
similar ['sɪmɪlə] ähnlich **II**
similarity [ˌsɪmɪ'lærəti] Ähnlichkeit; Gemeinsamkeit **IV**
simple ['sɪmpl] einfach; simpel **III**
simple past [ˌsɪmpl 'pɑ:st] Vergangenheitsform **II**
simple present [ˌsɪmpl 'preznt] Gegenwart; Präsens **I**
simply ['sɪmpli] einfach nur **IV**
since [sɪns] da **IV**
since *(+ Zeitpunkt)* [sɪns] seit; seitdem **III**
Yours **sincerely** [ˌjɔ:z sɪn'sɪəli] Mit freundlichen Grüßen **V U2**, 51
*to **sing** [sɪŋ] singen **I**
*to **sing** along [ˌsɪŋ‿ə'lɒŋ] mitsingen **III**
*to **sing** out loud [ˌsɪŋ‿aʊt 'laʊd] laut vorsingen **III**
singer ['sɪŋə] Sänger/-in **II**
to **single** out [ˌsɪŋgl‿'aʊt] herausgreifen; auswählen ⟨**V U2**, 62⟩
single ['sɪŋgl] einzeln; einzig; alleinstehend **IV**
single ticket ['sɪŋgl ˌtɪkɪt] einfache Fahrkarte **II**
singlet ['sɪŋglɪt] ärmelloses Trikot; Unterhemd ⟨**V U1**, 28⟩
singular ['sɪŋgjələ] Singular °**V U3**, 93
singular ['sɪŋgjələ] einzigartig ⟨**V U2**, 62⟩
*to **sink** [sɪŋk] untergehen; sinken **III**
to **sip** [sɪp] schlürfen; schluckweise trinken ⟨**V U3**, 101⟩
sir [sɜ:] mein Herr *(Anrede)* **V U2**, 64
Dear **Sir** or Madam [dɪə ˌsɜ:r‿ɔ: 'mædəm] Sehr geehrte Dame, sehr geehrter Herr **II**
sister ['sɪstə] Schwester **I**
half-**sister** ['hɑ:fˌsɪstə] Halbschwester **I**
*to **sit** [sɪt] sitzen **I**
*to **sit** down [ˌsɪt 'daʊn] sich hinsetzen; sich setzen **I**
*to **sit** face to face [ˌsɪt feɪs tə ˌfeɪs] sich gegenüber sitzen **I**
Sit! [sɪt] Sitz! *(Befehl für Hunde)*; Platz! *(Befehl für Hunde)* **I**
site [saɪt] Website **II**; Ort; Gelände; Schauplatz **V U1**, 17
situation [ˌsɪtju'eɪʃn] Situation **I**
six [sɪks] sechs **I**
size [saɪz] Größe; Kleidergröße **I**
roller **skate** ['rəʊlə ˌskeɪt] Rollschuh; Rollschuh- ⟨**V U3**, 92⟩
to **skate** [skeɪt] Inlineskates fahren; Schlittschuh laufen **I**
skateboard ['skeɪtbɔ:d] Skateboard **II**
skateboarder ['skeɪtbɔ:də] Skateboardfahrer/-in **V U3**, 84
skateboarding ['skeɪtbɔ:dɪŋ] Skateboardfahren **I**
skatepark ['skeɪtpɑ:k] Skateboardanlage **V U3**, 85
skates *(pl)* [skeɪts] Inlineskates; Rollschuhe; Schlittschuhe **I**
(inline) **skating** ['ɪnlaɪn ˌskeɪtɪŋ] Inlineskatefahren **I**
skill [skɪl] Fertigkeit; Geschick **I**
people **skills** *(pl)* ['pi:pl ˌskɪlz] soziale Kompetenz **V U2**, 50
skilled [skɪld] Fach-; qualifiziert ⟨**V U1**, 20⟩
to **skim** [skɪm] überfliegen **II**
skin [skɪn] Haut; Fell **IV**
skinny ['skɪni] dünn; mager **IV**
to **skip** [skɪp] auslassen; schwänzen **IV**
skirt [skɜ:t] Rock **II**
sky [skaɪ] Himmel **III**
skyscraper ['skaɪskreɪpə] Wolkenkratzer **IV**
to **slam** [slæm] niedermachen ⟨**VTS3**, 113⟩
to **slap** [slæp] schlagen; einen Klaps geben ⟨**V U3**, 100⟩
slave [sleɪv] Sklave/Sklavin **III**
sled [sled] Schlitten ⟨**V U2**, 64⟩
sleep [sli:p] Schlaf **III**
*to **sleep** [sli:p] schlafen **I**
sleepingroom ['sli:pɪŋrʊm] Schlafzimmer; Schlafraum ⟨**V U2**, 63⟩
sleepover ['sli:pˌəʊvə] Übernachtung **I**
to **slice** [slaɪs] in Scheiben schneiden **I**
slide [slaɪd] Rutschbahn **I**; Folie °**V U3**, 97
water **slide** ['wɔ:tə ˌslaɪd] Wasserrutsche **I**
*to **slide** the shutter [ˌslaɪd ðə 'ʃʌtə] die Blende einstellen ⟨**V U3**, 100⟩
slight [slaɪt] gering; leicht **V U3**, 95
slightly ['slaɪtli] etwas; ein wenig ⟨**V U3**, 100⟩
to **slip** into [slɪp‿'ɪntə] schlüpfen in **IV**
slogan ['sləʊgən] Slogan; Werbespruch **II**
time **slot** ['taɪm slɒt] Zeitfenster **II**
to **slow** [sləʊ] langsamer werden; bremsen ⟨**V U1**, 30⟩
to **slow** down [ˌsləʊ 'daʊn] langsamer werden; bremsen **V U2**, 65
slow [sləʊ] langsam **I**
to step into a story **slowly** [stepˌɪntʊ ə ˌstɔ:ri 'sləʊli] eine Geschichte langsam entwickeln **III**
slum [slʌm] Slum; Elendsviertel **V AC1**, 8
small [smɔ:l] klein **I**
small talk ['smɔ:l ˌtɔ:k] Smalltalk **III**
smart [smɑ:t] schlau; klug; intelligent **III**
smartcard ['smɑ:tkɑ:d] Chipkarte **II**
smartphone ['smɑ:tfəʊn] Smartphone **II**
to **smash** [smæʃ] zerschlagen; zerschmettern **III**
to **smear** [smɪə] schmieren; beschmieren ⟨**V U1**, 30⟩
smell [smel] Geruch; Duft; Gestank **V U3**, 95
*to **smell** [smel] riechen; duften **III**
smile [smaɪl] Lächeln **I**
to force a **smile** [ˌfɔ:s‿ə 'smaɪl] sich zu einem Lächeln zwingen ⟨**V U1**, 29⟩
to **smile** [smaɪl] lächeln **I**
to **smirk** [smɜ:k] grinsen; süffisant lächeln ⟨**V U1**, 29⟩
smog [smɒg] Smog ⟨**V U3**, 96⟩
smoke [sməʊk] Rauch **III**
smoky ['sməʊki] verraucht **III**
to **smooth** [smu:ð] glatt streichen ⟨**V U2**, 62⟩
smooth [smu:ð] glatt; weich; geschmeidig **V U3**, 97
smug [smʌg] selbstgefällig ⟨**V U1**, 28⟩
smuggler ['smʌglə] Schmuggler/-in **III**
snack [snæk] Snack; Imbiss **I**
snack bar ['snæk ˌbɑ:] Café; Imbissstube **I**

snake [sneɪk] Schlange **V U1**, 14
word **snake** ['wɜ:d ˌsneɪk] Wortschlange **I**
*to **sneak** [sni:k] schleichen; schmuggeln **IV**
*to **sneak** around [ˌsni:k‿ə'raʊnd] herumschleichen **II**
to **snore** [snɔ:] schnarchen **I**
snow [snəʊ] Schnee **III**
snow tire *(AE)* ['snəʊ ˌtaɪə] Winterreifen **IV**
snow-capped ['snəʊkæpt] schneebedeckt **IV**
so [səʊ] so; also **I**
so far [ˌsəʊ 'fɑ:] bis jetzt **II**
so is ['səʊ ɪz] ebenso wie **III**
so (that) [ˌsəʊ 'ðæt] damit; so dass **IV**
to **soak** up [səʊk‿'ʌp] aufsaugen **III**
soccer *(AE)* ['sɒkə] Fußball **IV**
social ['səʊʃl] sozial; gesellschaftlich **IV**
social media [ˌsəʊʃl 'mi:diə] soziale Netzwerke **IV**
social network [ˌsəʊʃl 'netwɜ:k] soziales Netzwerk **II**
society [sə'saɪəti] Verein; Gesellschaft **II**
soda pop *(AE)* ['səʊdə ˌpɒp] Limo **IV**
sofa ['səʊfə] Sofa; Couch **I**
soft [sɒft] weich; sanft **V U1**, 29
software ['sɒftweə] Software *(Computerprogramme)* **IV**
software manual ['sɒftweə ˌmænjuəl] Softwarehandbuch **III**
soil [sɔɪl] Erde; Boden **V U1**, 22
soldier ['səʊldʒə] Soldat/-in **III**
solution [sə'lu:ʃn] Lösung **II**
to **solve** [sɒlv] lösen **II**
Somali [sə'mɑ:li] Somali **III**
some [sʌm; səm] einige; ein paar; etwas **I**
somebody ['sʌmbədi] jemand **I**
someone ['sʌmwʌn] jemand **II**
something ['sʌmθɪŋ] etwas **I**
sometimes ['sʌmtaɪmz] manchmal **I**
somewhere ['sʌmweə] irgendwo **II**
son [sʌn] Sohn **III**
song [sɒŋ] Song; Lied **I**
*to break into a **song** [ˌbreɪk‿ɪntʊ‿ə 'sɒŋ] plötzlich anfangen zu singen °**VTS1**, 44
theme **song** ['θi:m sɒŋ] Titelmelodie **IV**
soon [su:n] bald **II**
as **soon** as [əz 'su:n‿əz] sobald **II**
no **sooner** [nəʊ 'su:nə] kaum **V U2**, 59
Sorry! ['sɒri] Entschuldigung!; Tut mir leid! **I**
*to be **sorry** [bi 'sɒri] leid tun **I**
*to feel **sorry** for [ˌfi:l 'sɒri fɔ:] Mitleid haben mit; bedauern **III**
I'm **sorry**! [ˌaɪm 'sɒri] Tut mir leid! **I**
a **sort** of nonstop repetition [ə ˌsɔ:t‿əv ˌnɒnstɒp ˌrepɪ'tɪʃn] eine Art Dauerschleife ⟨**V U3**, 101⟩
to **sort** [sɔ:t] sortieren **IV**
to **sort** into [sɔ:t 'ɪntʊ] einsortieren; sortieren nach **III**
soul [səʊl] Seele **IV**
You've got no **soul**! [ju:v ˌgɒt nəʊ 'səʊl] *hier:* Du hast kein Feingefühl! **IV**
sound [saʊnd] Ton; Geräusch; Klang **I**
to **sound** [saʊnd] klingen **I**
soundtrack ['saʊndtræk] Soundtrack; Filmmusik **VTS1**, 45
soup [su:p] Suppe **III**
source [sɔ:s] Quelle **II**
south [saʊθ] Süden; Süd- **II**
South Korean [ˌsaʊθ kə'ri:ən] Südkoreaner/-in; südkoreanisch; Südkoreanisch **II**
southern ['sʌðən] südlich; Süd- **V AC1**, 10
(the) **Southwest** [ˌsaʊθ'west] (der) Südwesten; im Südwesten; südwestlich **IV**
souvenir [ˌsu:vn'ɪə] Souvenir; Andenken **II**
space [speɪs] Raum; Fläche; Platz; Ort **II**
*to leave **space** [li:v 'speɪs] Platz lassen **I**
space [speɪs] Weltraum; Weltall **IV**
space program ['speɪs ˌprəʊgræm] Raumfahrtprogramm **IV**
spaceship ['speɪsʃɪp] Raumschiff **II**
Spanish ['spænɪʃ] spanisch; Spanisch; die Spanier **III**
to **spark** [spɑ:k] entzünden; entfachen ⟨**V U1**, 17⟩
sparkling ['spɑ:klɪŋ] glitzernd; funkelnd **IV**
sparse [spɑ:s] dünn; spärlich **IV**
*to **speak** [spi:k] sprechen **I**
*to **speak** out (about sth) [ˌspi:k‿'aʊt] seine Meinung (über etw.) deutlich vertreten; sich (zu etw.) äußern **VTS3**, 108
speaker ['spi:kə] Redner/-in; Sprecher/-in **I**
native **speaker** [ˌneɪtɪv 'spi:kə] Muttersprachler/-in ⟨**V AC1**, 11⟩
speaking ['spi:kɪŋ] Sprechen **I**
spear [spɪə] Speer **II**
special ['speʃl] besonders; speziell **I**
special effect [ˌspeʃl‿ɪ'fekt] Spezialeffekt **IV**
special offer [ˌspeʃl‿'ɒfə] Sonderangebot **I**
with **special** needs [wɪð ˌspeʃl 'ni:dz] behindert **II**
to **specialize** in *(AE)* ['speʃlaɪz‿ɪn] sich spezialisieren auf **V U3**, 100
specialty *(AE)* ['speʃlti] Spezialität; Besonderheit **IV**
specific [spə'sɪfɪk] spezifisch; speziell **III**
spectacular [spek'tækjələ] spektakulär **III**
spectator [spek'teɪtə] Zuschauer/-in ⟨**V U3**, 97⟩
speech [spi:tʃ] Rede **III**
direct **speech** [ˌdɪrekt 'spi:tʃ] direkte Rede **III**
indirect **speech** [ˌɪndɪrekt 'spi:tʃ] indirekte Rede **III**
speech bubble ['spi:tʃ ˌbʌbl] Sprechblase **I**
speed [spi:d] Geschwindigkeit **IV**
*to **spell** [spel] buchstabieren **I**
spelling ['spelɪŋ] Rechtschreibung **I**
*to **spend** [spend] ausgeben *(Geld)* **I**; verbringen *(Zeit)* **II**
to **spice** up [ˌspaɪs‿'ʌp] aufpeppen **IV**
spicy ['spaɪsi] würzig; pikant **IV**
spider ['spaɪdə] Spinne **III**
spike [spaɪk] Spitze; Stachel **IV**
*to **spill** [spɪl] verschütten; auslaufen **III**
spirit ['spɪrɪt] Geist; Stimmung **IV**
*to break sb's **spirit** [ˌbreɪk sʌmbədiz 'spɪrɪt] jmdn. entmutigen ⟨**VTS3**, 109⟩
spiritual ['spɪrɪtjuəl] spirituell; geistig **IV**
spirituality [ˌspɪrɪtʃu'æləti] Spiritualität **V AC1**, 9
in **spite** of [ɪn 'spaɪt‿əv] trotz **IV**
spoken ['spəʊkn] gesprochen **II**
spokesperson ['spəʊksˌpɜ:sn] Sprecher/-in; PR-Sprecher/-in **V U1**, 15
sponge [spʌndʒ] Rühr-; Biskuit- **I**
spontaneous [spɒn'teɪniəs] spontan **II**
spoon [spu:n] Löffel **III**
sport [spɔ:t] Sport; Sportart **I**
sportsperson ['spɔ:tspɜ:sn], **sportspeople** ['spɔ:tspi:pl] *(pl)* Sportler/-in ⟨**V U1**, 13⟩
sporty ['spɔ:ti] sportlich **VTS3**, 111
spot [spɒt] Fleck; Ort **IV**
urban **sprawl** [ˌɜ:bn 'sprɔ:l] Urbanisierung; Zersiedelung; Ausuferung des Stadtgebiets ⟨**V U3**, 96⟩
to **spray-paint** ['spreɪpeɪnt] mit Farbe besprühen **V AC3**, 114
*to **spread** [spred] (sich) verbreiten **V AC2**, 83
spring [sprɪŋ] Frühling **III**
to **spy** on ['spaɪ‿ɒn] nachspionieren; bespitzeln °**V U2**, 67
square [skweə] Quadrat; Quadrat- **V AC1**, 8
to **squat** down [ˌskwɒt 'daʊn] in die Hocke gehen; sich hinhocken ⟨**V U1**, 29⟩
squirrel ['skwɪrəl] Eichhörnchen **I**
to **stack** [stæk] stapeln **V U2**, 56
stadium ['steɪdiəm] Stadion **II**
staff writer ['stɑ:f ˌraɪtə] festangestellter Journalist/festangestellte Journalistin ⟨**VTS3**, 111⟩
stage [steɪdʒ] Bühne **III**
stage direction ['steɪdʒ dɪˌrekʃn] Regieanweisung **III**
to **stage** [steɪdʒ] aufführen **III**; inszenieren **IV**
stairs *(pl)* [steəz] Treppe **III**
to **stalk** sb [stɔ:k] jmdn. stalken; jmdm. nachstellen **V U3**, 101
food **stall** ['fu:d stɔ:l] Essensstand; Fressbude ⟨**V U3**, 97⟩
*to **stand** [stænd] stehen **I**
*to **stand** in line *(AE)* [ˌstænd‿ɪn 'laɪn] anstehen; Schlange stehen; (sich) anstellen **IV**
*to **stand** in the way of sb/sth [ˌstænd ɪn ðə 'weɪ‿əv] jmdm./etw. im Weg stehen **III**
*to **stand** out (from) [ˌstænd‿'aʊt] sich abheben (von); herausragen (aus) **V U2**, 49
*to **stand** up [ˌstænd‿'ʌp] aufstehen *(von einer Sitzgelegenheit)* **I**
*to **stand** up for sb/sth [ˌstænd‿'ʌp fə] jmdn./etw. verteidigen; für jmdn./etw. einstehen **V U1**, 28
standard ['stændəd] Standard °**V U2**, 51

standard of living [ˌstændəd_əv 'lɪvɪŋ] Lebensstandard **IV**
to **standardize** *(AE)* ['stændədaɪz] standardisieren; vereinheitlichen **V U2**, 62
standpoint ['stænpɔɪnt] Standpunkt; Haltung °**VTS3**, 112
star [stɑ:] Star; Stern **I**
to **stare** [steə] starren; anstarren **I**
start [stɑ:t] Anfang; Start **III**
to **start** [stɑ:t] anfangen; beginnen; starten **I**; *hier:* gründen **III**
*to get **started** [ˌget 'stɑ:tɪd] anfangen **II**
to **start** all over again [ˌstɑ:t_ɔ:l_'əʊvər_əˌgen] ganz von vorn beginnen **IV**
to **start** off [ˌstɑ:t_'ɒf] anfangen; beginnen; starten **IV**
starting place ['stɑ:tɪŋ pleɪs] Startpunkt **II**
startled ['stɑ:tld] alarmiert; verblüfft ⟨**V U2**, 62⟩
startling ['stɑ:tlɪŋ] alarmierend; verblüffend ⟨**V U2**, 63⟩
start-up company ['stɑ:tʌp ˌkʌmpəni] Start-up(-Unternehmen); Unternehmensgründung **V U3**, 90
state [steɪt] Staat; Bundesstaat; Land **IV**
head of **state** [ˌhed_əv 'steɪt] Staatsoberhaupt **II**
to **state** [steɪt] darlegen; darstellen **IV**; nennen °**V U2**, 50
statement ['steɪtmənt] Aussage; Behauptung; Erklärung **II**
station ['steɪʃn] Haltestelle; Bahnhof; Station **I**; Sender **II**
bus **station** ['bʌs ˌsteɪʃn] Busbahnhof **I**
statistics *(pl)* [stə'tɪstɪks] Statistik **IV**
statue ['stætʃu:] Statue; Standbild **IV**
to **stay** [steɪ] bleiben **I**; übernachten **II**
to **stay** away from [ˌsteɪ_ə'weɪ frəm] fernbleiben von; meiden **II**
to **stay** in touch (with) [ˌsteɪ ɪn 'tʌtʃ wɪð] in Kontakt bleiben (mit) **II**
to **stay** with ['steɪ wɪð] wohnen bei **II**
Stay the way you are. [ˌsteɪ ðə weɪ ju 'ɑ:] Bleib wie du bist. **III**
steady ['stedi] kontinuierlich; unaufhörlich **III**
steak [steɪk] Steak **I**
*to **steal** [sti:l] stehlen **II**
steam [sti:m] Dampf **III**
steam engine ['sti:m_endʒɪn] Dampfmaschine **III**
step [step] Stufe; Schritt **I**
step-by-**step** [ˌstepbaɪ'step] Schritt-für-Schritt- **II**
to **step** [step] treten; steigen **IV**
to **step** into a story slowly [step_ˌɪntʊ ə ˌstɔ:ri 'sləʊli] eine Geschichte langsam entwickeln **III**
stepmum ['stepmʌm] Stiefmutter **I**
stereotype ['steriəʊtaɪp] Klischee; Stereotyp **V U2**, 49
gender **stereotyping** ['dʒendə ˌsteriəʊtaɪpɪŋ] geschlechtsspezifische Klischees **V U2**, 49
steroid ['sterɔɪd] Steroide *(Pl.)* ⟨**VTS3**, 111⟩
*to **stick** out [ˌstɪk_'aʊt] hinausstrecken **IV**
*to **stick** with sb ['stɪk wɪð] zu jmdm. halten; bei jmdm. bleiben ⟨**V U1**, 31⟩
still [stɪl] Standbild **II**
still [stɪl] still **I**
*to keep one's feet or hands **still** [ˌki:p wʌnz 'fi:t_ɔ: 'hændz stɪl] die Beine und Hände ruhig halten **III**
still [stɪl] noch; immer noch **I**; dennoch **II**
*to **sting** [stɪŋ] stechen **III**
marine **stinger** [məˌri:n 'stɪŋə] Seewespe *(Würfelquallen-Art)* **V U1**, 14
stir [stɜ:] Bewegung; Erregung; Aufruhr ⟨**V U2**, 62⟩
to cause a **stir** [ˌkɔ:z_ə 'stɜ:] für Aufsehen sorgen **V U3**, 86
stomach ['stʌmək] Magen; Bauch **II**
my **stomach** churns [maɪ ˌstʌmək 'tʃɜ:nz] mir dreht sich der Magen um ⟨**V U1**, 28⟩
stomachache ['stʌməkeɪk] Bauchschmerzen; Bauchweh **II**
stone [stəʊn] Stein; Stein- **III**
stop [stɒp] Haltestelle; Halt **II**
to **stop** [stɒp] aufhören (mit); anhalten; stoppen **I**
Stop and think [ˌstɒp_ənd 'θɪŋk] Warte/Wartet und denk/denkt nach. **I**
to **stop** sb from doing sth ['stɒp frəm] jmdn. davon abhalten, etw. zu tun **VTS3**, 112
Stop it! ['stɒp_ɪt] Mach/Macht das aus!; Hör/Hört auf! **I**
store *(AE)* [stɔ:] Laden; Geschäft **IV**
storm [stɔ:m] Sturm **I**
story ['stɔ:ri], **stories** ['stɔ:riz] *(pl)* Story; Geschichte; Erzählung **I**
photo **story** ['fəʊtəʊ ˌstɔ:ri] Fotostory; Bildgeschichte **I**
to step into a **story** slowly [step_ˌɪntʊ ə ˌstɔ:ri 'sləʊli] eine Geschichte langsam entwickeln **III**
storyline ['stɔ:rilaɪn] Handlung **IV**
storyteller ['stɔ:riˌtelə] Geschichtenerzähler/-in **IV**
straight [streɪt] gerade; direkt; geradewegs **III**; heterosexuell **V AC2**, 82
straight away [ˌstreɪt_ə'weɪ] sofort; gleich **III**
straight on [streɪt_'ɒn] geradeaus **I**
to **straighten** up [ˌstreɪtn_'ʌp] aufräumen ⟨**V U3**, 101⟩
strange [streɪndʒ] fremd; seltsam; merkwürdig **I**
stranger ['streɪndʒə] Fremde/-r **IV**
strategy ['strætədʒi] Strategie **IV**
strawberry ['strɔ:bri] Erdbeere **V U3**, 93
to **stream** out [ˌstri:m_'aʊt] hinausströmen ⟨**V U1**, 29⟩
street [stri:t] Straße *(in der Stadt)* **I**
in the **street** [ˌɪn ðə 'stri:t] in der Straße; auf der Straße **I**
street fair ['stri:t feə] Straßenfest **V AC2**, 81
the high **street** [ðə 'haɪ ˌstri:t] die Haupteinkaufsstraße **III**
strength [streŋθ] Stärke; Kraft **V U1**, 28
stress [stres] Betonung **III**
to **stress** [stres] betonen; hervorheben **III**
*to be **stressed** out [bi ˌstrest_'aʊt] völlig gestresst sein **III**
stretchy ['stretʃi] Stretch-; elastisch ⟨**V U1**, 28⟩
strict [strɪkt] streng; strikt **III**
stripe [straɪp] Streifen **IV**
to **stroll** [strəʊl] schlendern; bummeln; spazieren **V U3**, 86
strong [strɒŋ] stark **II**
structure ['strʌktʃə] Struktur; Aufbau; Gliederung **III**
to **structure** ['strʌktʃə] strukturieren; gliedern **IV**
struggle ['strʌgl] Anstrengung; Kampf **IV**
to **struggle** ['strʌgl] kämpfen; Mühe haben; ringen **IV**
*to be **stuck** [bi 'stʌk] festsitzen; feststecken; hängen bleiben **IV**
stuck in the middle of … [ˌstʌk ɪn ðə 'mɪdl_əv] mitten in … stecken; feststecken in … **III**
student ['stju:dnt] Schüler/-in; Student/-in **I**
exchange **student** [ɪks'tʃeɪndʒ ˌstju:dnt] Austauschschüler/-in **III**
student council [ˌstju:dnt 'kaʊnsl] Schülerrat **V AC3**, 114
student exchange ['stju:dnt ɪksˌtʃeɪndʒ] Schüleraustausch **III**
studies *(pl)* ['stʌdiz] Studium; Lernen; Arbeit für die Schule **II**
studio ['stju:diəʊ] Studio; Atelier **IV**
recording **studio** [rɪ'kɔ:dɪŋ ˌstju:diəʊ] Aufnahmestudio; Tonstudio **I**
study ['stʌdi] Studie; Untersuchung **VTS2**, 77
to **study** ['stʌdi] studieren; lernen **III**
stuff [stʌf] Zeug **I**
stunt [stʌnt] Stunt **V AC3**, 114
stupid ['stju:pɪd] dumm; blöd **II**
style [staɪl] Stil **III**
stylistic [staɪ'lɪstɪk] Stil-; stilistisch **IV**
subject ['sʌbdʒɪkt] Schulfach; Subjekt; Satzgegenstand **II**; Thema **III**
sub-point ['sʌbpɔɪnt] Unterpunkt °**V U3**, 98
substance ['sʌbstns] Substanz; Gehalt **V U3**, 98
substitute ['sʌbstɪtju:t] Ersatz; Ersatz- **II**
suburb ['sʌbɜ:b] Vorort **IV**
suburban [sə'bɜ:bn] Vorstadt- **IV**
subway *(AE)* ['sʌbweɪ] U-Bahn **IV**
to **succeed** (in) [sək'si:d_ɪn] Erfolg haben (in/bei/mit) **III**
success [sək'ses] Erfolg **III**
successful [sək'sesfl] erfolgreich **III**

such [sʌtʃ] solch; solche/-r/-s **II**
such as ['sʌtʃ‿əz] (solche) wie; wie (zum Beispiel) ⟨**V AC1**, 11⟩
It **sucks**. *(slang)* [ɪt 'sʌks] Das ist zum Kotzen. **IV**
sudden ['sʌdn] plötzlich ⟨**V U2**, 62⟩
suddenly ['sʌdnli] plötzlich; auf einmal **I**
to **sue** sb for sth [su:] jmdn. wegen etw. verklagen ⟨**V U3**, 101⟩
to **suffer** (from) ['sʌfə frəm] leiden (unter) **IV**
sugar ['ʃʊgə] Zucker **III**
to **suggest** [sə'dʒest] vorschlagen **III**; andeuten; nahelegen **IV**
suggestion [sə'dʒestʃn] Vorschlag; Anregung **I**
suit [su:t] Anzug; Kostüm **IV**
to **suit** sb [su:t] (zu) jmdm. passen; jmdm. stehen **V U2**, 59
suitable ['su:təbl] geeignet; passend **V U3**, 86
suitcase ['su:tkeɪs] Koffer **III**
to **sum** up [ˌsʌm‿'ʌp] zusammenfassen **II**
to **summarise** ['sʌmraɪz] zusammenfassen **III**
to **summarize** *(AE)* ['sʌmraɪz] zusammenfassen **IV**
summary ['sʌmri] Zusammenfassung **III**
summer ['sʌmə] Sommer **II**
summer camp ['sʌmə kæmp] Sommerferienlager **II**
summit ['sʌmɪt] Gipfel; Berggipfel **IV**
sun [sʌn] Sonne **II**
Sunday ['sʌndeɪ] Sonntag **I**
sunflower ['sʌnflaʊə] Sonnenblume **III**
sunglasses *(pl)* ['sʌnˌglɑ:sɪz] Sonnenbrille ⟨**V U3**, 100⟩
sunny ['sʌni] sonnig **V U3**, 90
sunset ['sʌnset] Sonnenuntergang **IV**
super ['su:pə] super **IV**
superhero ['su:pəˌhɪərəʊ] Superheld **IV**
superlative [su:'pɜ:lətɪv] Superlativ **II**
supermarket ['su:pəˌmɑ:kɪt] Supermarkt **I**
supermodel ['su:pəˌmɒdl] Topmodel ⟨**V U3**, 100⟩
supernatural ['su:pəˌnætʃrl] übernatürlich **III**
superpower ['su:pəˌpaʊə] Supermacht **II**
superstar ['su:pəˌstɑ:] Superstar ⟨**V U3**, 101⟩
to **supply** [sə'plaɪ] versorgen **II**
support *(no pl)* [sə'pɔ:t] Unterstützung; Hilfe **IV**
to **support** [sə'pɔ:t] unterstützen **III**
supporting [sə'pɔ:tɪŋ] unterstützend °**VTS3**, 109
supporting role [sə'pɔ:tɪŋ ˌrəʊl] Nebenrolle **VTS1**, 38
*to be **supposed** to *(+ inf)* [bi sə'pəʊzd tə] sollen **V U2**, 48
sure [ʃʊə; ʃɔ:] sicher **I**
*to make **sure** [ˌmeɪk 'ʃɔ:] sich versichern **I**
I'm (not) **sure** … [ˌaɪm nɒt 'ʃʊə] Ich bin mir (nicht) sicher … **III**

surf instructor [ˌsɜ:f‿ɪn'strʌktə] Surflehrer/-in **V AC1**, 10
surface ['sɜ:fɪs] Oberfläche **IV**
surfer ['sɜ:fə] Surfer/-in; Wellenreiter/-in ⟨**V U3**, 92⟩
surfing ['sɜ:fɪŋ] Surfen **II**
surgery ['sɜ:dʒəri] Arztpraxis; Praxis; Praxisräume **I**
plastic **surgery** *(no pl)* [ˌplæstɪk 'sɜ:dʒəri] Schönheitschirurgie **V AC1**, 9
surprise [sə'praɪz] Überraschung **I**
to **surprise** [sə'praɪz] überraschen **II**
*to be **surprised** [bi sə'praɪzd] überrascht sein **II**
surprising [sə'praɪzɪŋ] überraschend **II**
to **surround** [sə'raʊnd] umgeben; umringen **IV**
surroundings *(pl)* [sə'raʊndɪŋz] Umgebung **VTS1**, 43
survey ['sɜ:veɪ] Umfrage; Studie **I**
survival [sə'vaɪvl] Überleben **V U1**, 15
to **survive** [sə'vaɪv] überleben **III**
survivor [sə'vaɪvə] Überlebende/-r **IV**
*to be **suspended** [bi sə'spendɪd] suspendiert werden; zeitweilig vom Unterricht ausgeschlossen werden **IV**
suspense [sə'spens] Spannung **II**
suspicious [sə'spɪʃəs] misstrauisch; argwöhnisch **III**; verdächtig **IV**
to **swap** [swɒp] tauschen **IV**
to **swap** roles [ˌswɒp 'rəʊlz] Rollen tauschen **I**
*to **swear** [sweə] schwören ⟨**V U3**, 101⟩
bead of **sweat** [ˌbi:d‿əv 'swet] Schweißperle ⟨**V U3**, 102⟩
sweatshirt ['swetʃɜ:t] Sweatshirt **VTS3**, 111
sweatshop ['swetʃɒp] Ausbeuterbetrieb **IV**
*to be **swept** out to sea [bi ˌswept‿aʊt tə 'si:] aufs offene Meer getrieben werden **V U1**, 14
sweet [swi:t] süß **I**
sweets *(pl)* [swi:ts] Süßigkeiten; Bonbons **I**
swim [swɪm] Schwimmen ⟨**V U1**, 30⟩
*to **swim** [swɪm] schwimmen **I**
swimming ['swɪmɪŋ] Schwimmen **I**
*to go **swimming** [ˌgəʊ 'swɪmɪŋ] Schwimmen gehen **I**
swimming pool ['swɪmɪŋ ˌpu:l] Swimmingpool; Schwimmbecken **III**
swirl [swɜ:l] Wirbel; Strudel ⟨**V U1**, 29⟩
swirly ['swɜ:li] wirbelnd ⟨**V U1**, 30⟩
switch [swɪtʃ] Schalter **III**
to **switch** [swɪtʃ] wechseln °**V U2**, 67
to **switch** off [ˌswɪtʃ‿'ɒf] ausschalten **IV**
syllable ['sɪləbl] Silbe **III**
symbol ['sɪmbl] Symbol **II**
symbolic [sɪm'bɒlɪk] symbolisch **IV**
to **symbolize** *(AE)* ['sɪmbəlaɪz] symbolisieren **IV**
symptom ['sɪmtəm] Symptom; Merkmal ⟨**V AC1**, 11⟩
system ['sɪstəm] System **IV**

T

table ['teɪbl] Tisch **I**; Tabelle **IV**
*to set the **table** [ˌset ðə 'teɪbl] den Tisch decken **IV**
the Round **Table** [ðə ˌraʊnd 'teɪbl] die Tafelrunde **II**
tablet ['tæblət] Tablet **II**; Tafel **IV**
tabloid ['tæblɔɪd] Boulevardzeitung **V U3**, 100
taekwondo [ˌtækwʌn'du:] Taekwondo **II**
question **tag** ['kwestʃən ˌtæg] Frageanhängsel; Bestätigungsfrage **II**
tail [teɪl] Schwanz; Schweif **I**
*to **take** [teɪk] nehmen; mitnehmen; wegnehmen; bringen; mitbringen **I**; dauern; (Zeit) brauchen **II**
*to **take** a breath [ˌteɪk‿ə 'breθ] Luft holen; Atem holen **III**
*to **take** a look at [ˌteɪk‿ə 'lʊk‿æt] einen Blick werfen auf **II**
*to **take** a message [ˌteɪk‿ə 'mesɪdʒ] eine Nachricht entgegennehmen; jmdm. etw. ausrichten **I**
*to **take** a risk [ˌteɪk‿ə 'rɪsk] ein Risiko eingehen **III**
*to **take** a test [ˌteɪk‿ə 'test] einen Test machen **II**
*to **take** a vote [ˌteɪk‿ə 'vəʊt] abstimmen **I**
*to **take** care of sb/sth [ˌteɪk‿'keər‿əv] sich um jmdn./etw. kümmern; für jmdn. sorgen **III**
*to **take** notes [ˌteɪk 'nəʊts] sich Notizen machen **I**
*to **take** off [ˌteɪk‿'ɒf] abnehmen; herunternehmen; ausziehen **I**
*to **take** part (in) [ˌteɪk 'pɑ:t (ɪn)] teilnehmen (an) **II**
*to **take** photos [ˌteɪk 'fəʊtəʊz] fotografieren; Fotos machen **I**
*to **take** place [ˌteɪk 'pleɪs] stattfinden **I**
*to **take** sth the wrong way [ˌteɪk‿ðə rɒŋ 'weɪ] etw. falsch auffassen; etw. in den falschen Hals bekommen **V AC2**, 83
*to **take** the day off [ˌteɪk ðə ˌdeɪ‿'ɒf] sich den Tag freinehmen **IV**
*to **take** the lead [ˌteɪk ðə 'li:d] die Führung übernehmen **V AC3**, 115
Take a deep breath. [ˌteɪk‿ə ˌdi:p 'breθ] Atme(t) tief ein. **II**
Take turns. [ˌteɪk 'tɜ:nz] Wechselt euch ab. **I**
take-off ['teɪk‿ɒf] Start; Abheben **III**
talent ['tælənt] Talent **I**
to showcase one's **talent** [ˌʃəʊkeɪs wʌnz 'tælənt] sein Talent unter Beweis stellen **V U3**, 86
talent show ['tælənt ˌʃəʊ] Talentwettbewerb **I**
talk [tɔ:k] Vortrag; Rede; Gespräch; Unterhaltung **IV**
*to give a **talk** [ˌgɪv‿ə 'tɔ:k] einen Vortrag halten **IV**

small **talk** ['smɔ:l ˌtɔ:k] Smalltalk **III**
to **talk** [tɔ:k] sprechen; reden **I**
to **talk** about … ['tɔ:k‿əbaʊt] sprechen über; erzählen von **I**
to **talk** sb out of sth [ˌtɔ:k‿'aʊt‿əv] jmdm. etw. ausreden °**V U3**, 103
to **talk** to ['tɔ:k tə] reden mit **I**
to **talk** with your mouth full [ˌtɔ:k wɪð jɔ: 'maʊθ fʊl] mit vollem Mund sprechen **III**
talker ['tɔ:kə] Sprecher/-in **III**
talking ['tɔ:kɪŋ] Sprechen **I**
tall [tɔ:l] groß; hoch **II**
tanker plane ['tæŋkə ˌpleɪn] Tankflugzeug **V U3**, 94
to **tap** [tæp] antippen **II**; klopfen ⟨**V U1**, 29⟩
target ['tɑ:gɪt] Ziel; Ziel- **IV**
tartan ['tɑ:tn] Schottenkaro *(bestimmtes Muster eines Clans)*; karierter Schottenstoff **III**
task [tɑ:sk] Aufgabe; Auftrag **I**
to **taste** [teɪst] schmecken; probieren **III**
tasteless ['teɪstləs] geschmacklos ⟨**V TS3**, 113⟩
tattoo [tæt'u:] Tattoo; Tätowierung **III**
tax [tæks] Steuer; Abgabe **V U2**, 56
taxi ['tæksi] Taxi **II**
tea [ti:] Tee **I**
tea bag ['ti: bæg] Teebeutel **III**
*to **teach** [ti:tʃ] unterrichten; lehren; beibringen **II**
*to **teach** somebody a lesson [ˌti:tʃ‿ə 'lesn] jmdm. eine Lehre/Lektion erteilen **II**
teacher ['ti:tʃə] Lehrer/-in **I**
team [ti:m] Team; Gruppe **II**
*to be a **team** player [ˌbi‿ə 'ti:m ˌpleɪə] gern im Team arbeiten **V U2**, 48
tear [tɪə] Träne **V TS1**, 40
to **tease** sb [ti:z] jmdn. aufziehen; jmdn. hänseln; jmdn. ärgern **III**
tech [tek] Technologie; Technik **IV**
techie ['teki] Technikfreak ⟨**V U3**, 101⟩
technique [tek'ni:k] Methode; Technik **IV**
narrative **technique** [ˌnærətɪv tek'ni:k] Erzähltechnik **IV**
technological [ˌteknə'lɒdʒɪkl] technisch; technologisch ⟨**V AC1**, 11⟩
Technology [tek'nɒlədʒi] Technik; Computerunterricht **II**
technology [tek'nɒlədʒi] Technologie **II**
teen [ti:n] Jugend- **II**; Teenager; Jugendliche/-r **III**
teenage ['ti:neɪdʒ] jugendlich; Jugend- **III**
teenager ['ti:nˌeɪdʒə] Teenager; Jugendliche/-r **I**
telegraph ['telɪgrɑ:f] Telegraf **IV**
telephone ['telɪfəʊn] Telefon **I**
*to **tell** [tel] erzählen; sagen; mitteilen **I**
Tell me about … ['tel mi:‿əˌbaʊt] Erzähle mir von … **I**
temperature ['temprətʃə] Temperatur **IV**
to **tempt** [tempt] in Versuchung führen; reizen **III**
temptation [temp'teɪʃn] Versuchung **IV**
tempted ['temptɪd] in Versuchung gebracht **III**
tempting ['temptɪŋ] verführerisch **III**
ten [ten] zehn **I**
ten times [ten 'taɪmz] zehnmal **I**
to **tend** to ['tend tə] neigen zu; tendieren zu ⟨**V AC1**, 11⟩
tendency ['tendənsi] Tendenz **V U3**, 85
tennis ['tenɪs] Tennis **I**
tense [tens] Zeit; Zeitform *(grammatisch)* **II**
term [tɜ:m] Begriff **III**
terrace ['terɪs] Terrasse **V U1**, 14
terrible ['terəbl] schrecklich; schlimm; furchtbar **IV**
territory ['terɪtri] Gebiet; Revier; Territorium **V U1**, 23
test [test] Test; Klassenarbeit; Prüfung **I**
*to take a **test** [ˌteɪk‿ə 'test] einen Test machen **II**
to **test** [test] testen; prüfen **II**
testimonial [ˌtestɪ'məʊniəl] Erfahrungsbericht **V U2**, 48
text [tekst] Text **I**
factual **text** [ˌfæktʃʊəl 'tekst] Sachtext **III**
text (message) ['tekst ˌmesɪdʒ] SMS; Kurznachricht **I**
wiki **(text)** ['wɪkɪ ˌtekst] Wikitext **IV**
to **text** [tekst] eine SMS schicken **II**
than [ðæn] als *(bei Vergleichen)* **II**
more … **than** ['mɔ: ðən] mehr … als **I**
*to give **thanks** [ˌgɪv 'θæŋks] danken **IV**
to **thank** [θæŋk] danken **II**
Thank you. ['θæŋk ju] Danke. **I**
thankful ['θæŋkfl] dankbar **I**
Thanks. [θæŋks] Danke. **I**
thanks to ['θæŋks tə] dank; wegen **V U3**, 94
that [ðæt] so *(Betonung)* **III**
that much [ðæt 'mʌtʃ] so viel **III**
that [ðæt; ðət] dass **I**
so **(that)** [ˌsəʊ 'ðæt] damit; so dass **IV**
that [ðæt] das; jenes **I**
after **that** [ˌɑ:ftə 'ðæt] danach **I**
like **that** [laɪk 'ðæt] so **I**
That was close! [ˌðæt wəz 'kləʊs] Das war knapp! **I**
that way [ˌðæt 'weɪ] so; auf diese Weise **V U3**, 86
That's … [ðæts] Das macht … **I**
that's how [ðæts 'haʊ] so **II**
That's what friends are for. [ˌðæts wɒt 'frendz‿ɑ: ˌfɔ:] Dafür sind Freunde da. **I**
that's why [ðæts 'waɪ] deshalb **II**
that [ðæt] der; dem; den; die; das *(Relativpronomen)* **II**
the [ðə; ði] der; die *(auch Pl.)*; das **I**
the others [ði‿'ʌðəz] die anderen **I**
the same [ðə 'seɪm] der-/die-/dasselbe; der/die/das gleiche **I**
the … **the** [ðə … ðə] je … desto **II**
theater *(AE)* ['θɪətə] Theater **IV**
movie **theater** *(AE)* ['mu:vi ˌθɪətə] Kino **IV**
theatre ['θɪətə] Theater **I**
their [ðeə] ihr/-e *(Pl.)* **I**
them [ðem] sie *(Pl.)*; ihnen **I**
theme [θi:m] Thema; Motto **I**
theme song ['θi:m sɒŋ] Titelmelodie **IV**
then [ðen] dann; danach **I**
back **then** [bæk 'ðen] damals **III**
theory ['θɪəri] Theorie **IV**
therapist ['θerəpɪst] Therapeut ⟨**V U3**, 101⟩
there [ðeə] da; dort; dahin; dorthin **I**
there is/are [ðər‿'ɪz/'ɑ:] da ist/sind; es gibt **I**
There's no need to … [ˌðeəz nəʊ 'ni:d tə] Es gibt keinen Grund zu … **III**
therefore ['ðeəfɔ:] deshalb; deswegen; daher; somit **V U2**, 51
these [ði:z] diese (hier) **I**
these days [ˌði:z 'deɪz] zurzeit **III**; heutzutage ⟨**V U3**, 101⟩
they [ðeɪ] sie *(Pl.)* **I**
It's …/**They**'re … [ɪts/ðeə] Es kostet …/Sie kosten … **I**
thick [θɪk] dick *(nicht für Personen)* **III**
thing [θɪŋ] Ding; Sache **I**
*to **think** [θɪŋk] denken; nachdenken; glauben **I**
Stop and **think** [ˌstɒp‿ənd 'θɪŋk] Warte/Wartet und denk/denkt nach. **I**
*to **think** of ['θɪŋk‿əv] halten von; denken über **I**; (sich) ausdenken; sich etwas einfallen lassen **II**
Think of … ['θɪŋk‿əv] Denke/Denkt an … **I**
*to **think** up [θɪŋk‿'ʌp] (sich) ausdenken; sich einfallen lassen **IV**
third [θɜ:d] dritte/-r/-s **I**
third person narrator [θɜ:d ˌpɜ:sn nə'reɪtə] Er/Sie-Erzähler/-in **III**
thirsty ['θɜ:sti] durstig **III**
thirteen [ˌθɜ:'ti:n] dreizehn **I**
this [ðɪs] dies; diese/-r/-s **I**
this afternoon [ðɪs 'ɑ:ftənu:n] heute Nachmittag **II**
this early ['ðɪs ˌɜ:li] so früh **III**
This is … ['ðɪs‿ɪz] Das (hier) ist … **I**
thistle ['θɪsl] Distel **III**
thongs *(pl)* [θɒŋz] Flip-Flops *(amerik.)* *(austral.)* ⟨**V U1**, 21⟩
those [ðəʊz] diese dort; jene **I**
those in power [ˌðəʊz ɪn 'paʊə] die Regierenden; die Herrschenden **III**
though [ðəʊ] doch; jedoch; obwohl **IV**
even **though** [ˌi:vn 'ðəʊ] auch wenn; obwohl **IV**
thought [θɔ:t] Gedanke **II**
thousands of ['θaʊzndz‿əv] tausende (von) **I**
three [θri:] drei **I**
thrilled [θrɪld] aufgeregt; außer sich vor Freude **IV**
thrilling ['θrɪlɪŋ] aufregend **IV**
through [θru:] durch **I**

throughout [θru'aʊt] während; überall in **V U2**, 62
*to **throw** (at) [θrəʊ] werfen (nach) **I**
*to **throw** away [ˌθrəʊ‿ə'weɪ] wegwerfen **I**
throw the dice twice [ˌθrəʊ ðə daɪs 'twaɪs] würfle zweimal **II**
to **thud** [θʌd] pochen ⟨**V U3**, 102⟩
thumb [θʌm] Daumen **II**
thunder *(no pl)* ['θʌndə] Donner **II**
Thursday ['θɜ:zdeɪ] Donnerstag **I**
to **tick** [tɪk] abhaken **II**
ticket ['tɪkɪt] Los; Ticket; Eintrittskarte **I**; Fahrschein **II**
one-way **ticket** ['wʌnweɪ ˌtɪkɪt] einfache Fahrkarte **II**
return **ticket** [rɪ'tɜ:n ˌtɪkɪt] Hin- und Rückfahrkarte **II**
single **ticket** ['sɪŋgl ˌtɪkɪt] einfache Fahrkarte **II**
ticket office ['tɪkɪt ˌɒfɪs] Kartenschalter **III**
high **tide** ['haɪ ˌtaɪd] Flut **II**
low **tide** ['ləʊ ˌtaɪd] Ebbe **II**
to **tidy** *(a room)* ['taɪdi] aufräumen; in Ordnung bringen **I**
to **tie** (to) ['taɪ tə] binden (an); fesseln (an) **III**
tight [taɪt] eng ⟨**V AC2**, 80⟩
till [tɪl] bis **I**
timber ['tɪmbə] Holz; Bauholz **IV**
time [taɪm] Zeit **I**; Mal **II**
all the **time** [ˌɔ:l ðə 'taɪm] die ganze Zeit **II**
at all **times** [ˌət‿ɔ:l 'taɪmz] immer; jederzeit; stets **V U2**, 48
at the same **time** [ət ðə ˌseɪm 'taɪm] zur selben Zeit; gleichzeitig **I**
at the **time** [ˌət ðə 'taɪm] damals **IV**
*to buy **time** [ˌbaɪ 'taɪm] Zeit gewinnen **IV**
by the **time** [ˌbaɪ ðə 'taɪm] bis *(zu dem Zeitpunkt)* **IV**
free **time** [ˌfri: 'taɪm] Freizeit **I**
on **time** [ɒn 'taɪm] pünktlich **II**
ten **times** [ten 'taɪmz] zehnmal **I**
time line ['taɪm ˌlaɪn] Zeitstrahl **I**
time slot ['taɪm slɒt] Zeitfenster **II**
I can't wait till next **time**. [aɪ kɑ:nt ˌweɪt tɪl nekst 'taɪm] Ich kann es bis zum nächsten Mal kaum erwarten. **II**
just in **time** [ˌdʒʌst‿ɪn 'taɪm] gerade rechtzeitig **IV**
Time to get up! [ˌtaɪm tə ˌget‿'ʌp] Es ist Zeit aufzustehen! **I**
What **time**? [ˌwɒt 'taɪm] Um wie viel Uhr? **I**
What's the **time**? [ˌwɒts ðə 'taɪm] Wie spät ist es?; Wie viel Uhr ist es? **I**
to **time** [taɪm] den richtigen Zeitpunkt wählen **IV**
timetable ['taɪmˌteɪbl] Stundenplan; Fahrplan **I**
timing ['taɪmɪŋ] Timing *(Wahl des richtigen Zeitpunkts)* °**V U3**, 97
tin [tɪn] Zinn **II**
tin can ['tɪn kæn] Blechdose **III**
tinned [tɪnd] Dosen-; aus der Dose **I**
tiny ['taɪni] klein; winzig **III**
tip [tɪp] Tipp; Ratschlag **I**; Trinkgeld **IV**
to **tiptoe** ['tɪptəʊ] auf Zehenspitzen gehen **II**
tire *(AE)* [taɪə] Reifen **IV**
snow **tire** *(AE)* ['snəʊ ˌtaɪə] Winterreifen **IV**
tired [taɪəd] müde **I**
*to be **tired** of [bi 'taɪəd‿əv] es müde sein (zu); es leid sein (zu); es satt haben (zu) **IV**
title ['taɪtl] Titel; Überschrift **II**
to [tʊ; tə] zu; nach; auf; in; vor *(bei Uhrzeitangaben)* **I**
from ... **to** [frəm ... tə] von ... bis **I**
quarter past/**to** ['kwɔ:tə pɑ:st/tə] Viertel nach/vor **I**
to the point [tə ðə 'pɔɪnt] prägnant; treffend **III**
toast [təʊst] Toast **I**
to **toast** it up *(coll)* [ˌtəʊst‿ɪt‿'ʌp] in Stimmung kommen *(auf einer Party)* ⟨**V U2**, 47⟩
tobacco *(no pl)* [tə'bækəʊ] Tabak **III**
today [tə'deɪ] heute **I**
together [tə'geðə] zusammen; miteinander; gemeinsam **I**
toilet ['tɔɪlət] Toilette **I**
tolerance ['tɒlrns] Toleranz **V AC2**, 80
tolerant ['tɒlrnt] tolerant **III**
to **tolerate** ['tɒlreɪt] tolerieren; dulden **VTS3**, 108
tomato [tə'mɑ:təʊ], **tomatoes** [tə'mɑ:təʊz] *(pl)* Tomate **I**
tomorrow [tə'mɒrəʊ] morgen **I**
tone [təʊn] Ton; Signalton **IV**
tonight [tə'naɪt] heute Abend; heute Nacht **III**
too [tu:] auch; zu **I**
Too bad! [ˌtu: 'bæd] Zu dumm!; Schade! **I**
You **too**? [ju: 'tu:] Du auch? **I**
tool [tu:l] Werkzeug; Gerät **II**
toothbrush ['tu:θbrʌʃ] Zahnbürste **V U2**, 58
toothpaste ['tu:θpeɪst] Zahnpasta **IV**
top [tɒp] Spitze; oberer Teil; oberes Ende **I**
on **top** [ɒn 'tɒp] oben; obendrauf **I**
to **top** up [tɒp‿'ʌp] aufladen **II**
top [tɒp] Spitzen-; oberster; bester **V U2**, 56
topic ['tɒpɪk] Thema **II**
to **topple** ['tɒpl] stürzen ⟨**V U3**, 100⟩
torch [tɔ:tʃ] Fackel; Taschenlampe **II**
to **toss** out [ˌtɒs‿'aʊt] ausstoßen; hinauswerfen **IV**
total ['təʊtl] Summe; Gesamtmenge °**V U3**, 98
a **total** of [ə 'təʊtl‿əv] insgesamt **IV**
total ['təʊtl] gesamt; Gesamt- **IV**
total crap [ˌtəʊtl 'kræp] völliger Quatsch ⟨**VTS3**, 110⟩
totalitarian [təˌtælɪ'teəriən] totalitär °**V U2**, 67
totally ['təʊtli] völlig; total **IV**
totem pole ['təʊtəm ˌpəʊl] Totempfahl **IV**
*to keep in **touch** [ˌki:p‿ɪn 'tʌtʃ] in Kontakt bleiben **IV**
to stay in **touch** (with) [ˌsteɪ ɪn 'tʌtʃ wɪð] in Kontakt bleiben (mit) **II**
to **touch** [tʌtʃ] berühren; antippen **IV**
to **touch** down [tʌtʃ 'daʊn] landen **IV**
tour [tʊə] Tour; Fahrt; Rundgang **II**
audio **tour** ['ɔ:diəʊ ˌtʊə] Audioführung **II**
tour company ['tʊə ˌkʌmpəni] Reiseanbieter **IV**
tourism ['tʊərɪzm] Tourismus **II**
tourist ['tʊərɪst] Tourist/-in **I**
tourist board ['tʊərɪst bɔ:d] Touristeninformation **II**
tourist information centre [ˌtʊərɪst ɪnfə'meɪʃn ˌsentə] Touristeninformation **I**
toward [tə'wɔ:d] in Richtung; auf ... zu; darauf zu ⟨**V U3**, 101⟩
towards [tə'wɔ:dz] in Richtung; auf ... zu; darauf zu **II**; gegenüber °**V U1**, 31
tower [taʊə] Turm **III**
town [taʊn] Stadt **I**
edge of **town** [ˌedʒ‿əv 'taʊn] Stadtrand **IV**
toy [tɔɪ] Spielzeug **I**
to **trace** [treɪs] verfolgen; nachspüren **I**
to **trace** back [ˌtreɪs 'bæk] zurückverfolgen **V U1**, 18
track [træk] Weg; Pfad **V U1**, 17; Spur; Fährte **V U1**, 22
tractor ['træktə] Traktor **IV**
trade [treɪd] Handel **V U2**, 53
to **trade** [treɪd] austauschen **II**
tradition [trə'dɪʃn] Tradition **I**
traditional [trə'dɪʃnl] traditionell **III**
traffic ['træfɪk] Verkehr **III**
trail [treɪl] Weg; Pfad **IV**
walking **trail** ['wɔ:kɪŋ treɪl] Wanderweg **II**
trailer *(AE)* ['treɪlə] Wohnwagen **V U3**, 86
train [treɪn] Zug **I**
to **train** [treɪn] trainieren **II**
trainer ['treɪnə] Turnschuh **III**
training ['treɪnɪŋ] Training **II**; Ausbildung **V U3**, 98
character **trait** [ˌkærəktə 'treɪt] Charaktereigenschaft °**V U3**, 86
traitor ['treɪtə] Verräter/-in **IV**
transition [træn'zɪʃn] Übergang **V U3**, 97
transitive ['trænsətɪv] transitiv *(ein Objekt nach sich ziehend)* **IV**
to **translate** [trænz'leɪt] übersetzen **I**
translation [trænz'leɪʃn] Übersetzung **I**
to **transmit** [trænz'mɪt] übertragen **V U2**, 64
transport ['trænspɔ:t] Verkehrsmittel; Transport **II**
public **transport** *(no pl)* [ˌpʌblɪk 'trænspɔ:t] öffentliche Verkehrsmittel **II**
to **transport** [træn'spɔ:t] transportieren; befördern **IV**
transportation *(AE)* [ˌtrænspɔ:'teɪʃn] Transport **IV**
*to be **trapped** [bi 'træpt] eingeschlossen sein; in der Falle sitzen **III**
trash *(AE)* [træʃ] Abfall; Müll **IV**
travel ['trævl] (das) Reisen; Reise **II**

travel agency ['trævl͜ˌeɪdʒnsi] Reisebüro **III**
travel agent's ['trævl͜ˌeɪdʒnts] Reisebüro **II**
travel report [ˌtrævl rɪ'pɔ:t] Reisebericht **II**
to **travel** ['trævl] fahren; reisen **II**
traveler *(AE)* ['trævlə] Reisende/-r **IV**
traveller ['trævlə] Reisende/-r **III**
travelling *(no pl)* ['trævlɪŋ] (das) Reisen **III**
treasure ['treʒə] Schatz **II**
treat [tri:t] *hier:* Leckerli; Belohnung **III**
It's my **treat**. [ɪts 'maɪ ˌtri:t] Das geht auf meine Rechnung. **IV**
to **treat** [tri:t] behandeln **IV**
tree [tri:] Baum **I**
family **tree** ['fæmli ˌtri:] Stammbaum **I**
palm **tree** ['pɑ:m ˌtri:] Palme **II**
redwood **tree** ['redwʊd ˌtri:] Mammutbaum **IV**
pony **trekking** ['pəʊni ˌtrekɪŋ] Ponyreiten im Gelände **II**
trend [trend] Trend; Entwicklung; Richtung **V U3**, 92
trendsetting ['trendˌsetɪŋ] zukunftsweisend °**V U3**, 92
trial [traɪəl] Qualifikation **II**
tribe [traɪb] Stamm; Volksstamm **III**
trick [trɪk] Trick; Streich **I**
to play a **trick** (on) [ˌpleɪ͜ə 'trɪk͜ɒn] einen Streich spielen **I**
to **trick** [trɪk] austricksen; täuschen **IV**
tricky ['trɪki] schwierig; kompliziert **V U2**, 60
trifle ['traɪfl] Trifle *(englischer Nachtisch)* **I**
trilogy ['trɪlədʒi] Trilogie °**V U2**, 67
trip [trɪp] Trip; Reise; Ausflug; Fahrt **II**
trouble ['trʌbl] Ärger; Probleme; Schwierigkeiten **II**
*to get into **trouble** [ˌget͜ɪntə 'trʌbl] in Schwierigkeiten geraten **IV**
*to make **trouble** [ˌmeɪk 'trʌbl] Ärger machen; in Schwierigkeiten bringen **I**
troublemaker ['trʌblmeɪkə] Unruhestifter/-in **IV**
trousers *(pl)* ['traʊzəz] Hose **II**
trowel ['traʊəl] kleiner Spaten **II**
truck *(AE)* [trʌk] *hier:* Wagen; Truck; Lastwagen **IV**
truckload ['trʌkləʊd] Lastwagenladung **IV**
true [tru:] wahr **II**
*to be **true** to oneself [bi 'tru: tu wʌnˌself] sich selbst treu bleiben **IV**
*to come **true** [ˌkʌm 'tru:] wahr werden; in Erfüllung gehen **IV**
trunk *(AE)* [trʌŋk] Kofferraum **IV**
trust [trʌst] Vertrauen ⟨**V U3**, 102⟩
to **trust** [trʌst] vertrauen **III**
truth [tru:θ] Wahrheit **III**
to **try** [traɪ] versuchen; probieren **I**
to **try** on [ˌtraɪ͜'ɒn] anprobieren **II**
to **try** out [ˌtraɪ͜'aʊt] ausprobieren **III**
T-shirt ['ti:ʃɜ:t] T-Shirt **I**
tsunami [tsʊ'nɑ:mi] Tsunami *(durch Seebeben ausgelöste Flutwelle)* ⟨**V U3**, 96⟩
the **Tube** [ðə 'tju:b] die Londoner U-Bahn **II**
tucker *(Aus)* ['tʌkə] Essen ⟨**V U1**, 21⟩
Tudor ['tju:də] Tudor- **III**
Tuesday ['tju:zdeɪ] Dienstag **I**
tune [tju:n] Melodie **III**
tunic ['tju:nɪk] Tunika; Kittel ⟨**V U2**, 65⟩
tunnel ['tʌnl] Tunnel **I**
turbulent ['tɜ:bjələnt] turbulent; aufgewühlt **IV**
It's your **turn**. [ˌɪts 'jɔ: tɜ:n] Du bist dran. **I**
Take **turns**. [ˌteɪk 'tɜ:nz] Wechselt euch ab. **I**
Your **turn**. ['jɔ: tɜ:n] Du bist dran. **I**
to **turn** [tɜ:n] einbiegen; abbiegen **I**; drehen; (sich) umdrehen **III**
to **turn** (a)round [ˌtɜ:n͜(ə)'raʊnd] (sich) umdrehen; wenden **II**
to **turn** away from sb/sth [ˌtɜ:n͜ə'weɪ frəm] sich von jmdm./etw. abwenden ⟨**V U3**, 100⟩
to **turn** back [tɜ:n 'bæk] umkehren; zurückgehen **II**
to **turn** into [ˌtɜ:n͜'ɪntə] ändern in; umwandeln in **III**
to **turn** off [ˌtɜ:n͜'ɒf] abschalten; ausschalten **II**
to **turn** on [ˌtɜ:n͜'ɒn] einschalten **V AC1**, 9
to **turn** out to be [ˌtɜ:n͜'aʊt tə] sich herausstellen als ⟨**V U1**, 21⟩; °**V U2**, 67
to **turn** to ['tɜ:n tə] sich wenden an; sich zuwenden **II**
turning point ['tɜ:nɪŋ ˌpɔɪnt] Wendepunkt **III**
It **turned** out that … [ɪt ˌtɜ:nd͜'aʊt ðæt] Es stellte sich heraus, dass … **III**
turned off [ˌtɜ:nd͜'ɒf] abgetörnt **V TS1**, 42
turn-off ['tɜ:nɒf] Abzweigung ⟨**V U1**, 30⟩
turtle ['tɜ:tl] Schildkröte ⟨**V U1**, 29⟩
tusk [tʌsk] Stoßzahn **III**
tutor ['tju:tə] Klassenlehrer/-in **I**
tutor group ['tju:tə ˌgru:p] Klasse *(in einer englischen Schule)* **I**
tutorial [tju:'tɔ:riəl] Tutorium; Tutorial **IV**
TV (= television) [ˌti:'vi: ('telɪvɪʒn)] Fernsehen; Fernseher **I**
to watch **TV** [ˌwɒtʃ ti:'vi:] fernsehen **I**
tweet [twi:t] Nachricht auf Twitter **IV**
twelve [twelv] zwölf **I**
twice [twaɪs] zweimal **IV**
twin [twɪn] Zwilling; Zwillings- **II**
to **twist** your ankle [ˌtwɪst jɔ:r͜'æŋkl] sich den Knöchel verrenken **II**
two [tu:] zwei **I**
the **two** of them [ðə 'tu:͜əv ðəm] beide **II**
two of which ['tu:͜əv wɪtʃ] zwei von ihnen **II**
type [taɪp] Typ; Art; Sorte **III**
typical ['tɪpɪkl] typisch **I**
typically ['tɪpɪkli] typisch **III**; typischerweise °**V U2**, 67
tyre [taɪə] Reifen **IV**

U

u *(= you)* [ju:; jə] du; Sie; ihr **I**
UFO [ˌju:ef'əʊ] UFO **II**
ugly ['ʌgli] hässlich **IV**
umbrella [ʌm'brelə] Regenschirm °**V TS2**, 75
*to be **unable** to do sth [bi͜ʌn'eɪbl tə] unfähig sein, etw. zu tun; nicht in der Lage sein, etw. zu tun **V TS2**, 75
unbelievable [ˌʌnbɪ'li:vəbl] unglaublich; unglaubwürdig **IV**
uncle ['ʌŋkl] Onkel **I**
uncomfortable [ʌn'kʌmftəbl] unwohl; unbehaglich; unbequem **V TS1**, 40
under ['ʌndə] unter **I**
underfloor heating *(no pl)* [ˌʌndəflɔ: 'hi:tɪŋ] Fußbodenheizung **III**
underground ['ʌndəgraʊnd] U-Bahn **II**
underground ['ʌndəgraʊnd] unterirdisch **V U1**, 22
to **underline** [ˌʌndə'laɪn] unterstreichen **III**
*to **understand** [ˌʌndə'stænd] verstehen **I**
understanding [ˌʌndə'stændɪŋ] Verständnis **II**
understanding [ˌʌndə'stændɪŋ] verständnisvoll **V TS1**, 44
undeveloped [ˌʌndɪ'veləpt] unentwickelt; unausgereift **IV**
unending [ʌn'endɪŋ] unendlich ⟨**V U3**, 101⟩
unexpected [ˌʌnɪk'spektɪd] unerwartet **IV**
unfair [ʌn'feə] unfair **II**
unfamiliar [ˌʌnfə'mɪliə] nicht vertraut; unbekannt **III**
unfortunately [ʌn'fɔ:tʃnətli] leider; unglücklicherweise **V U2**, 51
unfriendly [ʌn'frendli] unfreundlich **II**
uniform ['ju:nɪfɔ:m] Uniform **I**
uniformed ['ju:nɪfɔ:md] uniformiert ⟨**V U1**, 28⟩
unimportant [ˌʌnɪm'pɔ:tnt] unwichtig ⟨**V AC1**, 11⟩
uninhabitable [ˌʌnɪn'hæbɪtəbl] unbewohnbar ⟨**V U1**, 16⟩
unique [ju:'ni:k] einzigartig **IV**
uniqueness [ju:'ni:knəs] Einzigartigkeit °**V U3**, 92
unit ['ju:nɪt] Lektion; Kapitel; Einheit **I**
united [ju:'naɪtɪd] vereint; vereinigt **IV**
university [ˌju:nɪ'vɜ:səti] Universität **V U1**, 29
the **unknown** [ði ˌʌn'nəʊn] das Unbekannte **IV**
unless [ən'les] es sei denn, (dass) …; wenn nicht **IV**
*to be **unlucky** [bi͜ʌn'lʌki] Pech haben **I**
unnecessary [ʌn'nesəsri] unnötig °**V U3**, 98
unofficial [ˌʌnə'fɪʃl] inoffiziell **III**
unopened [ʌn'əʊpnd] ungeöffnet °**V U1**, 28
to **unpack** [ʌn'pæk] auspacken **IV**
unpleasant [ʌn'pleznt] unangenehm; unerfreulich ⟨**V AC1**, 11⟩
unpredictable [ˌʌnprɪ'dɪktəbl] unvorhersehbar ⟨**V U2**, 65⟩
unreal [ˌʌn'rɪəl] irreal **III**

unrealistic [ˌʌnrɪəˈlɪstɪk] unrealistisch **IV**
unrelated to [ˌʌnrɪˈleɪtɪd tə] unzusammenhängend mit ⟨**V U2**, 63⟩
unsafe [ʌnˈseɪf] unsicher; gefährlich ⟨**VTS3**, 113⟩
unsuccessful [ˌʌnsəkˈsesfl] erfolglos; ergebnislos °**VTS2**, 76
unsure [ʌnˈʃʊə] unsicher **III**
until [ʌnˈtɪl] bis; erst wenn **II**
not **until** [ˌnɒt ənˈtɪl] nicht vor; erst um/im **IV**
unusual [ʌnˈjuːʒl] ungewöhnlich **V U3**, 95
unwillingly [ʌnˈwɪlɪŋli] ungern; widerwillig **V AC2**, 81
to **unwrap** [ʌnˈræp] auswickeln; auspacken **I**
up [ʌp] hinauf; (nach) oben **II**
*to cut **up** [kʌt ˈʌp] zerschneiden **IV**
to end **up** [ˌend ˈʌp] enden; landen **II**
*to get **up** [ˌget ˈʌp] aufstehen *(aus dem Bett)* **I**
*to give **up** [ˌgɪv ˈʌp] aufgeben **III**
to look **up** [ˌlʊk ˈʌp] nachschlagen; nachschauen **I**
to look **up** to sb [ˌlʊk ˈʌp tə] zu jmdm. aufschauen; jmdn. bewundern **VTS3**, 111
up to [ˈʌp tə] bis zu **IV**
up the front [ˌʌp ðə ˈfrʌnt] ganz vorn ⟨**V U1**, 29⟩
What's **up**? [ˌwɒts ˈʌp] Was ist los? **III**
*to build **upon** [ˌbɪld əˈpɒn] sich türmen auf ⟨**V U2**, 64⟩
upright [ˈʌpraɪt] aufrecht **V U1**, 28
*to **upset** [ʌpˈset] aus der Fassung bringen **III**
upset [ʌpˈset] aufgebracht; bestürzt **II**
upstairs [ʌpˈsteəz] nach oben; im Obergeschoss; oben **II**
up-to-date [ˌʌptəˈdeɪt] modern; zeitgemäß; aktuell **IV**
urban [ˈɜːbn] städtisch; Stadt- **IV**
urban sprawl [ˌɜːbn ˈsprɔːl] Urbanisierung; Zersiedelung; Ausuferung des Stadtgebiets ⟨**V U3**, 96⟩
urbanisation [ˌɜːbnaɪˈzeɪʃn] Urbanisierung; Verstädterung ⟨**V U3**, 96⟩
urbanised [ˈɜːbnaɪzd] verstädtert; urbanisiert ⟨**V U1**, 16⟩
to **urge** sb to do sth [ɜːdʒ] jmdn. zu etw. drängen **V U3**, 90
us [ʌs] uns **I**
US [juːˈes] US-amerikanisch **IV**
use [juːs] Verwendung; Gebrauch; Nutzen **IV**
*to make **use** of [meɪk ˈjuːz əv] benutzen; verwenden **IV**
to **use** [juːz] benutzen; verwenden; gebrauchen **I**
*to be **used** to [bi ˈjuːs tə] gewöhnt sein an; gewohnt sein **III**
*to get **used** to sth [ˌget ˈjuːzd tə] sich an etw. gewöhnen **IV**
used to *(+ infinitive)* [ˈjuːst tə] pflegte(n) zu; tat(en) früher **V U1**, 18
useful [ˈjuːsfl] nützlich; hilfreich **I**
Useful phrases [ˌjuːsfl ˈfreɪsɪz] nützliche Ausdrücke **I**
useless [ˈjuːsləs] nutzlos **III**
user [ˈjuːzə] Benutzer/-in ⟨**V AC1**, 11⟩
usual [ˈjuːʒl] üblich **III**
usually [ˈjuːʒli] normalerweise; gewöhnlich; meistens **I**
utopia [juːˈtəʊpiə] Utopie °**V U2**, 67

V

vacation *(AE)* [vəˈkeɪʃn] Ferien; Urlaub **IV**
to **vacuum** [ˈvækjuːm] staubsaugen **IV**
valid [ˈvælɪd] gültig ⟨**V U1**, 20⟩
valley [ˈvæli] Tal **IV**
valuable [ˈvæljuəbl] wertvoll **V AC3**, 115
value [ˈvæljuː] Wert **V U1**, 22
variety (of) [vəˈraɪəti əv] Vielzahl (an); Vielfalt (von) **V U1**, 20
various [ˈveəriəs] verschieden; verschiedenartig **V AC2**, 80
vegetable [ˈvedʒtəbl] Gemüse **III**
vegetarian [ˌvedʒɪˈteəriən] Vegetarier/-in **III**
vegetarian [ˌvedʒɪˈteəriən] vegetarisch **III**
vending machine [ˈvendɪŋ məˌʃiːn] Automat **III**
verb [vɜːb] Verb **I**
verse [vɜːs] Vers; Strophe **III**
version [ˈvɜːʃn] Version **III**
cover **version** [ˈkʌvə ˌvɜːʃn] Coverversion **III**
versus (vs.) [ˈvɜːsəs] gegen **III**
very [ˈveri] sehr **I**
very much [ˌveri ˈmʌtʃ] sehr **I**
vet [vet] Tierarzt/Tierärztin **I**
victim [ˈvɪktɪm] Opfer **V U1**, 18
Victorian [vɪkˈtɔːriən] viktorianisch; Viktorianer/-in **III**
video [ˈvɪdiəʊ] Video **II**
video chat [ˈvɪdiəʊ ˌtʃæt] Videochat **II**
view [vjuː] Aussicht; Sicht; Ausblick; Blick **II**; Ansicht; Einstellung; Standpunkt **IV**
point of **view** [ˌpɔɪnt əv ˈvjuː] Standpunkt; Ansicht; Perspektive **II**
to **view** [vjuː] ansehen; anschauen °**VTS1**, 41
viewer [ˈvjuːə] Zuschauer/-in **II**; Display *(Kamera)* **V U3**, 102
viewing [ˈvjuːɪŋ] Hör-/Sehverstehen **I**
village [ˈvɪlɪdʒ] Dorf **I**
villain [ˈvɪlən] Bösewicht **II**
violence *(no pl)* [ˈvaɪəlns] Gewalt **III**
violent [ˈvaɪəlnt] gewaltsam; gewalttätig; brutal **III**
VIP (very important person) [ˌviːaɪˈpiː] VIP; Promi ⟨**V U2**, 47⟩
visa [ˈviːzə], **visas** [ˈviːzəz] *(pl)* Visum, Visa *(Pl.)*; Einreisebewilligung **III**
visit [ˈvɪzɪt] Besuch **I**
to **visit** [ˈvɪzɪt] besichtigen; besuchen **I**
visitor [ˈvɪzɪtə] Besucher/-in **I**
visual [ˈvɪʒuəl] Bild **IV**
visual [ˈvɪʒuəl] visuell; optisch **VTS1**, 38
vitamin [ˈvɪtəmɪn] Vitamin **III**
vocabulary [vəˈkæbjələri] Vokabular; Wortschatz **I**
voice [vɔɪs] Stimme **I**
*to have a **voice** [ˌhæv ə ˈvɔɪs] ein Mitspracherecht haben **V AC3**, 114
to lower one's **voice** [ˌləʊə wʌnz ˈvɔɪs] die Stimme senken ⟨**V U1**, 29⟩
*to make one's **voice** heard [ˌmeɪk wʌnz ˌvɔɪs ˈhɜːd] sich Gehör verschaffen **V AC3**, 114
volcano [vɒlˈkeɪnəʊ], **volcanoes** [vɒlˈkeɪnəʊz] *(pl)* Vulkan **IV**
volleyball [ˈvɒlibɔːl] Volleyball **I**
volunteer [ˌvɒlənˈtɪə] Freiwillige/-r; freiwillig; Ehrenamtliche/-r; ehrenamtlich **V U2**, 55
to **volunteer** [ˌvɒlənˈtɪə] eine ehrenamtliche Tätigkeit übernehmen **V U2**, 55
vote [vəʊt] Abstimmung; Stimme; Wahl **V AC3**, 114
*to take a **vote** [ˌteɪk ə ˈvəʊt] abstimmen **I**
to **vote** [vəʊt] abstimmen; wählen **I**
vulgar [ˈvʌlgə] vulgär; gewöhnlich **V AC2**, 83

W

wage [weɪdʒ] Lohn **V U2**, 56
minimum **wage** [ˌmɪnɪməm ˈweɪdʒ] Mindestlohn **V U3**, 93
wagon [ˈwægən] Wagen; Waggon; Planwagen; Karren **IV**
covered **wagon** [ˌkʌvəd ˈwægən] Planwagen **IV**
*to be worth the **wait** [bi ˌwɜːθ ðə ˈweɪt] das Warten wert sein ⟨**VTS1**, 41⟩
to **wait** (for) [weɪt] warten (auf) **I**
I can't **wait** till next time. [aɪ kɑːnt ˌweɪt tɪl nekst ˈtaɪm] Ich kann es bis zum nächsten Mal kaum erwarten. **II**
Wait and see! [ˌweɪt ənd ˈsiː] Warte ab! **I**
waiter [ˈweɪtə] Kellner/-in; Bedienung **IV**
*to **wake** up [weɪk ˈʌp] aufwachen; aufwecken **III**
walk [wɔːk] Gang **V U1**, 28
gallery **walk** [ˈgælri ˌwɔːk] Museumsrundgang; Vernissage **I**
*to go for a **walk** [ˌgəʊ fər ə ˈwɔːk] spazieren gehen **II**
night **walk** [ˈnaɪt wɔːk] Nachtwanderung **II**
to **walk** [wɔːk] gehen; laufen **I**
to **walk** the dog [ˌwɔːk ðə ˈdɒg] den Hund ausführen; mit dem Hund spazieren gehen **I**
walk-in closet [ˌwɔːkɪn ˈklɒzɪt] begehbarer Kleiderschrank **IV**
walking [ˈwɔːkɪŋ] Wandern **II**
walking trail [ˈwɔːkɪŋ treɪl] Wanderweg **II**
wall [wɔːl] Wand; Mauer **I**; Online-Pinnwand **III**

to **wander** ['wɒndə] gehen ⟨**V U3**, 101⟩
wanna *(= want to) (infml)* ['wɒnə] will/ wollen ⟨**VTS3**, 110⟩
wannabe *(infml)* ['wɒnəbi] Möchtegern; Möchtegern- **V U3**, 86
to **want** (to) ['wɒnt tə] wollen; mögen **I**
wanted ['wɒntɪd] gesucht **IV**
war [wɔ:] Krieg **III**
wardrobe ['wɔ:drəʊb] Kleiderschrank **I**
to **warm** up [ˌwɔ:m‿'ʌp] aufwärmen; sich aufwärmen **I**
warm [wɔ:m] warm **III**
warm-up ['wɔ:m‿ˌʌp] Aufwärmübung **I**
to **warn** [wɔ:n] warnen **III**
warrior ['wɒriə] Krieger **II**
to **wash** [wɒʃ] waschen; sich waschen **I**
to **wash** up [ˌwɒʃ‿'ʌp] angespült werden **II**
washing machine ['wɒʃɪŋ məˌʃi:n] Waschmaschine **II**
waste [weɪst] Verschwendung **IV**
to **waste** [weɪst] verschwenden **II**
wasteful ['weɪstfl] verschwenderisch **IV**
to **watch** [wɒtʃ] beobachten; (sich) ansehen; zuschauen **I**
to **watch** TV [ˌwɒtʃ ti:'vi:] fernsehen **I**
water ['wɔ:tə] Wasser **I**
drinking **water** ['drɪŋkɪŋ ˌwɔ:tə] Trinkwasser **IV**
water fountain ['wɔ:tə ˌfaʊntɪn] Wasserspender **IV**
water slide ['wɔ:tə ˌslaɪd] Wasserrutsche **I**
waterfront ['wɔ:təfrʌnt] Hafenviertel; Ufer **IV**
wave [weɪv] Welle **I**
to **wave** [weɪv] winken; schwenken **IV**
wavy ['weɪvi] wellig; gewellt ⟨**V U1**, 28⟩
wax [wæks] Wachs **II**
wax figure ['wæks ˌfɪgə] Wachsfigur **II**
way [weɪ] Weg; Art und Weise **I**
*to be in the **way** [ˌbi‿ɪn ðə 'weɪ] im Weg sein/stehen **I**
*to find one's **way** around [ˌfaɪnd wʌnz ˌweɪ‿ə'raʊnd] sich zurechtfinden **IV**
*to get in the **way** [ˌget‿ɪn ðə 'weɪ] stören; im Weg stehen **II**
*to take sth the wrong **way** [ˌteɪk‿ðə rɒŋ 'weɪ] etw. falsch auffassen; etw. in den falschen Hals bekommen **V AC2**, 83
in other **ways** [ɪn‿'ʌðə weɪz] auf andere Weise **II**
that **way** [ˌðæt 'weɪ] so; auf diese Weise **V U3**, 86
the other **way** around [ði‿ˌʌðə weɪ 'raʊnd] andersrum; umgekehrt ⟨**V U3**, 102⟩
the same **way** as [ˌðə seɪm 'weɪ æz] genauso wie **II**
way [weɪ] lange ⟨**V U3**, 100⟩
we [wi:; wi] wir **I**
We're from ... ['wɪə frəm] Wir sind aus ... **I**
weak [wi:k] schwach **IV**
weakness ['wi:knəs] Schwäche **V U2**, 49
wealth [welθ] Reichtum; Vermögen **V U3**, 90
wealthy ['welθi] wohlhabend; reich **IV**
weapon ['wepən] Waffe **III**
*to **wear** [weə] anhaben; tragen *(Kleidung)* **I**
weather ['weðə] Wetter **I**
weather forecast ['weðə ˌfɔ:kɑ:st] Wettervorhersage **II**
web [web] Netz; Spinnennetz **III**
web designer ['web dɪˌzaɪnə] Webdesigner **III**
website ['websaɪt] Website; Internetauftritt **I**
wedding ['wedɪŋ] Hochzeit **I**
Wednesday ['wenzdeɪ] Mittwoch **I**
week [wi:k] Woche **I**
weekday ['wi:kdeɪ] Wochentag **II**
weekend [ˌwi:k'end] Wochenende **I**
at the **weekend** [ət ðə ˌwi:k'end] am Wochenende **I**
to **weigh** [weɪ] wiegen **III**
weight [weɪt] Gewicht **III**
weighted ['weɪtɪd] beladen; belastet ⟨**V U2**, 64⟩
weird [wɪəd] merkwürdig; seltsam; sonderbar **II**
Welcome! ['welkəm] Willkommen! **II**
to **welcome** ['welkəm] willkommen heißen **II**
You're **welcome**. [jɔ: 'welkəm] Bitte schön.; Nichts zu danken.; Gern geschehen. **I**
*to do **well** [du: 'wel] gute Leistungen erbringen **III**
*to get **well** [ˌget 'wel] gesund werden **IV**
... as **well** as ... [əz 'wel‿əz] sowie; und (auch) **IV**
well-developed [ˌweldɪ'veləpt] gut entwickelt; ausgereift **IV**
well-known [ˌwel'nəʊn] (wohl) bekannt **VTS2**, 77
well-suited (to doing sth) [ˌwel'su:tɪd] geeignet (für/um zu); passend (für) **VTS2**, 77
well-written [ˌwel'rɪtn] gut geschrieben **IV**
well [wel] tja; nun **I**
Welsh [welʃ] walisisch; Walisisch; Waliser/-in **II**
west [west] Westen; West- **I**
in the far **west** [ɪn ðə fɑ: 'west] im äußersten Westen **II**
western ['westən] westlich; West- **IV**
wet [wet] nass **II**
whale [weɪl] Wal **IV**
what [wɒt] was; welche/-r/-s; was für ein **I**
What a ... ['wɒt‿ə] Was für ein/-e ... **IV**
What about ... ? ['wɒt‿əbaʊt] Wie wär's mit ...?; Was ist mit ...? **I**
What are ...? ['wɒt‿ɑ:] Welche ... sind es? **I**
What colour is ...? [ˌwɒt 'kʌlər‿ɪz] Welche Farbe hat ...? **I**
what else [ˌwɒt‿'els] was sonst; was noch **I**
What is missing? [ˌwɒt‿ɪz 'mɪsɪŋ] Was fehlt? **I**
What is ... about? [ˌwɒt‿ɪz ...‿ə'baʊt] Worum geht es in/im ...? **I**
what it's all about [ˌwɒt‿ɪts‿ɔ:l‿ə'baʊt] worum es geht **V U3**, 86
what it's like [ˌwɒt‿ɪts 'laɪk] wie das ist **II**
What luck! [wɒt 'lʌk] Was für ein Glück! **III**
What on earth ...? [ˌwɒt:‿ɒn‿'ɜ:θ] Was um alles in der Welt ...? **II**
What time? [ˌwɒt 'taɪm] Um wie viel Uhr? **I**
what to ... ['wɒt tə] was man ... **I**
What was it like? [ˌwɒt wɒz‿ɪt 'laɪk] Wie war es? **III**
What's going on? [wɒts ˌgəʊɪŋ‿'ɒn] Was ist los?; Was geht ab? **III**
what's more [ˌwɒts 'mɔ:] außerdem; überdies **IV**
What's that? [wɒts 'ðæt] Was ist das? **I**
What's the matter? [ˌwɒts ðə 'mætə] Was ist los?; Was hast du? **II**
What's the rule for ...? [ˌwɒts ðə 'ru:l fə] Was ist die Regel für ...? **I**
What's the time? [ˌwɒts ðə 'taɪm] Wie spät ist es?; Wie viel Uhr ist es? **I**
What's up? [ˌwɒts‿'ʌp] Was ist los? **III**
What's your favourite ...? ['wɒts jə ˌfeɪvrɪt] Was ist dein/-e Lieblings...? **I**
What's your name? [ˌwɒts jə 'neɪm] Wie heißt du?; Wie heißen Sie? **I**
whatever [wɒt'evə] wie auch immer; egal (was/welche) **IV**
wheat [wi:t] Weizen **IV**
wheel [wi:l] Rad; Steuerrad; Steuer **I**
great **wheel** [ˌgreɪt 'wi:l] Riesenrad **IV**
to **wheel** around [ˌwi:l‿ə'raʊnd] herumwirbeln ⟨**V U3**, 100⟩
wheelchair ['wi:ltʃeə] Rollstuhl **II**
when [wen] wenn; wann; als **I**
whenever [wen'evə] wann immer; jedes Mal, wenn; so oft **II**
where [weə] wo; wohin **I**
Where ... from? [ˌweə ... 'frɒm] Woher ...? **I**
where I belong [ˌweər‿aɪ bɪ'lɒŋ] wo ich hingehöre **III**
... **where** to go. [ˌweə tə 'gəʊ] ... wohin ich gehen kann. **II**
I go **wherever** the wind takes me. [aɪ ˌgəʊ weəˌrevə ðə wɪnd 'teɪks mi:] Ich lasse mich treiben. **III**
whether ['weðə] ob **IV**
which [wɪtʃ] welche/-r/-s **I**
which [wɪtʃ] der; die; das; dem; den *(Relativpronomen)* **II**
a **while** [ə 'waɪl] eine Weile **II**
while [waɪl] während **I**
to **whine** [waɪn] quengeln ⟨**V U3**, 100⟩
to **whip** [wɪp] schlagen **I**
whisky ['wɪski] Whisky **III**
to **whisper** ['wɪspə] flüstern **I**
white [waɪt] weiß **I**
white lie [ˌwaɪt 'laɪ] Notlüge **III**
who [hu:] wer; wem; wen **I**

Who … for? [ˌhu: 'fɔ:] Für wen …? **I**
Who is it? [ˌhu:‿'ɪz‿ɪt] Wer ist es? **I**
Who the hell cares? [ˌhu: ðə hel 'keəz] Wen zum Teufel interessiert's? ⟨**VTS3**, 110⟩
Who's in? [hu:z‿'ɪn] Wer macht mit?; Wer ist dabei? **II**
who [hu:] der; dem; den; die *(Relativpronomen)* **II**
whole [həʊl] ganz **I**
whom [hu:m] wem; wen **III**
whoosh [wʊʃ] wusch **I**
whose [hu:z] wessen **IV**
whose [hu:z] dessen; deren *(Relativpronomen)* **II**
why [waɪ] warum **I**
that's **why** [ðæts 'waɪ] deshalb **II**
wide [waɪd] breit; weit; ausgedehnt **II**
wide shot ['waɪd ʃɒt] Totale *(Kameraeinstellung)* **VTS1**, 38
wide-brimmed ['waɪdbrɪmd] breitkrempig ⟨**V U3**, 100⟩
widespread ['waɪdspred] weit verbreitet **V AC1**, 9
wife [waɪf], **wives** [waɪvz] *(pl)* Ehefrau **II**
wifi ['waɪfaɪ] WLAN **III**
wiki (text) ['wɪkɪ ˌtekst] Wikitext **IV**
wild [waɪld] wild **II**
wilderness ['wɪldənəs] Wildnis **IV**
wildfire ['waɪldfaɪə] Flächenbrand **V U3**, 94
wildlife ['waɪldlaɪf] Tierwelt *(in freier Wildbahn)* **II**
*to be **willing** to do sth [bi 'wɪlɪŋ tə] gewillt sein, etw. zu tun; bereit sein, etw. zu tun **V U3**, 94
willingly ['wɪlɪŋli] gern; freiwillig **V AC2**, 81
win [wɪn] Sieg °**V U3**, 98
*to **win** [wɪn] gewinnen; siegen **I**
*to **win** sb over [wɪn‿'əʊvə] jmdn. für sich gewinnen; jmdn. überzeugen **IV**
wind [wɪnd] Wind **II**
I go wherever the **wind** takes me. [aɪ ˌgəʊ weəˌrevə ðə wɪnd 'teɪks mi:] Ich lasse mich treiben. **III**
window ['wɪndəʊ] Fenster **I**
windsurfing ['wɪndsɜ:fɪŋ] Windsurfen **II**
wine [waɪn] Wein **I**
winner ['wɪnə] Gewinner/-in; Sieger/-in **I**
winter ['wɪntə] Winter **III**
wisdom *(no pl)* ['wɪzdəm] Weisheit; Klugheit **V U2**, 56
wish [wɪʃ] Wunsch **I**
*to make a **wish** [ˌmeɪk‿ə 'wɪʃ] sich etwas wünschen **I**
Best **wishes** [ˌbest 'wɪʃɪz] Viele Grüße; Herzliche Grüße **II**
to **wish** [wɪʃ] (sich) wünschen **IV**
with [wɪð] mit; bei **I**
as **with** ['æz wɪð] wie (auch) bei ⟨**V U3**, 97⟩
within [wɪ'ðɪn] innerhalb **IV**
without [wɪ'ðaʊt] ohne **I**
witness ['wɪtnəs] Zeuge/Zeugin **II**
wizard ['wɪzəd] Zauberer **II**
wobbly ['wɒbli] wackelig **II**
woe *(no pl) (liter)* [wəʊ] Kummer; Leid ⟨**V U1**, 24⟩
wolf [wʊlf], **wolves** [wʊlvz] *(pl)* Wolf **IV**
woman ['wʊmən], **women** ['wɪmɪn] *(pl)* Frau **I**
no **wonder** [ˌnəʊ 'wʌndə] kein Wunder **IV**
to **wonder** ['wʌndə] sich Gedanken machen; sich fragen **IV**
wonderful ['wʌndəfl] wunderbar **II**
wood [wʊd] Wald; Wäldchen; Holz **III**
wood [wʊd] Holz **III**
wooded ['wʊdɪd] bewaldet **IV**
wooden ['wʊdn] hölzern; aus Holz **III**
Woof! [wʊf] Wau! **I**
word [wɜ:d] Wort **I**
compound **word** ['kɒmpaʊnd wɜ:d] Kompositum *(zusammengesetztes Wort)* **II**
four-letter **word** [ˌfɔ:letə 'wɜ:d] Schimpfwort ⟨**VTS3**, 109⟩
key **word** ['ki: wɜ:d] Stichwort; Schlüsselbegriff **I**
linking **word** ['lɪŋkɪŋ ˌwɜ:d] Bindewort **I**
play on **words** [ˌpleɪ‿ɒn 'wɜ:dz] Wortspiel **III**
signal **word** ['sɪgnəl ˌwɜ:d] Signalwort **I**
word bank ['wɜ:d ˌbæŋk] Wortsammlung **III**
word cloud ['wɜ:d ˌklaʊd] Wörterwolke **II**
word order ['wɜ:d‿ˌɔ:də] Wortstellung; Satzstellung **I**
word snake ['wɜ:d ˌsneɪk] Wortschlange **I**
word-building ['wɜ:dˌbɪldɪŋ] Wortbildung **II**
work [wɜ:k] Arbeit **I**
pair **work** ['peə wɜ:k] Partnerarbeit **II**
to **work** [wɜ:k] arbeiten **I**; funktionieren **II**
to **work** out [ˌwɜ:k‿'aʊt] herausfinden; ausarbeiten **II**; funktionieren; klappen **III**
workbook ['wɜ:kbʊk] Arbeitsheft; Übungsheft **III**
worker ['wɜ:kə] Arbeiter/-in **V U2**, 49
construction **worker** [kən'strʌkʃn ˌwɜ:kə] Bauarbeiter/-in **V U2**, 49
workshop ['wɜ:kʃɒp] Workshop **I**
world [wɜ:ld] Erde; Welt **I**
outside **world** ['aʊtsaɪd ˌwɜ:ld] Außenwelt **IV**
from around the **world** [frɒm əˌraʊnd ðə 'wɜ:ld] aus aller Welt **II**
worldwide [ˌwɜ:ld'waɪd] weltweit **V U3**, 90
worm [wɜ:m] Wurm **I**
worn [wɔ:n] abgenutzt; abgewetzt ⟨**V U1**, 28⟩
worried ['wʌrid] beunruhigt; besorgt **III**
*to be **worried** [bi 'wʌrid] beunruhigt sein; besorgt sein **II**
No **worries**. [ˌnəʊ 'wʌriz] Kein Problem.; Gern geschehen. **V U1**, 18
to **worry** ['wʌri] sich Sorgen machen **II**
Don't **worry**! [ˌdəʊnt 'wʌri] Keine Sorge! **I**
the **worst** [ðə 'wɜ:st] der/die/das schlimmste; der/die/das schlechteste **II**
*to be **worth** [bi 'wɜ:θ] wert sein **I**
*to be **worth** the wait [bi ˌwɜ:θ ðə 'weɪt] das Warten wert sein ⟨**VTS1**, 41⟩
would [wʊd] würde/-st/-n/-t **III**
would like [wʊd 'laɪk] würde/-st/-n/-t gern; hätte/-st/-n/-t gern **I**
would love [wʊd 'lʌv] würde/-st/-n/-t sehr gern; hätte/-st-/-n/-t sehr gern **I**
Would you like …? [ˌwʊd jʊ 'laɪk] Möchtest du …?; Möchten Sie …?; Möchtet ihr …? **II**
wounded ['wu:ndɪd] verwundet; verletzt **III**
Wow! [waʊ] Wow! **I**
to **wrap** [ræp] einwickeln; einpacken **I**
wrapping ['ræpɪŋ] Verpackung; Hülle **I**
to **wreck** [rek] zerstören ⟨**V U3**, 102⟩
wrist [rɪst] Handgelenk **II**
*to **write** [raɪt] schreiben **I**
*to **write** down [ˌraɪt 'daʊn] aufschreiben **I**
writer ['raɪtə] Autor/-in; Verfasser/-in **III**
staff **writer** ['stɑ:f ˌraɪtə] festangestellter Journalist/festangestellte Journalistin ⟨**VTS3**, 111⟩
writing ['raɪtɪŋ] Schreiben **I**
wrong [rɒŋ] falsch **I**
*to be **wrong** [bi 'rɒŋ] unrecht haben; sich irren **I**
*to go **wrong** [ˌgəʊ 'rɒŋ] schiefgehen **I**

X

Xhosa ['kɔ:sə] Xhosa *(Sprache in Südafrika)* ⟨**V AC1**, 8⟩
XOXO [ˌhʌgz‿ən 'kɪsɪz] Umarmungen und Küsse *(am Ende von E-Mails und SMS)* **I**

Y

to **yank** [jæŋk] zerren (an) ⟨**V U3**, 100⟩
yapa ['jæpæ] Schwester *(australisch)* ⟨**V U1**, 29⟩
yard [jɑ:d] Garten; Hof **IV**
front **yard** *(AE)* [ˌfrʌnt 'jɑ:d] Vorgarten **IV**
yeah *(infml)* [jeə] ja **I**
year [jɪə] Jahr; Schuljahr **I**
gap **year** ['gæp ˌjɪə] *ein Jahr Auszeit (zwischen Schule und Ausbildung/Studium), das oft für einen freiwilligen ökologischen oder sozialen Dienst benutzt wird* **V U2**, 55
11-**year**-old [ɪˌlevn'jɪərəʊld] 11-Jährige/-r **II**
18-**year**-old [ˌeɪti:n 'jɪər‿əʊld] 18-jährig **II**
yearbook ['jɪəbʊk] Jahrbuch **II**
yellow ['jeləʊ] gelb **I**
yes [jes] ja **I**
yesterday ['jestədeɪ] gestern **II**
yet [jet] schon; noch **II**; doch; und trotzdem; und dennoch **IV**
not … **yet** [nɒt 'jet] noch nicht **II**
yoghurt ['jɒgət] Joghurt **I**
you [ju:; jə] du; ihr; Sie **I**
You know how to … [ju: 'nəʊ ˌhaʊ tə] Du weißt, wie man …; Ihr wisst, wie man … **I**

You too? [juː ˈtuː] Du auch? **I**
You'd better … *(= You had better)* [ˈjuːd ˌbetə] Du solltest lieber … **IV**
You're welcome. [ˌjɔː ˈwelkəm] Bitte schön.; Nichts zu danken.; Gern geschehen. **I**
young [jʌŋ] jung **I**
your [jɔː; jə] dein/-e; euer/eure; Ihr/-e **I**
What's **your** name? [ˌwɒts jə ˈneɪm] Wie heißt du?; Wie heißen Sie? **I**
Your turn. [ˈjɔː tɜːn] Du bist dran. **I**
yours [jɔːz] dein/-er/-e/-es; eure/-r/-s; Ihr/-e **II**
Yours … [jɔːz] Viele Grüße … *(am Ende von Briefen und Mails)* **II**
Yours sincerely [ˌjɔːz sɪnˈsɪəli] Mit freundlichen Grüßen **V U2**, 51
yourself [jɔːˈself] du/dir/dich/Sie/sich (selbst); selber **I**
yourselves [jɔːˈselvz] ihr/euch/Sie/sich (selbst); selber **II**
youth [juːθ] Jugend **III**
youth hostel [ˈjuːθ ˌhɒstl] Jugendherberge **V U1**, 14

Z

zero [ˈzɪərəʊ] null **I**
zone [zəʊn] Zone **IV**
zoo [zuː] Zoo; Tierpark **II**
zoom lens [ˈzuːm ˌlenz] Zoomobjektiv ⟨**V U3**, 100⟩
to **zoom** in (on) [ˌzuːm‿ˈɪn ɒn] heranzoomen (auf) **III**
zucchini [zʊˈkiːni] Zucchini ⟨**V U3**, 97⟩
Zulu [ˈzuːluː] Zulu *(Sprache in Südafrika)* ⟨**V AC1**, 8⟩

Boys' names

Abdoulaye [ˌabdʊˈlɛ] **V U2**, 53
Alex [ˈælɪks] **V U3**, 86
Ali [ˈɑːli] **V U1**, 29
Arnold [ˈɑːnld] **IV**
Arthur [ˈɑːθə] **V U1**, 21
Austin [ˈɒstɪn] **IV**
Ben [ben] **I**
Benjamin [ˈbendʒəmɪn] **V U2**, 63
Bill [bɪl] **V U1**, 18
Bob [bɒb] **I**
Brad [bræd] **III**
Brodie [ˈbrəʊdi] **IV**
Callum [ˈkæləm] **IV**
Carlos [ˈkɑːlɒs] **IV**
Charlie [ˈtʃɑːli] **V U1**, 22
Clayton [ˈkleɪtn] **IV**
Clifton [ˈklɪftən] **V U1**, 18
Connor [ˈkɒnə] ⟨**V U3**, 100⟩
Dan [dæn] **V U2**, 58
Daniel [ˈdænjəl] **IV**
Dave [deɪv] **I**
David [ˈdeɪvɪd] **I**
Dennis [ˈdenɪs] **V AC1**, 8
Desmond [ˈdezmənd] **I**
Diego [diˈeɪgəʊ] **IV**
Eddie [ˈedi] **III**
Ethan [ˈiːθn] **III**
Finn [fɪn] **III**
Frank [fræŋk] **II**
Gabriel [ˈgeɪbriəl] ⟨**V U2**, 66⟩
Harrison [ˈhærɪsn] **IV**
Henry [ˈhenri] **I**
Jack [dʒæk] **I**
Jake [dʒeɪk] **IV**
James [dʒeɪmz] **II**
Jamie [ˈdʒeɪmi] **I**
Jay [dʒeɪ] **I**
Jim [dʒɪm] **III**
John [dʒɒn] **II**
Jonas [ˈdʒəʊnəs] **V U2**, 62
Jonathan [ˈdʒɒnəθn] **V TS2**, 77
Josh [dʒɒʃ] **IV**
Lawrence [ˈlɔːrəns] **IV**
Lee [liː] **IV**
Liam [ˈliːəm] **V AC2**, 82
Luke [luːk] **I**
Mark [mɑːk] **IV**
Marley [ˈmɑːli] **II**
Marlon [ˈmɑːlən] **IV**
Matt [mæt] **III**
Matthew [ˈmæθjuː] **IV**
Max [mæks] **III**
Mick [mɪk] **II**
Mike [maɪk] **II**
Moses [ˈməʊzɪz] **IV**
Moshe [ˈmɒʃə] **V U1**, 14
Nasim [ˈneɪzɪm] ⟨**V U3**, 100⟩
Nathan [ˈneɪθn] **II**
Nick [nɪk] **II**
Paul [pɔːl] **V TS2**, 77
Peter [ˈpiːtə] **II**
Phil [fɪl] **V U2**, 60
Rick [rɪk] **III**
Rob [rɒb] **III**
Russell [ˈrʌsl] **V TS2**, 77
Ryan [raɪən] **V U2**, 49
Scott [skɒt] **IV**
Sean [ʃɔːn] **III**
Shahid [ʃɑːˈhiːd] **I**
Shane [ʃɑːn] **V TS3**, 109
Simon [ˈsaɪmən] **III**
Steve [stiːv] **I**
Stuart [ˈstuːət] **III**
Thomas [ˈtɒməs] **III**
Tim [tɪm] **IV**
Todd [tɒd] ⟨**V U3**, 102⟩
Tony [ˈtəʊni] **I**
Tristan [ˈtrɪstən] **IV**
Tyler [ˈtaɪlə] **I**
Wesley [ˈwezli] **IV**
Will [wɪl] **II**
Zach [zæk] **IV**

Girls' names

Abbie [ˈæbi] **IV**
Adriana [ˌeɪdriˈɑːnə] **V U3**, 93
Alice [ˈælɪs] **II**
Alicia [əˈlɪsiə; əˈlɪʃə] **I**
Amber [ˈæmbə] **I**
Amy [ˈeɪmi] **V U2**, 58
Anna [ˈænə] **I**
Anne [æn] **I**
Anne-Marie [ˌænməˈriː] ⟨**V U3**, 102⟩
Ashley [ˈæʃli] **IV**
Ava [ˈɑːvə] **IV**
Cam [kæm] **V U1**, 18
Carla [ˈkɑːlə] ⟨**V U3**, 102⟩
Carol [ˈkærəl] **I**
Carrie [ˈkæri] **V U1**, 23
Cassie [ˈkæsi] **V U2**, 56
Ceri [ˈkeri] **II**
Christine [krɪˈstiːn] **IV**
Cindy [ˈsɪndi] **V U1**, 22
Claire [ˈkleə] **I**
Courtney [ˈkɔːtni] **V U2**, 60
Daphne [ˈdæfni] ⟨**V U3**, 101⟩
Eileen [aɪˈliːn] **IV**
Ella [ˈelə] **V U2**, 49
Emily [ˈemɪli] **I**
Emma [ˈemə] **V U2**, 58
Erin [ˈɪərɪn] ⟨**V TS2**, 79⟩
Eva [ˈiːvə] **IV**
Fiona [fiˈəʊnə] **V U1**, 19
Frances [ˈfrɑːnsɪs] **I**
Gulwirri [ˈgʌlwɪrri] ⟨**V U1**, 30⟩
Gwen [gwen] **II**
Hayley [ˈheɪli] **III**
Harriet [ˈhæriət] **IV**
Helen [ˈhelɪn] **II**
Holly [ˈhɒli] **I**
Ivy [ˈaɪvi] **III**
Jean [dʒiːn] **III**
Jenna [ˈdʒenə] **IV**
Jenny [ˈdʒeni] **III**
Jessica [ˈdʒesɪkə] **IV**
Judith [ˈdʒuːdɪθ] **II**
Julie [ˈdʒuːli] **I**
June [dʒuːn] **IV**
Kate [keɪt] **II**
Kelly [ˈkeli] **IV**
Kim [kɪm] **IV**
Kirsty [ˈkɜːsti] **III**
Lara [ˈlɑːrə] **V TS3**, 108
Laura [ˈlɔːrə] **I**
Lauren [ˈlɔːrən] **II**
Libby [ˈlɪbi] **V U1**, 28
Lilly [ˈlɪli] **IV**
Lou [luː] **I**
Lucy [ˈluːsi] **I**
Madison [ˈmædɪsn] **IV**
Margaret [ˈmɑːgrət] **III**
Maria [məˈriːə] ⟨**V U3**, 101⟩
Martha [ˈmɑːθə] **V U2**, 48
Mary [ˈmeəri] **II**
Megan [ˈmegən] **II**

Meredith ['merədɪθ] **IV**
Nancy ['nænsi] **IV**
Ninja ['nɪndʒə] **V U3**, 87
Nisha ['nɪʃə] **VTS3**, 108
Nona ['nəʊnə] **V U1**, 28
Olivia [ɒl'ɪviə] **I**
Penelope [pə'neləpi] **IV**
Penny ['peni] **VTS1**, 39
Pia ['pi:ə] **I**
Pippa ['pɪpə] ⟨**VTS3**, 113⟩
Polly ['pɒli] **II**
Rani ['rɑ:ni] **V AC1**, 9
Rebecca [rɪ'bekə] **IV**
Rita ['ri:tə] **IV**
Rose [rəʊz] **I**
Rosie ['rəʊzi] **V U1**, 28
Ruby ['ru:bi] **II**
Rylee ['raɪli] **IV**
Saanvi ['sɑ:nvi] **V U2**, 60
Sally ['sæli] **I**
Sarah ['seərə] **IV**
Selena [sə'li:nə] **V U1**, 28
Sophie ['səʊfi] **IV**
Stella ['stelə] **VTS3**, 110
Sue [su:] **V U1**, 22
Susan ['su:zn] **IV**
Tamara [tə'mɑ:rə] **II**
Tanya ['tɑ:njə] **V U1**, 14
Tatiana [ˌtæti'ɑ:nə] ⟨**V U3**, 100⟩
Violet ['vaɪələt] **III**
Vivien ['vɪvjən] **II**
Waltjan ['wɒljən] ⟨**V U1**, 30⟩
Willow ['wɪləʊ] ⟨**V U3**, 101⟩

Surnames

Ashton ['æʃtən] **II**
Azad [ə'zɑ:d] **I**
Battiato [ˌbætɪ'eɪtə] **V AC1**, 10
Campbell ['kæmbl] ⟨**VTS3**, 113⟩
Carter ['kɑ:tə] **V U1**, 22
Chiku ['tʃɪkʊ] **V AC1**, 8
Cotter ['kɒtə] ⟨**VTS2**, 79⟩
Darshini [dɑ:'ʃi:ni] ⟨**V AC1**, 9⟩
Dolan ['dəʊlən] **VTS3**, 109
Eaton ['i:tən] **VTS3**, 109
Elliot ['eliət] **I**
Ford [fɔ:d] **IV**
Forester ['fɒrɪstə] **IV**
Foster ['fɒstə] **VTS2**, 77
Fox [fɒks] **VTS3**, 110
Francis ['frɑ:nsɪs] **III**
Fraser ['freɪzə] **I**
Frazee ['freɪzi:] ⟨**V U3**, 100⟩
Fuller ['fʊlə] **V U1**, 28
Green [gri:n] **I**
Harris ['hærɪs] **V U1**, 15
Hartley ['hɑ:tli] **V U2**, 53
Henry ['henri] **IV**
Hitchings ['hɪtʃɪŋz] ⟨**V AC1**, 11⟩
Jameson ['dʒeɪmsn] **IV**
Jones [dʒəʊnz] **III**
Kelley ['keli] **VTS2**, 77
King [kɪŋ] **III**
Kumani [ku:'mɑ:ni] **VTS3**, 108
Lee [li:] ⟨**VTS3**, 113⟩
Lewis ['lu:ɪs] **V U2**, 50
Llewellyn [lu:'elɪn] ⟨**VTS2**, 79⟩
Mahmoud [mæ'mu:d] **III**
Maldini [mɔ:l'di:ni] **VTS3**, 108
McDonald [mək'dɒnld] **V U1**, 23
Miller ['mɪlə] **III**
Morse [mɔ:s] **IV**
Nicholls ['nɪkəlz] **II**
Parker ['pɑ:kə] **II**
Philipp ['fɪlɪp] **V U1**, 21
Preston ['prestən] **I**
Ramirez [rə'mɪərez] **V U3**, 94
Reid [ri:d] **V U1**, 28
Richardson ['rɪtʃədsn] **I**
Ross [rɒs] **V U2**, 48
Shaw [ʃɔ:] **VTS3**, 111
Strasser ['stræsə] ⟨**V U3**, 102⟩
Sushruta ⟨**V AC1**, 9⟩
Swindon ['swɪndən] **I**
Thompson ['tɒmsən] **II**
Twine [twaɪn] ⟨**V U3**, 101⟩
Vail [veɪl] **IV**
Walker ['wɔ:kə] **I**
Watney ['wɒtni] **IV**
Webb [web] **VTS2**, 77
Woodruff ['wʊdrʌf] **III**
Wright [raɪt] **II**

Place names

Abengourou [aˌbɛngʊ'ru:] **V U2**, 53
Aberdeen [ˌæbə'di:n] *Stadt in Schottland* **III**
Baltimore ['bɔ:ltɪmɔ:] *Stadt in den USA* **IV**
Bankside ['bæŋksaɪd] *Stadtteil von London* **III**
Birmingham ['bɜ:mɪŋəm] **III**
Birritjimi [ˌbɪrrɪ'tjɑ:mi] *Ort in Australien* ⟨**V U1**, 29⟩
Bloemfontein ['blu:mfənteɪn] *Stadt in Südafrika* **V AC1**, 8
Boston ['bɒstn] *Stadt in den USA* **IV**
Bradford ['brædfəd] **II**
Brighton ['braɪtn] **V U2**, 50
Bristol ['brɪstl] **III**
Broadway ['brɔ:dweɪ] *Straße in NYC* **IV**
Brooklyn ['brʊklɪn] *Stadtteil von New York* **IV**
Cambridge ['keɪmbrɪdʒ] *Stadt in den USA* **IV**
Camden Market ['kæmdən ˌmɑ:kɪt] **II**
Cape Town ['keɪp ˌtaʊn] Kapstadt *(Stadt in Südafrika)* **V AC1**, 8
Chester ['tʃestə] **V U2**, 51
Chicago [ʃɪ'kɑ:gəʊ] *Stadt in den USA* **IV**
Cologne [kə'ləʊn] Köln **I**
Covent Garden [ˌkɒvnt 'gɑ:dn] **II**
Cracow ['krækɒv; 'krɑ:kaʊ] Krakau **I**
Dover ['dəʊvə] *englische Küstenstadt am Ärmelkanal* **III**
Dunstan ['dʌnstən] **V U2**, 50
Edinburgh ['edɪnbrə] **II**
Elcho Island [ˌeltʃəʊ‿'aɪlənd] *Insel vor Australien* ⟨**V U1**, 29⟩
Ellis Island [ˌelɪs‿'aɪlənd] *Insel vor New York City* **IV**
Florence ['flɒrns] Florenz **VTS2**, 74
Glasgow ['glɑ:zgəʊ] *Stadt in Schottland* **III**
Heathrow [ˌhi:θ'rəʊ] *Flughafen in London* **III**
Hollywood ['hɒliwʊd] **II**
Houston ['hju:stn] *Stadt in den USA* **IV**
Hyde Park [ˌhaɪd 'pɑ:k] **II**
Isle of Man [ˌaɪl‿əv 'mæn] **II**
Jamestown ['dʒeɪmztaʊn] *Stadt in den USA* **IV**
Larksdale Rise [ˌlɑ:ksdeɪl 'raɪz] **V U2**, 51
Leeds [li:dz] *Stadt in Nordengland* **VTS3**, 111
Liverpool ['lɪvəpu:l] **III**
London ['lʌndən] **I**
Los Angeles (LA) [lɒs‿'ændʒɪli:z (el'eɪ)] *US-amerikan. Stadt* **V U3**, 86
Manhattan [mæn'hætn] *Stadtteil von New York* **IV**
Melbourne ['melbən] *Stadt in Australien* **V U1**, 14
Miami [maɪ'æmi] *Stadt in den USA* **IV**
Mud Springs [ˌmʌd 'sprɪŋs] *Ort in Kalifornien* **V U3**, 90
Nashville ['næʃvɪl] *Stadt in den USA* **IV**
New Delhi [nju: 'deli] **V AC1**, 9
New York [ˌnju: 'jɔ:k] **III**
Nhulunbuy ['nʌlnbɔɪ] *Ort in Australien* ⟨**V U1**, 29⟩
Nottingham ['nɒtɪŋəm] **II**
Oxford ['ɒksfəd] *englische Universitätsstadt* **VTS2**, 77
Perth [pɜ:θ] *Stadt in Australien* **V U1**, 16
Philadelphia [ˌfɪlə'delfiə] *Stadt in den USA* **IV**
Pretoria [prɪ'tɔ:rɪə] *Stadt in Südafrika* **V AC1**, 8
Radford ['rædfəd] **VTS3**, 109
Salinas [seɪ'laɪnəs] *Stadt in Kalifornien* **V U3**, 85
San Diego [ˌsæn di'eɪgəʊ] *Stadt in den USA* **IV**
San Francisco [ˌsæn frən'sɪskəʊ] *Stadt in den USA* **V U3**, 91
Santa Monica [ˌsæntə 'mɒnɪkə] **V U3**, 92
Seattle [si'ætl] **III**
Silicon Valley [ˌsɪlɪkən 'væli] *bedeutender Standort der IT- und High-Tech-Industrie* **V U3**, 85
Stratford-upon-Avon [ˌstrætfədəpɒn'eɪvn] *Geburtsort Shakespeares* **III**
Sydney ['sɪdni] *Stadt in Australien* **V AC1**, 10
Vancouver [væn'ku:və] *Stadt in Kanada* **IV**
Varanasi [ˌværə'nɑ:zi] *Stadt in Indien* **V AC1**, 9
Venice ['venɪs] *Stadtteil von Los Angeles* **V U3**, 85

Washington, D.C. [ˌwɒʃɪŋtən ˌdiːˈsiː] *Hauptstadt der USA* **IV**
Wimbledon [ˈwɪmbldən] **I**
Yirrkala [ˈjɪrrkələ] ⟨**V U1**, 28⟩
York [jɔːk] *Stadt im Norden Englands* ⟨**VTS3**, 113⟩

Geographical names

Africa [ˈæfrɪkə] Afrika **III**
Alabama [ˌæləˈbæmə] *US-amerik. Bundesstaat* **IV**
America [əˈmerɪkə] Amerika **II**
the **Americas** [ðiˌəˈmerɪkəz] Nord- und Südamerika ⟨**V AC1**, 11⟩
Antarctica [ænˈtɑːktɪkə] Antarktis **V AC1**, 8
Arizona [ˌærɪˈzəʊnə] *US-Bundesstaat* **IV**
Asia [ˈeɪʒə] Asien **IV**
Atlantic Ocean [ətˌlæntɪk ˈəʊʃn] Atlantischer Ozean **II**
Australia [ɒsˈtreɪliə] Australien **II**
Austria [ˈɔːstrɪə] Österreich **II**
Ayers Rock [ˌeəz ˈrɒk] Ayers Rock *(= Uluru, heiliger Berg der Aborigines)* **V AC1**, 10
Bavaria [bəˈveəriə] Bayern **V U2**, 52
Ben Nevis [ben ˈnevɪs] *Berg in Schottland* **III**
Big Sur [ˌbɪg ˈsɜː] *Küstenstreifen in Kalifornien* **V U3**, 85
Blue Mountains [ˌbluː ˈmaʊntɪnz] *Gebirge in Australien* **V U1**, 16
Bondi Beach [ˌbɒndaɪ ˈbiːtʃ] *Strand in Sydney/Australien* **V AC1**, 10
Brazil [brəˈzɪl] Brasilien **V U3**, 90
Britain [ˈbrɪtn] Großbritannien **I**
British Empire [ˌbrɪtɪʃˌˈempaɪə] britisches Königreich **II**
British Isles [ˌbrɪtɪʃˌˈaɪlz] Britische Inseln **II**
California [ˌkælɪˈfɔːniə] Kalifornien *(US-amerik. Bundesstaat)* **IV**
Canada [ˈkænədə] Kanada **I**
China [ˈtʃaɪnə] China **I**
Cornwall [ˈkɔːnwɔːl] **II**
Cuba [ˈkjuːbə] Kuba **IV**
Death Valley [ˌdeθ ˈvæli] **IV**
Egypt [ˈiːdʒɪpt] Ägypten **III**
England [ˈɪŋglənd] England **I**
Europe [ˈjʊərəp] Europa **IV**
European Union (EU) [ˌjʊərəpiən ˈjuːnjən; iːjuː] Europäische Union **II**
Florida [ˈflɒrɪdə] *US-amerikan. Bundesstaat* ⟨**VTS3**, 113⟩
France [frɑːns] Frankreich **II**
Germany [ˈdʒɜːməni] Deutschland **I**
Great Britain (GB) [ˌgreɪt ˈbrɪtn] Großbritannien **II**
India [ˈɪndiə] Indien **II**
Iraq [ɪˈrɑːk] Irak **V U1**, 29
Ireland [ˈaɪələnd] Irland **IV**
Israel [ˈɪzreɪl] Israel **V U1**, 14
Italy [ˈɪtəli] Italien **II**
Ivory Coast [ˌaɪvri ˈkəʊst] Elfenbeinküste **V U2**, 53
Japan [dʒəˈpæn] Japan **V U3**, 90
Kenya [ˈkenjə] Kenia **III**
Latin America [ˌlætɪn əˈmerɪkə] Lateinamerika **IV**
Loch Ness [ˌlɒx ˈnes; ˌlɒk ˈnes] *See in Schottland* **III**
Maryland [ˈmeərilænd] *US-amerik. Bundesstaat* **IV**
Mexico [ˈmeksɪkəʊ] Mexiko **IV**
(the) **Midwest** [ˌmɪdˈwest] (der) Mittlere Westen **IV**
Milwaukee [mɪlˈwɔːki] *US-amerik. Bundesstaat* **IV**
Missouri [mɪˈzʊəri] *US-amerik. Bundesstaat* **IV**
Montana [mɒnˈtænə] *US-amerik. Bundesstaat* **IV**
New Jersey [ˌnjuː ˈdʒɜːzi] *US-amerik. Bundesstaat* **IV**
New Mexico [ˌnjuː ˈmeksɪkəʊ] *US-amerik. Bundesstaat* **IV**
New Zealand [ˌnjuː ˈziːlənd] Neuseeland **V U1**, 14
Normandy [ˈnɔːməndi] die Normandie **II**
North Sea [ˌnɔːθ ˈsiː] Nordsee **II**
Northern Ireland [ˌnɔːðnˌˈaɪələnd] Nordirland **II**
Oregon [ˈɒrɪgən] *US-amerik. Bundesstaat* **IV**
Oxfordshire [ˈɒksfədʃə] **VTS3**, 109
the **Pacific Northwest** [ðə pəˌsɪfɪk nɔːθˈwest] Pazifischer Nordwesten **IV**
Pakistan [ˌpɑːkɪˈstɑːn] **I**
Pennsylvania [ˌpensɪlˈveɪniə] *US-amerik. Bundesstaat* **IV**
Poland [ˈpəʊlənd] Polen **I**
Queensland [ˈkwiːnzlənd] *Staat in Australien* **V U1**, 14
Republic of Ireland [rɪˌpʌblɪkˌəvˌˈaɪələnd] Republik Irland **II**
the **Rockies** (= the Rocky Mountains) [ðə ˈrɒkiz] *Gebirge in the USA* **IV**
Russia [ˈrʌʃə] Russland **IV**
Scandinavia [ˌskændɪˈneɪviə] Skandinavien **III**
Scotland [ˈskɒtlənd] Schottland **II**
Somalia [səˈmɑːliə] Somalia **III**
South Africa [ˌsaʊθˌˈæfrɪkə] Südafrika **II**
Soviet Union [ˌsəʊviət ˈjuːnjən] Sowjetunion **IV**
Spain [speɪn] Spanien **II**
Sweden [ˈswiːdn] Schweden **IV**
Thailand [ˈtaɪlænd] Thailand ⟨**VTS3**, 113⟩
Thames [temz] **I**
Uluru [uːˈluːruː] Uluru *(= Ayers Rock, heiliger Berg der Aborigines)* **V AC1**, 10
United Arab Emirates [juːˌnaɪtɪd ˌærəb ˈemɪrəts] Vereinigte Arabische Emirate ⟨**V AC1**, 11⟩
United Kingdom (UK) [juːˌnaɪtɪd ˈkɪŋdəm; juːˈkeɪ] Vereinigtes Königreich von Großbritannien und Nordirland **I**
the **US** (= the United States) [ðə ˌjuːˈes] die USA (= die Vereinigten Staaten) **IV**
USA (United States of America) [ˌjuːesˈeɪ; juːˌnaɪtɪd ˌsteɪtsˌəvˌəˈmerɪkə] USA (Vereinigte Staaten von Amerika) **II**
Vietnam [ˌvjetˈnæm] Vietnam **V U1**, 18
Virginia [vəˈdʒɪnjə] *US-amerik. Bundesstaat* **IV**
Wales [weɪlz] **II**
Washington State [ˌwɒʃɪŋtən ˈsteɪt] *US-Bundesstaat* **IV**
Western Australia [ˌwestənˌɒsˈtreɪliə] *Bundesstaat in Australien* **V U1**, 15
Wisconsin [wɪˈskɒnsɪn] *US-amerik. Bundesstaat* **IV**
Wyoming [waɪˈəʊmɪŋ] *US-amerik. Bundesstaat* **IV**
Yellowstone National Park [ˌjeləʊstəʊn ˌnæʃnl ˈpɑːk] **IV**

Other names

1984 [ˌnaɪntiːnaɪtiˈfɔː] *Buchtitel* **V U2**, 67
Allegro [əˈlegrəʊ] **V U2**, 58
Arminder Singh Dhillon [ˌɑːmɪndə ˌsɪŋ dɪˈlɒn] *britischer Erfinder* **V U2**, 58
Aunty Rhonda Collard [ˌɑːnti ˌrɒndə ˈkɒləd] ⟨**V U1**, 23⟩
the **BBC** [ðə ˌbiːbiːˈsiː] *britische Rundfunkanstalt* **VTS2**, 77
Big Ben [ˌbɪg ˈben] **II**
Bixby Bridge [ˌbɪksbi ˈbrɪdʒ] *Stahlbeton-Bogenbrücke in Kalifornien* **V U3**, 85
Bollywood [ˈbɒliwʊd] Bollywood *(indische Filmindustrie: Bombay + Hollywood)* **V AC1**, 9
Brian Malarkey [ˌbraɪən məˈlɑːki] **V U3**, 98
Buckingham Palace [ˌbʌkɪŋəm ˈpælɪs] **II**
Cafazine [ˌkæfəˈziːn] *Name eines Cafés* ⟨**V U3**, 100⟩
Capital City Academy (CCA) [ˌkæpɪtl ˌsɪtiˌ əˈkædəmi] *Schule in London* ⟨**VTS2**, 79⟩
Census Bureau [ˈsensəs ˌbjʊərəʊ] *US-amerik. Bundesbehörde für Volkszählung* **IV**
Central Park [ˌsentrl ˈpɑːk] *Park in New York* **IV**
Central Plaza [ˌsentrl ˈplɑːzə] ⟨**V U2**, 65⟩
Cherokee [ˈtʃerəkiː] *Nordamerik. Indianerstamm* **IV**
Childwise [ˈtʃaɪldwaɪz] *Forschungsinstitut* ⟨**VTS2**, 79⟩
Church of England [ˌtʃɜːtʃˌəv ˈɪŋglənd] **III**
Cisco Systems [ˌsɪskəʊ ˈsɪstəmz] *US-amerikan. Unternehmen aus der Telekommunikationsbranche* **V U3**, 91
Daily News [ˌdeɪli ˈnjuːz] *Name einer Tageszeitung* **VTS2**, 75
Dirty Dancing [ˌdɜːti ˈdɑːnsɪŋ] *Filmtitel* **VTS1**, 45
Docklands Light Railway *(DLR)* [ˌdɒklændz ˌlaɪt ˈreɪlweɪ] *Regionalbahn im Osten Londons* **I**

Dragons' Den [ˌdrægnz ˈden] **V U2**, 58
Edinburgh Fringe Festival [ˌedɪnbrə ˈfrɪndʒ ˌfestɪvl] **III**
El Dorado [ˌel dəˈrɑːdəʊ] **V U3**, 90
Empire State Building [ˌempaɪə ˈsteɪt ˌbɪldɪŋ] *Wolkenkratzer in NYC* **IV**
En Vogue [en ˈvəʊg] *Bandname* **V AC2**, 80
Giants [dʒaɪənts] *Name eines Baseballteams* **V U3**, 97
the Globe Theatre [ðə ˌgləʊb ˈθɪətə] **III**
Goanna Lagoon [gəʊˌænə ləˈguːn] Goanna-Lagune ⟨**V U1**, 30⟩
God Save the Queen [ˈgɒd seɪv ðə ˌkwiːn] Gott schütze die Königin *(britische Nationalhymne)* **III**
Grease [griːs] *Filmtitel* **V TS1**, 45
Halloween [ˌhæləʊˈiːn] *Tag vor Allerheiligen* **I**
Hollywood Boulevard [ˌhɒliwʊd ˈbuːləvɑːd] *Straße in Los Angeles* **V U3**, 84
the Houses of Parliament [ðə ˌhaʊzɪz‿əv ˈpɑːləmənt] *britisches Parlamentsgebäude* **II**
The Hunger Games [ðə ˈhʌŋgə ˌgeɪmz] *Buchtitel* **V U2**, 67
Independence Day [ˌɪndɪˈpendəns ˌdeɪ] amerikanischer Unabhängigkeitstag **IV**
Industrial Revolution [ɪnˌdʌstriəl revlˈuːʃn] die industrielle Revolution **III**
Jackie Robinson [ˌdʒæki ˈrɒbɪnsn] *US-amerik. Baseballspieler* **V U3**, 98
Mardi Gras [ˌmɑːdi ˈgrɑː] Faschingsdienstag **V AC1**, 10
Mickey Mouse [ˌmɪki ˈmaʊs] **I**
Millennium Footbridge [mɪˌleniəm ˈfʊtbrɪdʒ] **II**
Natural History Museum [ˌnætʃrl ˈhɪstri mjuːˌziːəm] **II**
Navajo [ˈnævəhəʊ] *Nordamerik. Indianerstamm* **IV**
New York Weekly [ˌnjuː‿jɔːk ˈwiːkli] *US-Wochenzeitung* ⟨**V U3**, 100⟩
Ne-Yo [ˈniːjəʊ] *US-amerik. Sänger* ⟨**V U2**, 47⟩
Ngāpaki [ˈnɑːpəki] *Bezeichnung für weiße Australier* ⟨**V U1**, 29⟩
Nikon [ˈnɪkɒn] *finnisches Technologieunternehmen* ⟨**V U3**, 100⟩
Oracle [ˈɒrəkl] *US-amerikan. Soft- und Hardwarehersteller* **V U3**, 91
Orlando Cepeda [ɔːˌlændəʊ səˈpiːdə] *US-amerik. Baseballspieler* **V U3**, 98
Oz *(coll)* [ɒz] Oz *(Spitzname für Australien)* **V AC1**, 10
Pledge of Allegiance [ˌpledʒ‿əv‿əˈliːdʒns] *Treueeid auf die amerikanische Flagge* **IV**
Purnululu National Park [pɜːnəˌluːluː næʃnl ˈpɑːk] **V U1**, 15
Rainbow Cliff [ˈreɪnbəʊ klɪf] *Regenbogenklippe* ⟨**V U1**, 30⟩
Redhatch Road [ˌredhætʃ ˈrəʊd] **V U2**, 50
Revolutionary War [revlˌuːʃnri ˈwɔː] Amerikanischer Unabhängigkeitskrieg **IV**
Santa (Claus) [ˌsæntə ˈklɔːz] Nikolaus **V U1**, 19
Ski Beach [ˌskaɪ ˈbiːtʃ] ⟨**V U1**, 30⟩
Statue of Liberty [ˌstætʃuː‿əv ˈlɪbəti] Freiheitsstatue **IV**
Supreme Court [suːˌpriːm ˈkɔːt] Oberster Gerichtshof **V AC1**, 8
Sydney Cove [ˌsɪdni ˈkəʊv] *Bucht* **V U1**, 21
Sydney Opera House [ˌsɪdni ˈɒprə haʊs] **V U1**, 14
Thanksgiving [ˌθæŋksˈgɪvɪŋ] *amerik. Erntedankfest* **IV**
The Birds [ðə ˈbɜːdz] Die Vögel *(Filmtitel)* **V TS1**, 43
The Real Housewives of Orange County [ˌðə rɪəl ˌhaʊswaɪvz‿əv ˌɒrɪndʒ ˈkaʊnti] *Name einer Fernsehsendung* **V U3**, 98
The Taste [ðə ˈteɪst] *Name einer Fernsehsendung* **V U3**, 98
The Wind in the Willows [ðə ˌwɪnd ɪn ðə ˈwɪləʊz] *engl. Kinderbuchklassiker* **III**
Thirsty Merc [ˌθɜːsti ˈmɜːk] *australische Band* ⟨**V U2**, 47⟩
Thorny Devil Lizard [ˌθɔːni ˌdevl ˈlɪzəd] Dornteufel **V U1**, 17
Times Square [ˌtaɪmz ˈskweə] *Platz in New York* **IV**
Top Chef [ˌtɒp ˈʃef] *Name einer Kochsendung* **V U3**, 98
Top Chef Masters [ˌtɒp ʃef ˈmɑːstəz] *Name einer Kochsendung* **V U3**, 98
the Tower of London [ðə ˌtaʊər‿əv ˈlʌndən] **II**
Vine Street [ˈvaɪn striːt] *Straße in Los Angeles* **V U3**, 89
Walk of Fame [ˌwɔːk‿əv ˈfeɪm] **V U3**, 89
Whiteleaf [ˈwaɪtliːf] **V U2**, 50
Wikipedia [ˌwɪkɪˈpiːdiə] **V U3**, 98
the World Series [ˌwɜːld ˈsɪəriːz] *jährliches Endspiel zwischen den Gewinnern der beiden großen Baseballligen in den USA* **V U3**, 98
World War I [ˌwɜːld ˌwɔː ˈwʌn] Erster Weltkrieg **IV**
World War II [ˌwɜːld ˌwɔː ˈtuː] Zweiter Weltkrieg **II**
Yolnu [ˈjɒlnjuː] *(Volks-)Gruppe der Aborigines* ⟨**V U1**, 29⟩
Yosemite National Park [jəʊˌsemɪti ˌnæʃnl ˈpɑːk] **V U3**, 95

Famous names

Alfred Hitchcock [ˈælfrəd ˈhɪtʃkɒk] *US-amerik. Filmregisseur* **V TS1**, 43
Alison Lurie [ˌælɪsn ˈlʊəri] *US-amerik. Schriftstellerin* **V U3**, 85
Anne Boleyn [ˌæn ˈbɒlɪn] *Mutter von Elizabeth I.* **III**
Anne Hathaway [ˌæn ˈhæðəweɪ] *Shakespeares Frau* **III**
Annie Leibovitz [ˌæni ˈliːbəvɪts] *bekannte Fotografin* ⟨**V U3**, 102⟩
Arnold Schwarzenegger [ˌɑːnld ˈʃwɔːtsnegə] *38. Gouverneur Kaliforniens (2003–2011)* **V U3**, 85
Bobby Slayton [ˌbɒbi ˈsleɪtən] *US-amerik. Schauspieler* **V U3**, 85
Carl Laemmle [ˌkɑːl ˈlæmlə] *Gründer der Universal Studios* **V U3**, 89
Christopher Columbus [ˌkrɪstəfə kəˈlʌmbəs] **IV**
Edward Abbey [ˌedwəd ˈæbi] *US-amerik. Schriftsteller* **V U3**, 85
Elizabeth I [ɪˌlɪzəbəθ ðə ˈfɜːst] **II**
Francis Drake [ˌfrɑːnsɪs ˈdreɪk] **III**
Franklin D. Roosevelt [ˌfræŋklɪn diː ˈrəʊzəvelt] *32. Präsident der USA* **IV**
George Orwell [ˌdʒɔːdʒ ˈɔːwel] *englischer Schriftsteller* **V U2**, 67
George Washington [ˌdʒɔːdʒ ˈwɒʃɪŋtən] *1. Präsident der USA* **IV**
Henry Ford [ˌhenri ˈfɔːd] *US-amerik. Unternehmer* **IV**
Henry VIII [ˌhenri ði ˈeɪtθ] Heinrich VIII. **III**
Jacob Davis [ˌdʒeɪkəb ˈdeɪvɪz] *US-amerik. Schneider* **V U3**, 92
Jimmy Carter [ˌdʒɪmi ˈkɑːtə] *39. Präsident der USA* **V U3**, 85
John F. Kennedy (JFK) [ˌdʒɒn‿ef ˈkenədi; dʒeɪ‿ef keɪ] *35. Präsident der USA* **IV**
Kevin Rudd [ˌkevɪn ˈrʌd] *australischer Politiker* ⟨**V U1**, 23⟩
King George III [ˌkɪŋ‿ˈdʒɔːdʒ ðə ˌθɜːd] *britischer König (1760–1801)* ⟨**V U1**, 21⟩
Levi Strauss [ˌliːvaɪ ˈstraʊs] *Erfinder der Jeans* **V U3**, 92
Lois Lowry [ˌləʊɪs ˈlaʊri] *US-amerik. Schriftstellerin* ⟨**V U2**, 66⟩
Mark Twain [mɑːk ˈtweɪn] *US-amerik. Schriftsteller* **V U3**, 91
Nelson Mandela [ˌnelsn mænˈdelə] *1. südafrikan. Präsident nach Abschaffung der Apartheid* **V AC1**, 8
Pink [pɪŋk] *US-amerik. Sängerin* **V U3**, 85
Suzanne Collins [ˌsuːzæn ˈkɒlɪnz] *US-amerik. Schriftstellerin* **V U2**, 67
Thomas Jefferson [ˌtɒməs ˈdʒefəsn] *3. Präsident der USA* **IV**
William Shakespeare [ˌwɪljəm ˈʃeɪkspɪə] *englischer Dramatiker (1564–1616)* **III**
Woollarawarre Bennelong [wʊl.ləˌwɑːrə ˈbenəlɒŋ] ⟨**V U1**, 21⟩
Zelda Quakawoot [ˌzeldə ˈkwɒkəwuːt] ⟨**V U1**, 24⟩

Tip

Die Wörter und Ausdrücke auf diesen Seiten musst du nicht auswendig lernen. Aber in vielen Situationen im Klassenzimmer wirst du sie nützlich finden!

Vocabulary for instructions and activities

(Die mit * gekennzeichneten Begriffe werden im Fachlehrplan von mindestens einem Bundesland als Operatoren definiert. Die Verwendung der geforderten Operatoren in *Green Line* beginnt in Band 1 und wird Band für Band ausgebaut.)

Act (out) one of the scenes / the dialogues.	Spiele eine der Szenen / die Dialoge vor.
Add more words / ideas.	Füge weitere Wörter / Ideen hinzu.
***Analyse** the text.	Analysiere den Text.
Ask your partner questions.	Stelle deinem Partner / deiner Partnerin Fragen.
Answer your partner's questions.	Beantworte die Fragen deines Partners / deiner Partnerin.
***Characterise** the protagonist.	Charakterisiere die Hauptfigur.
Choose a character / one of the situations / options.	Wähle eine Figur / eine der Situationen / Optionen aus.
***Comment** on the statistics.	Kommentiere die Statistik.
***Compare** English and German.	Vergleiche das Englische und das Deutsche.
Complete the answers.	Vervollständige die Antworten.
***Contrast** the situation of the two teenagers.	Stelle die Situation der beiden Teenager einander gegenüber.
Copy the grid / the mind map.	Schreibe die Tabelle / die Mindmap ab.
Correct the wrong sentences.	Korrigiere die falschen Sätze.
***Describe** what you see / how it makes you feel.	Beschreibe, was du siehst / wie du dich dabei fühlst.
***Discuss** different ideas.	Diskutiert verschiedene Ideen.
Divide up into two groups.	Teilt euch in zwei Gruppen auf.
***Evaluate** the advert.	Bewerte die Anzeige.
***Examine** the author's intention.	Untersuche die Absicht des Autors.
Exchange your flyers / questions.	Tauscht eure Flyer / Fragen untereinander aus.
***Explain** your answer. / Explain why.	Erkläre deine Antwort. / Erkläre warum.
Fill in the grid / the form.	Fülle die Tabelle / das Formular aus.
Finish your brochure.	Mache deine Broschüre fertig.
Form expert groups.	Bildet Expertengruppen.
Get organised.	Organisiert euch.
Give reasons / examples.	Nenne Gründe / Beispiele.
Give feedback.	Gib ein Feedback.

Guess the new words.	Errate die neuen Wörter.
***Illustrate** the main points of the text.	Veranschauliche die Hauptpunkte des Textes.
Improve your text / part of the report.	Verbessere deinen Text / deinen Teil des Berichts.
***Interpret** the information.	Interpretiere die Informationen.
***Justify** your answer.	Begründe deine Antwort.
Listen to the sentences / the dialogue.	Höre dir die Sätze / den Dialog an.
***Look up** the words.	Schlage die Wörter nach.
Make a poster / a grid / a mind map / notes.	Fertige ein Poster / eine Tabelle / eine Mindmap / Notizen an.
***Match** the sentence parts.	Ordne die Satzteile einander zu.
Note down what is missing.	Notiere, was fehlt.
***Outline** the Information given in the text.	Skizziere die im Text enthaltenen Informationen.
Practise your scenes / the dialogues.	Übe deine Szenen / die Dialoge.
***Point out** what you find interesting.	Lege dar, was du interessant findest.
***Present** the information from your text.	Präsentiere die Informationen aus deinem Text.
Put in the correct forms.	Setze die richtigen Formen ein.
Put the verbs in the right / correct form.	Bringe die Verben in die richtige Form.
Read your text aloud. / Read your text out loud.	Lies deinen Text laut vor.
Record your final report / dialogue.	Nehmt euren fertigen Bericht / Dialog auf.
Repeat the sentences / the dialogues.	Wiederhole die Sätze / die Dialoge.
***Report** what the people say.	Berichte, was die Leute sagen.
Scan the text for details.	Suche den Text nach Details ab.
Share the information with your partner.	Teile die Informationen mit deinem Partner / deiner Partnerin.
***Show** what the letter is about.	Zeige, worum es in dem Brief geht.
Skim the text for the gist.	Überfliege den Text und finde die wichtigsten Aussagen.
***State** your reaction to the story.	Lege deine Reaktion auf die Geschichte dar.
***Sum up / Summarise** what happens in the story.	Fasse zusammen, was in der Geschichte passiert.
Swap roles.	Tauscht die Rollen.
Take notes.	Mache dir Notizen.
Take turns.	Wechselt euch ab.
***Talk** with / to your partner (about …).	Sprich mit deinem Partner / deiner Partnerin (über …).
***Tell** your partner about your experiences.	Erzähle deinem Partner / deiner Partnerin von deinen Erfahrungen.
Think about different problems.	Denke über verschiedene Probleme nach.
***Translate** the words / sentences.	Übersetze die Wörter / Sätze.
Underline the words that change.	Unterstreiche die Wörter, die sich ändern.
Use the ideas / the vocabulary.	Verwende die Ideen / die Vokabeln.
Work with a partner or in a group.	Arbeite mit einem Partner / einer Partnerin oder in einer Gruppe.
***Write** dialogues / a short text / a reply / a summary.	Schreibe Dialoge / einen kurzen Text / eine Antwort / eine Zusammenfassung.
Write about your friends.	Schreibe über deine Freunde.
Write down your ideas / key words.	Schreibe deine Ideen / Schlüsselwörter auf.

Find more online:
8c4nw3

■ ■ ■ Grundform, *simple past* und *past participle* sind identisch
■ ● ● Grundform unterscheidet sich vom *simple past* und *past participle*
■ ● ■ Grundform und *past participle* sind identisch, nur das *simple past* hat eine andere Form
■ ● ▲ Grundform, *simple past* und *past participle* haben alle eine andere Form

■ Grundform	■ simple past	■ past participle	Deutsch
bet [bet]	bet [bet]	bet [bet]	wetten
burst [bɜ:st]	burst [bɜ:st]	burst [bɜ:st]	bersten; platzen
cost [kɒst]	cost [kɒst]	cost [kɒst]	kosten
cut [kʌt]	cut [kʌt]	cut [kʌt]	schneiden
hit [hɪt]	hit [hɪt]	hit [hɪt]	schlagen, treffen
hurt [hɜ:t]	hurt [hɜ:t]	hurt [hɜ:t]	verletzen, sich weh tun
let [let]	let [let]	let [let]	lassen
put [pʊt]	put [pʊt]	put [pʊt]	legen, setzen, stellen
spread [spred]	spread [spred]	spread [spred]	(sich) verbreiten

■ Grundform	● simple past	● past participle	Deutsch
bring [brɪŋ]	brought [brɔ:t]	brought [brɔ:t]	(mit)bringen
build [bɪld]	built [bɪlt]	built [bɪlt]	bauen
burn [bɜ:n]	burnt [bɜ:nt] / burned [bɜ:nd]	burnt [bɜ:nt] / burned [bɜ:nd]	(ver)brennen
buy [baɪ]	bought [bɔ:t]	bought [bɔ:t]	kaufen
catch [kætʃ]	caught [kɔ:t]	caught [kɔ:t]	fangen; mitbekommen
dream [dri:m]	dreamt [dremt] / dreamed [dri:md]	dreamt [dremt] / dreamed [dri:md]	träumen
feel [fi:l]	felt [felt]	felt [felt]	fühlen
find [faɪnd]	found [faʊnd]	found [faʊnd]	finden
get [get]	got [gɒt]	got [gɒt] / gotten ['gɒtn]	bekommen; werden
hang [hæŋ]	hung [hʌŋ]	hung [hʌŋ]	hängen
have [hæv]	had [hæd]	had [hæd]	haben
hear [hɪə]	heard [hɜ:d]	heard [hɜ:d]	hören
hold [həʊld]	held [held]	held [held]	halten
keep [ki:p]	kept [kept]	kept [kept]	(auf)bewahren, behalten
lead [li:d]	led [led]	led [led]	(an)führen
lean [li:n]	leant [lent] / leaned [li:nd]	leant [lent] / leaned [li:nd]	(sich) lehnen
learn [lɜ:n]	learnt [lɜ:nt] / learned [lɜ:nd]	learnt [lɜ:nt] / learned [lɜ:nd]	lernen
leave [li:v]	left [left]	left [left]	(ver)lassen
lend [lend]	lent [lent]	lent [lent]	(ver)leihen
make [meɪk]	made [meɪd]	made [meɪd]	machen, tun
meet [mi:t]	met [met]	met [met]	treffen
pay [peɪ]	paid [peɪd]	paid [peɪd]	(be)zahlen
read [ri:d]	read [red]	read [red]	lesen
say [seɪ]	said [sed]	said [sed]	sagen
sell [sel]	sold [səʊld]	sold [səʊld]	verkaufen
send [send]	sent [sent]	sent [sent]	senden, verschicken
shoot [ʃu:t]	shot [ʃɒt]	shot [ʃɒt]	schießen (auf)
sit [sɪt]	sat [sæt]	sat [sæt]	sitzen
sleep [sli:p]	slept [slept]	slept [slept]	schlafen
smell [smel]	smelt [smelt]	smelt [smelt]	riechen, duften

spell [spel]	spelt [spelt]	spelt [spelt]	buchstabieren
spend [spend]	spent [spent]	spent [spent]	ausgeben, verbringen
spill [spɪl]	spilt [spɪlt]	spilt [spɪlt]	verschütten, auslaufen
stand (up) [stænd]	stood (up) [stʊd]	stood (up) [stʊd]	(auf)stehen
sting [stɪŋ]	stung [stʌŋ]	stung [stʌŋ]	stechen
teach [ti:tʃ]	taught [tɔ:t]	taught [tɔ:t]	lehren, unterrichten
tell [tel]	told [təʊld]	told [təʊld]	erzählen
think [θɪŋk]	thought [θɔ:t]	thought [θɔ:t]	(nach)denken, glauben
understand [ˌʌndə'stænd]	understood [ˌʌndə'stʊd]	understood [ˌʌndə'stʊd]	verstehen
win [wɪn]	won [wʌn]	won [wʌn]	gewinnen, siegen

■ Grundform	● simple past	■ past participle	Deutsch
become [bɪ'kʌm]	became [bɪ'keɪm]	become [bɪ'kʌm]	werden
come [kʌm]	came [keɪm]	come [kʌm]	kommen
run [rʌn]	ran [ræn]	run [rʌn]	laufen, rennen

■ Grundform	● simple past	▲ past participle	Deutsch
be [bi:]	was / were [wɒz / wɜ:]	been [bi:n]	sein
blow (out) [bləʊ]	blew [blu:]	blown [bləʊn]	(aus)blasen, (aus)pusten
break [breɪk]	broke [brəʊk]	broken ['brəʊkn]	(zer)brechen, kaputt machen
choose [tʃu:z]	chose [tʃəʊz]	chosen [tʃəʊzn]	(aus)wählen
do [du:]	did [dɪd]	done [dʌn]	machen, tun
draw [drɔ:]	drew [dru:]	drawn [drɔ:n]	zeichnen
drink [drɪŋk]	drank [dræŋk]	drunk [drʌŋk]	trinken
drive [draɪv]	drove [drəʊv]	driven ['drɪvn]	fahren
eat [i:t]	ate [et]	eaten [i:tn]	essen
fall [fɔ:l]	fell [fel]	fallen ['fɔ:lən]	fallen
fly [flaɪ]	flew [flu:]	flown [fləʊn]	fliegen
forget [fə'get]	forgot [fə'gɒt]	forgotten [fə'gɒtn]	vergessen
give [gɪv]	gave [geɪv]	given['gɪvn]	geben
go [gəʊ]	went [went]	gone [gɒn]	gehen, fahren
grow [grəʊ]	grew [gru:]	grown [grəʊn]	wachsen; anbauen
know [nəʊ]	knew [nju:]	known [nəʊn]	kennen, wissen
ring [rɪŋ]	rang [ræŋ]	rung [rʌŋ]	klingeln; anrufen
rise [raɪz]	rose [rəʊz]	risen ['rɪzn]	steigen, sich erheben
see [si:]	saw [sɔ:]	seen [si:n]	sehen
shake [ʃeɪk]	shook [ʃʊk]	shaken ['ʃeɪkn]	schütteln
show [ʃəʊ]	showed [ʃəʊd]	shown [ʃəʊn]	zeigen
sing [sɪŋ]	sang [sæŋ]	sung [sʌŋ]	singen
sink [sɪŋk]	sank [sæŋk]	sunk [sʌŋk]	sinken, untergehen
speak [spi:k]	spoke [spəʊk]	spoken ['spəʊkn]	sprechen
swim [swɪm]	swam [swæm]	swum [swʌm]	schwimmen
take [teɪk]	took [tʊk]	taken ['teɪkn]	nehmen
throw [θrəʊ]	threw [θru:]	thrown [θrəʊn]	werfen
wake up [ˌweɪk‿'ʌp]	woke up [ˌwəʊk‿'ʌp]	woken up [ˌwəʊkn‿'ʌp]	aufwachen; aufwecken
wear [weə]	wore [wɔ:]	worn [wɔ:n]	anhaben, tragen
write [raɪt]	wrote [rəʊt]	written ['rɪtn]	schreiben

Grammar solutions

Unit 1

G1 Has he been found yet?

Family of four rescued at sea
Two adults and two young children had to **be rescued** by a lifeboat on Saturday after their boat **had been caught** by a rip current and **pulled** out to sea.
They weren't very far from the shore when they suddenly noticed that they **were being carried** further and further away from the beach. Although there were four people on the boat, they had only one lifejacket and no other safety equipment with them. A lifeboat **was sent out** and the family **was found** about two kilometres down the coast, close to some dangerous rocks from where they **were brought** safely back to shore. Coastguard Tom Walsh said that people often didn't realise how easily these small boats can **be swept** out to sea and that this family had had a lucky escape. Nobody **was hurt** this time. But if their boat had crashed into the rocks, it would have been a very different story.

G2 They let her go to Australia

Good news. Mum and Dad are going to **let** me have the barbie at their house and they're going to **allow** us to use the pool too. But I can't **let** anybody sleep at the house and they're going to **make** me tidy up after the party. They're even going to **make** me cut the grass. Oh yeah, and we haven't **had** the pool cleaned this year yet. So guess who has to do that? I think they're getting a really good deal. I'm being **made** to do everything!

G3 I've been sent some brochures

1. We were in a jewellery shop and we were being shown some expensive rings when a woman in the street started to scream. 2. Her dog had been run over by a car.
3. The police were called. 4. When they arrived, they were given a photo of the car. 5. The owner of the dog hopes that the driver of the car will be found soon. 6. Anyone with any information is asked to contact the police.

G4 If I hadn't seen it for myself

Mike: Most snakes aren't aggressive. Normally, they'll only bite you if they feel threatened.
Jim: I know. So it was really lucky that I saw that snake in time. If I'd stepped on it, it would have bitten me.
Mike: Yes. And if it had bitten you, we'd have been in real trouble. The nearest hospital is miles away. Yesterday I heard that a tourist was attacked by a crocodile.
Jim: Yes, some people are really stupid. The crocodile probably wouldn't have attacked him if he hadn't thrown a stone at it.
Mike: Oh look! There's a baby kangaroo over there. Be quiet. If we make a noise, we'll frighten it and it'll jump away.

G5 I used to

1. I **used to live** in rural Australia, but now I live in Sydney.
2. At home we usually spoke our own language; we **didn't use to speak** English very often.
3. I **used to share** a room with my three sisters, but now I have my own room.
4. I **didn't use to drink / never used to drink** coffee, but now I drink it all the time.
5. I **didn't use to be / never used to be** interested in sport, but now I love surfing.

Unit 2

G6 How to sound more formal

1. Being a camp counsellor gives you an opportunity to lead groups, take on responsibility and to build your self-confidence. **Moreover**, it looks great on your CV. – Tom
2. **Personally**, I think that working as an assistant camp counsellor at a summer camp is the best experience any teenager can have. – Jane
3. It was really hard work. **In fact**, it was **probably** the hardest job I've ever had to do! – Brian
4. Spending 24 hours a day with a group of active young kids can be exhausting. **Nevertheless**, I wouldn't have missed the experience for the world. – Sarah
5. You don't have to be crazy to work as a camp counsellor, but it helps! It was the most amazing job I've ever had and I had a fantastic time. **Hopefully**, I can go back for more next year! – Marco

G7 I watched the kids ...

1. He always arrives really late for work and then he leaves early. Yesterday I saw him **arrive** at 9:30, **hang** his jacket on the chair, then **leave** again.
2. He prefers magazines to company reports. Today I noticed him **reading** a car magazine.
3. And he makes a lot of personal phone calls. This morning I was walking past his office when I heard him **telling** somebody all about his last holiday.
4. He also takes other people's equipment without asking. Yesterday I watched him **pick up** a pen from his colleague's desk, quickly **put** it into his pocket and then **walk away**.
5. Our boss isn't happy with him. As I was walking past her office today, I could hear her **shouting** at him.

G8 They arrived feeling exhausted

After a busy morning at work yesterday, I decided to spend my lunch break relaxing on the beach. But as I **lay reading** quietly, I soon **found myself wondering** if I had made the right choice. There weren't many people on the beach, just a few dog-walkers and two girls who were chatting quietly nearby as they **sat eating** ice creams. Then suddenly a large dog **came running** towards the two girls. He was barking loudly and the girls were scared. So they began to scream. When that didn't help, they threw stones. A moment later, the dog's owner **arrived shouting** angrily at the two girls. Then he **caught me watching** the drama, so he started shouting at me too! I **came hoping** for some peace on the beach. I **left thinking** the world had gone crazy!

G9 The Words-of-Wisdom Wall

I was walking past the pet shop, **which** I often do on my way into town, when I noticed a job advert in the window. They were looking for a student **who** could help them on Saturdays. It seemed the perfect job for me, so I went in. The shop manager, **who** was really busy, quickly explained everything **(that)** I needed to know and then offered me the position. I liked the other people **who** worked there and I liked the job. But it was *hard*. When the shop was full of people, **which** it usually was, it was difficult to find time to take a break. And the money **(that)** I earned wasn't enough for the hours **(which)** I had to put in. - Dan

G10 Not only was it super cold, but ...

No way should people be allowed to use mobile phones in public places. **Not only do they** make lots of noise, **but** they also force others to listen to their private conversations. Yesterday a woman on my bus talked non-stop. **Hardly had she** finished one call **when** she started again. **Never have I** heard such silly, unnecessary conversations! I was glad when she got off the bus. **Only then was I** able to read my book in peace.

G11 I do remember how it feels ...

1. I'm surprised. I do look really good in grey!
2. I do hope that you get the job.
3. So you did meet Tom yesterday!
4. You're right. The milk does taste strange.
5. I do know what you mean, but that isn't true / you're wrong.
6. Do let me know if I can bring you some more coffee.
7. She's heard so many good things about you and really does want to meet you!
8. Good evening, I'm glad you could come! Please do come in, the others are already here.
9. Mr Braxton, you do know that one should / that you should never be late for a job interview, but nevertheless you were late / you arrived late / you came late.
10. You didn't really enjoy yourself at the party. - No, I did enjoy myself. I just had to leave early.

Unit 3

G12 It starts at 8:00 but we're meeting at 6:00

Ella: What **are you doing** tomorrow?
Mia: I**'m meeting** my cousin at the new shopping mall. It **opens** tomorrow at 10:00. Why don't you come with us?
Ella: That sounds like a great idea. How **are you getting** there?
Mia: By bus or by subway. I haven't decided yet. The bus is cheaper but it **leaves** earlier and it **takes** a lot longer.
Ella: I've got a better idea. My brother **is driving** into town tomorrow morning. I'm sure he won't mind taking us with him. But let me ask him first what time he **is going**.

G13 What will Alex be doing by the time he's 30?

On Monday morning Alex **will be meeting** his agent. In the afternoon he**'ll be writing** a movie review for the internet. On Tuesday he**'ll be going** to an audition. On Wednesday he**'ll be interviewing** stars at a movie premiere on Hollywood Boulevard. On Thursday he**'ll be visiting** his buddy Dave. And on Friday his parents **will be coming** for the weekend so he**'ll be picking** them up from the airport.

G14 What will Alex have done by the time he's 30?

I really hope that by the time people read my blog I**'ll have gotten** my big break and that I**'ll be living** my dream. In six months' time, I'm sure I**'ll have become** a star and the reporters **will be wanting** to interview me. Then of course I'll be friendly and polite, but I'll tell them never to call me before 11:00 because I **won't have got up** by then. I**'ll still be sleeping**.

G15 California in the world

Sorry I didn't send you an e-mail earlier, but I was tired after all **the** fun we had at **the** movie premiere last night. When I got up, it was already 10:30. Then after **(–)** breakfast, I had to learn all about **the** history of California for **a** test on Wednesday. That took about **an** hour and **a** half. And I haven't even started to learn about **the** economy or **the** different landscapes yet. No, I haven't gone back to **(–)** college. **The** test is for a job with **the** Tourist Office. If I pass, I'll soon be able to work as **a** tour guide two or three times **a** week in-between my auditions. But I've already heard it's pretty difficult and **(–)** most people have to take it at least twice, so I'm not very hopeful. I haven't found **(–)** fame as **an** actor yet. But I can honestly say that I've found **(–)** happiness. L.A. is such **a** fantastic city and I just love **the** excitement of living here. For me, it's simply **the** most exciting city in **the** US.

G16 Should we be worried?

a) 1. If Mrs. Kent is late today, we **are to** wait for her in the hall. 2. Have you been to the new restaurant in West Street? It **is supposed to / is said to** be very good. 3. The plane landed early. It **was supposed to** land at 8:30. 4. If Lisa isn't feeling better soon, I think she **should / ought to** see a doctor. 5. Are you hungry? **Shall** I make us a sandwich? 6. We can take cell phones to school but we **aren't supposed to** use them in class.

b) 1. We've got plenty of time. We **needn't / don't need to** hurry. 2. It's not going to rain today, so we **won't need to** take an umbrella. 3. There were no trains or buses to the village, so I **was forced to** take a taxi. 4. There's no food in the cupboard. I**'ll need to** go shopping today. 5. Sometimes we **must / are forced to** make difficult decisions. We have no choice. 6. **Are** firefighters **obliged to / required to** rescue animals?

Unit solutions

Unit 1, Introduction → page 12, ex. 2

Look at these photos and describe the impression you get of Australia. Then compare it to the impression your partner got from the pictures on the Introduction pages.

A

B

C

D

E

Text smart 1, Station 1 → page 40, ex. 7

College Romance – The Musical (by Isabelle Sieb)

Boy 1: Coffee?
Penny: I'm Penny.
Boy 1: You OK?

Penny cries over spilled coffee (Boy 1).

Penny: Not again.

Oh no, I did it again. I let myself go.
And now, everyone's staring at me.
I feel rather uncomfortable.
What have I done to deserve this misery?

Since I was just a kid
I've had this problem that
I get a boo-boo or an ouchie
and I can't hold back
the tears I try to fight
when all that's on my mind
is finding true love
someone who understands.

Tell me girls, what can I do?

Girls: *We're reading self-help books. / We don't have a clue.*
Penny: *Oh teacher, what's my chance?*
A smile or just a glance?
I look at him, he looks at me.
Could it be true?
Is he the one for me?
I want it desperately.
Now act cool.
There's something on my back.
What's this?

Penny cries over picture on her back (Boy 2).

Penny: *Oh boy, what am I to do with this dreadful fate?*
The more I cry, the more I scare them away.
And now I'm dancing with books in the library.
What's become of me?

So what, I lost the plot.
So what, I'm out of luck.
Sometimes in life things
go a little wrong.
Maybe it's not too late.
Maybe he's worth the wait.

Girls: *Can you just pass the ball?*
Penny: *He's coming over here.*

Penny cries over being hit by a ball (Boy 3).

Penny: *Now I've had enough. I'm the master of my own fate.*
And who cares about romance in this day and age?
An independent woman is what I am.
And I don't need a man.

Girls: *You don't need a man.*
Penny: *I don't need a man.*
Choir: *She don't need no man.*

Boy 4 laughs.

Boy 4: Not again!

Unit 2, Introduction → page 46, ex. 1c)

Explain if one of the photos below or the photo on p. 46 comes closer to your 'good life'.

A

B

A look at the origins[1] of English

The Commonwealth

After the British Empire began to break apart following World War II, the former colonies became independent countries. But most of them remained 'together' in the British Commonwealth, or later simply the 'Commonwealth'. The countries in the Commonwealth are spread across Asia, Africa, Oceania and North America. Despite their differences, they have many strong cultural ties[2]. The strongest is surely their common language: English.

A look at the language

But what is this language that we call 'English'? It's perhaps ironic that this lingua franca, which is so closely associated with England, relies so heavily on words taken from French and Latin. (See pie chart.)

The origins of English vocabulary

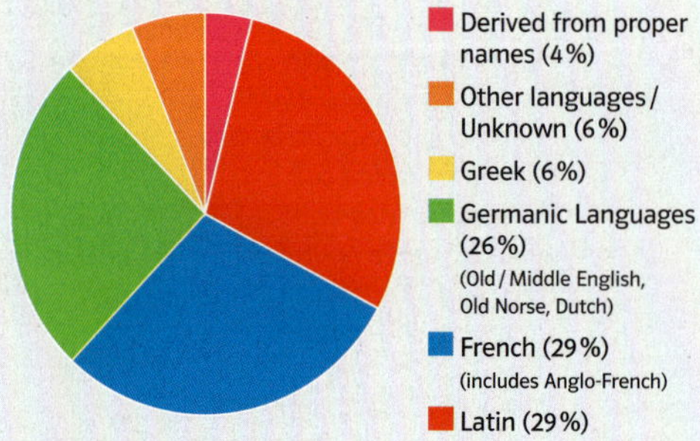

Formal vs. informal English

Interestingly, the English words which originate[3] from the Germanic language family (Old / Middle English, Old Norse, Dutch) are traditionally the ones which are often used in more informal, conversational contexts. For more formal contexts, it's more typical to use words taken from French and from the language that French originated from: Latin. Why is this so? The answer is actually quite simple: After the Normans conquered England in 1066, French took over as the language at court and for administration. The old form of English which was spoken at the time was ignored as a language for the lower classes. Eventually, the two languages merged[4], but the French-based terms remained favoured for a more formal style.

Surprising facts

- There are more words in English than any other language: between 450,000 and 650,000, depending on the dictionary.
- 4,000 new words are added to the English language each year; another record.
- English is the language for 80% of all the information stored in the world's computers.

Examples of common differences today:

Informal	Formal
- Can I **help** you?	- How may I **assist** you?
- I'm **asking** for your **help**.	- I'm **requesting** your **assistance**.
- **Sorry** for not **calling** you back.	- I **apologise** for not **returning** your call.
- Can you **give** us your address?	- Please **provide** us with your address.
- Could you please **check** that for me?	- Could you please **verify** that for me?
- Where do English words **come from**?	- Where do English words **originate**?

1 origin [ˈɒrɪdʒɪn] Ursprung; Herkunft | **2 tie** [taɪ] Verbindung | **3 to originate (from)** [əˈrɪdʒneɪt] stammen (aus) | **4 to merge** [mɜːdʒ] verschmelzen

Australia: Not always what you expect

There are several misconceptions[1] about Australia. What is myth? What is reality?

Myth no. 1:
"Australia is all just red desert and dusty outback."

The reality: Yes, Australia is dry. About 40 % of the country is desert, another 20 % is dry steppe land. But many don't realise that there are huge tropical rain forests all along the northern coastal regions, while the Southwest and Southeast have a temperate Mediterranean climate similar to what one finds in the South of France.

Green forests in the Blue Mountains

Myth no. 2:
"Australians are always at the beach, showing off their beach bodies."

The reality: Just as in other wealthy office-based societies, Australians spend a lot of time at work, so they can't always be at the beach. But even when they *do* go, you won't always see them 'showing off their bodies'. Instead, it's typical to find them swimming in long-sleeve shirts, long shorts and caps to protect them from skin cancer[2]: Australia and New Zealand have the world's highest rates of melanoma. And as for beach bodies: Although a major sports nation, Australia is also the 5th-fattest in the world, with a 28 % obesity[3] rate.

Myth no. 3:
"They don't have any problems in Australia. Life must be perfect down there."

The reality: The friendly people, cute koalas and spectacular scenery can distract from some real problems in Australian society. For example, there is white racism, and it isn't only directed towards Aboriginal Australians. Migrants from India and the Middle East have also been the victims of more and more frequent racist attacks; the Cronulla riots of 2005 are one particularly problematic example. On another front, environmental protection hasn't been one of Australia's strengths either: The country has major issues with the results of mining and deforestation[4], and also with extreme marine pollution.

In Great Otway National Park, home of many koalas

Surprising facts
- Australia is the only continent with no active volcano.
- Tasmania has the world's cleanest air.
- The word 'selfie' first appeared in Australia, in 2002.
- Melbourne is the world's second-largest Greek-speaking city, after Athens.

1 misconception [ˌmɪskən'sepʃn] falsche Vorstellung; Missverständnis | **2 cancer** ['kænsə] Krebs | **3 obesity** [ˌə'bi:səti] Fettleibigkeit | **4 deforestation** [di:ˌfɒrɪ'steɪʃn] Abholzung

A look at some career statistics

The UK's best-paying jobs

The UK Office for National Statistics publishes yearly rankings[1] of average salaries in nearly 350 professions. Here are some of the top jobs, followed by others further down the list. (For comparison: In parts of London, renting a small flat can easily cost £25,000 a year.)

Rank	English job title	German job title	Salary
1	**chief executive / senior official**	Geschäftsführer/-in; Firmenchef/-in	£ 118,065
2	**broker**	Börsenmakler/-in	116,104
3	**pilot**	Pilot/-in	86,342
4	**marketing / sales manager**	Marketingleiter/-in; Vertriebsleiter/-in	82,360
5	**financial institution manager**	Direktor/-in eines Geldinstituts / einer Versicherung	77,387
7	**air traffic controller**	Fluglotse/-lotsin	75,060
9	**medical practitioner (doctor)**	Arzt / Ärztin	72,315
10	**IT manager**	IT-Experte / Expertin	66,733
92	**secondary education teacher**	Lehrer/-in Sekundarstufe I	33,665
123	**web design professional**	Webdesigner/-in	30,339
135	**office manager**	Büroleiter/-in; Chefsekretär/-in	29,588
155	**business associate / professional**	Bürokaufmann/-frau	28,274
266	**secretary / personal assistant**	Sekretär/-in; Assistent/-in	19,295
291	**chef**	Koch / Köchin	17,531
339	**fitness instructor**	Fitnesstrainer/-in	11,054

Source: UK Office for National Statistics (2016)

An alternative ranking: The UK's most satisfying[2] jobs

A study conducted by the Cabinet Office of the Prime Minister, however, shows that the most satisfying jobs aren't always those that pay the best:

Rank	English job title	German job title	Salary
1	**clergy member**	Amtsträger/-in einer Kirche	£ 20,568
2	**chief executive / senior official**	Geschäftsführer/-in; Firmenchef/-in	118,065
3	**manager / proprietor in agriculture**	Leiter/-in; Eigentümer/-in in der Agrarwirtschaft	31,721
4	**secretary**	Sekretär/-in	19,295
5	**quality assurance professional**	Experte / Expertin für Qualitätskontrolle	42,898

Source: Cabinet Office (2014)

Surprising facts

- The world average for women in high management positions is just 24 %. Japan is near the bottom of the list at just 9 %, the UK comes in at 20 %, while Russia tops the list at 43 %.
- In English, a 'manager' can be just about anything: a powerful businessperson who earns millions, or a person who runs a small shop.
- In the US, if your employer hands you a 'pink slip', it means you're losing your job. (A 'slip' is a piece of paper.)

1 ranking ['ræŋkɪŋ] Rangliste | **2 satisfying** ['sætɪsfaɪɪŋ] zufriedenstellend; befriedigend

Contrasts: San Francisco and Los Angeles

San Francisco, the Bay, the Golden Gate Bridge

SAN FRANCISCO

Population: 860,000 (metro[1]: 4.6 million)
Area: 232 sq. mi (600 km²)
Economic profile: Long history as trade mecca (major port, railroad terminus); SF and nearby San José (= Silicon Valley) together form world capital of the IT / tech industry; tourism; wine country
Important historical dates:

- **Gold Rush:** Massive wealth discovered in the Bay Area, starting in 1849
- **Earthquake of 1906:** 80 % of city destroyed
- **'Summer of Love', 1967:** Heart of the world's alternative 'hippie' youth movement

Typical beach scene in Santa Monica, L.A.

LOS ANGELES

Population: 3.9 million (metro: 13 million)
Area: 503 sq. mi (1,302 km²)
Economic profile: World capital of the entertainment industry (film, TV & music); massive suburban sprawl[2] due to booming economy and year-round good weather; tourism; trendsetter in fitness, lifestyle
Important historical dates:

- Host city for **Summer Olympics** in 1932, 1984
- Violent, large-scale **race riots** in 1965, 1992
- The first ARPANET transmission was sent from the University of California in 1969; the **internet** was born.

At first glance, California's two most famous cities couldn't be more different. Up in Northern California, there's San Francisco with its historical Victorian architecture, its lively downtown, and its liberal tradition as a mecca for alternative lifestyles. And of course it also has a 'nerdy' reputation as the world's capital of IT / tech innovation. Then there's L.A., in Southern California, where the huge and powerful entertainment industry gives the city a sexy, glamorous, body-conscious[3] image as a place to be. But 'city' isn't really the right term here: L.A. is more like a collection of endless communities with no real centre for city life.

But a second glance might reveal that the two cities are just two sides of the same coin: Both are a magnet for Americans and foreigners who want to live their own 'California dream' in places of great natural beauty, with strong economies, and with residents who love the relaxed, freetime-oriented lifestyle that California invented.

Surprising facts

- It's about 200 km from one end of metropolitan L.A. to the other – the same distance as from Frankfurt to Stuttgart.
- The weather in San Francisco can get very cool in summer: First-time tourists are often surprised to find they need a jacket in July or August.

1 metro [ˈmetrəʊ] Großraum- | **2 sprawl** [sprɔːl] Ausdehnung | **3 body-conscious** [ˈbɒdi ˌkɒnʃəs] korperbewusst

Time line of Australian history

60,000–40,000 BC

The famous Ubirr rock paintings in Kakadu National Park: some of the oldest artworks in the world

The first people came to Australia from southeast Asia and spread across the red continent. The **Aboriginals** learned how to deal with the dry climate, and to find food and water where no one else could. They developed a rich culture of art and great spirituality.

1770

The statue of Captain Cook in Hyde Park, Sydney

For centuries, people had heard of a mythical southern continent. The English Lieutenant (later: Captain) **James Cook** believed the continent existed. He discovered Australia for Britain and **claimed it by order of King George III of England.** Cook named the eastern part of Australia 'New South Wales'.

1788

The **First Fleet**, under the command of British Navy captain Arthur Phillip, arrived at Botany Bay with about 800 convicts on board eleven ships. Their journey had taken them nearly eight months and many passengers had died because of the terrible conditions on board. Phillip founded the first British colony in Australia as a **penal colony**, and became its first governor.

1793

The first free settlers came to Australia in 1793. In the 1850s, the Australian Gold Rush brought more than 600,000 people to the country, especially from Britain, but also from America, Germany and China.

1860

In the mid-19th century the Australian outback was mostly unexplored. In 1860 **Robert Burke and William Wills** led an expedition which **crossed Australia from south to north.** The journey took nearly five months and most men died of starvation and exhaustion on their way back, including Burke and Wills.

1870

The surveyor John Forrest went on an **expedition from Perth to Adelaide.** It was the first west-to-east crossing of Western Australia.

1901

Australia first consisted of six British colonies. In 1901, the colonies were united and they now formed the **Commonwealth of Australia** with Canberra as its capital and the British monarch as head of state.

1901–1939

Governmental Protection Acts deprived the Aboriginal people of their legal and civil rights. Half-Aboriginal children (children with a white Australian father and an Aboriginal mother) were separated from their families and brought to missions or reserves in order to be 'assimilated' into white Australian society. These children were later called the **Stolen Generations**. The Australian government's assimilation policy lasted into the 1970s.

1945–2000

Almost 5.9 million immigrants settled in Australia after World War II, many of them came from Britain and Ireland. The peak of Asian immigration was in the early 1990s when more than half of the immigrants who arrived in Australia were from an Asian country.

1963

It wasn't until 1963 that the indigenous peoples received **full civil rights** as Australian citizens.
The Aboriginal flag was first introduced on National Aboriginal Day in 1971.
It represents Aboriginal identity: yellow symbolises the sun, red stands for the earth and black represents the Aboriginal people.

1986

With the **Australia Act** of 1986 the country, which was already self-governing, became fully independent of British Parliament.

2000

The **Summer Olympic Games** were held in Australian cities twice: in Melbourne in 1956 and in Sydney in 2000.
Cathy Freeman was the first Aboriginal to compete in the Olympic Games. In Sydney, she lit the Olympic Flame and won a gold medal in the 400 metres.

2001

Despite public pressure, Prime Minister John Howard refused to apologise to the Stolen Generations for the government's wrongdoings during its assimilation policy.

2007

The Sydney Opera House, built in 1973, became world cultural heritage in 2007. Two of the country's most well-known natural landmarks can also be found on the UNESCO list: Uluru ('Ayers Rock') and the Great Barrier Reef.

2008

Kevin Rudd, Prime Minister from 2007 to 2010, **officially apologised** to the Aboriginals and the Stolen Generations.

The UK Parliament today

House of Commons
One elected Member of Parliament (MP) for each of about 650 constituencies. Each MP has to be elected directly by the voters of a constituency. The candidate with the most votes in each constituency becomes its MP.

House of Lords
About 800 non-elected members. Most are appointed; about 90 members, however, are hereditary peers. There is now a strong movement in the House of Commons to allow only elected Lords (except the Law Lords).

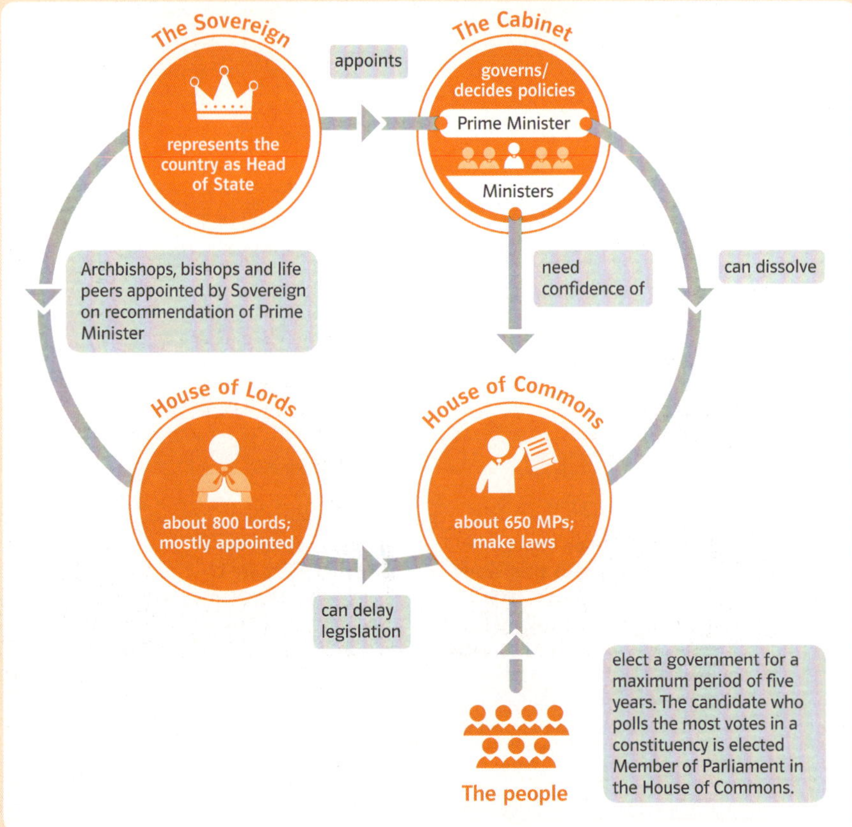

A history of Parliament

1

John, who became King of England in 1199, was unsuccessful in war. He lost most of his land in France. He asked his barons to give him more money, but they refused. When he tried to make them pay heavy taxes, they rebelled. In 1215 they formed an army, captured London and forced John to sign a treaty. It was called **Magna Carta** and is one of the most important documents in English history.

2

Most people at that time were not rich barons and churchmen, but poor peasants working on the barons' land. Magna Carta did not mention them. But the document was important because it did limit the king's power. Also, it formed the basis for the first Parliament, which was called by Edward I in 1295. This became known as the **Model Parliament** because it had so many of the features of later Parliaments.

3

King James II became king in 1685. He tried to rule alone, so Parliament invited James's daughter Mary and her Dutch husband William of Orange to come to England as King and Queen. Nobody wanted to fight for James, so it was a Glorious (and Bloodless) Revolution. William and Mary had to sign a document called the **Bill Of Rights** (1689), which made sure that Parliament was more important than the monarch.

Important articles from Magna Carta

- The English Church shall be free to choose its own bishops.
- No special taxes can be created unless the barons meet and agree to them.
- Freemen should only be imprisoned if they have had a proper trial.
- The barons shall choose 25 representatives to check that the king does not break these rules.

The Lords

- Barons
- Bishops
- Abbots

The King

- Parliament only met when the king wanted it to.
- Parliament could not tell the king what to do, but it could stop taxes if it disagreed with them.

The Commons

Representatives of the
- towns/ boroughs
- knights

Bill of Rights

- Parliament, not the monarch, passes laws and decides on taxes.
- Parliament keeps a check on the army.
- MPs have absolute freedom of speech.

The American government today

Congress

Senate
(100 senators: 2 from each state)

House of Representatives
(435 congressmen/women)

- can impeach and remove the president.
- may ignore the president's veto.
- The Senate approves the appointment of members of the Supreme Court.
- The Senate approves treaties made by the president.

The President

- controls foreign policy and makes treaties.
- may veto laws made by Congress.
- can recommend laws.
- appoints members of the Supreme Court; confirmation by the Senate is required.

The Supreme Court

- watches over the Constitution and interprets the laws.
- can call laws made by Congress unconstitutional.
- can call the president's decisions unconstitutional.

The people

- elect a president for four years, indirectly through the Electoral College
- elect senators for six years.
- elect one third of representatives every two years.

The American Constitution and the Bill of Rights

The War of Independence from Britain ('American Revolutionary War') ended in 1783 with an American victory. On September 17, 1787, delegates from the original 13 colonies signed the new **Constitution of The United States.**

In 1791 the **Bill of Rights** was added to the Constitution. This guaranteed:

The Constitution represents two basic beliefs:

- The individual is important and must be free.
- The people have the right to choose the officials of the government (government by 'consent of the governed').

Freedom of assembly

- Freedom to hold public meetings.
- Meetings must be peaceful and obey local laws.

Freedom of religion

- Freedom of worship.
- Freedom to belong to any religion, or to none.
- No official state religion is allowed.

Freedom of the press

- Freedom to print books, newspapers, and magazines.
- No one may print lies that harm other citizens ('libel').

Freedom of speech

- Freedom to express ideas and opinions.
- No one may use this freedom to tell lies in order to harm or to injure other citizens ('slander').

Freedom of petition

- Freedom to encourage the government to pass laws.
- Freedom to ask the government to take certain actions.

Freedom and security of citizens

- No unlawful search may be made of homes.
- Citizens may carry guns for self-defence.

Rights to equal justice

All persons accused of a crime must be treated fairly and equally in a court of law.

Bildquellen:
U1.1 Alamy stock photo (Vadym Drobot), Abingdon, Oxon; **U1.2** Getty Images RF (E+/narvikk), München; **2.1** Isabelle Sieb, London; **3.1** shutterstock (Mikadun), New York, NY; **4.1** iStockphoto (sturti), Calgary, Alberta; **5.1** shutterstock (De Visu), New York, NY; **7.1** shutterstock (oneinchpunch), New York, NY; **8.1** Dream Maker Software (RF), Colorado; **8.2** Getty Images (Universal Images Group), München; **8.3** shutterstock (Julian W), New York, NY; **8.4** Getty Images (Christian Science Monitor), München; **9.1** shutterstock (Radiokafka), New York, NY; **9.2** Thinkstock (Hemera), München; **9.3** shutterstock (Radiokafka), New York, NY; **9.4** shutterstock (Mikadun), New York, NY; **9.5** shutterstock (Tatiana Frank), New York, NY; **10.1** Getty Images (Universal Images Group), München; **10.2** Thinkstock (esancai), München; **10.3** Getty Images (Getty Images Entertainment), München; **10.4** Getty Images (Getty Images Entertainment), München; **10.5** shutterstock (amophoto_au), New York, NY; **11.1** shutterstock (IB Photography), New York, NY; **12.1** shutterstock (pisaphotography), New York, NY; **13.1** shutterstock (ChameleonsEye), New York, NY; **13.2** shutterstock (JonMilnes), New York, NY; **13.3** iStockphoto (Siwawut), Calgary, Alberta; **13.4** iStockphoto (robertcicchetti), Calgary, Alberta; **15.1** shutterstock (GybasDigiPhoto), New York, NY; **16.1** shutterstock (AridOcean), New York, NY; **17.1** Getty Images (Corbis Historical), München; **19.1** iStockphoto (Kokkai Ng), Calgary, Alberta; **20.1** Getty Images (Darrian Traynor), München; **21.1** Getty Images (Photolibrary), München; **21.2** Masterfile (R. Ian Lloyd), Düsseldorf; **21.3** shutterstock (ian woolcock), New York, NY; **21.4** © BBC Motion Gallery — British Broadcasting Corporation — Media Centre, London; **22.1** laif (Marc Dozier/hemis.fr), Köln; **23.1** Getty Images (Andrew Sheargold), München; **24.1** Getty Images (Richard Milnes/Pacific Press/LightRocket), München; **25.1** Getty Images (Corbis Historical), München; **26.1** Reuters (David Gray), Berlin; **27.1** iStockphoto (wdstock), Calgary, Alberta; **32.1** shutterstock (Rob Bayer), New York, NY; **34.1** Getty Images (Scott Barbour), München; **34.2** Getty Images (Fairfax Media), München; **35.1** www.CartoonStock.com (Goddard, Clive), Bath; **36.1** shutterstock (Jordi Prat Puig), New York, NY; **37.1** shutterstock (ChameleonsEye), New York, NY; **39.1–42.8** Isabelle Sieb, London; **43.1** Getty Images (John Springer Collection/CORBIS), München; **43.2** Getty Images (John Springer Collection/CORBIS), München; **43.3** Getty Images (Moviepix), München; **45.1** Isabelle Sieb, London; **45.2** Picture-Alliance (The Advertising Archives), Frankfurt; **45.3** Interfoto (Mary Evans / VESTRON PICTURES / Ronald Grant Archive), München; **46.1** shutterstock (View Apart), New York, NY; **48.1** Getty Images (E+/kali9), München; **49.1** shutterstock (Monkey Business Images), New York, NY; **52.1** AIFS in Bonn, Bonn; **53.1** laif (Daniel Rosenthal), Köln; **53.2** Getty Images (2011 Manfredi Caracausi/Moment), München; **55.1** iStockphoto (RapidEye), Calgary, Alberta; **55.2** Getty Images (Klaus Vedfelt/DigitalVision), München; **55.3** shutterstock (SpeedKingz), New York, NY; **55.4** Getty Images (Universal Images Group), München; **55.5** iStockphoto (asiseeit), Calgary, Alberta; **55.6** iStockphoto (FatCamera), Calgary, Alberta; **56.1** iStockphoto (sturti), Calgary, Alberta; **56.2** shutterstock (StockLite), New York, NY; **56.3** shutterstock (Nejron Photo), New York, NY; **57.1** shutterstock (Ema Woo), New York, NY; **58.1** Bulls Press (SWNS.com), Frankfurt; **60.1** Fosseway Films, London; **60.2** Fosseway Films, London; **60.3** Fosseway Films, London; **62.1** Interfoto (NG Collection), München; **65.1** Interfoto (NG Collection), München; **66.1** Interfoto (NG Collection), München; **67.1** Cover aus der Reihe Young Adult Literature: Klett English Editions, ISBN 978-3-12-578140-5, © Ernst Klett Sprachen GmbH, Stuttgart 1998, Stuttgart; **68.1** Masterfile, Düsseldorf; **70.1** Thinkstock (monkeybusinessimages), München; **70.2** Savage Chickens; **72.1** Masterfile, Düsseldorf; **73.1** Getty Images (Patrick Aventurier), München; **74.1** iStockphoto (georgeclerk), Calgary, Alberta; **77.1** shutterstock (Sabphoto), New York, NY; **79.1** shutterstock (pim pic), New York, NY; **80.1** www.CartoonStock.com (Reynolds, Dan), Bath; **80.2** Getty Images (ABC Photo Archives/ABC via Getty Images; EN VOGUE), München; **81.1** shutterstock (De Visu), New York, NY; **81.2** Getty Images (2003 Ulrich Baumgarten), München; **81.3** iStockphoto (svetikd), Calgary, Alberta; **82.1** Fosseway Films, London; **82.2** Fosseway Films, London; **82.3** Fosseway Films, London; **83.1** Fosseway Films, London; **83.2** Fosseway Films, London; **84.1** shutterstock (Sean Pavone), New York, NY; **85.1** shutterstock (Maks Ershov), New York, NY; **85.2** shutterstock (littleny), New York, NY; **85.3** Alamy stock photo (inga spence), Abingdon, Oxon; **85.4** Getty Images (Corbis News), München; **86.1** Alamy stock photo (Sunshine Pics), Abingdon, Oxon; **89.1** Getty Images (Bettmann), München; **90.1** Klett-Archiv-RF-HF, Stuttgart; **90.2** Dream Maker Software (RF), Colorado; **90.3** Geoatlas, Hendaye; **90.4** Klett-Archiv-RF-HF, Stuttgart; **90.5** Dream Maker Software (RF), Colorado; **90.6** Thinkstock (flowgraph), München; **90.7** Geoatlas, Hendaye; **90.8** Geoatlas, Hendaye; **90.9** Klett-Archiv-RF-HF, Stuttgart; **90.10** Klett-Archiv-RF-HF, Stuttgart; **92.1** iStockphoto (tomprout), Calgary, Alberta; **93.1** iStockphoto (rightdx), Calgary, Alberta; **94.1** shutterstock (Digital Media Pro), New York, NY; **95.1** shutterstock (Joseph Sohm), New York, NY; **96.1** Getty Images (Moment Mobile), München; **97.1** Getty Images (Major League Baseball), München; **98.1** Getty Images (Greg Gayne/NBC/NBCU Photo Bank), München; **99.1** shutterstock (oneinchpunch), New York, NY; **105.1** iStockphoto (LauriPatterson), Calgary, Alberta; **107.1** shutterstock (s_bukley), New York, NY; **107.2** laif (Polaris), Köln; **107.3** shutterstock (Kathy Hutchins), New York, NY; **108.1** Getty Images (Stefania D'Alessandro), München; **111.1** iStockphoto (RapidEye), Calgary, Alberta; **113.1** shutterstock (Monkey Business Images), New York, NY; **113.2** Getty Images (Westend61), München; **113.3** Alamy stock photo (Ray Evans), Abingdon, Oxon; **115.1** Fosseway Films, London; **115.2** Fosseway Films, London; **115.3** Fosseway Films, London; **117.1** Alamy stock photo (Jack Picone), Abingdon, Oxon; **118.1** Masterfile (R. Ian Lloyd), Düsseldorf; **119.1** Alamy stock photo (Moviestore collection Ltd), Abingdon, Oxon; **120.1** iStockphoto (SolStock), Calgary, Alberta; **120.2** iStockphoto (Koldunov), Calgary, Alberta; **120.3** shutterstock (Stefano Cavoretto), New York, NY;

120.4 iStockphoto (dcdp), Calgary, Alberta; **122.1** shutterstock (Uber Images), New York, NY; **123.1** Getty Images (Westend61), München; **124.1** iStockphoto (Stolk), Calgary, Alberta; **125.1** shutterstock (Arina P Habich), New York, NY; **128.1** Alamy stock photo (Kumar Sriskandan), Abingdon, Oxon; **131.1** shutterstock (Spectral-Design), New York, NY; **131.2** Alamy stock photo (Juice Images), Abingdon, Oxon; **139.1** Thinkstock (Tom Ackerman), München; **140.1** iStockphoto (clu), Calgary, Alberta; **143.1** PONS GmbH, Stuttgart; **145.1** iStockphoto (JohnnyGreig), Calgary, Alberta; **149.1** Getty Images (Hulton Archive), München; **151.1** shutterstock (dedoma), New York, NY; **151.2** shutterstock (Olga Kashubin), New York, NY; **151.3** shutterstock (Ivonne Wierink), New York, NY; **153.1** iStockphoto (Hermsdorf), Calgary, Alberta; **154.1** shutterstock (oliveromg), New York, NY; **161.1** Getty Images (DigitalVision), München; **162.1** Getty Images (E+/BraunS), München; **162.2** shutterstock (Phoenixns), New York, NY; **162.3** shutterstock (Monkey Business Images), New York, NY; **163.1** shutterstock (Syda Productions), New York, NY; **167.1** shutterstock (Ingus Kruklitis), New York, NY; **170.1** iStockphoto (subman), Calgary, Alberta; **170.2** shutterstock (Dobo Kristian), New York, NY; **179.1** shutterstock (GybasDigiPhoto), New York, NY; **179.2** Getty Images (Universal Images Group), München; **179.3** Alamy stock photo (Andrew Watson), Abingdon, Oxon; **179.4** Reuters (DANIEL MUNOZ/Reuters), Berlin; **188.1** shutterstock (FashionStock.com), New York, NY; **188.1** iStockphoto (RapidEye), Calgary, Alberta; **191.1** shutterstock (Hadrian), New York, NY; **195.1** iStockphoto (SoumenNath), Calgary, Alberta; **200.1** shutterstock (Galina Barskaya), New York, NY; **200.2** shutterstock (Vic Labadie), New York, NY; **203.1** shutterstock (ValeStock), New York, NY; **203.2** shutterstock (Chris Jenner), New York, NY; **260.1** Thinkstock (Creatas Images), München; **266.1** Getty Images (John van Hasselt/ Sygma), München; **266.2** Getty Images (Fairfax Media), München; **266.3** shutterstock (Holli), New York, NY; **266.4** shutterstock (Emma Jones), New York, NY; **266.5** iStockphoto (JohnCrux), Calgary, Alberta; **267.1** shutterstock (Dean Drobot), New York, NY; **267.2** shutterstock (Dean Drobot), New York, NY; **269.1** shutterstock (Chay Talanon), New York, NY; **269.2** iStockphoto (swissmediavision), Calgary, Alberta; **270.1** Getty Images (E+/RoBeDeRo), München; **271.1** iStockphoto (shelbyorme), Calgary, Alberta; **271.2** iStockphoto (oscity), Calgary, Alberta; **272.1** Getty Images (Artie/Moment), München; **272.2** iStockphoto (Hermsdorf), Calgary, Alberta; **272.3** shutterstock (G Tipene), New York, NY; **272.4** shutterstock (MagSpace), New York, NY; **273.1** Reuters (Mark Baker/Pool (AUSTRALIA)), Berlin; **273.2** shutterstock (Steve Allen), New York, NY; **273.3** Getty Images (2011 Gamma-Rapho), München; **273.4** dreamstime.com (Kaye Eileen Oberstar), Brentwood, TN; **274.1** Kessler-Medien, Saarbrücken; **275.1** MEV Verlag GmbH, Augsburg; **275.2** MEV Verlag GmbH, Augsburg; **275.3** Getty Images RF (Photodisc), München; **275.4** creativ collection Verlag GmbH, Freiburg

Textquellen:

11 "The Language Wars: A History of Proper English", Henry Hitchings, John Murray Publishers, 2011; **24** © Zelda Quakawoot, Mackay, Australia; **25** By Felicia, https://www.travelicia.de/australien-aborigines/; **28–30** "Nona & Me", by Clare Atkins (Black Inc. 2014); **37** www.college-contact.com; **47.1** Song: „Champagne Life", Text: Gough, David Dorohn/SMITH, SHAFFER, Verlag: EMI Blackwood Music Inc/Pen in the ground publishing/UniversalMusic Z-Tunes EMI Music Publishing Germany GmbH, Berlin/Musik Edition Discoton GmbH, Berlin; **47.2** Song: „The good life", Text: Hume, Jon Cobbe/Thistlethwayte, Rai Paul, Verlag: Sony ATV Music Publishing Australia P/L Sony/ATV Music Publishing (Germany) GmbH, Berlin; **49** By Richard Garner, *The Independent*, London, August 23, 2012; **52** Timo S., www.aifs.de; **62–66;** Excerpt from THE GIVER by Lois Lowry. Copyright © 1993 by Lois Lowry. Reprinted by permission of Houghton Mifflin Harcourt Publishing Company. All rights reserved.; **73** By Marleen, earthlink e.V., München, 2016; **77** By Jonathan Webb, BBC News, September 8, 2015, www.bbc.com, © 2015 BBC, London; **79** Copyright Guardian News & Media Ltd 2015; **80** Song: „Free your mind", Text: Foster, Denzil Delano/Levert, Gerald Edward/MC Elroy, Thomas Craig, Verlag: Two Tuff Enuff Publishing/Willesden Music Inc EMI Music Publishing Germany GmbH, Berlin/ Imagem Music GmbH, Berlin; **89** Stadt Bremerhaven, 2014; **92** Deutsche Welle, 2012; **100–102** From FAMOUS by Todd Strasser. Copyright © 2011 by Todd Strasser. Reprinted with the permission of Simon & Schuster Books for Young Readers, an imprint of Simon & Schuster Children's Publishing Division. All rights reserved.

Sollte es in einem Einzelfall nicht gelungen sein, den korrekten Rechteinhaber ausfindig zu machen, so werden berechtigte Ansprüche selbstverständlich im Rahmen der üblichen Regelungen abgegolten.

Alaska
(U.S.)
Aleutian Is.
(U.S.)
CANADA
UNITED KINGDO
IRELAND
Channel Is.
(U.K.)
UNITED STATES OF AMERICA
Gibraltar (U.K.)
Bermuda
(U.K.)
Hawaiian Islands
(U.S.)
BAHAMAS
Turks and Caicos Is. (U.K.)
Cayman Is.
(U.K.)
Virgin Is. (U.K./U.S.)
Anguilla (U.K.)
BELIZE
JAMAICA
Puerto Rico (U.S.)
ANTIGUA AND BARBUDA
DOMINICA
ST. CHRISTOPHER AND NEVIS
ST. LUCIA
Montserrat (U.K.)
BARBADOS
GRENADA
ST. VINCENT AND GRENADINES
TRINIDAD AND TOBAGO
GUYANA
GAMBIA
NIGER
SIERRA LEONE
LIBERIA
GHANA
CAMER
Palmyra Is.
(U.S.)
Howland Is.
(U.S.)
Jarvis Is.
(U.S.)
KIRIBATI
Ascension
(U.K.)
TUVALU
Tokelau Is. (N.Z.)
WESTERN SAMOA
American Samoa
(U.S.)
Cook Is.
(N.Z.)
Saint Helena
(U.K.)
NAN
TONGA
Pitcairn Is
(U.K.)
Tristan da Cunha
(U.K.)
Gough Is.
(U.K.)
Falkland Is./
Malvinas (U.K.)
Countries in which English is the / an official language
NAME Independent Commonwealth

ame Dependent territories of Commonwealth states (in brackets) SCALE 1 : 88,000,000

CALIFORNIA
OREGON
IDAHO
USA
NEVADA
ARIZONA
MEXICO
Goose Lake
Upper Lake
Redwood National Park
Coast Ranges
Redding
Lassen Peak 10,457 ft (3,187 m)
Pyramid Lake
Sacramento
Central
Sierra Nevada
Lake Tahoe
Napa Valley
Sacramento
Yosemite National Park
Mono Lake
San Joaquin
San Francisco
Silicon Valley
San Jose
Valley
Salinas
Big Sur
Pacific Ocean
Mount Whitney 14,505 ft (4,421 m)
Death Valley -282 ft (-86 m)
CALIFORNIA
Mojave Desert
CALIFORNIA REPUBLIC
Malibu
Santa Monica
Venice
Los Angeles
HOLLYWOOD
Palm Springs
Colorado
Salton Sea
San Diego

AUSTRALIA & NEW ZEALAND

NEW GUINEA
Coral Sea
Pacific Ocean
Cairns
Great Barrier Reef
Great Dividing Range
SYDNEY
Manly
Bondi Beach
Botany Bay
Brisbane
SOUTH WALES
Sydney
Australian Capital Territory
Canberra
CTORIA
Melbourne
Tasman Sea
Hobart
Auckland
NEW ZEALAND
Wellington
Christchurch